SINGLES

Six Decades of Hot Hits
& Classic Cuts

Thunder Bay Press

An imprint of the Advantage Publishers Group
5880 Oberlin Drive, San Diego, CA 92121-4794
www.thunderbaybooks.com

ISBN-13: 978-1-59223-651-0
ISBN-10: 1-59223-651-0

Library of Congress Cataloging in Publication Data available upon request.

WITH CONTRIBUTIONS FROM
Johnny Black
Mark Brend
Tony Burton
Sean Egan
Thomas Jerome
Joel McIver
John Morrish
Tamara Palmer

COMMISSIONING EDITOR: THOMAS JEROME
EDITOR: TONY BACON
DESIGN: BALLEY DESIGN LIMITED

Printed by Colorprint Offset Ltd. (Hong Kong)

SINGLES

Six Decades of Hot Hits

& Classic Cuts

THUNDER BAY
P·R·E·S·S

(We're Gonna) Rock Around The Clock

Bill Haley & His Comets

Released May 1954
Decca *9-29124* (U.S. #1) / Brunswick *05317* (U.K. #1)

The first rock'n'roll record to top the U.S. singles chart was, officially, a foxtrot. That's how Decca Records listed 'Rock Around The Clock' when it was released on May 13, 1954, tucked away discreetly on the B-side of 'Thirteen Women,' which Decca considered a more commercial waxing.

Clearly, the music business in 1955 had no more of an inkling that a new music was about to change the world than it would when The Beatles emerged in 1962, when punk arrived in 1976, or when Nirvana's grunge turned the '90s on its head. And that's enormously encouraging, because it means that despite the collective wisdom of the men in suits, despite their vast marketing budgets and their intensive audience research, the music belongs not to them but to the fans. Fans inject a healthy drop of unpredictability into the comforting formulas and tidy equations that the music industry lives by, and that is what made the triumph of 'Rock Around The Clock' so glorious.

It's like a classic detective story where all the clues are there for everyone to see – but they never come together until all is revealed at the end. In retrospect, it's obvious to us that Decca, RCA, and the other 1950s music-industry giants should have seen it coming. The electric guitar had been around since the 1930s, the term rock'n'roll was widely used as a musical description by the end of the '40s, and the spread of radio meant that white kids were increasingly exposed to black music.

Chuck Berry had been wowing live audiences with his guitar-fueled, countrified rhythm & blues since 1953, and on April 24, 1954, music trade magazine *Billboard* spelled out the future under the headline, 'Teenagers Demand Music With A Beat.' As Bill Haley himself said later: "The musical world was starved for something new. The days of the solo vocalist and the big bands had gone. About the only thing that was making noise was progressive jazz, but this was just above the heads of the average listener."

We should not judge Decca too harshly. Even if they had seen the signs, Haley was not the likeliest candidate to lead a teenage revolution. For much of his career he was billed as 'Yodeling Bill Haley – singing cowboy' and by 1954 he was already on the wrong side of 30. Nevertheless, he was ideally placed to fuse his western swing with the black roots of gospel and blues in a way that would take rock'n'roll to a mass audience. 'Rock Around The Clock' was not his priority on April 12, 1954, when Haley began a recording session in Decca's Pythian Temple Studio, a converted ballroom in New York City. The session's producer, Milt Gabler, said: "You could blow there, because there was this big, high ceiling. We had drapes hanging from the balconies, and a live wooden floor." Having worked with rhythm & blues pioneer Louis Jordan, Gabler knew how to achieve a dynamic, contemporary sound, and spent two-and-a-half hours to get a good take of 'Thirteen Women,' leaving just 30 minutes for the B-side.

'Rock Around The Clock,' written by James Myers and Max Freedman in 1952, had been recorded by Sonny Dae & His Knights as a jump jazz item, but when Haley heard it, he knew it was perfect for an idea he'd had for some while. "I felt that if I could take, say, a Dixieland tune and drop the first and third beats, and accentuate the second and fourth, and add a beat, the listeners could clap as well as dance; this would be what they were after." Unfortunately there was bad blood between

Myers and Dave Miller, head of Essex Records, to which Haley was contracted at the time. "Every time Miller would see it, he'd tear it up and throw it away," Haley recalled. "So I never could record it."

Haley's move to Decca cleared the way for recording the song, which the band re-fashioned at a rehearsal in his basement the night before the studio session. The saxophone player with Haley's group, The Comets, was Joey D'Ambrosia, who remembered: "First we listened to Sonny Dae's recording. Then we decided the record would have more bounce if we added staccato riffs throughout the song. The voicing on the riffs was three parts – sax, lead guitar, and steel [guitar]." Guitarist Danny Cedrone was uncertain about playing a guitar solo until bassist Marshall Lytle suggested he should simply re-use the one he'd played on Haley's earlier recording of 'Rock The Joint.'

Only one of The Comets, pianist Johnny Grandy, could read music, so once they were in the Pythian Temple, Gabler's years of studio experience came into play. To add zest to the backings, he would hum standard rhythm & blues riffs that the band copied by ear. It was also Gabler who told steel guitarist Billy Williamson to "take the steel bar and hit it across the strings of the guitar and make it arc. It'd make 'POW! POW!' I'd say, 'Give me some of those lightning flashes, Billy!'" Gabler also put three mikes on the drums to achieve a fuller sound and added

plenty of reverb to the track. For the final master he combined two tracks, one where Haley's voice had been drowned out by the musicians, and another on which the voice was clear.

The initial release of 'Rock Around The Clock' stiffed in the U.S., and it was not until March 1955, when it was used as the theme tune for the film *Blackboard Jungle*, that the song took off. "Kids started dancing in the aisles," explained Marshall Lytle. "Then it took the world by storm." It entered the U.S. Top 40 on May 14, 1955, and hit Number 1 on June 29. On November 25 it repeated the trick in the U.K. and became Britain's first million-selling single. Haley's subsequent U.K. tour inspired London schoolboy Cliff Richard to become Britain's first homegrown rock'n'roller, and Paul McCartney still vividly remembers seeing Haley's group at the Liverpool Odeon. "The lights went down and you had 'One, two, three o'clock, four o'clock – rock!' Bingo! There they were."

By the time Elvis Presley followed Haley to the U.S. Number 1 spot with 'Heartbreak Hotel' on April 21, 1956, it was clear that rock'n'roll was not just the most significant new musical form of the decade but a unifying force for youth of every color and creed. 'Rock Around The Clock' has by now notched up over 25 million sales worldwide, and while it was certainly not the first rock'n'roll record and arguably not the greatest, it was undeniably the one that changed everything.

FORTY-FIVE REVOLUTIONS PER MINUTE

RCA introduced the 45 rpm seven-inch vinyl disc in March 1949, probably as a panic response to the launch of a 33-1/3 rpm long-playing disc by its rival, CBS. RCA certainly rushed the little disc into production. The head of CBS had given RCA boss David Sarnoff a sneak preview of the LP only three weeks before its official launch in June 1948, hoping that RCA would start transferring its catalogue of recordings to the new medium. Instead, stung by CBS's coup, Sarnoff launched his own vinyl record.

CBS had taken the 33-1/3 speed from movie work, where it had provided a sound disc that ran as long as a standard reel of film. Using the new speed, the new vinyl, a narrower groove, and a smaller needle, the LP achieved a practical running time of 22 minutes, later extended to 30.

CBS's disc was developed by trial and error, but RCA developed the 45 using complex mathematics. Its engineers discovered that optimum sound quality came when the outside diameter of the playing area was twice that of the inner groove; that's why seven-inch records have a three-and-a-half-inch label. The 45 rpm speed gave the right frequency range and low distortion, resulting in a record with better fidelity at the end of a side than the LP.

One other factor was important: the duration of the 45 was identical to that of the old 78 shellac record, meaning RCA could simply transfer existing recordings to the new medium. In any case, the company had analyzed its catalogue and discovered that 96 per cent of its 'musical units' – songs or classical movements – were less than five minutes long. RCA thought that would answer any criticisms of the short playing time.

Singles were also cheaper to produce and sell. Not only did they use less vinyl, but they carried only two songs, meaning their musical content was much cheaper. The four-minute time limit proved absurd for classical music, but RCA coupled the discs with a new 'autochanger' record player that would play them one after the other (up to a claimed maximum of 50 minutes). The discs had a raised inner shoulder designed to protect the playing surface when they were stacked.

Early publicity for the seven-inch format made much of its convenience. The record player was smaller, and the discs would fit on shelves: 150 singles would supposedly fit into one foot of shelf space. At launch, records were issued in color-coded vinyl: black for popular music, but red for classical, green for country, yellow for children's music, and so on. This did not last long, although colored vinyl did not pose a technical problem and was revived many times in the single's long life.

The first single was a marketing tool, the 'Whirlaway Demonstration Record,' sent to dealers early in 1949, but by the time of the official launch, RCA had 76 albums (packages of singles) and 104 singles available. It soon became apparent that the LP was a better format for classical music, and RCA even considered abandoning its 45 rpm single.

In the event, it was saved by the teenage pop market, which liked the new format because it was cheap, unbreakable, and convenient. The jukebox clearly liked it too. By 1951, the other major record companies had adopted the 45 rpm play, although the old 78 did survive in parallel for a while, and RCA had gone over to the LP for classical music.

Throughout the life of the 45 rpm single, manufacturing techniques stayed the same. First the music is cut on a lathe on a blank acetate disc; that's then 'silvered,' meaning coated with a thin layer of metal, and the result plated thicker as the first stage of creating a metal 'stamper,' with a raised track matching the original groove.

A lump of vinyl, heated to make it soft, is then placed between two stampers, A and B side, in a press, and the record stamped out. The paper labels are added in the same process. Excess vinyl is then trimmed, leaving the single record. Although its sleeves are considerably more fragile, a CD is manufactured in much the same way, but covered with a protective coating.

Although it is no longer a mass-market product, the seven-inch vinyl single is still going strong as a promotional device and a magnet for collectors.

That's All Right
Elvis Presley

Released July 1954
Sun *209* (U.S.) / Not issued U.K.

Elvis Aaron Presley had visited Sam Phillips's Memphis Recording Services a couple of times in 1953 and '54 to cut a pair of double-sided acetates for his mother at $3.98 a throw. Phillips wasn't especially impressed but remarked: "We might call you sometime." That call finally came, and on Monday July 5, 1954, Elvis entered the home of Sun records on 706 Union Avenue, Memphis, Tennessee, for his first commercial recording session.

At first it was intended simply as an audition, and the recording of 'That's All Right' came about quite by accident. With Scotty Moore on guitar and Bill Black on stand-up bass, the ensemble kicked off with a rendition of 'Harbor Lights' before trying around a dozen takes of 'I Love You Because.' It was during a break in proceedings that Elvis launched into Arthur 'Big Boy' Crudup's blues 'That's All Right.' While Elvis jumped around and acted the fool, Moore and Black grabbed their instruments and joined in. The combination of Black's slapping bass and Moore's country licks was a shotgun marriage of country & western and rhythm & blues, now known as rockabilly.

It was a raw, authentic sound, but Presley's naive enthusiasm quickly evolved into quiet confidence as they made take after take, and Phillips soon realized that something new and exciting was happening. He'd finally found what he'd been looking for: a white boy who could sing the blues. As we now know, it was a defining moment in musical history, and the foundation stone of rock'n'roll was laid on that day. Asked a couple of years later about his music, the king replied: "The colored folk been singing it and playing it just the way I'm doin' now, man, for more years than I know. Nobody paid it no mind till I goosed it up."

Rose-Marie
Slim Whitman

Released April 1954
Imperial *8236* (U.S. #22) / London *HL 8061* (U.K. #1)

Cowboy yodeler Slim Whitman was discovered by Colonel Tom Parker, who later managed Elvis Presley. Whitman refused to sing about drinkin' or cheatin', in effect putting about half of all country songs out of his reach. Nevertheless, he done good: his first U.S. Top 10 came in 1951 with 'Indian Love Call,' drawn from the 1924 musical *Rose-Marie*.

The same musical's title song became his biggest international hit, spending a staggering 11 weeks at Number 1 in Britain, a record that would be unbroken until 1991. Movie mavens will know that it's Whitman's distinctive tenor-falsetto styling on 'Indian Love Call' that causes alien brains to explode in the 1996 sci-fi spoof *Mars Attacks*.

Shake Rattle And Roll
Joe Turner

Released April 1954
Atlantic *1026* (U.S. #22) / Not issued U.K.

Atlantic Records was formed in 1947 by Ahmet Ertegun, the son of Turkey's Ambassador to Washington, with a $10,000 loan from his dentist. The label became one of the prime outlets for 1950s rhythm & blues. Ertegun was in the business not so much to make money but more for the joy of the music. He said: "I wanted to make records like the records I loved, which were real blues records." By 1954 Atlantic was having great success with Ruth Brown, The Clovers, Ray Charles, and Kansas City-born blues shouter 'Big' Joe Turner, a former vocalist with Count Basie. Featuring Ertegun and Wexler on backing vocals, 'Shake Rattle And Roll' was especially written by Atlantic songwriter Jesse Stone under the pseudonym 'Charles E. Calhoun' and recorded at Atlantic's makeshift office-cum-studio on West 56th Street on February 9th, 1954. It reached Number 1 on *Billboard's* rhythm & blues chart. (What had been called 'Race' music became 'Rhythm & Blues' when Atlantic's Jerry Wexler renamed the relevant *Billboard* chart in 1949 – R&B records were still excluded from the main 'pop' chart.) Turner, meanwhile, made plenty of money for Atlantic but, despite all his hits, didn't make much himself and died penniless in 1987. Ertegun, one of the most respected men in the business, quietly paid for the funeral and settled the mortgage on Turner's widow's home.

Hey Senorita / Earth Angel (Will You Be Mine)
The Penguins

Released October 1954
DooTone *348* (U.S. #8) / Not issued U.K.

Music critics sometimes sarcastically describe records as "sounding as if they were recorded in a garage." Well, this one was. Producer Walter Williams remembered the session: "Every time the dog barked next door, I'd have to go out and shut him up, and then we'd do another take." This was the only U.S. Top 40 hit for The Penguins, a simple but elegant recording now judged by many to be one of the finest examples of what would become known as doo-wop. The group, whose name came from the picture of Willie the Penguin seen on packs of Kool cigarettes, was signed up on the strength of Curtis Williams's song 'Hey Senorita.' It was released as the A-side, but DJs soon flipped it for 'Earth Angel.' Legal complications added other names to the credits on the record, first issued as solely a Curtis Williams composition.

Once 'Earth Angel' got on the radio, the huge demand for the record nearly bankrupted DooTone. Williams again: "The record started selling so quickly, I ran out of paper for the label. That's why 'Earth Angel' was pressed on so many different colored labels." There were a number of covers by other artists, a common occurrence at the time, most notably by The Crew Cuts, a squeaky-clean white vocal group from Canada. Their version got higher up the U.S. charts and was the hit in Britain, but hindsight tells us now that the original by The Penguins – despite the cheap and amateurish production – is one of the great doo-wop records of all time.

Mr. Sandman
The Chordettes

Released October 1954
Cadence *1247* (U.S. #1) / Columbia *DB 3553* (U.K. #1)

Big-band leader Vaughn Monroe tucked away songwriter Pat Ballard's snappy 'Mr. Sandman' on the B-side of his minor 1954 hit 'They Were Doing The Mambo.' Luckily, Archie Bleyer of Cadence Records rescued the song with a recording by The Chordettes, a girl group from Sheboygan, Michigan. Bleyer's sparkling arrangement and the girls' energetic, jazzy harmonizing rocketed it past a competing version by The Four Aces to nab the U.S. Number 1 slot on November 27, 1954, for the first of seven weeks. By the time it entered the U.K. chart in January 1955 it was up against no fewer than three other versions but still destroyed the competition. In retrospect it's clear that The Chordettes were the stylistic bridge between the barbershop harmony vocalizing of predecessors such as The Andrews Sisters and the rhythm & blues pop of The Shirelles, which would spark the girl-group craze of the early 1960s.

Pledging My Love
Johnny Ace

Released December 1954
Duke *136* (U.S. #17) / Not issued U.K.

John Marshall Alexander was signed to Duke Records in 1952 and his first hit, as Johnny Ace With The Beale Streeters, was 'My Song,' which topped Billboard's rhythm & blues chart for nine weeks. Ace was just another sweet-voiced R&B singer with a sensitive baritone but earned eternal fame as the first rock'n'roll casualty. Drunk on vodka on Christmas Eve 1954, he shot himself – allegedly in a game of Russian roulette – backstage at a 'Negro Christmas Party' at the City Auditorium in Houston, Texas.

His posthumous hit 'Pledging My Love,' recorded in Houston on January 17, 1954, was co-written by Duke owner Don Robey and featured backup by Johnny 'Hand Jive' Otis & His Orchestra. There was a competing chart version by Teresa Brewer on Coral. The song has been much covered over the years, and in a bizarre coincidence was on the B-side of 'Way Down,' Elvis Presley's single at the time of his death.

White Christmas
Bing Crosby

Released October 1942
Decca *18429* (U.S.) / Brunswick *03384* (U.K) / Numerous chart entries

With a boost in popularity during 1954 thanks to its inclusion as the theme song of a Bing Crosby movie, it's no surprise that 'White Christmas' peaked at Number 13 in the U.S. *Billboard* chart that December. In fact, it had charted virtually every year since its first release in 1942 – and for some reason nearly always around December.

Indeed, until recently, Crosby's version of 'White Christmas' was the biggest selling single record of all time, having sold over 30 million copies over many, many years. It was Elton John who finally beat the record, with his version of 'Candle In The Wind,' specially recorded to mark the funeral of Diana, Princess Of Wales, and selling 33 million copies in just a few months.

Crosby was without doubt the biggest star of the first half of the 20th century, arriving when radio was entering its golden era and beginning his recording career just as the electric microphone was introduced, allowing for a close-up 'crooning' style of singing. He became America's greatest ever radio star, and appeared in over 50 Hollywood movies, including the famous *Road* series with his lifetime friend Bob Hope.

'White Christmas' was written by Irving Berlin for the 1942 Crosby movie Holiday Inn. For those who complain that "they don't write songs like they used to" and maintain that modern songwriters lack the requisite skills, it's interesting to note that Berlin could not read music and could only play the piano in one key, and only on the black notes. Recalling the day he first presented the song to the relaxed crooner, Berlin said: "When he read the song he just took his pipe out of his mouth and said to me, 'You don't have to worry about this one, Irving.'"

Crosby premiered the song on his radio show on Christmas Day 1941 and went into the studio to record it the following summer. It was May 29, 1942, and there was a 90-degree heatwave in Los Angeles. The air-conditioning had broken down, so Crosby stripped to the waist in the summer heat to sing: "I'm dreaming of a white Christmas." When the original masters of this 1942 recording wore out, Crosby made a new version, in March 1947, but the singer, the engineers, the John Scott Trotter Orchestra, and the Ken Darby Singers kept as close as possible to their original. No doubt it will still be selling strongly in 2042.

1955

Maybellene
Chuck Berry

Released July 1955
Chess *1604* (U.S. #5) / London *REU 1053* (U.K.)

Tutti-Frutti
Little Richard

Released October 1955
Specialty *561* (U.S. #7) / London *HLO 8366* (U.K. B-side)

When the saxman in boogie pianist Johnnie Johnson's band dropped out of a lucrative 1952 New Year's Eve gig at the last minute, Johnson hastily called in untried guitarist Chuck Berry as a stopgap replacement. That night, as Johnson remembered it later, Berry played a country song called 'Ida Red.' "The audience went crazy," said Johnson. "We had to play that song again, maybe two or three times." Some experts have pinpointed that moment as the beginning of rock'n'roll because, 17 months later, Berry re-worked 'Ida Red' and released it on Chicago-based Chess Records as 'Maybellene.' Chuck didn't know it, but the label's boss, Leonard Chess, arranged a payola kickback for DJ Alan Freed: the DJ would be credited as co-composer if he played the song regularly on his influential radio show, and if the record was a hit, Freed would earn massive royalties. With Freed's enthusiastic support, 'Maybellene' soared to Number 1 in the *Billboard* R&B chart and Number 5 on the pop chart, kick-starting the rock'n'roll revolution.

Down in J&M Studios, New Orleans, on September 14, 1955, barely a month after Berry started the commotion, the bizarrely pompadoured singer-pianist Richard Penniman recorded a cleaned-up version of a

filthy ditty with which he'd wowed club audiences for years. As he recalled: "It used to crack the crowds up when I sang it in the clubs, with those risqué lyrics, 'Tutti-Frutti good booty / If it don't fit, don't force it / You can grease it, make it easy.' I never thought it would be a hit."

Luckily his producer, Bumps Blackwell, knew better. Blackwell had aspiring local songwriter Dorothy La Bostrie come up with acceptable lyrics and, at the end of a fruitless session, captured Penniman's frantically cranked-up rendition of the song – complete with an improvised opening scream of "Awopbopaloobopalopbamboom." It was the scream that sold the track to Art Rupe, owner of Specialty Records, who later revealed: "The reason I picked it wasn't solely for the tempo. It was because of the wild intro; it was different, you know? Be Bop A Lop Bop! All that in front. You didn't hear things like that much on a record."

America's record-trade bible *Billboard* reviewed 'Tutti-Frutti' favorably as a "cleverly styled novelty with nonsense words" and on January 28, 1956, it entered the Top 40 singles chart, only to stall disappointingly at Number 17. "The white radio stations wouldn't play Richard's version," explained Blackwell. This was largely because, in a classic example of a white artist profiting from a black artist's inspiration, clean-cut teen crooner Pat Boone had rapidly knocked up an insipid cover version, which hogged the airplay and soared to Number 12. In the long run, of course, innovators like Chuck Berry and Little Richard would be recognized as the founding fathers of rock'n'roll. Indeed, the writing was already clearly on the wall in December 1955 when, at a copyright organization's awards dinner in New York City, 11 of the 23 prizes went to black-originated R&B songs, including Berry's 'Maybellene' and Johnny Ace's 'Pledging My Love.'

Cherry Pink And Apple Blossom White
Perez Prado

Released February 1955
RCA *5965* (U.S. #1) / HMV *B 10833* (U.K. #1)

In 1955 the mambo was an international outrage and 'king of the mambo' Perez Prado, with his goatee and lacquered pompadour, was just about the hippest thing on two legs. By adding swing jazz stylings to hot Latin music, Prado ruled the mambo roost in a world where the President of the Philippines declared it a 'national calamity' and church leaders threatened to deny absolution for anyone caught dancing it. 'Cherry Pink,' featuring sensational trumpet virtuosity from Billy Regis, was the biggest hit of the craze, spending ten weeks at Number 1 in the U.S. and inspiring countless cover versions worldwide. Technically, however, it's a cha-cha.

Unchained Melody
Les Baxter, His Chorus & Orchestra

Released March 1955
Capitol *3055* (U.S. #1) / Not issued U.K.

Before the proliferation of record players, sales of sheet music were more significant to the music business than sales of discs. Consequently, great songs rather than artists were regarded as the real money-spinners, and no song illustrates this better than the haunting evergreen 'Unchained Melody,' composed by Alex North and Hy Zaret.

It was first recorded by Al Hibbler for the soundtrack of the otherwise forgettable movie *Unchained*, but Les Baxter's version won the U.S. chart battle, peaking at Number 1, while a Roy Hamilton interpretation topped the rhythm & blues chart. Jimmy Young – who later became a BBC radio DJ – took it to Number 1 in the U.K. against fierce competition from no fewer than 13 other versions. The Righteous Brothers, Leo Sayer, and Will Young are just three artists among many for whom 'Unchained Melody' has delivered chart success in every decade since.

Pickin' A Chicken
Eve Boswell

Released December 1955
Not issued U.S. / Parlophone *R 4082* (U.K. #9)

Rarely, if ever, does Hungarian-born popular vocalist Eve Boswell's biggest hit, the cheerfully robust 'Pickin' A Chicken,' appear in lists of all-time great singles, but its significance is undeniable.

A young producer, George Martin, had joined EMI in 1950, working at EMI's studios on Abbey Road in north-west London on classical and light popular recordings. His gifts as a producer and arranger were quickly recognized so, five years later, he became Britain's youngest-ever record company head, at EMI subsidiary Parlophone. Impressive perhaps, but Parlophone was then regarded as EMI's Cinderella, a poor relation of the parent company. Nevertheless, when his production of 'Pickin' A Chicken' entered the U.K. pop singles chart on the last day of 1955, it signaled the start of a new era for the label. Martin soon secured more hits, mainly with imaginative and innovative novelty material by Bernard Cribbins, Peter Sellers, and others, but he was also instrumental in bringing rock'n'roll to the label with young vocalist Jim Dale.

By the early 1960s Martin was actively scouting for a young act that could push Parlophone to the top of the pile, and he found it when he signed The Beatles on June 4, 1962. Although Beatles productions dominated public perception of his work, he continued to make memorable hits for dozens of other acts, from the atmospheric 'Sun Arise' for Rolf Harris in late 1962 to Elton John's record-shattering 1997 re-interpretation of 'Candle In The Wind.' With no fewer than 30 Number 1 hit singles to his credit, Martin is one of the most successful producers of all time.

Hummingbird
Les Paul & Mary Ford

Released June 1955
Capitol *3165* (U.S. #7) / Philips *PB 498* (U.K.)

Les Paul's importance to rock guitar playing is hard to overstate. The Gibson guitar company's first solidbody electric guitar was its Les Paul Model in 1952, and his innovations in guitar design, multi-track recording, and tape speed manipulation created some of the most distinctive sounds ever put on disc. Beyond all this, however, Paul and his vocalist wife Mary Ford were able to make these new sounds accessible to the general public in a string of huge hit singles. 'Hummingbird' wasn't their biggest hit, but it finds Paul in sparkling form, brilliantly decorating Mary's elegant reading of the main melody.

Rock Island Line
The Lonnie Donegan Skiffle Group

Released November 1955
London *1650* (U.S. #8) / Decca *F 10647* (U.K. #8)

Hard though it may be to grasp today, the skiffle craze of the mid 1950s rivaled rock'n'roll as the favored sound of Britain's youth. It was simple, energetic music made with improvised and cheap musical instruments that thrived in a time of post-war austerity. Many British rock heroes of the 1960s – including John Lennon, Brian Jones, and Van Morrison – cut their musical teeth in skiffle bands, bashing out three chords on cheap acoustic guitars. Lonnie Donegan, skiffle's undisputed king, was their hero, and 'Rock Island Line,' his debut single, was skiffle's biggest hit.

The origins of skiffle lie in an earlier British music trend, the 'trad' jazz revival of the late 1940s and early 1950s, which nurtured a particular fondness for New Orleans jazz. Many of London's trad jazz bands introduced stripped-down, high-energy reworkings of old jazz, folk, blues, and jug tunes into their live sets, to which the term 'skiffle' was attached. In October 1954 popular trad jazzers The Chris Barber Band recorded an album called *New Orleans Joys*, which encapsulated the characteristics of the trad revival. The bulk of

the album was given over to the band's songs, but its banjoist and guitarist, Lonnie Donegan, was allowed two solo spots that represented the skiffle section of the band's live set. One of these was a primitive rendering of an old Huddie Ledbetter song, 'Rock Island Line.'

A full year after the album was first released, and after several singles had already been taken from it, Decca put out 'Rock Island Line' as a single (initially in 78 rpm form), originally credited to The Lonnie Donegan Skiffle Group. By January 1956 it was riding high in the British singles chart, establishing skiffle as a phenomenon in its own right, not just a sideshow to the trad-jazz movement. A shade under two-and-a-half-minutes long, with a lyric about negotiating railway tolls in New Orleans that would have meant precisely nothing to a British teenager, 'Rock Island Line' is one of the most primitive hit records ever. Donegan leads with three briskly strummed acoustic guitar chords and a yelping, hollering vocal, Chris Barber plucks a stand-up bass, and Beryl Bryden provides rhythmic accompaniment on a washboard. And that's it.

It was this simplicity that was the appeal of skiffle – like punk rock 20 years later, anyone could do it. But the craze was shortlived. Rock'n'roll was more glamorous, and by 1958 the callow, gauche teenagers who had imitated Donegan with cheap acoustics were trading up to cheap electric guitars and switching allegiance to rockers like Cliff Richard and Buddy Holly. Donegan, however, outlasted the craze he started. Unlike most other skiffle artists, he had hits in the U.S. and enjoyed British chart success into the 1960s. At his commercial peak – roughly early 1956 to mid 1958 – he was, in Britain, as big a star as Elvis and Little Richard. He died in 2002, not long after recording a final album with the help of many of the generation of rock stars he inspired.

Only You (And You Alone)
The Platters

Released July 1955
Mercury *70633* (U.S. #5) / Mercury *MT 117* (U.K. #18)

The Platters' deliciously smooth, rich vocal textures on 'Only You' owed something to swing-era outfits like The Mills Brothers and The Ink Spots, but it made them the first black combo of the rhythm & blues years to earn mainstream success with a song that was neither a novelty number nor a jump jive track. It was written by their manager, Buck Ram, and they'd first recorded it, complete with a whistling solo, for Federal Records in 1954. The superior Mercury version, with its gently insistent rock'n'roll beat and Tony Williams's ingenious vocal stutter, made them international stars and set them off on a run of twenty-three U.S. hits.

Darling, Je Vous Aime Beaucoup
Nat 'King' Cole

Released February 1955
Capitol *3027* (U.S. #7) / Not issued U.K.

The son of a Baptist Minister, Cole was the most successful black
American of the post-war period. After years of success as a jazz
pianist, he decided in 1946 to stake his future on his voice, rather than
his fingers. This delightful piece of *franglais* – complete with heavily
backing choir – was recorded on the 24th of August 1953, but not
issued until 18 months later. It was originally a hit for the American-born
cabaret star The Incomparable Hildegarde in 1943, having been written
for her by her manager, Anna Sosenko. Cole's version featured as the
closing song in the 1955 biographical movie *The Nat 'King' Cole Story*,
and on his 1956 album *Ballads Of The Day*.

Love And Marriage
Frank Sinatra

Released October 1955
Capitol *3260* (U.S. #5) / Capitol *CL 14503* (U.K. #3)

Born in Hoboken, New Jersey, on December 12, 1915, Francis Albert
Sinatra was probably the finest vocal interpreter of 20th-century popular
song. 'Love And Marriage' was specially written by Jimmy Van Heusen
and Sammy Cahn for an NBC-TV musical version of Thornton Wilder's
play *Our Town*, which starred Sinatra together with Paul Newman and
Eva Marie Saint. He recorded it under the guiding baton of Nelson
Riddle on August 15, 1955, at KHJ Studio in Hollywood and released it
as a single, between his albums *In The Wee Small Hours* and the
classic *Songs For Swingin' Lovers*. Cahn was one of the greatest
American wordsmiths – Sinatra recorded 87 of his songs. Speaking of
Sinatra's vocal interpretations, Cahn said: "He moved into a lyric like it
was his house." One of the most telling comments on Sinatra's talent
came from his own idol, Bing Crosby, who remarked: "Frank Sinatra is
the kind of singer who comes along once in a lifetime. But why did it
have to be in my lifetime?"

Heartbreak Hotel
Elvis Presley

Released January 1956
RCA *47-6420* (U.S. #1) / HMV *POP 182* (U.K. #2)

Hound Dog
Elvis Presley
Released July 1956
RCA *47-6604* (U.S. #1) / HMV *POP 249* (U.K. #2)

Blue Suede Shoes
Carl Perkins
Released January 1956
Sun *234* (U.S. #2) / London *HLU 8271* (U.K. #10)

Chuck Berry found mainstream success with 'Maybellene' in 1955 by marrying white country to black rhythm & blues, but white-trash teenager Elvis Presley had set off down the same route on July 5, 1954, when he covered bluesman Arthur 'Big Boy' Crudup's 'That's All Right' for Sun Records of Memphis. Elvis, however, didn't make much of an impact on the charts until April 21, 1956, when 'Heartbreak Hotel' hit Number 1.

The song was sparked to life by a *Miami Herald* story about an unidentified middle-aged man who had committed suicide leaving a note that said only "I walk a lonely street." Inspired by this grim tale, songwriter Mae Axton wrote 'Heartbreak Hotel' with Presley in mind. Having lately been bought from the independent Sun Records for an unprecedented $40,000 by the multi-national RCA, Presley was at a make or break point in his career. It was vital that his first recording session for RCA in their Nashville studios should go well. The company was providing a state-of-the-art recording environment and some of the

finest session players available, but they also wanted top-notch material and a great performance from their young rising star.

As well as Presley's Sun sidemen, guitarist Scotty Moore, bassist Bill Black, and drummer D J Fontana, the session was enhanced with the estimable Chet Atkins on rhythm guitar, the nimble-fingered Floyd Cramer on piano, and members of the top-rated gospel group The Jordanaires handling back-up vocals. Elvis rose to the occasion with a smoldering echo-drenched vocal that made the most of the song's melodramatic lyric – but it didn't exactly fly off the shelves when it was released in late January. It wasn't until April 3, when Presley sang it on NBC-TV's *Milton Berle Show*, with an audience estimated at a quarter of the entire U.S. population, that 'Heartbreak Hotel' finally took off.

Three weeks later it was at Number 1 and rock'n'roll was clearly becoming not just the most significant new musical form of the decade but a rallying point for youth of whatever color or creed. Not one but three Beatles – John Lennon, Paul McCartney, and George Harrison – subsequently cited 'Heartbreak Hotel' as a profound inspiration, and Bob Dylan said: "When I first heard Elvis's voice I just knew that I wasn't going to work for anybody; and nobody was going to be my boss. ... Hearing him for the first time was like busting out of jail."

Big Mama Thornton recorded the original version of 'Hound Dog' on August 13, 1952. Written by Jerry Leiber and Mike Stoller, who would become the most successful songwriting and production team of the 1950s, the song was released in at least six versions and a couple of parodies before Elvis turned it into a massive international smash.

It was in late March 1956, during a week-long engagement at the Frontier Hotel in Las Vegas, that Elvis dropped into the lounge to watch Freddie Bell & The Bellboys. He enjoyed their humorous treatment of 'Hound Dog' so much that he decided to include it in his own act. Presley's guitarist Scotty Moore recalled: "We stole it straight from them. He already knew it, knew the song, but when we seen those guys do it, he said, 'There's a natural.' We never did it in Las Vegas, but we were just looking on it as comic relief, if you will, just another number to do onstage."

Moore's recollection is confirmed by the fact that Presley performed the song twice on national TV shows before finally recording it, somewhat reluctantly, in July. Steve Allen, host of one of the shows on which Presley performed the song, reckoned: "It was television that made Elvis's success possible. What his millions of young fans responded to was obviously not his voice but Elvis himself. His face, his body, his gyrations, his cute country-boy persona."

Not everyone responded so favorably. U.S. Congressman Emanuel Celler, for one, was horrified. "Rock'n'roll has its place among the colored people," he ranted. "The bad taste exemplified by Elvis Presley Hound Dog music, with his animal gyrations, which are certainly most distasteful to me, are violative of all that I know to be in good taste." Nevertheless, what Leiber & Stoller had knocked up in nine minutes as a country-blues for Big Mama went on, thanks to Presley's supercharged rendition, to top the U.S. chart for 11 solid weeks.

Sun Records owner Sam Phillips later told of how, during the anxious weeks before Presley's 'Heartbreak Hotel' took off, RCA's A&R guru Steve Sholes began seriously wondering if he'd bought the wrong artist from Sun. Carl Perkins's version of 'Blue Suede Shoes' was looking like a much better bet for massive success. Perkins wrote it at a relatively slow tempo, but Phillips encouraged him to speed it up for the record and changed the lyric slightly but significantly. "When he said, 'Go, man,

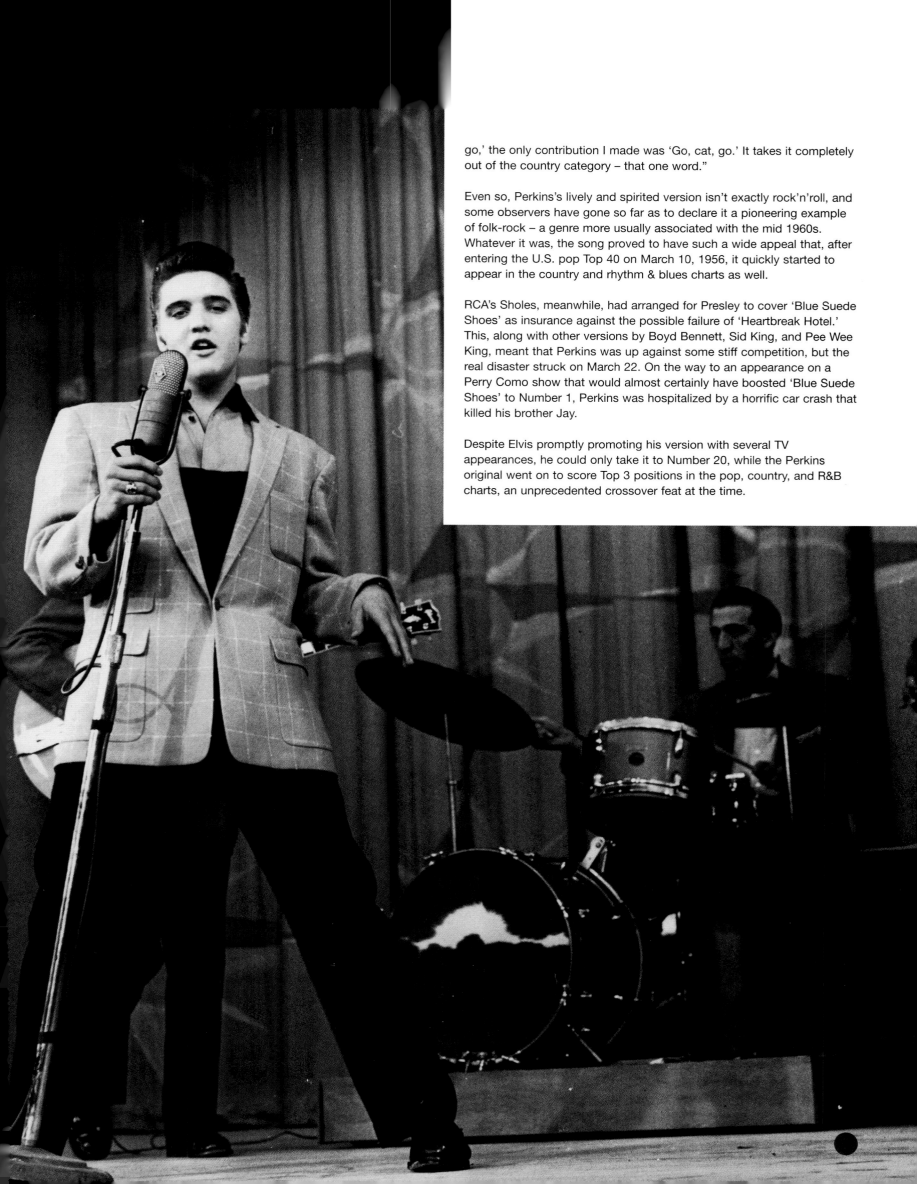

go,' the only contribution I made was 'Go, cat, go.' It takes it completely out of the country category – that one word."

Even so, Perkins's lively and spirited version isn't exactly rock'n'roll, and some observers have gone so far as to declare it a pioneering example of folk-rock – a genre more usually associated with the mid 1960s. Whatever it was, the song proved to have such a wide appeal that, after entering the U.S. pop Top 40 on March 10, 1956, it quickly started to appear in the country and rhythm & blues charts as well.

RCA's Sholes, meanwhile, had arranged for Presley to cover 'Blue Suede Shoes' as insurance against the possible failure of 'Heartbreak Hotel.' This, along with other versions by Boyd Bennett, Sid King, and Pee Wee King, meant that Perkins was up against some stiff competition, but the real disaster struck on March 22. On the way to an appearance on a Perry Como show that would almost certainly have boosted 'Blue Suede Shoes' to Number 1, Perkins was hospitalized by a horrific car crash that killed his brother Jay.

Despite Elvis promptly promoting his version with several TV appearances, he could only take it to Number 20, while the Perkins original went on to score Top 3 positions in the pop, country, and R&B charts, an unprecedented crossover feat at the time.

I Walk The Line
Johnny Cash

Released May 1956
Sun *241* (U.S. #17) / London *HL 8358* (U.K.)

Johnny Cash was the legendary Man In Black, the first 'outlaw' of country, and a member of the famous Million Dollar Quartet (Cash, Presley, Lewis, and Perkins). He auditioned for Sam Phillips at Sun Records in 1955 as part of The Tennessee Three, playing gospel. Phillips pointed out that they'd need to sing country if they wanted to succeed. Taking this on board, Cash swiftly delivered his own compositions 'Cry Cry Cry' and 'Folsom Prison Blues.' Their third single, 'I Walk The Line', released in May 1956, was the first to cross over to the pop charts. Cash had begun writing the song some years earlier when he first learned to play guitar in 1950 while stationed in Germany with the U.S. Air Force. He originally performed it as a slow ballad on the *Louisiana Hayride* TV show, but Phillips suggested speeding it up somewhat for the recording, and Cash's distinctive growl combined with some subtly clever key changes assured success. Cash stayed with Sun for three years before departing to Columbia and ultimately became an American icon. He continued to record and perform until his death in 2003, making some of his best recordings towards the end of his life, in particular the stunning, intense rendition of a Nine Inch Nails song, 'Hurt.'

Just Walkin' In The Rain
Johnnie Ray

Released August 1956
Columbia *40729* (U.S. #2) / Philips *PB 624* (U.K. #1)

They called him The Cry Guy, The Prince Of Wails, The Sultan Of Sob. All these nicknames were based on what the world considered Johnnie Ray's most remarkable feature: over-wrought, tear-jerking performances that bridged the gap between Sinatra's smooth crooning and Presley's riotous rock'n'roll. It's perhaps more remarkable, however, that Ray was practically deaf. Even wearing his hearing aid he could never hear his bass player, a disability that contributed to his unique phrasing. 'Just Walkin' In The Rain' was originally recorded by genuine Tennessee State Pen inmates The Prisonaires, in 1953, but it took Ray's trademark vocal anguish to turn it into an international sensation, topping the U.K. chart for seven weeks.

True Love
Bing Crosby & Grace Kelly

Released September 1956
Capitol *3507* (U.S. #3) / Capitol *CL 14645* (U.K. #4)

Even as rock'n'roll was eroding Tin Pan Alley's grip on the charts, this heartrendingly gorgeous Cole Porter song proved there was still plenty of life in the older generation. Crosby had sung it to Kelly in the 1954 film *High Society* so it was a natural choice for a single. Despite strong competition from blonde bombshell Jane Powell's version, Kelly and The Old Groaner scored Top 5 honors on both sides of the Atlantic, earning Bing his 21st gold disc and Kelly her first and last because, two months later, she quit the business to become Princess Grace of Monaco.

Banana Boat (Day-O)
Harry Belafonte

Released December 1956
RCA *6771* (U.S. #5) / HMV *POP 308* (U.K. #2)

Belafonte's second album, *Calypso*, spearheaded America's calypso craze in 1956. It was a bold move, a drastic switch of style from his folk-based debut, but cheap Caribbean holiday flights meant that thousands of middle-class Americans were familiar with this exotic new sound. Belafonte's timing was perfect. One track, 'Day-O,' which had been spontaneously knocked up in the studio as a filler, proved so catchy that it was released as a single, peaking at Number 5. Around the same time, the calypso 'Marianne' by The Hilltoppers reached Number 3. Before long, Ella Fitzgerald, Nat 'King' Cole, and other superstars of the era were recording calypsos. By the end of 1957, calypso accounted for a quarter of all records sold in the U.S.

Be-Bop-A-Lula
Gene Vincent & His Blue Caps

Released June 1956
Capitol *3450* (U.S. #7) / Capitol *CL 14599* (U.K. #16)

Long Tall Sally
Little Richard
Released March 1956
Speciality *572* (U.S. #6) / London *HLO 8366* (U.K. #3)

Blueberry Hill
Fats Domino
Released September 1956
Imperial *5407* (U.S. #2) / London *HLU 8330* (U.K. #6)

THE CAPITOL TOWER · HOLLYWOOD, CALIFORNIA, U.S.A.

The golden age of rock'n'roll is generally acknowledged as the period from July 1955 when 'Rock Around The Clock' hit Number 1 until Buddy Holly's death on February 3, 1959 – "the day the music died." By that time, Jerry Lee Lewis's career was in tatters, Little Richard had found religion, Chuck Berry had written his best tunes, Bill Haley was well past his sell-by date, and Elvis had joined the army. The classic year for the genre was 1956, awash with hits such as 'Blue Suede Shoes,' 'Hound Dog,' 'Tutti-Frutti,' 'See You Later Alligator,' 'Roll Over Beethoven,' and a few others that deserve a special mention.

Through the mists of time, the pedigree of 'Be-Bop-A-Lula' is difficult to see clearly. We'll stick with the legend that states that young Mr. Vincent (born Vincent Eugene Craddock) bought the song for $25 from a fellow marine while in naval hospital recovering from a motorcycle accident. He played it to 'Sheriff' Tex Davis, a DJ at WCMS, who saw some potential and coupled him with Cliff Gallup's band, and made a demo recording at the radio station.

That demo was then dispatched to Ken Nelson at Capitol Records, which was eagerly searching for its own Elvis. For his pains, Davis cut himself in as co-writer and would make off with half the royalties of what became a huge hit and a legendary recording. Capitol soon gave a positive reply, and a formal recording session was arranged at Owen Bradley's Nashville studios for May 4, 1956.

Mort Thomasson was the studio engineer responsible for the massive echo treatment on the session, when Gallup's band were officially renamed as The Blue Caps. Thomasson recalled that Vincent and his band "looked like a motorcycle gang." Unsure of their musical expertise, producer Ken Nelson had some session musicians on standby, but it quickly became apparent they wouldn't be needed. According to Thomasson: "They started playing and all hell broke loose – they didn't know nothing except to play loud and fast." Legend has it that Elvis's mum thought it was her own son when she first heard the recording on the radio.

It was a teenage girl, Enotris Johnson, who originally brought the rough lyrical idea for Little Richard's second hit to producer Robert 'Bumps' Blackwell at Specialty Records. (She also contributed to Richard's 1957 hit 'Jenny Jenny.') Many white American radio stations had refused to play 'Tutti-Frutti,' the first hit by this bizarre, black, camp figure who wore heavy make-up, loud clothes, and had his hair in a huge pompadour.

In an effort to beat Pat Boone, who'd had the bigger hit with 'Tutti Frutti,' when it came to Richard's second single, 'Long Tall Sally' (originally titled 'The Thing,' then 'Bald Headed Sally'), Blackwell encouraged him to sing the song at breakneck speed so that Boone wouldn't be able to catch the lyrics.

Boone covered the song nevertheless, but this time Richard beat him up the charts. The Beatles covered 'Long Tall Sally' and McCartney himself wrote an undisguised Little Richard-style screamer, 'I'm Down,' as the B-side of The Beatles' 1965 single 'Help!'

New Orleans-born pianist Antoine Domino was earning $3 a week playing in honky-tonks when he was spotted by Imperial Records producer Dave Bartholomew in 1949. Although not strictly a rock'n'roll artist, Fats had 60 Billboard Top 100 hits in less than ten years. But he nearly didn't record 'Blueberry Hill,' his biggest hit, at all.

Bartholomew was set against recording a song that had already been a hit several times, but fortunately for posterity Fats won the day. The song was written in 1940 for yodeling cowboy Gene Autry – who with his trusty horse Champion seemed to make his Westerns at the rate of about one per week – and was featured in Autry's 1941 movie *The Singing Hill*.

By that time the tune had already been a Number 1 hit for Glenn Miller. According to lyricist Larry Stock, a major publisher at first turned down his song because "blueberries don't grow on hills." Stock assured them they did, and since then it has been recorded by any number of artists, although there's little doubt that Fats made the definitive version.

I Put A Spell On You
Screamin' Jay Hawkins

Released November 1956
Okeh *7072* (U.S.) / Fontana *H 107* (U.K.)

Originally conceived as a simple ballad, 'I Put A Spell On You' became one of the most striking and unusual singles of the late 1950s. It is also one of the more notable banned records of the rock'n'roll era. Radio stations across the U.S. and abroad objected to Hawkins's suggestive, animalistic vocal performance and would only play a significantly edited version. Perhaps because of this, the single failed to chart on its release, but it has since become a cult classic, not to mention a favorite of compilers of scary-movie soundtracks.

This best-known version of 'I Put A Spell On You' is not, in fact, the original. Hawkins first wrote and recorded it in a more serene setting in 1949 but was encouraged by producer Arnold Maxon to update the song, with a performance more in keeping with its title. Legend has it that Hawkins and his band were drunk as skunks while recording the song, which goes some way to explain the opening half-minute of groaning and grunting. Hawkins's visceral baritone is offset effectively by a chorus of cooing backing vocalists and a spacious, bass-led arrangement.

Hawkins recorded a number of similarly maniacal follow-ups in subsequent years, although none is so well known as 'Spell' (since covered by everyone from Nina Simone to Marilyn Manson).

I'm Not A Juvenile Delinquent
Frankie Lymon & The Teenagers

Released November 1956
Gee *1026* (U.S.) / Columbia *DB 3878* (U.K. #12)

Diana
Paul Anka

Released May 1957
ABC-Paramount *9831* (U.S. #1) / Columbia *DB 3980* (U.K. #1)

Lymon's best-remembered hit is 'Why Do Fools Fall In Love,' but 'Delinquent' was easily his weirdest. With rock'n'rollers coming in for more than their share of harsh adult censure, this single was designed as a teenage counterblast. The harsh reality, however, was that fresh-faced Frankie was pimping and doing drugs on the streets of Harlem before he was 16, making him precisely what his heartfelt denial claimed he wasn't. His record label, Gee, was part-owned by Morris Levy, probably the most notorious gangster in the music business of the time. Levy used his muscle to have himself credited as the song's composer, although it was in fact written by Bobby Spencer of The Cadillacs, who would write Millie's ska novelty hit 'My Boy Lollipop.' Lymon died of a heroin overdose at the age of just 25 on April 30, 1968. Levy, meanwhile, landed ten years on extortion charges in 1988.

Unfair adult perceptions of teenage immaturity also fueled Paul Anka's lovelorn 'Diana,' the true tale of his 15-year-old lust for 20-year-old babysitter Diana Ayoub. Anka, however, was a clean-living boy signed to a reputable company, so when 'Diana' went on to sell over nine million copies worldwide and became one of the bestselling singles of all time, he was in clover. Somehow, Ayoub found the now-wealthy singer more appealing, but Anka himself was no longer smitten. In 1963, as all good rock stars should, he married a leggy blonde model in Paris, France.

Who Do You Love
Bo Diddley

Released March 1957
Checker *842* (U.S.) / Not issued U.K.

Hey! Bo Diddley
Bo Diddley

Released October 1957
Checker *860* (U.S.) / Not issued U.K.

Bo Diddley stands among the most influential early rock'n'roll performers, despite his failure to achieve the commercial success of many of his peers. After turning his back on a potentially lucrative boxing career, he signed to Checker Records in 1955 and immediately began to pile up an impressive body of work, characterized by insistent tremolo-laden guitar licks not entirely dissimilar to those of Chuck Berry.

'Who Do You Love' is set apart from a lot of Diddley's contemporary material by its shuffling drum pattern, while the call-and-response of the title's question and the instrumental answer stick in the brain long after the song has finished. It features some of Diddley's strongest and most surreal lyrics, taking in cobra snake neckties and a chimney "made out of human skull." Like many of his songs, it has been regularly covered in subsequent years, by artists including The Doors and Tom Rush. 'Hey! Bo Diddley' was just one of a number of his self-referential songs, which in a way predate a similar, widespread trend in modern rap lyrics. He began his career with the single 'Bo Diddley' in 1955 and soon followed it with titles like 'Diddley Daddy,' 'Bo's Guitar,' and 'Diddling.' It wasn't all self-love, however: another early single, 'Bring It To Jerome,' was named for one of his regular musical foils, bassist and maracas-shaker Jerome Green.

That'll Be The Day
The Crickets

Released May 1957
Brunswick *55009* (U.S. #1) / Coral Q *72279* (U.K. #1)

Oh Boy! / Not Fade Away
The Crickets

Released October 1957
Brunswick *55035* (U.S. #10) / Coral Q *72298* (U.K. #3)

A new John Wayne movie, *The Searchers*, opened at The State Theatre in Lubbock, Texas, on May 31, 1956. During its run, two local teenagers, Buddy Holly and Jerry Allison, were so taken by Wayne's catch-phrase, "That'll be the day," that they borrowed it for a song title. Two months later, having just recorded it for Decca in Nashville, Allison was crushed when the producer rubbished it as "the worst song I've ever heard in my life." Nevertheless, they persevered, investing $60 to re-record it as a demo on February 27, 1957 in Clovis, New Mexico.

Bob Thiele, a legendarily discerning A&R boss at Brunswick/Coral Records, signed them up and decided to release the demo as a single, credited to The Crickets to avoid breaching the terms of Holly's Decca contract. When Brunswick's version, pegged by *Billboard* as "medium-beat rockabilly," started to take off, Decca unearthed their version of the worst song their producer had ever heard and released it, but it was The Crickets who rocketed to Number 1 in the U.S. and U.K., where it became the first song John Lennon ever learned to play.

So prolific was Holly at this time that The Crickets' next release, 'Oh Boy,' featured a killer B-side, 'Not Fade Away,' which integrated Bo Diddley's famed hambone riff into a more accessible rock'n'roll song format. It would eventually provide the first Top 10 hit for The Rolling Stones in 1964, a debut single for Rush in 1973, and made regular appearances at Grateful Dead gigs.

Great Balls Of Fire
Jerry Lee Lewis & His Pumping Piano

Released November 1957
Sun *281* (U.S. #2) / London *HLS 8529* (U.K. #1)

There are many who believe that Jerry Lee Lewis was the true king of rock'n'roll. He certainly leads an uncompromising life, in contrast to the always demurring and polite Elvis Presley. Lewis began playing piano at age nine. His parents mortgaged their house to buy his first instrument, and legend has it that they lost their home when they couldn't meet the repayments. Expelled from preacher training college for playing hymns boogie-woogie style, he had been resident pianist at a number of brothels, and declared himself 'the greatest' long before Muhammad Ali.

Lewis had been married twice before he arrived at Sun Records for an audition in 1956, a trip financed by the sale of 33 dozen eggs. His second Sun release, 'Whole Lot Of Shakin' Goin' On,' was banned by many U.S. radio stations as obscene but sold a reputed six million copies across America.

He was something of a wild inferno both onstage and off. Kicking over his piano stool was at first an accident, but he soon incorporated it into his act. Before too long he was demanding to close the show on any tour on which he appeared, but on one memorable outing with Chuck Berry, he was forced to open the show. Setting fire to his piano as he departed,

he remarked: "I'd like to see any son of a bitch try to follow that!"

Lewis's greatest song was his third Sun single, 'Great Balls Of Fire,' which sold a million copies in its first ten days of release, but was held at Number 2 on the U.S. chart by 'At The Hop' by Danny & The Juniors. 'Great Balls Of Fire' was written by Otis Blackwell and the aptly named Jack Hammer, whose sole contribution amounted to the title itself. Blackwell wrote a number of key rock'n'roll anthems including 'All Shook Up,' 'Don't Be Cruel,' and 'Return To Sender' for Elvis, 'Handy Man' for Jimmy Jones, and 'Fever' for Little Willie John.

Jerry Lee's career plummeted in the wake of bad publicity following the revelation that he had married his 13-year-old cousin Myra. Although such marriages weren't uncommon in the American South, Lewis was on tour in Britain when the news broke, and the U.K. papers voiced their outrage. A 37-date tour was canceled after just three engagements, and Lewis returned to the U.S., his career in shreds. It took the best part of ten years for him to get back on track.

Relentlessly living up to the sex and drugs and rock'n'roll lifestyle, Lewis has been on the critical list on a number of occasions. Following emergency surgery for a ruptured stomach ulcer in 1981, he was given a 50-50 chance of survival. On leaving hospital his immediate response was to buy a new customized Cadillac, a big cigar, and a bottle of his favorite whiskey, claiming: "As long as they gimme a piano I'll be out there. They try to take that away, I'm gonna kick some ass."

Peggy Sue
Buddy Holly

Released September 1957
Coral *61885* (U.S. #3) / Coral Q *72293* (U.K. #6)

Can a song change the course of events in the real world? Of course it can. This Holly classic started life as 'Cindy Lou' in honor of Buddy's niece, but Crickets' drummer Jerry Allison, who had recently broken up with his girlfriend, Peggy Sue Gerron, suggested the name-change as a way of getting back into her good books.

Probably the best-remembered song in Holly's catalogue, 'Peggy Sue' was recorded on July 1, 1957, at producer Norman Petty's studio in Clovis, New Mexico. When the session kicked off, the backing had a calypso feel, not unlike Harry Belafonte's then-popular 'Banana Boat (Day-O),' but it just wasn't working.

When Allison was asked to play a consistently rolling paradiddle, which he did on a snare drum with the snares turned off, the song took on a dynamic rock'n'roll aspect, which Holly intensified by playing his rhythm guitar part entirely with speedy downstrokes. The result was a song of unusually propulsive, throbbing intensity that soared to Number 3 in the U.S. and Number 6 in Britain.

It also had the desired effect of bringing Allison and Peggy Sue together again – so effectively that they eloped on July 22, 1958, to Honey Grove, Texas, and got married. That might have been the end of it had Holly's father not suggested that there might be some mileage in writing a sequel. Buddy agreed and recorded 'Peggy Sue Got Married' on December 5 in his New York City apartment. Released as a single after Holly's tragic death, it reached Number 13 in Britain.

I'm Walking / A Teenager's Romance
Ricky Nelson

Released April 1957
Verve *10047* (U.S. #2) / HMV *POP 355* (U.K.)

Ricky Nelson was the first teen pop star created by a television series. Many would follow in his footsteps, notably The Monkees in the 1960s and David Cassidy in the '70s. Nelson had played himself in his parents' radio and TV sitcom *The Adventures Of Ozzie And Harriet* since 1949. Spotted there by famed jazz guitarist and Verve A&R chief Barney

Kessel, he was wheeled in for a recording session where Kessel suggested a cover of Fats Domino's recent hit 'I'm Walking' coupled with the custom-written throwaway 'A Teenager's Romance.'

Nelson's version of 'I'm Walking' got national TV exposure when he performed it on the family show and swiftly flew up the charts. When the song peaked, radio stations began playing the other side, which rose even higher. Nelson recorded one further single for Verve, but the lack of a binding contract coupled with the company's reluctance to cough up royalties resulted in a move to Imperial. Nelson's career really took off and he enjoyed an impressive run of hits until 1964.

At The Hop
Danny & The Juniors

Released November 1957
ABC-Paramount *9871* (U.S. #1) / HMV *POP 436* (U.K. #3)

Danny Rapp first put together his Philadelphia high-school group in 1955 as The Juvenairs. Philly was the home of America's most influential television show of the period, *American Bandstand*, which Dick Clark began hosting for WFIL-TV in 1956. Clark became an extremely powerful man in American popular music, although he skillfully managed to avoid the payola scandal of the early 1960s that ruined DJ Alan Freed. Producer Arthur Singer took a song called 'Do The Bop' to Clark, who suggested a change of title since the bop dance craze was on the wane. Duly re-titled, 'At The Hop' sold 7,000 copies in Philadelphia when first released by Danny & The Juniors on Singer's local Singular label and was soon picked up for national distribution by ABC-Paramount. The final piece of the puzzle fell into place when another group failed to turn up for *Bandstand* and Danny & the Juniors hopped in at the last moment.

Mr. Lee
The Bobbettes

Released June 1957
Atlantic *1144* (U.S. #6) / London *HLE 8477* (U.K.)

Maybe
The Chantels

Released December 1957
End *1005* (U.S. #15) / London *HLU 8561* (U.K.)

The Shirelles, who ascended to the U.S. Number 1 slot in 1961 with Carole King's 'Will You Love Me Tomorrow,' are now usually thought of as the starters of the girl-group sound. So where does that leave New York's Bobbettes, who made their U.S. Top 40 chart debut with 'Mr. Lee' on August 12, 1957? As the first all-female doo-wop group to hit Number 1 on the rhythm & blues chart, they surely deserve some kind of recognition.

They were followed almost immediately by another all-female quintet, The Chantels, who recorded 'Maybe' in a disused Manhattan church to take advantage of the building's superb acoustics. It worked, and 'Maybe' hit Number 15 on the national charts and Number 2 on the R&B chart. The Shirelles paved the way, but only after The Bobbettes and The Chantels had blazed the trail.

CHARTING THE BESTSELLING SINGLES

Record charts have been around for more than 60 years and are always a source of fascination for music fans, but they exist primarily as a tool for the music industry. *Billboard* began life as a magazine for the advertisement-hoarding industry and then turned to show business in the broadest sense, including circuses and carnivals. In the 1930s, however, it started to concentrate on music, encouraged by jukebox manufacturers, who became important advertisers.

In 1936, *Billboard* introduced the ancestor of the modern pop chart when it created a list of the songs most commonly played on three major radio stations. Earlier in the century, the music publishers who were *Billboard*'s customers had been ambivalent about radio, fearing it would destroy home performance and the associated sheet-music market. But they were already earning money from so-called 'mechanicals,' meaning fees for the reproduction of songs on player-pianos, cylinders, records, and jukeboxes, and from public performances. They soon realized that radio had huge potential for promoting both sheet music and record sales.

As a result, the music publishers changed from opposing the playing of their songs on radio to promoting the idea, through a network of 'pluggers' who were paid according to the number of plays their songs achieved. The new chart assisted those pluggers as well as the record shops, which could now stock the popular discs of the day.

By 1940, however, the magazine realized that records were now the most important means of selling publishers' wares. So in July that year *Billboard* introduced its Music Popularity Chart. This brought together existing charts of 'Records most popular on music machines' (jukeboxes, in other words), 'Sheet Music Best Sellers,' an alphabetical list of 'Songs With Most Radio Plugs,' and a new chart of 'Best selling retail records' based on a survey of stores around the U.S. The various charts reflected the way the interest of the readership continued to be

split between sheet music and records. In 1945, *Billboard* introduced its Honor Roll Of Hits, which combined both elements in an attempt to discover "the nation's top 10 tunes." The record sales chart dominated, however, and in 1958 it formed the basis of the celebrated Hot 100 singles chart, although that has always combined record sales with radio airplay. Over the years, the number of charts expanded, to reflect different genres. Most importantly, the first chart of black music, the Harlem Hit Parade, based on sales in that New York district, was introduced in 1942. In 1945 its name was changed to Race Records, finally becoming Rhythm & Blues in 1949. It would retain that name until the late 1960s. Country, meanwhile, made its *Billboard* debut in a jukebox chart of 'Folk Records' in 1944. The magazine currently features charts for R&B, country, Latin, Christian, dance, rock, adult contemporary, international, and others, including digital and cell-phone downloads.

Billboard charts were never the only charts. *Cash Box*, another American trade magazine, offered its own versions, which had a slightly different methodology and consequently gave different results. The trades produced geographical charts, but there were also local charts, compiled by small record stores or based on radio-station plays. These often showed quite different patterns of popularity than the national charts and allowed artists to claim local hits. For instance, the first Beach Boys single, 'Surfin',' reached Number 2 in the Los Angeles area when originally released on the tiny Candix label and enabled them to secure a deal with Capitol, a major label.

In the U.K., charts began with the *New Musical Express*'s Top Twelve, in 1952. A survey of only 20 shops at the beginning, it became the Top Twenty in 1954, and spawned imitators from *Melody Maker*, *Record Mirror*, and *Disc*. For the trade market, *Record Retailer* started a Top 50 in 1960. The BBC's chart began as a combination of the charts published by the consumer magazines, but from 1969 it employed the British Market Research Bureau to compile what is now the pre-eminent chart in Britain.

Jailhouse Rock
Elvis Presley

Released September 1957
RCA *47-7035* (U.S. #1) / RCA *1028* (U.K. #1)

Jerry Leiber and Mike Stoller were commissioned to write two songs for Presley's second movie, *Loving You* (1957). Later that year, they gravitated to writing and producing the entire score for his next movie, *Jailhouse Rock*, and for a brief period their names became synonymous with that of the king.

Although *Jailhouse Rock* is considered by many as the high water mark of Presley's generally disappointing movie career, Jerry Leiber, tasked with writing the words of the songs that would accompany the movie's action, was not impressed by the script. However, Leiber had got used to looking for a nugget within Presley's film vehicles that would allow him to do something exciting. Sometimes this involved turning a scenario on its head.

Leiber found a scene where a song was prescribed and which he thought ridiculously feeble for a prison setting, so instead he delivered 'Jailhouse Rock,' fully expecting the producers to reject it. Instead he was rewarded with such a positive response that the song became the title track of the movie.

To partner Stoller's melody, Leiber provided a lyric depicting a prison playing host to a wild party. There was even a slight hint of homosexual activity in the couplet: "Number 47 said to number 3 / You're the cutest jailbird I ever did see." Presley meanwhile contributed a typically committed vocal to a stop-start backing, where the walking bassline was a highpoint. In the relevant sequence of the movie Presley provided some accompanying choreography – shimmying in prison stripes and sliding down a pole – that has become indelibly associated with the song.

LEIBER & STOLLER: IS THAT ALL THERE IS?

Jerry Leiber and Mike Stoller were the first important non-performing songwriters of the rock era. Leiber has always provided lyrics and Stoller the melodies to their songs. Precociously gifted, they were still in their teens when their compositions were recorded by Jimmy Witherspoon and The Robins. By 1952, Stoller had become bored with generic blues and insisted on a more specific melody for 'Kansas City,' originally recorded by Little Willie Littlefield as 'K.C. Lovin" but which would go on to be covered by more than a hundred artists, including Wilbert Harrison (who hit the top in the U.S. with the song in 1959), Little Richard, and The Beatles.

Leiber & Stoller's lives were changed by accident. Their song 'Hound Dog' – a 12-bar diatribe against a feckless man – had been a hit on the rhythm & blues charts in 1953 for Big Mama Thornton. In 1956 it was covered by a white singer they'd never heard of – one Elvis Presley. The pair found Presley's bowdlerized version laughable, but did not object to the fame and the money that his transatlantic smash earned them. They would provide Presley with many songs over the next few years, including some of his best known: 'Loving You,' 'Jailhouse Rock,' 'Trouble,' 'King Creole,' and 'Baby I Don't Care.' They got on well with Presley but the relationship foundered in a business wrangle with his manager Tom Parker.

The pair's stream of records for black vocal-group The Coasters, meanwhile, saw them employing narratives, comic-book imagery, and funny voices to create records unique for the era, including 'Searchin',' 'Young Blood,' 'Yakety Yak,' 'Charlie Brown,' 'Along Came Jones,' and 'Poison Ivy.' Another song intended for The Coasters was 'Love Potion No. 9,' but instead it was given as a favor to a similar group, The Clovers.

They didn't write much for The Drifters, but 'There Goes My Baby' was not only a U.S. Number 2 but also massively influential for two things never heard before on a rhythm & blues or rock recording: classical strings and Latin rhythms. They also hit big with ex-Drifters vocalist Ben E. King in 1961. But their productivity declined when they set up their own Red Bird label in 1963, leaving them burdened by administration.

After selling the label three years later they were never the same force again, but remained in demand as producers and songwriters. 'Is That All There Is' was a spoken-word hit for Peggy Lee influenced by Kurt Weill and Bertolt Brecht. 'Pearl's A Singer' saw them rewrite an old song for Elkie Brooks to create a 1977 Top 10 U.K. hit. In 1995, delivering 'The Girls I Never Kissed' to Frank Sinatra, they provided material to just about the only major artist who had never recorded one of their songs.

Catch A Falling Star / Magic Moments
Perry Como

Released January 1958
RCA 7128 (U.S. #1) / RCA 1036 (U.K. #1)

This was a double-sided hit, and while 'Catch A Falling Star' was the chart-topper in America, in Britain it was 'Magic Moments' that spent eight weeks at the top. Former barber and king of laidback, Pierino Como had been singing with bands since 1933 and signed with RCA in '43. 'Magic Moments' is of particular significance since it was one of the first hits written by Burt Bacharach and Hal David. In fact their very first hit, 'The Story Of My Life,' a U.S. hit for Marty Robbins, was a U.K. Number 1 for Michael Holliday the week before 'Magic Moments.' Meanwhile, 'Catch A Falling Star' won the first ever official Gold Disc for sales of one million copies and a Grammy for Best Male Vocal Performance. (RCA first dreamed up the Gold Disc idea as a gimmick, in 1940, awarding one to Glenn Miller for 'Chattanooga Choo Choo.') Como enjoyed something of a revival in the early 1970s covering contemporary material such as Don McLean's 'And I Love You So,' by which time he'd racked up an impressive 150 U.S. chart entries.

Tom Hark
Elias & His Zigzag Jive Flutes

Released March 1958
Not issued U.S. / Columbia DB 4109 (U.K.)

The influence on pop of black American music – jazz, blues, rhythm & blues – is well documented. Caribbean calypso and South American cha-cha also had a big effect on the 1950s charts, but the influence of Africa itself is often overlooked. The Weavers, for example, had taken the Zulu folk song 'Wimoweh' into the U.S. charts in 1952. 'Tom Hark' was a much more authentic proposition. Elias and his Flutes were a proper kwela band made up of buskers from the streets of Johannesburg, South Africa, and led by penny-whistle virtuoso Big Voice Jack Lerole. Remarkably, such effervescent, high-pitched, rhythmically-driven music would not gain international acclaim until Paul Simon included kwela musicians on his 1986 album Graceland.

Witch Doctor
David Seville

Released March 1958
Liberty 55132 (U.S. #1) / London HLU 8619 (U.K. #11)

The Purple People Eater
Sheb Wooley

Released May 1958
MGM 12651 (U.S. #1) / MGM 981 (U.K. #12)

Les Paul had been doing it with his guitar for years, but when David Seville decided to use the studio's tape recorder to speed up his vocals, he unwittingly established a new musical sub-genre. Seville's humorous song, with its unforgettable hook, "Oo-ee-ooh-ah-ah ting-tang walla-walla-bing-bang," used the speeding-up technique to create the weird

voice of 'Witch Doctor' and land him a Number 1 smash. Before long, singing cowboy Sheb Wooley rehashed the idea for the alien voices in his Number 1, 'The Purple People Eater,' and The Chipmunks, another Seville creation, topped the chart in December. The U.K.'s singing piglet puppets, Pinky & Perky, also found success with the technique, which remains a staple of novelty discs even now.

Return To Me
Dean Martin

Released March 1958
Capitol 3894 (U.S. #4) / Capitol CL 14844 (U.K. #2)

Former shoeshine boy, casino croupier, and amateur boxer Dino Paul Crocetti first found gainful employment as a singer in 1941. Five years later he teamed up with comedian Jerry Lewis for one of the most successful entertainment partnerships in U.S. history. In 1957 the pair broke up somewhat acrimoniously and Martin stepped out alone, introducing his new 'drunk' persona. Many thought he wouldn't make it on his own, but he proved them all wrong with a highly successful film and recording career. 'Return To Me' was co-written by bandleader Guy Lombardo's brother Carmen in 1957 and first recorded by Guy's Orchestra with vocals by Don Rodney, but became Martin's first hit after the split with Lewis. Dean Martin was Elvis Presley's favorite vocalist, and according to author Peter Guralnick, Elvis purchased a copy of this very record the week before he enlisted in the U.S. Army.

All I Have To Do Is Dream / Claudette
The Everly Brothers

Released April 1958
Cadence 1348 (U.S. #1) / London HLA 8618 (U.K. #1)

The Everly Brothers were one of the pivotal acts in popular music history. Don Everly (born 1937) and Phil Everly (1939) grew up in a musical family and made their first performance on their parents' radio show when Don was eight and Phil just six. Their close-harmony country-rock became an enormous influence on the wave of artists who found fame in the 1960s. A teenage Paul McCartney bought all the Everlys singles as soon as they were released, and Bob Dylan was a staunch Everlys fan. Dylan said: "We owe those guys everything. They started it all."

They got their record deal through an introduction by family friend and Nashville heavyweight Chet Atkins, coupling the duo with husband-and-wife songwriting team Felice and Boudleaux Bryant. The combination was to become one of the most successful in pop music history. The Bryants were by no means teenagers – Boudleaux was born in 1920, Felice in 1925. The couple met and married in 1945, at which point

Boudleaux began putting music to Felice's poems, and one of Nashville's most successful songwriting partnerships was born. The first song the Bryants presented to the Everlys was 'Bye Bye Love,' one that had already been given the thumbs-down by everyone in Nashville, including Elvis Presley.

Although the Everlys had been signed as a country act, Atkins gave them more of a rock'n'roll sound coupled with those close-harmony vocals. This combination proved to be the perfect vehicle for the brothers, and 'Bye Bye Love' became a huge international hit. The Bryants followed up with a string of gems including 'Wake Up Little Susie' and 'All I Have To Do Is Dream,' which Boudleaux claims was written in 15 minutes. 'Dream' became the duo's best loved song and their biggest seller, topping the charts on both sides of the Atlantic. It was also a double-sided hit, marking Roy Orbison's arrival as a hit songwriter with 'Claudette,' written for his wife. Orbison had recorded the song a couple of years previously while at Sun Records but it had not been released.

Fever
Peggy Lee

Released July 1958
Capitol 3998 (U.S. #8) / Capitol CL 14902 (U.K. #5)

'Fever' was Peggy Lee's crowning achievement – almost two decades into her singing career – and remains one of the definitive moments in late-1950s swing. Lee was notable during the decade as one of the few female singers who contributed to her own material. She co-wrote 'Mañana (Is Soon Enough For Me),' which was later a hit for Dean Martin, and 'He's A Tramp,' as featured in Disney's *Lady And The Tramp*.

'Fever,' however, was not one of Lee's own compositions. It was written in 1956 by Eddie Cooley and Otis Blackwell, although at the time Blackwell took the more 'white sounding' name of his stepfather, John Davenport, most likely to avoid any potential racial prejudice. His other writing credits – as Davenport – include the Elvis Presley hits 'All Shook Up' and 'Don't Be Cruel,' and Jerry Lee Lewis's 'Great Balls Of Fire.'

'Fever' was a hit first for Little Willie John in a more straightforward rock'n'roll setting. Lee made the song her own by adapting the lyrics, suggesting the slower, jazzier arrangement, and offering up a typically sultry vocal performance. None of the subsequent cover versions – by artists including Madonna and Ella Fitzgerald – have come close to Lee's.

Tom Dooley
The Kingston Trio

Released August 1958
Capitol 4049 (U.S. #1) / Capitol CL 14951 (U.K. #5)

This deftly modernized Blue Ridge Mountains ballad was based on the exploits of Tom Dula, hanged for murder in 1868, and it changed America's folk-music scene forever. What had been a determinedly purist, avowedly non-commercial, left-wing liberal ferment was suddenly represented at Number 1 in the pop charts by The Kingston Trio. Few denied their artistry, but to be this successful approached heresy. Because of The Kingston Trio, the next generation of folkies, including Joan Baez and Bob Dylan, and folk-rockers like The Byrds and The Band, knew that their music could resound beyond the basket-houses of Cambridge, Massachusetts, and New York City's Greenwich Village. Folk music was now, officially, big business.

Smoke Gets In Your Eyes
The Platters

Released November 1958
Mercury 71383 (U.S. #1) / Mercury AMT 1016 (U.K. #1)

This timelessly beautiful Otto Harbach-Jerome Kern standard first became a Number 1 hit for Paul Whiteman's Orchestra back in 1934. It would score again for Bryan Ferry in 1974 and John Alford in 1996, but few would dispute that The Platters created the definitive recording.

The group had chosen the song against the advice of Mercury Records boss Art Talmadge, who thought they needed contemporary material, and they faced an injunction from Jerome Kern's widow who tried to prevent them releasing it. But in the end, quality won out and The Platters' immaculately serene rendition scored a Number 1 on both sides of the Atlantic.

Rumble
Link Wray & His Ray Men

Released April 1958
Cadence *1347* (U.S. #16) / London *HLA 8623* (U.K.)

One of the great debut singles of the 1950s, 'Rumble' inaugurated a pioneering guitar style that went on to influence everything from blues-rock to heavy metal. If anybody can lay claim to inventing the power chord – that distorted beast so prevalent in rhythm guitar playing ever since – then it's Link Wray. No less an authority than Pete Towshend of The Who admitted: "If it hadn't been for Link Wray and 'Rumble' I would never have picked up a guitar."

'Rumble' is dominated by Wray's dirty, thick guitar chords, which gradually deteriorate into a soup of tremolo effects as the song moves to its conclusion, underpinned by the unfussy playing of his drumming brother Doug and bassist Shorty Horton. 'Rumble' reached Number 16 in the U.S. chart on its release but ended up as the trio's only recording for the Cadence label.

The song's title, inspired by the fight scenes in *West Side Story*, was taken by many to be an incitement to teenage violence. Bowing to pressure, Cadence boss Archie Bleyer asked the group to clean up its act and work with The Everly Brothers' producers in Nashville. Wray refused and moved to Epic Records, but he would never again record anything that matched the power of 'Rumble.'

Although his career dwindled through the next three decades, Wray enjoyed a resurgence of interest after 'Rumble' was included in the beyond-cool soundtrack to Quentin Tarantino's *Pulp Fiction* movie, but even then found himself overshadowed by another guitar instrumental used in the same film, Dick Dale's surf classic 'Miserlou.'

Johnny B. Goode
Chuck Berry

Released April 1958
Chess *1691* (U.S. #8) / London American *HLM 8629* (U.K.)

Chuck Berry's songs have been an unparalleled influence upon pop musicians of the last 45 years. While Bill Haley and Elvis changed the music, it was artists such as Berry and Buddy Holly who inspired the beat bands of the 1960s to write their own songs.

Berry was once called "the folk poet of the 1950s" but there have been some recent attempts to show that at least some of the classic songs credited to him were partially written by his pianist, Johnnie Johnson. However, a 2002 judgment dismissed any claim that Johnson might have had, principally because he waited some 35 years to stake his claim in the construction of these seminal tunes, over 30 of which Johnson claimed that he and Berry had created together.

'Johnny B. Goode' was recorded on February 28, 1958, and was allegedly written by Berry in honor of Johnson, although it was mostly about himself. In his autobiography Berry says: "I'd guess my mother has as much right to be declared the source of 'Johnny B. Goode' as any other contender in that she was the one that repeatedly commented that I would be a millionaire someday." 'Goode' was a reference to Goode Street, the street on which Berry grew up. The song has

become the most covered in Berry's extensive catalogue – and could well be one of the first songs from our planet that alien beings will hear. It was dispatched on copper disc upon the Voyager probe launched into outer space in 1977. Remarkably, Berry only ever had one Number 1 record throughout his career, the abysmal 'My Ding-A-Ling,' a transatlantic chart-topper in 1972 filled with double entendres that, purely from a historical perspective, somewhat detracts from the man's unique contribution to popular music.

Summertime Blues
Eddie Cochran

Released June 1958
Liberty *55144* (U.S. #8) / London *HLU 8702* (U.K. #18)

Cochran is not often remembered as one of the great stars of rock'n'roll, mainly because of his brief career, but nonetheless he left us with some classic songs of the genre. Following a couple of hillbilly singles in 1955, he teamed with songwriter Jerry Capehart and together they wrote most of his biggest hits. Like many of the best songs of the rock'n'roll era, 'Summertime Blues' was a success thanks to its simplicity and honesty. Together with his other major hit, 'C'mon Everybody,' it celebrated teenage life – the parties, the music, the cars, and the rebellion against increasingly uncomprehending parents.

Cochran and Capehart had been working on 'Summertime Blues' for some time before recording the song in May 1958. It was originally intended only as a B-side to an A composed by Sharon Sheeley, 'Love Again.' Sheeley, a teenage songwriter, later became Cochran's girlfriend and had just written Ricky Nelson's American Number 1, 'Poor Little Fool.' She and Cochran wrote another of his best songs, 'Somethin' Else,' later covered by Tom Petty, Showaddywaddy, and The Sex Pistols. However, it was in 'Summertime Blues' that Cochran found his trademark style, and as an A-side it became his biggest hit, reaching the Top 20 in both America and Britain and turning Cochran into an overnight star.

Move It
Cliff Richard

Released August 1958
Not issued U.S. / Columbia *DB 4178* (U.K. #2)

Rock'n'roll was an exclusively American phenomenon until September 12, 1958, when Cliff Richard entered the U.K. charts with 'Move It.'

A former member of the Dick Teague Skiffle Group, Cliff had switched to rock'n'roll after hearing Elvis Presley. By the middle of 1958, he and his band The Drifters (later renamed The Shadows) were playing regularly at London's hip 2Is coffee bar. They were snapped up by EMI Records, on the prowl for homegrown rock'n'roll talent. Their first single was to be 'Schoolboy Crush,' but they had no B-side until Cliff's guitarist Ian Samwell, infuriated by a smug feature in U.K. music weekly *Melody Maker* predicting the imminent demise of rock'n'roll, poured his righteous rage into a song, 'Move It.'

Samwell started by trying to imitate a Chuck Berry-style riff. "I came up with this little introduction," he said, "and then the words just popped into my head – 'C'mon pretty baby, let's a-move it and a-groove it' –

deliberately making it as American as possible. Remember, people in Britain simply didn't call each other 'baby' back then, and moving it and grooving it was considered positively obscene."

Released as the B-side of 'Schoolboy Crush' on EMI's Columbia label, the song was only switched over when TV producer Jack Good refused to allow Cliff to sing the A-side on his show, *Oh Boy!*. Good wanted 'Move It' or nothing – and the British public agreed with him, sending the single to Number 2. After Cliff, the floodgates opened, and by the mid 1960s British rock ruled the world.

To Know Him Is To Love Him
The Teddy Bears

Released September 1958
Dore *503* (U.S. #1) / London *HLN 8733* (U.K. #2)

Phil Spector bought his first guitar after hearing British skiffle star Lonnie Donegan sing the old Huddie Ledbetter song 'Rock Island Line' and started his first band, The Sleepwalkers, at Hollywood's Fairfax High. He was barely 18 when he composed 'To Know Him Is To Love Him' for his next combo, The Teddy Bears. The song was somewhat morbidly inspired by the inscription on his father's tombstone and became a hit right out of the box, securing the top spot on December 1, 1958. The group never had another hit, but Spector moved into production, created the Wall Of Sound, and masterminded the careers of The Ronettes, The Crystals, and many more.

Lonely Teardrops
Jackie Wilson

Released November 1958
Brunswick *55105* (U.S. #7) / Coral *Q 72347* (U.K.)

Night
Jackie Wilson

Released February 1960
Brunswick *55166* (U.S. #4) / Not issued U.K.

Jackie Wilson was based in Detroit but his first success came in Britain when the vibrant 'Reet Petite,' written by Motown founder Berry Gordy, reached Number 6 there late in 1957. However, Wilson's follow-ups didn't click with the Brits, but his luck held when another Gordy composition, the calypso-doowop-gospel styled 'Lonely Teardrops,' secured his first U.S. Top 10 placing.

In his autobiography, *To Be Loved*, Gordy recounted the song's origins. "I created a story about a guy crying, begging a lost love to come back. I started with 'My eyes are crying lonely teardrops.' I liked it, but not exactly. Too common. I changed 'My eyes are crying' to 'My heart is crying.' I liked it."

So did the American public, who bought over a million copies, keeping it at Number 1 in the R&B chart for seven weeks. After that, Wilson could do no wrong, notching up a further 20 hits by the end of the 1960s. The biggest of these was 'Night,' peaking at Number 4 in April 1960. Given that the U.K. had dried up on Wilson, it might seem curious that 'Night,' an obviously commercial proposition, was never released there. The reason? Wilson's U.K. label, Coral, apparently reasoned that the British

public might disapprove of a pop song based on the aria 'My Heart At Thy Sweet Voice' from the Saint-Saens' opera *Samson & Delilah*. Wilson's luck hadn't quite run out, however, because when his American hits dried up in 1968, Britain came on stream again, giving him major triumphs with 'Higher And Higher' and 'I Get The Sweetest Feeling.'

Donna / La Bamba
Ritchie Valens

Released November 1958
Del-Fi *4110* (U.S. #2) / London *HL 8803* (U.K. #29)

It Doesn't Matter Anymore
Buddy Holly

Released January 1959
Coral *62074* (U.S. #13) / Coral *Q 72360* (U.K. #1)

As with Bill Haley's 'Rock Around The Clock' and Cliff Richard's 'Move It,' Richie Valens's seminal rocker 'La Bamba' was tucked away on a B-side. The A-side was a nicely crafted affirmation of undying love for his girlfriend Donna Ludwig and did well, reaching Number 2 in the *Billboard* chart, but it was ultimately eclipsed by a rocked-up Mexican folk tune.

Valens was reluctant even to record 'La Bamba,' fearing that the all-important white audience wouldn't understand the lyrics, which were entirely in Spanish. Underpinned by the throb of an unusual and relatively new instrument, the electric bass, 'La Bamba' thrashed along with a rock'n'roll spirit – and one that inspired songwriter Bert Berns to re-shape it, with English lyrics, as 'Twist And Shout.' A significant hit for The Isley Brothers and The Beatles, Berns's song became a staple live number for virtually every 1960s beat group. 'La Bamba' itself would hit Number 1 as the title song for a 1987 Valens biopic.

Buddy Holly was so struck by the Paul Anka-composed 'It Doesn't Matter Anymore' that he recorded it on the day he first heard it, October 21, 1958. It would bring him his first British chart topper but, tragically, he and Valens both died in a plane crash on February 3, 1959, so neither saw the fruits of their final works. The following day, delivery boy Don McLean cut open a bundle of newspapers in New Rochelle, New York, and was heartbroken to read of Holly's death. Years later, in 'American Pie,' he would immortalize that crash as "the day the music died."

1959

There Goes My Baby
The Drifters

Released April 1959
Atlantic *2025* (U.S. #2) / London *HLE 8892* (U.K.)

Shout
The Isley Brothers

Released August 1959
RCA *7588* (U.S.) / RCA *1149* (U.K.)

The Drifters' first hit had Ben E. King on lead vocals and Jerry Leiber and Mike Stoller as producers, and was a landmark in the development of popular music. King composed 'There Goes My Baby' and brought it to a session, but lead vocalist Charlie Thomas wasn't getting it. So King stepped up to the mic and delivered an impeccable performance.

Leiber & Stoller, keen not to simply replicate the hit-making formula they had used with The Coasters, saw The Drifters as a more sophisticated project and introduced a swaying Brazilian baion rhythm and an elegantly swirling string section. As Carole King later observed: "It had the guts of R&B and the 'head' of classical music." Rhythm & blues was now firmly on the road to becoming soul.

'Shout' by The Isley Brothers was a much less sophisticated proposition but proved equally important in shaping the future of R&B. During a rousing rendition of Jackie Wilson's 'Lonely Teardrops' in Washington, D.C., one of the Isleys threw in the line: "You know you make me want to shout." The crowd shouted back so enthusiastically that they decided to build that line into a blockbuster audience-response song.

When Ernie Maresca secured a Top 10 smash in April 1962 with 'Shout! Shout! (Knock Yourself Out)' the Isleys saw an opportunity to revive Bert Berns's composition 'Twist And Shout,' which had been a minor hit for The Top Notes during the early-1960s twist craze. By the time The Beatles took it to a U.S. Number 2 in 1964, the merger of rock'n'roll and R&B was official.

above > Clockwise from top left: Zeke Carey, Terry Johnson, Nate Nelson, Jake Carey, and Paul Wilson of The Flamingos c. 1960.
left > Left to right: Ben E. King, Charlie Thomas, Dock Green, and Elsbearry Hobbs of The Drifters.

I Only Have Eyes For You
The Flamingos

Released April 1959
End *1046* (U.S. #11) / Top Rank *JAR 263* (U.K.)

'I Only Have Eyes For You' remains one of the most memorable hits of the doo-wop era and, like much of The Flamingos' catalogue, was a clear influence on the Motown Sound of the 1960s.

The Flamingos formed around cousins Jake and Zeke Carey, who in 1950 relocated from Baltimore to Chicago, where they met fellow choristers Paul Wilson and Johnny Carter, and later lead vocalist Sollie McElroy. After recording several unsuccessful singles for the Chance label, the group signed to Checker, scoring their first hits in 1956 with 'I'll Be Home' and 'A Kiss From Your Lips.' That year they also starred in the *Rock, Rock, Rock* movie and performed with Bill Haley and The Platters as part of the first racially-integrated rock'n'roll tour.

By this stage, as well as being tremendous vocalists, The Flamingos had become accomplished musicians and honed their onstage dance routines in the manner of 1960s groups like The Temptations. Their success was soon put on hold, however: there were contractual wrangles with Checker, and Jake Carey and Johnny Carter were called up for military service. Carey returned to the group in 1958, but Carter made a clean break and joined another vocal group, The Dells.

In late 1958 The Flamingos signed to End Records and hit their commercial and artistic peak, first with 'Lovers Never Say Goodbye' and then 'I Only Have Eyes For You.' Originally recorded by bandleader Eddy Duchin in 1934, the song soared into the upper reaches of the chart on the strength of its warm, ethereal backing vocals, the gently nagging, piano-led arrangement, and, most importantly, McElroy's lilting lead vocal about a love that "must be a kind of blind love."

Peter Gunn
Duane Eddy

Released March 1959
Jamie *1122* (U.S. B-side; A #27) / London *HLW 8879* (U.K #6)

Duane Eddy began playing guitar when he was five years old, had his first hit in 1958 with 'Rebel Rouser,' and became one of the most successful instrumental artists in pop history. His famous 'twangy' guitar sound was inspired by Bill Justis's 1957 hit 'Raunchy.' Eddy's sound came from his habit of playing lead on the bass strings of his Gretsch guitar, aided by the studio expertise of producer Lee Hazlewood, including a novel 'drainpipe' echo chamber.

'Peter Gunn' was written by Henry Mancini for the late-1950s American TV detective series of the same name and was originally a U.S. hit for the Ray Anthony Orchestra. Eddy's recording was originally released in the U.S. as the B-side of his 1959 Top 30 hit 'Yep!', although in Britain it was flipped and 'Peter Gunn' became his first Top 10 hit. Eddy recorded most of his hits with Lee Hazlewood's band, including top-notch session musicians Larry Knechtel (organ, bass) and Jim Horn (saxophone), later full-time members of Phil Spector's so-called Wrecking Crew. 'Peter Gunn' was reissued in America as an A-side and made number 27 in 1960. Eddy was invited to record the tune again in 1986 with London studio band Art Of Noise when it reached number 8. Shortly after this he recorded a comeback album produced by ELO leader Jeff Lynne and with guest appearances by Eddy fans Ry Cooder, Paul McCartney, and George Harrison.

Quiet Village
Martin Denny

Released early 1959
Liberty *55162* (U.S. #4) / London *HLU 8860* (U.K.)

Denny's instrumental hit is the best known 'exotica' record, a genre that resists easy definition. It imagines what Polynesian, Afro-Caribbean, and Hawaiian music might sound like, and caught the attention of a newly-affluent American middle-class beginning to warm to the idea of foreign travel. But it was not in any sense the real music of those cultures. Its 'exotic' credentials depended to a great extent on its packaging, with jackets featuring a dusky bikini-clad beauty in an appropriate setting; the music itself owed more to jazz, swing, and easy listening.

It all started in 1951 when musician, composer, and arranger Les Baxter recorded an album on Capitol, *Le Sacre Du Sauvage (Ritual Of The Savage)*. It included 'Quiet Village,' which in Denny's hands a few years later became an engagingly insistent piano-led instrumental. Denny was a former child prodigy already into his 40s when he moved to Hawaii in 1954. There he formed a piano-and-vibes group that included percussionist Augie Colon. The band usually played in the open air and became accustomed to performing to a background chorus of croaking bullfrogs and screeching birds. As a joke, Colon began imitating the bird calls onstage, a ruse that fitted well with the band's ersatz tropical style. Throwing in a few Southern Pacific and Eastern percussion instruments, Denny arrived at the sound heard on 'Quiet Village.' He recorded the song in mono in 1956, to little success, but when he tried again with a stereo version in 1959 he scored a major hit.

Mack The Knife
Bobby Darin

Released August 1959
Atco *6147* (U.S. #1) / London *HLK 8939* (U.K #1)

'Mack The Knife,' or 'Moritat' as it was originally entitled, was written by Kurt Weill and Bertolt Brecht for their 1928 *Threepenny Opera*, itself based upon the first opera in English, *The Beggar's Opera*, written by John Gay in the early 18th century. *The Threepenny Opera* was first performed on Broadway in 1933 but was revived in 1955, after which the song became a hit for Dick Hyman. Louis Armstrong released the first version with the title 'Mack The Knife' in 1956.

Bobby Darin signed to Decca Records shortly before his 20th birthday and recorded four singles without success before switching to Atlantic's Atco label. Producer Ahmet Ertegun recalled: "I thought he was a fantastic artist, and just needed to be recorded properly." Under Ertegun's supervision Darin recorded his first hit, 'Splish Splash,' a novelty song that he had written in 15 minutes. But Darin wasn't satisfied to be a fly-by-night pop star and yearned respect as a 'real singer,' which explains his switch in 1959 to covering standards with Sinatra-like swinging arrangements.

Since 'Mack' had been a hit so many times before, Darin didn't consider it as a single, but when his label decided to release the song, Darin informed Dick Clark that he would perform it on Clark's influential TV show *American Bandstand*. The producer allegedly commented: "If he wants to turn his career into chopped liver, so be it." In fact it was probably the smartest career move that Darin ever made. While his version became the sixth to hit the U.S. charts it was also the most successful: his only American Number 1, and the biggest hit of the year, spending nine weeks at the top and winning two Grammy awards.

What'd I Say (Part 1) / What'd I Say (Part 2)
Ray Charles

Released June 1959
Atlantic *2031* (U.S. #6) / London *HLE 8917* (U.K.)

'What'd I Say' was the record that introduced the world to the genius of Ray Charles and remains one of his finest individual achievements. It was considered so long at six-and-a-half minutes that it had to be spread over two sides of a single, which explains the addition of 'Part 1' and 'Part 2' to the title.

Charles studied composition at the St. Augustine School For The Deaf And The Blind, moved to Seattle, and made his recording debut with 'Confession Blues' in 1949 as part of The Maxim Trio. He spent the next few years honing his sound on a series of singles for the Downbeat, Swingtime, and Atlantic labels, gradually developing his celebrated amalgam of blues and gospel that in essence became a template for 1960s soul. By the mid 1950s he was making regular use of a horn quintet on such epochal recordings as 'I've Got A Woman' and 'Hallelujah I Love Her So,' lending the songs a raucous, euphoric backdrop.

The story goes that 'What'd I Say' began at a live performance early in 1959. By the end of a long show, Charles found himself short of material. Undeterred, he started to improvise – first with a series of 12-bar blues-based runs on the electric piano and then by starting a call-and-response with his female backing singers, The Raelettes.

On February 18th, 1959, Charles went to New York City to cut the song with Atlantic engineer Tom Dowd. 'What'd I Say' begins, as it had on that night of inspiration a few weeks earlier, with Charles's electric piano. Bassist Milton Garrard and drummer Milt Turner soon join in, and the three of them take time to feel their way around the song's simple but captivating structure. The riffs and licks Charles plays might sound traditional to modern ears, but it's no exaggeration to suggest that, at the time, he was in the midst of formulating a blueprint for R&B-soul keyboard playing.

Charles's vocal doesn't arrive until just over a minute and a half into the track – all the more remarkable given that many pop records of the time were not much longer than that. He leads the band through a half dozen verses of suggestive couplets about a girl in a red dress who can "do the Birdland all night long," and is eventually joined by the now-mandatory horn section before the song comes to what seems like a sudden stop after four-and-a-half minutes. The Raelettes then make an appearance, first to plead with Charles to continue, and then, when he agrees, to trade moans and groans with him to the song's close.

All this added up not only to a landmark record but also to a great pile of controversy. 'What'd I Say' was one of the most sexually charged single releases of the time, but that didn't stop it climbing to Number 6 on the U.S. pop chart and to the top of the R&B chart. After the furore died down, the recording inspired numerous covers by artists including Roy Orbison and Elvis Presley (in his 1964 movie *Viva Las Vegas*).

Venus
Frankie Avalon

Released February 1959
Chancellor *1031* (U.S. #1) / HMV *POP 603* (U.K #16)

A song with the title 'Venus' topped the American charts on three separate occasions. The first was composed by songwriter Ed Marshall, who presented it to Frankie Avalon after popping round to the singer's Philadelphia home one afternoon. Avalon liked it, was sure it was a hit, but was worried when he heard that Marshall had just hotfooted it from Al Martino's place. Martino thought it was more likely just an album cut, but Avalon wasn't taking any chances and recorded the song within three days. Avalon had a further U.S. Number 1, but was robbed in Britain when the second, 'Why,' was covered by Anthony Newley and hit the top there.

'Venus' version two was composed by Robbie van Leeuwen and reached Number 1 for Dutch group Shocking Blue in 1969. Covered by British trio Bananarama, it topped the charts yet again in 1986 – and can be credited with yet another chart-topping appearance when it formed the basis of the 'Stars On 45' medley, a Number 1 in 1981.

Puppy Love
Dolly Parton

Released early 1959
Goldband *45-8213* (U.S.) / Not issued U.K.

One of 12 children brought up in poverty, Parton began making up songs as a child, and by her early teens was an accomplished singer and regular performer on local radio and television in Knoxville, Tennessee. It was her uncle Bill Owens who gave her a guitar when she was seven years old. He also offered some songwriting assistance for her first recording, 'Puppy Love' / 'Girl Left Alone,' taped at Goldband Records in Lake Charles, Louisiana, in 1959 when Parton was just 13.

Studio owner Eddie Shuler remembers that little Dolly had to use the highest stool in the studio to get close enough to the microphone. (The original tape of this recording now resides at the Country Music Hall Of Fame in Nashville.)

It would be another five years before Parton recorded again, but it must have been something she was particularly looking forward to. The day after she graduated from High School in 1964, she packed her bags, took the first Greyhound to Nashville, and never looked back.

A Teenager In Love
Dion & The Belmonts

Released April 1959
Laurie *3027* (U.S. #5) / London *HLU 8874* (U.K. #28)

Dion DiMucci and his Belmonts – Freddy Milano, Angelo D'Aleo, and Carlo Mastrangelo – were one of many groups of Bronx-based Italian-American teenagers singing doo-wop in the late 1950s. 'Teenager In Love' was the biggest of their several hit singles, a record that ably demonstrates the group's gift for imbuing standard teen-pop fluff with a sense of yearning for transcendence. This was largely due to Dion himself, a blue-eyed-soul singer a decade before the term was coined. Marty Wilde covered the song for the British market and grabbed a bigger slice of the U.K. sales, but his pale imitation serves only to underline Dion's status as one of rock's great voices.

Tiger
Fabian

Released June 1959
Chancellor *1037* (U.S. #3) / HMV *POP 643* (U.K.)

From the 'blink and you'll miss them' brigade, Fabian saw 'Tiger' become the biggest of his eight American Top 40 hits in a 13-month whirlwind career. Originally hired purely on the basis of his good looks, Fabian Forte was just 15 years old when he recorded his debut, a Doc Pomus and Mort Shuman song with the unlikely title 'I'm A Man.' The songwriting duo also delivered his second hit, 'Turn Me Loose,' which Fabian debuted on the TV show *American Bandstand* in March 1959.

'Tiger' was a U.S. Number 3, with the unforgettable line "Hey, lumpa sugar, you look kinda sweet," before his movie debut in *Hound Dog Man*, the title song of which was his only British hit. A reviewer noted that in the movie "Fabian is surprisingly good" but then added: "Of course, he also sings." Three more hits followed with diminishing returns, but by April 1960 Fabian had become embroiled in the payola scandal, and when it was revealed that his recordings had been "significantly doctored" to improve his voice, his career was over.

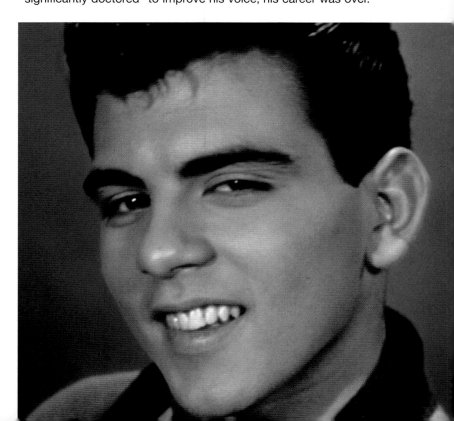

ALAN FREED AND THE PAYOLA SCANDAL

Payola is as old as the music industry. It means the payment of incentives to people to sing your songs or play your records. In the sheet-music days, pluggers handed out cash to performers to promote the songs they were trying to sell. Later, they would hand out gifts to early DJs to play the tunes they had for sale. By the time the 'payola' scandal broke in the U.S. in the late 1950s, the practice was well established and no one seemed to be unduly concerned. But people were annoyed and scared by rock'n'roll music, which had been championed on radio, and in particular by New York City DJ Alan Freed. Ostensibly a campaign against corruption, the payola scandal was also a way of attacking rock and its promoters.

Freed had begun his career as a classical music DJ in Cleveland, Ohio. In 1951 he was encouraged to change to playing rhythm & blues, which he began to call "rock'n'roll" to distance it from its black origins. While his claims to have invented the term were an exaggeration, Freed enthusiastically promoted the music it described. In 1954, having outgrown Cleveland, Freed moved to New York where he was recognized as the most influential DJ in the country. Calling himself Moondog, howling into the microphone, and speaking in a deep, gravelly voice, he won over a huge audience both by his musical choices and his on-air personality. He enraged the conventional morality of the day by organizing concerts that attracted a mixed-race crowd and by playing the original versions of songs by black artists rather than innocuous white cover versions.

The payola scandal began when a congressional committee that had been investigating quiz-show rigging in television turned its attentions to practices in the record and radio industries. Payola was seen as another symptom of a corrupt society. But it was not a crime; it was just unpopular within the record and music-publishing industries, mainly among those who thought that rock'n'roll was only being played because DJs had been bribed. It was certainly the case that payola had made DJs more receptive to the output of the small independent labels who championed the new music.

The committee began hearings in February 1960, and immediately the major record companies and radio stations disowned the practice, which was being viewed as 'unfair competition.' Employees were immediately required to sign affidavits to say they had never taken payola. Alan Freed refused and was sacked by WABC Radio. In the committee's hearings, he admitted that he had been on the payroll of several record companies, but had never taken "a dime" to play a record. "I'd be a fool to," he said. "I'd be giving up control of my program." His argument was that he was paid to advise record companies on the music that would sell well, rather than helping sell the music they had made. Either way, it brought him a handsome income. He had also benefited from another common practice of the era and was credited as co-composer of some 15 songs, including Chuck Berry's 'Maybellene' and 'Sincerely' by The Moonglows.

Nonetheless, despite cooperating with the committee, Freed was charged – not for payola, which did not become an offence until later in 1960, but for the New York State offence of 'commercial bribery.' His crime was to take inducements without informing his employer. After a plea bargain, he was fined $500 and given a suspended six-month jail sentence. However, by this time, partly as a result of his heavy drinking, his career was on the skids. An indictment for tax evasion during the payola years arrived in 1964, by which time he was out of work and broke. Within a year, at age 43, he was dead.

Wonderful World
Sam Cooke

Released May 1960
Keen *8-2112* (U.S. #12) / HMV *POP 754* (U.K. #27)

Cooke was 'the man who invented soul music' and an influence on so many others – Marvin Gaye, Otis Redding, Al Green, the list is almost endless. But this extremely talented singer, writer, arranger, and producer would surely have produced even greater work had he not died in somewhat mysterious circumstances at the tragically young age of 29 in 1964.

At first he recorded gospel music for Art Rupe's Specialty label, but the two fell out when Cooke and producer Bumps Blackwell recorded the poppy 'You Send Me' in 1957. Rupe, in a magnanimous but costly decision, allowed Cooke and Blackwell to depart, with the song and Cooke's contract, to Keen Records – and watched as 'You Send Me' shot to Number 1.

While with Keen, Cooke's songs just got better and better. Among the other classic sides he recorded for the label were 'Only Sixteen' and 'Wonderful World,' recorded at his last session for the label in Los Angeles on March 2, 1959. 'Wonderful World' became one of his best loved and most covered songs. Surprisingly, this inspired slice of pop songwriting was looked upon as something of a throwaway at the time and wasn't released until over a year later, by which time Cooke had moved on to RCA. The song was originally written by Lou Adler and Herb Alpert, but Cooke added the finishing lyrical touches, and the trio used the songwriting pseudonym 'Barbara Campbell.' It became a huge hit in Britain in 1986, reissued in conjunction with a TV advertisement for jeans.

Cause I Love You
Carla & Rufus

Released August 1960
Satellite *102* (U.S.) / Not issued U.K.

Way back in the 1930s, Rufus Thomas was a comedian working with a traveling revue, The Rabbit Foot Minstrels. He made his first recording, 'I'll Be A Good Boy,' in 1949, but his rise to fame coincided with a stint as a DJ on the Memphis-based WDIA, one of the era's few black-owned stations. While at WDIA he launched his first hit, 'Bear Cat' (1953), an answer song to Big Mama Thornton's 'Hound Dog' and, more significantly, the first national chart hit for Sun Records.

Come 1959, Rufus and his daughter Carla proved significant in launching another vitally important Memphis label, Stax Records. ''Cause I Love You,' based largely on the New Orleans-style rhythm of Jessie Hill's 'Ooh Poo Pah Doo,' was the first track recorded in a converted theatre at 926 East McLemore, the brand new studio of country-music based Satellite Records. When the song broke out locally, Satellite owner Jim Stewart realized that his label's future lay with rhythm & blues. "It was like a blind man who suddenly gained his sight," he later explained. The success of the duet, which also featured 16-year-old Booker T. Jones on saxophone, convinced Atlantic Records producer Jerry Wexler to invest a $5,000 advance to secure a five-year option on the pair which, in turn, led to the re-launching of Satellite as Stax.

Stax went on to become the world's coolest soul and rhythm & blues label, while Rufus's raw but upbeat vocals and starkly simple proto-funk grooves made him almost as big a star as Carla, who was rarely out of the U.S. R&B charts for the rest of the decade.

Bye Bye Baby
Mary Wells

Released December 1960
Motown *1003* (U.S.) / Not issued U.K.

Former Ford Motor Company employee Berry Gordy was the man behind Motown Records, a business he would build up from an $800 loan in 1959 to one of the most successful black-run corporations in America, selling out 29 years later in 1988 for $61 million. (Gordy wisely held on to the valuable Jobete song catalogue, later selling a 50 per cent share in the company for a whopping $132 million.) Along the way he brought us such artists as The Supremes, featuring Diana Ross, Smokey Robinson, The Four Tops, Stevie Wonder, The Temptations, The Jackson 5, featuring 12-year-old Michael Jackson, and Marvin Gaye.

One of Gordy's first major artists was Mary Wells. She has been somewhat forgotten in the mists of time, despite giving Motown many early hits. Gordy originally got started in the music business writing hits for Jackie Wilson, and 17-year-old Mary Wells had Wilson in mind for her song 'Bye Bye Baby,' which she took to Gordy. Now with his own company to run, Gordy immediately suggested she record the song herself.It was not a major pop hit, but Wells went on to provide Motown with eleven Top 40 hits between 1961 and 1964, culminating in her international hit 'My Guy,' penned by Smokey Robinson. Ironically, 'My Guy' came out just as she was preparing to join 20th Century Fox for a large advance with talk of movie projects, but nothing ever came of the plans, and her Motown hits remain her greatest successes.

Stuck On You

Elvis Presley

Released March 1960
RCA *47-7740* (U.S. #1) / RCA *1187* (U.K. #3)

'Stuck On You' is far from Elvis's greatest recording, but as his first release after his Army service it assumed huge significance, racking up 1,250,000 advance sales before its title had even been announced. It was also the first stereo single to hit Number 1 in the U.S. and the first in RCA's new policy of releasing all singles in stereo. Domenico Modugno's 1958 Number 1, 'Volaré,' sparked a lasting taste for classy Italian songs, which Presley plugged into with 'It's Now Or Never,' based on the 1901 composition 'O Sole Mio.' There had already been successful versions of the song, but it still became Presley's biggest seller ever – 20 million copies and counting – and opened the door to the adult market for many upwardly mobile rock'n'rollers.

Three Steps to Heaven

Eddie Cochran

Released May 1960
Liberty *55242* (U.S.) / London *HLG 9115* (U.K. #1)

Cochran recorded this on January 8, 1960, at Gold Star studios in Hollywood, California, during his last recording session, alongside 'Cherished Memories' and 'Cut Across Shorty.' Cochran then flew to the U.K. to headline a tour with Gene Vincent. Following a final concert at the Bristol Hippodrome on April 16, Cochran, his girlfriend Sharon Sheeley, and Vincent hired a taxi to return to London. In the early hours of the morning near Chippenham, Wlitshire, the taxi hit a lamp-post. Cochran was thrown through the windshield and died later in hospital, while Vincent, Sheeley, and the taxi driver were seriously injured. In an ironic conclusion to Cochran's sadly short career, 'Three Steps To Heaven' became a posthumous Number 1 in Britain in June 1960, but surprisingly was not a hit in America. The song was later covered by British rock'n'roll revival band Showaddywaddy, becoming a Number 2 U.K. hit in 1975.

above > Clockwise from top left: Otis Redding, Stax Records owner Jim Stewart, Rufus Thomas, Booker T, and Carla Thomas, pictured at the Stax headquarters in Memphis, Tennessee, in the mid 1960s.

My Old Man's A Dustman
Lonnie Donegan

Released March 1960
Not issued U.S. / Pye *7N 15256* (U.K. #1)

Tie Me Kangaroo Down Sport
Rolf Harris
Released May 1960
Epic *9596* (U.S. #3) / Columbia *DB 4483* (U.K. #9)

Itsy Bitsy Teeny Weeny Yellow Polka Dot Bikini
Brian Hyland
Released June 1960
Kapp *342* (U.S. #1) / London *HLR 9161* (U.K. #8)

Lonnie Donegan was not content merely to be Britain's king of skiffle in the 1950s, but carved out a new career for himself as a fresh decade dawned by tapping into a rich vein of cockney music-hall humor. Despite the handicap of having been born in Scotland, he convincingly portrayed a London barrow-boy stereotype in 'My Old Man's A Dustman,' his biggest U.K. hit, while 'Does Your Chewing Gum Lose Its Flavour' restored him to the American charts where he'd last been seen in 1956. Similar Brit humor was adopted by beat-boom bands such as The Small Faces and The Kinks and remains present in post-millennium groups inlcluding The Arctic Monkeys.

Shortly after Donegan's 'Dustman' and on the other side of the globe, all-round entertainer Rolf Harris hit the Australian top spot by parodying Aussie idiosyncrasies in 'Tie Me Kangaroo Down Sport,' which (and this is true) he adapted from a Harry Belafonte calypso with the lyric: "Tie me donkey down there, let him bray let him bray." Storming out of Australia into the British and American Top 10s, Harris embarked on a diverse career that thrives to this day.

Brooklyn schoolboy Brian Hyland's entry into the 1960 novelty-hit stakes came with 'Itsy Bitsy Teeny Weeny Yellow Polka Dot Bikini,' a cutely catchy ditty composed by Paul Vance after watching his two-year-old daughter playing on the beach. Fortunately, Hyland was able to transcend his novelty status and scored subsequent hits including 'Ginny Come Lately' and 'Sealed With A Kiss,' which established him as a class act.

Only The Lonely (Know How I Feel)
Roy Orbison

Released May 1960
Monument *421* (U.S. #2) / London *HLU 9149* (U.K. #1)

It is one of the great mysteries of popular music. The "ooh-eeh-ooh-ah-ah" gibberish in David Seville's 'Witch Doctor' is rib-ticklingly funny. But somehow when 'Only The Lonely' opens up with the equally nonsensical "Dum dum dum dummy doo wah, woh yeah yeah woh-woh, oh-woh-woh-woh-woh-oh-ooh-wah-ah-ah" every syllable sounds like a ripple of sorrow. Orbison's astonishing voice, swooping and soaring, tear-stained yet unbroken, was a major factor, and although 'Only The Lonely' fell just short of the U.S. Number 1 position it went all the way in the U.K. and transformed Orbison, a struggling rock'n'roll hopeful, into The Big O, master of the heart-stopping ballad.

Walk – Don't Run
The Ventures

Released May 1960
Dolton *25* (U.S. #2) / Top Rank *JAR 417* (U.K. #8)

Apache
The Shadows

Released July 1960
ABC-Paramount *10138* (U.S.) / Columbia *DB 4484* (U.K. #1)

The Ventures didn't invent rock guitar instrumentals – Link Wray and Duane Eddy pioneered that field years earlier. Nor did they invent surf music – Dick Dale & The Del-Tones did that during their late 1950s residency at the Rendezvous Ballroom in Balboa, California. Nevertheless it's hard to deny that their restlessly churning 'Walk – Don't

Run,' which peaked at Number 2 in August 1960, sparked America's early-1960s surf instrumental craze. In its wake came The Chantays with 'Pipeline,' The Surfaris with 'Wipe Out,' and many more.

'Walk – Don't Run' started life as a smooth, jazzy confection by guitarist Johnny Smith in 1954, which The Ventures discovered in a 1957 version on a Chet Atkins album, *Hi-Fi In Focus*. By the time they had stripped it back to a minimalist rock'n'roll chord sequence overlaid by a single-note melody line, it was virtually a new song. Johnny Smith himself later told the band that if they hadn't named it 'Walk – Don't Run' he wouldn't have recognized it.

Meanwhile, over in Britain, Cliff Richard's backing group The Shadows were about to score their first Number 1 with 'Apache,' a titanic tower of twang underpinned by pounding war drums, the first of more than 30 chart hits for the group over the next two decades. No other instrumental outfit came close to matching The Shadows' consistency and longevity, and their leader, Hank B. Marvin, is one of the most influential rock guitarists of all time, cited as a primary influence by Eric Clapton, Mark Knopfler, Neil Young, and dozens of other top axemen.

Shakin' All Over
Johnny Kidd & The Pirates

Released June 1960
APT-ABC *25040* (U.S.) / HMV *POP 753* (U.K. #1)

There wasn't much of any lasting quality that emerged from British recording studios in the early 1960s, but 'Shakin' All Over' was a notable exception. The song, written by Kidd (a.k.a. Frederick Heath) and his manager Gus Robinson, was allegedly thrown together in about half an hour the night before it was recorded at EMI's Abbey Road studios on May 13, 1960. The group were scheduled to record a cover of 'Yes Sir, That's My Baby' and needed a B-side. 'Shakin'' was recorded in one take. To the record company executives it was obvious that this should be the A-side, much to Kidd's surprise and joy. Clem Cattini was the

drummer with Kidd's band. He later played on dozens of 1960s hits by The Tornados, The Kinks, Donovan, and T.Rex, and claims to have played on 45 Number 1 hits. Johnny Kidd's chart career ground to a halt in 1964 when a new wave of beat groups arrived. Cattini recalled that Walter Ridley, who was credited with this production, "didn't know anything about rock'n'roll," and was apparently not even at the session, in fact produced by Ridley's assistant, Peter Sullivan.

The Twist
Chubby Checker

Released June 1960
Parkway *811* (U.S. #1) / Columbia *DB 4503* (U.K.)

In 1958, Detroit-based rhythm & blues singer Hank Ballard was watching his band improvising some dance steps as they played and he decided to write a song based on their moves. He called it 'The Twist' but his label, King Records, didn't think it was good enough to release as a single, so it was relegated to the B-side of a ballad, 'Teardrops On Your Letter.' Kids who came to see Ballard started picking up on 'The Twist,' and by the summer of 1960 the influential TV presenter Dick Clark noticed dancers twisting on his show, *American Bandstand*.

A shrewd operator, Clark arranged for Chubby Checker to cover Ballard's song, duplicating the original so precisely that when Ballard heard it on the radio he thought it was his own recording. Boosted by appearances on *Bandstand*, Chubby's version hit Number 1 on September 19, 1960, returning to the top more than a year later when the dance caught on among older music fans.

Chubby's follow-up, 'Let's Twist Again,' spread the fever to Europe, hotly pursued by a flood of twist-related releases, from Joey Dee's 'Peppermint Twist' to Sam Cooke's 'Twistin' The Night Away' and The Isley Brothers' 'Twist And Shout.' It became evident on November 14, 1961, that Ballard's B-side had penetrated the highest echelons of society when the U.S. Presidential Press Secretary, Pierre Salinger, officially denied that anyone had danced the twist during a recent party in the White House. The shake, the hully-gully, and the watusi were just around the corner – but let's not mention the funky chicken.

Oh Carolina / I Met A Man
The Folkes Brothers

Released late 1960
Buster Wild Bells *ZSP 52833* (Jamaica) / Blue Beat *BB 30* (U.K.)

This is arguably the most significant recording in Jamaican musical history and is often touted as the first ska record. The Folkes Brothers made just this one record, produced by vocalist and DJ Prince Buster in 1960. He'd been fascinated by the Rastafarian drumming of Count Ossie (Oswald Williams), which he incorporated into the single alongside featured teenage brothers John, Mico, and Junior Folkes on vocals. Buster supplied clapping and imitation horn sounds, and the whole thing was recorded with one microphone. Written by John Folkes in 1958, the track was released on the Blue Beat label in Britain in 1960, where it later became a club favorite. However, when Shaggy made 'Oh Carolina' internationally famous some 33 years later and the cash started rolling in, it prompted a number of lawsuits, and Prince Buster claimed that he had written the song. In a November 1994 decision, the British High Court decided otherwise, thus guaranteeing John Folkes a happy retirement. Mr. Folkes himself denies the ska tag and calls this a "heritage folk song."

Spanish Harlem
Ben E. King

Released January 1961
Atco *6185* (U.S. #10) / London *HLK 9258* (U.K.)

Stand By Me
Ben E. King

Released May 1961
Atco *6194* (U.S. #4) / London *HLK 9358* (U.K. #27)

Legendary producers Jerry Leiber and Mike Stoller had been working for Atlantic Records since 1956 writing and producing a slew of hits for The Coasters and The Drifters. They also wrote some of Elvis Presley's biggest hits including 'Hound Dog' and 'Jailhouse Rock.'

When lead vocalist Ben E. King left The Drifters in 1960, he recorded four songs in a remarkable three-hour session on October 27, including 'Spanish Harlem' and 'Stand By Me.' Phil Spector was also in the studio that day: he had written 'Spanish Harlem' with Leiber after pestering him for ages about writing a song together. 'Stand By Me' was put together in the studio and inspired by several gospel songs, including an early Sam Cooke record. King had suggested recording a version with The Drifters, but they weren't interested. Arriving at the session early, he sang what he had – some lyrics and a few bars of music – and worked with Leiber to complete the song. When Mike Stoller arrived, he came up with the defining bassline, and a classic was born.

'Stand By Me' was not a major British hit the first time around, but topped the U.K. chart in 1987 after appearing in a movie of the same name and a jeans commercial. Muhammad Ali, when he was still Cassius Clay, made a recording of 'Stand By Me,' on the B-side of his 1963 single, 'I Am The Greatest.' John Lennon had a hit with the song in 1975, taken from his *Rock'N'Roll* album in which, coincidentally, Phil Spector was involved.

Crazy
Patsy Cline

Released October 1961
Decca *31317* (U.S. #9) / Brunswick *05861* (U.K.)

'Crazy' was written by up-and-coming songwriter Willie Nelson and recorded under unusual circumstances. Two months before the session, Cline had been in a near-fatal automobile accident. Consequently she recorded the song while still on crutches and had problems sustaining notes because her ribs hurt when she tried to hold her breath.

She also had some difficulty grasping the song, and in an unusual move for the time producer Owen Bradley suggested that the backing track should be recorded first, and then Cline could return at a later date to record her vocal. This of course became normal practice, but back in the early 1960s it was more common to record several versions of a song 'live' in the studio with band or orchestra and then release the best take. The 'Crazy' session featured Nashville session legend Floyd Cramer on piano and The Jordanaires, most famous for their work with Elvis, on backing vocals.

Cline had been presented with two new Willie Nelson songs by fellow country artist Billy Walker. The other one was 'Funny How Time Slips Away' and was Cline's preference. However, fate stepped in when Walker refused to let her have it. She settled for 'Crazy,' and a classic recording was born.

According to Bradley, when she did indeed return to the studio a few days later to record her vocal, she nailed it on the first take. 'Crazy' was not a hit in Britain at the time but became a surprise chart entry there in 1990. It has the additional honor of being the most played jukebox hit of all time.

DANCING THE JUKEBOXE JIVE

The idea of a machine that would play music in return for small change is almost as old as recorded music itself. Thomas Edison's cylinder-based phonograph was patented in 1877, and only 12 years later a coin-operated version of the machine was first demonstrated, in a restaurant in San Francisco.

The 'nickel-in-the-slot phonograph,' so called because it charged 5¢ a play, was an immediate and astonishing success. Its inventor, Louis Glass, told a convention of phonograph operators that in the first six months of operation, his first 15 machines took $4,000, worth something like $80,000 today. Glass's machines bore little resemblance to later jukeboxes: they only played one record, which would be changed every day or two, and with no amplification, only four customers could listen at one time, through crude acoustic earphones. (Interestingly, a Brit, Charles Adam Randall patented an 'automatic parlophone' in London a year earlier, but there is no evidence it was ever built.)

The early machines tended to be electrically driven, either by battery or the early AC power supply. Reliable spring-driven machines came later and were a boon because they could be used in areas without electric power. The modern jukebox began to take shape at the turn of the 20th century with the arrival of the Automatic Entertainer, which offered 24 selections, on disc, played through a 40-inch acoustic horn on the top.

The year 1925 saw the first electrically-recorded 78 rpm discs, but record players remained purely acoustic for several more years. Because a large acoustic horn could fill a domestic living room, manufacturers thought that electrical amplification was unnecessary. Jukeboxes, however, were installed in noisy public spaces and needed much more volume, especially for dancing. The turning point came with the National Automatic Selective Phonograph of 1927. This electrically-amplified machine could select from 20 songs on 10 records. It is usually recognized as the first real jukebox and was made by the forerunner of the Automatic Musical Instrument company, one of the most celebrated names in the business. Another famous company, Wurlitzer, launched its first real jukebox in 1933.

Jukeboxes only began to acquire their classic look in the late 1930s, when J.P. Seeburg introduced colorful plastics. The last of the 'big four' manufacturers, Rock-Ola, entered the market in 1939. Its name is often associated with rock'n'roll, but that's entirely accidental. It was owned by a man called David Rockola.

In the late 1940s and early 1950s, great efforts went into increasing the available selections on the machines. The 200-selection machine was introduced by Seeburg in 1955. That marked a high-point for the conventional machine. In the 1950s, Seeburg had introduced the first jukebox that played 45s, although in poor black areas the old 78 standard lived on as late as 1958, not least because operators had moved the redundant machines to those neighborhoods. Some see the jukebox as the savior of the 45 single in the 'war of the speeds' in the early 1950s. (No jukebox ever played 12-inch 33 rpm albums.) The dominance of jukebox sales as an outlet for 45 rpm production also ensured that jukebox hits did well in the charts.

The word 'jukebox' is first recorded in 1939, in a *Time* magazine article on Glenn Miller, who attributed his success to his popularity on the machines. 'Jukes' or 'juke-joints' were roadhouses or bars frequented by black plantation workers in the Southern states of the U.S., while 'to juke' meant to dance. The word is believed to come from a West African term meaning 'disorderly' or 'wicked.' The early coin-operated phonographs were too expensive for the black bars, but by the 1930s they had become established as a cheap replacement for live musicians.

In the 1940s and 1950s, when radio was effectively off-limits to black artists, jukeboxes were a key part of the burgeoning rhythm & blues scene. Independent operators would take their records direct to the juke joints and even provide the owners with coins so they could promote their records. There was thus a close connection between record makers and listeners; many in the early independent rock'n'roll record companies began in the jukebox business.

In the 1950s, jukeboxes led the youth trend taking rhythm & blues and then rock'n'roll music out of the purely black marketplace, by enabling white listeners to hear the authentic originals rather than the white cover versions that were so prominent on radio. Jukeboxes have always catered to a wide range of tastes, however. A poll of jukebox operators in 1996 declared that the 'number 1 jukebox single of all time' was Patsy Cline's 'Crazy.'

After the glory days, later innovations were less far-reaching, including stereo and CD operation. Today the jukebox is still going strong, in digital versions that hold some 5,000 songs on hard disk while allowing customers to download their choices from a catalogue of at least 150,000 songs held on a central server. They won't be getting those for a nickel, however. Many of the new machines accept credit cards.

Are You Sure
The Allisons

Released February 1961
London *1977* (U.S.) / Fontana *H 294* (U.K. #2)

The Eurovision Song Contest was established in 1956 but, although it boosted sales and built careers in Europe, Britain still hadn't won the competition by 1961. The Allisons were Bob and John, and with their optimistic, self-composed Everly Brothers soundalike 'Are You Sure' seemed to be serious contenders. But they returned from the Contest in France mere runners-up, and headed smack into a press storm over revelations that – gasp! – they were not brothers. In fact they were Colin Day and Brian Alford. Nonetheless, the publicity helped them all the way to Number 2 in Britain where they were held off the top spot by – who else? – The Everly Brothers, with 'Walk Right Back.'

Blue Moon
The Marcels

Released February 1961
Colpix *186* (U.S. #1) / Pye *7N 25073* (U.K. #1)

Pity The Collegians, whose vocal arrangements on their 1957 doo-wop classic 'Zoom Zoom Zoom' provided the inspiration for The Marcels' dramatic restructuring of the 1934 Rogers & Hart standard 'Blue Moon.' Despite the blatant plagiarism, rarely have the opening seconds of any record been as arresting as Fred Johnson's tongue-twisting bass vocal that introduces the Pittsburgh vocal quintet's greatest moment. Not only did 'Blue Moon' top the charts on both sides of the Atlantic and start a doo-wop revival, it inspired two tribute hits, Johnny Cymbal's 'Mr. Bassman' and Barry Mann's 'Who Put The Bomp,' both saluting Johnson's vocal prowess.

Runaway
Del Shannon

Released March 1961
Big Top *3067* (U.S. #1) / London *HLX 9317* (U.K. #1)

Sharp good looks, a strong voice, and songwriting ability put Del Shannon into the charts in 1961 and kept him there until the middle of the decade. 'Runaway' was Shannon's first hit, and his biggest. It is a true pop classic: engagingly catchy without being trite, and unusual yet accessible.

The first thing that set 'Runaway' apart is the way Shannon uses his falsetto so effectively and prominently. Then there's the song's unusual structure, which abandoned conventional verse-chorus repeats. And there's the instrumental break played by Shannon's keyboard player, Max Crook, on an instrument he dubbed the Musitron, which was in fact a modified Clavioline, a small, three-octave electronic keyboard invented in France in 1947.

Although we hear 'Runaway' as a flawless pop capsule, the session at which it was recorded was fraught. The producer was concerned about the song's unconventional shape, and after it was recorded he speeded up the tapes to make them sound more commercial (and, some say, to disguise Shannon's wayward pitching).

The released record, originally recorded in A minor, is pitched somewhere just below B flat minor. Yet for all this, 'Runaway' became one of those records that transcends its time and origins. It was a massive international hit, and still sounds good today.

Although Shannon never scored as big a hit again after 'Runaway,' he remained a major worldwide star for several years. By the end of the decade he had drifted into management, production, and cabaret work, punctuated with occasional comebacks. Reputedly depressed at his inability to re-launch his pop career, he took his own life in February 1990.

Halfway To Paradise
Billy Fury

Released April 1961
Not issued U.S. / Decca *F 11349* (U.K. #3)

Ronald Wycherley was signed up to the stable of the famous U.K. impresario Larry Parnes, affectionately known by the British press as 'Mr. Parnes, Shillings, and Pence.' Parnes renamed the boy Billy Fury and reckoned he was "the most important rock'n'roll singer Britain ever produced." This is not particularly apparent on 'Halfway To Paradise,' one of several Fury hits that made the Top 3 in Britain, although he never managed a number 1. (To hear Fury at his rock'n'roll best, check out his 1960 album *The Sound Of Fury*.) 'Halfway To Paradise' was a cover of a U.S. Number 39 hit by Tony Orlando (who would later find international fame fronting Dawn on such ditties as 'Tie A Yellow Ribbon Round The Ole Oak Tree'). Renowned U.K. session guitarist Big Jim Sullivan played on 'Paradise,' one of the first hit compositions of Gerry Goffin and Carole King.

Quarter To Three
U.S. Bonds

Released May 1961
Legrand *1008* (U.S. #1) / Top Rank *JAR 575* (U.K. #7)

Following his first hit, 'New Orleans,' Gary 'U.S.' Bonds threw a party and invited label-mates The Church Street Five. They weren't as merry as Bonds because their saxophone-based instrumental, 'A Night With Daddy G,' had flopped. Astutely, their leader, Gene Barge (a.k.a. Daddy G), asked Gary if he'd write some lyrics for the track, and the inebriated vocalist rattled off 'Quarter To Three' in ten minutes. They recorded it that night and by June 26 it was Number 1 in *Billboard*. Bonds never again hit the top, but he did bank a substantial out-of-court settlement when he sued Chubby Checker in 1963 because Chubby's 'Dancin' Party' bore uncanny resemblances to 'Quarter To Three.'

Take Five
Dave Brubeck Quartet

Released September 1961
Columbia *31769* (U.S. #25) / Fontana *H 339* (U.K. #6)

It isn't often that a jazz artist has a hit single, but pianist Dave Brubeck and his Quartet managed several in the early 1960s, of which 'Take Five' was the biggest. Composed by Quartet saxophonist Paul Desmond, 'Take Five' gains much of its distinctive flavor from its 5/4 time and is one of many Brubeck songs in unconventional time signatures (unconventional meaning anything other than 4/4, 3/4, or 6/8). Although Brubeck is sometimes disdained by jazz purists – mainly because he enjoyed this crossover pop success – the pianist has been one of the genre's most productive artists. Now in his 80s, he still composes, performs, and records.

Runaround Sue
Dion

Released September 1961
Laurie *3110* (U.S. #1) / Top Rank *JAR 586* (U.K. #11)

The Wanderer
Dion

Released December 1961
Laurie *3115* (U.S. #2) / HMV *POP 971* (U.K. #10)

Dion split from his backing group The Belmonts in 1960 and went on to achieve even greater chart success as a solo act. 'Runaround Sue' and 'The Wanderer' were the two biggest hits in this stage of a career that continues to this day. In the first song he is the wounded lover; in the second all macho swagger and braggadocio. His voice is flexible enough to serve him perfectly in both roles. Heroin addiction would later derail his career for a while, but he reinvented himself first as an acoustic singer-songwriter, then a gospel act, then a street-smart New York hipster, unique among 1950s rockers in his ability to remain artistically vibrant through the decades. "Nobody is hipper than Dion," Lou Reed once said – and he was right.

There's No Other (Like My Baby)
The Crystals

Released October 1961
Philles *100* (U.S. #20) / Parlophone *R 4867* (U.K.)

In the three years after Phil Spector wrote and performed on his first hit, 'To Know Him Is To Love Him' by The Teddy Bears, he learned the crafts of record production and musical arrangement as he worked on classic singles for Ben E. King, Gene Pitney, and others. As the first release on his newly formed Philles label, 'There's No Other' ignited the fire that Spector had started as a Teddy Bear. The Crystals had six consecutive hits and established Philles as a major chart force. Two years later they were the group with which Spector perfected his awesome Wall Of Sound production technique, which can be heard on such landmark singles as 'Da Doo Ron Ron' and 'Then He Kissed Me.'

Telstar
The Tornados

Released August 1962
London *9561* (U.S. #1) / Decca *F 11494* (U.K. #1)

The early 1960s were a golden age for instrumental rock, with artists like The Shadows, Duane Eddy, and The Ventures all thriving. But their best efforts were eclipsed by 'Telstar,' a record credited to The Tornados but which was more the work of its composer and producer, Joe Meek.

The story of 'Telstar' starts in July 1962 when the Telstar 1 satellite was rocketed into orbit. It provided the first transatlantic television broadcast, and hundreds of thousands of viewers huddled around their televisions, captivated when the ghostly, indistinct image of a man sitting at a desk finally appeared on the screen. Joe Meek was one of them.

Meek was already fascinated with the idea of space travel and loved electronic gadgetry. Those two passions meant he could not miss the Telstar broadcast; later, dwelling on the night's events, he was struck with a tune. He then began his idiosyncratic method of composing, which involved singing a very vague approximation of his tune over a backing track that he'd already recorded for another song. One of Meek's associates, Dave Adams, was charged with deciphering the music encrypted in Meek's wailing, and gradually the 'Telstar' melody emerged.

A few days later The Tornados came to Meek's unique home studio and began work on the song. The band were part of Meek's stable of artists, worked as an instrumental rock group, and backed British rock'n'roll star Billy Fury. They labored with Meek for a day and a half, and by the end had a backing track recorded, but the melody line was yet to be added. The Tornados then had to leave for an engagement with Fury, so Meek worked on with another collaborator, Geoff Goddard, who had co-written an earlier Meek-produced hit, 'Johnny Remember Me,' for John Leyton. Meek sat Goddard down at a Clavioline, a small electronic keyboard, to lay down the melody line. Between them, the two strange friends – united in their belief that Buddy Holly spoke to them from beyond the grave – completed the record.

The end result was the most radical British rock'n'roll single yet recorded, distinguished by a simple, rousing tune – Goddard's Clavioline part – and Meek's peculiar production. The record is peppered with Meek's homespun ingenuity: electronic static for an intro; harp-like arpeggios performed on a piano with tacks stuck in the hammers; swathes of echo and reverb. Yet for all its oddness, it is an immediately accessible pop record.

'Telstar' went on to become one of the biggest hits of 1962, not only topping the charts in Britain but also in the U.S. – the first British rock record to do so. It sold more than five million copies worldwide on first release, remained in Decca's catalogue continually until the mid 1980s, and is still the best-selling rock instrumental single ever.

JOE MEEK: THE ORIGINAL INDEPENDENT PRODUCER

The producer and songwriter Joe Meek was an unlikely candidate for pop success. From a very early age he didn't fit in. His mother had wanted a girl, and it is said that Meek wore dresses until he went to school. As he grew up he became sensitive and often bad tempered. Although well built, he avoided sports and other typically boisterous boyhood activities in favor of the solitude of a garden shed. Here his fascination with sound and electronics was born as he dismantled old radios and gramophones.

As a young man, Meek found his way to London and worked his way through a series of jobs in recording studios. These rarely lasted very long as Meek usually quarreled with his employers over some sleight, real or imagined. But he seemed to have a knack, and was involved in the making of several big hits of the time, including Lonnie Donegan's 'Cumberland Gap' and Frankie Vaughan's 'Green Door.'

Despite this success, Meek was frustrated with the unwritten rules and established hierarchy of the music business of the 1950s, and he yearned for independence. He eventually found this in his home studio, in a rented flat above a leather goods shop in Holloway Road, north London. Here he wrote and recorded dozens of songs for his roster of artists, making finished masters that he then hawked around to major labels under the aegis of RGM Productions (named for the initials of his given name, Robert George Meek). Although commonplace now, independent production companies were unknown at the time.

Many of the recordings Meek made were indifferent, some simply awful. But a few were touched with a true, strange greatness. The classic death disc, 'Johnny Remember Me' by John Leyton (1961), has ghostly female voices singing from a deep well of reverb, representing the dead heroine's pleas from beyond the grave. 'Have I The Right' by The Honeycombs (1964) features bass drum augmented by the band stamping on the stairs at Holloway Road. Both were British Number 1 hits.

But 'Telstar' was Meek's greatest triumph, although it also contributed to his downfall. A French composer, Jean Ledrut, claimed that Meek had stolen the tune from a piece of film music Ledrut had written in 1960. He sued, and Meek's royalties for 'Telstar' were frozen while the case meandered through the French courts. Eventually Meek got his money, but the anxiety further damaged what was already a fragile state of mind.

Although Meek had hits after 'Telstar,' eventually his career faltered. Always unstable and prone to fits of temper, he became increasingly paranoid, believing that his competitors, among them Phil Spector, were bugging his studio to learn his tricks. He took pills to stay awake as he worked too hard, which increased his jumpiness. A gay man at a time when homosexuality was illegal, he was arrested for importuning, and was terrified that his family would find out. His interest in the occult became an obsession. Then, on February 3, 1967, Meek argued with his landlady and shot her dead, before reloading and blowing his own head off. He was 38 years old. It was eight years to the day since his hero, Buddy Holly, had died.

Shout – Part 1
Joey Dee & The Starliters

Released March 1962
Roulette *4416* (U.S. #6) / Columbia *DB 4842* (U.K.)

This is one of the all-time rhythm & blues classics, and had been a hit for The Isley Brothers, who recorded their original in July 1959. The two records indicate the segregation that still existed between R&B and pop in the U.S. – the Isleys' recording was a great production by Hugo Peretti and Luigi Creatore, yet due to the lack of radio exposure it made only Number 47 on the pop charts.

Joey Dee & The Starliters were the house band at New York City's Peppermint Lounge in 1960, which led to a contract with Roulette Records. They recorded the cash-in 'Peppermint Twist,' an American Number 1 in early 1962, directly following Chubby Checker's 'The Twist.' The group gave the twist another shot with their second single, 'Hey, Let's Twist,' before trying something different with their Isleys cover.

If I Had A Hammer (The Hammer Song)
Peter Paul & Mary

Released August 1962
Warner *WB 5296* (U.S. #10) / Warner *WB 74 51911* (U.K.)

This Greenwich Village trio were brought together by Bob Dylan's manager Albert Grossman to capitalize on America's lucrative early-1960s folk-music market. They scored their first hit with 'Lemon Tree,' a late entry in the calypso stakes, but really made their mark when their Grammy-winning performance of folk doyen Pete Seeger's 'The Hammer Song' got to Number 10. An even more successful version by Trini Lopez peaked at Number 3 just over a year later, and it went on to achieve a status many great songwriters only dream of: most people think it is a traditional song.

Green Onions
Booker T. & The M.G.s

Released August 1962
Stax *127* (U.S. #3) / London *HLK 9595* (U.K.)

Booker T. and the M.G.s were the house band for Stax Records, soul's biggest hit factory after Motown, and as such were one of the most listened-to bands of the 1960s: they played on hits by the likes of Otis Redding, Wilson Pickett, and Sam & Dave, to name just a few. The four-piece of organist Booker T. Jones, guitarist Steve Cropper, drummer Al Jackson, and bassist Donald 'Duck' Dunn also recorded a series of instrumental hits under their own name – it stands for Memphis Group.

'Green Onions,' a mid-paced organ groove punctuated by Cropper's clipped, brash guitar chords, set a million toes a-tapping. But the song was a musical accident, a simple warm-up jam committed to tape while the band were waiting in vain for a singer to turn up for a session. It was first released as the B-side to 'Behave Yourself,' a coupling ignored until the sides were flipped. Originally a U.S. hit in 1962, it remained an underground favorite on the British mod scene through the 1960s. With the resurgence of that movement in the late 1970s, 'Green Onions' then made a belated appearance in the U.K. charts.

Monster Mash
Bobby 'Boris' Pickett & The Crypt-Kickers

Released September 1962
Garpax *44167* (U.S. #1) / London *HLU 9597* (U.K.)

This classic novelty hit tapped into an early-1960s revival of the great monster movies – *Dracula*, *Frankenstein*, and so on – and has become a perennial Halloween favorite. The song's title was inspired by the mashed potato dance, a close relative of the twist.

The song itself was the work of an aspiring actor, Bobby Pickett, who performed the spoken vocal in the style of horror movie star Boris Karloff. His backing group included noted session player Leon Russell. Pickett followed up two months later with the less successful festive-themed 'Monster's Holiday.' In 2005 he recorded 'Climate Mash' as a protest against the U.S. Government's failure to respond adequately to the threat of global warming. 'Monster Mash' only became a hit in Britain in 1973.

The Lonely Bull (El Solo Torro)
The Tijuana Brass Featuring Herb Alpert

Released October 1962
A&M *703* (U.S. #6) / Stateside *SS 138* (U.K. #22)

Herb Alpert's Tijuana Brass was something of a phenomenon on the American album charts during the 1960s, clocking up several years' worth of chart action and five Number 1 LPs, quite a remarkable achievement in the golden age of pop.

Alpert originally recorded 'The Lonely Bull' in his garage as 'Twinkle Star' in 1962 and said that he was inspired by a trip to Tijuana, Mexico, where he experienced his first bullfight. He incorporated the sound of live bullfight effects, but still couldn't find a record company interested in releasing the track, so he set up his own A&M Records with Jerry Moss. The Tijuana Brass was an instant success. At first Alpert shipped copies of the record out of his garage, and the single soon sold 700,000 copies. In 1990 Alpert and Moss cashed in their chips, selling their A&M label to Polygram for a cool $500 million.

Zip-A-Dee Doo-Dah
Bob B. Soxx & The Blue Jeans

Released November 1962
Philles *107* (U.S. #8) / London *HLU 9646* (U.K.)

This children's song, written in 1945 by Ray Gilbert and Allie Wrubel for the Disney movie *Song Of The South*, was recorded by Phil Spector on August 24, 1962, and was among the first sessions where the producer achieved the huge sound he had been looking for. Not surprising: there were two guitarists, three bass players (including legendary session player Carole Kaye), two pianists, a drummer, and a percussionist. The studio was Gold Star in Los Angeles, and from this point until Tina Turner's 'River Deep' in 1966 Spector would record everything there. Spector rehearsed the band for three hours until he finally got what he wanted, recording the track in one take and adding the vocals of Bobby Sheen, Darlene Love, and Fanita James.

It Might As Well Rain Until September
Carole King

Released July 1962
Dimension *2000* (U.S. #22) / London *HLU 9591* (U.K. #3)

In 1961 Carole King was a staff songwriter for New York City publishers Aldon Music, and together with her lyricist Gerry Goffin composed two U.S. Number 1s, The Shirelles' 'Will You Love Me Tomorrow' and Bobby Vee's 'Take Good Care Of My Baby.' When King presented Aldon supremo Don Kirshner with a new demo for Vee, 'It Might As Well Rain Until September,' Kirshner decided it was good enough to release as it stood, under King's name. It did well in America and even better in the U.K., but almost a decade passed before King charted again, with 'It's Too Late,' which established her as the brand leader for the rising generation of female singer-songwriters.

1963

She Loves You
The Beatles

....

Released August 1963
Swan *4152* (U.S. #1) / Parlophone *R 5055* (U.K. #1)

I Want To Hold Your Hand
The Beatles

....

Released November 1963
Capitol *5112* (U.S. #1) / Parlophone *R 5084* (U.K. #1)

Paul McCartney made it sound so simple. "We just sat up in one of our hotel rooms for a few hours and wrote it." That's how he explained the phenomenon that was 'She Loves You.' To be more precise, the room was in Turk's Hotel, Newcastle Upon Tyne, a shipbuilding town in the north-east of England, where he found himself immediately after a gig at the Majestic Ballroom. "I got the idea for doing one of those answer-type songs where someone says, 'She loves you,' and the other person says, 'Yes' or 'Yeah, Yeah.' John and I thought it was a stupid thing – and it really was, when you think about it."

Stupid or not, 'She Loves You' fairly exploded out of its grooves from the second the needle hit the vinyl. Banging straight into the chorus, dispensing with the formality of an opening verse, gave the song instant impact, but repeated plays revealed plenty of delicious subtleties, including those weird 'Yeah, yeah, yeah' vocal harmonies. Producer George Martin explained they were "a major sixth with George Harrison doing the sixth, and the other two the third and fifth. It was just the way Glenn Miller wrote for the saxophone."

It became their second U.K. Number 1 on September 12, 1963, at which point The Beatles were a household name in Britain but virtually unknown in America. Capitol Records, the customary home for Parlophone product in the U.S., was steadfastly refusing to release Beatles records, so 'She Loves You' appeared there later that month on the Swan label – to massive public indifference. Beatles manager Brian Epstein was quite used to this sort of reaction in America. It had been the same when they'd put out 'Please Please Me' and 'From Me To You' on Vee-Jay Records.

Back in Britain, meanwhile, there was no stopping them. After four triumphant weeks, 'She Loves You' slipped off the top, on October 10, only to re-appear at Number 1 on November 28 for another two weeks before being replaced by their next release, 'I Want To Hold Your Hand,' which hogged the summit for five solid weeks. The Beatles had become the first artists ever to replace themselves at the top of the U.K. singles chart.

Finally, Capitol in America began to waver. Maybe The Beatles did have something to offer after all. On December 26 they rush-released 'I Want To Hold Your Hand' and eight days later America had its first glimpse of Beatlemania when they were featured on TV's *Jack Paar Show*. On February 1, 'I Want To Hold Your Hand' was Number 1 in America, until, in a bizarre reversal of the British situation, it was replaced at the top by 'She Loves You' on March 21. Then, incredibly, on April 4, 'Can't Buy Me Love' made it three in a row – an unprecedented achievement in chart history. America was now, officially, a suburb of Liverpool.

Summer Holiday
Cliff Richard & The Shadows

Released February 1963
Not issued U.S. / Columbia *DB 4977* (U.K. #1)

Diamonds
Jet Harris & Tony Meehan

Released January 1963
London *4589* (U.S.) / Decca *F 11563* (U.K. #1)

Before the arrival of The Beatles, Cliff Richard and his backing group The Shadows dominated the U.K. charts. By the early 1960s Cliff, like his American rival Elvis, had moved into the movie business, though on a somewhat smaller scale. 'Summer Holiday,' the theme song of his 1963 movie, became his seventh British Number 1, although those chart-toppers would become less frequent with the arrival of The Beatles and the rest. Cliff did perform the song in America on the Ed Sullivan TV show in April, but it was not released in the States, and consequently a cover appeared by one Jimmy Griffin, later to find success in the 1970s as a member of Bread.

Tony Meehan (drums) and Jet Harris (bass) left The Shadows in 1961 and 1962 respectively, and although at first they did not intend to work together, Meehan saw Harris at Decca Records where Meehan was now working in A&R. Their big hit 'Diamonds' (with Harris playing lead bass) was composed by Jerry Lordan, who had already delivered three massive hits for The Shadows: 'Apache' (on which both Harris and Meehan had performed), 'Wonderful Land,' and 'Atlantis.' In one of those musical twists of fate, The Shadows' British chart-topper 'Dance On!' was replaced by Harris & Meehan's 'Diamonds' in January 1963. Following a couple of further hits, the duo's career was curtailed when Harris was injured in an automobile accident. Cliff Richard, Britain's most consistently successful chart artist, has had only had a handful of U.S. hits, but it seems remarkable that The Shadows, hugely popular in Europe and the rest of the world, have had none whatsoever.

Sweets For My Sweet
The Searchers

Released June 1963
Mercury *72172* (U.S.) / Pye *7N 15533* (U.K. #1)

The Searchers paid their dues on the same Continental circuit as The Beatles, performing at the Star Club in the notorious Reeperbahn district of Hamburg, Germany. Reckoned as second only to the Fab Four on Merseyside in terms of musicianship and local popularity, and named for the same John Wayne movie in which the big man's repetition of the phrase "That'll be the day" inspired the Buddy Holly classic, they were duly signed to Pye Records in 1963. Their first record was this cover of a Drifters U.S. hit from 1961 that took them straight to the top of the U.K. charts. The group delivered a string of Top 10 hits, including 'When You Walk In The Room' and 'Needles And Pins,' under the guidance of writer-producer Tony Hatch, and it was Hatch himself who wrote the group's second hit, 'Sugar And Spice.' While the group were highly competent musically, their sound never progressed and their chart career was cut short by a lack of original material.

You'll Never Walk Alone
Gerry & The Pacemakers

Released September 1963
Laurie *3218* (U.S.) / Columbia *DB 7126* (U.K. #1)

When Gerry & The Pacemakers became the first Liverpool group to reach Number 1 in Britain, with 'How Do You Do It,' it seemed as if they might outshine The Beatles as Liverpool's biggest pop band. And their powerful cover of 'You'll Never Walk Alone,' the 1945 Rodgers & Hammerstein classic, became their third consecutive U.K. Number 1 single at a time when The Beatles had only managed two.

That also gave them three Number 1s with their first three singles, a feat unequalled in Britain until another Liverpool band, Frankie Goes To Hollywood, did the same in 1984. Remarkably, Gerry took 'You'll Never Walk Alone' to Number 1 again, as lead vocalist of The Crowd in 1985, to raise funds for victims of a fire at Bradford soccer stadium that claimed the lives of 56 football fans.

I Wanna Be Your Man
The Rolling Stones

Released November 1963
London *9641* (U.S.) / Decca *F 11764* (U.K. #12)

John Lennon and Paul McCartney offered The Rolling Stones a helping hand by giving them 'I Wanna Be Your Man' before recording it themselves. Lennon and McCartney later offered different accounts of how the song was handed over to the Stones. Did they play an incomplete version to Jagger in a club where the Stones were performing and finish it off for him right there? Or did the two soon-to-be-pop-superpowers meet in a taxi cab in London? However they got hold of it, the Stones managed to inject some of their patented bad-boy attitude into what – in the hands of The Beatles, with Ringo singing – was a pretty tame song. It became the Stones' second U.K. hit after their cover of Chuck Berry's 'Come On.'

Within months of RCA having introduced its new 45 rpm seven-inch single back in the late 1940s, it must have been apparent that the short playing time was a problem. The result was the 'extended play' or EP record, a triumph in the art of getting quite a lot into a small space.

Introduced in late 1951, the seven-inch EP boasted two songs and a running time of just over seven minutes on each side. The extra time was achieved by compressing the music to reduce its dynamic range and cutting the disc at a low level so that the grooves could be closer together. The result was a reduction in fidelity and volume, but it proved acceptable to most listeners.

In the early 1950s the standard pop LP was a ten-inch disc holding about eight songs. Two EPs, packaged together in a similar pictorial sleeve, made a satisfactory alternative. RCA, committed to its own 45 rpm seven-inch format, initially produced just EPs and singles for its own artists. But other companies hedged their bets, sometimes releasing one set of songs as an LP, twin EPs, or multiple singles.

When the 12-inch LP became standard in pop music, midway through the 1950s, the idea of the EP as a replacement for LPs fell by the wayside. From that point on, EPs became a sampler of the LP for those who could not afford the real thing, which was certainly the case for young pop fans. They had already embraced the 45 format, and the fact that EPs came in a sleeve with a picture of their idol on the front only enhanced the appeal of these records.

Elvis Presley was one of the first artists to exploit the EP, to the extent that some thought that EPs were named for his initials. RCA issued an EP of four tracks from his LP, at the same time and in the same sleeve (later imitated by The Clash for *London Calling*). The EP went to DJs, who immediately began playing its opening track, 'Blue Suede Shoes,' giving Elvis his third hit and keeping Carl Perkins's original off the top of the chart. There was also an eight-song double-EP pack.

Eight further Elvis EPs were released in his first year with RCA. The format proved especially suitable for the soundtrack to his first film, *Love Me Tender*, since that only included four songs. Other artists and labels

followed up, and *Billboard* magazine introduced an EP chart in 1957, although it only ran for three years, by which time the format was starting to fade in the U.S. Some indication of its early demise was that while The Beatles released hundreds of EPs in markets around the world, only two official Capitol releases made it on to the U.S. market. Similarly, The Monkees issued only two EPs, and those just for jukebox owners.

In less affluent Britain, however, the EP had a much longer life. It was a cheap alternative to the LP: most of The Beatles' many British EPs served that function. EPs of original material were rarer. The Beatles' *Long Tall Sally* EP of June 1964 was one example, as was The Who's *Ready Steady Who* of 1965.

Sometimes, it was a way of cashing in on artists who had achieved a hit or two and who weren't expected to have any more. The EP might contain just two hits and two B-sides. One further function was to launch a new act, test its market potential, or cash in quickly on chart success. In January 1964, after The Rolling Stones had gained two modest hits, Decca released an EP of cover versions while they were in the studios recording their first album. Other important Stones EPs included *Five By Five* and *Got Live If You Want It*, containing bluesy material that appealed to a more dedicated audience than their singles. Many 1960s EPs have since become hugely collectable, not least because of their attractive packaging.

Perhaps the artistic high-point of the whole EP story was The Beatles' *Magical Mystery Tour* of 1967. A double EP reminiscent of the earliest EP albums, it contained six songs in elaborate packaging, including a 32-page full-color booklet. EPs had a second coming during Britain's punk-rock era. They made good commercial sense. Many of the innumerable bands launched in that shortlived era only had a couple of good songs in them. The EPs also allowed small or homemade labels to showcase several of their artists. Later, the format mutated into the maxi-single, usually on 12-inch vinyl running at 45 rpm.

Today, the EP continues to have a nominal existence through short CDs or on 12-inch vinyl and has been favored by acts including My Bloody Valentine, Belle & Sebastian, and Radiohead. Indeed, Radiohead's first commercial release, *Drill*, was an EP on CD and 12-inch vinyl. When the original format surfaces today, it is usually as a promotional stunt. Early in 2006, Paul Weller released his *As Is Now* album on two CDs. At the same time, he issued four tracks from it as a 45 rpm EP on seven-inch vinyl, for one week only.

left > The Rolling Stones' *5x5 EP*, featuring five songs recorded at Chess Studios during the group's first trip to the U.S., and The Beatles' *Magical Mystery Tour*, which includes the much loved 'I Am The Walrus.'

1963

Da Doo Ron Ron
(When He Walked Me Home)
The Crystals

Released April 1963
Philles *112* (U.S. #3) / London *HLU 9732* (U.K. #5)

Be My Baby
The Ronettes

Released August 1963
Philles *116* (U.S. #2) / London *HLU 9793* (U.K. #4)

There are those who maintain that Gene Pitney's 1961 single 'Every Breath I Take' was Phil Spector's first fully-realized Wall Of Sound production, but the cavernous depths from which The Crystals 'Da Doo Ron Ron' seems to emerge is the record that introduced America to The Wall. Spector once explained: "I was looking for a sound so strong that if the material was not the greatest, the sound would carry the record."

To achieve that sound, Spector began by putting together a hand-picked session-player elite featuring guitarists Glen Campbell, Sonny Bono, and Barney Kessel, pianist Leon Russell, and drummer Hal Blaine, to name just a few. He would augment this basic core with additional players, often cramming 30 or more musicians into a tiny studio at Gold Star in Hollywood, California, and then opening up the echo chambers to their fullest extent. While most producers were seeking a clean, clearly defined sound with lots of separation between instruments, Spector was creating a huge swirling sonic soup.

'Da Doo Ron Ron' thundered into the U.S. Top 40 on May 11, 1963, peaking at Number 3, but in purely sonic terms it was dwarfed by the signature drum lick that opened 'Be My Baby' and the swoon-inducing orchestral parts that soared through its gargantuan soundscape. Beach Boys genius Brian Wilson would later admit that 'Be My Baby' was "where I learned how to produce records." After Phil Spector, the sound of a record could be every bit as important as its melody, lyric, or performance.

PHIL SPECTOR AND HIS WALL OF SOUND

Phil Spector first appeared on the scene in 1958 with his Number 1 composition for The Teddy Bears, 'To Know Him Is To Love Him.' He then spent two years learning about record production under the expert guidance of Jerry Leiber and Mike Stoller. Spector was present at most of their sessions between 1959 and 1961, although he would later make some wild claims about his input, hotly denied by the duo. He set up his Philles label in late 1961, and the acclaimed recordings he made between 1963 and 1966 were all taped at Gold Star studios in Los Angeles.

To create his famous Wall Of Sound, Spector used a regular team of local session musicians, who became known as The Wrecking Crew. Despite the advent of stereo and multi-track facilities, he insisted on releasing his records in mono: that way, he argued, they would sound the same way on radio and record as he heard them in the studio. Using multiple combinations of instruments and rehearsing his musicians for hours, and sometimes days on end, he would then record everyone as an ensemble. This resulted in considerable leakage of sound between microphones but it gave his three-minute slices of magic their unique sound. Spector called these anthems of the generation his "little symphonies for the kids."

After an early incident when DJs flipped one of his records, he began putting somewhat second-rate instrumentals on his B-sides to ensure this would never happen again. Spector used the best writers he could find to compose his material, beginning with Jeff Barry and Ellie Greenwich, with whom he wrote 'Da Doo Ron Ron' and 'Then He Kissed Me' for The Crystals and 'Be My Baby' and 'Baby I Love You' for The Ronettes. He later teamed up with Barry Mann and Cynthia Weil for further hits, including the classic Righteous Brothers' 1964 smash 'You've Lost That Lovin' Feelin'.'

His masterwork was Ike & Tina Turner's 'River Deep, Mountain High,' a monster of a record that featured over 20 musicians in the cramped studio and an additional 20 background vocalists. Hailed as a work of genius in Britain, it was virtually ignored by American radio and the song only reached Number 88. This rejection so enraged Spector that he closed down his Philles label and went into semi-retirement. He returned at the end of the 1960s to salvage The Beatles' album *Let It Be* (or, if you ask Paul McCartney and many others, to ruin it) and produced albums for John Lennon (*Imagine*) and George Harrison (*All Things Must Pass*).

Puff (The Magic Dragon)
Peter Paul & Mary

Released February 1963
Warner *5348* (U.S. #2) / Warner *WB 95* (U.K.)

Peter Paul & Mary were the most popular folk-based group of the 1960s, scoring ten albums in the American Top 20 between 1962 and 1970. They mixed children's songs, comedy, and folk material, and were partially responsible for Bob Dylan's first popularity thanks to their hit recordings of his songs 'Blowin' In The Wind' and 'Don't Think Twice It's All Right' in 1963. Following the trio's first two hits in 1962, 'Lemon Tree' and 'If I Had A Hammer,' they reached Number 2 on the U.S. chart with 'Puff The Magic Dragon,' which became a children's favorite, despite some rumored drug connotations. It was based on a poem written by Leonard Lipton in 1959. Group member Paul Stookey said later: "Puff never was anything except a song about the innocence of childhood and the sadness of the passing of that kind of innocence that we all feel."

Ring Of Fire
Johnny Cash

Released May 1963
Columbia *42788* (U.S. #17) / CBS *AAG 159* (U.K.)

'Ring Of Fire' was the single that cemented Cash's reputation as the outsider anti-hero of country music. Like many of his hits of the time, it spent several weeks atop the country chart, but also reached Number 17 on the U.S. pop chart, making it Cash's biggest mainstream success since 'Ballad Of A Teenage Queen' and 'Guess Things Happen That Way,' which both made the Top 20 in 1958. With its jaunty rhythm offset by that memorably ominous vocal delivery, the song has all the hallmarks of classic Cash, even if its toughest critics find the breezy Mariachi trumpet break to be at odds with lyrics about falling "down, down, down."

Unlike many of his other most famous recordings, 'Ring Of Fire' was not one of Cash's own compositions. It was written for him by his future wife June Carter – a big country music star in her own right as part of the second incarnation of The Carter Family – and singer-songwriter Merle Kilgore. Carter and Kilgore most likely had Cash in mind when they wrote the song, however: it sounds today as well-suited to the Man In Black as any of his self-penned hits, from 'I Walk The Line' to 'Folsom Prison Blues.'

Surfin' U.S.A.
The Beach Boys

Released March 1963
Capitol *4932* (U.S. #3) / Capitol *CL 15305* (U.K. #24)

Given their shaky start, it's a miracle The Beach Boys survived. Their sparky 1961 debut single, 'Surfin',' wiped out at Number 75 and earned them so little money that guitarist Al Jardine quit to study dentistry. Although the follow-up, 'Surfin' Safari,' took them into the Top 20, their third single, 'Ten Little Indians,' couldn't struggle beyond Number 49.

Things looked very promising when a fourth release, 'Surfin' U.S.A.,' soared to Number 3. Then, when Jan & Dean hit Number 1 two weeks later with 'Surf City,' written by head Beach Boy Brian Wilson, the group

began to look like the biggest new musical force in America. Ultimately, though, 'Surfin' U.S.A.' plunged them into an embarrassing and costly fracas when Chuck Berry sued because the song was almost identical to his 1958 hit 'Sweet Little Sixteen.' (Evidently Chuck had forgotten that 'Maybellene,' which made him a star, was little more than a re-write of Bob Wills's 'Ida Red.')

Despite their ups and downs, The Beach Boys persevered and, by the end of 1963, they were the biggest group in America. And then The Beatles showed up. "They eclipsed a lot of what we'd worked for," said Brian Wilson. "I just couldn't handle the fact that there were these four guys from England coming over here to America to invade our territory."

Wilson hit back with the brilliantly arranged and masterfully performed teen epic 'I Get Around,' delivering The Beach Boys their first U.S. Number 1 and serving notice on The Beatles that America's surf kings were here to stay. The most exciting chart battle of the decade was on.

Can't Get Used To Losing You
Andy Williams

Released March 1963
Columbia *42674* (U.S. #2) / CBS *AAG 138* (U.K. #2)

Certain M.O.R. songs transcend the schmaltz of that genre, and this hauntingly restless Doc Pomus-Mort Schuman composition is one of the best. It was Williams's 14th chart entry, peaking at Number 2 on both sides of the Atlantic, but more significantly it made Williams hip with a younger audience. A ska-punk treatment of the song by The Beat restored it to the U.K. Top 3 in 1983, and when Enya's debut single, 'Orinoco Flow,' hit the British Number 1 spot in 1988 it was impossible not to notice the resemblance between her synthesized string arrangement and the pizzicato violins that drive 'Can't Get Used To Losing You.'

Fingertips – Pt. 2
Little Stevie Wonder

Released June 1963
Tamla *54080* (U.S. #1) / Oriole *CBA 1853* (U.K.)

The marketing of Steveland Morris Judkins was highly imaginative. Having signed the precociously gifted multi-instrumentalist in 1962, Motown Records had to work out how to present him to the world. First, he needed a name. He was just five feet tall, so 'Little' linked him nicely to Little Richard, Little Walter, and other rhythm & blues greats. Stevie was an appropriately diminutive connection to his given name, and Wonder had the edge over Judkins.

After his first album, Motown wanted to capitalize on the energy of his live shows, so they released *Little Stevie Wonder – The 12-year-old*

Genius. Stevie was now 13, but Motown wasn't about to let mere facts get in the way of a great title. Better yet, Stevie was blind, black, and soulful, so the word Genius slyly implied a younger version of Ray Charles, widely known as The Genius.

All of this, however, would count for nothing if Stevie couldn't live up to Motown's carefully contrived hype. 'Fingertips – Pt. 2,' a hand-clappin', foot-stompin', harmonica-based call-and-response riot, recorded live in Chicago, proved beyond a shadow of a doubt that he could. "It was the first time he had ever performed it," remembered Motown producer Hank Cosby, who had written the music but left the words to Stevie. "As he was singing, half the song was ad-libbed right there."

On August 24, 1963, the single and album made Stevie the first artist ever to top America's three key charts – pop singles, rhythm & blues singles, and LPs – all in the same week. Enough said.

Blue Velvet
Bobby Vinton

Released August 1963
Epic *9614* (U.S. #1) / Columbia *DB 7110* (U.K.)

Vinton was yet another student of the Dick Clark college of pop stars and one of a whole string of Bobbys who appeared on the American pop scene at the time, alongside Vee, Rydell, and Darin. He may well have inspired the 1962 Marcie Blane-Susan Maughan hit 'Bobby's Girl,' but this particular Bobby was the most successful chart act with a run of U.S. hits from 1962 to 1975, although in Britain he was much less popular and only had three hits.

'Blue Velvet' was originally recorded by Tony Bennett and The Percy Faith Orchestra back in 1951, but Vinton's U.S. chart-topper is now considered to be the definitive version. It wasn't a hit in Britain, though, until 1990, when it was used in a TV advertisement for a face cream. The recording also featured in David Lynch's critically acclaimed 1986 movie of the same name.

Louie Louie
The Kingsmen

Released September 1963
Wand *143* (U.S. #2) / Pye *7N 25231* (U.K. #26)

An undisputed triumph of style over substance, 'Louie Louie' provided a blueprint for every garage-rock band that followed. Originally by Richard Berry, the song was given a new lease on life by The Kingsmen's loose, lugubrious arrangement, in particular the stuttering third beat. This offbeat, now commonplace, was unusual at the time and apparently arose when frontman Jack Ely muddled the rhythm while teaching the song to the rest of the band.

Another important part of the appeal of 'Louie Louie' is its primitive sound. It was The Kingsmen's second single, recorded in a budget studio for less than $50 with just three microphones. One was on the bass drum, one was overhead – which vocalist Jack Ely strained on tiptoe to reach and which was also charged with picking up the rest of the band – and one was in front of Mike Mitchell's guitar amp and switched on only for his solo.

'Louie Louie' failed to make much of an impression on its first release on the Jerden label in June 1963 but started to climb up the charts after a reissue three months later on Wand. By the beginning of 1964 it had climbed to Number 2 on the U.S. singles chart and peaked at Number 26 in Britain.

The success rather went to the group's heads, particularly drummer Lynn Easton, who took the copyright on the group's name and insisted he take over on vocals. Two members left the band – a dissatisfied Ely, whose raunchy warble was another key ingredient in the song's success, along with bassist Bob Nordby – and The Kingsmen were never the same again.

Dominique
The Singing Nun (Soeur Sourire)

Released November 1963
Philips *40152* (U.S. #1) / Philips *BF 1293* (U.K. #7)

The Singing Nun must rate as one of the most unusual acts ever to grace the charts. Aside from qualifying as a one-hit wonder, she was the first artist with a simultaneous Number 1 single and album on the American charts. She even won a Grammy award, for Best Gospel Or Other Religious Recording. Born Jeanine Deckers in Belgium in 1933, she became a Dominican nun and adopted the name Sister Luc-Gabrielle in the 1950s.

In 1961, accompanied by her Mother Superior, she visited Philips Records headquarters in Brussels. Could the company arrange to record her and manufacture a few hundred records to be given as gifts to the other nuns?

Philips agreed to a private recording, but when the company's executives heard the material, they offered her a contract, with all proceeds going to the Dominican order. They also suggested she be known on record as Soeur Sourire (Sister Smile). Following large sales throughout Europe, her recordings were released in Britain and America, where she was billed as The Singing Nun.

'Dominique,' sung mostly in French, was written as a tribute to St Dominic, founder of her Catholic order. The Singing Nun's album spent a remarkable ten weeks at Number 1 in America and was replaced in early 1964 by the arrival of The Beatles' first U.S. collection, *Meet The Beatles*. It was the beginning of a new era, and it's unlikely that the she would have been so successful had she arrived after 1963.

Jeanine Deckers continued with missionary work throughout her life but was later hounded by the Belgian tax authorities for back-taxes relating to her income as Soeur Sourire. In 1985, in despair over her tax difficulties, she took her own life in a suicide pact with a close friend.

House Of The Rising Sun
The Animals

Released June 1964
MGM *13264* (U.S. #1) / Columbia *DB 7301* (U.K. #1)

Maybe this 1964 recording really did make Bob Dylan decide to put down his acoustic guitar and pick up an electric, to the disgust of many of his folk fans. The Animals started as The Alan Price Combo, a rhythm & blues band from a working-class neighborhood of Newcastle Upon Tyne in north-east England. Relocating to London, they became The Animals and were coupled with up-and-coming record producer Mickie Most, on EMI's Columbia label.

Most used to fly to the U.S. every couple of weeks to pick up the latest songs from the leading Brill Building songwriters, and was keen for the group to record the poppy 'Can't You Hear My Heartbeat' (later a hit for Herman's Hermits). The Animals refused, though, insisting instead on taping 'House Of The Rising Sun,' a traditional folk blues of uncertain heritage that was first recorded in the 1920s.

The Animals began their session for the song one morning at 8:00am. Following just one run-through, it was promptly taped and the work was over by 8:30. Total recording cost? Just £4/10/- (£4.50, about $12.50 at the time). With the song in the can, Most was now convinced that it would be a hit, despite its lyric about a brothel and its four-and-a-half-minute length at a time when most singles clocked in at about two-and-

a-half. EMI weren't so easily convinced, but following the Top 30 appearance of The Animals' debut, 'Baby Let Me Take You Home,' Most persuaded them to release the powerful performance. In America, where radio play for such a lengthy song was impossible, MGM released an edited version.

In the wake of the song's success there was considerable disagreement within the group as to who had arranged this traditional number. The only name that appeared on the label credit was that of Alan Price, although all The Animals had contributed, notably Hilton Valentine, who provided the distinctive guitar riff. The rest of the group, somewhat naive in the ways of the music industry, were informed that there wasn't enough room on the label for all of their names – a pretty lame excuse.

Because
Dave Clark Five

Released July 1964
Epic *9704* (U.S. #3) / Not issued U.K.

British drummer Dave Clark was an astute businessman from the very beginning. He managed the group himself, and it was Clark who arranged and produced the group's hits, leasing the masters to EMI's Columbia label in the U.K. (and Epic in the U.S.). and setting up his own music-publishing company to oversee royalties. With full control over all aspects of his career, and negotiating an unusually high royalty deal with record companies, Clark was a millionaire by his early 20s and invested his money wisely. In America, the group rivaled The Beatles, enjoying sixteen Top 30 hits between 1964 and 1967. Following their massive success with 'Glad All Over,' 'Bits And Pieces,' and 'Do You Love Me,' this ballad – written by Dave Clark and keyboardist Mike Smith – was an American-only release and became their biggest U.S. hit so far.

A Hard Day's Night
The Beatles

Released July 1964
Capitol *5222* (U.S. #1) / Parlophone *R 5160* (U.K. #1)

The Beatles first arrived on American soil on February 3, 1964, and immediately took the country by storm. By the time they released this single they had already scored eleven Top 40 hits and four Number 1s in America in just four months. This notched up their fifth Number 1, on both sides of the Atlantic. At this point in their career the group could probably have recorded the weather report put to music and still have a chart-topper – but of course they delivered yet another gem.

It was the title track of their debut movie and accompanying album, which was their first to contain entirely original material (although on the abbreviated and rearranged U.S. edition, two tracks were instrumentals, performed by The George Martin Orchestra). The title was a Ringo-ism, uttered after a long day's filming, and the song was created literally overnight. While making the film, loosely based around a 'typical' day in the life of the group, producer Walter Shenson mentioned to John Lennon that it would be great to have a song called 'A Hard Day's Night' to play over the credits. Lennon said he'd think about it, and at 8:30 the following morning, he and Paul McCartney turned up and sang Shenson the finished article. They recorded it at Abbey Road studios on April 16, 1964. It is especially notable for George Harrison's strident opening chord, the subject of much debate among guitarists ever since, and for winning The Beatles their first Grammy award, for Best Vocal Performance By A Vocal Group.

You Really Got Me
The Kinks

Released August 1964
Reprise *0306* (U.S. #7) / Pye *7N 15673* (U.K. #1)

One of the landmark hits of the British Invasion, 'You Really Got Me' is cited by many commentators as the birthplace of heavy rock – an argument given further credence 14 years later when a cover of the song launched the metal quartet Van Halen.

With its simple two-chord riff and snarling vocal, the third single from The Kinks is a world apart from the gentler, psychedelic material that singer-songwriter Ray Davies would devise in subsequent years. Nonetheless, it proved to be the making of the group, topping the U.K. singles chart and climbing into the U.S. Top 10 a month later – no mean feat for a fledgling British quartet that had only formed a year earlier. The record's defining aspect is the dirty, distorted guitar sound, provided by Ray Davies's 17-year-old brother Dave (and not, despite persistent rumors to the contrary, by future Led Zeppelin axeman Jimmy Page).

Dave achieved this revolutionary sound by cutting slits in the speaker of his Elpico amplifier, and used it not just for the main power-chord riff but also during his juddering, ferocious guitar solo that, like the song itself, is reminiscent of The Kingsmen's lo-fi 1963 classic 'Louie Louie.'

The Kinks went on to become one of the most internationally successful British groups of the next decade, later inspiring not just heavy rock but also the mid-1990s Britpop scene.

Time Is On My Side
The Rolling Stones

Released September 1964
London *9708* (U.S. #6) / Not issued U.K.

Little Red Rooster
The Rolling Stones

Released November 1964
Not issued U.S. / Decca *F 12014* (U.K. #1)

'Time Is On My Side' was a powerfully soulful cut squirreled away on the B-side of 'Baby Don't Come On With Me,' a 1963 single by trombone virtuoso Kai Winding with the song credited to Norman Meade. It remained a humble B-side when Irma Thomas released her version the following year, but the Stones spotted its potential to be something bigger.

At London's Regent Sound studio in June 1964 they recorded the slow, smoldering version, complete with gospel-style organ, that delivered their first U.S. Top 10 entry – and still crediting Meade as composer. Just as they knew nothing of the Kai Winding original, they had no idea that 'Norman Meade' was really acclaimed American songsmith, producer, and arranger Jerry Ragavoy. The Stones didn't release 'Time' in the U.K., probably because they felt that it didn't suit the wild-men-of-rock image they had cultivated at home. As Stones guitarist Keith Richards said: "In America we were basically known for heavy, slow-ish ballads. 'Time Is On My Side,' 'Tell Me,' 'Heart Of Stone.'"

But this doesn't explain why, towards the end of 1964, they similarly failed to release in America their chart-topping British version of the Willie Dixon composition 'Little Red Rooster.' It was, after all, heavy and slow-ish – just what their Stateside fans were lapping up. But the group's reasoning was probably right. They'd picked up on the song from the Sam Cooke version, which had already done well enough in the U.S. charts (Number 11) to significantly reduce the sales potential of their own attempt.

Here I Go Again
The Hollies

Released May 1964
Imperial *66044* (U.S.) / Parlophone *R 5137* (U.K. #4)

As Merseybeat gathered momentum, Britain's record companies began looking beyond Liverpool for talent. The Hollies from nearby Manchester were among the first beneficiaries of that policy. After four chart entries, each bigger than the last, they consolidated their success with their vibrant performance of 'Here I Go Again,' confirming them as the U.K.'s best vocal harmony group. Even so, they didn't secure a Number 1 until the unstoppable 'I'm Alive' did the trick on June 24, 1965, prompting Hollie and working-class lad Graham Nash to declare that they had escaped the cycle of "work 40 years, get a gold watch, and then die." He concluded: "Music saved our ass."

DICK CLARK: THE AMERICAN BANDSTAND MAN

Dick Clark is one of the most important figures in the early development of rock'n'roll and its transformation into the innocuous pop of the early 1960s. Clark was a radio DJ in Philadelphia in 1956 when he was invited to take over a local pop-music TV show after its original host had been arrested for drunken driving.

The format of *Bandstand* was simple. Records were played, clean-cut well-dressed and impeccably-behaved teenagers danced, and the stars of the day made brief personal appearances, though there was no live playing. In August 1957, following phenomenal local success, the show went national, appearing on ABC-TV for 90 minutes every weekday afternoon, just as teenagers were coming home from school.

The renamed *American Bandstand* gave early national exposure to many important artists, including Chuck Berry, Jerry Lee Lewis, Buddy Holly, and Chubby Checker. It was racially integrated, with a modest number of black teenagers dancing alongside their white peers and even, on occasions, interviewed on air. The show made Philadelphia the most important market for the music industry, with particular benefits to local labels such as Cameo-Parkway, Swan, and Chancellor. Clark had financial involvement in them all, as well as 30 more companies involved in publishing, distribution, artist management, and record manufacture.

This cozy relationship inevitably drew the attention of the payola investigation, which looked into the practice of record companies buying airtime. But while the scandal ended the career of the more threatening Alan Freed, it did no great harm to that of Clark, although he was forced to give up his music-business interests.

In a public hearing, he told the congressional investigation into payola that he had merely been trying to secure his financial future. Indeed, he always maintained that his interest in rock'n'roll had been primarily commercial: his own tastes ran more to big-band music. Backed by his employers and respectful to the committee, Clark walked away with his reputation effectively intact, despite admitting he had received jewelry and a fur stole from a record-company executive.

A clean-cut, avuncular figure, 27 years old when his TV series went national, Clark successfully moderated the element of threat in rock'n'roll music, paving the way for the bland teen-idol period of the early 1960s. He would host *American Bandstand* until 1989, by which time his broadcasting career had moved on to quiz-shows, variety, and production.

That year he told *Rolling Stone* magazine that he had learned an important lesson from the payola hearings: "Protect your ass at all times."

Walk On By
Dionne Warwick

Released April 1964
Scepter *1274* (U.S. #6) / Pye *7N 25241* (U.K. #9)

Florence Greenberg, head of Scepter Records, thought so little of 'Walk On By' that she relegated it to a B-side. DJ Murray The K disagreed with the decision to put 'Any Old Time Of The Day' on the A-side and began playing the flip, creating the momentum that would take 'Walk On By' into the U.S. Top 10. The record scored similarly in Britain.

Without wishing to beat the unfortunate Greenberg over the head, it's certainty difficult to understand her initial decision. 'Walk On By' is perhaps the greatest ever collaboration between composers Bacharach & David and vocalist Dionne Warwick.

Subtle piano and chinka-chinka guitars form the opening before Warwick, always close to sobbing, begins gently enunciating a lyric in which the narrator tells her ex that, should he come across her, he should ignore the devastation he has wreaked by leaving her. As she sings that self-flagellating title refrain, it is counterpointed by flugelhorn.

The end of each verse in which the title refrain is set is followed by a rumbling piano run, to stunning effect, and the instrumental break is given over to the velvet strings heard briefly in the second verse.

There have been many cover versions of the song, the most noteworthy probably Isaac Hayes's 12-minute vamp and The Stranglers' more aggressive rendition. The definitive performance remains Warwick's original, a recording that possesses utter class and utter soulfulness, a difficult balance for many – including, often, Bacharach & David.

left > Burt Bacharach (left) and his regular lyrical collaborator, Hal David.
below left > Dionne Warwick, flanked by autograph-hunters, on a trip to New York in August 1964.

THE COCKTAIL-LOUNGE CLASS OF BACHARACH & DAVID

It was perfectly appropriate that Burt Bacharach, a classically trained musician, should meet professional lyricist Hal David in the Brill Building, where so many pop songwriting partnerships flourished. They immediately had hits together – with 'The Story Of My Life,' recorded by Marty Robbins, and Perry Como's jaunty 'Magic Moments,' both in 1957 – but did not immediately become exclusive partners. That happened around the time they began writing a string of hits for Dionne Warwick.

The gifted black vocalist was originally hired merely to sing the duo's demos, but they soon gave Warwick her own career, starting with the seething 'Don't Make Me Over' (1963) and continuing through the dramatic 'Anyone Who Had a Heart,' the masochistic 'Walk On By,' the blissful 'I Say a Little Prayer,' and the deceptively pretty tale of crushed ambition, 'Do You Know the Way to San Jose?' These songs – like so many of Bacharach & David's – were notable for their lyrical maturity, musical sophistication, and often an ability to convey a convincing female perspective.

Gene Pitney and Jackie DeShannon – good songwriters themselves – benefited from the magic touch of Bacharach & David, Pitney with 'True Love Never Runs Smooth' and 'Twenty Four Hours From Tulsa' and DeShannon with 'What The World Needs Now Is Love.' That magic touch ensured the duo were hired to work on movies, devising the title themes to What's New Pussycat? – its nonsensical lyric sung with ludicrous enthusiasm by Tom Jones – and Alfie. The latter is Bacharach's

favorite of his own songs, but Cilla Black's impassioned version was rejected by the producers of the movie while still managing to go Top 10 in the U.K. charts. Herb Alpert recorded Bacharach & David's theme for the spoof Bond flick Casino Royale, but their biggest movie-related triumph was 'Raindrops Keep Falling On My Head.' Although this euphoric creation seemed lost in the sometimes gritty post-modernist western Butch Cassidy And The Sundance Kid, it had enough feel-good quality to ensure that B.J. Thomas's single became a U.S. Number 1. Sacha Distel had the biggest of three simultaneous U.K. hit versions.

Casino Royale also saw the unveiling of the duo's 'The Look Of Love,' sung by Dusty Springfield, the first song they gave to her after she had hit big with Bacharach & David material by issuing her own takes on the original versions of 'Wishin' And Hopin'' and 'I Just Don't Know What To Do With Myself.' Herb Alpert meanwhile achieved a U.S. Number 1 with the pair's 'This Guy's In Love With You,' and The Carpenters inaugurated their chart career with 'Close To You.'

Bacharach & David's partnership and friendship was frayed in the early 1970s as their work for the soundtrack to Lost Horizon was poorly received and then pulled apart by publishing-related lawsuits. Some have suggested that their compositions too often stray uncomfortably close to cocktail-lounge music in pursuit of class – Warwick's excepted, there was little grit in their songs – but there is no doubting that Bacharach & David brought a genuine sophistication to post-Elvis popular music.

Where Did Our Love Go
The Supremes

Released June 1964
Motown *1060* (U.S. #1) / Stateside *SS 327* (U.K. #3)

Baby Love
The Supremes

Released September 1964
Motown *1066* (U.S. #1) / Stateside *SS 350* (U.K. #1)

With these two singles, The Supremes began a remarkable run of Number 1 hit singles that made them the most successful girl group of the 1960s and the most bankable stars on the Motown books.

Surprisingly, however, their career didn't have a particularly auspicious start. None of the trio's first half-dozen singles made it beyond the lower reaches of the U.S. Top 100, but Motown boss Berry Gordy kept his faith in The Supremes, and in late 1963 allocated them to crack songwriting and production team Holland-Dozier-Holland as a special project.

The effect was almost instantaneous: in less than a year came a pair of landmark singles that shot The Supremes to the top of the pop firmament. 'Where Did Our Love Go' was originally offered to, and rejected by, The Marvelettes, and even The Supremes themselves, still bereft of a genuine hit, were unsure about the song. But along with 'Baby Love' it was cast from the classic Motown pop-soul mold: each is led by bright drums, strident bass, and tinkly keys. And in front of that perfect backdrop sit a pair of sumptuous Diana Ross vocals, backed with restraint and elegance by Florence Ballard and Mary Wilson. The producers had in fact argued over whether Ross or Wilson should take the lead vocal.

Not only did The Supremes sound brilliant but also they looked and acted the part, putting their peers to shame in almost every area. It's a measure of how hot The Supremes – and Holland-Dozier-Holland – were at this point in their careers when you consider the B-sides: they too are nearly faultless, particularly 'Ask Any Girl' on the flip of 'Baby Love.'

Oh Pretty Woman
Roy Orbison & The Candy Men

Released August 1964
Monument *851* (U.S. #1) / London *HLU 9919* (U.K. #1)

Many of Roy Orbison's hits seemed to be tales of woe and heartbreak with unhappy endings – although Roy concluded: "On balance, I'd say it was at least 50-50." This was probably his most upbeat song. Orbison, who adopted his trademark dark glasses one night after mislaying his regular reading specs, had bought himself out of his Sun Records contract after writing 'Claudette' for The Everly Brothers. He then recorded 'Only The Lonely' himself, after it had been turned down by Elvis and the Everlys, and it became his first major hit.

Looking for a follow-up to his June 1964 U.K. Number 1 'It's Over,' Orbison and his writing partner Bill Dees were dabbling in the studio when his wife Claudette announced that she was going shopping. Orbison: "I said, 'Do you have any money?' And Bill Dees said, 'Pretty woman never needs any money!' Then he said, 'Would that make a great song title?' I said, 'No, but 'Pretty Woman' would.' So I started playing guitar, and he was slapping the table for drums, and by the time she got back – which was about 40 minutes later – we had the song."

Orbison's life was filled with tragedy. Claudette was killed in a motorcycle accident in 1966, and two of his three children died in a house fire in 1968. Some 20 years later, when he was on the verge of a major comeback after renewed success with the Traveling Wilburys, and with a new album ready for release, he died of a heart attack, on December 6, 1988. We should be thankful that his voice and his music, at least, are still with us.

Dancing In The Street
Martha & The Vandellas

Released August 1964
Gordy *7033* (U.S. #2) / Stateside *SS 345* (U.K. #28)

Surely in the Top 5 all-time Motown classics, this is the song from which Keith Richards claims he stole the idea for his 'Satisfaction' riff. Martha Reeves and her Vandellas always played second fiddle to The Supremes in the corridors of Motown, but they still got a fair slice of the action with some classic songs, including 'Heat Wave,' 'Nowhere To Run,' and 'Jimmy Mack.'

'Dancing In The Street' was originally slated for Kim Weston, but Martha Reeves – who was working part-time as a secretary for the company – got lucky and recorded what was supposed to be the demo. There was no contest. This was the Motown sound at its very best, with the tambourine mixed so far upfront it cracked like a whip. Motown boss Berry Gordy reckoned: "My goal to hook people in the first 20 seconds was never accomplished better. The intro was a hit before Martha even opened her mouth."

Downtown
Petula Clark

Released October 1964
Warner *5494* (U.S.) / Pye *7N 15722* (U.K.)

Petula Clark was one of Europe's most popular *chanteuse* of the 1960s. Born in Epsom, Surrey in 1932, she was encouraged to sing from an early age. By 1943 she had her own radio show and during the 1940s and 1950s appeared in over 20 movies. She began recording in 1949 and was a regular chart visitor until 1972. Enter Tony Hatch, one of the U.K.'s big backroom boys of 1960s pop. As A&R manager for Pye Records in Britain he delivered hits for Emile Ford and Mark Wynter as well as writing material for American acts Bobby Rydell, Connie Francis, and Pat Boone, and arranging for Lonnie Donegan. In 1963 he traveled to Liverpool and signed The Searchers, producing all their material and writing their second big hit, 'Sugar And Spice' under the pseudonym 'Fred Nightingale.'

By this time Hatch was writing and producing for Ms. Clark. He was inspired to write 'Downtown' during a 1964 trip to New York City and his first walk down Broadway. He originally wrote the song with The Drifters in mind, but when he played the melody to Clark she told him that if he could come up with a set of lyrics to match the quality of the melody and his title 'Downtown,' she would record it.

According to Hatch, he was still writing the lyrics half an hour before it was recorded. Remarkably, 'Downtown' won a Grammy award as 'Best Rock'n'Roll Recording' and in 2003 the record won a prestigious Grammy Hall Of Fame Award. Such awards are given only to "recordings of lasting qualitative or historical significance that are at least 25 years old."

Leader Of The Pack
The Shangri Las

Released October 1964
Red Bird *10-014* (U.S. #1) / Red Bird *RB 10014* (U.K. #11)

This is a wrought-up teen drama telling the story of a girl's love for a motorbikin' boy from the wrong side of down. Spoken word sections and dramatic piano flourishes lead into impassioned call-and-response vocals before the record peaks with revving engines and screeching tires, signaling the tragic end of the bad boy with the heart of gold.

Those engine noises and tire squeals reputedly came from producer George 'Shadow' Morton's Harley Davidson, which he drove into the studio. But that might just be another example of the self-mythologizing that Morton revelled in. An enigmatic figure, he later worked with artists as diverse as Vanilla Fudge, Janis Ian, and The New York Dolls, before drug addiction drove him into obscurity. Which is where – fittingly, perhaps, given his self-cultivated aura of mystery – he remains.

The Shangri-Las had several other hits under Morton's guidance, all carefully constructed mini-operas high on kitsch but nonetheless strangely affecting. Whether the group were the embodiment of sassy street-girl cool or mere puppets in Morton's hands is difficult to assess. But it hardly matters. Between them, Morton and The Shangri-Las constructed a unique pop legacy.

Transistor radios are always associated with pop music, but their impact was slow in coming. To begin with, their relatively high price placed them well out of the reach of teenagers. True portable radios only became possible with the arrival of the transistor, invented by Bell Laboratories in 1947. Initially the new technology was used only in hearing aids, but in the early 1950s hobbyists began to experiment by using them in radios, which until then had depended on heavy, expensive, power-guzzling tubes.

Texas Instruments, one of the first companies to manufacture transistors, went looking for a partner to make a radio it had designed, but most manufacturers saw no point in undercutting their existing products. A small company in Indianapolis, known as IDEA, decided to go ahead. These were the Cold War years, and IDEA's president apparently believed that a battery radio would become an essential of life in the event of a nuclear attack.

The result was a small radio known as the Regency TR-1. It appeared on the market in November 1954, priced at $49.95 (£18), equivalent to some $350 (£200) today. Batteries were extra. It used only four transistors, and its performance was poor. A much better eight-transistor radio was produced by Raytheon in February 1955, at $80. This American manufacturing activity was a false dawn, however. In August 1955 a Japanese company called Totsuko (later Sony) produced its first transistor radio, the TR-55. Its real breakthrough came with the TR-63, the first 'pocketable' radio. In truth, it was slightly too large for a normal shirt pocket, so Sony ordered a batch of special shirts with enlarged pockets, to be worn by its sales force.

At first both Japanese and American-built transistor radios were expensive. Only in the 1960s, when U.S. prices dropped below $20, they did become readily available to the teenagers with whom they are always associated. Previously, radios had been large objects in the family living room, which meant that young people's music was subject to parental scrutiny, criticism, and mockery. Now it became possible for the young to listen to music away from their parents, which created a whole new market. It was a turning point in the development of pop music and the music industry.

You've Lost That Lovin' Feelin'
The Righteous Brothers

Released December 1964
Philles *124* (U.S. #1) / London *HLU 9943* (U.K. #1)

'You've Lost That Lovin' Feelin" is officially the most broadcast record of the 20th century in America (at least according to the BMI performing rights organization). But, perhaps more importantly, it is also a record of incredible sophistication and innovation – attributes that aren't always reflected in the amount of radio plays a single receives.

The Righteous Brothers were a West Coast vocal duo consisting of the unrelated Bill Medley and Bobby Hatfield. Medley was an able songwriter himself, penning 'Little Latin Lupe Lu,' covered by Mitch Ryder in 1966. Nonetheless, it was frustration at their own chart failure that prompted The Righteous Bothers in the early 1960s to seek out legendary producer and idol-maker Phil Spector, a trek that so many other would-be stars would make. Spector recognized great raw material in the duo, in particular the magical combination of Medley's deep baritone and Hatfield's skilful tenor and falsetto lines.

Spector approached songwriters Barry Mann and Cynthia Weil, with whom he'd already had some success with The Paris Sisters and The Crystals. The husband-and-wife team decided that Medley and Hatfield's voices would be suited to a ballad and set about writing one, inspired by a favorite song of the moment, 'Baby I Need Your Loving' by The Four Tops, written by Holland-Dozier-Holland. Mann & Weil played two verses and the chorus to Spector over the telephone. The producer was extremely enthusiastic. How could he not be? The song contained one of the great opening lines of all time, written by Mann, who did not usually provide the lyrics: "You never close your eyes any more when I kiss your lips."

The pair finished the song with Spector. His contributions were valuable: Spector came up with the idea for the descending refrain at the end of each chorus, "Gone, gone, gone – whoa-oh-ohhh," and for the Latin-style riff leading into the bridge, which made it highly distinctive for the time.

The finished record was revolutionary. Part of this was deliberate: it was nearly four minutes long, usually a real obstacle to radio airplay in those days. Mostly it was accidental: the artists and writers would find themselves credited with inventing a new genre, blue-eyed soul. While they took their initial creative cue from The Four Tops, Mann & Weil never imagined they would help bridge the gap between white and black musical styles.

Despite all this, the record did not mark the start of an especially fruitful relationship between composers and artist. Although Mann & Weil did provide another U.S. Number 1 for The Righteous Brothers in 1966, with '(You're My) Soul And Inspiration,' that song is far behind 'Unchained Melody' among the Brothers' best remembered records. Both writers and artists, however, would reap the financial dividends of 'Lovin' Feelin'' for some time to come and enjoy the record's artistic glory forever.

left > Barry Mann and Cynthia Weil, captured in the midst of composing one of their many hit songs.
right > The Brill Building in New York City, where many of the duo's songwriting peers were based.

BARRY MANN & CYNTHIA WEIL: NEW YORK SONGWRITING

Budding New York songwriters Cynthia Weil and Barry Mann met when Weil deliberately engineered a meeting at the offices of Aldon Music Publishing for reasons more romantic than professional. Weil was a writer from a Broadway tradition. Mann had turned to songwriting almost in desperation after dropping out of an architecture course. He had dabbled with performing, scoring a Top 10 hit in 1961 with 'Who Put The Bomp (In The Bomp, Bomp, Bomp).' Vinny Monty's 'Painting The Town With Teardrops' was the first song Mann & Weil wrote together and their first collaboration successfully placed with an artist, while 'Bless You' by Tony Orlando was the duo's first hit, in 1961, the same year they married.

Mann handed over all the lyric writing to Weil, and the two settled on a technique of melody-first from which they almost never deviated. They loved the atmosphere at Aldon Music on New York City's Broadway, writing nearly half of their songs in one of the spartan cubicles there and often overhearing the works-in-progress of other Aldon writers such as Neil Sedaka & Howard Greenfield and fellow man-and-wife team Gerry Goffin & Carole King. This is often referred to as the Brill Building scene, although Aldon was in offices a block away from the Brill Building, which was at 1619 Broadway.

Phil Spector was one of the first to spot their abilities and they repaid his faith with a couple of early-1960s hits for his girl group The Crystals, 'Uptown' and 'He's Sure The Boy I Love.' The former was a pointer to the quietly revolutionary lyrics that Weil would write, its proletarian tableau depicting a man taking solace from his lack of fulfillment and power at work through the joy of his domestic life. Spector declined to release 'On Broadway,' another song the pair had provided for The Crystals, so they approached Leiber & Stoller and their four-way rewrite became a hit for The Drifters in 1963. Evidently Spector had no hard feelings: in 1964 Mann, Weil, and Spector collaborated on the phenomenally successful Righteous Brothers hit 'You've Lost That Lovin' Feelin'.'

Weil was now in her stride as a social commenter as the pair provided The Animals with the angry-young-man anthem 'We've Gotta Get Out Of This Place' and Paul Revere & The Raiders with the anti-drugs diatribe 'Kicks.' However, their anti-segregationist song 'Only In America,' designed for The Drifters, was considered too controversial for radio airplay, and so they censored themselves for a version that became a patriotic chart success for Jay & The Americans. As if to prove that not all issues are black and white, they wrote the reflective 'Shades Of Gray,' recorded by The Monkees.

The golden age of the Brill Building sputtered to an end towards the close of the 1960s, but Mann & Weil's own success continued into the 1970s, with Elvis Presley covering 'I Just Can't Help Believing' and Dolly Parton recording 'Here You Come Again.' The next decade saw them branching out into soundtracks, including the animated movies *An American Tail* (1986) and *Muppet Treasure Island* (1996). This remarkable team entered the 21st century proving they still had chart appeal by working with Hanson.

WHEN JACKIE DESHANNON WALKS IN THE ROOM

Jackie DeShannon seemed destined for stardom as a recording artist. Not only could she write songs, but she was a powerful singer possessed of a quite incandescent beauty. For reasons that remain unfathomable, she secured only a couple of significant hits as an artist, one of which was by another writer. But she has had a very successful career as a freelance songwriter and contributed some memorable compositions to the rock canon.

Born in Kentucky, DeShannon was a singer from the start of her career, but at the same time she was placing songs with artists, often co-written with her friend Sharon Sheeley. Among these early works were two U.S. hits for Brenda Lee – 'Dum Dum,' Number 4 in 1961, and 'Heart In Hand,' Number 15 in 1962 – and '(He's) The Great Impostor,' which reached Number 30 in 1961 for The Fleetwoods.

Over in Britain, The Searchers had two hits in 1964 with songs associated with DeShannon: 'Needles And Pins,' which she had recorded, although it was written by Sonny Bono and Jack Nitzsche, and her own composition 'When You Walk In The Room.' Both of the Searchers recordings feature 12-string guitar riffs and a chiming ambience more commonly associated with folk rather than rock. DeShannon imported a little of folk's intellectual gravitas, too: not many songs of the era featured the word "nonchalant," but there it is in 'When You Walk In The Room.'

DeShannon was responsible for Marianne Faithfull's 'Come And Stay With Me,' a U.K. Number 4 and U.S. Number 26 in 1965. Her links to the British scene did not end there. A pre-Led Zeppelin Jimmy Page collaborated with her on several songs, and a Page B-side, 'Keep Movin',' featured her vocals. It has been rumored that the Led Zeppelin song 'Tangerine' was written about DeShannon.

Also in 1965, DeShannon scored her first major hit as an artist when she took 'What The World Needs Now Is Love,' an idealistic Bacharach & David song that Dionne Warwick had rejected, into the U.S. Top 10. The same year saw the appearance of The Byrds' debut album, which contained an excellent DeShannon song, 'Don't Doubt Yourself Babe,' a thank-you for the support she'd shown the band. DeShannon also wrote the erotically-charged theme song for the movie *Splendor In The Grass*.

She achieved her biggest solo hit in 1969 with 'Put A Little Love In Your Heart,' a song DeShannon wrote with Jimmy Holiday and her brother Randy Myers, full of hippie-inflected idealism and almost a bookend to 'What The World Needs Now Is Love,' but with some funky undertones. It went to Number 4. The same team was responsible for the U.S. Top 40 song 'Love Will Find A Way' later that year, marking DeShannon's last hit as an artist. Although she made several singer-songwriter albums in the 1970s, her performing career ground to a halt for two decades thanks to a lack of artistic control. However, as if to prove the utter unpredictability of fate, she found herself with a transatlantic smash in 1981 when gravel-throated singer Kim Carnes unexpectedly covered the smoky, atmospheric 'Bette Davis Eyes' that DeShannon had written with Donna Weiss.

(I Can't Get No) Satisfaction
The Rolling Stones

Released May 1965
London *9766* (U.S. #1)/ Decca *F 12220* (U.K. #1)

As Tears Go By
Marianne Faithfull

Released July 1964
London *9697* (U.S. #22)/ Decca *F 11923* (U.K. #9)

The Rolling Stones started out by reinventing Chicago electric blues for a British teen audience, but their far-sighted manager, Andrew Loog Oldham, realized that the key to longevity lay in persuading the band to write their own material. The story goes that he locked an initially reluctant Mick Jagger and Keith Richards into a room to compose their first songs, which they later dismissed as commercial pap. But after these inauspicious beginnings, the two rapidly matured into a hit-making machine to rival Lennon & McCartney.

One of the first Jagger-Richards songs the world heard was 'As Tears Go By,' as performed by Marianne Faithfull. A poignant folk ballad perfectly suited to Faithfull's fragile voice, it was a big American and British hit a year before the Stones released their own version (which became a U.S. hit single) and a year before the group really got into their stride recording their own material. Around the same time that Faithfull made her chart debut with 'As Tears Go By,' in summer 1964, they scored a minor U.S. hit with the self-penned 'Tell Me (You're Coming Back)' but followed it with a couple of covers, 'Time Is On My Side' and 'It's All Over Now.' It wasn't until 1965 and 'The Last Time' that the famous run of big Jagger-Richards hits started. 'Satisfaction,' perhaps the most famous of them all, went to the top in the middle of the year.

Although it has come to be considered as a 'rock' archetype, 'Satisfaction' is a record crammed with pop hooks: Richards's simple fuzz guitar riff, Charlie Watts's drum break before the chorus, and the shouting frustration of the chorus itself. Jagger and Richards chanting "I can't get no! Satisfaction!" seemed to embody the anger of teenagers kicking against the constraints of the staid adult world, just at a time when they were becoming a real social force. Soul legend Otis Redding scored a minor hit with his cover of the song in 1966, a version which the Stones themselves professed to prefer to their own. For most of us, however, it's their original that satisfies the most.

Faithfull went on to have a number of wistful folk-pop hits during the next few years before drug addiction sent her into what seemed like an irreversible tailspin in the early 1970s. To her considerable credit, she re-emerged at the very end of that decade, her voice transformed to a husky growl, with a classic rendition of 'The Ballad Of Lucy Jordan.' This heralded a second phase of her career that continues still. These days, Faithfull is the grande dame of rock chicks, releasing occasional albums assisted by a host of younger, mainly male, musicians. The Stones, of course, just never stopped rolling. The hits, mostly written by Jagger-Richards, keep coming, and the band remain the biggest live draw in rock.

Yesterday
The Beatles

Released September 1965
Capitol *5498* (U.S. #1) / Not issued U.K.

'Yesterday' is perhaps the best known song in The Beatles' extensive canon of popular music standards. It stands among the most performed and covered songs of all time and was the most played record on U.S. radio for eight consecutive years, from 1965 to 1972. It is one of Paul McCartney's finest moments. It topped the U.S. chart, but its release as a U.K. single was blocked by the other three Beatles, who didn't think much of it. This might have had something to do with the fact that 'Yesterday' was the first Beatles song to feature only its author and none of the other members of the band. McCartney is backed by a string quartet, scored by producer George Martin.

McCartney maintains that 'Yesterday' arrived, near enough fully formed, in a dream, and that he leapt out of bed on the morning in question to play it straight into a tape recorder, lest he forget it. Amazed at its effortless birth, he was sure he must have unconsciously plagiarized another writer's work, and spent the next month playing the song to various music-industry figures, expecting that eventually somebody would identify it. Nobody did – although some have since suggested a likeness to Ray Charles's 'Georgia On My Mind' – so McCartney polished off the lyric, dropping the working title of 'Scrambled Eggs,' and recorded the song during the *Help!* sessions. 'Yesterday' was the eighth of 19 American Number 1 hits for The Beatles and has since been recorded by over 3,000 artists, from Frank Sinatra to Boyz II Men.

I Got You Babe
Sonny & Cher

Released July 1965
Atco *6359* (U.S. #1) / Atlantic *AT 4035* (U.K. #1)

Salvatore 'Sonny' Bono had been hustling his songs in Los Angeles for some years before he met 16-year-old Cherilyn Sarkisian in 1963. Sonny was an assistant to producer Phil Spector while Cher began working as a back-up singer on Spector sessions, and the two became lovers. After much persuasion from Sonny, she was allowed to record one single for Spector in 1964, a cash-in on The Beatles' success, 'Ringo I Love You,' on which she was credited as Bonnie Jo Mason. Sonny had already enjoyed some songwriting success with Spector's studio arranger, Jack Nitzsche. The pair had written 'Needles And Pins' for Jackie DeShannon, and this became an international hit for British group The Searchers.

When Spector refused to entertain the idea of recording further material with Sonny's girlfriend, the couple left and recorded a couple of unsuccessful singles as Caesar & Cleo for Reprise. They mostly sang duets: although Sonny wanted to record Cher alone, she was nervous behind the microphone and insisted that Sonny join her. Reprise had neglected to sign the duo to a binding contract and Atlantic, who stepped in with a better offer, were rewarded when Bono came up with the hippie-lovers duet, 'I Got You Babe.' It was recorded at Gold Star studio in Los Angeles, home of Spector's hits and using the same session musicians. Atlantic originally scheduled the B-side, 'It's Gonna Rain,' for release, so Bono, a former promotions man, had to outsmart his own record company. He quickly arranged some heavy airplay for 'I Got You Babe' and Atlantic were forced to change their plans.

Mr Tambourine Man
The Byrds

Released June 1965
Columbia *43271* (U.S. #1) / CBS *201765* (U.K. #1)

Turn! Turn! Turn! (To Everything There Is A Season)
The Byrds
Released October 1965
Columbia *43424* (U.S. #1) / CBS *202008* (U.K. #26)

Eight Miles High
The Byrds
Released April 1966
Columbia *43578* (U.S. #14) / CBS *202067* (U.K. #24)

Although more credit tends to go to The Beatles, The Beach Boys, and the Stones, The Byrds were one of the most influential and consistent bands of the 1960s. Almost permanently blighted by in-fighting and factionalism, Roger McGuinn and his ever-changing cast of colleagues all but invented folk-rock, psychedelic-rock, and country-rock, were the single most important factor in bringing Bob Dylan to the attention of the rock audience, and remain one of the few bands to have a guitar sound named after them – the jangle of a picked 12-string Rickenbacker will forever be termed 'Byrdsian' by rock writers.

The band's breakthrough hit was 'Mr Tambourine Man.' Dylan's original was a multi-versed acoustic meander through typically elliptical wordplay. The Byrds stripped the song back to one verse and a few chorus repeats, in doing so introducing folk to Merseybeat and creating folk-rock, and opening a door into the charts for artists like Simon & Garfunkel and The Mamas & The Papas. McGuinn, with his heavily-compressed Rickenbacker guitar, was the only member of the band to play on the record; other instrumental duties were taken by tightly drilled sessionmen. But the serene, uplifting three-part harmonies of the chorus were the work of band members McGuinn, Gene Clark, and David Crosby. (The other two original members were bassist Chris Hillman and drummer Michael Clarke.)

'Turn! Turn! Turn!,' with lyrics lifted from the Old Testament book of Ecclesiastes, was another folk-rock classic and another big hit. This time it was the turn of traditional folkie and activist Pete Seeger to have his song reinvented. But by the time of 'Eight Miles High,' which came a year after the band's breakthrough, The Byrds were already moving on from folk-rock. A band composition of considerable sophistication, it boasts one of the most avant-garde guitar solos ever to make the charts. McGuinn's apparently free-form freak-out was, he said, carefully constructed and inspired by the playing of jazz saxophonist John Coltrane.

'Eight Miles High' aroused considerable controversy for the supposed drug references in the lyrics. In those days, the merest mention of the word 'high' was enough to have the moral guardians of the popular press in a frenzy of disapproval. To this day, McGuinn and other surviving band members insist the song is about nothing more than the band's flight to Britain for a tour.

After 'Eight Miles High,' various Byrds began to leave, although the band continued to record in various configurations into the 1970s. Later incarnations rarely troubled the singles charts, although their albums are now revered, particularly *Sweetheart Of The Rodeo*, one of the first country-rock records. Meanwhile David Crosby, who left the band in 1967, went on to form the massively successful Crosby Stills Nash & (sometimes) Young.

Wooly Bully
Sam The Sham & The Pharaohs

Released April 1965
MGM *13322* (U.S. #2) / MGM *1269* (U.K. #11)

'Wooly Bully' opens with a joyous cry to "dance rock'n'roll" and is – like its near namesake, 'Louie Louie' by The Kingsmen – an irresistibly primitive slice of 1960s garage rock. It was a multi-million-selling international hit, despite being banned by numerous radio stations who couldn't follow the unintelligible vocal and were worried that flamboyant Texan frontman Domingo 'Sam' Samudio might be singing something risqué. Sam and his cronies followed it with a number of other U.S. chart hits – mostly novelty songs like 'The Hair On My Chinny Chin Chin' – but none sticks in the memory like 'Wooly Bully.'

The Sounds Of Silence
Simon & Garfunkel

Released November 1965
Columbia *43396* (U.S. #1) / CBS *201977* (U.K.)

On February 19, 1964, Paul Simon was in his bathroom with the water running and the light off. Why? "Because the bathroom had tiles, so it was a slight echo chamber," he said. "I'd turn on the faucet so that water would run – I like that sound, it's very soothing to me – and I'd play. In the dark." The song he completed that day, which he'd started three months earlier, was 'The Sounds Of Silence.' It was a haunting rumination on man's inability to communicate with man, and it found its way onto aspiring folk duo Simon & Garfunkel's debut album, *Wednesday Morning, 3AM*. But when that record didn't sell, Art Garfunkel went back to university and Simon went to live and work in Europe.

However, one Boston radio station doggedly playlisted 'The Sounds Of Silence,' drumming up so much audience response that Columbia Records producer Tom Wilson was assigned to upgrade the song from a simple folksy acoustic duet to fully fledged electric folk-rock. Wilson was then working with Bob Dylan on his new electric music so, naturally, he used Dylan's musicians to overdub electric guitar and drums onto the track. Listen closely and you'll hear them trying to keep in time with the duo's original idiosyncrasies.

On December 4, 1965, Wilson's studio-augmented version of 'The Sounds Of Silence' entered the U.S. Top 40, and by the time it hit Number 1 on New Year's Day, Simon & Garfunkel were back in business, set to become the biggest popular music duo of the 1960s.

My Generation
The Who

Released October 1965
Decca *31877* (U.S.) / Brunswick *05944* (U.K. #2)

In 1965, Who guitarist and songwriter Pete Townshend had recently come into the possession of a Packard hearse. Parked outside his home in London's Chesham Place, it was spotted one day by the Queen Mother, who was immediately adjacent in Buckingham Palace. "Her husband had been buried in a similar vehicle and it reminded her of him," Townshend said later. With one imperious wave of an over-privileged arm, the car was towed away.

That and another incident, when a posh lady made a snooty comment when he was out driving a different car, inspired Townshend to pen a composition that constituted an explosion of frustration with the sorry lot of the young and non-posh in grey, drizzly, rigidly hierarchal 1960s Britain. Each verse culminated in the line "Hope I die before I get old!" This was true jaw-socking bluntness in those times of socially decorous entertainers.

While the song started out as a slow blues, Townshend's colleagues eventually settled on an arrangement that was entirely sympathetic with the snarling lyric. The rhythm section of John Entwistle (bass) and Keith Moon (drums) provided a relentless, charging, bruising ambience. Singer Roger Daltrey stutters the lyric like a buffoon, alluding to a physical effect of purple hearts, the mod constituency's drug of choice. Entwistle meanwhile contributes the first ever bass solo on a pop record. It somehow spoils the perfection of 'My Generation' that it didn't go to Number 1 in any of the four competing U.K. pop charts of the day. But make no mistake: on this record, The Who were the mouthpiece for millions.

California Dreamin'
The Mamas & The Papas

Released December 1965
Dunhill *4020* (U.S. #4) / RCA *1503* (U.K. #23)

The Mamas & The Papas were leaders of the West Coast folk-rock movement of the middle 1960s, part of a social circle that included Scott McKenzie, Barry McGuire, Lovin' Spoonful leader John Sebastian, and Roger McGuinn of The Byrds. They had sprung from the Greenwich Village folk scene over in New York City, as John Phillips, his wife Michelle, Cass Elliot, and Denny Doherty worked their way through a number of folk groups, including The Smoothies, The Journeymen, and The Mugwumps, before joining forces to form The New Journeymen. The group then relocated to Los Angeles where they lived in the house of their friend Barry McGuire, who had recently enjoyed a worldwide hit with his apocalyptic 'Eve Of Destruction.'

McGuire decided to use the group as backing singers on his album *This Precious Time* – at which point they called themselves The Magic Circle – and among the songs he recorded was John and Michelle's 'California Dreamin'.' When Dunhill Records owner Lou Adler heard the album, and particularly that song, he was so impressed that he signed The Magic Circle. The group was re-christened The Mamas & The Papas, and their first single release was their own interpretation of 'California Dreamin'' using McGuire's backing track. The only difference was that McGuire's gruff voice was erased from the tape and The Mamas & The Papas recorded a new set of lead vocals. It became a huge international hit in 1966 and was one of the songs responsible for ushering in the hippie era.

It's Not Unusual
Tom Jones

Released January 1965
Parrot *9737* (U.S. #10) / Decca *F 12062* (U.K. #1)

Tom Jones (born Thomas Woodward) was discovered in 1964 by Gordon Mills, singing at the Top Hat Club in Merthyr Tydfil, Wales. Performing as the frontman of Tommy Scott & The Senators, he was hailed as "the twisting vocalist from Pontypridd." Mills had co-written 'It's Not Unusual' for barefoot songbird Sandie Shaw, intended as a follow-up to her recent Number 1, '(There's) Always Something There To Remind Me.' Mills used Jones and his band to record a demo of the song, and the singer tried to persuade him to hand it over, but Mills was adamant that it would go to Shaw. However, when Jones persisted, Mills finally said, "I'll tell you what, if Sandie Shaw turns it down, I'll let you have it." Fortunately for Jones that's exactly what happened, and he went into the studio to make a proper recording. Apparently he was so enthusiastic about the song that his vocal completely drowned out the studio musicians, and a few days later a third recording had to be made, this time with a louder horn section and with Jones singing in the tape-storage closet. It was definitely third time lucky, and his vigorous interpretation was soon rewarded when 'It's Not Unusual' flew to Number 1 on the British charts.

Stop! In The Name Of Love
The Supremes

Released February 1965
Motown *1074* (U.S. #1) / Tamla Motown *TMG 501* (U.K. #7)

The Supremes were Motown's most successful act of the 1960s, with no fewer than 12 American Number 1s between 1964 and the departure of lead singer Diana Ross at the end of 1969. No other American act achieved so many Number 1s during the 1960s. It was a phenomenal achievement for the trio of women who, before their smash hit 'Where

Did Our Love Go,' were known around the corridors of Motown as the 'no-hit' Supremes. 'Stop!' was the fourth in a series of five consecutive American chart-toppers for the group, all written by Holland-Dozier-Holland, and the first single released on the custom Tamla Motown label in Britain. Lamont Dozier recalled that the title sprang from an argument with his girlfriend. She was about to walk out the door and the phrase "stop in the name of the law" came into his head. Dozier said: "I just changed it slightly to 'stop in the name of love' and there was my song."

I Can't Help Myself
The Four Tops

Released May 1965
Motown *1076* (U.S. #1) / Tamla Motown *TMG 515* (U.K. #23)

When Motown songwriter Lamont Dozier was a child, his grandmother ran a beauty parlor from home. Her flirtatious husband would call out greetings to the arriving customers: 'Hi sugar pie,' and 'Hi, honey bunch.' The young Dozier's brain evidently filed away the scene. In 1965, as he attempted to write with the brothers Holland their second hit for The Four Tops following 'Baby I Need Your Loving,' he incorporated the phrases into the chorus of this brisk-paced song of romantic devotion. The trio's next effort for the Tops was so similar that many erroneously thought that the same backing track was employed. Its title? 'The Same Old Song.'

Papa's Got A Brand New Bag Part 1
James Brown

Released July 1965
King *5999* (U.S. #8) / London *HL 9990* (U.K. #25)

I Got You (I Feel Good)
James Brown

Released November 1965
King *6015* (U.S. #3) / Pye International *7N 25350* (U.K. #29)

Just as Motown was becoming slick and sophisticated and Bob Dylan was writing the most complex lyrics ever heard in popular music, James Brown re-invented square one. The razor-sharp guitar rhythms and shattering horn riffs of 'Papa's Got A Brand New Bag' were simultaneously primitive and brand spanking new. He recorded it on February 1, 1965, and claimed: "When I saw the speakers jumping, vibrating in a certain way, I knew that was it – deliverance. What I started on 'Out Of Sight' I took all the way on 'Papa's Got A Brand New Bag.'"

The lyrics seemed largely gibberish, but for sheer, unbridled energy nothing else came close in the mid 1960s. Brown had been scoring hits since the late 1950s, but 'Brand New Bag' wrote his name large on the map. Now recognized as the template for funk, it reached Number 1 in the American R&B chart, Number 8 on the pop chart, and collected a Grammy as the year's Best Rhythm & Blues Recording.

The follow-up, 'I Got You,' was a barely-disguised re-write of Brown's earlier composition, 'I Found You,' which had flopped when recorded by his girlfriend, Yvonne Fair, in 1962. Mick Jagger said at the time that it was "a good record" but rightly qualified his praise by observing that it didn't compare with 'Brand New Bag.' Nevertheless, using the success of 'Bag' as a springboard, 'I Got You' went on to become Brown's biggest-ever hit, peaking at Number 3 in the U.S. pop chart.

In The Midnight Hour
Wilson Pickett

Released July 1965
Atlantic *2289* (U.S. #21) / Atlantic *AT 4036* (U.K. #12)

Atlantic tagged their new signing as 'the Wicked Pickett' in 1965. He had already recorded for a couple of labels before landing at the company, notably as a member of The Falcons, singing lead on their 1962 R&B hit 'I Found A Love.' It was another Falcons member, 'Sir' Mack Rice, who would later deliver one of Wilson's other memorable hits, 'Mustang Sally.'

Following a couple of flops for Atlantic recorded in New York City, Pickett found himself coupled with Booker T. & The MGs and the Memphis Horns at Stax studios. Producer Jerry Wexler had decided to try cooking up a Memphis soul stew for the singer. This combination would usher in a looser, funky soul sound that became the hallmark of Stax and Atlantic's soul sides during the mid 1960s.

MGs guitarist Steve Cropper did his homework when he heard Pickett was coming to town. Checking out some earlier records, he noticed that Pickett had a habitual routine of repeating phrases such as: "See my Jesus in the midnight hour." Cropper said: "He'd start preaching this 'midnight hour' thing on the fade-outs." When Pickett arrived in town, he and Cropper retired to the Lorraine Hotel where they found an immediate empathy and quickly wrote a couple of songs, including the one that would become his theme song, 'In The Midnight Hour.' When it came to recording and the band couldn't quite get the right groove, Wexler danced the jerk around the studio, much to the musicians' amusement, and a classic soul anthem was swiftly in the can.

Respect
Otis Redding

Released August 1965
Volt *128* (U.S. #35) / Atlantic *AT 4039* (U.K.)

R&B of the 1950s turned into soul in the 1960s through Sam Cooke and James Brown and two of the major labels most associated with the music, Stax and Atlantic. Otis Redding began his career in the early 1960s and had his first R&B hit in 1963 with his own composition, 'These Arms Of Mine,' on the Stax subsidiary label, Volt. Redding soon became Stax's biggest artist and was one of the Southern States' best soul singers.

He was a great interpreter of covers but often wrote his own material, notably 'Respect,' which together with 'I've Been Loving You Too Long' and his cover of the Temptations 'My Girl' were his first three pop hits of 1965, all appearing on his classic album *Otis Blue*. Remarkably, all three were recorded on the very same day and the entire album was cut during a single weekend between tour dates.

'Respect' may well have been written that very weekend. MGs drummer Al Jackson recalled the song's inspiration. Redding had apparently been complaining about a recent grueling tour, and Jackson said to him: "What are you griping about? You're on the road all the time. All you can look for is a little respect when you come home."

Famously, 'Respect' was later covered by Aretha Franklin, who created a powerful new arrangement and turned a song written by a man into a feminist anthem. Upon hearing Franklin's completely re-worked version, recorded a couple of years after his original, Redding is reported to have said: "That little girl done took my song away!"

The Carnival Is Over
The Seekers

Released October 1965
Capitol *5531* (U.S.) / Columbia *DB 7711* (U.K. #1)

The Seekers were an Australian quartet fronted by vocalist Judith Durham who played a crossbreed of folk and white gospel. Like many antipodeans, they traveled to London, England, to find fame and fortune. At first they were signed by EMI to their mail-order division, World Record Club, before being transferred to the company's Columbia label. They were managed by Tom Springfield, brother of Dusty and former member of British folk trio The Springfields, who composed many of the group's hits, including the first three: 'I'll Never Find Another You,' 'A World Of Our Own,' and 'The Carnival Is Over.' The latter song was based on an old Russian folk-song, a pedigree it shared with at least two other major hits, Mary Hopkin's 'Those Were The Days' and Kenny Ball's 'Midnight In Moscow.' It tells the story of a 17th century Cossack rebel leader named Stenka Razin. (Pete Seeger had used the same melody in 1950 for a song he called 'River Of My People.') It became the group's second British Number 1 but was not a hit in America. When they split up in 1968, guitarist Keith Potger managed the successful New Seekers.

Uptight (Everything's Alright)
Stevie Wonder

Released November 1965
Tamla *54124* (U.S. #3) / Tamla Motown *TMG 545* (U.K. #14)

The word 'genius' has been much overused in the music business, but one man who undoubtedly deserves the title is Stevie Wonder. Here is a musician who writes all his own material, plays virtually most of the instruments on his records – harmonica, guitars, drums, and keyboards – and is in possession of a marvelous voice. As if that weren't enough, he arranges and produces his own records.

Kicking off a chart career with a Number 1 single and album is always going to be hard to follow, especially when you're 13 years old, as 'Little' Stevie Wonder was when 'Fingertips' hit the top of the American charts. It took him over two years to find his voice, but during that period he was constantly hanging around the Motown studios, learning all the tricks as an apprentice in America's top hit factory of the era. Wonder had formed a songwriting partnership with Henry Cosby and Sylvia Moy that was to produce many of his 1960s hits, including 'I Was Made To Love Her,' 'I'm Wondering,' 'My Cherie Amour,' and 'Uptight,' his second hit as plain Stevie Wonder. 'Uptight' was inspired by 'Satisfaction' by The Rolling Stones (which itself was inspired by Motown's own 'Dancing In The Street') and featured some ferocious drumming by Benny Benjamin, backbone of the Motown house band, The Funk Brothers. Showcasing the by now familiar Motown sound, it reached Number 1 on the R&B chart and Number 3 in the pop chart, forming a solid foundation stone for what would be a remarkable career.

Like A Rolling Stone
Bob Dylan

Released July 1965
Columbia *43346* (U.S. #2) / CBS *201811* (U.K. #4)

In 1964 there had been no reason to think that Bob Dylan was doing anything other than purveying the sound he wanted to. His format was one man, one guitar, and a head full of grievances about the conduct of his supposed elders and betters. It made his reputation and led some to call him the Voice Of A Generation. Others who had known him longer knew better. The kids with whom Dylan had played in amateur bands back in Hibbing, Minnesota, where he grew up knew that he was a rock'n'roll kid. Even his high-school teachers – had they been interested in such things – would have been able to put right the folkies who thought Dylan was loyal to their cause. In his high-school yearbook, Dylan – then Robert Zimmerman – had written that his ambition was to "join Little Richard."

Dylan must have been gratified to be lauded by critics, to play to adoring audiences, and to see several of his zeitgeist-encapsulating songs such as 'Blowin' In The Wind' recorded in lucrative covers. But he wasn't satisfied. The trouble was, it wasn't that easy for Dylan to do what he now wanted to do. It is difficult to convey to today's audience the extent of the division between rock-pop and folk that existed in the early to mid 1960s. There was something like a Berlin Wall between the genres. Dylan's folk fans considered their music as having intellectual weight and socio-political import and viewed rock'n'roll and pop as adolescent trash. His own audience could very well turn against him if he made a record that displayed his true tastes. And there might not be a new audience there to take up the slack: the idea that the kids buying 'A Hard Day's Night' or 'It's All Over Now' might be able to relate to a man who penned such literate songs as 'To Ramona' was not necessarily a plausible one.

However, emboldened by The Animals' stunning, shimmering electric hit arrangement of 'The House Of The Rising Sun' – a standard he had included on his debut album – Dylan booked into Columbia Studio A in New York City in January 1965 with a full band. This was not the type of band that had accompanied folk-scene contemporaries such as Fred Neil or Tim Hardin. Dylan instructed these people to play rhythm & blues and rock'n'roll. They did not appear on all the tracks of the resulting album, *Bringing It All Back Home* (March '65), which was divided neatly down the middle: the first side featured tracks with band accompaniment, the second Dylan's familiar voice-guitar-harmonica format. Nonetheless, it was one of the rock tracks – the hip-talking Chuck Berry update 'Subterranean Homesick Blues' – that became a Top 10 hit for Dylan in Britain when he toured there in the spring.

Dylan took a band to the Newport Folk Festival in July 1965, where he was booed by parts of the audience – perhaps because he had seemingly turned his back on folk in favor of rock music, or maybe just because the sound was too loud. Folkies were beginning to perceive him as a mercenary betrayer of the folk idiom. It soon didn't matter. It was at this juncture that a new Los Angeles group called The Byrds took an electric version of his song 'Mr. Tambourine Man' to Number 1 on both sides of the Atlantic. The week before Newport saw the release of Dylan's new single, 'Like A Rolling Stone.' Its subsequent success proved he had access to pop's mass market, not just through cover versions by the likes of The Byrds; its extraordinary grittiness and length proved that he did not have to compromise his art one jot to reach that mass market. Many consider it the finest single ever made.

The song had started out as what Dylan described as "this long piece of vomit." Certainly on the finished record Dylan seemed to be throwing up all the bile and hatred in his system, spitting out his satisfaction at the downfall of an over-privileged character who had wronged him. While Dylan had clearly labored hard in writing the lyric and editing it down, the recording process was extremely quick. Al Kooper – a guitarist who bluffed his way into playing organ on the record – has even said that the first complete take was the one used.

Kooper had never played organ before and Dylan strummed his electric guitar like it was an acoustic, but this rawness only added to the song's gritty ambience. The lyrics were as poetic and dazzling as Dylan's always were, but were also utterly street-level. The record proved that, just like a film or novel, popular music could be a window on real life. Dylan's vocal performance was mesmerizing, raising goosebumps on your flesh as he capped every malice-dripping verse with the accusatory refrain "How does it *feel*?" Just to drive home the point that pop-rock had never heard anything like it, the record ran to six minutes, double the standard single length for the time. Now we think nothing of it, but it's astonishing that such an all-round revolutionary release should become a smash.

The Berlin Wall that divided folk and rock was destroyed by 'Like A Rolling Stone.' With one release, Dylan had proved that moon-in-June conventions did not have to inform the lyrics of records aimed at the hit parade. Giants like The Beatles, the Stones, The Beach Boys, and the countless pop minnows who copied the moves of those giants were suddenly liberated. The financial and artistic success of 'Like A Rolling Stone' had effectively given them permission to write about anything they wanted to, in whatever format they chose, and to ignore misgivings about controversy or of rendering themselves uncommercial. 'Like A Rolling Stone' had no less an effect than to turn rock'n'roll into rock, causing a kids' medium to grow up overnight and to be seen as just as valid and important as any other art form.

These Boots Are Made For Walkin'
Nancy Sinatra

Released January 1966
Reprise *0432* (U.S. #1) / Reprise *R 20432* (U.K. #1)

Somethin' Stupid
Nancy Sinatra & Frank Sinatra

Released March 1967
Reprise *0561* (U.S. #1) / Reprise *RS 23166* (U.K. #1)

Although often compared, unfairly, to her legendary father, Nancy Sinatra recorded a number of seminal hits in the late 1960s, most of them in collaboration with the cult singer-songwriter Lee Hazlewood. 'These Boots Are Made For Walkin'' was her breakthrough release, and topped the charts on both sides of the Atlantic. Hazlewood apparently instructed his young protégé to sing the song as if she was a young girl giving the brush-off to a middle-aged man. This gives her vocal a detached insolence perfectly in keeping with the lazy cool of the backing track. Hazlewood called in The Wrecking Crew to record 'Boots' and their playing is exemplary, particularly Hal Blaine's deft, uncluttered drumming and the neat combination of Carol Kaye on electric bass and Ray Pohlman on stand-up acoustic bass.

Sinatra followed 'Boots' with several more Hazlewood-penned hits and the James Bond theme 'You Only Live Twice' before recording the duet for which she is best known. 'Somethin' Stupid' set her sweet, youthful voice against her father's older, knowing croon, and provided him with his first ever Gold-certified single in America. After that, Nancy resumed her work with Hazlewood, recording two further classic singles in 1968, both of which feature on their collaborative album *Nancy & Lee*. 'You've Lost That Lovin' Feelin'' is perhaps the only subsequent version to do justice to the timeless original by The Righteous Brothers, while 'Some Velvet Morning' was recently named by the U.K.'s *Daily Telegraph* newspaper as the greatest duet of all time.

When A Man Loves A Woman
Percy Sledge

Released April 1966
Atlantic *2326* (U.S. #1) / Atlantic *584 001* (U.K. #4)

This classic love song began life as an on-stage jam when Sledge was depressed at the loss of a girlfriend, and originally it had the working title 'Why Did You Leave Me?' Sledge and his musicians worked to improve it for several months before coming up with the new title, but due to the basic facilities in the studio, the major part of the song had to be recorded in mono in one take, with the horns and background vocals recorded at one later overdubbing session. The finished recording was down on tape just before Christmas 1965, but the musicians weren't particularly impressed with the result, especially since Sledge was

The Sun Ain't Gonna Shine (Anymore)
The Walker Brothers

Released February 1966
Smash *2032* (U.S. #13) / Phillips *BF 1473* (U.K. #1)

Americans Scott Engel, John Maus, and Gary Leeds – a.k.a. The Walker Brothers – relocated to Britain in 1965 to launch a pop career that engendered hysteria on a level with Beatlemania in their adopted homeland, although in America the response was more muted. Tall and handsome to a man, they released a string of epic, orchestrated ballads powered by Engel's resonant baritone, ensuring the band were chart regulars from 1965 until 1967. Engel was always the musical focus of the group, although Maus occasionally took lead vocals. Leeds, nominally the band's drummer, didn't do much, as most of the music on the band's records was cut by session players. 'The Sun Ain't Gonna Shine' was one of their two British chart-toppers and one of just two of their singles that also charted well in America.

After the band split, only Engel – as Scott Walker – was able to sustain a career in music, albeit an unusual one. For several years in the late 1960s and early 1970s he vacillated between two extremes. On one hand there were dark, existential solo albums full of Jacques Brel covers and his own compositions; on the other, mainstream readings of MOR standards, a TV series, and cabaret appearances. He surprised everyone – maybe even himself – by regrouping with Maus and Leeds in the mid 1970s and returning to the British charts with a version of Tom Rush's 'No Regrets.'

decidedly off key. The overdubbed horn section was also painfully out of tune, but producer Quinn Ivy felt the recording had a certain something, and a copy was sent to Jerry Wexler at Atlantic Records. He agreed, but insisted that a new recording be made, this time in tune, at Atlantic's expense. Several weeks and a lot of dollars were spent to create a totally new version of the song, but due to a mix-up, Atlantic released the first version, out-of-tune horns and all.

Mr, Sledge had come up with the original idea for the song but he somewhat unwisely waved goodbye to a fortune by giving writing credit to organist Arthur Wright and bassist Cameron Lewis. The song generated millions of dollars in royalties over the years, although poor Percy probably saw very little of it.

River Deep – Mountain High
Ike & Tina Turner

Released May 1966
Philles *131* (U.S.) / London *HL 10046* (U.K. #3)

By 1966, the marriage of Ellie Greenwich and Jeff Barry had come to an end. Amongst many other hits, their joint songwriting credits included 'Baby I Love You,' 'Be My Baby,' 'Chapel Of Love,' 'Da Doo Ron Ron,' 'Do Wah Diddy Diddy,' and 'Leader Of The Pack.' Professional separation seemed to be inevitable too. To this day, Greenwich is unsure if producer Phil Spector, with whom they'd had considerable success, knew that the two were no longer involved when he contacted them about collaborating on new material. They agreed, and proceeded to stitch together three song fragments that each of them had devised, creating in the process an almost orgasmic hymn of romantic devotion.

Naturally there were variations in tempo and melody in such a process, and Spector appropriately applied an operatic tone when he came to record it with Tina Turner. (The brandname established with her husband was retained, but Ike does not appear on the record.) As if trying to claw back his status after recent flops, Spector poured everything – including a then mind-boggling $22,000 – into a track of extraordinary grandiosity.

While the record went Top 3 in the U.K. it flopped in the States, and a devastated Spector retired, albeit temporarily. Today the recording enjoys a legendary reputation at odds with its original chart placing, and is much covered and revered as the apotheosis of the Spector Wall Of Sound.

Mellow Yellow
Donovan

Released November 1966
Epic *10098* (U.S. #2) / Pye *7N 17267* (U.K. #8)

Irish singer Donovan had suffered during the early part of his career after he was labeled a 'Dylan copyist,' but when top producer Mickie Most took over, his folk ditties were transformed into pop hits. Their first effort together, 'Sunshine Superman,' hit number 1 on the U.S. charts. But

U.K. contractual disputes meant that 'Superman' and this follow-up were released in America many months before they came out in Britain.

Donovan was part of The Beatles' inner circle, and fab-four links to his music were numerous. 'Sunshine Superman' had originally been titled 'For John And Paul,' while 'Mellow Yellow' featured background whispering by Paul McCartney. Donovan featured as a background vocalist on the group's 'Yellow Submarine' and supplied its author with a couple of lines for the song when McCartney got stuck. He also appeared on the worldwide live-by-satellite performance of 'All You Need Is Love' in August 1967, and his hit of the same year, 'Jennifer Juniper,' was written for Jenny Boyd, younger sister of George Harrison's wife Patti. The lyric of 'Mellow Yellow' mentioned an "electrical banana," and in the U.S. Country Joe McDonald allegedly started a rumor that you could get high by smoking dried banana skins, which gave the song a whole new meaning – one which Donovan has always refuted.

I'm A Believer
The Monkees

Released November 1966
Colgems *1002* (U.S. #1) / RCA *1560* (U.K. #1)

Last Train To Clarksville
The Monkees

Released August 1966
Colgems *1001* (U.S. #1) / RCA *1547* (U.K. #23)

American TV producers Bob Rafelson and Bert Schneider had a great idea: why not make a series about a zany pop quartet that combined the attributes of The Beatles and The Marx Brothers? After considering The Lovin' Spoonful, they opted instead to advertise in the movie biz bible *Variety*. From over 400 auditioners they selected four personable young men – Michael Nesmith, Peter Tork, Mickey Dolenz, and Davy Jones – blessed with varying degrees of musical and acting talent. Screen Gems bought the idea, and music publishing mogul Don Kirshner was drafted in to find songs for the show. The reliable duo of Tommy Boyce and Bobby Hart (who also composed *The Monkees* theme) came up with the lively 'Last Train To Clarksville,' apparently inspired by a mis-hearing of the lyrics to The Beatles' 'Paperback Writer.' With Monkees' vocals dubbed on top of a backing track played by top New York sessioneers, the song was virtually guaranteed its Number 1 placing on November 5, 1966, amongst all the publicity generated by the TV show.

Their next single, 'I'm A Believer,' did even better. Written by aspiring young songsmith Neil Diamond, this was a marginally more rock-oriented track with a hint of blue-eyed gospel. The success of 'Clarksville' was largely limited to America, but with the TV series now being broadcast overseas, *Billboard* magazine was able to report on March 11, 1967, that Europe too was now "gripped by Monkeesteria." It was a blatantly patriotic attempt to bestow a whiff of Beatlemania on America's young pretenders, but it was also true.

Good Vibrations
The Beach Boys

....

Released October 1966
Capitol *5676* (U.S. #1) / Capitol *CL 15475* (U.K. #1)

Brian Wilson picked up the phone and called long-distance from Western Recorders studio, Los Angeles, to his brother Carl. It was Monday August 15, 1966. That night, The Beach Boys were playing half way across America in the Municipal Auditorium at Minot, North Dakota. "The first time I ever heard the music to 'Good Vibrations,'" remembered Carl many years later, "I came back to my hotel room and the phone rang, and it was Brian. He called from the recording studio and played this really bizarre-sounding music over the phone."

At this point in their career, The Beach Boys were a group divided into two distinct entities. Their emotionally unstable creative genius, Brian, had withdrawn from live performances and spent his time working on new music for the group in a string of Los Angeles studios. The other five members maintained the public face of The Beach Boys. They did the touring, the radio and TV appearances, and the promotional visits to record stores, while Brian remained cocooned in L.A. with The Wrecking Crew, an elite cadre of America's top session players.

Wrecking Crew bassist Carol Kaye was in Hollywood's Gold Star Studios on February 18, 1966. when Brian supervised recording of the first track for 'Good Vibrations.' She recalled: "He'd come in and play piano to give us the feel for the tune, then go in the booth. Brian would give us instructions from the booth where he'd experiment with sounds. I never knew Brian was a bass player until much later; he never played bass in front of me." Kaye also noted that The Wrecking Crew were routinely expected to create musical parts for the other artists they worked with, but Brian usually had their contributions already written for them. "He'd let the rhythm guitars and drums play what they want, with direction from the booth sometimes, but it was all Brian in the production," she said. "We were in awe of Brian."

Brian once defined 'Good Vibrations' as a pocket symphony and justified that description by explaining that within its three minutes and thirty-five seconds he oversaw "a lot of riff changes … it had a lot of movements. … Changes, changes, changes. Building harmonies here, drop this voice out, this comes in, bring the echo chamber in … bring the cello up a little louder here … a series of intricate harmonies and mood changes."

As well as controlling every musical note in 'Good Vibrations,' Wilson took one vital step further. He was one of the first rock musicians to use the unique characteristics of individual studios to enhance his musical vision. As one example, he explained how "we recorded the 'Ah I love the colorful clothes she wears' sections at Gold Star, and the 'I'm pickin' up good vibrations' at Columbia."

Although he did work on other songs at this time, Brian's top priority was 'Good Vibrations' through the spring and summer of 1966. To those around him, however, his working methods seemed outlandish. "They were in the studio and they had an idea of what they wanted, but they didn't know how to find it right off," recalled country music star and former L.A. session player Glen Campbell. "And, gosh, Brian, he'd be in there doing that theremin line for 'Good Vibrations,' tryin' to get that thing right. I think it cost him $105 a man just to sit there trying to do that for three hours." Brian had previously used an electro-theremin – a primitive electronic instrument – on the *Pet Sounds* track 'I Just Wasn't Made For These Times' but it came into sharp relief on 'Good Vibrations,' providing the high-pitched ethereal howl of 'oo-wee-ooh' that adds a spine-tingling touch to the already catchy chorus.

Brian remained completely on top of the music during these complex sessions but the one thing he did lose sight of was the world outside 'Good Vibrations.' Come May of 1966, the other Beach Boys and the executives at Capitol Records were becoming increasingly concerned about the disproportionate amount of time and money he was investing into just one song – a song none of them had even heard yet. Capitol's anxiety was grounded in good, solid business practice. "In those days," admitted Brian, "you could record a single for $1,500. 'Good Vibrations' cost about $15,000." No record in the history of popular music had ever cost so much or taken this long, and Capitol execs were well aware of the prodigious amounts of dope being consumed during the studio sessions.

The Beach Boys, however, were more concerned about their working relationship with Brian. He had established, on the *Pet Sounds* album, his pattern of creating tracks without them, merely calling them in at the last minute to add their vocals. With 'Good Vibrations,' it was beginning to look as if that call might never come. Did he really need them at all? They need not have worried. Just nine days after the long-distance conversation with Carl in North Dakota, Brian invited the others to join him in Sunset Sound. As lead vocalist Mike Love remembered: "It was kind of a cliffhanger. Brian said, 'We need some words,' and I said, 'Well, OK. Let's see.'" Ten minutes before the session started, Mike was barreling down Hollywood freeway dictating lyrics.

It was an intense day, during which Love recalls 25 to 30 overdubs being applied to just one small section. But, working to Brian's guide vocal, they made substantial progress and, on September 21, 1966, at Columbia Studio A, Brian finally completed 'Good Vibrations.' He remembered: "When I dubbed it down, made the final mix, it was a feeling of power. It was a rush, a feeling of exaltation. I remember saying, 'Oh, my God.'"

Released on October 10, 'Good Vibrations' reached Number 1 in the U.S. and U.K. and went on to become the first million-selling Beach Boys single. It was nominated for the music industry's highest honor, a Best Contemporary Rock'n'Roll Recording Grammy but, astonishingly, the expert Grammy judges decided it wasn't quite as good as 'Winchester Cathedral' by The New Vaudeville Band. Time, however, has rectified that mind-boggling decision and 'Good Vibrations' is now acknowledged not just as an all-time classic single but as a recording that changed the course of popular music.

major labels who wanted to distribute the single nationally. The band signed with Cameo-Parkway, allegedly because their label was ?'s favorite color, orange. '96 Tears' eventually climbed all the way to the top of the national charts, followed by several lesser hits, before changing times rendered the band's primitive rock obsolete. ? has resurfaced periodically since then, recording, gigging, and claiming to hail from Mars.

The Shadows Of Knight added another twist to the cultural exchange that first saw the Stones and The Yardbirds reinterpreting Chicago electric blues. They delved into the same influences, but through the British bands' interpretations rather than the American originals. Their albums were peppered with revved-up blues standards, but their breakthrough single was a reasonably faithful cover of Them's 'Gloria.'

Thanks to the inclusion of the psychedelic pop classic 'I Had Too Much To Dream (Last Night)' on the later *Nuggets* compilation, The Electric Prunes are remembered as typical 1960s garage punks. In fact, the band – or at least, the name – enjoyed a curious, varied career that stretched to five albums. At first most Prunes material, including 'Too Much To Dream,' was provided by the commercial songwriting team of Annette Tucker and Nancie Mantz. In the hands of the band and their producer, Dave Hassinger, who had engineered some Rolling Stones sessions in the mid 1960s, this raw material was lent a measure of sonic adventure by experiments with reverb, backwards guitar, and other effects that fitted well with the 1960s penchant for pop weirdness.

A similar follow-up hit, 'Get Me To The World On Time,' and an album including both singles marked this first phase in the band's history. A second album, *Underground*, saw the band briefly wresting control of their destiny, writing their own material as they continued with the odd noises. But the hits stopped, and The Electric Prunes fell into the hands of composer David Axelrod. This proved to be an ill-starred marriage that led to the gradual disintegration of the band. Eventually it became little more than a name-badge to put on recordings made by other people. A religious concept album in Latin ensued, and by the time of the appositely-titled *Just Good Old Rock'n'Roll*, the final album to bear the Prunes' name, no original members remained.

96 Tears
? & The Mysterians

Released February 1966
Cameo *428* (U.S. #1) / Cameo Parkway *C 428* (U.K. #37)

Gloria
The Shadows Of Knight
Released January 1966
Dunwich *116* (U.S. #10) / Atlantic *AT 4085* (U.K.)

I Had Too Much To Dream (Last Night)
The Electric Prunes
Released November 1966
Reprise *0532* (U.S. #11) / Reprise *RS 20532* (U.K.)

The youth of America responded to the Beatles and Stones-led British invasion of 1964 with a musical mobilization on a vast scale. Across the land, in garages, bars, schools, and youth clubs, countless teenagers tore through 'Louie Louie' with more enthusiasm than expertise. For most of these garage bands, a locally released independent single was the absolute peak of their achievements. Yet a few went beyond that, scoring national, even international hits, touring, and even making albums.

The Mysterians were fronted by ?, previously one Rudy Martinez, who had legally changed his name to ? (and not 'Question Mark'). He permanently wore shades. The group's debut hit was driven by a two-chord organ riff, over which ? wailed about "too many teardrops for one heart to cry." It was first recorded for a small label, Pa-Go-Go, and became a regional hit, in the process attracting the attention of several

Wild Thing
The Troggs

Released April 1966
Fontana *1548* (U.S. #1) / Fontana *TF 689* (U.K. #2)

The Troggs seemed like an unlikely proposition for international pop stardom. They hailed from unfashionable Andover in the south-west of England and were fronted by a bricklayer-turned-singer, Reg Ball, who with comic audacity had been renamed Reg Presley. Yet they scored an impressive run of pop-rock hits in the 1960s, all basic in the extreme, and 'Wild Thing' was the first.

In many ways it is an eccentric record – replete with an incongruous ocarina solo and pauses that defiantly fall out of step with the song's rhythmic pulse – but it caught the imagination of millions. Including Jimi Hendrix, who later fashioned a greedy, unsubtle version of his own. Hendrix and the rest of us might never have heard the song if The Troggs hadn't come across it in the office of their manager Larry Page in the form of a demo by writer Chip Taylor. Looking for something unusual to kick-start their career, they felt it was worth a shot. If nothing else, the story of how 'Wild Thing' was recorded tells a story about how singles were sometimes made in those far-off, simple times. Presley recalled that producer Larry Page was recording an orchestral session. "He said we had to be up there waiting outside the studio in case there was any time left at the end. As it turned out there was 45 minutes to get our gear in, get a sound, record it, and get out. And we did the B-side as well."

Somebody Help Me
The Spencer Davis Group

Released March 1966
Atco *6416* (U.S.) / Fontana *TF 679* (U.K. #1)

The Spencer Davis Group were named after their guitarist, but are more associated with two entirely different names, Jackie Edwards and Stevie Winwood. The latter was the band's bizarrely gravel-throated teenage singer-keyboardist, while the former was not a member of the Group at all but a Jamaican songwriter who composed a couple of their early hits. The first hit Edwards provided for them, 'Keep On Running,' is the best known but this follow-up was another good record, even if it rather shamelessly adhered to the template of its predecessor in its grittily impassioned singing and identikit guitar licks.

Kicks
Paul Revere & The Raiders Featuring Mark Lindsay

Released March 1966
Columbia *43556* (U.S. #4) / CBS *202205* (U.K.)

The name of Paul Revere & The Raiders doesn't resonate so much today – especially in the U.K. where they failed to register on charts or public radar – but the group secured a dozen *Billboard* Top 40 placings in the U.S. during the 1960s. Mostly their records were infectious and earthy enough to sideline their gimmicky revolutionary war costumes – even if they did seem to be inordinately and permanently angry at girls. The denunciatory tone of this particular number was more understandable: it was written by Barry Mann & Cynthia Weil as a wake-up-call to a friend who was destroying himself with drugs.

Paperback Writer / Rain
The Beatles

Released June 1966
Capitol *5651* (U.S. #1) / Parlophone *R 5452* (U.K. #1)

This single marked the point at which The Beatles moved from pop group to rock band. The a cappella fronted A-side was recorded during sessions for *Revolver* in mid-April 1966 and featured a heavier guitar sound from the group. The B-side, 'Rain,' had plenty of studio trickery with some of The Beatles' earliest experimentation with backwards tapes and vocals and what Ringo considers his best ever performance. After much interference with their releases, from here on Beatles singles were duplicated on both sides of the Atlantic, with the same A and B-sides.

The Beatles popularity in America was marred that summer following John Lennon's comment in an interview with the London *Evening Standard* that "we're more popular than Jesus right now." Though this remark went unnoticed in Britain, all hell broke loose in America with

public burnings of the group's records – even the Ku Klux Klan got in on the action. The Beatles were about to retreat permanently into the studio and played their last live gig at Candlestick Park in San Francisco (with the exception of the famous rooftop 'concert' in 1969). These final live performances must have been excruciating for Lennon, who had already recorded *Revolver*'s otherworldly 'Tomorrow Never Knows' yet still had to go on stage singing "she loves you, yeah, yeah, yeah."

Sunny Afternoon
The Kinks

Released June 1966
Reprise *0497* (U.S. #14) / Pye *7N 17125* (U.K. #1)

The Kinks virtually invented heavy rock with 'You Really Got Me' in 1964 but had proved themselves equally able at affecting ballads with the lovely, melancholic 'Tired Of Waiting For You,' a talent consolidated by 'Set Me Free,' 'See My Friend,' and then in summer 1966 'Sunny Afternoon.'

Kinks supremo Ray Davies wrote the song while recuperating from a nervous breakdown. The lugubrious, descending introduction marks it out as one of those numbers recognizable from its first notes, while the opening line – "The taxman's taken all my dough" – was a real grabber.

Ray's colleagues provide deft backing and sweetly cooing harmonies, but it is his own lead voice that really lifts this track into the ranks of the immortal. His tale of a man broken financially and romantically is sung to exquisite effect in a voice that drifts between conventional pop and the vaudeville stylings of a Jimmy Durante or an Al Jolson. The breadth of The Kinks' talents are displayed on the B-side, which offers up the smoldering hard-rock of 'I'm Not Like Everybody Else.'

I Feel Free
Cream

Released December 1966
Atco *6462* (U.S.) / Reaction *591 011* (U.K. #11)

When guitarist Eric Clapton, bassist Jack Bruce, and drummer Ginger Baker formed a new band in summer 1966 they were aware that they were pooling talents considered significant, to say the least. Suitably boastful, they titled themselves Cream because of this fact. As if that wasn't enough, they proceeded to explore a musical style that was quite new. Their super-amplified blues shot through with virtuoso playing swiftly made them one of the biggest and most important groups of the era, as they helped to prove that rock could be about more than pretty melodies and banal lyrics and could contain the improvisation and virtuosity that jazz, for instance, took for granted.

Singles were not really their forte. Cream's style thrived more on albums and especially the live concert. But at the same time they did not disdain singles in the same way that Led Zeppelin soon would. 'I Feel Free' is like much of their studio work in that it exhibits a discipline usually lacking from their live sets, which typically included very long drum and guitar solos. With a melody from Bruce and a lyric supplied by non-band-member Pete Brown, it featured a pretty 'bomp bomp' vocal riff, a hummed vocal counter riff, and a concise pop melody. Clapton's powerful lead guitar work meanwhile hints at the group's 'other' identity, and the delicious way that the anguished, double-time verses contrast with the whimsy of the rest of the composition point to heavier inclinations held in check.

Reach Out I'll Be There
The Four Tops

Released August 1966
Motown *1098* (U.S. #1) / Tamla Motown *TMG 579* (U.K. #1)

By the fall of 1966, writers Holland-Dozier-Holland had secured five *Billboard* hits for black vocal outfit The Four Tops. While these included the chart-topper 'I Can't Help Myself,' the fact that the last two had stalled in the lower reaches of the Top 20 indicated that they might be losing their touch with the group. Perhaps this was partly the reason that, at a Motown quality-control meeting, a company employee insisted that 'Reach Out' would not sell. "Too different," was his conclusion. However, this was the very quality that Motown boss Berry Gordy liked about it, causing him to take the executive decision to release it.

Certainly the record was singular in its grandiosity. The kids would no doubt be able to empathize with the customarily passionate vocal from Levi Stubbs, but the singing was also tinged with an epic pathos they might find risible. Meanwhile, what were they to make of the flute, oboe, and exotic percussion of the instrumentation? Just because Lamont Dozier and Brian Holland were weaned on a mixture of gospel and classical music, it didn't mean that young Americans would want to know about a fusion of those styles.

As it turned out, they very much did want to know about it. And so did British kids – they, like their American counterparts, sent it to the top. "We just wanted to keep striving for something different to make people listen to Holland-Dozier-Holland," Brian Holland said later. "It was a gem of a song."

HOLLAND-DOZIER-HOLLAND: THE MOTOWN HIT MACHINE

In 1963, Freddie Gorman made it clear to his Motown songwriting colleagues Brian Holland and Lamont Dozier that his job as a postman was making it too difficult to continue writing with them. Holland's brother Eddie – hitherto a recording artist – was drafted in to take up the slack, and one of the most famous publishing credits of all time was born.

Each of the team's members would give you a different story about why the names are credited in the order Holland-Dozier-Holland (often abbreviated to H-D-H) but they all agreed on the way they worked as a unit. Brian and Lamont would come up with the initial idea or title and write a melody, which would then be passed on to Eddie, who would devise a lyric. Regardless of contribution, credit and royalties would be divided up in exact thirds. It was a streamlined process that yielded the trio, and their label, record sales estimated at 73 million over five years. And as if to prove that factory methods do not necessarily equate with philistinism, they produced classic song after classic song.

'Come And Get These Memories' was the first song credited to the trio, although Lamont had written most if it already. He has said that their first true collaboration was either Mary Wells's 'You Lost The Sweetest Boy' or The Marvellettes' 'Locking Up My Heart' – both *Billboard* Top 50 entries in 1963. That same year they gave Martha & The Vandellas a brace of Top 10 U.S. singles, 'Heat Wave' and 'Quicksand,' as well as

one for Smokey Robinson's Miracles in the gimmicky 'Mickey's Monkey.' In 1964 H-D-H secured their first Number 1, for female vocal trio The Supremes, in the shape of 'Where Did Our Love Go?' A song of almost nursery-rhyme simplicity, it was ridiculed by the group as a Marvellettes cast-off, but their attitude changed when it topped the chart. An astonishing nine further *Billboard* chart-toppers followed, including 'Baby Love,' 'Come See About Me,' 'Stop! In The Name of Love,' 'Back In My Arms Again,' 'You Can't Hurry Love,' and 'You Keep Me Hangin' On.'

Vocal quartet The Four Tops were also granted the H-D-H magic touch, starting with 'Baby I Need Your Loving' and continuing through 'I Can't Help Myself' and its soundalike but still superb 'It's The Same Old Song.' The songwriters moved into epic territory with the Tops for the ornate 'Reach Out I'll Be There,' a 1966 transatlantic Number 1, and 'Standing In The Shadows Of Love.' Marvin Gaye didn't use them quite so often, but they did give him 'How Sweet It Is To Be Loved By You' – which is probably better known now in its 1975 cover version by James Taylor, a hit ten years after Gaye charted with the song.

While Holland-Dozier-Holland continued to have big hits on their own labels after parting company with Motown in the late 1960s following a financial dispute, neither they nor Motown were ever quite the same force again.

Penny Lane / Strawberry Fields Forever
The Beatles

Released February 1967
Capitol *5810* (U.S. #1) / Parlophone *R 5570* (U.K. #2)

The Beatles' finest and most accomplished single, this double A-side release provides a perfect summation of the two sides of the group. Both songs were conceived as evocations of their authors' childhoods and are named for parts of their hometown of Liverpool, England. But while Paul McCartney's 'Penny Lane' is a breezy, immaculately recorded singalong, John Lennon's flipside, 'Strawberry Fields Forever,' is ominous and hypnotic, and more concerned with mood than melody.

'Penny Lane' and 'Strawberry Fields Forever' were the first new Beatles songs released since *Revolver*, which had been issued six months earlier in August 1966. This constituted the longest pause between releases of the group's career, although they had managed to plug a gap in the Christmas market with the thoroughly unnecessary compilation *A Collection Of Beatles Oldies*. These two songs, though, were anything but oldies: intended originally as part of the *Sgt. Pepper* album, they showcase the group's growing mastery of the recording studio and Lennon & McCartney's apparently effortless affinity for song.

Of the pair, 'Strawberry Fields Forever' was recorded first, beginning on November 24, 1966, at Abbey Road Studio 2. The Beatles hadn't convened in a recording studio since June, having spent the summer on their final concert tour and the intervening months working on individual projects: Lennon took an acting role in *Help!*-director Richard Lester's *How I Won The War*; McCartney composed the score to *The Family Way*; George Harrison traveled to India to study the sitar; and Ringo Starr did nothing of importance.

As such, initial work on 'Strawberry Fields' was filled with false starts and regularly interrupted by other projects, whether it be the recording of the fan-club-only single 'Pantomime: Everywhere It's Christmas' or Lennon's appearance on the TV comedy show *Not Only . . . But Also* alongside legendary funny-men Peter Cook and Dudley Moore.

By the end of November, The Beatles had completed seven takes of 'Strawberry Fields' with Lennon on acoustic guitar and vocals, Harrison playing an electric slide-guitar part, Starr on drums, and McCartney on bass and Mellotron. A forerunner of the sampler, the Mellotron was a keyboard instrument containing tape loops of brass, string, and woodwind sounds, each triggered by different keys. McCartney played the song's distinctive introductory bars on the instrument.

Lennon, though, was unhappy with these recordings but, equally, was unsure as to what needed to be done to improve them. After a week's contemplation (during which time work commenced on McCartney's 'When I'm Sixty-Four') he enlisted George Martin to score 'Strawberry Fields' for trumpets and cellos. The Beatles recorded a new, faster version of the song on December 8 and 9, with a much more complex arrangement that included backwards cymbals and an Indian instrument, the surmandal, on which Harrison plays the unusual scale that links the later choruses back to the verse. The brass and string parts were added a week later, and 'Strawberry Fields Forever' was completed.

Or so everyone thought. After a further week of mulling over the song, Lennon decided he liked the first minute of the slower, sparser version, but also the remaining couple of minutes of the busier, orchestrated rendition. He called George Martin and engineer Geoff Emerick back to the song, asking them to create a composite mix of the two. This wasn't entirely straightforward, particularly as the two versions were recorded in different keys. But by speeding up the first and slowing down the second, Martin was able to create a seamless edit at about the one-minute mark. And with that, 'Strawberry Fields' was finally finished.

Lyrically, 'Strawberry Fields Forever' finds John Lennon at his most oblique and unsure of himself. Like the hazy, spellbinding music, the words bear the hallmarks of a mind opened up but also thrown into confusion by LSD. In recalling childhood memories of the Strawberry Fields park, located just around the corner from where he was brought up, Lennon uses the narrative device of a young girl, wandering and wondering absentmindedly. Lines about how "no one I think is in my tree" are intentionally stuttering and contradictory, and ultimately reveal little more than that "living is easy with eyes closed."

While 'Strawberry Fields' has the sound and feel of a memory about to slip away, 'Penny Lane' displays a much more definite, detailed recall. It does possess a certain wistfulness but paints a much more cheerful picture: in five neatly constructed verses, McCartney reminisces about barbers and bankers and children laughing, under a blanket of "blue suburban skies." Musically, 'Penny Lane' is clearly inspired by Brian Wilson's widescreen production of The Beach Boys' *Pet Sounds* album. Driven by jolly, staccato piano and the by now de rigueur walking bassline,

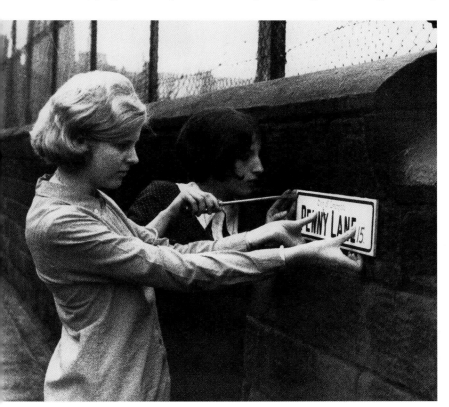

the song grows over its tight three minutes with the addition of several other keyboard parts, rousing trumpets, flugelhorn, and – in the most explicit indicator of The Beach Boys' influence – a melancholy flute.

The recording of 'Penny Lane' was much more straightforward than that of 'Strawberry Fields Forever.' McCartney taped the basic tracks alone four days after Christmas before inviting the other Beatles to add to it in the first week of 1967. While it might not outwardly display the technical wizardry of 'Strawberry Fields,' 'Penny Lane' is in fact packed with clever studio tricks.

Most notable are the various piano parts, which were recorded at different speeds and then synchronized together to create unusual overtones. During the second week of January, a whole host of additional instruments were overdubbed by guest musicians, including flute, oboe, cor anglais, and double bass. McCartney decided on the final finishing touch – a piccolo-trumpet solo – after watching a performance of Bach's *Brandenburg Concerto Number Two in F Major* on BBC television.

With 'Penny Lane' completed, The Beatles continued work on what would become *Sgt. Pepper*, turning next to 'A Day In The Life.' By this stage, however, the group's label was in need of a new Beatles single. With only three tracks completed since November (the other one was 'When I'm Sixty-Four'), they opted for a double A-side, consisting of 'Penny Lane' and 'Strawberry Fields Forever,' thus disqualifying both from inclusion on any as-yet unfinished new album. George Martin has always considered this to be a huge mistake, claiming – quite rightly – that *Sgt. Pepper* would have been a much stronger album with the inclusion of these two songs.

At the end of January, as had become customary The Beatles shot a short promo film for each side of the single, with the Swedish director Peter Goldmann. (They had been doing this since late 1965, in part to avoid having to turn up to perform on *Top Of The Pops* and other TV music shows.) The single itself was released in mid February and quickly climbed to Number 1 on the U.S. singles chart. In the U.K., however, it was held off the top spot by Engelbert Humperdinck's 'Release Me.'

Happy Together
The Turtles

Released February 1967
White Whale *244* (U.S. #1) / London *HL 10115* (U.K. #12)

This whimsical pop classic was turned down by a number of artists, including The Vogues and Gary Lewis & The Playboys, before The Turtles took it to Number 1. It replaced The Beatles' glorious double A-side 'Penny Lane' / 'Strawberry Fields Forever' at the top of the U.S. singles chart – rather fittingly, as The Turtles had been inspired to move away from their earlier folk-rock material towards the richer sound of 'Happy Together' by the fab four's recent experimental offerings.

Silence Is Golden
The Tremeloes

Released April 1967
Epic *10184* (U.S. #11) / CBS *2723* (U.K. #1)

With their erstwhile leader, Brian Poole, The Tremeloes had the distinction of signing to Decca instead of The Beatles; the two bands had auditioned on the same day. A solid run of beat-pop chart singles followed, until 1966 when Poole left for a solo career, eventually returning to his family butchers business. His former backing band did better without him, having hits into the 1970s. 'Silence Is Golden,' an old Four Seasons B-side, was the biggest. It's a finely executed slice of gentle, mid-paced harmony pop that gave the band a British chart-topper, although the musical sweetness disguised a darker lyric: "Talking is cheap, people follow like sheep / Even though there is nowhere to go," sang lead vocalist Len 'Chip' Hawkes. Within a few years, changing tastes meant there was nowhere for The Tremeloes to go. Tiring of their pop image, they alienated their fans by disowning their back catalogue and 'going progressive.' When this stunt failed, the band quickly reclaimed their old hits again and took them out on to the cabaret circuit, where a version of the band performs 'Silence Is Golden' to this day.

Born Under A Bad Sign
Albert King

Released May 1967
Stax *217* (U.S.) / Stax *601 015* (U.K.)

Like his contemporaries Freddy and B.B. King, blues guitarist Albert King was a crucial influence on many rock guitarists, including Eric Clapton, Jimi Hendrix, and Stevie Ray Vaughan. Though he began recording in 1953, King didn't find any real success until he joined Stax Records in 1966 and was coupled with Booker T. & The MGs, creating a blues sound coated with Memphis soul. MGs guitarist Steve Cropper recalled that King could neither read nor write, and it was difficult to persuade him to record songs with which he was unfamiliar. Among the sides he recorded at Stax were 'Laundromat Blues,' 'Crosscut Saw,' and 'Born Under A Bad Sign,' specially written for King by Booker T. Jones and singer William Bell, and later notably covered by Clapton's band Cream. King had a unique playing style, often using his left-handed Flying V guitar strung 'upside down' and with his unorthodox tuning that resulted from his first attempts to play on a homemade guitar.

Light My Fire
The Doors

Released June 1967
Elektra *45615* (U.S. #1) / Elektra *EKSN 45014* (U.K.)

It is Jim Morrison's beauty, akin to that of Michelangelo's David, that has become the image most associated with The Doors. Consequently, many are under the impression that it was he who wrote this, the band's most famous song. Others assume it was written by keyboardist Ray Manzarek, the musical star of the record. In fact it was guitarist Robbie Krieger who came up with the number after a meeting during the group's early days when Morrison encouraged his colleagues to compensate for the paucity of their original material.

Knowing of Morrison's "very heavy" lyrical tastes, as Kreiger described them, the guitarist decided to write a song that would incorporate one of the four elements. Morrison loved the smoldering sensuality of the creation, tweaking the lyric only a little. The group worked up the song and emerged at the end with a six-and-a-half-minute epic featuring lengthy instrumental passages, with Manzarek's manic organ runs particularly prominent, alternating with a somber yet desirous vocal.

Those lengthy instrumental passages were mostly jettisoned for the edit of the song that was considered necessary for a single release. Even in chopped form, the song sounded like little else in mainstream rock, particularly with its blatant drug reference in the line "We couldn't get much higher," recitation of which got them banned from the influential *Ed Sullivan* TV show forever. The record still spent three weeks at the top of the U.S. chart. José Feliciano's 1968 cover was at first the more popular version in Britain, where The Doors' original would have to wait until 1991 to go Top 10.

Purple Haze
The Jimi Hendrix Experience

Released March 1967
Reprise *0597* (U.S.) / Track *604 001* (U.K. #3)

This was the first self-composed single by The Jimi Hendrix Experience, full of quality and epoch-marking innovation, and yet when manager Chas Chandler had signed the guitarist months previously, he had no idea whether Hendrix could write songs or not.

Chandler had bridged the gap between Hendrix the dazzling guitarist and Hendrix the proficient songwriter – he'd only composed scraps and generic exercises before – by getting him to record his live staple 'Hey Joe,' and a very good record it made too. But 'Purple Haze' was the fundamentally important single that proved he was not some kind of 'guitar Elvis' – an iconic figure but still a mere interpreter – but really had become a significant artistic force.

It's difficult to convey just how barrier-smashing 'Purple Haze' was in the first quarter of 1967. So it is fitting that this utterly alien-sounding record was partly inspired by a science fiction story, namely *Night Of Light* by Philip José Farmer, in which the phrase "purple haze" is used to describe the disorienting effects of sunspot activity on a planet called Dante's Joy.

The lyric was appropriately surreal, its discussion of the hazy state capped by bizarre interrogatives like "Is this tomorrow or just the end of time?" and, deliciously, "'Scuse me while I kiss the sky." The music was even more arresting in its freshness, propelled by a ferocious guitar riff that made even 'You Really Got Me' sound tame and yet somehow always retaining a melodic commerciality.

White Rabbit
Jefferson Airplane

Released June 1967
RCA *9248* (U.S. #8) / RCA *1631* (U.K.)

With a lyric inspired by *Alice In Wonderland,* the disquietingly catchy 'White Rabbit' was one of the defining singles of late-1960s U.S. psychedelic rock. Jefferson Airplane had formed in 1965; their debut album of the following year failed to chart, but like many of their contemporaries the group benefited from an appearance at the 1967 Monterey International Pop Festival.

The arrival of vocalist and songwriter Grace Slick gave the group a stronger focus. Her rich, powerful vocal belied a sweet, almost childlike image. Slick also contributed the two songs that made Jefferson Airplane the first truly internationally successful West Coast psychedelic rock group: the rousing 'Somebody To Love' and its insidious follow-up, 'White Rabbit.'

While the words to 'White Rabbit' are clearly from Lewis Carroll's *Alice In Wonderland*, the music came to Slick, according to later interviews, after a day spent listening again and again to Miles Davis's *Sketches Of Spain* while under the influence of LSD. There is also a suggestion of Ravel's *Bolero* in the insistent, militaristic rhythms and the way the song gradually builds to its menacing peak, over which Slick implores the listener, somewhat amusingly, to "remember what the dormouse said."

As well as its obvious musical charm, 'White Rabbit' was aided in its ascent up the *Billboard* singles chart by a memorable performance of the song on the *Ed Sullivan* TV show. The group was filmed using then cutting-edge chroma key technology (also known as 'blue screen') that gave the song a suitably hallucinatory visual backdrop.

Heroes And Villains
The Beach Boys

Released July 1967
Brother *1001* (U.S. #12) / Capitol *CL 15510* (U.K. #8)

Although it was never completed to bandleader Brian Wilson's satisfaction, 'Heroes And Villains' remains one of The Beach Boys most accomplished singles. A second pocket symphony in the vein of 'Good Vibrations,' the single version is significantly shorter and less complex than Wilson had in mind.

In fact Wilson handed it over to Capitol as a compromise as sessions for the (ultimately abandoned) *Smile* album ran over time. Nonetheless, its rousing verses and elegant chorus – not to mention the sublime middle eight – are vastly superior to most of the popular music of the time.

Four decades later, a longer, more extravagant 'Heroes And Villains' was included on a newly re-recorded version of Smile, put together by Wilson, original lyricist Van Dyke Parkes, and Darian Sahanaja of the Beach Boys-inspired group The Wondermints.

A Whiter Shade Of Pale
Procol Harum

Released May 1967
Deram *7507* (U.S. #5) / Deram *DM 126* (U.K. #1)

With its haunting, Bach-derived melody and impenetrable lyrics, 'A Whiter Shade Of Pale' is one of the all-time great debut singles. It was also one of the few things that Beatles John Lennon and Paul McCartney could agree upon in 1967: the former is said to have listened to it on endless repeat during long limo rides, while the latter has since named it one of his favorite songs of the 1960s.

Before fronting Procol Harum, Gary Brooker led The Paramounts, an R&B covers band who had a minor U.K. hit in 1963 with a version of The Coasters' 'Poison Ivy.' By 1966 the group had dissolved, and Brooker began writing songs with lyricist Keith Reid.

Reid and Brooker originally saw themselves as a professional songwriting partnership in the manner of the classic Brill Building teams of the time, but after struggling to find artists to record their songs they decided there was nothing else for it but to put together a band of their own. Reid remained with Procol Harum (named for their manager's cat) as a 'non-musical' member, contributing the lyrics to each of the group's 11 studio albums.

Procol Harum recorded 'A Whiter Shade Of Pale' in 1967 with producer Denny Cordell, who worked with The Moody Blues, The Move, and Joe Cocker. Musically, the song's main chord progression and melody bears a resemblance to a section of Johann Sebastian Bach's *Suite No. 3 in D Major*, more commonly known as *Air On A G String*. Reid and Brooker have always been listed as the song's composers, but at the time of writing the group's keyboardist, Matthew Fisher, had instigated legal action against the pair, claiming to have come up with the distinctive organ riff himself.

Lyrically, the single is a maze of confusing couplets about skipping "the light fandango," vestal virgins, turning cartwheels, and ghostly faces. Neither Reid nor Brooker has ever explained what the words mean, prompting years of over-eager analysis, particularly in the current age of nitpicking everything to the nth degree on the internet. Ultimately, it's probably no more or less than a love song packed full of intentionally bewildering nautical metaphors.

Whatever it meant then or means now, 'A Whiter Shade Of Pale' struck a chord with listeners across the world in 1967, topping the U.K. singles chart for six weeks during the Summer of Love and peaking at Number 5 in America. Coupled with the similar success of 'Nights In White Satin' by The Moody Blues, the single marked out the Deram label as the home of British progressive rock. It ended up as Procol Harum's only release for Deram, however, as by the fall of the same year they had moved to Regal Zonophone in Britain and A&M in the States. Although the follow-up single, 'Homburg,' gave them a second international hit, Procol Harum would never again match the success of their debut.

Brown Eyed Girl
Van Morrison

Released June 1967
Bang *545* (U.S. #10) / London *HLZ 10150* (U.K.)

In April 2005 the White House revealed that 'Brown Eyed Girl' was one of George W. Bush's favorite songs, featuring on his iPod selection. Quite how this will affect the song's popularity is unknown, although Irish singer Van Morrison's response was: "I would have preferred it if it was a new song."

Following a particularly grueling American tour in 1966, Morrison left Them and accepted a one-way-ticket to New York City and a solo contract from Bert Berns's Bang Records. Berns had produced Them in London – 'Here Comes The Night' was a Berns composition – and was a major player in 1960s pop music as a producer, publisher, and songwriter.

Of course, Berns wanted Morrison to record hits, which was not at all what Morrison had in mind, and most of his material for Bang was about as uncommercial as it gets. However, one song that emerged from the sessions turned into a big hit in America. Morrison's original title was 'Brown Skinned Girl.' Beginning life as a "calypso thing" it somehow got changed along the way. None too happy at this 'commercial' turn of events, Morrison returned to Belfast before he had completed his vocals for the song, and consequently Jeff Barry (writer of dozens of hits with Ellie Greenwich) had to overdub the "sha la la" chorus at the end of the record. (The line "making love in the green grass" was edited out of the third verse for radio purposes.)

While it was never a hit in the U.K., 'Brown Eyed Girl' has since become something of a classic summer anthem, and despite Morrison's anger over his contractual circumstances in 1967 (yes – he was a grumpy young man too), this was the song that launched his solo career.

Itchycoo Park
The Small Faces

Released July 1967
Immediate *501* (U.S. #16) / Immediate *IM 057* (U.K. #3)

Together with The Who, The Small Faces were one of the most popular groups with the British mod movement of the middle 1960s. Like The Who they began as an R&B outfit, but as their career progressed, and with unlimited studio time at their disposal, they ventured into broader musical areas. Prior to joining erstwhile Rolling Stones manager Andrew Loog Oldham's Immediate label in 1967, they had recorded a string of hits for Decca. Oldham allegedly paid former manager Don Arden £25,000 for this transaction (about $60,000 at the time), which was delivered in cash in a brown paper bag

The group's first single for Immediate, 'Here Come The Nice,' was released in May 1967 and rose to Number 12 in Britain, quickly followed by 'Itchycoo Park,' a song with a surrealistic lyric that contained a number of relatively undisguised drug references. The BBC gramophone committee, charged with banning unsuitable records from the corporation's airwaves, seemed to be gloriously unaware of this, and were probably more used to stimulants of the liquid variety, although they had earlier objected to a number of The Small Faces' Decca singles because of sexual innuendo.

‘Itchycoo Park’ rose to Number 3 in Britain and became the group’s sole American hit. According to drummer Kenny Jones: “Itchycoo Park wasn’t really a park, it was an overgrown bombsite full of stinging nettles in Ilford [east London] which ran down to the railway lines.” The recording was particularly notable for its use of phasing, a technical effect that produced a strange ‘whooshing’ sound. While their two psychedelic singles are undeniably good, The Small Faces were in fact one of Britain’s most accomplished R&B bands and Marriott one of the country’s finest R&B vocalists, as he would prove on their next and perhaps best single, ‘Tin Soldier.’

Hole In My Shoe
Traffic

Released August 1967
United Artists *50218* (U.S.) / Island *WIP 6017* (U.K. #2)

Considering that Stevie Winwood left The Spencer Davis Group to participate in a band with a little more musical gravitas, it’s ironic that Traffic are now remembered mostly for this record, written by the frequently-fired band member Dave Mason. Despite its Eastern ambience, backwards effects, and hallucinogenic lyric, it boasted the type of sing-song melody that made it attractive to children. To underline its lightweight aura, it became even better known when Neil – a hippie character from the TV comedy series *The Young Ones* – took a not entirely serious rendition to Number 2 in Britain in 1984.

Nights In White Satin
The Moody Blues

Released November 1967
Deram *85023* (U.S. #2) / Deram *DM 161* (U.K. #9)

When Justin Hayward and John Lodge joined The Moody Blues in 1966, they joined an R&B group that had already enjoyed their moment of fame with the 1965 Number 1 ‘Go Now’ and were back to playing gigs for small change. With two new songwriting members, the group decided they had little to lose by changing their image and created a sequence of songs based around a normal day, in which Hayward’s ‘Nights In White Satin’ formed an integral part.

At this point Decca approached the group and suggested they record a rock version of Dvorak’s *New World Symphony*. This wasn’t exactly what they had in mind, but it certainly suited their purposes. Demanding a week ‘alone’ in the studio, the Moodys proceeded to record their new material and the result was *Days Of Future Passed*, a song suite interwoven with orchestral links written by Peter Knight.

Presenting the finished product to Decca’s executives, the group was met with a stunned silence. It certainly wasn’t Dvorak, but since a good deal of money had been spent making the album, it proved to be something of a fait accompli. While the album took some time to find an audience, its high point, ‘Nights In White Satin,’ was the song that finally began to attract attention.

Of the group’s breakthrough song, Hayward said: “I knew when I wrote it that it was like nothing I’d ever done before. I was just a 19-year-old kid … and there’s actually a lot of wisdom there that I never noticed at the time.” ‘Nights In White Satin’ remains their best-loved and most successful song. It made its mark on the British Top 20 on three separate occasions but did not reach the U.S. charts until 1972.

I Can See For Miles
The Who

Released October 1967
Decca *32206* (U.S. #9) / Track *604 011* (U.K. #10)

“To me it was the ultimate Who record,” Pete Townshend once pronounced of this psychedelic hard-rock single. It certainly sounds like it was intended that way. Despite the sparse instrumentation there is a grandness about the sound and the vaguely science-fiction-like lyric. Keith Moon’s drums sound absolutely gigantic and Townshend’s fretboard slashings are epic. It was almost a running joke that, despite their massive significance, The Who never had a Number 1 U.K. or U.S. single. That joke turned sour here, with Townshend bitter at the record’s modest chart achievements. “I spat on the British record buyer,” he said.

Pictures Of Matchstick Men
The Status Quo

Released November 1967
Cadet Concept *7001* (U.S. #12) / Pye *7N 17449* (U.K. #7)

A clever pastiche of the British psychedelic rock of the time, 'Pictures Of Matchstick Men' would give Status Quo their only U.S. hit (next year), although the group was a mainstay on the U.K. charts for the rest of the century. Driven by wah-wah guitar, organ, and crashing drums, the single was The Status Quo's first for the Pye label in Britain. After several similarly trippy releases, the group dropped the definite article from its name and turned to a more simplistic style based on 12-bar blues, with which they stuck doggedly for the next three decades. Despite an often unfashionable sound – and image – Status Quo continued to score hit after hit in the U.K., including 'Rockin' All Over The World' (1977) and 'In The Army Now' (1986).

Arnold Layne
Pink Floyd

Released March 1967
Tower *333* (U.S.) / Columbia *DB 8156* (U.K. #20)

See Emily Play
Pink Floyd

Released June 1967
Tower *356* (U.S.) / Columbia *DB 8214* (U.K. #6)

Pink Floyd's debut single, 'Arnold Layne,' was written by their guitarist-vocalist Syd Barrett and banned by British radio, never rising above Number 20 in the charts.

Nonetheless, its influence was significant. The young Phil Collins was a big fan of the song, and Cream's bassist Jack Bruce recalled it as "the first truly English song about English life with a tremendous lyric. It certainly unlocked doors and made things possible."

Given that Arnold is a thief specializing in stealing ladies' lingerie from washing lines, it should be stressed that what the song made possible was not knicker nicking but a homegrown approach to psychedelia that would ultimately free British bands from merely imitating the American pioneers.

With the eerie sounds of their second single, 'See Emily Play,' the Floyd took psychedelia to the masses, peaking at Number 6 in the British chart. Mind-blowing though the record sounded back then, Floyd keyboardist Rick

Wright insisted in retrospect that much of its groundbreaking sonic landscape was achieved by a relatively simple means. "That 'Hawaiian' bit at the end of each verse," he noted, "was just Syd using a bottleneck through echo."

Tragically, Barrett would become one of rock's first acid casualties. His chemically-enhanced musical vision powered the band through their innovative first album, but as his friend (and replacement) David Gilmour recalled, Barrett was already burning out when Gilmour visited him in London's Sound Techniques on May 23, 1967. "I went down to the studio," said Gilmour, "and he didn't even recognize me – and that was the day they were making 'See Emily Play.'"

On radio, the Summer of Love was marred by storm clouds and downpours. Those hot, heady months coincided with a transition in British broadcasting, which meant that sometimes, when you tuned to your favorite station, all you got was static. Indeed, the only way you could be sure to hear the pop hits of the day was by turning the dial on your transistor radio to 'the great 208,' Radio Luxembourg. That commercial station had been broadcasting popular music around Europe for decades with short, fast-moving shows sponsored by eager advertisers. Since the 1950s Luxembourg had actively courted the youth audience and was well established amongst British teenagers as the best place to hear rock'n'roll.

The BBC, on the other hand, was slow to respond to the new music and teen culture. Since the late 1940s it had operated three main radio stations: the Home Service, which broadcast news and current affairs; the Third Programme, for classical music; and the Light Programme, on which pop competed for air time with easy listening and comedy. This restrictive set-up was constrained even further by an archaic agreement that meant the Light could only play up to five hours of commercial recordings a day. This led to a strange position where current hit records were often performed live, rather than the single being played. What is more, most of these live performances were dire cover versions by BBC musicians rather than performances by the original artists playing their own songs.

With the staid BBC marginalizing itself, and no British commercial radio, Luxembourg's pre-eminence in pop broadcasting was unchallenged. Until 1964, that is, with the launch of the first pirate radio stations. The maritime allusion in the name was appropriate: these stations broadcast into the British mainland from high-powered transmitters fitted into battered old merchant ships moored just outside British territorial waters – and therefore just out of reach of the law. Unhampered by arcane regulations, these stations played an almost constant stream of rock and pop – chart hits and underground sounds – interrupted only by the advertisements that funded the stations and the DJs' quick-fire patter. They became immensely popular with British youth.

The first pirate to take to the seas was Radio Caroline, which by 1966 was boasting more than six million listeners. Radio London was even more successful, with nearly eight-and-a-half-million tuning in. There were others, too: Radio City, Radio Essex, Radio Scotland, even the shortlived Radio Sutch, the vehicle of novelty rock'n'roller and relentless self-publicist Screaming Lord Sutch.

It wasn't just the open broadcast policies that attracted millions to the pirates. The stations were illegal – loathed by the broadcast establishment and the subject of much hand-wringing in the British

parliament. The music business itself was forced into a position of awkward ambivalence: it appreciated the massive exposure that the pirates gave to new records, but resented the fact that they didn't pay airplay royalties. So in tuning the dial to Caroline or London, you were guaranteed not only some great music, but also a frisson of outlaw excitement – an irresistible combination for any rebelliously-minded teenager. But it couldn't go on.

At the very peak of pirate radio's success, a new bill was going through parliament that would extend the arm of the law sufficiently to ensure that the pirate ships were within its reach. At the same time, plans were set in motion to revamp BBC radio. The plans involved creating both a national pop station, which became Radio One, and local BBC stations. The first of these measures came into effect at the height of the Summer of Love with the passing of the Marine Offences Act on August 15, 1967. Radio London broadcast its last record that same day, The Beatles' 'A Day In The Life.' Thousands of fans gathered outside a London railway station to welcome the station's DJs as they returned home from their doomed vessel. Caroline kept going, denying the law, until 1968, until it too bowed to the inevitable.

Six weeks or so after the passing of the act, the BBC launched its new pop station. For much of that intervening period the corporation had been frantically interviewing dozens of applicants for jobs on the new station, most of them recently disembarked from the pirate ships plus a few who'd come over from Luxembourg. So when the station was launched, the DJs in that first roster were names already familiar to Britain's teenagers, including Tony Blackburn (who had worked on radios Caroline, London, and Luxembourg) and John Peel (Radio London).

The momentous day of the launch came on September 30 when, at 5:30am, the Light Programme opened for the last time. It broadcast for a mere one and a half hours, before a new specially-written Radio One theme tune was played, 'Theme One' by The George Martin Orchestra. Then, at 7:00am, Tony Blackburn opened the first ever show on Radio One, playing 'Flowers In The Rain' by The Move.

Release Me (And Let Me Love Again)
Engelbert Humperdinck

Released January 1967
Parrot *40011* (U.S. #4) / Decca *F 12541* (U.K. #1)

Raised in Leicester, England, Gerry Dorsey recorded his first single, 'Mr. Music Man,' for Decca in 1958, and then found himself going nowhere fast. By 1966 he and his wife were living in poverty in a small apartment, but it was a long-time friendship with Gordon Mills that was to be his salvation. Mills had successfully guided Tom Jones to superstardom.

With Jones's career doing nicely, Mills decided to assist his old friend Dorsey. The first matter of business was to kill off 'Gerry Dorsey' and come up with a new name. They settled on the unlikely Engelbert Humperdinck, a name borrowed from an old German composer. It was a mouthful – but certainly likely to attract attention. (Later on, when Mills signed Ray O'Sullivan and changed his first name to Gilbert, Humperdinck had the audacity to remark that it was "a ridiculous name.")

'Release Me' was Engelbert's third single under Mills's guidance. It was written in 1946 and became a country standard, earning hits on the Country charts for Jimmy Heap, Ray Price, and Kitty Wells in 1954, as well as a Number 8 *Billboard* pop hit for Esther Phillips in 1962. Engelbert's version hit home in Britain after the singer performed it on the highly popular nationally televised entertainment show *Sunday Night At The London Palladium*. The record famously kept The Beatles' classic double-A-side 'Penny Lane' / 'Strawberry Fields Forever' from reaching Number 1 in Britain. During some of Engelbert's early shows in 1967, where new acts with major hits would play so-called package tours, among his unlikely fellow travelers was The Jimi Hendrix Experience.

For What It's Worth (Stop, Hey What's That Sound)
Buffalo Springfield

Released January 1967
Atco *6459* (U.S. #7) / Atlantic *584 077* (U.K.)

Neil Young is the most celebrated ex-member of Buffalo Springfield, but it was Stephen Stills who wrote this one iconic song of the group's (admittedly brief) career. It sprang out of the civil war in miniature that Stills was witnessing on Los Angeles's Sunset Strip at the time. A couple of clubs, Pandora's Box and the Whisky A Go Go, became beacons to some particularly troublesome youngsters. Not that they were causing trouble in the conventional sense – violence was hardly the currency when Love & Peace was the vibe and grass the stimulant of choice – but young and old seemed at their farthest apart during the late 1960s. White L.A.P.D. cops, many from the deep South, found the sight of teens and 20-somethings with hair hanging to their shoulders, swathed in outlandish clothes and brandishing joints, akin to an invasion from another planet. Soon, batons were whistling through the air. Stills had recently returned from Latin America and was horrified at how similar the tensions in that region on the brink of revolution were to those in a developed democracy. He concocted this brooding creation about what he saw, flecked with eerie, ringing guitar harmonics and, despite the song's ambivalence, boasting an ominous, unforgettable chorus that sounded like a generational call to arms: "Stop, hey, what's that sound? / Everybody look – what's going down?"

The Guns Of Navarone
The Skatalites

Released April 1967
Not issued U.S. / Island *WI 168* (U.K. #36)

Nothing could be further removed from ska, the Jamaican predecessor of reggae, than a World War II movie starring the very proper David Niven. But then it's unlikely that much thought went into this jaunty instrumental recording of the theme to *The Guns Of Navarone* in the first place: it was simply one of hundreds laid down by the loose aggregation of musicians who played under the Skatalites banner in the mid 1960s. By the time the record climbed the charts in the U.K. the band had ceased to exist, mainly because leader Don Drummond had been convicted of killing his wife in 1965.

San Francisco (Be Sure To Wear Flowers In Your Hair)
Scott McKenzie

Released May 1967
Ode *103* (U.S. #4) / CBS *2816* (U.K. #1)

The definitive flower-power anthem, 'San Francisco' gave its singer Scott McKenzie a brief moment of fame in the hippie summer of 1967. The folk-rock movement was big business at the time and The Mamas & The Papas were the movement's key figures, so it's no surprise to discover that Mamas & Papas leader John Phillips wrote this song. He did so at McKenzie's suggestion, as a song for all the hippies attending the 1967 Monterey Pop Festival. According to McKenzie, Phillips wrote the song within 20 minutes. Phillips and his manager Lou Adler were the principal arrangers of the Festival, and the blanket airplay that 'San Francisco' received on the West Coast leading up to the concert was nothing short of free advertising. In contemporary interviews, McKenzie was very sincere about his flower-power philosophy. He certainly did wear flowers in his hair during the recording of the song.

Can't Take My Eyes Off You
Frankie Valli

Released May 1967
Philips *40446* (U.S. #2) / Philips *BF 1580* (U.K.)

The Four Seasons had been cranking out hits for three years before frontman Frankie Valli started a solo career in parallel with the Seasons in 1965. He began with 'The Sun Ain't Gonna Shine (Anymore),' which flopped for him but became familiar through The Walker Brothers' version. That had been composed by the Seasons' writing team of Bob Crewe and Bob Gaudio, who also supplied Valli's major solo success with 'Can't Take My Eyes Off You.' The success seemed somehow pointless: it sounded like cocktail-lounge music compared to The Four Seasons' much-loved recipe of pop gems garnished with operatically intense vocals.

You Keep Me Hangin' On
Vanilla Fudge

Released June 1967
Atco *6495* (U.S. #6) / Atlantic *584 123* (U.K. #18)

Previously known as The Pigeons, Vanilla Fudge played what they called "psychedelic-symphonic rock" and their initial idea was to play sloweddown and lengthy re-arrangements of recent hits. This version of the 1966 Supremes Number 1 was their only major hit and quite impressed co-writer Brian Holland, who said: "They did a brilliant re-adaptation – I was happy to hear it like that." The Fudge's version only managed to reach Number 67 on its first release in 1967 but when reissued the following year made Number 6. (Kim Wilde would take the song to Number 1 in America in 1987.) In 1968 Jeff Beck had plans to form a group with Rod Stewart and two Fudge members, bassist Tim Bogert and drummer Carmine Appice, but the plans were put on hold, only to be resurrected in 1973 and leading to the creation of Beck Bogert & Appice.

The Letter
The Box Tops

Released August 1967
Mala *565* (U.S. #1) / Stateside *SS 2044* (U.K. #5)

Chips Moman, who had been instrumental in the success of the legendary soul label Stax, ran American Sound Studios in Memphis, a hotbed of hit-making in the 1960s with a core group of elite session musicians. Among the many hits recorded at American were Dusty Springfield's 'Son Of A Preacher Man,' Presley's 'In The Ghetto' and 'Suspicious Minds,' and hits by Neil Diamond, B.J. Thomas, and this gem by The Box Tops, a local group who got their name at the session itself. Written by Wayne Carson Thompson, composer of 'Always On My Mind,' this must be one of the shortest records to top the charts, clocking in at under two minutes. Moman said that between 1967 and 1971 over 100 hits were recorded at his studio and claimed that during one particular week there were 28 hits on the *Billboard* Hot 100 that had all been recorded at American – and all featured the same musicians.

Soul Man
Sam & Dave

Released August 1967
Stax *231* (U.S. #2) / Stax *601 023* (U.K. #24)

It's a well known rule of rock music that every anthem intended to celebrate rock'n'roll somehow manages to end up bereft of the musical qualities it is aimed to convey. However, 'Soul Man' perfectly conveyed the rousing passion, delightful brass work, and instant singlalongability of the best soul music. And it was not surprising, considering that the song was written by Isaac Hayes and Dave Porter and featured the impeccable backing of Booker T. & The MGs. On the other hand, the theory is probably blown to pieces by the fact that The Blues Brothers reputedly sold more copies of the song with their anodyne cover of 1979.

What A Wonderful World
Louis Armstrong

Released November 1967
ABC-Paramount *10982* (U.S.) / HMV *POP 1615* (U.K. #1)

If this was the only recording you ever heard by Louis Daniel Armstrong you could be forgiven for not realizing that he was one of the most important and influential musicians of the 20th century. At 66 years of age he became the oldest person to top the U.K. charts when 'What A Wonderful World' hit Number 1 early in 1968. (Of course, there's every possibility that Cliff Richard might beat this record – any time after June 2007.) There are many scholars who believe that popular music as we know it might not have existed without the pioneering vocal techniques of Louis Armstrong back in the 1920s.

Armstrong was no stranger to the charts, although his forays became somewhat more limited in the age of rock'n'roll. Some might describe 'Wonderful World' as a sentimental load of old bunkum, but it was especially written for Louis, and he loved it. A chart-topper in Britain, it comes as something of a surprise to discover that the 45 was not a hit on first release in America. This may have had something to do with the stringent Top 40 radio formatting that would have excluded such a middle-of-the-road performance, but the main reason was the fact that ABC Records chief Larry Newton hated the record and refused to have it promoted. It finally charted in the States after featuring in the 1987 movie *Good Morning Vietnam*, peaking at Number 32.

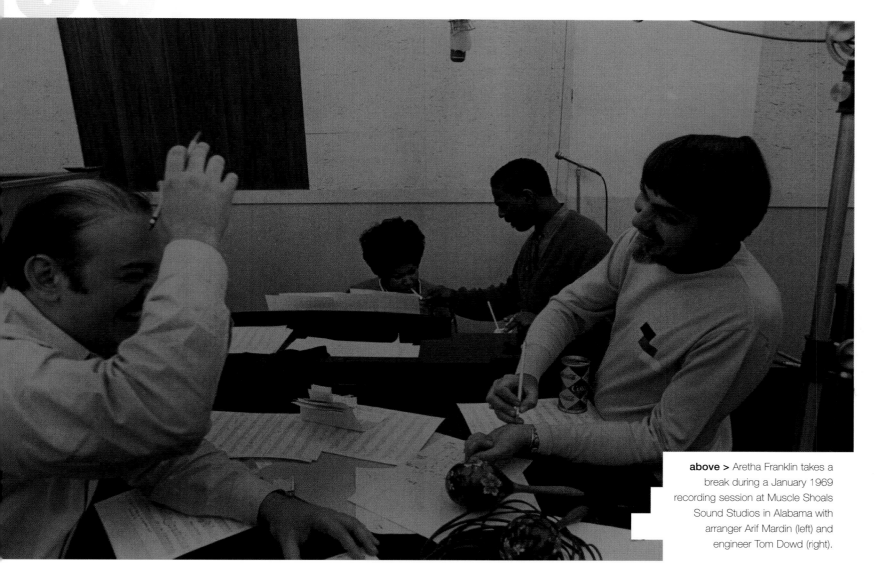

above > Aretha Franklin takes a break during a January 1969 recording session at Muscle Shoals Sound Studios in Alabama with arranger Arif Mardin (left) and engineer Tom Dowd (right).

Respect
Aretha Franklin

Released March 1967
Atlantic *2403* (U.S. #1) / Atlantic *584 115* (U.K. #10)

I Say A Little Prayer
Aretha Franklin

Released July 1968
Atlantic *2546* (U.S. #6) / Atlantic *584 206* (U.K. #4)

Aretha Franklin – or The Queen Of Atlantic Soul as she became known – scored a peerless run of hits during the mid to late 1960s. She made her first recordings as a gospel singer during the late 1950s before being signed by John Hammond to Columbia Records at the age of 18, in 1960. Hammond's attempts to push her as a blues singer failed, and she left the left the label six years later without a Top 30 hit to her name.

Franklin's fortunes changed in late 1966 when she found herself a new home at Atlantic Records and a behind-the-boards team that couldn't possibly fail: producer Jerry Wexler, who had worked with Wilson Pickett, Rufus Thomas, and Solomon Burke; engineer Tom Dowd, whose previous clients included everyone from John Coltrane to The Drifters; and arranger Arif Mardin, who went on to work with The Bee Gees and Dusty Springfield among others.

The remarkable metamorphosis in Franklin's sound – and her commercial appeal – was apparent from the outset with her first single for Atlantic, the U.S. Top 10 hit 'I Never Loved A Man (The Way I Love You).' That song was almost immediately overshadowed by its follow-up, however, a staggering rendition of Otis Redding's 'Respect.' Redding's 1965 original is still considered among the best Southern blues-soul records of the era, but Franklin took the song much further. She cut her version of 'Respect' on Valentines Day 1967 with her sisters Carolyn and Erma on backing vocals. Drummer Gene Chrisman, bassist Tommy Cogbill, pianist Dewey Oldham, and a trio of saxophonists provided the perfect musical backdrop, but the real masterstroke was Franklin's adaptation of the lyric for the unforgettable "R-E-S-P-E-C-T" refrain. The 45 shot to the top of the U.S. charts and into the U.K. Top 10.

Franklin then embarked on a mazy run of great singles, including 'Baby I Love You,' 'A Natural Woman (You Make Me Feel Like),' and 'Chain Of Fools.' The pick of the bunch, however, was 'I Say A Little Prayer.' Like 'Respect' it had already been a hit for another artist, Dionne Warwick, in the summer of 1967. But again, Franklin recorded the definitive version. Warwick's reading of the Burt Bacharach-Hal David song is fast and breezy, and indeed Bacharach considered it to be too fast – which explains why, as producer of the Franklin version, he gave the song a slower tempo and a jazz-soul arrangement, stripping it back to piano, bass, drums, and acoustic guitar. The vocal delivery is, as ever, flawless. 'I Say A Little Prayer' was twinned with the upbeat 'The House That Jack Built' as a double A-side single on its release in the U.S., while in the U.K. it was backed with 'See Saw.'

Time Of The Season
The Zombies

Released April 1968
Date *1628* (U.S. #3) / CBS *3380* (U.K.)

The Zombies burst to public prominence in 1964 with the transatlantic success of 'She's Not There,' but later their musical sophistication and silky electric organ runs seemed to fall out of favor with the record-buying public. By the time they came to cut this track to round off their album *Odessey And Oracle* they had tired of the commercial freefall and decided to split. 'Time Of The Season' saw The Zombies displaying unusual sensuality, with smooth but urgent instrumentation and singer Colin Blunstone asking to "give it to me easy." The words were completed by composer-keyboardist Rod Argent on the morning that the band came to rehearse the song for the first time and he had to send his colleagues down the pub while he added the final touches.

The recording session was conducted in an extremely fractious atmosphere. Thoughts were on the future, not on completing this contractual obligation. "The language was as extreme as you can imagine," said Blunstone. But perhaps this was as nothing compared to the language employed by people in and around The Zombies when the record was released later in the States, after the band's dissolution, and proceeded to march into the Top 3. Argent had already set up his own band and refused point blank to reform The Zombies and take advantage of the success, feeling it would be a step backwards. Bizarrely, while Argent stuck to his principles, a fake Zombies began playing gigs to fill the gap in the market.

Jumpin' Jack Flash
The Rolling Stones

Released May 1968
London *908* (U.S. #3) / Decca *F 12782* (U.K. #1)

'Jumpin' Jack Flash' is one of the Stones' greatest performances on record and marked a decisive return to form for the group in 1968 following a lengthy period in the musical wilderness. Its arrival highlighted a period of transition for the group: it was the first Stones recording produced by Jimmy Miller, but one of the last to feature founding member Brian Jones. The year before had been marred by a series of drug busts and, amid these legal problems, the Stones, like just about everybody else, had been attempting to compete with The Beatles' landmark *Sgt. Pepper* album. This resulted in *Their Satanic Majesties Request*, a pseudo-psychedelic mess with an expensive three-dimensional jacket illustration, put together while three Stones – Jagger, Richards, and Jones – were in and out of court and prison.

According to bass guitarist Bill Wyman, 'Jumpin' Jack Flash' was based upon a piano riff that he came up with after arriving early at rehearsals one day. Together with Charlie Watts and Brian Jones, he expanded the idea until Jagger and Richards arrived and exclaimed: "Keep playing that, and don't forget it – it sounds great!" The song soon came together, and Jagger wrote one of his most savage sets of lyrics, including the line: "I was raised by a toothless, bearded hag." Quite what his mother thought about this is unknown. Keith Richards has confirmed in interviews that 'Flash,' his favorite Stones song, was Wyman's idea. But the bassist never received a writer's credit for his efforts. He magnanimously admitted that he didn't worry about it at the time

because "the song only contributed to the band's continued success." However, in retrospect, he probably wishes he'd put his foot down and claimed his share of the royalties of one of the Stones' greatest songs.

Fire
The Crazy World Of Arthur Brown

Released June 1968
Atlantic *2556* (U.S. #2) / Track *604022* (U.K. #1)

Opening with a cry of "I am the God of hellfire," this was one of the more unlikely British Number 1 hits of the 1960s. The crazed vocal is matched by an insistent, apocalyptic Hammond organ and sharp bursts of trumpet. Although Brown was never able to repeat its success, this single was more than enough to earn him a place in pop history. He became notorious for his onstage antics, which included (seemingly) setting his head on fire and performing naked. Such behavior inspired countless other shock-rockers, from Alice Cooper to Marilyn Manson.

Hey Jude / Revolution
The Beatles

Released August 1968
Apple *2276* (U.S. #1) / Apple *R 5722* (U.K. #1)

Clocking in at over seven minutes, 'Hey Jude' became the first release on The Beatles' new Apple label. It is one of Paul McCartney's more soulful compositions – which explains a cover version by Wilson Pickett featuring Duane Allman on guitar – and was the group's first recording outside EMI's Abbey Road. Work on it did begin at EMI's studios until the group discovered that London's Trident studios had an 8-track recorder, whereas Abbey Road only had 4-track at the time. When EMI heard about this they demanded the recording continue at Abbey Road, but because the machine at Trident was faulty, this proved impossible.

McCartney had written the song with John Lennon's son Julian in mind as he drove down to Lennon's home. The recording was made during sessions for the double 'White Album,' during which George Harrison was playing answering phrases to McCartney's lines, something that annoyed the composer, who wanted to keep it simple. McCartney later recalled saying: "George, do us a favor, man. Don't play that. We'll have a solo later or something. But don't answer every phrase; it's going to get boring very soon."

'Revolution' was taped a couple of weeks before 'Hey Jude' and remains one of the band's most powerful recordings. Lennon had hoped his song would be the A-side, but as so often happened McCartney had come up with something better – and 'Hey Jude' was one of Lennon's favorite McCartney songs. The double-headed single became their most successful American 45, spending nine weeks at Number 1.

Abraham, Martin And John
Dion

Released October 1968
Laurie *3464* (U.S. #4) / London *HLP 10229* (U.K.)

Five years after his last chart entry, Dion returned, artistically rejuvenated, with this hymn to Abraham Lincoln, Martin Luther King, John F Kennedy (and Bobby Kennedy too, although he didn't make it into the title). The rock'n'roll and doo-wop styles of the Dion of old were replaced by an easy, mid-paced folk-rock groove, over which Dion's voice swoops and glides with characteristic grace. Dion hasn't had a hit since this, but he still records well-received albums. In 1970 Marvin Gaye slowed the song down and took it into the charts again.

Eloise
Barry Ryan

Released October 1968
Not issued U.S. / MGM *1442* (U.K. #2)

Paul and Barry Ryan were sons of Marion Ryan, who had scored a British hit single in 1958. As a duo the brothers had eight minor British hits of their own between 1965 and '67, before Paul volunteered for a backseat role, writing for his brother. The rearranged partnership scored a spectacular success with their first single, 'Eloise,' easily the Ryan family's biggest hit. An orchestral epic that sprawled well past the regulation three minutes, it pushed Ryan to the very edge of his rather limited vocal range and beyond, and the song ends with a fade-out over which the singer breaks down into near hysterics. British punks The Damned scored their biggest hit with a cover version in 1986.

Wichita Lineman
Glen Campbell

Released November 1968
Capitol *2302* (U.S. #3) / Ember *EMBS 261* (U.K. #7)

After scoring a Top 30 hit with 'By The Time I Get To Phoenix,' Glen Campbell contacted the song's composer, Jimmy Webb, with a request for a follow-up, suggesting that it too should have a place-name in the title. From such an apparently mercenary prompt came the second installment of a trilogy that, with another single, 'Galveston,' marked collectively one of the more haunting and subtle musical creations of the 1960s. The lonesome plight of the narrator, a telegraph-pole repairman, is underlined by Webb's organ work in a somehow vast and yet empty soundscape, alongside the memorable line: "And I need you more than want you / And I want you for all time."

JIMMY WEBB: PLAYING CHECKERS BY THE TREES

Songwriter Jimmy Webb was born in Elk City, Oklahoma, in 1946, the son of a minister. As a young man he worked for Jobete, Motown's music publishing company, and the first song of his to be recorded was a track on a Supremes Christmas album. His first hit was 'Up – Up And Away' a Top 10 hit for The 5th Dimension in the U.S., and The Johnny Mann Singers in Britain. The song is destined to be cued every time a TV show runs something about Superman.

That same year, Glen Campbell covered Webb's song 'By The Time I Get To Phoenix' and it made the U.S. Top 30. The cleft-jawed, wholesome artist was a simple man, as happy to record characterless versions of 'Dock Of The Bay' as sophisticated fare like 'Phoenix,' but Webb wasn't going to agonize about Campbell being little more than a cipher in the process. Among the other Webb songs Campbell released are 'Wichita Lineman and 'Galveston,' which, with 'Phoenix,' form a triumvirate of exquisite bleakness. (Campbell has said Webb told him all three were about the same character.)

The Association turned down a Webb song called 'Macarthur Park' and, in a bizarre move, Webb decided to ask his friend, the hard-drinking actor Richard Harris, to become a recording artist for this ornate and often effete extravaganza, boasting such risible lines as: "Someone left

the cake out in the rain / I don't think that I can take it / 'Cos it took so long to bake it / And I'll never have that recipe again." Yet the record often has a vast sweep and even majesty – one writer compared it to Gershwin's *Rhapsody In Blue* – and it was certainly an achievement to take a seven-minutes-plus record into the Top 3 in both the U.K. and U.S. charts in 1968. It should also be noted that at this point Webb was just 21 years old.

Webb has cited his song 'The Moon Is A Harsh Mistress,' recorded by several artists including Judy Collins and Joe Cocker, as a personal favorite, despite its harrowing subject matter: it concerns a manipulative married woman with whom the narrator embarks on an affair. His song 'Highwayman' was recorded by The Highwaymen – an illustrious line-up of Waylon Jennings, Willie Nelson, Johnny Cash, and Kris Kristofferson. Webb's creation was superbly appropriate to these peddlers of mythical outlaw tales and was a U.S. Country Number 1 in 1985. Meanwhile, Linda Ronstadt had a U.S. Adult Contemporary hit in 1990 with Webb's 'Adios.'

Webb's music became less orientated towards the hit parade as he turned his attention with increasing frequency to film, theatre, and TV scores and themes, but his imaginative and never simple music has regularly pointed to new possibilities for rock and pop.

Mrs. Robinson
Simon & Garfunkel

Released April 1968
Columbia *44511* (U.S. #1) / CBS *3443* (U.K. #4)

Although The Lovin' Spoonful had written two soundtracks by the time director Mike Nichols used Simon & Garfunkel's music as part of the score for *The Graduate*, it was the phenomenal commercial success of the resulting album that really kicked off the whole pop soundtrack industry. Previously, the idea of getting 'kids' who weren't classically trained to provide the mood-setting music for motion pictures was considered absurd.

Ironically, that soundtrack album was almost worthless. Nichols merely used previously-released Simon & Garfunkel records, with the exception of one new Paul Simon song, 'Mrs. Robinson.' And while the song is generally considered as great as any of the duo's other hits, the version you'll probably hear on the radio is not the one featured in the movie, which is a prototype version barely longer than a minute. Simon fleshed out the song for inclusion on *Bookends*, the Simon & Garfunkel album released simultaneously with *The Graduate* soundtrack.

The song began life as an instrumental for which Simon could not find words. Art Garfunkel suggested inserting the name of the film's main female character, and Simon developed that to include a memorable verse employing baseball star Joe DiMaggio as a symbol of America's turmoil. Another memorable feature of the hit version is the twining acoustic guitar figure that introduces the record and recurs pleasantly throughout. 'Mrs. Robinson' later served to break The Lemonheads when they released a power-pop version of the song in 1992.

Sunshine Of Your Love
Cream

Released February 1968
Atco *6544* (U.S. #5) / Polydor *56 286* (U.K. #25)

Cream and The Jimi Hendrix Experience were similar in that they were power trios with blues leanings and each had virtuoso musicians, so it's appropriate that 'Sunshine Of Your Love' was not only inspired by Hendrix, but influenced him too.

Cream bassist Jack Bruce devised the song's Kalashnikov riff specifically as a tribute to the guitarist after seeing the Experience in concert in London in 1967. Lyricist Pete Brown and guitarist Eric Clapton also got composer credits on this roaring anthem to romance. When Cream announced their split in 1969, Hendrix hijacked his appearance on Lulu's TV show to perform a tribute to them. He played 'Sunshine Of Your Love.'

Born To Be Wild
Steppenwolf

Released June 1968
Dunhill-ABC *4138* (U.S. #2) / Stateside *SS 8017* (U.K. #30)

Steppenwolf's frontman John Kay would never have made a biker. Always afflicted by bad eyesight, he was registered blind while still a young man. This didn't stop him from composing a song that became the anthem of leather-clad Harley Davidson owners all over America's highways. While Steppenwolf went on to enjoy a long career and a dozen further U.S. hits, most notably 'Magic Carpet Ride,' this staple of gold radio remains the one song of theirs that most people know. No disgrace in that, for 'Born To Be Wild' is a great record. It also gave a name to a new genre.

The song was written by Mars Bonfire, a.k.a. Dennis Edmonton, brother of Steppenwolf's drummer and a member of Sparrow. Edmonton found inspiration in a motorcycle poster bearing the legend Born To Ride. When he used the phrase "heavy metal thunder" to describe the roar of a motorcycle, his words passed into the language, so applicable did they seem to the menacing and distorted sounds then in vogue. The song portrays the motorcycle as transport for the man who refuses to be tied by straight society's chains. Kay's hedonistic vocal is given a smooth if throbbing ride by a bed of growling guitar and waves of organ. The song's anti-establishment credentials were cemented by its inclusion in the movie *Easy Rider* in 1969.

On The Road Again
Canned Heat

Released July 1968
Liberty *56038* (U.S. #16) / Liberty *LBS 15090* (U.K. #8)

On first hearing, 'On The Road Again' sounds like a simple collection of blues mannerisms. With repeated listens, however, the constituents come to seem collectively not a bag of clichés but a validation of the form. There's the 12-bar progression as old as the hills, the guitar and harp riff, the chugging melody that is almost not a melody at all but a sustained groove, and the blues lyrics' staple phrase, "One morning down the road I'm gone." Folky solo artist Katie Melua recorded a most unlikely cover version in 2005.

Suzie Q. (Part 1) / Suzie Q. (Part 2)
Creedence Clearwater Revival

Released September 1968
Fantasy *616* (U.S. #11) / Not issued U.K.

'Suzie Q' was the only Creedence hit not composed by John Fogerty; nonetheless, this four-man group's success was clearly down to one person. Sole writer, arranger, and producer of all the band's hits except this cover of a Dale Hawkins song, Fogerty had the voice and the guitar style that became the CCR trademark.

This is underlined by the sound of his later, more infrequent solo recordings, and the fact that the band's final studio album *Mardi Gras* was a relative flop. Known as 'Fogerty's Revenge,' it had songwriting duties split equally among the band. Rock critic Jon Landau described it as "the worst album by a major group that I have ever heard." This was a sad end for the band that had a string of nine million-selling singles in America in just 29 months.

They formed as The Blue Velvets in San Francisco in 1959, nowhere near the Mississippi delta that Fogerty liked to sing about so much. They became The Golliwogs on signing to Fantasy in 1964. Several hitless years followed until the end of 1967 when they became Creedence Clearwater Revival. Beginning with a mixture of covers and originals, Fogerty soon moved into top songwriting gear and delivered 'Proud Mary,' followed by 'Bad Moon Rising,' 'Green River,' 'Down On The Corner,' and a further five million-sellers (not to mention some great B-sides and album tracks). Creedence were the most successful band of the period, whether you measure them by sales or as a concert attraction. The only surprise was that in America their 45s always stranded at Number 2; they never enjoyed a U.S. Number 1 single.

Following the demise of the band in 1972, Fogerty discovered that not only had contractual obligations virtually robbed him of his songs, but also he was obliged to deliver a further eight albums to Fantasy. He refused to work under these conditions, and many years of legal battles and recriminations ensued between him and Fantasy boss Saul Zaentz.

Fogerty even refused to perform any of his Creedence hits for over 20 years because most of the money went to Zaentz. Finally, in the mid 1990s, he was able to sort out his legal difficulties and regained control of his songs – although the seemingly endless re-issues of Creedence material in the intervening years must surely have cost him several million dollars in lost earnings.

All Along The Watchtower
The Jimi Hendrix Experience

Released September 1968
Reprise *0767* (U.S. #20) / Track *604 025* (U.K. #5)

In Hendrix's pre-fame days his friends and acquaintances were amazed by his obsession with Bob Dylan. In an era when the idea of 'crossover' was little known, it seemed remarkable that a black kid should be so into a white artist. However, Hendrix was not interested in sociological ghettos. He loved Dylan's dazzling song-words – and he didn't do a bad pastiche in his own song, 'The Wind Cries Mary,' with lines such as: "After all the jacks are in their boxes / And the clowns have all gone to bed."

When Dylan returned to music after sitting out 1967 following his motorcycle accident, it was with the acoustic-flavored album *John Wesley Harding*, whose stand-out track 'All Along The Watchtower' summed up the record's tone of vague foreboding, right down to the way the song apparently ended on a cliff-hanger: "Two riders were approaching / The wind began to howl."

By the time The Jimi Hendrix Experience knuckled down to recording a version of the song at Olympic studios in London, covering Dylan songs was a lucrative tradition. But Hendrix was breaking the mold a little, because he was already successful as an artist with his own songs. He broke the mold of the song itself, too. Where Dylan's original was a finely detailed, sepia-toned sketch, Hendrix used big, bold brush strokes – power chords, castanets, and surround-sound production techniques – to create a dazzling alternative version. Dylan was so impressed that he started playing it like the Experience in concert.

Albatross
Fleetwood Mac

Released November 1968
Epic *10436* (U.S.) / Blue Horizon *57 3145* (U.K. #1)

Upon its release, 'Albatross' had few friends. "Peter Green's Fleetwood Mac are already too commercial and have lost their original guts," fulminated BBC Radio One DJ Mike Raven. His colleague John Peel played the B-side instead, while the BBC's *Top Of The Pops* TV chart show initially wouldn't give 'Albatross' a break.

It's not difficult to understand their surprise. Fleetwood Mac's eponymous first album was stuffed to the gills with 12-bar blues. They had quickly moved beyond covers, but tracks like the slinky 'Black Magic Woman' were still informed by the gritty spirit of the blues. By comparison the instrumental 'Albatross' sounded like background music for a wildlife documentary – for which purpose it has often been used subsequently. This tranquil meld of languorous guitar work and subtle cymbal washes was inspired by a combination of a 1950s oldie called 'Sleepwalk' by Santo & Johnny, the Coleridge poem *The Rime Of The Ancient Mariner*, which features an albatross that brings a curse down on sailors who kill it, and a group of notes from an Eric Clapton solo, although played more slowly.

The U.K. public did get a chance to hear 'Albatross' when *Top Of The Pops* needed something to play over the end credits nearly a month after the record's release, and as many as 60,000 orders were placed for the single in the next 24 hours. By Christmas it was Number 1 in Britain. No less than The Beatles were fans, borrowing its guitar work for *Abbey Road*'s 'Sun King.'

I Heard It Through The Grapevine
Marvin Gaye

Released November 1968
Tamla *54176* (U.S. #1) / Tamla Motown *TMG 686* (U.K. #1)

'Grapevine' was one of the greatest Motown singles, but it was recorded by a number of the label's other acts before Marvin Gaye released the definitive version. Written in 1967 by Norman Whitfield and Barrett Strong, the song had something of an uneasy gestation. Whitfield recorded it twice, with Smokey Robinson & The Miracles and The Isley Brothers, but neither version made it past Motown's stringent quality-control committee, which met on Fridays to decide if new songs were fit for release. Undeterred, Whitfield presented the song to Gaye, and spent most of April and May 1967 working on a new recording of the song with him.

This time, he gave 'Grapevine' a slower, spookier arrangement, built around voodoo drums, tense electric piano, and a nightmarish string arrangement, much more in keeping with its lyrical theme, the sudden realization of a romantic betrayal. As on many of the great Motown records of the 1960s, the bulk of the instrumentation was provided by the label's peerless house band, The Funk Brothers. Gaye's wounded vocal is pitched just outside his normal register, giving it a suitably raw edge. Set against him are the sweet, soothing tones of The Andantes: Jackie Hicks, Marlene Barrow, and Louvain Demps.

It seems inconceivable now, but this version too failed to impress when first aired at a quality-control meeting. Motown head Berry Gordy was by now sick of the song, but Whitfield persevered, taking it next to Gladys Knight & The Pips. Their version recast the song – somewhat dubiously – as an upbeat, pop-gospel number, in the manner of Aretha Franklin's recent U.S. hit 'Respect.' It climbed to Number 2 on the *Billboard* Hot 100 at the tail end of 1967 and spent six weeks on top of the R&B chart.

Despite turning 'Grapevine' into a big hit, Whitfield still felt that Gaye's tortured reading of the song better captured its mood and throughout 1968 continued to pressure Gordy to release it. The Motown boss eventually relented, agreeing to its inclusion on Gaye's *In The Groove* album but not to its issue as a single. He thought that, having recently been a hit for Knight, it was unlikely that it would do so well so soon for Gaye. But when the album was sent out to radio stations, 'Grapevine'

was the most played and most requested song, forcing Gordy to release it against his better judgment. Lo and behold, it was an instant smash hit, spending seven weeks on top of the *Billboard* pop singles chart in December 1968 and January 1969, and reached Number 1 in Britain too. It was, until the release of The Jackson 5's 'I'll Be There' in 1970, the most successful Motown single ever.

With what remains the definitive reading in the can and at the top of the charts, Whitfield still found it necessary to cut the song again, with both The Temptations, in 1969, and The Undisputed Truth, in 1971. Neither comes close to Gaye's version, however, and nor do the many subsequent covers by artists as diverse as Credence Clearwater Revival and The Slits.

I'm Gonna Make You Love Me
Diana Ross & The Supremes & The Temptations

Released November 1968
Motown *1137* (U.S. #2) / Tamla Motown *TMG 685* (U.K. #3)

In 1968 Motown hit upon the financially lucrative idea of teaming up The Supremes, whose fans were mostly white, with The Temptations, who had a largely black following. This came as a welcome reunion for the two groups, who both hailed from Detroit and had worked together regularly, pre-fame, in the early 1960s. 'I'm Gonna Make You Love Me' was originally a hit on Mercury Records in 1967 for Dee Dee Warwick (little sister of Dionne) and as such marked one of the first occasions that Motown put out a record not written by one of the label's own songwriting stable. It was the biggest of several hits for the Supremes-Temptations pairing and was only stopped from hitting the Number 1 spot in the U.S. by Marvin Gaye's colossal 'I Heard It Through The Grapevine.' In 1970 The Supremes repeated the trick alongside The Four Tops, with whom they dueted on 'River Deep – Mountain High.'

(Sittin' On) The Dock Of The Bay
Otis Redding

Released January 1968
Volt *157* (U.S. #1) / Stax *601 031* (U.K. #3)

On December 6, 1967, Otis Redding began a two-day recording session at Stax Records in Memphis, Tennessee, which was intended to launch an ambitious new phase of his career. Earlier hits such as 'Respect' and 'Fa-Fa-Fa-Fa-Fa (Sad Song)' had established him alongside Wilson Pickett as America's premier hard R&B vocalist, but 'Dock Of The Bay' was planned as the first of his new black folk songs. "Otis and I spent a lot of time talking about his image," said Al Bell, then vice president of Stax Records. "We started moving him into some kind of black folk-singer image, which might advance him to where we would get more than just Southern black radio play."

The idea for the song had come to Otis while he was staying on a houseboat in Sausalito, California. "When he brought it to Memphis," remembered Stax house-band guitarist Steve Cropper, "it had this little intro and about one verse. He said, 'What do you think of this?' And I said, 'It's great.'" Much as he liked it, Cropper had reservations. "It had no R&B in it whatsoever. I thought it might even be detrimental." Redding remained adamant that the song would be a big hit. But before it could be released he died when his plane crashed into the icy waters of Lake Monoma in Wisconsin. Three months later, 'Dock Of The Bay' became America's first posthumous Number 1 single, proving Redding right and going on to win two Grammys.

I've Gotta Get A Message To You
The Bee Gees

Released August 1968
Atco *6603* (U.S. #8) / Polydor *56 273* (U.K. #1)

Barry, Robin, and Maurice Gibb have one of the richest back-catalogues in pop music history. Their songs are regularly recorded by new artists and appreciated by new generations, and seem set to do so for many years to come. They have certainly had a see-saw career, with more comebacks than Frank Sinatra. From reaching the mountain-top after the *Saturday Night Fever* movie in the late 1970s they found themselves virtually ostracized in the disco backlash that followed. American radio stations even promoted 'No Bee Gees' weekends.

Following their first string of hits, including 'New York Mining Disaster 1941,' 'To Love Somebody,' '(The Night The Lights Went Out In) Massachusetts,' and 'Words,' and shortly after 'I've Gotta Get A Message To You,' the egos began to clash. Perhaps this was the price of fame at such an early age – Barry was 21, twins Robin and Maurice just 19 – and the brothers parted temporarily. Robin was 'persuaded' to pursue a solo career. Barry and Maurice continued as a duo, but the magic was gone, and the three soon realized that their greatest strength lay in writing and performing together. By this time, however, their popularity had waned, and there followed some lean years in the early 1970s, culminating in the rejection of an entire album of material by their record company in 1974.

'I've Gotta Get A Message' was a somewhat unusual song, about a man awaiting his execution, and was recorded the same day it was written. In a contemporary interview, Robin Gibb explained that the song was about someone who has "killed a man who's been carrying on with his wife, and he wants to get a message to her before he dies." That the subject bordered on the distasteful did not seem to bother the record-buying public, and the single became the group's second British Number 1.

Dream A Little Dream Of Me
Mama Cass With The Mamas & The Papas

Released July 1968
Dunhill *4145* (U.S. #12) / RCA *1726* (U.K. #11)

Recorded in the midst of the demise of The Mamas And The Papas, 'Dream A Little Dream Of Me' originally featured on the group's fourth and final album but was re-credited by the Dunhill label as the debut single release of its new solo star. Arranged and produced by the group's manager, Lou Adler, the song is remembered for its lilting vocal melody, but it also bears the influence of musique concrète. Cass's voice emerges from a collage of disparate sounds – bass and flute alongside crashing waves and radio tuning – before it is eventually whisked away, and up the charts, by what sounds like a Hawaiian bar band.

Everyday People
Sly & The Family Stone

Released November 1968
Epic *10407* (U.S. #1) / Direction *58 3938* (U.K. #36)

'Everyday People' was the first of three U.S. Number 1 hits for Sly and delivered on the promise of the same year's 'Dance To The Music,' showcasing a sound that mixed evangelical soul with psychedelic funk. As well as spending four weeks atop the *Billboard* singles chart, 'Everyday People' inspired a whole host of other musicians, particularly Motown producer Norman Whitfield, who would give The Temptations' *Cloud Nine* a similarly widescreen, genre-bending sheen. The success of the single helped cement Sly & The Family Stone's position as the first hit act with a fully racially-integrated line-up, while the group's Larry Graham maintained that it features the first example of 'slap bass' playing on a record.

Son-Of-A Preacher Man
Dusty Springfield

Released November 1968
Atlantic *2580* (U.S. #10) / Philips *BF 1730* (U.K. #9)

It was Dusty's recording of one of Carole King's songs, 'Some Of Your Lovin',' that attracted the attention of legendary producer and founder of Atlantic Records, Ahmet Ertegun, and since her U.S contract with Philips had expired he was eager to sign her. Ertegun arranged for her to record at American Studios in Memphis, and Dusty was put together with production godfathers Arif Mardin, Jerry Wexler, and Tom Dowd to record what is without doubt her finest album, *Dusty In Memphis*.

'Son-Of-A Preacher Man' was first offered to Aretha Franklin, but the Queen of Soul apparently turned it down on the grounds of the somewhat risqué lyrics. Ms. Franklin was herself the daughter of a preacher man. After Dusty's version had become a hit, Franklin later changed her mind and recorded the song.

The sessions in Memphis weren't without problems. When Wexler first met Dusty to present the material that he had gathered for her to record, she turned down everything and promptly returned to London. This was not unusual for the often moody vocalist, and having gathered her thoughts she returned some weeks later in a more enthusiastic frame of mind. Dusty was also used to performing her vocals after the musicians had cut the finished instrumental tracks, though this was not the system at American Studios, where vocalists and musicians normally worked together. Dusty stood her ground, and while she was present at the Memphis sessions, she recorded her vocals later at Atlantic's studio in New York City.

Hooked On A Feeling
B.J. Thomas

Released November 1968
Scepter *12230* (U.S. #5) / Pye International *7N 25481* (U.K.)

Thomas was a highly successful artist in America with a string of hits between 1966 and 1977, most of which were recorded at American Studios in Memphis and produced by Chips Moman. It was a hotbed of activity, particularly in the late 1960s, and there was plenty of songwriting talent around to deliver hit material.

'Hooked' was written by Mark James, who composed Elvis Presley's 'Suspicious Minds,' and features an appealing guitar-sitar sound, becoming a U.S. Number 5 for Thomas early in 1969. Though not a hit in Britain, it was revived there in 1971 by eccentric pop personality Jonathan King, who introduced the "ooga-choogas" later used by Swedish outfit Blue Swede who covered the song in 1974 and were rewarded with a surprise American Number 1. (The same week that Blue Swede reached the top, Abba won the Eurovision Song Contest in Britain, marking a great seven days for Swedish pop.) That might have been the end of the story, but the song enjoyed a revival many years later when it featured in the popular TV series *Ally McBeal* for some notorious 'dancing baby' sequences.

Je T'aime ... Moi Non Plus
Jane Birkin & Serge Gainsbourg

Released July 1969
Fontana *TF 1042* (U.S.) / Major Minor *MM 645* (U.K. #1)

While it may sound as if Jane Birkin and Serge Gainsbourg are having a fairly good time in the studio recording this song, in fact they were in separate booths, and the decadent piece wasn't recorded in France, either, but in a studio in central London. Gainsbourg had originally recorded this erotic little number with his previous beau, Brigitte Bardot, a couple of years before, and that recording was reputed to be the real thing. However, after some persuasion from Bardot's husband, the 'session' remained unreleased. In the meantime Gainsbourg met Jane Birkin while making a movie in France, and once they became lovers it didn't take him long to persuade her to record the song anew with him.

Released in Britain on the Fontana label it was, not surprisingly, immediately banned by the BBC. A breathless Birkin (who definitely hadn't just dashed back from the drugstore with a pack of Gitanes for Serge) was serenaded by muttered sweet-nothings from Gainsbourg that few in Britain understood, though they certainly got the picture. The ensuing publicity helped the record sell quickly, and before long it had reached Number 2. At this point, Fontana suddenly woke up to the record's risqué content and swiftly removed it from their catalogue. Following Fontana's withdrawal … an independent label, Major Minor, took over the rights and the record returned to the charts, this time going all the way to Number 1 in Britain. In America, where airplay was even more restricted, the recording appropriately rose no higher than number soixante-neuf (69).

Saved By The Bell
Robin Gibb

Released July 1969
Atco *6698* (U.S.) / Polydor *56337* (U.K. #2)

In February 1969 The Bee Gees were two years into their first run of hits when Robin Gibb split from his brothers Maurice and Barry over a dispute about which song should be the band's next single. Polite sniping in the music press ensued, while Robin Gibb quickly plunged into life as a solo artist, taking this self-penned ballad to the upper reaches of the British and German singles charts.

The record is notable not only as an example of just how epic a pop song could get with an orchestra behind it, but also for the first use of an electronic drum machine on a hit record. You can clearly hear the primitive device chugging away under Gibb's trademark vibrato and the lush strings. It was a quietly revolutionary moment that passed unnoticed at the time, but by the 1980s the drum machine would be an accepted and significant part of the pop musician's musical palette.

After this strong start, Gibb's career faltered. He released an intriguing and highly original solo album, *Robin's Reign*, that failed commercially, although it has since attracted a cult following. Another was recorded and left unreleased, but has since leaked onto the internet. In 1971 Gibb rejoined his brothers in The Bee Gees for a few years in the commercial doldrums before disco gave them a new lease on life.

In The Year 2525 (Exordium & Terminus)
Zager & Evans

Released June 1969
RCA *0174* (U.S. #1) / RCA *1860* (U.K. #1)

In 1968, Denny Zager and Rick Evans were a folk-rock duo scratching a living in the finest motel lounges of Lincoln, Nebraska. "We were looking for up-tempo material," recalled Zager some years later, "because most of the stuff we did was ballads." Serendipitously, Evans had spent an entire 30 minutes knocking up the apocalyptic sci-fi epic 'In The Year 2525' four years earlier, but his previous band, The Eccentrics, wouldn't record it. Released on local label Truth Records in 1968, it attracted the attention of RCA, who sold a million copies within two months and four million overall. "We tried everything to come up with that second hit," said Zager, "but it never happened."

Marrakesh Express
Crosby Stills & Nash

Released July 1969
Atlantic *2652* (U.S. #28) / Atlantic *584 283* (U.K. #17)

He Ain't Heavy, He's My Brother
The Hollies

Released September 1969
Epic *10532* (U.S. #7) / Parlophone *R 5806* (U.K. #3)

Graham Nash left The Hollies in December 1968 in disagreement over the proposed recording of a collection of Dylan covers (which they later recorded as *Hollies Sing Dylan*) and their alleged rejection of his own song 'Marrakesh Express.' Nash had made a number of new friends in America, more in keeping with his own musical ambitions. David Crosby had been a fan of Nash's harmony vocals for some time, and in June 1968, while The Hollies were touring America, he had taken Nash to meet Stephen Stills.

Crosby and Stills sang a new Stills composition, 'You Don't Have To Cry,' to Nash, and after just two listens the Hollie instinctively added a third harmony. Apparently the three then looked at each other in disbelief. Nash described the moment as "nothing short of musical magic." Purely by accident they had discovered a unique harmony sound that became the hallmark of Crosby Stills & Nash, initially heard by many music fans on CSN's first hit, 'Marrakesh Express.'

Nash was replaced in The Hollies by former Escorts and Swinging Blue Jeans guitarist Terry Sylvester, and the group's chart success continued, despite Nash's departure. 'He Ain't Heavy, He's My Brother' hit in 1969, featuring Elton John on piano. The song was also a U.S chart entry for Neil Diamond, in 1970, and eventually made number 1 for The Hollies in Britain in 1988 after featuring in a TV advertisement for beer.

I Want You Back
The Jackson 5

Released November 1969
Motown *1157* (U.S. #1) / Tamla Motown *TMG 724* (U.K. #2)

The fact has now been obscured by the headline-guzzling train-wreck of Michael Jackson's private life and the multi-platinum success of his solo career, but the names of Jermaine, Jackie, Michael, Marlon, and Tito Jackson once collectively tripped off the tongue of young record purchasers worldwide. The Jackson 5 were a phenomenon: their first four singles went to the top of the U.S. chart and they spawned their own cartoon series.

It was a phenomenon that was very important to Motown. The label had just lost Holland-Dozier-Holland in a dispute about royalty rates. While no one songwriting team is bigger than a label, Motown supremo Berry Gordy was clearly stung by their defection, and gained an injunction preventing them from working elsewhere. He pointedly depersonalized the songwriting and production credits on this Jackson 5 debut – "The Corporation," read the label – lest these workers also became too big for their boots.

In fact Deke Richards, Fonce Mizel, and Freddie Perren were the creative team behind 'I Want You Back,' originally written for Gladys Knight & The Pips. Gordy, once a songwriter himself, wasn't satisfied with lyric or arrangement. The words were overhauled and the key lowered. The result was a passionate declaration of regret at a fractured relationship, plainly absurd from such children. But listeners ceased to think about that once they heard the utter commitment in main lead-singer Michael's voice and witnessed the preternaturally slick dance routines of the combo on TV.

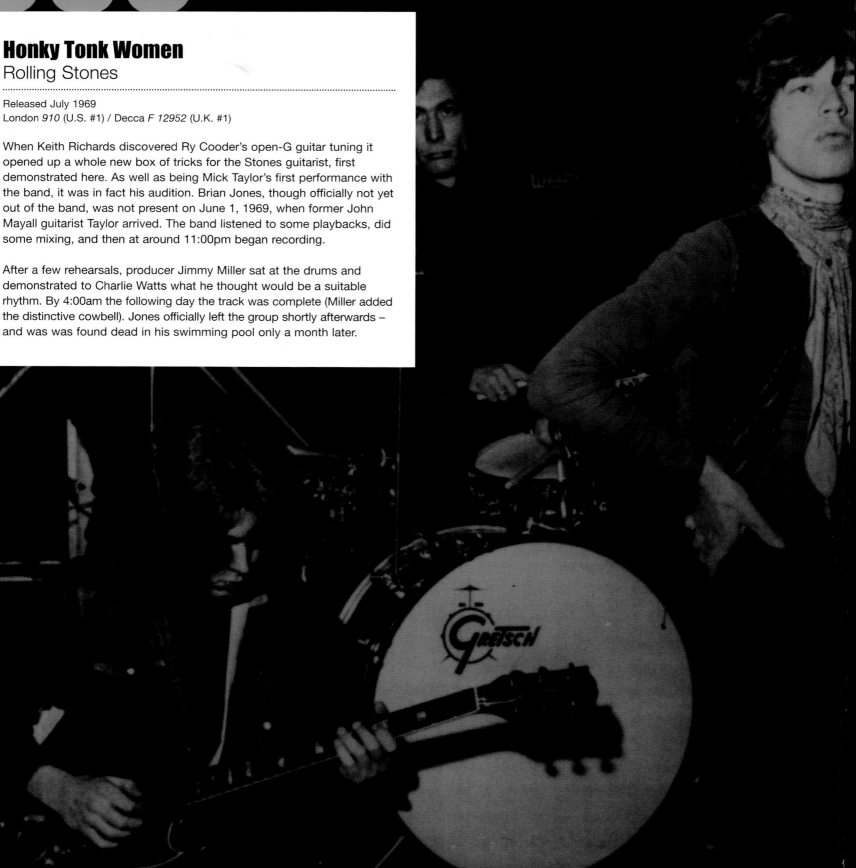

1969

Honky Tonk Women
Rolling Stones

....

Released July 1969
London *910* (U.S. #1) / Decca *F 12952* (U.K. #1)

When Keith Richards discovered Ry Cooder's open-G guitar tuning it
opened up a whole new box of tricks for the Stones guitarist, first
demonstrated here. As well as being Mick Taylor's first performance with
the band, it was in fact his audition. Brian Jones, though officially not yet
out of the band, was not present on June 1, 1969, when former John
Mayall guitarist Taylor arrived. The band listened to some playbacks, did
some mixing, and then at around 11:00pm began recording.

After a few rehearsals, producer Jimmy Miller sat at the drums and
demonstrated to Charlie Watts what he thought would be a suitable
rhythm. By 4:00am the following day the track was complete (Miller added
the distinctive cowbell). Jones officially left the group shortly afterwards –
and was was found dead in his swimming pool only a month later.

The B-side, 'You Can't Always Get What You Want,' was one of the group's most unusual tracks, featuring the London Bach Choir and an orchestration by former Phil Spector arranger Jack Nitzsche, alongside keyboards played by Al Kooper. This would be the Stones' last single for Decca before they signed a new custom deal with Atlantic. The degree of animosity between the Stones and Decca is best revealed by their parting of the ways when their contract expired in 1970: with one final single owing to the company, they delivered the un-releasable 'Cocksucker Blues.'

Whole Lotta Love
Led Zeppelin

Released November 1969
Atlantic *45-2690* (U.S. #4) / Not issued U.K.

Had this book been restricted to singles released only in an artist's home territory then Led Zeppelin would not feature in it at all. In an era when a band could gain kudos by spurning singles – which at the time were beginning to be seen by rock's maturing audience as kid's fodder – they made sure that no Zeppelin 45 ever came out in Britain.

Vocalist Robert Plant had learned the song after seeing The Small Faces play in his native Midlands. Their 'You Need Loving' was a rip-off of bluesman Willie Dixon's lustful song 'You Need Love.' When Zeppelin guitarist Jimmy Page presented Plant with a brilliant, instantly memorable guitar riff, the singer lashed the Dixon-Small Faces song onto it – although it wasn't until 1985 that Dixon's daughter brought the steal to his attention.

Whatever the moral dubiousness of Zeppelin's plagiarism, it can't be doubted that they added profoundly to what they appropriated: not just through Page's riff but the characteristic collective muscle and swagger with which they rendered the song. Radio stations began playing a version that omitted the lengthy instrumental middle section (and Plant's vaguely embarrassing orgasm sounds) and Atlantic Records promptly created their own radio-edit version. Almost as if God were mocking Zeppelin for their hold-out on U.K. singles, the song would achieve a bizarre afterlife as the theme tune to Britain's *Top Of The Pops* TV chart show.

Israelites
Desmond Dekker & The Aces

Released February 1969
Uni *55129* (U.S. #9) / Pyramid *PYR 6058* (U.K. #1)

Leslie Kong, one of the great early reggae producers, was a Chinese-Jamaican ice-cream café proprietor turned record producer. Desmond Dekker composed 'Poor Me Israelite' while out walking in the park one afternoon. Overhearing a couple arguing about money, an opening line came into his mind, "Get up in the morning slaving for bread," and by the time he'd walked home he had the whole song worked out.

The song was originally released in Jamaica in 1968 as 'Poor Me Israelite' and was only a small local hit, but it attracted some dance-floor attention in Britain. Graeme Goodall released the record there on his Pyramid Records, but was told by the BBC after just one broadcast that the record was too badly produced for further radio plays. So Goodall had the tapes sent over from Jamaica and remixed the track, shortening the title to 'Israelites.' The BBC then agreed to play the new version and it immediately took off.

It hit the British charts in March 1969 and launched a big wave of reggae popularity. The music was adopted by skinheads, who wore braces (suspenders) and boots and liked to look for some 'bovver,' or trouble. Dekker remains one of the most popular Jamaican artists of all time in Britain, and a re-recording of the song went Top 10 again there in 1975.

One of the most popular reggae tracks of all time, the song is in fact a blues, a cry of despair for survival, and was the first truly international reggae hit. (Johnny Nash's hits of the previous year were in the rock-steady style, and while they were recorded in Jamaica, Nash was from Texas.)

The Boxer
Simon & Garfunkel

Released April 1969
Columbia *44785* (U.S. #7) / CBS *4162* (U.K. #6)

They say the devil has all the best songs but, just occasionally, inspiration can come from a more elevated plane. Paul Simon has claimed that much of the lyric of 'The Boxer' came about because "I was reading the Bible around that time. That's where phrases such as 'workman's wages' came from, and 'seeking out the poorer quarters.'"

Simon & Garfunkel had enjoyed hits since 1965, but the runaway success of the infectiously upbeat 'Mrs. Robinson,' boosted by its use in the 1968 movie *The Graduate*, had brought them unprecedented levels of fame. 'The Boxer,' with its rippling guitar and melancholic lyric, was an unlikely follow-up but is arguably their quintessential musical statement. The elegant synthesizer solo and the dramatic percussive slaps are remarkably innovative touches in an arrangement that evolves like a flower opening in a stop-motion film, each new element blending in unobtrusively as the verses rise and fall around the "lie-la-lie" vocal hook.

This was remarkably cerebral pop, far too metaphysically inclined to have any hope of matching the success of 'Mrs. Robinson,' but then that's exactly what Paul Simon intended. "I think the song was about me," he said. "Everybody's beating me up, and I'm telling you now I'm going to go away if you don't stop." It didn't even make the Top 5 in

Billboard, floundering at Number 7. A year later, the melodramatic gospel schmaltz of 'Bridge Over Troubled Water' would restore them to Number 1, becoming their signature song and, regrettably, eclipsing 'The Boxer.'

Aquarius–Let The Sunshine In (The Flesh Failures)
The 5th Dimension

Released February 1969
Soul City *772* (U.S. #1) / Liberty *LBF 15193* (U.K. #11)

This vocal quintet based in Los Angeles had their first major hit a couple of years earlier with 'Up – Up And Away,' giving songwriter Jimmy Webb his first Top 10 single and enough royalties to purchase his first piano. The group also helped to popularize the songs of contemporary writer Laura Nyro. Their biggest worldwide hit was this medley of two songs from the hippie musical *Hair* which had opened on Broadway in 1968. Notorious for its explicit language and on-stage nudity, *Hair* also supplied hits for Oliver with 'Good Morning Starshine' and Nina Simone performing 'Ain't Got No – I Got Life.' Husband-and-wife Dimension members Marilyn McCoo and Billy Davis Jr. had a 1977 Number 1 with 'You Don't Have To Be A Star (To Be In My Show).'

Get Back
The Beatles With Billy Preston

Released April 1969
Apple *2490* (U.S. #1) / Apple *R 5777* (U.K. #1)

This song, which briefly gave its name to the project in which The Beatles attempted to return to the days of no overdubs, marked a couple of rarities. One was the unique co-credit given to elegant keyboardist Billy Preston. The other was a switching of roles by Lennon and Harrison. While Lennon's lead guitar work was rather watery, Harrison's brilliant rhythm guitar gave the track a rock solid, razor sharp groove that helped to prove the intended point that, ornate masterpieces like *Sgt. Pepper* notwithstanding, The Beatles were still at heart a fabulous rock'n'roll band.

Space Oddity
David Bowie

Released July 1969
Mercury *72949* (U.S.) / Philips *BF 1801* (U.K. #5)

Released to coincide with Neil Armstrong's giant leap for mankind, 'Space Oddity' gave David Bowie his first U.K. hit single, launching a career that continues into the 21st century. The lead track from his second album, 'Space Oddity' was Bowie's first release for Philips/Mercury following several years of unsuccessful recordings for the Deram label. George Martin turned down the opportunity to produce the single, as did Tony Visconti (who went on to make numerous albums with Bowie). Visconti considered 'Space Oddity' to be too gimmicky and handed it over to his assistant, Gus Dudgeon, who cut the single with Bowie on June 20, 1969, at Trident Studios in London, England. It was rush-released just three weeks later, in time for the Apollo 11 moon landing.

'Space Oddity' is one of Bowie's finest narrative songs, spinning a tale over its five minutes about an astronaut, Major Tom, who gets lost – perhaps intentionally – on an intergalactic mission. Driven by Bowie's acoustic guitar, the song leaps from slow, atmospheric verses through soaring choruses and several instrumental breaks. The other musicians include noted session bassist Herbie Flowers and keyboardist Rick Wakeman, who went on to join the progressive rock group Yes. Bowie plays a Stylophone on the song, a tiny, oscillating keyboard sold mostly as a children's toy. Bowie and the single benefited from his appearance in press ads for the instrument around the time of the release of 'Oddity.'

What really helped push the single up the U.K. charts, however, was the BBC's decision to use the song during its coverage of the moon landing. 'Space Oddity' remained a favorite both of its author and his audience. The single returned to the British charts in 1975, to make Number 1, and in the U.S. two years earlier had reached Number 15. Bowie returned to the Major Tom character for his 1980 U.K. Number 1 hit 'Ashes To Ashes' and on the 1995 single, 'Hello Spaceboy.'

Something In The Air
Thunderclap Newman

Released May 1969
Track *2656* (U.S. #37) / Track *604 031* (U.K. #1)

This trio escaped the one-hit wonder tag by earning a week at Number 46 for the follow-up to this British chart-topper in the summer of 1969. They had got to know Pete Townshend after vocalist Speedy Keen's composition 'Armenia City In The Sky' opened The Who's Sell Out album in 1968. Townshend produced and played bass guitar as 'Bijou Drains' on 'Something In The Air,' originally titled 'Revolution.' But as John Lennon had already done that, Townshend gave the song its new title, and his involvement generated the necessary publicity to send it all the way to Number 1 in Britain, complete with magical piano interludes by Andy Newman.

A Boy Named Sue
Johnny Cash

Released July 1969
Columbia *44944* (U.S. #2) / CBS *4460* (U.K. #4)

That 'A Boy Named Sue' sounds unlike anything else in Johnny Cash's generally brooding canon is down to the fact that it was written by Shel Silverstein, the gifted but comedy-inclined composer of, among others, 'The Cover Of Rolling Stone' and 'Freakin' At The Freakers Ball.' His 'Boy Named Sue' is the tale of a man who grows up mean because of the ridicule inspired by his feminine name – which doesn't make sense. Why doesn't he just change it? But it provides some good laughs. Cash recorded it at San Quentin prison and does a remarkable job, considering that he was reading the unfamiliar lyric from a sheet of paper.

Sugar Sugar
The Archies

Released July 1969
Calendar *1008* (U.S. #1) / RCA *1872* (U.K. #1)

Music publishing mogul Don Kirshner, who masterminded the songs for The Monkees, was somewhat embittered when that manufactured quartet deprived him of a share of their profit by deciding to write their own songs. Reasoning that cartoons don't have egos, he invented *The Archies*, an animated TV series based on a popular comic book, and supplied songs for that instead. A guaranteed party floor-filler, 'Sugar Sugar,' written by Jeff Barry and Andy Kim, was performed by top-notch studio sessioneers, including vocalist Ron Dante, who around the same time was in the U.S. Top 10 singing lead on 'Tracy' by The Cuff Links. 'Sugar Sugar,' the best-selling single of 1969, remains the definitive bubblegum hit.

Everybody's Talkin'
Nilsson

Released August 1969
RCA *0161* (U.S. #6) / RCA *1876* (U.K. #23)

Nilsson had spent many years as a successful songwriter, with his compositions covered by the likes of Three Dog Night, The Yardbirds, and The Monkees, so it was somewhat ironic that his debut hit was written by someone else. The reclusive folk-rock innovator Fred Neil composed 'Everybody's Talkin'' and was the first to record it. Neil retired from music in the early 1970s, funded for the rest of his life by the proceeds from the song, which has been much covered.

An insouciant shrug-of-the-shoulders of a record, Nilsson's version was taken at a faster pace than Neil's original, and had more pop appeal. It was chosen for inclusion on the soundtrack of the Dustin Hoffman movie *Midnight Cowboy*, which helped the single into both the U.S. and U.K. charts. It has remained lodged in pop's collective consciousness ever since and in the U.S. it remains one of the most-played singles on oldies radio. A few year's later, Nilsson scored a second big hit with a cover version, 'Without You,' written by two members of British band Badfinger.

Is That All There Is?
Peggy Lee

Released September 1969
Capitol 2602 (U.S. #11) / Capitol CL 15614 (U.K.)

Written by Jerry Leiber and Mike Stoller, this magnificent single proved that they and the song's vocalist, Peggy Lee, could still cut it, well after their 1950s heyday. Although Lee had recently recorded well-chosen covers of songs by such contemporary songwriters as Jimmy Webb and Carole King, 'Is That All There Is?' is far removed from the rock-orientated sounds of the time. Against a backdrop of delicate piano and whimsical orchestrations, arranged and conducted by Randy Newman, Lee offers a suitably lugubrious vocal performance that ponders whether there is any more to life. If there isn't, she concludes, we should "break out the booze and have a ball." It was the only one of her recordings to win her a Grammy, for Best Contemporary Vocal Performance, although in 1995 she was given a Lifetime Achievement Award.

Suspicious Minds
Elvis Presley

Released August 1969
RCA 47 9764 (U.S. #1) / RCA 1900 (U.K. #2)

Aside from his early recordings at RCA's Nashville studios, the few weeks that Presley spent at the American Sound Studios in Memphis during January and February 1969 must rate as the most rewarding and productive of his career. It was the first time Elvis had recorded in a Memphis studio since his pre-RCA days at Sun in 1955.

'Suspicious Minds' was recorded between 4:00 and 7:00am on the last day of the first ten-day session and was considered the song with the biggest hit potential. The basic track took just four takes, although it was many months until the song was released, mainly due to a lengthy dispute over the publishing royalties. As was the custom with the Presley organization, Freddie Bienstock, who looked after Elvis Presley Music, demanded a cut of the publishing rights, but there was no way that songwriter Mark James was going to agree to a royalty split.

It was a lengthy conflict, and consequently 'Suspicious Minds' didn't appear on the original *From Elvis In Memphis* album. Under normal circumstances the song might never have been released at all. However, all were agreed that the recording was the highlight of the sessions, and once Elvis began performing it at his summer appearances at the Las Vegas Hilton, it was finally released in August 1969. Following the Number 3 success of 'In The Ghetto' (recorded in Memphis two days before 'Suspicious Minds') Elvis was on a roll, and the record became his first American Number 1 record for seven years, and the last in his lifetime. In a 2002 poll by the *New Musical Express*, readers voted it the best Elvis song of all time.

My Way
Frank Sinatra

Released March 1969
Reprise 0817 (U.S. #27) / Reprise RS 20817 (U.K. #5)

Although Frank Sinatra's years with Capitol during the 1950s were the most productive and successful of his career, in 1961 he established his own record label, Reprise, and enjoyed continuing chart success throughout the decade. However, 'My Way' would be his last American hit single for 11 years and preceded the first of his endless retirements. With this in mind, Sinatra had long been trying to persuade Paul Anka to compose an appropriate song, and Anka came up with the goods while on holiday in France. There he heard the song 'Comme d'Habitude' by Claude François and, recognizing the potential in the melody, he bought the rights and composed a new English lyric with Sinatra in mind.

Recorded December 30, 1968, in Hollywood, 'My Way' was released the following spring and soon became a big hit in Britain, although in America it only reached Number 27. Though latter-day Sinatra fans often cite 'My Way' as their favorite, Ol' Blue Eyes himself grew to hate the song that became his signature tune. It was infamously covered by Sid Vicious and The Sex Pistols in 1978, but David Bowie had tried his hand at a translation of the French original before Anka. Bowie wrote his version in 1968 and titled it 'Even A Fool Learns To Love,' but it was never released and may not even have been recorded, although Bowie's lyrics have become available on various internet sites.

1970

Funky Drummer (Part 1)
James Brown

Released February 1970
King *6290* (U.S.) / Not issued U.K.

Get Up (I Feel Like Being Like A)
Sex Machine (Part 1)
James Brown

Released July 1970
King *6318* (U.S. #15) / Polydor *2001 071* (U.K. #32)

James Brown's recorded output in the 1960s and 1970s was prodigious by anybody's standards. In 1969 alone he released 15 singles and five albums, including the landmark 'Say It Loud – I'm Black And I'm Proud.' While he wasn't quite so prolific in 1970, the year did throw up a pair of epochal singles, both among the most important recordings of his career.

Cut on November 20th, 1969, in Cincinnati, Ohio, 'Funky Drummer' was one of Brown's last recordings with his backing group The Famous Flames. While the song itself isn't as instantly memorable as some of his earlier hits, the drum break – played by Clyde Stubblefield – has become one of the most sampled beats in hip-hop and electronic music. Everyone from Public Enemy to TLC and The Beastie Boys to Vanilla Ice has built a rhythm track out of Stubblefield's funky drumming.

By the summer of 1970 Brown had disbanded The Famous Flames and put together a new group, The JB's, with a membership that included future funk legend Bootsy Collins. The new group's first release was the breathtaking 'Get Up (I Feel Like Being Like A) Sex Machine,' driven by Collins's extraordinary bass playing and his brother Catfish's slick guitar licks. Both Collins brothers were also integral members of George Clinton's groups Parliament and Funkadelic. 'Sex Machine' provided Brown with his first U.K. hit since 'It's A Man's Man's Man's World' back in 1966, and the disc paved the way for almost every funk record of the 1970s.

War
Edwin Starr

Released June 1970
Gordy *7101* (U.S. #1) / Tamla Motown *TMG 754* (U.K. #3)

In the early 1970s, Motown Records was in a period of transition. It had recently lost the prolific writing and production team of Holland-Dozier-Holland, and somehow the label had to fill the void. For Norman Whitfield, a successful Motown house producer since the early 1960s, HDH's departure precipitated a golden age. Inspired by Sly & The Family Stone's psychedelic soul innovations, Whitfield helmed extraordinarily ambitious singles such as The Temptations' 'Cloud Nine' and Marvin Gaye's 'I Heard It Through The Grapevine.'

'War' was produced and written by Whitfield, establishing a curious new hybrid: the psychedelic-soul freak-out protest song, and all built around the ever-reliable 'Louie Louie' riff. "None of us thought after we cut it that it would be such a big hit," Starr admitted in 1971. "And, although it sounds a real complicated thing on the single, it wasn't as hard as that to get together." Originally recorded as an album track by The Temptations, 'War' had prompted hundreds of letters from students asking the Temps to release it as a single, but they were already committed to another Whitfield production, 'Ball Of Confusion.'

Now that he was alerted to the song's commercial potential, Whitfield was unwilling to let 'War' languish as just another album track, and he offered it to Starr, whose powerhouse performance rocketed the song to Number 1 and justly earned a Grammy for Best Male R&B Vocal Performance. The song has a wider significance, too: along with Marvin Gaye's 'What's Going On' it marked Motown's emergence as a politically active label.

Give Me Just A Little More Time
Chairmen Of The Board

Released January 1970
Invictus *9074* (U.S. #3) / Invictus *INV 501* (U.K. #3)

Band Of Gold
Freda Payne

Released April 1970
Invictus *9075* (U.S. #3) / Invictus *INV 502* (U.K. #1)

Holland-Dozier-Holland, the songwriting and production engine that powered Motown's hit factory, fell out spectacularly with Motown boss Berry Gordy as the 1960s ended. Unhappy with their share of the royalties from their dozens of hits, they quit Motown and started their own label, Invictus. The launch of this new venture was stalled, though, by a lengthy legal battle that put the team out of action for the best part of two years when they were at the top of their game.

The Chairmen Of The Board, formed to be a new Four Tops for Invictus, helped Invictus off to a flying start with 'Give Me Just A Little More Time,' which peaked at Number 3 in *Billboard*. It still stands as the band's defining moment, featuring an extraordinarily powerful virtuoso vocal performance by 'General' Norman Johnson who, fittingly, first found fame as the vocalist on The Showmen's 1961 rock'n'roll anthem, 'It Will Stand.'

By no means an overnight success, Freda Payne was a seasoned vocalist who had sung jazz with both Duke Ellington and Quincy Jones and appeared on Broadway before renewing an old friendship with Brian Holland in 1969 and signing up with Invictus. This was one of the first songs she recorded for the label, although Payne wasn't keen on the lyrical content of this honeymoon melodrama, essentially a story of non-consummation of wedding vows – an unusual subject for a pop single. She needn't have worried: 'Band Of Gold' swiftly became a major international hit, proving that HDH had not lost their magic touch in the intervening years.

All of which brings us to the most interesting revelation about 'Band Of Gold.' At the time, HDH were still under a Motown restraining order and could therefore not write for other labels. While 'Band Of Gold' had songwriting credits to Ronald Dunbar and Edith Wayne, there were always industry suspicions that HDH were the real authors, an accusation rigorously denied at the time. In recent years, however, with the Motown lawsuits long forgotten, the trio have finally admitted that they did indeed write the song, and that company employees Dunbar and Wayne's names were used as a cover.

Ain't No Mountain High Enough
Diana Ross

Released July 1970
Motown *1169* (U.S. #1) / Tamla Motown *TMG 751* (U.K. #6)

Berry Gordy had been fine-tuning his plans for Diana Ross's solo career for some years before her departure from The Supremes at the end of 1969. The group's final single with Ross, 'Someday We'll Be Together Again,' was intended to be her solo debut, but ultimately it was decided that it would be more appropriate as a Supremes swansong, and it topped the U.S. charts at the turn of the decade. Now, the most important task was to find a song to launch Ross as a solo artist.

After an unsuccessful attempt to produce some hits with outside producer Bones Howe, responsible for Number 1s by The Association and The 5th Dimension, Gordy put Ross together with one of Motown's own teams, Nickolas Ashford and Valerie Simpson. Among the songs they recorded with her was this completely rearranged version of 'Ain't No Mountain,' a song they had recorded with Marvin Gaye & Tammi Terrell in 1967.

For Ross's version they added some newly-composed spoken segments, but the only problem was that the result was six minutes long, and Gordy had no intention of releasing it as a single. That changed when U.S. radio DJs began to feature the song, forcing Motown to release an edited version, which soared to the top of the charts in September 1970 and became Ross's first major solo triumph.

Bridge Over Troubled Water

Simon & Garfunkel

Released February 1970
Columbia *45079* (U.S. #1) / CBS *4790* (U.K. #1)

Bridge Over Troubled Water was an apt title for what would be Simon & Garfunkel's last studio album together: they certainly went through some extremely troubled times making the record. During much of the recording Art Garfunkel was absent from the studio, busy filming *Catch 22* in which he starred. Paul Simon spent a good deal of time working alone, writing and recording the songs, some of which were aimed directly at the absent Garfunkel. For example, 'Why Don't You Write Me' and 'The Only Living Boy In New York' addressed 'Tom' – Garfunkel had been 'Tom' in their earlier incarnation, Tom & Jerry – and referred to Garfunkel's frequent trips to Mexico for the filming.

'Bridge Over Troubled Water' was one of the few songs on the album where the duo spent much time working together. Simon, who originally envisaged the song as a gospel hymn, wrote it on guitar, recording a demo that he played to Garfunkel. (This demo eventually surfaced on Simon's *1964/1993* boxed set.) It was only later that the song turned into a tour de force, highlighting Garfunkel's angelic voice and the piano of Larry Knechtel, in a grandiose arrangement inspired by Phil Spector's production of 'Ol' Man River' for The Righteous Brothers.

At first there were only two verses, but Garfunkel felt that the song needed a third and persuaded Simon to write one. In later years, perfectionist Simon regretted these events, feeling that the final verse was not as good as the first two. Talking in a 1972 interview, he said: "[Garfunkel] didn't want to sing it himself – he felt I should have done it, and many times I think I'm sorry I didn't do it." About the album itself, Simon recalled: "On several tracks there's no Artie at all – it's a Simon & Garfunkel record, but there are many songs where you don't hear Simon & Garfunkel singing together."

There was much bickering in the studio, and Garfunkel's refusal to record a song Simon had written, 'Cuba Si, Nixon No,' coupled with Simon's refusal to complete 'Feuilles-O' (which later appeared on Garfunkel's debut solo album) reduced the *Troubled Water* album to 11 tracks, marking the end for the duo who then went their separate ways.

Surprisingly, and considering the amount of effort put into the recording, neither Simon nor Garfunkel thought 'Bridge Over Troubled Water' was a potential hit single. However, when the album was completed, Columbia Records chief Clive Davis decided it should be both the first single and the title of the album.

Upon release, the single went straight to Number 1 on the U.S. charts. Massive radio exposure helped lift the album to the top spot seven days later, while the title song won the Grammy for Song Of The Year.

AIRING THE HITS: THE TOP 40 RADIO FORMAT

AM, which stands for Amplitude Modulation, is the original and simplest form of radio. Although it has now largely been supplanted by FM (Frequency Modulation) and digital radio, which provide better sound and less interference, AM was the home of music radio through most of the 20th century and in the golden era of rock and pop.

Before television, radio in America was dominated by national stations providing live music, drama, comedy, serials, and news. When television arrived, most of these forms of programming migrated to the new medium, leaving radio with music but a limited income. While the national stations declined, local stations made the most of their modest budgets by playing records, chosen by DJs (disc jockeys) and catering to local and specialized tastes, notably country and rhythm & blues.

These DJs rapidly developed vivid on-air personalities, and because of the quirks of AM transmission (especially late at night) developed audiences far outside their local areas. In the world of rock'n'roll, they included Alan Freed, most famously, but also Danny 'Cat Man' Stiles, Tommy 'Dr. Jive' Smalls, Douglas 'Jocko' Henderson, George 'Hound Dog' Lorenz, Ken 'Jack The Cat' Elliott, and others. What many of the white DJs had in common was that they did their best to sound black, using jive talk and black slang to accompany the black music they were playing.

Perhaps the most celebrated was Wolfman Jack, real name Bob Smith, who began broadcasting from a station just across the border in Mexico in 1962. Because the station was not subject to U.S. broadcast power restrictions, it had a huge reach across the U.S., and the Wolfman, with his gravel voice, howls, and innuendo, became a cult. He did not reveal his true identity until 1973, when he appeared in a pivotal scene in the George Lucas film *American Graffiti*.

As time went by, many of the local stations were bought by regional operators and formed into chains, which began to develop a new format called Top 40. There had long been weekly chart shows, but in the 1950s a chain owner called Todd Storz took things much further. Observing the way jukebox customers chose the same songs repeatedly, he limited the music output of his stations to just the top 40 songs sold in local stores, and then arranged for the top 10 records to be played more frequently than the others. This was called 'rotation.' The idea was that the casual listener would never have to wait more than a few minutes for one of the major hits of the day.

But there was more to the Top 40 concept than that. News bulletins and commercials now appeared at fixed times, and jingles, DJ patter, and audience competitions and promotions were introduced. The idea, above all, was to avoid any sort of silence, known as 'dead air' in radio jargon.

Although the DJs' personalities were still an essential part of the mix, they now had to squeeze themselves into a rigid format, and had lost the ability to express their own musical tastes. Those who were primarily motivated by music moved on to FM. Escapees from AM included Murray 'The K' Kaufman, who had become famous as 'the fifth Beatle' when he attached himself to the band on their first tour of the States. A new, album-based type of music programming, known as freeform or progressive rock, began to blossom on FM in the mid 1960s.

Both Top 40 and AM radio continue to thrive today, however. *American Top 40* is a nationally syndicated chart show, launched in 1970 by Casey Kasem (the voice of Shaggy in the Scooby-Doo cartoons) and continuing to this day. Unlike classic Top 40 radio, it uses a countdown format and includes snippets of biographical information about the featured artists, as well as requests and audience queries. While AM radio is now primarily the home of U.S. talk radio it still hosts some music stations in the States and elsewhere in the world.

Mama Told Me (Not To Come)
Three Dog Night

Released May 1970
Dunhill/ABC *4239* (U.S. #1) / Stateside *SS 8052* (U.K. #3)

As strange as it might seem to think it today, from 1969 to 1975 Three Dog Night were one of the most successful bands in the U.S. During that period the group – essentially a vocal trio – had twenty-one Top-40 *Billboard* chart entries, with three chart-toppers among them. The group's biggest hits were all covers, but they were no bland copyists. Not only did they devise interesting arrangements but also they covered songs by people not normally associated with the charts, including Laura Nyro and, in this case, Randy Newman. In its depiction of a youth horrified by the decadent goings-on at a party, the song could not have been more out of tune with the supposedly liberated spirit of the times.

All Right Now
Free

Released May 1970
A&M *1206* (U.S. #4) / Island *WIP 6082* (U.K. #2)

By 1970, Free had two albums behind them but seemed little more than a group following uncertainly in the footsteps of Peter Green's Fleetwood Mac and their bluesy hard rock. It was precisely because the band realized there were limits to 12-bar laments, however authentic, that led to this song's creation.

A gig in Durham, England, had seen the band leaving the stage to the sound of their own footsteps. "It was obvious that we needed an up-tempo number, a rocker to close our shows," drummer Simon Kirke said later. Bassist Andy Fraser began dancing around the dressing room singing the phrase "all right now" and proceeded to write the song on the spot. The process took him ten minutes. The lyric was a sparkling tale of flirtation leading to sexual congress, driven home by one of the all-time great rockin' guitar riffs.

The band then applied their considerable skills of extemporization to the raw material, ending up with a track lasting over five minutes as the finale of their third album, *Fire And Water*. Ironically, after all that work, the song had to be edited for single release. While such measures are usually considered sacrilege, the song was given greater punch and power after the shortening of its lengthy instrumental section. 'All Right Now' was one of two great singles kept from the top of the British charts by the (admittedly fine) Mungo Jerry song 'In The Summertime.' The other one was T. Rex's 'Ride A White Swan.'

Lola
The Kinks

Released June 1970
Reprise *0930* (U.S. #9) / Pye *7N 17961* (U.K. #2)

Like many successful groups of the 1960s, The Kinks ran out of steam a little as the new decade arrived, not least due to Ray Davies's predilection for writing a series of concept albums. This was the last of a lengthy run of hits in America, and with the exception of the follow-up, 'Apeman,'

their last ever U.K. Top 10 hit. The group did, however, enjoy a second round of success in the States in the late 1970s, and hit Number 13 in Britain in 1983 with 'Come Dancing.'

The Kinks had been one of Britain's most successful pop groups of the 1960s. When leader Ray Davies found his songwriting feet, he created some of the best typically British popular music of the era. He produced a classic series of cleverly written songs, including 'Dead End Street,' 'Sunny Afternoon,' 'Dedicated Follower Of Fashion,' and 'Waterloo Sunset' (originally titled 'Liverpool Sunset' but changed when The Beatles released 'Penny Lane' / 'Strawberry Fields'). Davies continues to be recognized as one of the most intuitive pop writers of the period.

The inspiration for 'Lola' came to Davies from a male colleague who thought he was on to a good thing in a dingy London nightclub. As the night wore on, his dancing partner's chin-stubble became increasingly apparent, leading to the song's clever punchline: "I'm glad I'm a man … and so's Lola."

The single was banned in Australia for its sexual imagery, and was about to be banned by the BBC in Britain: the lyric mentioned Coca-Cola, and product advertising was not allowed on the Corporation's airwaves. Davies was in the U.S. when this news arrived and made a swift 24-hour trip back to London to replace the offending line with "cherry-cola."

My Sweet Lord
George Harrison

Released November 1970
Apple *2995* (U.S. #1) / Apple *R 5884* (U.K. #1)

Many fans were surprised when George Harrison became the first ex-Beatle to hit the top of the singles chart following the group's demise at the beginning of 1970. His songwriting talents had always been overshadowed by those of Lennon and McCartney – and Harrison can't have been particularly happy when Frank Sinatra repeatedly introduced 'Something' as "the best song Lennon & McCartney have written."

While a judge would later decide otherwise, Harrison said that 'My Sweet Lord' was inspired by The Edwin Hawkins Singers' 1969 hit 'Oh Happy Day.' He originally gave the song to Billy Preston with the intention that Preston should release it as a single. However, having recorded his own version together with producer Phil Spector, he earmarked it as the debut single from his triple album *All Things Must Pass*, and the Preston single was withdrawn.

After 'My Sweet Lord' had topped charts around the world and sold in excess of five million copies, it became apparent that the melody was not unlike The Chiffons' 1963 hit, 'He's So Fine,' written by Ronnie Mack. A protracted lawsuit began, which George Harrison eventually lost some five years later, although he always maintained that the similarity was purely coincidental. An American district court judge agreed that Harrison's so called 'plagiarism' might well have been sub-conscious, but still awarded in favor of the plaintive to the tune of $587,000.

Harrison topped the *Billboard* Hot 100 on two further occasions over the years – with 'Give Me Love' in 1973 and 'Got My Mind Set On You' in 1987 – but neither single matched the enduring popularity of 'My Sweet Lord.' After his death in November 2001 this, his most successful solo recording, returned to the top of the U.K. charts in January 2002.

Paranoid
Black Sabbath

Released August 1970
Warner Bros. *7437* (U.S.) / Vertigo *6059 010* (U.K. #4)

'Paranoid' is the Black Sabbath song that even people who normally detest the group actually like. Part of the reason for this is because it doesn't sound like them at all, but rather their contemporaries in the heavy-metal world, Deep Purple.

Throughout their career, Sabbath have played the slow, grinding, menacing music they had pioneered on their eponymous 1970 debut and that arguably gave them the right to claim the title of founders of the HM genre. (Led Zeppelin fans may think otherwise.) On 'Paranoid' the group retained their gloomy subject matter but speeded up the tempo to create that most unlikely of beasts, a Sabbath smash hit: not only did it achieve a U.K. Top 5 in 1970 but a decade later climbed to Number 14.

Perhaps the uncharacteristic Purple-like speed happened because the group didn't agonize much about the track. With work almost completed on their second album, producer Roger Bain pointed out that an extra three or four minutes of material was needed to round it off. Guitarist Tony Iommi devised a riff, singer Ozzy Osbourne a melody, and bassist 'Geezer' Butler a lyric, the latter prompted by the fact that people kept accusing him of being paranoid. Within ten minutes the band had on their hands a creation that would ensure they achieved what most heavy metal men never managed: a hit single primed for the pop-loving masses.

Your Song
Elton John

Released November 1970
UNI *55265* (U.S. #8) / DJM *DJS 233* (U.K. #7)

Reginald Kenneth Dwight became Elton John in December 1967 when he left his group Bluesology. By that time he'd begun writing with lyricist Bernie Taupin after joining up through an ad for talent in *New Musical Express* placed by Liberty Records.

It's important to appreciate the importance of Taupin in John's career, as he pointed out in a 1970 interview: "Without Bernie, there'd be no songs. I get very annoyed when people ignore him." The duo were signed to a writing deal by Dick James, whose impressive publishing empire included administration of The Beatles' catalogue. Taupin received £10 per week, John £15 (about $25/$35). Soon afterwards Elton John was signed as a recording artist.

DJM released three albums, *Empty Sky*, *Elton John*, and *Tumbleweed Connection*, and five singles, before his breakthrough hit, 'Your Song,' was released towards the end of 1970. Between the recording of this song and its release, John continued to supplement his income by recording cover versions of current hits for Hallmark on the budget label's *Top Of The Pops* series. He can be heard performing such 1970 hits as 'Spirit In The Sky,' 'Young Gifted And Black,' and 'In The Summertime.' In more recent years these ancient recordings have resurfaced, collected on the album *Reg Dwight's Piano Goes Pop*.

'Your Song,' which Taupin now calls "wonderfully naive," was released to coincide with John's second visit to America. Taupin wrote the lyrics over a scrambled-egg breakfast at John's mother's house in north-west London when he was just 17 years old.

Spirit In The Sky
Norman Greenbaum

Released February 1970
Reprise 0885 (U.S. #3) / Reprise RS 20885 (U.K. #1)

No one can have been more surprised than American singer Norman Greenbaum when his quasi-religious 'Spirit In The Sky' reached Number 1 in Britain in 1970. One of the all-time one-hit-wonders, Greenbaum made a few albums for Warner Brothers in the States that produced nothing of note and he swiftly disappeared into the annals of pop history. He had in fact visited the U.S. charts on one previous occasion as a member of Dr West's Medicine Show & Junk Band, in 1966, with the unlikely titled 'Eggplant That Ate Chicago' that reached Number 52.

Greenbaum's 'Spirit In The Sky' came about when he felt inclined to write a gospel-tinged song, influenced by country singer Porter Wagoner. Greenbaum noted that Wagoner always ended his television show with a gospel number, one of which was a song about a preacher. So it was that Greenbaum wrote his own religious rock song. Recorded in the autumn of 1969, the single had a distinctive fuzz-guitar intro and unusual lyrics. While Greenbaum's chart career may have been short, his song has continued to pay the bills. Dr & The Medics took their cover version to Number 1 in Britain in 1986, while the original version has appeared on dozens of oldies compilation albums, in several movies, and on numerous television advertisements.

(They Long To Be) Close To You
The Carpenters

Released May 1970
A&M 1183 (U.S. #1) / A&M AMS 800 (U.K. #6)

When 'Close To You' was first recorded way back in 1963 by television's Dr. Kildare, alias Richard Chamberlain, it failed to make any impression on the charts. But The Carpenters were lucky that the song hadn't been a hit. In 1964, Dusty Springfield made a recording that was scheduled as a follow-up to her Bacharach & David U.K. hit 'I Just Don't Know What To Do With Myself.' However, it was left on the shelf and didn't appear until her 1967 album *Where Am I Going*?

Brother and sister duo Richard and Karen Carpenter were one of the most popular easy-listening acts of the 1970s, with their distinctive vocal sound and a combination of original material and contemporary covers. Composer Burt Bacharach had earlier suggested that Herb Alpert record 'Close To You' after Alpert's success with another Bacharach & David song, 'This Guy's In Love With You,' but Alpert thought the lyric was too sugary. He passed it on to Richard Carpenter, who didn't like the song much either but

eventually agreed to record it, although there was a considerable difference of opinion regarding the record's potential. Lyricist Hal David wasn't impressed at all, and recalled: "When A&M sent over the [Carpenters] record I didn't think it was a hit. Not that Karen Carpenter didn't sound great – I just thought it didn't have what it took to really catch on. It shows that nobody, myself included, knows a hit until it becomes a hit."

In The Summertime
Mungo Jerry

Released May 1970
Janus 125 (U.S. #3) / Dawn DNX 2502 (U.K. #1)

Some 35 years down the line, 'In The Summertime' has become one of the best-loved summer anthems of all time. You only need to write one hit like this and you're set for life, as Ray Dorset has discovered. Looking back to 1970, Mungo Jerry frontman Dorset recalled that his music then was "a hobby that became a job, but I never imagined music would become my career." The former Good Earth Band played their first gig as Mungo Jerry at the Hollywood Pop Festival in Newcastle-under-Lyme, England, in May 1970, and their good-time blend of skiffle and jug-band blues stole the show.

In what looks retrospectively like a wise decision, the group had apparently turned down an £8 ($20) gig that weekend to appear at the festival. The following week 'In The Summertime' shot to the top, where it remained for seven weeks, and it soon topped charts around the world, shifting several million copies in the process and becoming the group's only U.S. hit. Dorset and his bank manager must have been thrilled when Shaggy took a new version of the song up the charts in 1995. Shaggy's album on which the song appeared, *Boombastic*, was a multi-million seller. Let's face it: in Ray Dorset's household it must be summertime all year round.

Black Magic Woman
Santana

Released October 1970
Columbia 45270 (U.S. #4) / CBS 5325 (U.K.)

Santana were originally signed to Columbia in 1969, and it was label boss Clive Davis who also engineered an impressive comeback 30 years later with the multi-platinum *Supernatural*. Mexico-born Carlos Santana is one of the world's most distinctive guitarists, and his band had their major breakthrough in 1969 at the Woodstock festival, where their Latin-rock fusion 'Soul Sacrifice' was one of the event's highlights. The movie and soundtrack album arrived the following summer, just in time for their second album *Abraxas*, which is still considered their finest collection.

One of the major hits from the album, 'Black Magic Woman,' was not a Santana original but had been composed by Peter Green, a minor U.K. hit for his band Fleetwood Mac in April 1968. Santana recorded the song at the urging of the group's keyboard player and vocalist Greg Rolie, although he said it took about a year to persuade them. *Abraxas*, a million-selling Number 1 album in America, also gave the group a U.S. hit with 'Oye Como Va,' while another track, 'Samba Pa Ti,' became their first British hit in 1974.

What's Going On
Marvin Gaye

Released January 1971
Tamla *54201* (U.S. #2) / Tamla Motown *TMG 775* (U.K.)

Among the finest of the many classic Motown singles of the 1960s and early 1970s, 'What's Going On' signposted Marvin Gaye's move from a merely great pop singer to a serious musical artist. In the late 1960s, Gaye had released the biggest hits of his career to date, including 'I Heard It

Through The Grapevine' and 'Too Busy Thinking About My Baby,' but increasingly felt that he wanted to make music in a more spiritual, socially conscious vein. He was also deeply affected by the death of his singing partner, Tammi Terrell, from a brain tumor in March 1970, aged just 24. The melancholy tone of the U.K. single he released next, 'Abraham, Martin, And John,' gave some indication of where Gaye would soon be headed.

The initial idea for 'What's Going On' came from The Four Tops' Obie Benson, who worked on it with Motown songwriter Al Cleveland before bringing it to Gaye. At this point Gaye was in such a state of depression that he considered retiring, but Benson and Cleveland convinced him to record the song himself rather than produce it for another group, The Originals, as Gaye had originally intended.

With David Van DePitte on production duties, Gaye and various members of Motown house band The Funk Brothers recorded the basic tracks of 'What's Going On' (and its eventual B-side, 'God Is Love') at Hitsville U.S.A. Studio A on June 1st, 1970. Gaye returned to the studio during the second week of July to add various vocal parts, while the strings were taped in September.

'What's Going On' introduced a new vocal style for both Gaye and Motown. Although the label had been using a primitive form of multi-tracking since the mid 1960s – particularly to add power to vocal tracks, as on The Supremes' 'You Keep Me Hanging On' – Gaye took the process a step further. Singing in a softer, more soulful voice than on his earlier hits, he added his own backing harmonies to each of his vocal parts, resulting in the subtle, graceful sound that became a hallmark of his later releases. He added to the song's sense of spiritual dislocation by including background sounds of partygoers, utterly at odds with his own lament about the state of the world.

While Gaye was certain he had created his masterpiece, Motown head Berry Gordy was not so sure and was initially reluctant to release it. Gaye countered by refusing to record any more music for Motown. When Gordy eventually relented, in early 1971, the song began its swift climb up the Billboard singles chart, prompting the label head to order a whole album of similar material. That album is, of course, *What's Going On*, generally recognized as both Motown and Gaye's finest artistic statement, and one of the landmark recordings of the early 1970s. Surprisingly, however, given the earlier success of Gaye's hits like 'I Heard It Through The Grapevine,' neither single nor album charted in Britain.

Tired Of Being Alone
Al Green

Released May 1971
Hi *2194* (U.S. #11) / London *HLU 10337* (U.K. #4)

Let's Stay Together
Al Green

Released November 1971
Hi *2202* (U.S. #1) / London *HLU 10348* (U.K. #7)

Having languished in obscurity for years as a sub-Sam & Dave soul shouter, Al Green finally achieved mainstream success with his own composition, 'Tired Of Being Alone,' a laidback Southern soul groove telling the story of his unhappy romance with singer Laura Lee. "This lady used to leave me all the time," he revealed. "She was the busiest woman I'd ever seen. Always had something to do – her nails, hair, shopping. Consequently, I was alone a lot, and that's why I wrote that song."

Producer Willie Mitchell, who started out as a Hi Records artist in the early 1960s, was vital in changing Green's direction and, between them, the pair established Hi as second in the Southern soul stakes only to Stax, with whom they shared many session players. 'Tired Of Being Alone' entered *Billboard*'s U.S. Top 40 chart on August 21, 1971, and peaked at Number 11. It did even better in the U.K. where it soared to Number 4 in October, the same month that it earned a gold disc in the States.

Having scored a major hit, Green was keen to try his luck with another up-tempo hard-soul workout, but Mitchell prevailed on him to remain in the smooth soul vein and the result was the sublime 'Let's Stay Together,' which gave Green his only U.S. Number 1, on February 12, 1972, and established Willie Mitchell's Hi Records sound as the new benchmark in soul: finely tuned percussion, laidback rhythm, and tough but understated brass stabs.

Imagine
John Lennon Plastic Ono Band

Released October 1971
Apple *1840* (U.S. #3) / Apple *R 6009* (U.K. #1)

'Imagine' is the record that saved John Lennon's post-Beatles reputation. There is much talk of Lennon writing songs with an edge that was profoundly lacking in Paul McCartney's solo material. Yet if this song was removed when assessing the quality of Lennon's post-Beatles career, there would be a remarkably threadbare catalogue left behind and – notwithstanding his five-year sabbatical and early demise – precious few truly top quality songs, let alone iconic ones.

Lennon once described his *Imagine* album as a sugar-coated version of the preceding LP, the confessional and raw *Plastic Ono Band*. The title track, 'Imagine,' was certainly a sweetened variant of the political songwriting that Lennon engaged in before and after. This is not just due to the pretty, stately melody and Lennon's simple but hypnotic piano playing. 'Power To The People' (1971) and the *Sometime In New York City* album (1972) had the sort of agitprop lyrics loved by people with posters of Che Guevara on their walls. 'Imagine' was a song geared to such people's utopian ideals but designed to be palatable to the masses. So palatable, apparently, as to be opaque for some. How else to explain the British Conservative party using it at an annual conference during their most right-wing phase in modern history?

Many have pointed to the easy sentimentality and platitudinous nature of lines such as: "Imagine all the people living life in peace." Easy for some, perhaps, but they marked the culmination of a difficult journey that Lennon had taken from his time as a surprisingly violent young man – including violence against women and, allegedly, ex-Beatle colleague Stuart Sutcliffe – into his later years as a pacifist and feminist. However, he could have done more to stifle qualms about the apparent hypocrisy in the line "Imagine no possessions / I wonder if you can?" simply by changing that 'you' to 'we.' Despite that wrinkle, the end result was quite remarkable: a song that almost instantly achieved status as a mass rallying cry among such similarly gentle, abstract left-wing anthems as 'We Shall Overcome' and 'Blowin' In The Wind.'

There can be little doubt that the impact of 'Imagine' on the popular consciousness was increased by Lennon's murder, manifested since by its regularly topping public polls to find the greatest song of the 20th century or of all time. There is a poetic act of defiance involved in voting for it, a display of confidence in the utopianism of the lyric and a mark against the type of evil that led to his death. Nonetheless, 'Imagine' did have a significant resonance when Lennon was still with us.

It went unreleased as a single in Britain until 1975 – amazingly, there were no contemporaneous 45s issued from the *Imagine* album in Lennon's homeland – and effortlessly sailed to Number 6 there despite the fact that Lennon was now on the cusp of his half-decade withdrawal from the music business. Following his death in December 1980 it went all the way to a U.K. Number 1.

Layla
Derek & The Dominos

Released March 1971
Atco *6809* (U.S. #10) / Polydor *2001 148* (U.K. #7)

Eric Clapton wrote this song for George Harrison's wife, Pattie Boyd, whom Clapton had "fallen madly in love with." Ms. Boyd is one of the most famously serenaded women in rock history, with Harrison's 'Something' and Clapton's later 'Wonderful Tonight' also to her credit. By the time of 'Wonderful Tonight' Clapton had successfully won Pattie's heart and married her.

Following his stints with Cream and Blind Faith, Clapton was anxious to escape his guitar-hero image and disappear into the background. He toured America with Delaney & Bonnie And Friends before stealing the backbone of Delaney's band and retiring to Criteria Studios in Miami, Florida, to record his next project, as Derek & The Dominos. He deliberately intended this to be a low-profile affair, fronting the band as 'Derek' and refusing to have his name on the resulting album.

Tom Dowd was hired to co-produce the sessions, and it so happened that Dowd was currently engaged in producing an album for The Allman Brothers. Guitarist Duane Allman swiftly became friends with Clapton and joined the Dominos sessions to play slide guitar. The full version of 'Layla' was recorded in two distinctively separate sessions.

The first, with one of the all-time great power-guitar riffs, was written by Clapton and recorded in September 1970, while the instrumental second part was written by drummer Jim Gordon and recorded in October. The two sections were then spliced together at the mixing stage. The song became the title track of the Dominos album, released in December, and was first issued as a single early in 1971 but did not chart until 1972.

Won't Get Fooled Again
The Who

Released June 1971
Decca *32846* (U.S. #15) / Track *2094 009* (U.K. #9)

Rescued from the abandoned *Lifehouse* project, Townshend's planned successor to *Tommy*, 'Won't Get Fooled Again' was a stunning climax to what was undoubtedly The Who's best studio album. Following a false start at New York City's Record Plant studio in March 1971, where drummer Keith Moon's drug intake seriously alarmed the rest of the group, recording was switched to Britain and supervised by Glyn Johns. Townshend had been experimenting at home with an early synthesizer and came up with the sequence that formed the basis of the song.

Recorded in the main hall of Mick Jagger's house Stargroves in April using the Rolling Stones mobile studio, the song is not, as many assume, a revolutionary anthem. According to Townshend, it was "a song against the revolution. The first verse sounds like a revolution song and the second like somebody getting tired of it." With The Who playing at their very best, this eight-and-a-half-minute epic, hacked down to under four as a single, was cleverly programmed as the last track on side two of *Who's Next*. Other songs from *Lifehouse* including 'Let's See Action,' 'Relay,' and 'Join Together' were released as singles in the following years, while the entire project eventually came to fruition nearly 30 years later.

Get It On
T. Rex

Released July 1971
Reprise *1032* (U.S. #10) / Fly *BUG 10* (U.K. #1)

'Get It On' is the best known and most successful single by one of the leading lights of the British early-1970s glam-rock scene. In the U.S. it was given a slightly elongated title, 'Bang A Gong (Get It On),' in part to distinguish it from a similarly titled single by the jazz-rock outfit Chase, but also so as not to offend American listeners' delicate sensibilities. It was the group's only American Top 40 hit.

Marc Bolan formed the original, folk-rock Tyrannosaurus Rex in late 1967. The duo's long-winded debut album, *My People Were Fair And Had Sky In Their Hair But Now They're Content To Wear Stars In Their Brows*, marked the start of a career-long association with producer Tony Visconti, who also worked on a number of key David Bowie albums. By the dawn of the 1970s Bolan had abbreviated the Tyrannosaurus in the group's name, switched to electric guitar, and brought in three new backing musicians to replace original percussionist Steve Took.

These changes resulted in 'Ride A White Swan' and 'Hot Love,' both becoming unexpected U.K. hits and the second reaching Number 1. With T. Rex now a full-on touring machine, Visconti was forced to record *Electric Warrior*, the group's defining fifth LP, on the run at various British and American studios. The album was preceded by the release of 'Get It On,' an exultant piece of dirty blues with a guitar riff later 'borrowed' wholesale by the 1990s retro rock act Oasis. It came third in a run of ten consecutive U.K. Top 5 chart entries for T. Rex, including such later gems as '20th Century Boy' and 'Metal Guru.'

Maggie May
Rod Stewart

Released July 1971
Mercury *73224* (U.S. #1) / Mercury *6052 097* (U.K. #1)

Rod Stewart has an anonymous Cleveland DJ to thank for superstardom. In 1971, a rendition of Tim Hardin's 'Reason To Believe' was chosen as the single to promote Stewart's third solo album, the magnificent *Every Picture Tells A Story*. The DJ preferred the flip and began playing it. 'Reason to Believe' was quite lovely, but you could see his point.

'Maggie May' was a composition by Stewart and a guitarist, Martin Quittenton, who had worked on Stewart's first two albums. The two wrote the song when Quittenton was staying at Stewart's house for the purpose of playing on the third LP. Quittenton devised the famous 12-string acoustic guitar intro on the subway on his way to the studio one day.

While 'Maggie May' was, like most Stewart music of the time, essentially rustic, it was a quite extraordinary extravaganza. Its close to six minutes of playing time takes in the coming-of-age tale of a boy who falls for and is then spurned by an older woman and features not only great backing and the usual fine, raspy singing from Stewart but some exquisite moments, those little crescendos of brilliance or spontaneity that make repeated listening a pleasure. This is especially so of the concluding verse, in which the narrator juggles his options – school, or careers as a pool player or (he wishes) a singer – while a celeste ratchets up the poignancy behind him. The single became a Number 1 in Britain and America, and the parent album simultaneously proceeded to replicate that transatlantic chart-topping feat, a history-making first.

I'd Like To Teach The World To Sing
The New Seekers

Released December 1971
Elektra *45762* (U.S. #7) / Polydor *2058 184* (U.K. #1)

The New Seekers were assembled in 1969, logically enough by a former member of The Seekers, Keith Potger. At first performing with the group, he soon withdrew into a management role, selecting their material. In 1970 they were hired by American Coca-Cola executive Bill Backer to record a number of advertising jingles for the company. Arriving in Britain, Backer had come up with the line: "I'd like to buy the world a coke and keep it company." Together with Roger Cook and Billy Davis, who had written hits with Berry Gordy, they put together the new lyric the night before the session. The tune was based on a melody by Cook and Roger Greenaway, entitled 'True Love And Apple Pie,' and the result became perhaps the most successful advertising jingle of all time.

The TV advertising campaign began in 1971, and featured a crowd of youngsters on a hilltop miming to The New Seekers' vocals. The tune was so successful that listeners phoned U.S. stations asking where they could buy the record. At this point Backer arranged for Cook and Greenaway to rewrite the lyric, and since The New Seekers were unavailable, recorded it with a group appropriately named The Hilltop Singers. Shortly afterwards, The New Seekers rushed into a New York studio to record the new lyrics over their original version. New Seekers vocalist Lyn Paul said: "I remember thinking I wasn't very keen on it. How wrong can you be?" Both versions made the U.S. Top 20, although The New Seekers climbed higher, and in Britain their version reached Number 1. Brit-pop band Oasis later hijacked part of the melody for their 1994 single 'Shakermaker,' which resulted in an expensive plagiarism case.

Ain't No Sunshine
Bill Withers

Released June 1971
Sussex *219* (U.S. #3) / A&M *AMS 858* (U.K.)

Bill Withers began writing songs because, as he recalled, "I figured if I was going to be a singer, I'd have to have some tunes." As he hawked his material around the Los Angeles labels, a chance meeting with Booker T. Jones got him a deal with the small Sussex label. His debut album, *Just As I Am*, was produced by Jones, and the musicians included three members of the world's greatest house-band: the impressive studio line-up of Booker T. & The MGs minus guitarist Steve Cropper and supplemented by Stephen Stills.

Among the songs recorded was 'Ain't No Sunshine,' a concise performance at just over two minutes. The lengthy repetition of "I know, I know…" was a result of Withers forgetting the words, but it sounded so good it was left in. 'Sunshine' was at first released as the B-side of 'Harlem,' but DJs soon found the gem on the other side and the song rose to Number 3 on the U.S. charts in the fall of 1971 and won Withers a Grammy award for Best Rhythm & Blues Song. It was not a hit in Britain, where the song was covered by a young Michael Jackson, reaching Number 8 a year later.

Riders On The Storm
The Doors

Released June 1971
Elektra *45738* (U.S. #14) / Elektra *K 12021* (U.K. #22)

'Riders On The Storm' seemed to mark a return to form for The Doors after a couple of years of lesser recordings. Sadly, however, it became the group's swan song, as vocalist Jim Morrison died just as the single began to climb up the charts.

The recording is driven by session player Jerry Scheff's walking bassline and Ray Manzarek's energetic electric piano, and has a more mature, blues-derived sound compared to The Doors earlier work. The group arrived at this refined sound alongside Bruce Botnick, who was promoted from his usual role of engineer to produce the album *L.A. Woman* after Paul Rothchild dropped out, unhappy with the group's apparent direction. Far from being what Rothchild considered "cocktail music," however, the resulting album was one of The Doors' finest, second only perhaps to their eponymous 1967 debut.

'Riders On The Storm' was the second single release from *L.A. Woman* and followed 'Love Her Madly' into the upper reaches of the U.S. *Billboard* chart. Like the earlier Doors classic, 'Light My Fire,' the rambling album cut – which stretched beyond the seven-minute mark – had to be edited down for the singles market but lost little of its mesmeric, foreboding charm. Featuring one of Morrison's strongest vocal performances, it was already on its way to becoming a hit when the singer died suddenly of a drug-induced heart attack at his home in Paris, France, on July 3, 1971.

Theme From Shaft
Isaac Hayes

Released September 1971
Enterprise *9038* (U.S. #1) / Stax *2025 069* (U.K. #4)

When Isaac Hayes was asked to provide music for the ground-breaking blaxploitation movie *Shaft*, the former Stax Records songwriter simply dug up a track he had knocked up a year earlier. "I pulled it out," he explains, "and told Skip, my guitarist, 'Man, put the wah-wah on this.'" The resulting combo of sharp-edged wah-wah guitar and rapidly clattering hi-hat not only won an Academy Award for Best Song and a Best Instrumental Arrangement Grammy, but 'Shaft' went to Number 1 in *Billboard* and established the blueprint for an influential new funky stew. Hayes, who later found even greater fame as Chef in the cult TV series *South Park*, was inducted into the Rock & Roll Hall Of Fame in 2002.

Family Affair
Sly & The Family Stone

Released October 1971
Epic *10805* (U.S. #1) / Epic *EPC 7632* (U.K. #15)

'Family Affair' is the work of a musical genius on the verge of a meltdown. It was the third and last of the group's U.S. Number 1 hits, and the Family Stone – not to mention Sly Stone himself – began to disintegrate soon afterwards. The group marked the end of the first phase of their career – which culminated in the chart-topping 'Thank You (Fallettinme Be Mice Elf Again)' – with a *Greatest Hits* compilation in late 1970. Sly spent much of the next year pulling together his masterpiece, the *There's A Riot Goin' On* album, in something of a drugged haze, re-recording some of the tracks so many times that the tapes began to warp.

'Family Affair' was the first fruit of the lengthy, disorganized *Riot* sessions. Although it didn't exactly prepare the group's fans for what was to come on the full-length vinyl, it does have a markedly hazier sound compared to the Family Stone's earlier hits. It was the first ever Number 1 hit to be underpinned by a programmed drum track, for which Stone used a Maestro Rhythm King machine. He also played the bass himself – Larry Graham was still in the group at this point, but his parts were wiped by the paranoid bandleader. The other instruments were played by session men, with Billy Preston contributing Rhodes electric piano and Bobby Womack adding wah-wah-laden guitar. Sly shares the vocal with his sister, Rose, the only other member of the Family Stone to feature on the single.

Have You Seen Her
The Chi-Lites

Released October 1971
Brunswick *55462* (U.S. #3) / MCA *MU 1146* (U.K. #3)

Like Detroit, Memphis, and Philadelphia, Chicago too was a hotbed of R&B and soul music, home to such artists as Curtis Mayfield, Jackie Wilson, Jerry Butler, The Delfonics, and Gene Chandler. The Chi-Lites were formed in 1959, led by vocalist-writer Eugene Record, and while their chart debut was the funky '(For God's Sake) Give More Power To The People,' they staked out a place with a string of smooth-soul plaintive ballads including 'The Coldest Days Of My Life,' 'Oh Girl' (a U.S Number 1), and 'Have You Seen Her,' co-written by another of the Windy City's finest, Barbara Acklin, and later updated by M.C. Hammer. The Chi-lites' chart career in Britain lasted beyond its 1973 American conclusion, with 'Have You Seen Her' again scaling the U.K. Top 10 in 1975, together with a number of non-U.S. pop hits including 'Homely Girl' (later covered by UB40), 'Too Good To Be Forgotten,' and 'It's Time For Love.'

A Horse With No Name
America

Released December 1971
Warner Bros. *7555* (U.S. #1) / Warner Bros. *K 16128* (U.K. #3)

This was so much in the contemporarily popular style of Crosby Stills Nash & Young that on first hearing many listeners thought that this was indeed Neil Young – and coincidentally it replaced Young's 'Heart Of Gold' at Number 1 in the U.S. Though American, these three sons of U.K.-based Air Force officers got together in England where they recorded their first album. The record included this track, which became a hit in Britain before a U.S. release saw it topping the American charts in March 1972. Their debut album spent five weeks at the top of the *Billboard* album charts and the group won the Grammy for Best New Artist. Riding on the popular early-1970s singer-songwriter wave, America followed up with several appealing acoustic-based hits, including 'I Need You' and 'Ventura Highway.' Their later recordings were overseen by former Beatles producer George Martin, resulting in a second American Number 1 with 'Sister Golden Hair' in 1975.

Without You
Nilsson

Released December 1971
RCA *0604* (U.S. #1) / RCA *2165* (U.K. #1)

Few songs have a history as sad as this sweet ballad. Its compositional division was unusually neat: Badfinger's Pete Ham supplied the lilting verses while his fellow guitarist Tom Evans provided the soaring chorus ("I can't live, if living is without you").

Originally it was just a track on the band's second album, but hard-boozing rocker Nilsson surprised the group by releasing an incongruously delicate version that went Top 5 in the States at the same time as Badfinger's own 'Day After Day.' The millionaire status one would expect for the composers never materialized: legal wrangles prevented them receiving their due. Both musicians eventually committed suicide.

Morning Has Broken
Cat Stevens

Released December 1971
A&M *1335* (U.S. #6) / Island *WIP 6121* (U.K. #9)

Before embracing Islam in 1979 and changing his name to Yusuf Islam, Cat Stevens enjoyed two successful musical careers. The first was as a pop star in the late 1960s with the hits 'Matthew And Son,' 'I Love My Dog,' and 'I'm Gonna Get Me A Gun.'

Following a year in recuperation from tuberculosis he returned as Britain's premier singer-songwriter, recording a string of million-selling albums and hits including 'Lady D'Arbanville,' 'Father And Son,' 'Moonshadow,' and 'Morning Has Broken.' 'Father And Son' was one of a number of songs that Stevens wrote for a proposed musical, *Revolussia*, about the Russian Tsarist dynasty, telling the story of a peasant farmer's son who goes off to join the revolution.

Most of Stevens's hits were self-composed, but 'Morning Has Broken' was an old English hymn, written by Eleanor Farjean and often sung at morning assemblies in British schools. Stevens had rediscovered the song in the religious section of a London bookstore and recorded it in March 1971 for his *Teaser And The Firecat* album.

Keyboard virtuoso Rick Wakeman played piano and assisted Stevens with the arrangement, and according to later interviews never received his session fee for the job. Wakeman recalled that when the song became a hit and the record company had difficulty in finding a pianist to appear on British TV chart show *Top Of The Pops*, the musician's reply on being contacted was: "Tough!" An exchange of correspondence in *Q* magazine finally resolved the situation almost 30 years later, and Wakeman duly received a check for £9.50 (about $15) from Yusuf Islam to settle his long-overdue session fee.

American Pie

Don McLean

Released November 1971
United Artists *50856* (U.S. #1) / United Artists *UP 35325* (U.K. #2)

Don McLean was by no means a one-hit wonder, but his international hit 'American Pie' has certainly overshadowed the rest of his work. McLean himself has often complained that its huge success has meant that a lot of his other songs have been largely overlooked.

A folk singer since 1963, McLean began to attract attention when he became 'The Hudson River Troubadour' in 1968, a job given to him by the New York State Council on the Arts. This entailed playing to Hudson River communities up to three times a day for a month and brought him to the attention of folk singer Pete Seeger, who later called McLean "the finest singer and songwriter I have met since Bob Dylan." American record companies didn't necessarily share this opinion.

While McLean's popularity among folk audiences was increasing, 34 record companies turned down his demo tapes before he finally got a deal with the small Mediarts label, who released his debut album *Tapestry* in 1970. The record didn't sell particularly well, but McLean kept touring and performing, and during this period he began writing 'American Pie.' It was at this point that the large United Artists company bought Mediarts.

Over the years, much has been read into the lyrical content of the song, which takes as its starting point the death of Buddy Holly in 1959, "the day the music died." It was Holly who had inspired McLean to pick up a guitar in the first place. "I was in love with Buddy Holly and his music," he recalled, "and I remember sadly that by 1964 you didn't hear anything about Buddy Holly. He was completely forgotten. But I didn't forget him. I think this song helped make people aware that Buddy's legitimate musical contribution had been overlooked."

It is generally assumed to be a nostalgic look at the growth of popular contemporary music in the 1960s, but according to McLean the theme of this eight-and-a-half-minute epic was that "commercialism is the death of inspiration." This negative trend was perhaps reflected in McLean's own difficulty in obtaining a record contract. One positive outcome of the song's success was a renaissance for the recordings of Buddy Holly.

Because of its length, 'American Pie' was split into two parts on the single, but most U.S. radio stations soon featured the entire song, and it became one of the most-played records of the time, swiftly rising to Number 1. McLean's follow-up, 'Vincent,' a tribute to painter Vincent Van Gogh, did nearly as well, reaching Number 1 in Britain where 'Pie' had stalled at 2.

However, the huge success of 'American Pie' had taken McLean somewhat by surprise, and contrary to his record company's wishes, he didn't see himself as a hit songwriter, preferring to return to his folk roots. Consequently, record-buyers generally overlooked his later recordings, and apart from a brief return in 1980 with a cover of Roy Orbison's 'Crying' – a British Number 1 which his American record company had rejected in 1978 – McLean's chart success has been limited.

Me And Bobby McGee

Janis Joplin

Released January 1971
Columbia *45314* (U.S. #1) / CBS *7019* (U.K.)

Part-time helicopter pilot, part-time recording studio janitor, and full-time aspiring songwriter Kris Kristofferson picked up his phone one day to hear a Mr. Fred Foster saying: "I've got a song title for you." Foster owned the Nashville building where Felice and Boudleaux Bryant, composers of quality hits for The Everly Brothers and others, worked alongside their secretary, Bobbie McFee. Foster evidently liked the sound of the name and suggested that Kristofferson should write a song called 'Me And Bobbie McFee.'

It took Kristofferson three months, and he tinkered a little with the title, but not everyone immediately recognized it as a classic. "Some of my songwriting friends wanted me to take the line 'Freedom's just another word for nothing left to lose' out of the song," he recalled. "They said, 'You got these great concrete images and then you change to this philosophical statement in the chorus.'"

When Johnny Cash heard it, however, he knew better. First he convinced Roger Miller to record it, then he offered Kristofferson a slot at the 1969 Newport Folk Festival, which got his career off and running. Come 1970, Kristofferson was a successful Columbia Records artist and, on the night of October 3, his girlfriend, Janis Joplin, recorded what is now recognized as the definitive version of the song in one brilliant take. The following day she died of a heroin overdose. It hit Number 1 in *Billboard* on March 20, 1971, and still regularly appears in critics' polls of all-time great songs.

You've Got A Friend

James Taylor

Released June 1971
Warner Bros. *7498* (U.S. #1) / Warner Bros. *WB 16085* (U.K. #4)

When Carole King moved over to the West Coast at the turn of the 1970s she ended up quite spectacularly in the right place at the right time. As her generation entered a new decade, exhaustion at the ceaseless concern with the problems of others that had characterized the 1960s began to set in. Introspection became the order of the day. Musically, this was manifested in the singer-songwriter movement.

Not entirely as expected, King, a New Yorker and Brill Building pop merchant, became the queen of the laidback and mainly acoustic songs of Pacific adult reflection that characterized the genre. Her breakthrough album *Tapestry* – at one point the second biggest-selling album of all time – featured a song that perfectly encapsulated that style, 'You've Got A Friend.' It was a mature song about friendship, sounding like it was meant as a comforting message from one divorced woman (which King now was) to another – although there was a token 'baby' at the close.

James Taylor brought forward the romantic element of this almost gender-neutral song when he decided to cover it. Taylor knew it well: he had played acoustic guitar on King's version. King returned the favor by contributing backing vocals to his own recording, which was more guitar-heavy, with some subtle conga work. The result was Taylor's sole U.S. Number 1 – and a not unpleasant reminder for King of the days when she used to provide hits for others.

TAKE GOOD CARE OF CAROLE KING

Carole King enjoys a rare distinction. She is one of the few non-performing composers to have reinvented herself as an artist. Once synonymous with Brill Building pop through her songwriting partnership with husband Gerry Goffin, she subsequently stepped triumphantly into the spotlight herself with the album *Tapestry*, a record that seemed to reside in every home during the early 1970s.

Goffin & King were almost a mirror image of their friends and fellow Aldon Music writers Barry Mann & Cynthia Weil. Whereas Mann & Weil had a man who wrote melodies and a woman who gave them lyrics, Goffin & King had the reverse operational procedure. In fact, this produced one of the more intriguing head-scratchers of rock history: when the pair achieved their first success by providing The Shirelles with a U.S. chart-topper in 1961 with 'Will You Love Me Tomorrow' – a will-he-still-respect-me-in-the-morning rumination with a beautiful pizzicato string arrangement – many were amazed that Goffin could write with such sensitivity from a female perspective.

Before embarking on that career as a freelance writer, King had tried it as a solo without success – and one of her discs, 'Oh Neil,' was an answer-song to 'Oh Carol,' which Neil Sedaka had written for her. A selection of her collaborations with Goffin constitutes an almost ridiculously familiar litany of catchy and memorable songs: 'Crying In The Rain' (The Everly Brothers); 'Don't Bring Me Down' (The Animals); 'I'm Into Something Good' (Herman's Hermits); 'The Loco-Motion' (Little Eva); 'One Fine Day' (The Chiffons); 'Pleasant Valley Sunday' (The Monkees); 'Take Good Care Of My Baby' (Bobby Vee); 'Up On The Roof' (The Drifters); and 'A Natural Woman (You Make Me Feel Like)' (Aretha Franklin). 'The Loco-Motion' was a U.S. Top 3 in three successive decades: Grand Funk and Kylie Minogue successfully resurrecting it in the 1970s and '80s. Meanwhile, 'Chains' by The Cookies only made a U.S. Number 17 but was later covered by The Beatles on their first album, a lucrative occurrence for Goffin & King.

King had secured a solo hit in '62 with 'It Might As Well Rain Until September' but her career as a recording artist did not take off until she and Goffin parted company in the late 1960s, following which she formed part of a trio called The City. Now forgotten, they put out an album containing 'Hi-De-Ho,' a hit for Blood Sweat & Tears, and 'I Wasn't Born To Follow,' which became not only a highlight of The Byrds' *Notorious Byrd Brothers* album but also a key song in the movie *Easy Rider*.

In 1971, James Taylor had a transatlantic hit with King's song 'You've Got A Friend.' It had been Taylor who encouraged her to record solo material, and phenomenal success ensued from that suggestion. From that point on King's career was really as an albums artist, although it included a U.S. Number 1 single in 'It's Too Late.' *Tapestry* was the longest charting album of all time by a female artist.

below > Carole King, producer Lou Adler (center), and James Taylor (right), pictured during sessions for King's hugely successful *Tapestry* album at A&M studios in 1970.

Heart Of Gold
Neil Young

Released February 1972
Reprise *1065* (U.S. #1) / K *14140* (U.K. #10)

Neil Young's only U.S. Number 1 hit single remains a classic of the early 1970s singer-songwriter genre. Ever contrary, however, its author spent the ensuing years – until he began to mellow slightly in the 1990s – doggedly making anything but a follow-up.

Young was a member of the seminal country-rock group Buffalo Springfield and also part of a 'supergroup' alongside David Crosby, Stephen Stills, and Graham Nash before his solo career began to take off. His first truly great album was his third full-length effort, *After The Gold Rush*, which yielded the minor hit 'Only Love Can Break Your Heart.' The follow-up was *Harvest*, from which 'Heart Of Gold' was taken, and this album was a strange assortment of disparate recordings made with different musicians, ranging from the heavily orchestrated 'A Man Needs A Maid' to the hard rock 'Words (Between The Lines Of Age).'

Stuck slap-bang in the middle of this, like the proverbial diamond in the rough, is this sweet, country-tinged single. 'Heart Of Gold' is driven by Young's strident acoustic guitar and the drumming of noted session player Kenny Buttrey (whose other credits include Bob Dylan's *Blonde On Blonde* album). Added color is provided by steel guitarist Ben Keith and backing vocals from Linda Ronstadt and James Taylor.

Topped off by one of Young's most haunting, memorable melodies, sung in his usual broken voice, the single became his biggest hit in Britain and the U.S. but served only to make him determined not to record anything else with such a mainstream sheen. As he wrote in the sleevenotes to his *Decade* anthology: "This song put me in the middle of the road. Traveling there soon became a bore so I headed for the ditch. A rougher ride, but I met more interesting people there."

Take It Easy
The Eagles

Released May 1972
Asylum *11005* (U.S. #12) / Asylum *AYM 505* (U.K.)

Ironically, 'Take Is Easy' – the record that broke The Eagles – is really more of a Jackson Browne song. He penned the bulk of this number, including that unforgettable opener about running down the road trying to loosen his load with seven women on his mind: "Four that wanna own me / Two that wanna stone me / One says she's a friend of mine."

At the time Browne was living in the apartment below that of Glenn Frey, whose band The Eagles were just out of the blocks. Browne's somewhat anxious and self-deprecating verses were balanced out by a new verse from Frey in which he boasts about a woman noticeably taking an interest in him. Few probably noticed the 'join,' distracted by the streamlined and feel-good vibe of this perfect highway-cruising music.

A George Jones fan would probably not consider the record to be anything other than straightahead rock, but there was a noticeable 'twanginess' to it that would have surprised the average rock-radio listener. It is possibly The Eagles' greatest achievement that pretty soon the surprise at such rural inflections on the pop charts would be something that people didn't even think about – indicated by the fact that *Their Greatest Hits 1971-1975* would become the biggest-selling album of the 20th century. Up to the late 1960s, rock was so associated with radicalism and country with conservatism that country-rock was a tag that made as much sense as communist-fascism.

Listen To The Music
The Doobie Brothers

Released August 1972
Warners *7619* (U.S. #11) / Warners K *16208* (U.K. #29)

The Doobies' second album *Toulouse Street* adhered to their previous formula of soft boogie but intensified the punch, in part thanks to their recruitment of a second drummer. The LP led off with 'Listen To The Music.' The riff had been used on 'Feelin' Down Farther,' a track on the group's debut album, but was transferred here to acoustic guitar, now strapped to a lyric celebrating the soothing qualities of music and given a little gimmick with a dash of a whoosing 'phased' sound effect. A version that edited out the virtuosity was released as a single (two years later in Britain) and lucratively established the band as competitors to soft rock acts such as The Eagles.

You're So Vain
Carly Simon

Released November 1972
Elektra *45824* (U.S. #1) / Elektra K *12077* (U.K. #3)

Along with Carole King, Carly Simon was in the vanguard of a new generation of female singer-songwriters that emerged in the early 1970s: confessional, literate, mature, yet pop-savvy. She had been seen in the charts before 'You're So Vain' but it was this single that really established her reputation. It had an irresistible chorus paired with a lyric that shines an unforgiving light on the self-obsession of celebrity, and became a huge international hit.

The frank tone of the words seemed to leave little doubt that the song was autobiographical, but who was she singing about? Was it Mick Jagger? Or Warren Beatty? Or Kris Kristofferson, maybe? Rumors abounded, while Simon herself kept teasingly quiet, dropping the odd hint and red herring. More than 30 years later she still won't say. One person she said it definitely wasn't about, though, was fellow singer-songwriter James Taylor, whom she married one month before the song hit number 1 in America.

The First Time Ever I Saw Your Face
Roberta Flack

Released February 1972
Atlantic *2864* (U.S. #1) / Atlantic *K 10161* (U.K. #14)

Scottish-born folk artist Ewan MacColl composed this song for his wife Peggy Seeger (half-sister of the folk singer Pete) in 1957. Peggy was performing in a play in the U.S. at the time, and legend has it that MacColl, who'd written this eulogy of undying love in under an hour, sang it to his wife down the telephone. MacColl was probably just as surprised as Roberta Flack when his song went to Number 1 in America some 15 years after it had been composed.

Recorded in 1969, the song became a hit in 1972 after it had featured in the Clint Eastwood movie *Play Misty For Me*. In the wake of Flack's success with the song came a number of sugary cover versions by artists such as Engelbert Humperdinck, Andy Williams, and Mantovani. MacColl is on record as particularly hating Elvis Presley's version. 'The First Time Ever I Saw Your Face' won two Grammy awards, for Song Of The Year and Record Of The Year, awards Ms. Flack was to win again the following year for her next big hit, 'Killing Me Softly With His Song.'

Puppy Love
Donny Osmond

Released February 1972
MGM *14367* (U.S. #3) / MGM *2006 104* (U.K. #1)

Behind the lightweight image of The Osmonds there was real musical talent. They all played instruments and wrote some of their own material. In fact, the family would probably be outraged that this single – a Donny solo 45 that was a syrupy cover of an old Paul Anka song – is the sole representation in this book of the Osmonds phenomenon of the early 1970s. It became the best known song associated with any of them, and thus marked the point at which they took an irrevocable step, after which they would be remembered not as purveyors of classy rock songs like 'Crazy Horses' but of fodder for teenyboppers.

Amazing Grace
The Pipes & Drums & Military Band Of
The Royal Scots Dragoon Guards

Released March 1972
RCA *0709* (U.S. #11) / RCA *2191* (U.K. #1)

Perhaps the most surprising thing about this British Number 1 is that it also made the U.S Top 20. While bagpipes arouse some nationalistic emotions in Britain (or more specifically, in Scotland) they are not often heard on American Top 40 radio. The song was composed in 1779 by the Reverend John Newton and had already been a transatlantic hit in a stunning a cappella version by Judy Collins that spent 67 weeks lingering in the U.K charts between 1970 and 1972. Formed in 1678, The Royal Scots Dragoon Guards can take pride in being the oldest established act ever to hit the charts. Those 294 years it took them to get a hit will certainly take some beating. Unfortunately, they won't be having any more hits since they were amalgamated into another unit in 1994. Younger readers will be familiar with this tune because it forms the basis of All Saints' late-1990s hit 'Never Ever.'

My Ding-A-Ling
Chuck Berry

Released August 1972
Chess *2131* (U.S. #1) / Chess *6145 019* (U.K. #1)

Chuck Berry might have written some of the greatest and most covered entries in the rock canon, but his biggest hit as a performer was with this novelty song. 'My Ding A Ling' was edited from a longer live recording made in the distinctly un-rock'n'roll setting of Coventry, England, and is a faintly sinister combination of infantile singalong and risqué lyric. Who could resist one of the founding fathers of rock'n'roll inviting us to play with his 'ding-a-ling'? Hardly anyone, it seems, as the song topped the U.K. and U.S. charts and went gold, giving Berry an unexpected second commercial wind well into the middle years of his career. A second transatlantic Top 30 hit, 'Reelin' & Rockin',' taken from the same live recording, followed in early 1973.

In A Broken Dream
Python Lee Jackson

Released September 1972
GNP Crescendo *449* (U.S) / Youngblood *YB 1002* (U.K. #3)

If the vocalist on this song sounds naggingly familiar, that's because it is none other than Rod Stewart. Back in 1968, British DJ John Peel signed Australian band Python Lee Jackson to his Dandelion label and asked his friend Rod Stewart to record a guide vocal for them. The track remained unreleased because the band's singer, Dave Bentley, never got around to recording his own vocal. The producer of the session, Miki Dallon, bought the tapes from Peel, sensing their worth, and released the song as a single on his own Youngblood label in 1970. It was ignored, but two years later Stewart was a major international star – enough to push a re-released 'In A Broken Dream' high up the U.K. charts.

The Cover Of Rolling Stone
Dr. Hook & The Medicine Show

Released November 1972
Columbia *45732* (U.S. #6) / CBS *1037* (U.K.)

Written by band manager Shel Silverstein, the song documents the frustration of a generically stoned and decadent rock group who fail to ever make the prestigious appearance on the front of the rock journal. Its non-appearance on the U.K. chart was due to the BBC refusing to play a track they considered to be advertising (despite Dr. Hook playfully recording a special promo version, 'The Cover Of Radio Times,' referring to the BBC's listings magazine). Ironically, Dr. Hook did appear on the cover of *Rolling Stone* in March 1973, after the single became a hit. When the band dropped 'Medicine Show' from their name and no longer recorded Silverstein songs, they became purveyors of the type of soporific weepie that Silverstein had intended to parody with their debut, 'Sylvia's Mother.'

Rockin' Robin
Michael Jackson

Released March 1972
Motown *1197* (U.S. #2) / Tamla Motown *TMG 816* (U.K. #3)

He would become the biggest-selling solo artist of all time, but Michael Jackson was already something of a chart veteran when he first struck out on his own, at the age of just 13, in late 1971. His second solo single – following the international hit ballad 'Got To Be There' – was 'Rockin' Robin,' a classic of 1970s Motown.

Most of Jackson's full-length debut album, *Got To Be There*, was overseen by The Corporation, the team of Motown writers, arrangers, and producers that included the label's founder, Berry Gordy. 'Rockin' Robin,' however, was the work of a relatively unknown duo, Mel Larson and Jerry Marcellino, who took Bobby Day's 1958 novelty hit and turned it into a bright, funky, pop smash.

While Michael continued to record and perform with The Jackson 5 throughout the 1970s, the future King Of Pop scored three further hits in 1972, including his first solo U.S. Number 1, 'Ben.'

Papa Was A Rollin' Stone
The Temptations

Released October 1972
Gordy *7121* (U.S. #1) / Tamla Motown *TMG 839* (U.K. #14)

During Motown's 1960s domination of the black-music market, The Temptations were the main male rivals to The Four Tops, their hits stretching from 1964 until 1985, by which time the Tops had long since left the company.

During the early part of the Temps' career, the hits were supplied by Smokey Robinson, one of Motown's most prolific and respected writers, but by 1966 their recordings fell under the guiding hands of rising writer-producer Norman Whitfield. After Whitfield teamed up with co-writer Barrett Strong in 1967, the duo delivered some classic hits for the group. 'Cloud Nine' was the first of a string of psychedelic-soul songs with politically aware lyrics by Whitfield and Strong, who followed through with 'I Can't Get Next To You,' 'Psychedelic Shack,' and 'Ball Of Confusion (That's What The World Is Today).'

Whitfield's funk masterpiece is without doubt his 1972 creation, 'Papa Was A Rollin' Stone.' Clocking in at almost seven minutes, the song runs for almost two minutes before the vocals begin.

Dennis Edwards, lead vocalist on the song, was far from happy at the recording session. He recalled: "It upset me. I kept asking: When do I come in, when do I come in? I got so mad that I sang [the song's opening lines]: 'It was the third of September / That day I'll always remember' very tightly, not my usual style. But Norman was real good at psyching us up, and I realized it was the attitude he wanted. I was wrong about that record – I'm glad I was wrong."

The end result is best described as a soul symphony, the fine vocal arrangement combining with Whitfield's subtle production to make it one of The Temptations' most successful records – and even the era-identifying wah-wah guitars have failed to date this remarkable recording.

Superstition
Stevie Wonder

Released October 1972
Tamla *54226* (U.S. #1) / Tamla Motown *TMG 841* (U.K. #11)

'Superstition' is an R&B-funk classic that captures Stevie Wonder in the midst of his prolific early-20s. It was his first U.S. Number 1 for almost a decade, following his 1963 breakthrough hit 'Fingertips (Part 2).' He had spent the 1960s as a fairly typical – albeit highly talented – Motown star, chalking up hits like 'I Was Made To Love Her' and 'My Cherie Amour.' After his initial contract with the label expired on his 21st birthday, in May 1971, he was at first reluctant to sign again: like Marvin Gaye, he was dissatisfied at the lack of creative control the label offered him. By the end of the year, however, he had convinced Motown head Berry Gordy of his abilities and was given permission to write, arrange, record, and produce the subsequent *Music Of My Mind* LP himself.

Music Of My Mind was the first of five classic albums recorded by Wonder in an intensive five-year period that demonstrated his abilities as one of the most dazzlingly inventive musicians and songwriters of the 1970s. Soon after, he started work on *Talking Book*, for which one of his principal collaborators was guitarist Jeff Beck. 'Superstition' arose while the pair were jamming in the studio. Beck came up with the drum groove, Wonder the distinctive clavinet riff. Wonder originally offered the song to Beck, but saw so much promise in the guitar man's version that he decided to issue it as a single himself, much to the annoyance of Beck's label.

'Superstition' has a blend of funk, rock, and R&B that opened up Wonder's appeal to a white audience, and with the single on top of the *Billboard* Hot 100 he received an invitation to tour with and regularly jam onstage alongside The Rolling Stones. A host of other great singles followed over the next few years, but the double-Grammy-winning 'Superstition' remains the pick of the bunch.

Superfly
Curtis Mayfield

Released November 1972
Curtom *1978* (U.S. #8) / Buddah *2011 156* (U.K.)

During the racially explosive 1960s, Curtis Mayfield, as a member of The Impressions, delivered some of the finest musical social-commentaries of the age, including his compositions 'People Get Ready,' 'Keep On Pushing,' and 'Choice Of Colors.' What is more, these were songs filled with optimism. He continued on the same path after leaving The Impressions in 1970, and his solo debut album included his later U.K. hit 'Move On Up,' which inexplicably was not released as a single in America.

Following the success of *Shaft* and its accompanying soundtrack by Isaac Hayes there was a rash of what we now call blaxploitation movies. *Superfly* may not have been the best of these – it concerned the morally questionable and not particularly original story of a Harlem dealer out one last coup – but it certainly fielded the finest soundtrack.

Rather than glorifying the *Superfly* story, Mayfield, who felt the movie was something of an infomercial for cocaine, chose to deliver a series of anti-drug messages that were beautifully arranged and orchestrated, in stark contrast to the on-screen activities. 'Freddie's Dead,' which did not in fact appear in the movie, was a bigger hit, while the title track rose to Number 8 in America and the soundtrack LP spent four weeks at Number 1. The cornerstone blaxploitation soundtrack, regardless of the movie it was made to enhance, *Superfly* is a classic album that stands as Mayfield's finest creation.

Virginia Plain
Roxy Music

Released August 1972
Reprise *1124* (U.S.) / Island *WIP 6144* (U.K. #4)

Roxy Music's debut single sounded like nothing else in 1972, and still doesn't, despite a host of imitators. In their formative years, the group was often lumped in with the British glam-rock scene of the time, but it was evident from the opening bars of 'Virginia Plain' that Roxy had a much more cultured, intellectual sound than that of the bulk of their contemporaries.

The single opens with frontman Bryan Ferry frantically stabbing at his piano and Phil Manzanera beating ugly sounds from his fuzz-toned guitar. Drummer Paul Thompson and bassist Rik Kenton (who was only in the band for six months, and as such appeared only on this single) give the song a firm rhythmic foundation before Ferry introduces his unusual warbling croon, giving voice to a lyric that's part Lou Reed street hustle and part F. Scott Fitzgerald glitz and glamor. What pushes the song even further from the standard fare of the time are the contributions of the group's other two members: Andy Mackay flits between saxophone and oboe, while sound-manipulator and keyboardist Eno coaxes all manner of unearthly sounds from his banks of high-tech machinery.

Roxy Music benefited from a visual appeal to match their ambitious sound, particularly in the case of Ferry, the dapper fop, and the ever-eccentric Eno, who spent much of the period dressed like a futuristic peacock. Although it would take some time for significant American success to arrive, 'Virginia Plain' gave the group a debut hit in the U.K., where their first LP *Roxy Music* also reached the Top 10. They followed it early in 1973 with 'Pjamarama' and a second, equally successful album, *For Your Pleasure*.

right > Roxy Music performing on the BBC TV show *Full House* on November 25th, 1972. Left to right: Phil Manzanera, Eno, Andy Mackay, Rik Kenton, Bryan Ferry, and Paul Thompson (hidden behind a cymbal).

Rock And Roll (Part 1) /
Rock And Roll (Part 2)
Gary Glitter

Released March 1972
Bell *45237* (U.S. #7) / Bell *1216* (U.K. #2)

Paul Gadd had leapt on every passing bandwagon during the 1960s before finally finding a place for his over-the-top showmanship as British glam-rock icon Gary Glitter (other names under consideration were Stanley Sparkle, Terry Tinsel, and Vicky Vomit). Between 1960 and 1971 he'd recorded unsuccessfully for Decca, Parlophone, and MCA and worked as a warm-up act on British television's *Ready Steady Go!* pop show. In 1971 he teamed up with producer Mike Leander, with whom he'd been associated since 1961, and created a 15-minute stomp-and-shout piece of nonsense, edited down to a two-part single as 'Rock And Roll (Parts 1 & 2).'

It was the mostly instrumental 'Part 2' that hit the charts after some three months on release, assisted by Gary's performance in glitter suits, ludicrously tight trousers, and platform boots, all the while displaying his hairy chest and wearing a permanently astonished expression. A stream of similar follow-ups included three British Number 1s, although this would be his only sizeable hit in the U.S., where 'Part 2' was used widely as a sports anthem. The one time 'Leader Of The Gang' has since fallen out of favor following his conviction in the U.K. for possession of child pornography in 1999 and subsequent imprisonment in Vietnam on charges of sexual abuse of minors in 2006.

Tumbling Dice
The Rolling Stones

Released April 1972
Rolling Stones *19103* (U.S. #7, U.K. #5)

By 1972, The Rolling Stones were past masters at the classic single. Which is why many were bewildered when they unleashed 'Tumbling Dice,' a seemingly lethargic, slovenly, almost tuneless recording with indecipherable lyrics. On first hearing, everything sounds inadequate, particularly as it lurches through three different tempos in its opening bars and mixes different elements like female backing coos and guitar lines that fall in and out of focus. That the track marched into the upper reaches of the world's charts was ascribed by many to the goodwill that the group's back-catalogue had engendered in the buying public.

When the song's parent album, *Exile On Main Street*, emerged the following month, the single begun to make a bit more sense. It was certainly representative of that long player's exhausted, sluggish, and frayed timbre. This was due to the fact that part of the album (not all, as has often been assumed) was recorded in stultifying conditions in the basement of Keith Richards's rented French mansion Nellcote – and then sometimes overdubbed in his crowded, clattering kitchen. 'Dice' started life as 'Good Time Women' in 1970 at Jagger's English house. It was re-recorded at Nellcote in the summer of 1971, with a new lyric and a drunken ambience that – irony of ironies given later personnel changes – was reminiscent of the style of Stones wannabes The Faces. 'Tumbling Dice' began to make further sense as the fans realized that, like the album, its scuffed, inchoate nature assumed a real charm once the listener got used to such unprofessional methods.

School's Out
Alice Cooper

Released May 1972
Warner Bros. *7596* (U.S. #7) / Warner Bros. *K 16188* (U.K. #1)

For a brief period, Alice Cooper (then a band, not a person) were considered to be as scandalous as Elvis or The Sex Pistols at the height of their respective notoriety. One reason was the genuinely disturbing streaked mascaraed face of their frontman. Another was the group's macabre stage shows, involving guillotines and snakes. And another was this record. Although its anti-education sentiment now sounds dated, at the time it still bothered a generation who had been in power before the 1960s became permissive and who were not yet retired.

Cooper frontman Vince Furnier was inspired to write the lyric of 'School's Out' when he saw an old movie in which a character called Mugs whacked someone around the head while enunciating the phrase. The cartoon-like nature of this bad boy's anthem is illustrated by the line at the end of a litany of boasts about their rebellious acts: "We can't even think of a word that rhymes!" Guitarist Glen Buxton provided a fine dirty-guitar riff while producer Bob Ezrin kept the metal this side of pop.

Despite the quality of the record, it was a surprise when its commercial success and scandal-mongering carried over to Britain (where moral guardian Mary Whitehouse wanted it banned). "We got no class / And we got no principles" was a pun that made no sense in the U.K., where heads of schools were not principals but headmasters or headmistresses. And the phrase "school's out" is not part of the lexicon in Britain, where schools instead "break up."

Silver Machine
Hawkwind

Released June 1972
United Artists *50949* (U.S.) / United Artists *UP 35381* (U.K. #3)

If ever a band was known for just one song, it's Hawkwind. Yet while they have rarely troubled the chart compilers since the release of 'Silver Machine,' the group has enjoyed a successful career for three decades, courtesy of a fanatical following for their virtually unique 'space rock.'

'Silver Machine' was a co-write between Dave Brock and Bob Calvert, who had joined the group in the month that the song was recorded at a Greasy Truckers party at London's Roundhouse in February 1972. It posits the titular spacecraft as a girl-pulling device on the level of a Porsche.

Hawkwind had begun life as Group X in 1969, springing from the thriving hippie community then in Notting Hill Gate, west London. Yet it was the distinctly un-hippie Lemmy who sang the vocal on 'Silver Machine.' Calvert, poet-in-residence and sometime vocalist, had been sectioned under mental health legislation for 28 days and the band, who found his BBC English vocal style laughable, took advantage of this by wiping his singing and having the future Motorhead frontman replace it.

It was the prevailing tradition (in the U.K., at least) rather than hippie idealism that led the band to not include the track on their next album, although the full Roundhouse version – with Calvert on vocals and running to eight minutes – appeared on the contemporary various-artists triple LP *Glastonbury Fayre*.

Hocus Pocus
Focus

Released October 1972
Sire *704* (U.S. #9) / Polydor *2001 211* (U.K #20)

Focus was one of a handful of Dutch groups including Shocking Blue and Golden Earring who found chart success on both sides of the Atlantic in the early 1970s. Featuring Jan Akkerman on guitar and Thijs van Leer on flute, keyboards, and vocals, the mostly instrumental group had classical leanings, with flavors of The Nice and Jethro Tull. 'Hocus Pocus' was recorded in London with British blues producer Mike Vernon as something of a joke that came about during a studio jam session. On the spur of the moment, not wishing to be outdone by the rest of the band's improvisation, Leer decided to yodel, something he claimed he had never done before. Vernon recalled: "It used to look more painful than it was in reality – he was bright red by the time he'd finished yodeling the high bit." This edited version of the six-and-a-half-minute original recorded in 1971 became a hit when a later single, 'Sylvia,' climbed the British charts early in 1973. The U.S. version of 'Hocus Pocus' was a completely different mix.

The Jean Genie
David Bowie

Released November 1972
RCA *0838* (U.S.) / RCA *2302* (U.K. #2)

This playfully androgynous hit cemented David Bowie's position among the leading lights of British music and capped a remarkable 12 months for its author. In the final weeks of 1971 he issued the slow-burning *Hunky Dory* LP and its resplendent single, 'Changes,' quickly following them both with the landmark concept album *The Rise And Fall Of Ziggy Stardust And The Spiders From Mars*. For that album he 'became' the title character, blurring – or perhaps erasing – the line between the performer and his songs.

Like the album *Aladdin Sane* that it trailed, 'The Jean Genie' is a more robust, refined take on the *Ziggy Stardust* material. Bowie's backing trio – still trading as The Spiders From Mars – had by now achieved an incredible synchronicity with their leader and, noting this, producer Ken Scott refrained from any unnecessary sonic bells and whistles, limiting his contribution to capturing a great band and song. The single is propelled forward by Mick Ronson's corrosive lead guitar and Trevor Bolder's swaggering bass, underpinned by Mick Woodmansey's tight, uncluttered drumming. Bowie himself contributes intermittent harmonica as well as a fervent vocal, pleading with the Jean Genie to "let yourself go!"

'The Jean Genie' was Bowie's highest charting single so far in the U.K., arriving just as glam-rock began to dominate the airwaves there. As it hung around on the charts in the early months of 1973, it was joined by significant hits for artists including T. Rex, The Sweet, and Slade. While most of his peers' careers would fall into decline by the mid 1970s, Bowie's went from strength to strength as he recorded a series of diverse, innovative albums throughout the decade and beyond.

Whiskey In The Jar
Thin Lizzy

Released November 1972
London *20076* (U.S.) / Decca F *13355* (U.K. #6)

Irish rockers Thin Lizzy scored their debut hit with this reworking of a traditional folk song. At the time the band was a three-piece fronted by bassist and singer Phil Lynott, whose gruff but tender tones give the single much of its appeal. But the record's dominant feature is a melodic electric guitar refrain and a ringing solo by Eric Bell. He left Thin Lizzy shortly after 'Whiskey' charted in Britain, complaining that the band was becoming too commercial. Lynott, meanwhile, waited three years before returning to the singles charts with his reconfigured group and 'The Boys Are Back In Town,' with Bell replaced by not one, but two lead guitarists.

Walk On The Wild Side
Lou Reed

Released November 1972
RCA *0887* (U.S. #16) / RCA *2303* (U.K. #10)

The history of popular music is overflowing with records that might have become big hits were it not for their 'obscene' lyrics and the ensuing radio ban. But 'Walk On The Wild Side' managed to slip through the censors' nets, despite its reference to "giving head," and became Lou Reed's greatest solo success.

Few expected much of a solo career from Reed after he left The Velvet Underground in 1970. His former group had yet to gain the recognition it holds today, and Reed himself seemed unlikely to buck that trend by setting out on his own. One of his few fans at the time, however, was David Bowie, the rising star of British glam-rock, who helped Reed get a deal with RCA. (Bowie gave another of his cult heroes, Iggy Pop, a similar leg-up the following year.)

Bowie and his guitarist, Mick Ronson, then produced Reed's second solo album, *Transformer*. Cleaner and more melodic than any of Reed's earlier work, the album contains some of his best-loved solo work, including 'Perfect Day' and 'Satellite Of Love.' Even more memorable is 'Walk On The Wild Side.' Pretty much everything about the song is exactly right, from Herbie Flowers's lugubrious bass to the "colored girls" cooing backing vocals and, of course, Reed's straight-talking lyric, which didn't deviate much from the subject matter of his Velvet Underground output – drugs, gender confusion, and so on – but was well served by a refined, calmer setting.

All Because Of You
Geordie

Released March 1973
MGM *14539* (U.S.) / EMI *2008* (U.K. #6)

Geordie would be remembered simply as glam-rock also-rans if it wasn't for the presence of one Brian Johnson on lead vocals. After his first band's 15 minutes of fame, Johnson re-emerged in 1980 as the replacement for Bon Scott, recently-deceased vocalist of AC/DC. The Australian metal monsters became one of a very few big bands not only to survive the death of a totemic member but also to get even bigger afterwards. "Just look at me now I'm shouting," pronounced Johnson on this, the biggest of Geordie's four minor U.K. hits. Over 30 years later he is still shouting, his gritty tones having graced some of rock's best-selling albums.

I Wish It Could Be Christmas Everyday
Wizzard

Released November 1973
Not issued U.S. / Harvest *HAR 5079* (U.K. #3)

Merry Xmas Everybody
Slade

Released December 1973
Warner Bros. *7759* (U.S.) / Polydor *2058 422* (U.K. #1)

This year saw two of the kings of British glam-rock tussling for the top of the charts with Christmas records. By now, Wizzard's frontman Roy Wood was on his third noteworthy band. He had made his name with pop-psychedelic outfit The Move and helped form the Electric Light Orchestra. With Wizzard he married grandiose Spector-pop to an image that brought to mind a simian antecedent of Ziggy Stardust.

Blockbuster
The Sweet

Released January 1973
RCA *45361* (U.S.) / RCA *2305* (U.K. #1)

Someone once described the British glam-rock bands of the 1970s as "bricklayers in leotards." Never was this description more apt than in the case of The Sweet, four out-of-condition, beer-drinking journeymen done up in sequins, satin, and make-up. Although the band had been doing the rounds as Sweetshop in the 1960s, it wasn't until 1971 and with their newly truncated name that they started to get some chart action with their hybrid of bubblegum pop and heavy metal. A string of 15 British hit singles lasted through most of the decade, many penned by glam-rock's songwriting maestros, Nicky Chinn and Mike Chapman.

Some British glam acts found that their style just didn't translate into American, but The Sweet were an exception, becoming a big live draw and chart act there. The truth was, leaving aside the comically garish presentation, the band's records were well-crafted, catchy pop-rock that sat well on U.S. playlists, not a million miles from Alice Cooper or even very early Aerosmith.

'Blockbuster' was the band's biggest U.K. hit and a conundrum for those whose musical judgments were too influenced by notions of what was and wasn't critically acceptable, and who would otherwise dismiss The Sweet as pop lightweights. The song was based on an old blues riff, the same one that the ultra-hip David Bowie had pinched for 'The Jean Genie' just a few months earlier.

Slade, meanwhile, were the biggest band of the British glam-rock era, notching up an impressive seventeen Top-20 singles in a five-year stretch in the 1970s, plus a few more during their second coming in the 1980s. Among the best of these was 'Cum On Feel The Noize,' with its deliberately misspelled title (a Slade trademark) and shout-along chorus reinforcing the band's cartoon yob image. But where close rivals like The Sweet gamely tapped into the international language of rock androgyny and saw chart action outside their homeland, Slade, with their soccer-terrace rock, remained a peculiarly British phenomenon.

The title of Wood's creation is the almost verbatim sentiment expressed by children, and indeed many adults, as they bask in spiritual mellowness (and gifts) each Yuletide. But that didn't make the record any less a stroke of quasi-genius. Wood insisted that a kids' choir was transported from his native Birmingham for chorus work on the recording session.

Slade's record started life as a psychedelic leftover from the 1960s called 'Ride Yourself A Rocking Chair,' the tune of which was cannibalized when bassist Jim Lea's grandmother lamented the fact that nobody wrote Christmas songs any more. No doubt granny Lea was pleased at the sudden plenitude of Christmas records – and the fact that it was Slade who won the battle for Number 1.However, both Wizzard and Slade emerged in artistic triumph, each having managed to create a song that perfectly captured the tearfully happy atmosphere of the holiday season.

above left > The Sweet performing on *Top Of The Pops* in 1973.
below left > Slade on the same show.
right > Wizzard frontman Ron Wood.

TOP OF THE POPS: THE BRITISH CHARTS ON TV

Nothing has had more influence over single sales in the U.K. than the BBC's long-running television show, *Top Of The Pops*. Over 2,000 editions of the chart program aired between 1964 and 2006, but it was not considered very promising when it began. It was first shown on January 1, 1964, commissioned for a run of just six shows. Nonetheless, it was a hit from the start, thanks to a tight format that has been imitated in numerous countries across the world. Each show includes a rundown of the week's bestselling records, in reverse order, and ends with the current Number 1. In between, there are live appearances by acts, miming to their records with different degrees of accuracy and enthusiasm, and filmed sequences. In the heyday of the show, various troupes of dancers – of which the most famous was Pan's People – would perform choreographed sequences to accompany records by acts who were not available to appear and had not supplied films.

Thanks to its huge family audience – for many years the show was a fixture in the main BBC-1 evening schedule – *Top Of The Pops* succeeded in attracting the big names right from the beginning. The very first edition, broadcast from a converted church hall in Manchester, opened with The Rolling Stones performing 'I Wanna Be Your Man' and continued with Dusty Springfield, The Dave Clark Five, The Hollies, and The Swinging Blue Jeans. There were filmed items from Cliff Richard & The Shadows, Freddie & The Dreamers, and, in the Number 1 slot, The Beatles with 'I Want To Hold Your Hand.'

In 1967, the program moved to the BBC's London studios, and DJs from the broadcaster's new pop channel, Radio One, took over presentation duties. The format remained the same, however, and it proved remarkably accommodating to successive generations of artists. Even at the height of rock's album-led self-importance, *TOTP* retained its central role in the teenage market.

While some artists refused to appear because of the show's insistence on miming, others turned up but mocked the process: Les Gray of Mud once brought a ventriloquist's dummy on stage to 'sing' his lead vocal. However, an attempt in 1991 to introduce live vocals over pre-recorded backing tracks proved shortlived, thanks to atrocious performances. Nirvana's only appearance on the show, performing 'Smells Like Teen Spirit,' was during this era. Kurt Cobain sang in a low, mournful voice that he later claimed was a homage to Morrissey.

Over the years, the BBC extended the *Top Of The Pops* brand to take in various spin-off programs, a magazine, and separate programing for BBC Prime, the Beeb's satellite channel for Europe, Africa, and the Middle East. But as sales of singles fell, the show began to decline in popularity. After 40 years, it was moved in 2004 to BBC-2, the Corporation's second TV channel. Two years later, with a sad inevitability, it was announced that *Top Of The Pops* would be broadcast for the very last time on 30th July, 2006.

Frankenstein
The Edgar Winter Group

Released February 1973
Epic *10967* (U.S. #1) / Epic *EPC 1440* (U.K. #18)

Keyboardist Edgar Winter had played with his guitarist brother Johnny and in his own brass-based outfit White Trash before forming The Edgar Winter Group in 1972, kicking off with his debut Epic album *They Only Come Out At Night*. 'Frankenstein' was one of the greatest all-time rock instrumentals, featuring some nifty ARP synthesizer effects, and began life as a lengthy on-stage jam entitled 'The Double Drum Solo.' In the studio it was just as lengthy, and Winter and producer Rick Derringer spent hours chopping and editing down the master tape to an acceptable length. In fact it became something of a monster – which explains its final title. At first it was released as the B-side to the album's first single, 'Hangin' Around,' but was soon flipped by radio DJs and began a three-month climb to the summit of the U.S. charts.

Reelin' In The Years
Steely Dan

Released March 1973
ABC *11352* (U.S. #11) / Probe *PRO 587* (U.K.)

Led Zeppelin's Jimmy Page has said his all-time favorite guitar solo is the astonishingly euphoric confection of arpeggiated triads, multi-bends, pull-offs, slides, and hammer-ons immaculately executed by Elliott Randall on 'Reelin' In The Years.' And when Eric Clapton first heard it, he was so blown away that he wanted to meet the man responsible. Steely Dan was a pair of jobbing musos based in New York, Donald Fagen and Walter Becker. They fashioned a peerless catalogue of rock classics by the simple expedient of writing great songs, hiring only the finest session players to play them, and then testing these hapless virtuosi to distraction with endless re-takes in pursuit of perfection.

Famously, Becker & Fagen were huge jazz fans, but their working methods would obliterate the spontaneity essential to the creation of good jazz. Fagen countered that songs like 'Reelin' In The Years' were "composed and then improvised on." Randall seemed to confirm this, reporting that on his first day in the studio they simply asked him to pull off a solo that their regular guitarist hadn't managed in two days. However, the song is much more than a tune and some words hung around a killer solo. Fagen perfectly nails a near-impossible stream of inscrutable lyrics, the rhythm section is permafrost solid, and the whole construction is architecturally brilliant. Mind you, it must break Clapton and Page's hearts to learn that, in Randall's opinion, "The first solo I did on 'Reelin' In The Years' should have been the keeper. Unfortunately the record button wasn't on."

Yesterday Once More
The Carpenters

Released May 1973
A&M *1446* (U.S. #2) / A&M *AMS 7073* (U.K. #2)

This was just one of an impressive twenty American Top 40 hits that The Carpenters scored between 1970 and 1981, ten of which made the Top 3. At the height of their popularity in 1973 they shrewdly took advantage

of a nostalgia boom by recording a medley of 1960s hits on their album *Now & Then*. They had been doing the same thing during recent concerts to a very favorable response. The medley was cleverly linked together like a '60s U.S. radio show with a DJ adding inserts. Richard Carpenter recalled: "The 'oldies' were enjoying a resurgence in popularity during the early 1970s, much to the delight of Karen and me. I thought it would be nice to write a song about this and use the piece to bookend the [album's] oldies medley." The result was 'Yesterday Once More.'

Smoke On The Water
Deep Purple

Released May 1973
Warner *7710* (U.S. #4) / Purple *PUR 132* (U.K. #21)

'Smoke On The Water' was famously recorded in Montreux, Switzerland, following a fire at the Montreux Casino where Deep Purple were intending to tape their new album on the Rolling Stones mobile studio. The song was inspired by the sight of smoke from the fire drifting over Lake Geneva. Purple bassist Roger Glover came up with the title, and the lyric of this self-explanatory tale was completed by vocalist Ian Gillan. The track was cut when the band relocated to the Grand Hotel, closed for the winter season, and recorded in a hotel corridor with mattresses brought in for soundproofing.

Guitarist Ritchie Blackmore recalled that they were recording at such a high volume that "we were waking up the neighbors about five miles away." Police arrived en masse to put a stop to the session, but the group didn't let them in until they had finished the track to their satisfaction. Organist Jon Lord remembered the song's working title was 'Durh Durh Durh,' unsurprising given its guitar riff, probably the most famous in rock history. But the huge success of the song came as something of a surprise to the band.

Deep Purple had specifically written another track, 'Never Before,' as a likely single, and Gillan said he thought it was "the most commercial thing we'd ever done." However, it only reached Number 35 in the U.K. charts. Gillan also claimed that 'Smoke' was only recorded as a last-minute filler when they discovered they were a little short of material. Even with the finished recording in the can, the group didn't think it was anything out of the ordinary until U.S. radio DJs started highlighting the track. It became an American hit in 1973, with a live-in-Japan version on the B-side, but was not released as a single in Britain until 1977, by which time the legendary Mark 2 Deep Purple line-up had long since disbanded.

Let's Get It On
Marvin Gaye

Released June 1973
Tamla *54234* (U.S. #1) / Tamla Motown *TMG 868* (U.K. #31)

Following Marvin Gaye's stream-of-social-consciousness album, *What's Going On,* and his blaxploitation movie soundtrack *Trouble Man*, he returned to the subject closest to his heart for 'Let's Get It On.' This celebration of sex was inspired by his new love, Janis Hunter, the woman who would become wife number two. Co-writer Ed Townsend's original framework for the song had been about "getting on with life," but Gaye cut to the basics, leaving no doubt what he was talking about. The song spent two weeks atop the U.S. charts – showing how much had changed in just two years since Marc Bolan's 'Get It On' was considered too risqué a title for the American market and modified to 'Bang A Gong.'

Shortly afterwards Gaye made an album of duets with Diana Ross, and his career for the remainder of his lifetime was troubled, to say the least. He married Ms. Hunter in 1977, but the following year a slight disagreement with the I.R.S. over several million dollars in back taxes resulted in a particularly acrimonious divorce, which in turn led to Gaye's 1979 double album, *Here, My Dear*. This was literally presented to his departing wife as part of their divorce settlement. There then followed a severe drug problem for Gaye, and he eventually left Motown in 1981. Retreating to Ostend, Belgium, of all places (partly to avoid the I.R.S.), he managed to resurrect his career and return to the world's charts with the equally explicit 'Sexual Healing' in 1982.

While his career fluctuated between soul perfection (*What's Going On*) and willful self-indulgence (*Here, My Dear*), there's no doubt that Gaye possessed one of the finest voices in popular music. Sadly, his troubled life reached a bizarre conclusion when he was shot dead by his own father on April 1, 1984.

Knockin' On Heaven's Door
Bob Dylan

Released August 1973
Columbia *45913* (U.S. #12) / CBS *1762* (U.K. #14)

Following the release of *New Morning* (1970) the only official new Bob Dylan album in the next four years was his soundtrack to the Sam Peckinpah movie *Pat Garrett & Billy The Kid.* Dylan had a small but telling role as the eccentric Alias. He had also been approached to write a score, and was triumphant in this capacity. 'Knockin' On Heaven's Door,' a dark but beautiful composition for a death scene, not only obtained the producers more publicity than they may have hoped for, but also reassured Dylan fans despairing at his prolonged absence that his talent remained very much intact.

Rock On
David Essex

Released August 1973
Columbia *45940* (U.S. #5) / CBS *1693* (U.K. #3)

David Essex made many records following this inaugural 1973 hit but none has sounded like this echo-drenched and vaguely menacing creation. Essex wrote the song for the movie *That'll Be The Day*, in which he starred, but it was turned down by the producers on the grounds that its strangeness did not fit the film's 1950s retro tone, despite namechecking the likes of James Dean and 'Blue Suede Shoes.' Essex recorded it and gained a solo record that went Top 5 in the U.K. and U.S., surely one of the most skeletal and spooky concoctions to do so.

Hello It's Me
Todd Rundgren

Released September 1973
Bearsville *0009* (U.S. #5) / Bearsville *K 15513* (U.K.)

Rundgren had originally recorded this song with his 1960s power-pop band The Nazz, but re-worked it as a solo vehicle for his album *Something/Anything?*. Rundgren described his song as "just a dense arrangement of simple parts," built around a chord sequence lifted from jazz organist Jimmy Smith's version of 'When Johnny Comes Marching Home.'

It brought him his biggest chart success, but the ease with which he could knock off hits like this and 'I Saw The Light' soon led him to reject commercial music. After it peaked at Number 5 in *Billboard*, Rundgren refused to release anything else from the album and pursued cultish credibility instead.

Seasons In The Sun
Terry Jacks

Released December 1973
Bell *45432* (U.S. #1) / Bell *1344* (U.K. #1)

Hated and loved in equal intensity due to its unashamed sentimentality, this song is about a dying man saying his goodbyes to friend, father, and wife, with a pseudo-profound chorus kiss-off: "The hills that we climbed / Were just seasons out of time." The lyrics were an English translation by Rod McKuen of a Jacques Brel song, and the result was originally recorded by The Kingston Trio. Jacks had been upset by a friend's death and decided to put out his rendition on his own label, with huge success. It was not too much of a surprise when boy-band Westlife later recorded a U.K. chart-topping take of the song, but the version by grunge-meisters Nirvana amazed many fans. It turned out that the Terry Jacks single had been the first record Kurt Cobain ever bought.

Jungle Boogie
Kool & The Gang

Released November 1973
De-Lite *559* (U.S. #4) / Polydor *2001 500* (U.K.)

For those wishing to get down on the early-1970s pre-disco dancefloors there were no better records than those made by Kool & The Gang. The group delivered a string of strutting classics including 'Funky Stuff,' 'Jungle Boogie,' 'Hollywood Swingin',' and 'Spirit Of The Boogie,' horn-and-chant driven workouts that were an inspiration to many in the disco age. Surely K.C. & The Sunshine Band would never have existed without the groundwork of Kool & The Gang? The group would have even greater success some five years later with glossy, commercial, watered-down funk such as 'Celebration' and 'Ladies Night,' but these early sides were the genuine article. (U.K.-label sales suffered as the group's British company was slow to get records to market, allowing imports to sell instead.) 'Jungle Boogie' was the biggest of the Gang's early hits, and would feature in John Travolta's comeback movie *Pulp Fiction*. Now, blow that whistle and get down with the genies!

Tiger Feet
Mud

Released January 1974
Not issued U.S. / RAK *166* (U.K. #1)

British quartet Mud were merely a jobbing covers band when songwriters Nicky Chinn and Mike Chapman took them under their wing. At first the group were mere puppets, but at least they were afforded the privilege of playing on their own records after the first couple of releases. The decision was vindicated by their contributions to this U.K. Number 1 of early 1974.

While the bedrock of the record was the songwriting team's soccer-terrace chant melody and a lyric that reveled in its own meaninglessness and stupidity, the quite thunderous rhythm section and the sublime twin-guitar runs after each chorus, provided by Mud, contributed hugely to what is surely the quintessential Chinnichap glam-rock anthem.

Devil Gate Drive
Suzi Quatro

Released February 1974
Not issued U.S. / RAK *167* (U.K. #1)

Another major beneficiary of the Chinnichap midas touch was the American singer-bassist Suzi Quatro, who burst onto the U.K. singles chart in 1973 with a Number 1 hit, 'Can The Can,' penned by the songwriting duo. In the late 1960s Quatro had been a member of garage-rock girl group The Pleasure Seekers – which later became Cradle – alongside her sisters, Arlene, Patti, and Nancy. She moved to London in 1971 after being discovered by 1960s pop producer and RAK label boss Mickie Most. After 'Can The Can,' 'Devil Gate Drive' gave her a second U.K. chart-topper, and was one of 11 British Top 40 hits. While her records had little impact in the U.S., she did achieve a brief period of fame there in the late 1970s as a semi-regular guest star on *Happy Days*, and was a clear influence on later female rockers, among them Joan Jett.

A BALLROOM BLITZ WITH CHINN & CHAPMAN

Nicky Chinn and Mike Chapman were the premier songwriters and star-makers in Britain between 1973 and 1975 and became indelibly associated with a genre that came to be known as glam-rock. They had nothing to do with the glitter and sequins that adorned some of the acts for whom they wrote, but glam was also about a sound, and for this they certainly were responsible – although a nod should be given to Slade, one of the bands they didn't handle. Glam songs almost always sounded like anthems, shot though with the distinctly British flavor of a soccer-crowd singalong, with chanted vocals and thumping percussion. When the glam craze ended, the pair moved on effortlessly to other musical styles, with similar success.

Chinn was British, Chapman Australian, and they met in London in 1970. Chinn was a non-musician embarking on a career as a lyricist; guitarist Chapman was a member of a struggling band, Tangerine Peel. They had

a comfort zone thanks to the wealth of Chinn's family – Chinn financed their early demos – and they set about devising songs informed by what Chinn described as an "essential commerciality. Very, very pop indeed."

Early hits included an Archies-flavored jingle-pop number 'Funny Funny' (U.K. Top 20 for Sweet in 1971) and the downbeat and folk-ish 'Tom Tom Turnaround' (U.K. Number 6 for New World around the same time). Chinn & Chapman provided further hits for Sweet in 'Little Willy,' 'Co-Co,' and 'Poppa Joe,' but when they took the band into a more raucous style with the crunching 'Hellraiser,' 'Ballroom Blitz,' and 'Blockbuster' they began – unknowingly – to define an era in Britain.

The duo developed a formula of nonsensical but undeniably catchy and galvanizing rock'n'roll records, with lyrics chosen more for alliteration than linear coherency, which they gave to Mud ('Crazy,' 'Dyna-Mite,' and the titanic 'Tiger Feet' among them), Suzi Quatro ('Can The Can,' '48 Crash,' 'Devil Gate Drive') and Arrows ('A Touch Too Much').

Chinn & Chapman – or 'Chinnichap' as they became known collectively – came up with an Elvis-alike ballad, 'Lonely This Christmas,' which not only was a U.K. Yuletide Number 1 for Mud in 1974 but also proved they could write beyond the glam template. This versatility came in handy as glam started to fade in '74. Chinnichap were by now working on the start of a succession of fine hits for Smokie, boasting mellow tones and sophisticated words far removed from their earlier creations.

In the late 1970s, having racked up five U.K. chart-toppers as writers, the pair relocated to the States, a market that had proved largely immune both to glam and their songs. They secured U.S. chart placings with Huey Lewis, Tina Turner, and Exile, but before long the pair's partnership and friendship was ending. Chapman moved with great success into record production. Chinn experimented with different songwriting partners but, finding he wasn't enjoying the work as much as he had with Chapman, retired to tend a back catalogue that has continued to be lucrative, testament to the success of that "very, very pop indeed" sensibility.

Waterloo
Abba

Released April 1974
Atlantic *3055* (U.S. #6) / Epic *EPC 2240* (U.K. #1)

When Abba won the Eurovision Song Contest with 'Waterloo' it provided the group with a breakthrough international hit and set them on their way to become the quintessential singles act of the 1970s. Abba was formed in 1971 around the songwriting duo of Benny Andersson and Björn Ulvaeus and their partners Agnetha Fältskog and Anni-Frid Lyngstad. The following year, Andersson and Ulvaeus were encouraged by their manager to write a song for Lena Anderson, the Swedish entrant in the Eurovision Song Contest (usually just called 'Eurovision'). The pan-European televised event was first held in 1956 with the idea that each participating nation performs a song, with the winner chosen by viewers across the continent who vote by telephone. The contest is held in the country that provided the previous year's victor.

Having caught the Eurovision bug, Andersson and Ulvaeus entered Abba into the 1973 contest. Their song, 'Ring Ring,' failed to make it beyond the preliminary stages of the competition but gave a glimpse of what was to follow. It demonstrated for the first time the potent combination of Andersson and Ulvaeus's knack for a catchy tune, Fältskog and Lyngstad's sugary-sweet voices, and the Phil Spector-influenced production talents of Michael B. Tretow.

The following year found Abba (and Tretow) determined to win Eurovision and to use it as a launch-pad for international stardom. For 1974's performance the group wrote and performed 'Waterloo,' an inspired blend of the proto-disco-pop of 'Ring Ring' and the glam-rock sound that currently dominated the British charts. 'Waterloo' stole the show at the 1974 contest, becoming such a favorite that in 2005 it was named as the greatest song in the history of the competition. More importantly for Abba, however, it topped the U.K. singles chart and reached the U.S. Top 10, laying the foundations for a career that would yield such classic hits as 'The Winner Takes It All,' 'Take A Chance On Me,' and 'Dancing Queen.'

This Town Ain't Big Enough For Both Of Us
Sparks

Released April 1974
Island *001* (U.S.) / Island *WIP 6193* (U.K. #2)

'This Town Ain't Big Enough For Both Of Us' is one of the most memorably off-the-wall singles of the glam-rock era. It introduced the eccentric Mael brothers to the pop world – wild-eyed vocalist Russel and Hitler-mustached keyboardist Ron – and packed more into its three minutes than a lot of bands managed in their entire careers. The Maels

formed the first incarnation of Sparks (at first known as Halfnelson) in the late 1960s in America and recorded two albums for Todd Rundgren's Bearsville label. Neither was a success, prompting the brothers to dismantle the band and move to London, England. Recruiting a new set of British musicians, they set about recording a third album, *Kimono My House*, with producer Muff Winwood, elder brother of Traffic frontman Steve.

'This Town Ain't Big Enough For Both Of Us' was the first single to be drawn from the album, and the debut release of Sparks Mark 2. It fades in over a backdrop of pulsating, hypnotic keyboards, as Russel intones the beginnings of a lyric about "stampeding rhinos, elephants, and tacky tigers." The words grow more bizarre as the song progresses – "You are a khaki-colored bombardier, it's Hiroshima that you're nearing" – but are matched by the ever-changing music, which evokes nothing much else except perhaps Queen with attention deficit disorder. Indeed, in some ways 'This Town' is a punchier prototype for 'Bohemian Rhapsody,' particularly given its numerous key and time-changes and the pseudo-operatic vocals. Sparks's single was a huge hit in the U.K. during the summer of 1974, and while there were a few respectable follow-ups, such as 'Amateur Hour' from the same year, Sparks were never able to match its success.

When Will I See You Again
The Three Degrees

Released June 1974
Philadelphia *3550* (U.S. #2) / Philadelphia *PIR 2155* (U.K. #1)

Although they did not quite live up to the billing, The Three Degrees had a good try at taking on the mantle of top female pop-soul vocal group, worn so elegantly and for so long by The Supremes. In fact, The Three Degrees had a history almost as long as their Motown rivals: they had formed in the early 1960s, but by the time 'When Will I See You Again' went platinum in 1974, none of the original line-up remained. The group was said to be a favorite of Prince Charles, a fact confirmed when he booked them to play at his 30th birthday party at Buckingham Palace. Later, they were guests at his wedding to Princess Diana, although she preferred Status Quo. (British pop act Brother Beyond had a minor hit with a cover of 'When Will I See you Again' in 1989.)

Emma
Hot Chocolate

Released March 1974
Big Tree *16031* (U.S. #8) / RAK *168* (U.K. #3)

The ominous two-chord riff that underpins 'Emma' is the perfect foundation for a lyric telling the story of a young woman who takes her own life, disillusioned after a failed search for fame and fortune. It features one of pop's most memorable fade-outs, with lead singer Errol Brown screaming the title over a descending five-note guitar riff. Hot Chocolate had a knack for that sort of thing, and their polished pop-rock served them well. Between 1970 and 1984 they had at least one British chart single every year, and a few U.S. hits too. 'Emma' was the first to chart in both countries, reaching its U.S. peak a year after it hit in Britain.

The Air That I Breathe
The Hollies

Released January 1974
Epic *11100* (U.S. #6) / Polydor *2058 435* (U.K. #2)

This hit marked the end of the road for The Hollies as a regular chart force. With a string of chart singles dating back to 1963 – all produced by George Martin's former Parlophone deputy Ron Richards – they were one of Britain's most consistently successful singles groups, with twenty-six Top-30 hits between 1963 and 1974. But an unexpected return to Number 1 in Britain in 1988 with 'He Ain't Heavy, He's My Brother' ensured that their U.K. Number 1s spanned an impressive 23 years. In America they enjoyed some of their biggest hits in the early 1970s. 'He Ain't Heavy' reached Number 7 in 1970, while the Creedence-like 'Long Cool Woman In A Black Dress' was their biggest ever U.S. hit, making Number 2 in August 1972.

Following the departure of Graham Nash and the break-up of the group's songwriting team of Nash, Tony Hicks, and Allan Clarke, The Hollies had used mostly contemporary pop writers such as Roger Cook, Roger Greenaway, and Tony Macaulay. Clarke wrote 'Long Cool Woman' with Cook and Greenaway. The group found 'The Air That I Breathe' on *Star Spangled Banner*, a 1973 solo album by Phil Everly, and the song was written by Albert Hammond and Mike Hazelwood. Hammond would become one of the world's most successful songwriters over the next 20 years. 'Air' had originally appearing on Hammond's own album, *It Never Rains In Southern California*, in 1972, and would become a U.K Top 10 hit again in 1998 when it was covered by Simply Red.

Sweet Home Alabama
Lynyrd Skynyrd

Released July 1974
MCA *40258* (U.S. #8) / MCA *160* (U.K.)

Lynyrd Skynyrd wrote this breakthrough hit, at least in part, in response to Neil Young's scathing 'Southern Man.' Young's song, included on his third solo album, *After The Gold Rush* (1970), was an attack on what he perceived as prevalent racist attitudes in the Southern United States. He warmed to the theme further on 'Alabama,' which featured on the subsequent *Harvest* (1972). Lynyrd Skynyrd frontman Ronnie Van Zant wrote 'Sweet Home Alabama' shortly thereafter. It was included on the group's sophomore album, *Second Helping*, and as a single.

While 'Sweet Home' does mention Young by name – "I hope Neil Young will remember / Southern Man don't need him around anyhow" – its role at the center of a supposed feud between the two parties is often exaggerated. Young and Van Zant might not have agreed about the politics of the South, but they were still mutual fans of each other's work. Young has even covered 'Sweet Home Alabama' live on a number of occasions. Speaking in 1992, he decided that "they didn't really put me down. [Not] in a way that matters. Shit, I think 'Sweet Home Alabama' is a great song."

Lynyrd Skynyrd had a further hit later in 1974 with the rock staple 'Free Bird' and continued to tour and record successfully until October 1977, when Van Zant and fellow band-members Steve and Cassie Gaines were killed in a plane crash.

You Are So Beautiful
Joe Cocker

Released December 1974
A&M *1641* (U.S. #5) / Fly *BUG 57* (U.K.)

With a voice that sounded as if he gargled gravel for breakfast, Joe Cocker has had something of a see-saw career. Born in Sheffield, England, Cocker enjoyed a breakthrough at home with his cover of The Beatles' 'With A Little Help From My Friends' in 1968 and went on to extensive American success with his 1970 tour and album *Mad Dogs And Englishmen*. Tour exhaustion put Cocker out of action for a period during which he was temporarily refused entrance to the U.S. following an Australian drugs charge. He had his biggest American success of the 1970s with this somewhat out-of-character but eloquently simple love song, composed by Billy Preston and Bruce Fisher. The song had originally appeared on Preston's 1974 album *The Kids & Me*. After Cocker had a Number 5 U.S. hit with his interpretation, he would have to wait another seven years for a Top 40 hit on either side of the Atlantic, when he topped the American charts with 'Up Where We Belong' in a duet with Jennifer Warnes.

You're The First, The Last, My Everything
Barry White

Released October 1974
20th Century *2133* (U.S. #2, U.K. #1)

An unlikely sex symbol, and sadly with us no more, Barry White weighed in at 300 pounds, sported a goatee beard, and had long curly hair. But of course, he didn't always have that voice. Unlikely as it now seems, White recalled: "Until I was 14 years old I had a sound not unlike the high-pitched voice of Michael Jackson." However, when he reached puberty his voice broke overnight, "like a drop off the Empire State Building," as he put it. "I woke up, and spoke to my mother – and scared us both to death."

White's highly orchestrated recordings, often accompanied by long erotic monologues, gave him a string of Top 10 hits during the 1970s as well as success with his Love Unlimited trio and The Love Unlimited Orchestra. Of the transatlantic hits he racked up between 1973 and 1979, 'You're The First' was the most successful, reaching Number 1 in Britain and Number 2 in America. White, and this song in particular, enjoyed something of a renaissance in 2000 when featured in the hit TV series *Ally McBeal*. The Man was back, and even made a cameo appearance on the show.

Apart from creating music, Mr. White was much in demand for his advice with regard to the intricacies of relationships, and particularly the creation of seductive circumstances. White advised that to get in the mood, a romantic song is a must (preferably one of his), saying that a red-hot evening should include a candlelit dinner and plenty of time. He suggested that at the end of a relationship one should "get back out there A.S.A.P. and find someone else to love."

In a bizarre turn of events, marine center officials in Britain hoped that White's seductive songs would do for sharks what they have done for countless humans. Staff at the Great Yarmouth Sea Life Centre played his music to their sharks in an effort to spice up their sex life, and this practice has now spread to other marine establishments around the country. Perhaps they should reconfigure the song as 'You're The First, The Last, My Every Fin'?

Bohemian Rhapsody
Queen

Released November 1975
Elektra *45297* (U.S. #9) / EMI *2375* (U.K. #1)

One of the most adventurous and innovative recordings in pop music history, 'Bohemian Rhapsody' was not at first intended as a single because, among other things, some considered it far too long. A six-minute mini-rock-operetta was hardly going to compete for airtime with Hot Chocolate and John Denver, ran the argument.

Queen vocalist Freddie Mercury first played his new, only half completed composition to producer Roy Thomas Baker, on piano. With a royal flourish, he then stopped and said: "Now dear, this is where the opera section comes in." Recording of the multi-part backing track commenced at Rockfield studio in Wales in the spring of 1975. Baker recalled: "The beginning section was pretty spot on, and the end section was fairly similar, although we obviously embellished it with guitars and overdubs. But the opera section ended up nothing like the original concept because we kept changing it and adding things to it."

These 'embellishments,' recorded at Scorpion studio in London, consisted of Mercury, guitarist Brian May, and drummer Roger Taylor spending around 12 hours every day for a week adding 180 vocal overdubs. Baker had left about half a minute of blank tape between the first and third sections for what was intended to be a short operatic interlude – including the odd "Scaramouche" and "fandango." But Mercury kept putting in new bits and would arrive at the studio declaring: "I've added a few more Galileos here, dear."

There were so many edits on the tape that Baker remembered it looking "like a zebra-crossing whizzing by." Mercury: "That middle section got longer and longer and longer. ...We were all in hysterics when it was being recorded. ...We had to sit there going, 'No, no, no, no, no, no, no, no!' about 150 times." This wasn't the only problem. Even using 24-track technology, the many overdubs meant the engineers had to employ tricks such as track 'bouncing' to accommodate the increasing number of vocals, and even a number of complete tape-to-tape transfers. Baker said the making of the song "was basically one continuous track bounce."

There is an oft-repeated myth that by this time the master tape was "almost transparent," but when the tapes were recently retrieved for conversion to surround-sound, the "transparent" claim was proved untrue. The tape also exhibited no physical edits, which would indicate that the original master tape must have been transferred at some stage. (The conversion did reveal that there were three alternative takes for the lead vocals.) Baker reckoned that the total recording time was about three weeks, including two days for the basic backing track, seven days for all the vocal overdubs, a few more for guitar overdubs, and two days of mixing. For most acts, this was enough time to record an entire album, and the total cost was astronomical.

Since their third album, *Sheer Heart Attack*, the band had fallen out with their previous management, Trident, and signed a new deal with Elton John's manager John Reid in time for *A Night At The Opera*, named after a Marx Brothers movie that the group had watched during work at Rockfield. In one of his first directives as the group's manager, Reid insisted that EMI release 'Bohemian Rhapsody' as a single, although both Queen and EMI thought radio DJs would not be interested. According to Reid, Elton John told Queen that they were crazy even to consider releasing a single of such length. This seems odd, however, since three of Elton's own recent singles were just as lengthy. Baker recalled that he was ready for this argument and noted that songs of equal length such as Richard Harris's 'MacArthur Park' and 'Eloise' by Barry Ryan, both issued in 1968, had been readily played by the BBC in Britain. Surely it was the quality of the product that mattered?

Queen rather cleverly circumvented EMI's reluctance by giving a copy of the completed track to London's Capital Radio DJ Kenny Everett, a friend of Mercury's. With a nod and a wink, they gave Everett strict instructions not to play the record. That certainly did the trick: Everett played it 14 times in two days on his weekend radio show, claiming on-air that his "finger had slipped." With this amount of exposure, a Number 1 record was pretty much guaranteed, and EMI were persuaded.

Realizing that live performance of the song was going to be tricky, the group decided to make a promotional video that could be screened to promote the single. Roger Taylor said: "We only did it because we had to be in Liverpool and couldn't do [TV singles show] *Top Of The Pops*." The ground-breaking video has often been described as the first of its kind, but the idea of promo clips dates back at least to the 1960s and had been used by The Beatles after they ceased touring. Brian May said: "Everyone thought the film was a huge production. But it was really easy to do, and since then we've spent a lot of time on films which probably aren't as good, and certainly didn't get the exposure."

What is true is that this innovative clip cost a meager £4,500 (about $10,000 at the time) and was screened for nine consecutive weeks on *Top Of The Pops* while the song was Number 1. It ushered in the age of video clips and, ultimately, the arrival of MTV. Ironically, Queen would later criticize the importance of video presentation versus musical content in their 1984 hit 'Radio Ga Ga.'

So what was 'Bohemian Rhapsody' all about? Mercury was never particularly forthcoming. Roger Taylor said: "Freddie had the whole song mapped out in his head. Don't ask me to explain what it's about because I haven't got a fucking clue. It's the vibe that's important." According to Kenny Everett, Mercury told him it was "random rhyming nonsense."

Does it really matter? From the opening 15 seconds of a cappella voices to the closing gong, this was Queen's finest moment on record. Their greatest performance on stage was the 17-minute medley of hits they delivered in front of millions worldwide at Live Aid ten years later in the summer of 1985. In his usual no-nonsense vocabulary, Live Aid organizer Bob Geldof secured the services of Freddie Mercury and his band by phoning their manager and saying: "Tell the old faggot it's gonna be the biggest thing that ever happened." Showman Freddie Mercury could hardly turn down an offer like that, and the group didn't disappoint. Following the show, Geldof said: "Queen were absolutely the best band of the day."

'Bo-Rap' topped the U.K. charts for nine weeks from November 1975 and a further five from December 1991, following Mercury's death. Reigning over the new year on both occasions meant that the song gained the unique distiction of being Number 1 in four separate years.

The original Number 9 placing in America was eclipsed by a 1992 Number 2 in the wake of the song's central role in the hilarious head-banging scene from the movie *Wayne's World*. Strangely, the Abba song that followed Queen to Number 1 in early 1976 may have gained some subliminal promotion since its title, 'Mamma Mia,' also appeared in the Queen hit.

Many commentators at the time thought that 'Bohemian Rhapsody' was symptomatic of the excess of 1970s progressive rock, but time and wisdom have drawn different conclusions. It is the third biggest selling single of all time in Britain, and in a 2002 survey undertaken by the *Guinness Book Of British Hit Singles* to discover the U.K. public's favorite all-time 45, 'Bohemian Rhapsody' was the runaway Number 1 choice.

Autobahn
Kraftwerk

Released February 1975
Vertigo *203* (U.S. #25) / Vertigo *6147 012* (U.K. #11)

With the benefit of hindsight, we can recognize the German synthesizer band Kraftwerk as true pioneers of pop. The band's influence has spread through hip-hop, techno, and the New Romantic movement, and bled into virtually all mainstream rock and pop. Many are the hits by artists as diverse as Madonna, New Order, and Afrika Bambaataa, to name just a few, that simply wouldn't have been made if it wasn't for the impeccably drawn sonic blueprint that emerged from Kraftwerk's Kling Klang studio more than 30 years ago.

The album *Autobahn,* which included a lengthy version of the title track from which the single was edited, was Kraftwerk's fourth, and the first to be issued in America. Until that point the band were thought of as little more than marginal German eccentrics, and even after 'Autobahn,' their breakthrough single, it was a while before their importance was understood. The mix of precision electronic rhythms, pulsing synthesizers, and deadpan vocals simply had not been heard before. Even though 'Autobahn' the single and then the album were big international hits, for some time afterwards many considered Kraftwerk as little more than a novelty act.

The song is a hymn to the straight-line speed and efficiency of the German freeway network, itself an apposite image of the new music of Kraftwerk (the group's name means 'power station'). Sounds surge into the mix and hit a crescendo before fading out again, evoking a sleek Mercedes passing at 100 mph, while a detached voice intones: "Wir fahr'n fahr'n fahr'n auf der Autobahn." To some ears, this sounded like "Fun, fun, fun on the Autobahn," leading a handful of critics to conclude that Kraftwerk were engaged in some Teutonic spoof of The Beach Boys. They weren't, of course: they were just being themselves. And although there have been many imitators, still no one else sounds quite like Kraftwerk.

Roadrunner
Jonathan Richman & The Modern Lovers

Released June 1975
Beserkley *5701* (U.S.) / United Artists *36006* (U.K. #11)

This classic of proto-punk garage rock took the long route to success. It was recorded in 1973, not issued as a single until 1975 in Britain and '76 in America, and did not chart until 1977. It was produced by former Velvet Underground member John Cale and featured guitarist Jerry Harrison, who had joined Talking Heads by the time 'Roadrunner' reached the U.K. singles chart. Opening with a cry of "one-two-three-four-five-six!" the song is a frenetic, two-chord paean to driving down the highway while listening to the radio. It remains Richman's defining moment, although more people may be aware of him – probably without realizing – for his musical role in the 1998 comedy movie *There's Something About Mary.*

No Regrets
The Walker Brothers

Released October 1975
Not issued U.S. / GTO *GT 42* (U.K. #7)

They were teen-idol balladeers of the 1960s, but when they reformed unexpectedly in 1975, The Walker Brothers adopted a more mature, country-rock sound. They immediately reaped rewards from the change of direction with a hit version of Tom Rush's classic break-up song, 'No Regrets.'

Rush had originally recorded the song with an acoustic arrangement on his 1968 album, *Circle Game*, and he came back to it in 1974, recasting it with sweeping strings and a searing guitar solo for his *Ladies Love Outlaws* album. It was this that caught the ears of the reformed Walkers, and they copied the arrangement virtually note-for-note: same string part, same guitar solo. 'No Regrets' was given title billing for the band's first comeback album and was released as a single, briefly competing for airtime with a single of Rush's version in the arrangement the Walkers had covered.

Scott, John, and Garry – who weren't brothers at all – won the battle for a chart place, but Rush earned his composer's royalties and reasoned that imitation was the sincerest form of flattery. Another twist in the tale came in 1982 when Midge Ure had a hit with yet another version of the song. Although Ure made heavy use of drum machines and synthesizers it was clear that his version still owed much to The Walker Brothers cut, and thereby to the Tom Rush take.

Lady Marmalade (Voulez-Vous Coucher Avec Moi Ce Soir?)
LaBelle

Released January 1975
Epic *50048* (U.S. #1) / Epic *EPC 2852* (U.K. #17)

'Lady Marmalade' was released a mighty 13 years after Patti 'Patricia Holt' LaBelle and her band had scored their first hit, and made it to Number 1 on the U.S. Billboard charts, staying around for months and refusing to budge either from the listings or from the brain of anyone who heard it. Damn, those girls were funky, with their coy invitations of "Voulez-vous coucher avec moi ce soir?" and what sounded like some sort of sexual voodoo chant in the immortal verse "Itchi gitchi ya ya da da / Itchi gitchi ya ya here / Mocha-choca-lata ya ya / Creole Lady Marmalade!" Musically, it's pure fatback funk, with a huge bass and piano part playing that awe-inspiring backing lick in full, those vocal improvisations and interjections from the singers lending a grind that seems positively rude.

The trio's outlandish image made the impact of the song all the more forceful: they wore silver Funkadelic-like apparel and came up with futuristic soundbites that could have come straight from the sci-fi-meets-Black-Panther world of George Clinton and Bootsy Collins. Little wonder that the song has been covered with varying degrees of success by modern acts such as All Saints and a collective of high-stepping R&B females, Christina Aguilera, Lil' Kim, Mya, & Pink. 'Lady Marmalade' remains one of the finest moments of the classic girl-group era – and, remarkably, it's not even a love song. Patti LaBelle herself couldn't match its success, and she slipped into AOR blandness in the 1980s, in the following decade espousing causes such as diabetes awareness. But as career highs go, this is one to cherish.

Bye Bye Baby
The Bay City Rollers

Released March 1975
Arista *0120* (U.S.) / Bell *1409* (U.K. #1)

'Bye Bye Baby' was the start of a new era for The Bay City Rollers. With five U.K. Top 10 hits under their belt, they decided that the time was ripe to play on their own records, instead of giving way again to the sessioneers who had fulfilled that function, and to write their own singles. It took a little longer to achieve the latter objective than the former – and even that was shortlived – but 'Bye Bye Baby,' as the band's first U.K. Number 1, constituted a vindication of sorts.

The song was an old Four Seasons number, although the Rollers knew it from a version by British harmony group The Symbols, who had secured the only U.K. hit for the song so far. The Rollers could not hope to match Frankie Valli's vocal gymnastics or the musicianship of the original, but their rendition was pleasant enough. That could be said about their entire catalogue, and hardly seemed to explain the global domination that briefly followed. America succumbed later in 1975 when 'Saturday Night' became a chart-topper there, following the Stateside failure of 'Bye Bye Baby.' The group's trick seemed to be their ability to hold teens and pre-teens in their thrall thanks to a set of genuinely personable natures. They were not, as has been erroneously alleged, precursors of the boy-band genre: the Rollers were musicians, not a vocal group.

However, none of the retrospective credibility that has been afforded Abba will go to them, for The Bay City Rollers were, quite simply, the definition of lightweight.

Jive Talkin'
The Bee Gees

Released May 1975
RSO *510* (U.S. #1) / RSO *2090 160* (U.K. #5)

Following their first string of 1960s hits, The Bee Gees saw their popularity slowly declining. There followed some lean years in the early 1970s culminating in the rejection of an entire album of material by their record company in 1974. That unreleased album, *A Kick In The Head Is Worth Eight In The Pants*, was the group's turning point – and a kick in the pants was exactly what they needed, and got, when their manager, Robert Stigwood, connected them with veteran producer Arif Mardin. The trio's songwriting magic returned for *Main Course*, the 1975 album that marked a dramatic return by the group who many thought were past their best.

'Jive Talkin'' was originally inspired by a daily trip that the brothers Gibb took over a metal bridge to and from the studio. The metallic rhythm that the bridge produced inspired an idea that began as "Drive talking…" but quickly evolved into the more famous title. Upon presenting their new song to Mardin, the group were surprised to discover what it actually meant. They'd been thinking in terms of dancing, whereas Mardin was quick to point out that in the context of the song it was black slang for talking rubbish. This didn't worry the group, who quickly changed their original lyric "you dance with your eyes" into "you're telling me lies." They were swiftly rewarded with their second U.S. Number 1 and repeated the success with 'You Should Be Dancing' in 1976. Little did they know that in a couple of years the whole world would be dancing to their new R&B music.

I'm Not In Love
10cc

Released May 1975
Mercury *73678* (U.S. #2) / Mercury *6008 014* (U.K. #1)

It was always easy to admire 10cc but difficult to love them. After all, few people love a smart-ass. Or to put it more scientifically, 10cc had unquestionable musical and production abilities, but their songs were so self-conscious and post-modern that it seemed as though they were above all this. By 1975, the quartet had racked up five Top 10 U.K. hits, including the rip-roaring 'Rubber Bullets' but also 'Donna,' a pastiche of a 1950s oldie that was so knowing as to be somehow insufferable, and considered by many to be part of the problem. Depending on your taste, 'I'm Not In Love' either rectified a deficiency of soullessness, or confirmed it.

The song started life with 10cc guitarist Eric Stewart, whose girlfriend of the time complained to him that he didn't tell her he loved her often enough. His response was not so cruel as the song title – he replied that it was meaningless if he said so every day – but the idea for a song was born. The group piled on vocal harmony after vocal harmony and had a slightly speech-impaired studio receptionist intone "big boys don't cwy" in an interlude. One highly unusually effect came from the fact that the recording has no drums. Once the record was complete, the band lay on the studio floor in the dark listening to the creamy result. The single, edited down from the LP version, was massively popular, even among those cynical enough to perceive it as sheer form and artifice.

That's The Way (I Like It)
K.C. & The Sunshine Band

Released June 1975
T.K. *1015* (U.S. #1) / Jayboy *BOY 99* (U.K. #4)

K.C. was Harry Wayne Casey, and as a commercial disco artist he understood the value of repetition just as well as his punk contemporaries The Ramones. The title of 'That's The Way I Like It' is repeated 17 times during the course of the song, with the truncated phrase "that's the way" turning up another eight times. But it wasn't just endless chorus repeats that gave K.C. and his Sunshine Band this smash hit – it was the memorable tune, the eminently danceable groove, and the stabbing horn interjections. Together they made a record still guaranteed to send even the most reluctant and ungainly of dancers onto the floor. It was a formula that served the band well and gave them many more hits. One of the last was 'Give It Up,' where the title was repeated 22 times.

Rhinestone Cowboy
Glen Campbell

Released June 1975
Capitol *4095* (U.S. #1) / Capitol *CL 15824* (U.K. #4)

This is a masterpiece of songwriting economy, performed with great gusto by one of the most popular country singers of the 1960s and '70s. 'Rhinestone Cowboy' tells the maudlin tale of a Broadway entertainer who has "been walkin' these streets so long / Singin' the same old song" and knows at heart that he is never destined for glory. But the show must go on, and as the song continues, the melody expertly ascends, mirroring the chest-beating optimism of the pay-off line: "But I'm gonna be where the lights are shinin' on me." It has become the song that Campbell is most associated with and, although it was not his own composition, he clearly empathized with its lyrical content, even going so far as to title his 1994 autobiography *Rhinestone Cowboy*.

It Only Takes A Minute
Tavares

Released July 1975
Capitol *4111* (U.S. #10) / Capitol *CL 15832* (U.K.)

Like the Jacksons, the Osmonds, and the Isleys, Tavares were a family R&B group, this one consisting of five brothers from New Bedford, Massachusetts. Originally called Chubby & The Turnpikes, they reverted to the family name before signing to Capitol in 1973. The first album was produced by Johnny Bristol and the group then teamed up with writer-producers Dennis Lambert and Brian Potter, who had recently enjoyed major success with the post-Motown Four Tops. 'It Only Takes A Minute' was an R&B Number 1 and their biggest of eight Top-40 pop hits in America, reaching Number 10 on the regular chart. It was not a hit at the time in Britain, despite heavy disco play, and the following year was covered there by Jonathan King, man of many hats, under the guise One Hundred Ton And A Feather, making Number 9. Tavares's most enduring hit in the U.K. was 'Heaven Must Be Missing An Angel,' a Number 4 in 1976 and Number 12 when remixed in 1986.

Sailing
Rod Stewart

Released August 1975
Warner Bros. *WB 8146* (U.S.) / Warner Bros. *K 16600* (U.K. #1)

For his first Warner Brothers album, *Atlantic Crossing*, Rod Stewart had engaged renowned R&B producer Tom Dowd to record with the famous Muscle Shoals rhythm section in Alabama. When Stewart was introduced to the musicians, he was convinced Dowd was playing a joke on him, exclaiming: "That can't be the Muscle Shoals rhythm section, they're all white!" It wasn't until he heard the band play that he was convinced. 'Sailing' was written by Gavin Sutherland of British group The Sutherland Brothers, who had released it as a single without success. Stewart made the song his own and its singalong chorus soon made it popular with soccer crowds throughout Britain, where it remains a firm favorite. Stewart said: 'I recorded it in Alabama, a partially 'dry' state. I was asked to sing live at 10:30 in the morning with no lubrication for the vocal chords on hand – get my drift?' A U.K. Number 1 in 1975, it returned to the Top 3 the following year when featured in a BBC documentary series about the aircraft carrier Ark Royal. Surprisingly, 'Sailing' flopped in the States, only making Number 58, although the following year Stewart would enjoy a U.S. Number 1 with 'Tonight's The Night.'

You Sexy Thing
Hot Chocolate

Released November 1975
Big Tree *16047* (U.S. #3) / *RAK 221* (U.K. #2)

An ardent chorus, a chattering conga pattern, and a memorable six-note guitar riff are just a few of the hooks in Hot Chocolate's biggest hit. Lead singer Errol Brown was just the man for the mildly suggestive lyrics, too. Smooth, snake-hipped, and usually dressed in a silk shirt unbuttoned almost to the waist, Brown had a carefully cultivated ladies-man image that was a major factor in the band's success. A little dangerous, maybe, but not really bad. "Oh touch me, you sexy thing," he screamed as the song seductively slinked to a close – and millions wished they could. Panties were thrown, singles were bought, and 'You Sexy Thing' became a huge U.S. and U.K. hit, charting again in Britain in the 1980s and 1990s.

No Woman, No Cry
Bob Marley & The Wailers

Released August 1975
Island *037* (U.S.) / Island *WIP 6244* (U.K. #8)

Eternally misinterpreted as meaning "you're better off without a woman" when in fact the title means the much more sympathetic "woman, please don't cry," this song was the first British hit for Bob Marley & The Wailers. It is one of the few songs best known as a live version, and was edited down from the take on the band's *Live!* LP (although the original version on the *Natty Dread* album, also released in '75, is worth checking out). While Marley is usually assumed to have written the song, the credit was given to Vincent Ford, a friend of Bob's who ran a soup kitchen in Kingston, Jamaica. Revenue from the song kept Ford's charitable operation running for years.

In 'No Woman, No Cry' Marley demonstrates his mastery of storytelling, laying down his sentiments of political despair and encouragement within a format that is almost a hymn. Over an organ backing simultaneously hypnotic and stirring, he sings: "I remember when we used to sit / In the government yard in Trenchtown / Observing the hypocrites / As they would mingle with the good people we meet." His backing singers gently raise their voices in angelic harmony, before the song takes off half way through and evolves into a funkier, almost gospel invocation of "everything's gonna be all right" that, you can safely assume, everyone in the world can sing. It's remarkably effective, and a perfect route into the otherwise more challenging Marley canon.

Born To Run
Bruce Springsteen

Released September 1975
Columbia *10209* (U.S. #23) / CBS *3661* (U.K.)

This was probably the most important recording in Springsteen's career. It was make or break time for the future Boss after his first two albums had sold poorly. He later described 'Born To Run' as "my shot at the title. A 24-year-old kid aimin' at 'the greatest rock'n'roll record ever.'" He re-wrote and re-wrote the song over a period of about six months, filling up 50 pages in his notebook until he was satisfied with the lyric.

It took a further three months to complete the recording of this one song, which cost $10,000. The original take was overdubbed with everything imaginable, including female back-up vocals and a string arrangement, by which time Springsteen had completely lost the plot. He recalled: "I was striving for something very specific that I didn't know how to get." Fortunately, Jon Landau did. He was brought on board in an advisory capacity and boiled down all the overdubs to the basic ingredients that had featured on the original version.

Landau had witnessed Springsteen's first live performance of the song on May 9, 1974, in Cambridge, Massachusetts, and wrote a review ("I saw the future of rock'n'roll") that has since become famous. Even when completed, 'Born To Run' had a lukewarm reception at Columbia Records, so manager Mike Appel sent cassettes to a number of radio jocks – and Columbia was furious. Appel said: "People were coming into the stores – in Cleveland, Dallas, Boston, all over – looking for the new Springsteen album, which didn't exist. All we'd cut to that point was a single that hadn't been released." All the hype eventually paid off and secured cover stories on Springsteen in *Newsweek* and *Time* during the same week. In the U.K. that hype was detrimental, and 'Born To Run' wasn't a hit until a live version finally made the charts in 1987.

The Boys Are Back In Town
Thin Lizzy

Released April 1976
Mercury *73786* (U.S. #12) / Vertigo *6059 139* (U.K. #8)

'The Boys Are Back In Town' was the apotheosis of Thin Lizzy's tandem guitar attack. The riff following the fist-punching choruses saw Brian Robertson and Scott Gorham playing in harmony what sounded like a speeded-up, dirtied-down version of Woody Woodpecker's laugh. It made for one of the most unforgettable licks in rock history.

Also memorable was the opening guitar lick, which, ingeniously, was adapted from the horn chart in a lesser-known Bruce Springsteen song called 'Kitty's Back.' There is still a trace of Springsteen about the song's blue-collar ambience and anthemic properties. The lyrics by Lizzy bassist and frontman Phil Lynott started out with "G.I. Joe's back in town" before he decided to jettison the idea of a returning Vietnam vet for a song based on a disreputable Manchester mob, the Quality Street Gang. The words possess a cartoon quality and at least appear to make sense ("If that chick don't wanna know, forget her!") but any misgivings about the song are swept aside by a chorus so infectious as to be ludicrous, even though it does consist merely of the title phrase repeated over and over by a voice performing a call-and-response with itself in each speaker.

Jon Bon Jovi has admitted that he based his band's entire style on Lizzy. Their continuing impact is underlined by the fact that Dan Hawkins, guitarist with The Darkness, is rarely seen in public without a Lizzy T-shirt.

Devil Woman
Cliff Richard

Released April 1976
Rocket *40574* (U.S. #6) / EMI *2458* (U.K. #9)

The perpetual bachelor boy was already 20 years into his career and looking a bit tired when he emerged rejuvenated with 'Devil Woman.' Hailed at the time as a return to Cliff's rock'n'roll roots and considered in questionable taste by his Christian fans, 'Devil Woman' in fact sounds pretty tame. But it is perfectly executed mature pop and set the tone for a run of late-1970s / early-1980s chart hits, including 'We Don't Talk Anymore' and 'Wired For Sound.' Most of Cliff's dozens of U.K. hit singles have missed the mark in America, but 'Devil Woman' charted very respectably there.

A Little Bit More
Dr. Hook

Released June 1976
Capitol *4280* (U.S. #11) / Capitol *CL 15871* (U.K. #2)

Formed in 1968 as Dr. Hook & The Medicine Show, this country-pop outfit featured two lead singers, Ray Sawyer (the one with the eye-patch, added after he lost an eye in an automobile accident) and Dennis Locorriere. Their first success came with songs written by *Playboy* cartoonist Shel Silverstein. 'Sylvia's Mother' was a worldwide hit after Columbia chief Clive Davis put the company's promotional muscle

behind it, followed by 'The Cover Of Rolling Stone.' Legal problems and the departure of Davis from Columbia led to a switch to Capitol and decidedly more middle-of-the-road country material recorded in Nashville – and to far greater success, particularly internationally. 'A Little Bit More,' composed by the unlikely-named Bobby Gosh, was co-produced by Waylon Jennings and gave Dr. Hook a worldwide hit, leading to a new wave of success that culminated in 1979 with a U.K. Number 1 for 'When You're In Love With A Beautiful Woman.'

Let's Stick Together
Bryan Ferry

Released June 1976
Atlantic *3351* (U.S.) / Island *WIP 6307* (U.K. #4)

Roxy Music's distinctive vocalist Bryan Ferry began his parallel solo career after the band's second album in 1973. For his early projects he stuck to covers while keeping original material for the Roxy albums, and he wrote or co-wrote nearly all of Roxy Music's hits. His first U.K. solo hit in October 1973 was a cover of Bob Dylan's 'A Hard Rain's A-Gonna Fall' and he followed through the following year with remakes of Dobie Gray's 'The In Crowd' and The Platters' 'Smoke Gets In Your Eyes' before his biggest solo success in 1976 with 'Let's Stick Together.' None of these were hits in America, and indeed neither Roxy Music nor Ferry on his own have enjoyed much U.S. chart action.

For his solo career, Ferry adopted a suave dinner-jacket-and-bow-tie image, something like a modern day crooner, in contrast to his more bohemian appearance in Roxy Music. His third solo album, bearing the same title as this hit, was simply a hotchpotch of B-sides and a couple of current singles of which this, a full-throttle three minutes with an effective saxophone lead, was the standout track. While the song was perhaps best known as 'Let's *Work* Together,' a hit for blues band Canned Heat in 1970, writer Wilbert Harrison had originally recorded it in 1962 as 'Let's Stick Together' before later re-recording it in 1969 as 'Let's Work Together.' Ferry made a second chart appearance in Britain in 1988 with the song, given considerably more punch in a remix by Bob Clearmountain.

Harvest For The World
The Isley Brothers

Released June 1976
T-Neck *2260* (U.S.) / Epic *EPC 4369* (U.K. #10)

Although only a minor hit in the U.S., the international success of 'Harvest' provided evidence of how soul-folk fusion, pioneered by Otis Redding's 'Dock Of The Bay' in 1968, was coming of age in the mid 1970s. The Isleys had weathered pop's changing fashions from their early-1960s R&B successes, through a rock-oriented approach as the decade ended, to their generally folkier leanings on 1973's *3+3* album. Now they were delivering an ecological message through an artful blend of strummy guitars, keyboards, and handclaps. Enduringly popular, 'Harvest' has been covered by artists as diverse as Power Station (1985), The Christians (1988), and Kirsty MacColl (1999).

If You Leave Me Now
Chicago

Released July 1976
Columbia *10390* (U.S. #1) / CBS *4603* (U.K. #1)

Like the similarly brass-driven Blood Sweat & Tears (with whom they shared a producer), Chicago signed to Columbia in 1969. The group elongated their name to Chicago Transit Authority after threatened legal action by the mayor of the Windy City. At first they scored only in Britain, with 'I'm A Man' and '25 Or 6 To 4' in 1970, but soon racked up a wall full of platinum albums Stateside and over a dozen hit singles before a mid-1970s switch to AOR ballads.

'If You Leave Me Now' gave them their first Number 1 on both sides of the Atlantic. Written and sung by bass guitarist Peter Cetera, the song featured fine acoustic guitar solos played by producer James Guercio. They continued in similar style, later enjoying further ballad success, with 'Hard To Say I'm Sorry' and 'You're The Inspiration' in the early 1980s, both composed by Cetera together with the group's later producer David Foster, before Cetera's departure for a solo career in 1985.

(Don't Fear) The Reaper
Blue Öyster Cult

Released July 1976
Columbia *10384* (U.S. #12) / CBS *6333* (U.K. #16)

Considering the lawsuits that heavy metal bands have attracted from parents of distressed or dead teenagers for their alleged backwards messages and gloomy lyrics, it is surprising that Blue Öyster Cult's signature song has not thus far led to the same. Buck Dharma, the Cult guitarist who wrote it, denies that it celebrates suicide, claiming its subject is a love that transcends the physical. The musical backing is

suitably epic and stately, and boasts a typical Öyster airbrushed polish. It's intelligent heavy metal – even if the song is not quite as disquieting or magisterial as it's clearly intended to be.

More Than A Feeling
Boston

Released September 1976
Epic *50266* (U.S. #5) / Epic *EPC 4658* (U.K. #22)

Boston marked a phenomenon that really only became possible in the 1970s: a faceless band. Hitherto, record consumers would not tolerate pop or rock bands with whom they could not associate a face, so bound up was popular music with good looks – or at least with image. By the '70s, the audience for rock had grown with the medium. To record purchasers older than teens, the only requisite was good music. This makes it all the more interesting that Boston was the kind of band disdained by punk, a movement that was shifting onto the public radar in Britain just as Boston secured a transatlantic hit with this, their debut.

The boast of punk was that it was liberating for performers, especially females, because nobody cared what they looked like, but Boston were ahead of them on that score. Also ironic is that, although Boston have always suffered from a 'corporate' image, they in fact have always supported and aligned themselves with left and liberal causes. The group is essentially Tom Scholz, the one mainstay of the group and the mastermind behind their multi-tracked extravaganzas.

Scholz touched all bases in this song: a crunching guitar riff, soaring melody, a lyric of music-inspired nostalgia, and an airbrushed, widescreen production. The result was FM immortality. Its parent album became one of history's all-time biggest sellers.

Livin' Thing
Electric Light Orchestra

Released October 1976
United Artists/Jet *888* (U.S. #13) / Jet *UP 36184* (U.K. #4)

The Electric Light Orchestra was originally conceived as "a band with strings" in the late 1960s by Birmingham musicians Roy Wood and Jeff Lynne. By 1976, Wood was long gone and Lynne was the sole writer, singer, guitarist, and producer of all ELO's material. 'Livin' Thing' was the first of three hit singles on both sides of the Atlantic from *A New World Record*, ELO's first million-selling U.S. album.

One of Lynne's major problems was recording all his string overdubs with studio orchestras, particularly in Britain where archaic Musicians' Union rules continued to frustrate him. Lynne recalled: "We'd be coming to the end of a song and the clock would be going just over the minute, and they'd just stop. Unless you booked them for another three hours to play this extra minute, they were gone."

Lynne eventually discovered Musicland studios in Munich, Germany, and took his business there. "Orchestras in Munich were totally different," he concluded. "They'd all crowd into the control room and go, 'Wow, that's good! Let's try it again. Maybe we can make it better.'" (The Beautiful South had a U.K. hit with a re-make of 'Livin' Thing' in 2004.)

December 1963 (Oh What A Night)
The 4 Seasons

Released January 1976
Warner Bros./Curb *8168* (U.S. #1) / Warner Bros/Curb *K 16688* (U.K. #1)

The Seasons were one of America's most successful vocal acts of the 1960s, with twenty-seven U.S. Top-40 hits between 1962 and 1968, including four Number 1s, but were not nearly so popular in the U.K., with only nine Top-40 hits there in the same period, the biggest of which were 'Sherry,' Let's Hang On,' and 'Rag Doll.' It was a slightly reformatted group that returned in the 1970s, although the main ingredients were still on board: vocalist Frankie Valli and writer-producer Bob Gaudio.

This song was originally written about the repeal of prohibition in America in December 1933, an unlikely subject for a pop song, which was why the story was updated to 1963. The Seasons had a couple more hits during this revival, but it was Valli who made the most of the opportunity, enjoying two solo U.S. Number 1s with 'My Eyes Adored You' and 1978's Barry Gibb-composed theme for the *Grease* movie.

Save Your Kisses For Me
Brotherhood Of Man

Released March 1976
Pye *71066* (U.S. #27) / Pye *7N 45569* (U.K. #1)

The group was originally formed by Tony Hiller as a studio session outfit in 1969 and had a transatlantic hit with 'United We Stand,' something of a gay anthem. The name was then resurrected for an entirely new group in 1976 to front this composition at the Eurovision Song Contest. The song was an odds-on favorite and won the contest by a large margin. Unsurprisingly, the victorious Brotherhood, with their popular two-boy two-girl line-up, were labeled as Abba copyists, and scored in Britain and Europe with a number of further Abba-flavored concoctions, including the U.K. Number 1s 'Angelo' and 'Figaro.' Ironically, justice was seen to be done when Abba's own 'Fernando,' a definitively superior product, replaced 'Save Your Kisses' as Britain's Number 1.

Play That Funky Music
Wild Cherry

Released June 1976
Epic *50225* (U.S. #1) / Epic *EPC 4593* (U.K. #7)

In the mid 1970s Wild Cherry was just another heavy rock band that suddenly found itself playing to disco audiences who were demanding a different beat. This track was inspired by a cry of, "Play that funky music, white boy," from the audience. Guitarist-vocalist Robert Parissi rose to the challenge and wrote the song, initially slated as the B-side of their cover of The Commodores' 'I Feel Sanctified.' Their record company decided otherwise, and rightly so: it's a decidedly funky track that stands up well today and ain't half bad for a bunch of white boys. The group got its name from the flavor of a box of cough drops, but despite a few other minor U.S. hits, this was their only big international success. The song was covered in 1991 by Robert Van Winkle, alias Vanilla Ice, as a follow-up to his chart-topping 'Ice Ice Baby.'

Dancing Queen
Abba

Released August 1976
Atlantic *3372* (U.S. #1) / Epic *EPC 4499* (U.K. #1)

There are a couple of myths that have endured about Abba. One is that they bowed out at their artistic and commercial peak. In fact, the recordings at the end of their career had begun to pall, with unlovely and lazy synthesized arrangements replacing their organic if ultra-slick instrumentation. This decay seemed to be reflected by chart positions: it's shocking to realize that, come the end, their singles were stalling outside the Top 30 in the U.K., always one of their most lucrative territories.

Similarly foggy memory surrounds success at the beginning of their career. Contrary to the recollections of many, it was not all plain sailing once the immortal 'Waterloo' had won the 1974 Eurovision Song Contest. It was only with the sensual 'S.O.S.' well over a year later that the group began to claw their way back to respectable chart positions. While the following 'Mamma Mia' and 'Fernando' were both U.K. chart-toppers, it was with 'Dancing Queen' that they really secured more than a foothold in rock history. Alongside 'Waterloo' it has become their signature song. America occasionally allowed the group into its Top 10 but was always uneven in its affections for the Swedish singers. But for 'Dancing Queen' the nation succumbed unequivocally, granting Abba their sole Stateside Number 1.

A mini-myth surrounds this song itself. Because Abba performed it two months before its official release at a gala to celebrate the nuptials of the king of Sweden, many assumed that it was written specifically for the occasion. In fact, it started life in August 1975 as a track provisionally titled 'Boogaloo,' which authors Björn Ulvaeus and Benny Andersson had vague visions of giving a 'dance' feel. Their session musicians – and how strange it is to contemplate that Abba was never a self-contained entity but a vocal group with a resident guitarist and keyboardist – achieved the result with a self-conscious cross of disco smash 'Rock Your Baby' by George McCrae and a Dr. John album. Only then was the lyric added, and with subject matter concerning a 17-year-old queen of the disco, the song was destined to endear itself to dancefloor-addicted teenagers everywhere.

One half of Abba's female vocal pairing, Agnetha Fältskog, has said that the group knew instantly that the song was going to be "massive," but the track did not gain an immediate release. It's a testament to how strong were the act's compositions at this point that they were able to put 'Dancing Queen' on the back burner and instead release as a single 'Fernando' – and a testament to their pop craftsmanship that 'Fernando' became a smash despite its almost surreally unlikely subject matter of Latin American revolutionaries. When 'Dancing Queen' was issued it did indeed become the "massive" hit foreseen by Fältskog – and seemed to know it was destined for immortality by giddily announcing its arrival with surely the most famous piano glissando in pop history.

Blitzkrieg Bop
The Ramones

Released May 1976
Sire *725* (U.S.) / Sire *6078 601* (U.K.)

New Rose
The Damned

Released October 1976
Not issued U.S. / Stiff *BUY 6* (U.K.)

Some earlier bands such as The Stooges may have displayed many of the characteristics later associated with punk, but The Ramones were the first punk-rock band, and 'Blitzkrieg Bop' was the first punk-rock single. Formed in 1974, 'da brudders' Joey, Johnny, Dee Dee, and Tommy donned ripped drainpipe jeans, battered sneakers, and biker jackets, adopted the surname Ramone, and started playing to initially hostile audiences in the clubs of New York City.

Although The Ramones took their musical cues from the past, they used them to create the future. Rock'n'roll, surf, Phil Spector, and 1960s garage-rock were the inspirations. The music was stripped back to the barest of essentials: no drum fills, no guitar solos, just short, fast, four-chord songs with catchy tunes and the dumbest of lyrics. Today, it doesn't seem like the recipe for a revolution, such is the extent to which The Ramones' aesthetic has become common currency. But in an era gorged on musical excess, it was indeed revolutionary.

The band signed to Sire Records in late 1975 and recorded their debut album for under $6,000 (about £3,300) early the following year, from which 'Blitzkrieg Bop' was lifted as a single. Opening with a refrain of "Hey, ho, let's go!" shouted (not sung) over brutalized tom toms, it was a wake-up call for a generation. Not that everyone instantly opened their eyes. 'Blitzkrieg Bop' was not a hit, nor did it get a great deal of airplay, and in an era when conspicuous musicianship was revered, most critics and many rock fans were simply baffled by the starved pop minimalism.

STIFF: THE WORLD'S MOST FLEXIBLE RECORD LABEL

The rise of 'New Rose' by The Damned helped establish one of the key British independent labels of the punk era, Stiff Records, and its in-house producer, Nick Lowe. The label was founded in 1976 by Dave Robinson and Jake Riviera, ex-managers of pub-rock groups Brinsley Schwarz and Dr. Feelgood respectively. Lowe had been the bassist and vocalist in the former group, and released the first Stiff

single, 'So It Goes.' He then took on the role of producer of much of the label's initial output, most notably the landmark punk single 'New Rose' by The Damned. He was at the helm of all Elvis Costello's 1970s work, including the singles 'Less Than Zero' and 'Watching The Detectives.' He also continued his own recording career, which included the formation of Rockpile with Dave Edmunds. Because they were signed to different labels, only one of the albums the duo recorded together was credited to Rockpile; the rest masqueraded as solo albums by Lowe and by Edmunds.

Although the label's output was more diverse than is often thought, stretching way beyond three-chord punk-rock, for the first couple of years their releases were very much of a type. The regular deployment of Lowe as producer was integral to this, as was the series of iconic jackets designed by graphic artist Barney Bubbles. Stiff also maintained a relentless – and often somewhat controversial – marketing strategy, which included arranging for Costello to be "arrested for busking" outside CBS Records (who later signed him to a lucrative long-term contract).

As was the case with almost everything punk, Stiff didn't last long in its original incarnation. Riviera left to form the shortlived Radar Records in early 1978, taking Costello and Lowe with him. Robinson responded by diversifying the Stiff roster further, and in the process scoring greater commercial success with artists including Ian Dury & The Blockheads, Madness, and Kirsty MacColl.

The criticism leveled at The Ramones in the early days was that they "couldn't play," and if musicianship is about nothing more than deft fingerwork, then that was true. But what The Ramones could do was drill straight to the very heart of what made rock'n'roll so exciting in the first place.

They first played in Britain in July 1976, galvanizing the nascent London punk scene. In the audience to see them were members not only of The Clash and The Sex Pistols but also the band that would release the official first British punk single, The Damned. Like The Ramones, The Damned played loud, fast, and basic, and like their American counterparts they too had a well-tuned pop sensibility, all heard on their debut single, 'New Rose.' Released on British independent label Stiff, 'New Rose' was an attention-grabber from the moment the band's singer – Bela Lugosi lookalike Dave Vanian – posed the question: "Is she really going out with him?" before standing back for a flurry of drums and some quick-fire chord changes. Like 'Blitzkrieg Bop' it was all over in two minutes.

At odds with their reputations for brevity, both The Ramones and The Damned forged enduring careers. The Ramones toured and recorded relentlessly for another 20 years, while The Damned still appear in one configuration or another. But any quibbles about failing to grow old gracefully should be set aside in the face of these two masterful distillations of the very essence of rock'n'roll

Anarchy In The U.K.
The Sex Pistols
....

Released November 1976
Not issued U.S. / EMI *2566* (U.K. #38)

The music of The Sex Pistols was driven by the singular dissatisfaction of the young in mid-1970s Britain. The economy was stagnant and the national atmosphere was one of conflict and discontent, epitomized by the labor strikes that seemed to erupt every single day. Combine that with the perpetually drizzly weather that has always afflicted the country and things seemed to assume a permanent grayness. It was even grimmer for the kids. Clearly the stars of the 1960s had all long passed their peak, their somnambulant albums reeking of the blunted artistic ambition engendered by success, their gigs reeking of self-regard in the form of interminable extemporization.

It was their contempt for their dreary culture and moribund music scene that underpinned the Pistols' music. Singer Johnny Rotten was the last to join the band. While primarily invited into the fold because the group liked his short hair and distressed clothes sense (both then rare), his diseased, wheezy voice was quite unusual too. By astonishing fortuitousness, this young man, picked for reasons of surface flash, transpired to have a unique ability for writing lyrics, steeped in disgust at both himself and the world, that was the missing piece in their brand of alt rock, whose reference points were The Velvet Underground, The Stooges, and The New York Dolls. The Pistols were soon outraging London and then the country with music that was as snotty and sneering as their demeanor, and they were already semi-mythical before they released this, their first record, the only one ever to be issued by the group's original line-up.

Such was the myth – they inspired concert violence, wore swastikas, and had a reputation for studied musical incompetence – that when this debut did appear, it came as a surprise to those who had not seen them live. It was relatively conventional. Rotten's lyric may have started with the chilling conversational gambit, "I am an anti-Christ!" and ended with the equally disturbing, "Destro-o-oy!" and his menacing vocal certainly gave it a demented kink. But otherwise it was all comparatively familiar, highly competent hard-rock, complete with two nifty guitar breaks. The band had labored hard and agonized long over the record, the ultimate product of sessions stretching from July to October 1976 supervised by two different producers, Dave Goodman and Chris Thomas. Despite the joint group composing credit, the song was a collaboration between Rotten and bassist Glen Matlock. Matlock had devised the melody after guitarist Steve Jones had suggested the band needed an anthem. Rotten wrote the lyric following a pub conversation in which band friend and sleeve designer Jamie Reed contributed several ideas.

The record eventually made Number 38 on the British chart. Rotten has said that had it not been for their scandal-making, record-deal-ending appearance on tea-time TV that December, it would have made the top spot. While that does seem unlikely, it is exactly what happened (in some charts) to their controversial follow-up, 'God Save The Queen.'

God Save The Queen
Sex Pistols

Released May 1977
Not issued U.S. / Virgin *VS 181* (U.K. #2)

By early 1977 The Sex Pistols and their media-manipulating manager Malcolm McLaren had managed to relieve two major record companies of considerable amounts of money for agreeing not to release their records.

It was EMI who first signed up Johnny Rotten and his sneering crew in October 1976, releasing their first single, 'Anarchy In The UK.' The relationship didn't last long, and following a scandalous appearance on an early-evening British television show and other acts of public disorder, EMI dumped the group alleging "adverse publicity," deleting 'Anarchy' after sales of 55,000, and letting the band keep the £40,000 advance (about $70,000 at the time).

McLaren next cut a deal with A&M. 'God Save The Queen' – originally entitled 'No Future' – was to be their next single, and with the track's title in mind and Queen Elizabeth's Silver Jubilee celebrations fast approaching, an official signing ceremony was staged outside Buckingham Palace on the March 10th 1977. Just six days later the A&M contract was also terminated, making this possibly the shortest recording contract in pop-music history.

This was the result of a riotous party at A&M's headquarters to celebrate the signing, at which the company's employees were so disgusted by the group's behaviour that they were dropped before any product was released. The Pistols and McLaren received another golden handshake, this time a princely £75,000 (about $132,000) for doing absolutely nothing. By this time, however, A&M had already pressed 25,000 copies of the single, which had to be destroyed, although some remain in circulation and are among the most collectable of rarities. (An A&M copy of 'God Save The Queen' was sold for £2,820 – about $4,085 – at a Sotheby's auction in 2001.)

Now desperate to get the single out in time for the Jubilee in June, McLaren then signed with Richard Branson's Virgin for further £15,000 (about $26,000), and 'God Save The Queen' was officially released on May 27th. While this controversial single received minimum radio play, the wave of publicity surrounding the group made sure that it sold 150,000 copies in five days, reaching Number 2 on the officially recognized BBC/British Market Research Bureau chart, although it's always been alleged that the British Phonographic Industry managed to rig its own chart so that they would not suffer the embarrassment of having 'God Save The Queen' at Number 1 in Jubilee week.

left > The Sex Pistols and Malcolm McLaren sign a short-lived deal with A&M outside Buckingham Palace, London.
below > The group onstage in the U.S. in January 1978.

Marquee Moon
Television

Released March 1977
Not issued U.S. / Elektra *K 12252* (U.K. #30)

Blank Generation
Richard Hell & The Voidoids
Released September 1977
Sire *SRE1003* (U.S.A.) / Sire *6078608* (U.K.)

Psycho Killer
Talking Heads
Released December 1977
Sire *1013* (U.S.A.) / Sire *6078610* (U.K.)

White Riot
The Clash

Released March 1977
Not issued U.S. / CBS *5058* (U.K. #38)

In August 1976, Clash frontman Joe Strummer, bassist Paul Simonon, and manager Bernard Rhodes attended the annual festival in west London's Notting Hill Gate. Always a lively affair, in this instance the carnival became literally incendiary as black youths – who had long accused the city's police of racial harassment – erupted into spontaneous violence. Strummer and Simonon enjoyed the civil disobedience enough to pitch in themselves, but the experience was of more importance because it provided the nascent group with its first signature song. Written by Strummer and lead guitarist Mick Jones, 'White Riot' proposed that the Caucausian working class youth should express their dissatisfaction in a similar fashion, with a "White riot / A riot of my own!"

Overlaid with the sound of stomping boots, breaking glass, and police sirens, 'White Riot' was the first single recorded by The Clash for CBS under the terms of a £100,000 deal (about $175,000) that some saw as a betrayal of the very principles of U.K. punk. Others were amazed that such a growling, brutal song could become a semi-hit – especially with little radio play or promotion. But as it climbed into the British Top 40, 'White Riot' proved that punk had become the street-level voice-of-real-youth.

Less than a year after The Ramones lit the fuse under a stagnant rock scene, New York punk had evolved into something more arch and intellectual, characterized by angular, spidery guitars and obtuse, diffident lyrics.

First out of the blocks was Television, who had formed from the ashes of The Neon Boys in 1973. The group's first single for Elektra, 'Marquee Moon,' seemingly broke all the rules of the fledgling punk movement: it has key changes and guitar solos, and runs to almost eleven minutes. While that might sound like a recipe for progressive rock – anathema to any punk worth his salt – Television did, nonetheless, share a visceral urgency with their punk peers, and in Tom Verlaine they had one of the great atonal singers.

Before rounding up the Voidoids, Richard Hell was the bassist in an early incarnation of Television, and co-wrote 'Chinese Rocks' with former New York Doll Johnny Thunders for the latter's new group The Heartbreakers. The Voidoids second single – following '(I Could Live With You In) Another World' – 'Blank Generation' is pitched somewhere between the sound of Hell's previous bands: more raw and primal than Verlaine's bunch, but still knowingly playful.

Although both retain ever-growing cult followings, Richard Hell and Television found their careers waning by the end of the 1970s. Talking Heads, meanwhile, were only just getting started in 1977, and would remain active – and dazzlingly creative – well into the 1980s. 'Psycho Killer' is one of several early gems that, in David Byrne's "fa-fa-fa-fa-fa-fa-fa-fa-fa" breakdown, contains the greatest pop stutter since The Who's 'My Generation.'

Do Anything You Wanna Do
Eddie & The Hot Rods

Released August 1977
Island *IS 093* (U.S.) / Island *WIP 6401* (U.K. #9)

A hymn to the perpetual adolescent struggle for freedom, 'Do Anything You Wanna Do' is a perfect marriage of lyrics and music. The simplistic yearning of lines such as "Searching for adventure / It's the kind of life to find" sound like profound spiritual truths when pitted against a wall of ringing Telecaster chords. Eddie & The Hot Rods had the misfortune to fall between two British styles of the time – too fast and basic for pub rock, and just a little too old for punk. But they made a series of strong singles, of which 'Do Anything' was the biggest and best. The band's ambiguous status was underlined when, at the height of punk, they appeared on the *Top of The Pops* TV singles show to promote the single. Singer Barrie Masters unwittingly committed the ultimate fashion crime of the time – he wore white flares.

Hotel California
The Eagles

Released February 1977
Asylum *45386* (U.S. #1) / Asylum *K 13079* (U.K. #8)

A lot had happened to The Eagles in the years since their 1972 debut single 'Take It Easy,' during which time they had become one of the biggest acts on the planet, notching up six U.S. Top 10 hits (including three Number 1s) in the process, and turned into a symbol for some for everything that was 'wrong' in music. Punks didn't consider them quite the sell-out acts that Rod Stewart and The Rolling Stones had become in their eyes, but The Eagles were frequently cited by the new wave as representatives of a self-satisfied rock elite who had jettisoned grit in favor of soporific tempos, vapid production techniques, and self-satisfied lyrics.

Added to the alleged crimes of The Eagles was the fact that their success made them the de facto leaders of the country-rock genre, whose roots in Californian cocaine culture and Me Generation ethics were anathema to those who held that contemporary popular music should exhibit a concern for the issues of the day. "It's our job to get people off," Eagles drummer Don Henley had shrugged in a 1975 interview, "not to get them crazy and militant." The same interview had seen him splutter: "I hate those stupid labels! I hate when people call us a country-rock band, because they are so full of it. We can do anything!"

Hotel California was the album that saw The Eagles move away from country rock and start to embrace social commentary. The former may have had something to do with a change of personnel, with Bernie Leadon replaced on guitar by Joe Walsh. The album's title track sets the sunny State as a metaphor for the condition of America. A traveler checks into the Hotel California and finds himself in a decadent nightmare. The lyrics are brilliantly constructed and in places genuinely spooky, as in the line "You can check out any time you like but you can never leave." Musically, the crux of the record is its stunning guitar finale. Played by Don Felder and Joe Walsh alternately and then in tandem, the guitars twine, snake, yowl, and cool across the space of two endlessly fascinating minutes. Inexplicably, many DJs opted to fade the record at this point.

'Hotel California' is what 'Stairway To Heaven' is to Led Zeppelin, and 'Bohemian Rhapsody' to Queen: the grand statement of their career, an opus whose self-consciousness generates a degree of ridicule and accusations of pompousness, but at the same time underlines an intense dedication to craft that lifts the recording to the stature, quite simply, of a classic piece of work.

American Girl
Tom Petty & The Heartbreakers

Released May 1977
Shelter *62007* (U.S.) / Shelter *WIP 6403* (U.K. #40)

The Byrd's Roger McGuinn once heard this song on the radio and sat trying to remember when he'd recorded it. Petty certainly had captured McGuinn's jangling guitar and quavering vocal style, but it would be unfair to dismiss the song as a Byrds pastiche. While it was probably inspired by the patriotic ambience of the year of the bicentennial – it was recorded on July 4, 1976 – there is more to the lyric than the rousing celebration of American womanhood that it at first appears to be. Petty, however, denies an urban myth that the song is about a student's suicide.

Dreams
Fleetwood Mac

Released April 1977
Warner Bros. *8371* (U.S. #1) / Warner Bros. *K 16969* (U.K. #24)

Fleetwood Mac's only American Number 1 single was written on a black velvet bed in Sly Stone's cocaine pit. The group was formerly a successful Brit-blues combo but had long since relocated to California, now re-energized by the incorporation of two estimable and romantically entwined young songwriters, Lindsey Buckingham and Stevie Nicks. The Mac's eponymous 1975 album had restored the ailing band to the top spot in the *Billboard* album chart. 'Dreams' arrived while they were squirreled away in the Record Plant in Sausalito, California, recording what would become the mega-platinum follow-up album, *Rumours*.

One afternoon while the rest of the band was busy in the main studio, Nicks lugged her Fender Rhodes piano into a smaller studio, favored by Sly of Sly & The Family Stone, and settled down on a bed in a sunken pit that, according to Mac founder-member Mick Fleetwood, "was usually occupied by people we didn't know, tapping razors on mirrors." Seated Indian-style on the bed, Nicks recalled how she simply "found a drum pattern, switched my little cassette player on, and wrote 'Dreams' in about ten minutes."

According to Fleetwood Mac's other female songwriter, Christine McVie, the ten-minute wonder song consisted of "just three chords and one note in the left hand," and it had to be dramatically refashioned into three distinct sections by Buckingham before it came to life. Sadly, this professional camaraderie masked the fact that the song was about the agonizing break-up of Nicks's romance with Buckingham following her dalliance with Don Henley of The Eagles.

Mull Of Kintyre / Girls' School
Wings

Released November 1977
Capitol *4504* (U.S.) / Capitol *R 6018* (U.K. #1)

A mull in Scotland is a promontory, and the Mull of Kintyre is at the south-western tip of the Kintyre peninsula – a few miles from Paul McCartney's Scottish farm where this song was recorded using a mobile studio in a barn. It was a deliberate attempt to write a modern Scottish anthem, and McCartney, who hired seven pipers and ten drummers from the Campbell Town Pipe Band to assist him, described it as a cross between 'Sailing' and 'Amazing Grace.' He thought 'Mull' was something of a throwaway but was proved quite wrong when it became the biggest-selling record of all time in Britain, spending nine weeks at Number 1, selling over two million copies, and beating the previous record holder – his own 'She Loves You' for The Beatles. It was McCartney's first British post-Beatles Number 1 (although in America he'd already had five chart-toppers: 'Uncle Albert,' 'My Love,' 'Band On The Run,' 'Listen To What The Man Said,' and 'Silly Love Songs'). 'Mull' was part of a double A-side in Britain but didn't hit in America, where 'Girls' School,' the B-side, made the running and reached a modest Number 33. 'Mull Of Kintyre' was co-written with fellow Wings member Denny Laine, who later sold his rights back to McCartney when he was declared bankrupt.

I Feel Love
Donna Summer

Released July 1977
Casablanca *884* (U.S. #6) / GTO *GT 100* (U.K. #1)

The first British Number 1 hit to be constructed entirely from synthesized electronic sounds, 'I Feel Love' is a landmark in the evolution of the pop single. It was the brainchild of production duo Giorgio Moroder and Pete Bellotte, setting Summer's euphoric vocal against a futuristic backdrop of unrelenting programmed bass and drums.

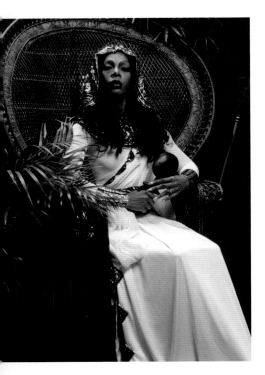

Donna Summer stood among the most popular performers of the disco era, achieving a level of success exceeded only by The Bee Gees. Like them, she began her career before the disco boom and continued to score hits beyond it. Born Donna Andrea Gaines in Boston, Massachusetts, Summer moved to Germany as a teenager in the late 1960s and performed there in the musicals *Hair* and *Godspell*. She spent the early 1970s working on the fringes of the music industry before meeting Moroder and Bellotte, who produced her first European hit, 'The Hostage,' in 1974.

Summer, Moroder, and Bellotte developed a signature sound over the next couple of years. The sultry, funky 'Love To Love You

Baby' (1976) gave Summer her first U.S. hit, despite radio bans brought on by her suggestive heavy breathing. Her album of the same name included a dazzlingly exploratory 17-minute version of the title track. Summer was unusual among disco artists in that she focused just as much on albums as singles, notably the conceptual set *Four Seasons Of Love*. She latched onto the trend for issuing lengthy mixes on 12-inch vinyl – aimed mostly at dance clubs – alongside shorter versions, edited down for the singles market.

By 1977 Summer and her producers had begun to tire of the lush string arrangements and rich production jobs that had come to characterize disco (and which they had helped to popularize). Trailing the release of her fifth full-length album, *I Remember Yesterday*, 'I Feel Love' introduced a sleeker, sparser, ultra-modern sound driven by squelching, programmed bass and loops of overlapping electronic drums, with the sweeping strings of old replaced by a single droning synthesizer.

One of the most important electronic recordings of the 1970s, 'I Feel Love' showed that a huge international hit could be achieved without having to use conventional instrumentation or backing musicians, and effectively drew up the blueprint for much of the techno and house music of the 1980s and 1990s. While other records could claim to be more innovative – 'Trans Europe Express' by Kraftwerk, perhaps, or Brian Eno's album *Another Green World* – none had the commercial clout of 'I Feel Love.' The most crucial element in its mainstream success, however, is the exultant vocal melody, which gives a much-needed human counterpoint to the harsh, robotic backing track.

'I Feel Love' gave Donna Summer her first Number 1 hit in the U.K. and was the first of her singles to reach the U.S. Top 10 since 'Love To Love You Baby.' Her star continued to rise for the remainder of the 1970s, earning her the title The Queen Of Disco. In 1978 and '79 she released four chart-topping singles in the U.S. – 'MacArthur Park,' 'Hot Stuff,' 'Bad Girls,' and 'No More Tears (Enough Is Enough)' – but 'I Feel Love' remains her most important recording.

12-INCH SINGLES: ACCOMMODATING THE MEGAMIX

The 12-inch single was introduced out of musical necessity and economic acumen. For the previous three decades there had been few challengers to the 7-inch 45rpm disc, which had been in use since 1949. The 7-inch had been devised to hold up to five minutes of music, which was more than ample at the point of its introduction, when the average popular song tended to last around two minutes. In the 1950s, with the arrival of the EP (extended play), the discs could hold up to seven minutes per side.

The extended-play format was achieved by cutting thinner, tighter grooves into the vinyl. This lowered the signal-to-noise ratio, resulting in a decrease in sound quality and volume. It didn't seem to matter a great deal to the record-buying public of the 1950s, but in subsequent decades there was a marked increase in the quality of record production and home stereo equipment. As a result, listeners expected a better quality of sound. The arrival of disco music in the mid 1970s made the need for a new format even more pressing. Record makers had begun to produce extended mixes of songs, aimed predominantly at club DJs. Thus a new format was required, one that could accommodate longer songs without any noticeable depreciation in fidelity and volume.

There was no real point in attempting to enhance the 7-inch single as, by this point, there was little difference in the production costs of that or a 12-inch disc. A 12-inch 45rpm single would be able to hold more music and, just as crucially, reproduce it at a higher fidelity, because it allowed for wider, deeper grooves to be cut. From an economic standpoint, a 12-inch record looked like a bigger, better product and could thus be marketed and priced as such. It also allowed record labels to sell two different versions of a single – the conventional 7-inch pop single and a 12-inch version, sometimes referred to as a 'maxi single,' which was labeled as containing extended club mixes. The idea was that the devoted fan would have to buy both.

The first commercially released 12-inch single was Walter Gibbons's remix of 'Ten Percent' by the Philadelphia-based disco act Double Exposure. The format quickly grew in popularity, notably with releases by disco acts such as Boney M and Donna Summer. It became a staple of independent record labels during the 1980s, notably Factory Records, which in 1983 issued the biggest-selling 12-inch single of all time, 'Blue Monday' by New Order.

"Heroes"
David Bowie

Released October 1977
RCA *11211* (U.S.) / RCA *PB 1121* (U.K. #24)

Although it wasn't a major chart success, '"Heroes"' has come to be recognized as perhaps the finest moment in the career of one of the stalwarts of British music. It was the title track from Bowie's second album of 1977 and arrived in the midst of the most experimental period of his career. After going through a series of stylistic changes that took him from proto-metal to glam-rock to plastic soul in the earlier 1970s, Bowie moved to Berlin, Germany, in 1976 and made three albums there – *Low*, *"Heroes,"* and *Lodger* – with his regular producer Tony Visconti and the pioneering electronic musician Brian Eno.

These albums contain some of Bowie's best and most adventurous work, but much of it finds him at his least commercial. '"Heroes"' is the one song from this period that stands up as a classic pop song. Bowie was inspired to write the lyric after catching sight of Visconti and backing singer Antonia Maass canoodling by a wall. It was given a suitably widescreen backing, dominated by Robert Fripp's searing lead guitar parts, which were played through Eno's EMS synthesizer. Fripp flew in from the U.S. to record all of his parts for *"Heroes"* in one brief session.

The most striking aspect of the song is Bowie's vocal. Easily the most powerful of his career, it begins in a soft, conversational tone but gradually rises and by the song's close has become a passionate cry. The ever-inventive Visconti captured Bowie's vocal in one pass by setting up three microphones in the studio at different distances from the singer. Each had a 'noise gate' attached so that it would only switch on when Bowie reached a certain level of volume. For the opening verses his voice was picked up only by the first, closest mike, lending it a gentle intimacy, but the full-throated pleas of the latter part of the song were captured by all three microphones, allowing the sound to swirl and echo in the distance.

Surprisingly, given its anthemic qualities, '"Heroes"' failed to match the chart success of earlier Bowie singles like 'Space Oddity' or 'The Jean Genie.' It was a hit across Europe, in part because it was also issued in German and French-language versions (as '"Helden"' and '"Héros"' respectively). Despite its continual use in advertising and at sporting events, the single has lost none of its original power and remains constant at the top end of many a list of the Greatest Singles Of All Time.

below > David Bowie (right) at Hansa By The Wall studios in Berlin, Germany, where he recorded '"Heroes"' with former King Crimson guitarist Robert Fripp (left) and sonic alchemist Brian Eno (center).

Stayin' Alive
The Bee Gees

Released December 1977
RSO *885* (U.S. #1) / RSO *2090 267* (U.K. #4)

How Deep Is Your Love
The Bee Gees
Released September 1977
RSO *882* (U.S. #1) / RSO *2090 259* (U.K. #3)

Night Fever
The Bee Gees
Released January 1978
RSO *889* (U.S. #1) / RSO *002* (U.K. #1)

More Than A Woman
Tavares
Released April 1978
Capitol *4500* (U.S. #32) / Capitol *CL 15977* (U.K. #7)

On December 24, 1977, 'How Deep Is Your Love' became the first of six consecutive singles on RSO Records to hit the U.S. Number 1 slot, giving rock, theatre, and movie mogul Robert Stigwood's label a resounding five months' domination of the American chart. 'How Deep Is Your Love' was followed to the top by Player's 'Baby Come Back,' The Bee Gees' 'Stayin' Alive,' Andy Gibb's 'Love Is Thicker Than Water,' The Bee Gees yet again with 'Night Fever,' and finally 'If I Can't Have You' by Yvonne Elliman.

Tidy as it would be to explain away this phenomenal achievement as simply the magic of The Bee Gees, the reality is a much more complex tale involving the brothers Gibb, their canny manager, the emergence of a new dance craze, and a low-budget teen movie starring an unknown but charismatic young hopeful.

In the summer of 1976 on both sides of the Atlantic punk rock was beginning to emerge as a powerful new musical force. Meanwhile, the hopelessly old-fangled Bee Gees were ensconced in the Chateau

D'Herouville outside Paris, France, working on their next album. Stigwood, their manager, was in New York City where his gaze fell upon a feature by Nik Cohn in *New York* magazine. Cohn eloquently described the music, attitudes, and fashions that surrounded the emerging culture of the Big Apple's discotheques. Stigwood immediately saw an opportunity to make a killing with a movie about disco-obsessed teens. His clients The Bee Gees had already scored chart-toppers with dance-oriented material, including 'Jive Talkin'' and 'You Should Be Dancing,' so he made a transatlantic call to Barry Gibb.

"All of those songs in *Saturday Night Fever* were for our own album," Barry remembered later. "They weren't for Fever at all. Robert just happened to hear those four or five songs and said he wanted them for the movie." His brother Maurice recalled Stigwood telling them precious little about the project. "All we knew was that it was about this guy who works in a paint shop, blows his wages every Saturday night, and wins a dance competition."

Stigwood's name is familiar to most serious music fans, but few know very much more about this powerful entertainment entrepreneur. Ruddy faced and notoriously stubborn, Stiggy had arrived in London from Australia in 1959 as a backpacker with just £3 ($8) in his pocket. After an unsuccessful attempt to be a pop singer, he switched to artist management, guiding British teen idol John Leyton. By 1967 Stigwood was working with Beatles manager Brian Epstein and learned enough to build The Bee Gees up to the point where they became significant rivals to the Liverpool group. An astute talent-spotter, Stigwood secured a roster of very successful acts, including Cream, and was a millionaire by the age of 30. When he quit Britain in the early 1970s to avoid punitive taxation, he was already one of the most powerful men in the music business.

During the first week of December 1977, American cinema audiences were treated to a 30-second trailer for *Saturday Night Fever*. It was largely unmemorable, consisting mainly of the feet of the movie's unknown leading man, John Travolta, striding down a New York street – but pounding away behind those feet was 'Stayin' Alive,' a song that had started life as a few lines scrawled by Robin Gibb on his Concorde ticket. It was 'Stayin' Alive' that brought the trailer vibrantly to life. When Stigwood first heard 'Stayin' Alive' he was adamant that the Gibbs should change the title to 'Saturday Night' but Barry refused. "We said, 'There are so many songs out there called 'Saturday Night.' It's corny. It's a terrible title.'"

The movie premiered in New York City on December 14, 1977, and 'How Deep Is Your Love,' which Barry Gibb confidently predicted would flop in the face of the rising tide of punk, was at Number 1 before Christmas, initiating a run of *Saturday Night Fever*-related chart successes that broke all previous records. Aside from the chart-toppers by The Bee Gees and Yvonne Elliman already mentioned, the movie was also responsible for the success of 'Boogie Shoes' by K.C. & The Sunshine Band (U.S. Number 35) and 'Disco Inferno' by The Trammps (Number 11).

A peculiarity of the *Fever* soundtrack was that it included two versions of 'More Than A Woman,' one by The Bee Gees and one by Tavares. When the Tavares version came out as a single in America it floundered at Number 32, probably because it was already available on the album and as the B-side of The Bee Gees' 'Night Fever.' However, on May 6, 1978, it entered the U.K. charts, where it peaked at Number 7, reviving Tavares's flagging fortunes on the international stage.

By the end of the 1970s, the *Saturday Night Fever* soundtrack had sold 25 million copies, and the movie, made for just $7 million, has since grossed well over $300 million, transforming Stigwood, in his own words,

"from a minor millionaire into a minor billionaire." In the early 1990s he left his 26-acre estate in Bermuda and returned to live on his 55-acre Barton Manor on the Isle Of Wight in southern England. A recent estimate of his personal fortune put it at £170 million and rising.

Despite the large sums of money that *Saturday Night Fever* deposited into the Bee Gee coffers, it continues to irritate them that the movie's astonishing impact radically altered perceptions of their music. "We were being called blue-eyed soul," Maurice said shortly before his unexpected death in 2003, "but when the film came out we were the kings of disco. 'How Deep Is Your Love' was an R&B ballad but, when the film came out, it somehow became a disco ballad."

As well as making Stigwood, Travolta, and The Bee Gees filthy rich, *Saturday Night Fever* also transformed the lives of countless teenagers worldwide, among them London lad Georgios Panayiotou, now better known as George Michael. "Before *Saturday Night Fever* I was blind to that kind of music," he said. "You didn't hear a lot of dance on the radio, everybody was still into the 1960s and early-1970s idea of getting into your own thing at home. Saturday Night Fever got me out to the clubs."

Chanson D'Amour
Manhattan Transfer

Released January 1977
Atlantic *3374* (U.S.) / Atlantic *K 10886* (U.K. #1)

When Manhattan Transfer's first album wasn't much of a U.S. success, spending just four weeks on the album Top 40, Atlantic wheeled in super-producer Richard Perry – against the highly talented vocal ensemble's wishes – for album number two, *Coming Out*. 'Chanson D'Amour' was recorded as an afterthought at the end of a session in which little else had been accomplished and nailed in one take. The song had originally been a Number 6 *Billboard* hit for husband-and-wife team Art & Dotty Todd in 1958. While not particularly representative of Mantran's usual material, it was their biggest hit, and is particularly notable for its slight lyrics (there are in fact just four lines), questionable Anglo-French rhyming (encore, more, je t'adore), and those catchy 'rah-tah-tah-tah-tah' interjections.

Oxygène Part IV
Jean-Michel Jarre

Released July 1977
Polydor *PD 14425* (U.S.) / Polydor *2001 721* (U.K. #4)

Electronically-generated musical sounds had been incorporated into hit singles since the early 1960s, usually for their novelty value, and some massive international hits such as 'Telstar' by The Tornados and 'Reflections' by The Supremes had prominently featured electronics.

Robert Moog's new generation of controllable synthesizers inspired artists as diverse as The Beatles, The Byrds, and Stevie Wonder to increase the electronic content of their songs, and by the early 1970s German bands including Tangerine Dream and U.S. innovators such as Tonto's Expanding Head Band used nothing but synths to create their music. What much of this electronic music lacked, though, was worldwide popular appeal. Alongside Kraftwerk and Donna Summer, Jean-Michel Jarre took the final step of making music that was as danceable as it was cerebral.

His first album, an eight-part suite entitled *Oxygène*, was recorded during August 1976 in the 28-year-old French composer's studio, converted from his dining room, near the Champs-Elysées in Paris, with not a guitar in sight, and using state-of-the-art ARP, AKS, and RMI synthesizers plus a Mellotron and a 'rhythmic computer.'

'Oxygène Part IV' was released as a single in the late summer of 1977, in the midst of the punk boom, and became one of the first internationally successful 45rpm fusions of the undeniably futuristic sounds of synth technology with some infectiously memorable tunes and disco beats. It would prove to be the way that much music was made from now on, with Jarre ushering in the age of popular synthesized music that provided, at last, a viable alternative to the electric guitar.

Float On
The Floaters

Released July 1977
ABC *12284* (U.S. #2) / ABC *4187* (U.K. #1)

Disco and R&B act The Detroit Emeralds deservedly scored well with their spin-off group The Floaters as the languid ballad 'Float On' became an enormous hit on both sides of the pond. While the song, all icy guitar flicks and organ washes, insinuated itself into everyone's minds, the image of the band – Afro hairdos, polite suits, and all – was just right for the times. Unfortunately they couldn't sustain any momentum and 'Float On' remained a one-off. But if you're going to join the ranks of one-hit wonders, you might as well have a smash hit.

Cold As Ice
Foreigner

Released July 1977
Atlantic *3410* (U.S. #6) / Atlantic *K 10986* (U.K. #24)

Heavy metal with touches of synth might be de rigueur today, but back in the late 1970s only a few bands were dabbling with such blasphemy. However, New York outfit Foreigner achieved the right blend of silky electronics and polite riffs and scored massive sales as a result. This little ditty was memorable solely for its "You're as cold as ice" line (which goes up a tone and back again, memorably) and made a good impression in Middle America – the Brits were less keen –ensuring a few years of touring success for Lou Gramm and his chums. Foreigner's eponymous debut LP from this year remains an AOR classic.

Uptown Top Ranking
Althia & Donna

Released December 1977
Warner Bros. *17098* (U.S.) / Lightning *LIG 506* (U.K. #1)

Althia Forrest and Donna Reid were a pair of Jamaican teenagers who topped the U.K. chart through a combination of pure luck and naive charm. While 'Uptown Top Ranking' was a semi-credible slice of warmed-up reggae, with their harmonies taken from the Bananarama school (in other words not really in harmony at all), it was the song's lyrics about a night out on the town that fuelled the imagination. "Shoulda see me and the ranking dread / Check how we jamming and ting!" intoned the twosome, and while only those familiar with Jamaican patois understood it, the feel-good vibe came through clear and strong.

Wuthering Heights
Kate Bush

Released January 1978
EMI America *8003* (U.S.) / EMI *2719* (U.K. #1)

This stunning debut single announced the arrival of the 19-year-old Kate Bush, perhaps the most naturally gifted British female musician of the modern era. At 15, Bush caught the attention of Pink Floyd's Dave Gilmour, who helped record the demo tape that earned her a deal with EMI. The label allowed Bush to spend the next two years studying music, dancing, and mime before she started work on her debut album, The Kick Inside. EMI at first chose 'James And The Cold Gun' to be her first single, but the precocious singer insisted that it should be this dazzling adaptation of Emily Bronte's classic mid-19th century novel of the same name.

'Wuthering Heights' opens with Bush's twinkly piano playing, quickly joined by her siren-like vocal, which weaves in and out of a complex melody and chord progression. Voice and piano are joined by warm synths, soaring strings, and, eventually, a lyrical guitar solo, as the song rises to a glass-shattering crescendo. Bush's choice of debut single was vindicated when it brought her unexpectedly immediate success, giving her a British Number 1 at the first attempt. The follow-up, 'The Man With The Child In His Eyes,' wasn't quite so popular in the U.K. but did provide the singer with a minor U.S. hit.

Bush continued an almost unbroken run of critical and commercial successes throughout the 1980s and early 1990s. Along the way she re-recorded 'Wuthering Heights' – for her 1986 anthology The Whole Story – but there is little doubt that the original remains the definitive version and one of the most striking debuts in the history of pop.

Mr. Blue Sky
Electric Light Orchestra

Released January 1978
Jet *5050* (U.S. #35) / Jet *UP 36342* (U.K. #6)

The definitive Electric Light Orchestra single, 'Mr. Blue Sky' demonstrates all of the group's strengths but also shows off the comical excesses that have regularly seen them dismissed as a bloated Beatles tribute act. Frontman Jeff Lynne – formerly of The Move – might just have got the last laugh, however, when he worked as producer with Paul McCartney, George Harrison, Ringo Starr, and, in effect, John Lennon on the two Beatles 1990s 'comeback' singles, 'Free As A Bird' and 'Real Love.'

Formed in 1971, ELO went through various changes of line-up in the early 1970s before eventually reaching a relatively settled membership that included Lynne, drummer Bev Bevan, bassist Kelly Groucutt, keyboardist Richard Tandy, violinist Mik Kaminski, and cellists Hugh McDowell and Melvyn Gale. The latter trio of string players was crucial to the group's sound, which drew most explicitly on Beatles songs like 'A Day In The Life' and 'I Am The Walrus.'

Prior to selection as a single, 'Mr. Blue Sky' made up the final part of 'Concerto For A Rainy Day,' a four-song suite that filled the third side of the double-disc set Out Of The Blue (1977). The most conventionally structured of the four songs, 'Mr. Blue Sky' does nonetheless stretch beyond five minutes, taking in the obligatory big string arrangement, a choir, vocoder'd vocals, and an extended false ending. An international chart hit, it has also become the unofficial theme tune of Lynne's hometown soccer club, Birmingham City.

Baker Street
Gerry Rafferty

Released February 1978
United Artists *1192* (U.S. #2) / United Artists *UP 36346* (U.K. #3)

The other song for which Gerry Rafferty is well known is Stealer's Wheel's 'Stuck In The Middle With You,' and while that was a good song, it was chiefly notable as an absolutely uncanny imitation of Bob Dylan. With 'Baker Street' Rafferty revealed a more original vision. It is an exquisite song about self-delusion and loneliness in the big city with a cleverly realistic lyric ("One more year and then you'll be happy…"). Rafferty devised instrumental parts for the song and Raphael Ravenscroft was brought in to transpose them to saxophone. The result was the cherry on the cake, perfectly complementing the air of aching melancholy.

Sultans Of Swing
Dire Straits

Released May 1978
Warners Bros. *8736* (U.S. #4) / Vertigo *6059 206* (U.K. #8)

The Out were a late-1970s power-pop band who once opened for the up-and-coming Dire Straits. Mark Knopfler, frontman and guitarist of Dire Straits, admired the great sound that Out guitarist George Borowski obtained from his ridiculously battered instrument. Knopfler wondered why Borowski didn't play solos. "I can't really play solos," came the guileless response, "I just play chords."

Not long afterwards, Knopfler was working on 'Sultans Of Swing,' a song about a "crap little band" he had seen playing when drinking in a pub, and he decided to put in a verse about the incident: "Check out Guitar George / He knows all the chords / Mind, he's strictly rhythm, he doesn't want to make it cry or sing / And an old guitar is all he can afford / When he gets up under the lights to play his thing."

It was this song that secured Dire Straits a record deal after a demo played on DJ Charlie Gillett's London radio show Honky Tonk in summer 1977 provoked record-company interest. However, it was not plain sailing after the band released 'Sultans Of Swing' as their debut single. The American record company barely promoted it or the group's first album, on which could be found a different, slightly smoother version of the track. Radio stations loved the band, however, and eventually the single climbed into the Top 10 in February 1979. This Stateside success prompted U.K. stations to play the record, even though BBC Radio 1 had declined previously on the grounds that the song had too many words, and the single went Top 10 at home too.

Le Freak
Chic

....

Released October 1978
Atlantic *3519* (U.S. #1) / Atlantic *K 11209* (U.K. #7)

While the punk wars raged and the roots of electro and hip-hop spread, Chic knocked out an effortless sequence of timeless disco singles, each of which evoked images of a night-time club existence that unified races and nations under one ineffable groove. This was an illusion, of course, but it says much for the super-clean, super-euphoric music of Nile Rodgers and Bernard Edwards that to this day the songs sound as if they come from another planet.

Guitarist Rodgers and bassist Edwards formed Chic in 1976 and soon recruited fellow New Yorker Tony Thompson, a drummer who had previously worked with LaBelle. The trio's earliest work, including the international debut hit 'Dance Dance Dance,' featured vocalist Norma Jean Wright, but she was forced to quit in 1978 due to complications with her recording contract. 'Le Freak' was the first Chic single to feature new vocalist Luci Martin, but it was inspired, in a sense, by another, more famous singer.

On new year's eve, 1977, Rodgers and Edwards were invited to meet Grace Jones at the world famous New York City disco club Studio 54 to discuss the possibility of the duo producing her next album. On arriving at the club's entrance, however, Rodgers and Edwards were stopped from entering by the venue's bouncers. Understandably irritated, they went back to Rodgers's nearby apartment and decided to vent their anger by composing a new song together. In its initial incarnation, the funky, chicken-scratch guitar riff was overlaid by a repeated cry of "Aaaaah, fuck off!" Sensibly, Rodgers later changed the lyric to "Freak out," and a disco classic was born.

'Le Freak' is more than just a fun song: as with so many of Chic's works, the world-class bass playing of Edwards inspired a swathe of rappers, samplers, and producers to improve their game. It formed the basis of The Sugarhill Gang's 'Rapper's Delight,' generally considered to be the first charting hip-hop single. 'Le Freak' quickly rose to the top of the *Billboard* Hot 100. It was followed midway through 1979 by another seminal Chic Number 1, 'Good Times,' which had the distinction of being the source material for Grandmaster Flash's landmark single 'Adventures On The Wheels Of Steel.' Together, these two songs represent a funkier, more colorful era in pop music, which was the most enduring legacy of disco (John Travolta's white suit notwithstanding).

NILE RODGERS: A CHIC PRODUCTION STYLE

Nile Rodgers formed Chic with Bernard Edwards in 1976, but the group's popularity began to dwindle at the start of the 1980s, and it was at that point that Rodgers's second career as one of the decade's biggest and most important record producers began to take off. He had already worked with Sister Sledge and Diana Ross, for whom he produced the smash hit 'I'm Coming Out,' and was invited to update the sound of 1970s pop chameleon David Bowie for his *Let's Dance* album (1983). Rodgers looms large over the record, painting its eight concise songs with a palette of shiny synthesizers, funky bass, and disco guitar licks. Let's Dance remains the biggest commercial success of Bowie's career and spawned three international hits: the title track, 'Modern Love,' and 'China Girl.'

Rodgers then turned his attentions to Madonna, for whom he produced the hits 'Material Girl' and 'Like A Virgin.' After that it was Mick Jagger and Duran Duran. In 1986 he finally got the chance to work with Grace Jones, on her I*nside Story* album; he also worked on movie soundtracks, including *Alphabet City* (1984) and *Coming To America* (1988).

Most of the albums Rodgers worked on during the 1980s were made at The Power Station in New York City (now known as Avatar Studios), with his one-time Chic bandmates Bernard Edwards and Tony Thompson regularly providing bass and drums. In 1992, Rodgers and Edwards reformed Chic (without Thompson) to make the *CHIC-ism* album and for a world tour. Rodgers was named Top Producer In The World by *Billboard* magazine in 1996, but a series of celebratory gigs in Japan was marred when Edwards contracted pneumonia and died suddenly.

During the 1990s and beyond Rodgers's work-rate slowed, but he continues to produce hit records, both for artists he has worked with previously in the early part of his career, including David Bowie and Duran Duran, and the likes of Samantha Cole and All-4-One.

After the U.S. terrorist attacks of September 11, 2001, he organized an all-star re-recording of the Sister Sledge classic 'We Are Family' and shortly thereafter founded the We Are Family Foundation to promote cultural and religious tolerance.

Rivers Of Babylon
Boney M

Released April 1978
Sire *1027* (U.S. #30) / Atlantic-Hansa *K 11120* (U.K. #1)

Rasputin
Boney M
Released September 1978
Sire *1049* (U.S.) / Atlantic-Hansa *K 11192* (U.K. #2)

Mary's Boy Child – Oh My Lord
Boney M
Released November 1978
Sire *1036* (U.S.) / Atlantic-Hansa *K 11221* (U.K. #1)

One of the most successful European pop acts of the 1970s, Boney M recorded two of the ten biggest-selling singles of all time in the U.K., a feat unmatched by any other group. Despite finding little success in the U.S., Boney M is one of a select few groups that could claim to have a truly global fan-base, with a following that stretches across Africa, India, and South-East Asia. Boney M was the brainchild of the German music producer Frank Farian, who recruited four West Indian session vocalists to front the group. They began to hit their stride with three U.K. Top 10 hits in 1977 before topping the charts early the following year with 'Rivers Of Babylon.' Originally a hit for the Jamaican rock-steady band The Melodians in 1969, the song set biblical lyrics – taken from Psalm 137 – against a gentle disco backbeat. In Britain, Boney M's version has been outsold only by Elton John's 'Candle In The Wind,' 'Do They Know It's Christmas?' by Band Aid (both of which were charity singles), Queen's 'Bohemian Rhapsody,' and 'Mull Of Kintyre' by Wings. It was also the group's only American hit.

Boney M followed 'Rivers Of Babylon' with the equally memorable 'Rasputin' – essentially a Russian history lesson set to four-to-the-floor drums and swooping strings. But that was soon eclipsed by the festive hit 'Mary's Boy Child – Oh My Lord,' Boney M's second U.K. chart-topper and the tenth best-selling single of all time in Britain. Despite their remarkable successes in 1978, the group had fallen into a steady decline by the end of the decade and split in 1981.

You're The One That I Want
John Travolta & Olivia Newton-John

Released March 1978
RSO *891* (U.S. #1) / RSO *006* (U.K. #1)

'You're The One That I Want' was the biggest of several international smash hits to be drawn from the *Grease* soundtrack album, which has sold in excess of 30 million copies worldwide.

The original stage version of *Grease*, written by Jim Jacobs and Warren Casey, first appeared in 1971. Six years later, when Robert Stigwood obtained the movie rights, it had notched up more than 2,000 Broadway performances. Newton-John was already an established singer with a string of hits and awards to her name, while John Travolta had found fame and fortune for his part in Stigwood's previous production, *Saturday Night Fever*, and had also toured in a stage production of *Grease*.

For the purposes of the movie version, Stigwood commissioned some new songs. Not surprisingly, given the success of *Fever*, he called on Barry Gibb of The Bee Gees to write the title song, while Gibb in turn invited former Four Seasons vocalist Frankie Valli to sing it. In addition, John Farrar, Olivia Newton-John's musical director, wrote her solo hit, 'Hopelessly Devoted To You' and the duet, 'You're The One That I Want,' which spent an impressive nine weeks at Number 1 in Britain. The follow-up, another Travolta/Newton-John duet, 'Summer Nights' (from the original *Grease* score), was Number 1 in Britain for seven weeks, making the couple one of the most successful double-acts of all time.

Miss You
The Rolling Stones

Released May 1978
Rolling Stones *19307* (U.S. #1) / Rolling Stones *EMI 2802* (U.K. #3)

The Rolling Stones didn't look like a good bet for a classic single in 1978. The band were viewed by most punks as bloated, indulgent parodies, and with guitarist Keith Richards facing long-term imprisonment for drug offences in Canada, the end of the one-time World's Greatest Rock'n'Roll Band looked a real possibility. But Richards paid his debt to society by playing a concert for the blind, thereby escaping prison, and the band regrouped for 'Miss You' and its parent album, *Some Girls* – their best work since 1972's *Exile On Main Street*.

With Bill Wyman's walking octave bass part and Mick Jagger's mincing, falsetto vocal, 'Miss You' took some tricks not from the new wave but from the other musical phenomenon of the time, disco. In many ways this was a re-run of how the band had started out – taking black music styles and regurgitating them with a sleazy panache and a carefully offhand pop sensibility. The single came not only in a standard 7-inch picture sleeve but also as a limited-edition pink vinyl 12-inch, a ploy that no doubt helped to secure its high chart placing.

Three Times A Lady
The Commodores

Released June 1978
Motown *1443* (U.S. #1) / Tamla Motown *TMG 1113* (U.K. #1)

The Commodores were formed by students attending the Tuskegee Institute in Alabama in 1967, including Lionel Richie, and chose their name at random from a dictionary. Chart success began with the instrumental 'Machine Gun' in 1974. Since all the other members of the group were writing up-tempo material, Richie made a conscious decision to write ballads since this would guarantee his material a place on their albums. Of course, he never expected them to be so successful, but following major chart hits with 'Sweet Love,' 'Just To Be Close To You,' and 'Easy,' Richie realized he had established a winning formula.

'Three Times A Lady' was the result of a conversation Richie had with his father at a party to celebrate his parents' 37th wedding anniversary. He recalled: "My father told me that in 37 years of marriage he'd never told my mother how much she meant to him. I decided I wasn't going to wait 37 years to tell my wife, Brenda." Richie sat down with the express intention of writing a declaration of love to his wife, and 'Three Times A Lady' was the result. He recalled how the song was written at the height of the 1970s disco phenomenon and that one radio programmer told him: "You are either the craziest man who ever lived, or the bravest, for releasing this song now." History proves that Richie was certainly not crazy, and the song swiftly rose to Number 1 on both sides of the Atlantic.

An Everlasting Love
Andy Gibb

Released July 1978
RSO *904* (U.S. #5) / RSO *015* (U.K. #10)

Andy Gibb, the younger brother of The Bee Gees, could hardly have picked a better time to launch his solo career. During 1977 and '78 the group were at the top of their game, their compositions dominating the charts and helping manager Robert Stigwood's RSO Records enjoy a remarkable 30 weeks at Number 1 on the *Billboard* singles charts in '78.

Andy's first three singles, 'I Just Want To Be Your Everything,' '(Love Is) Thicker Than Water,' and 'Shadow Dancing,' were all U.S. Number 1s. The first two were composed by Barry Gibb within two hours on the same evening, while 'Shadow Dancing' was a Barry-Robin-Maurice-Andy composition. 'Thicker Than Water' also carried an Andy Gibb composition credit, although apparently his sole contribution was the title. Barry co-produced the majority of Andy's biggest hits, to which he also often added his distinctive falsetto backing-vocals.

In the pre-*Saturday Night Fever* U.K. punk landscape, Andy's singles had not fared so well, and it was his fourth American hit, 'An Everlasting Love' (a Barry solo composition, and the first not to top the U.S. charts), that was his most successful single in Britain, reaching Number 10. Andy's instant success ultimately led to numerous personal and drug-related problems that in turn led to his untimely death in 1988 at the age of 30.

I Will Survive
Gloria Gaynor

Released December 1978
Polydor *14508* (U.S. #1) / Polydor *2095 017* (U.K. #1)

This marks one of many instances where a throwaway B-side has turned into an international hit. The A-side, recorded at a session overseen by veteran producer Freddie Perren, was a cover of a recent British Number 2, 'Substitute' by Clout. However, Perren had agreed to produce the record on condition that he and partner Dino Fekaris would supply the B-side, a move that would guarantee them 50 per cent of the royalties should 'Substitute' become a hit.

With this in mind, 'I Will Survive' was especially tailored for Gaynor, and Fekaris consulted her about subject matter that might appeal. However, when he arrived at the session he'd forgotten to bring the lyrics and had to quickly jot them down on a brown paper bag. As soon as she read them, Gaynor was immediately attracted to the defiant words. She was also stunned. How could this be a B-side? Surely it was a major hit. Her record company disagreed, and 'Substitute' was duly released with 'I Will Survive' hidden away on the back.

Gaynor decided to take matters into her own hands, persuading club DJs to flip the record. The breakthrough followed when 'Survive' became a favorite at New York's influential Studio 54 discotheque. Finally, after months of persuasion (and when it became apparent that 'Substitute' wasn't going to repeat its U.K. success), 'Survive' was re-released as the A-side and promptly shot to the top of the charts worldwide, selling several million copies and winning a Grammy for Best Disco Record. Gaynor has never been able to better this career blockbuster, a song that has since become a gay and feminist anthem and is recognized as something of a modern classic. 'I Will Survive' returned to the U.K. Top 5 in a 1993 remix, and anyone who has been near a karaoke bar will certainly have heard some awful versions as the song is one of the most-performed karaoke tunes.

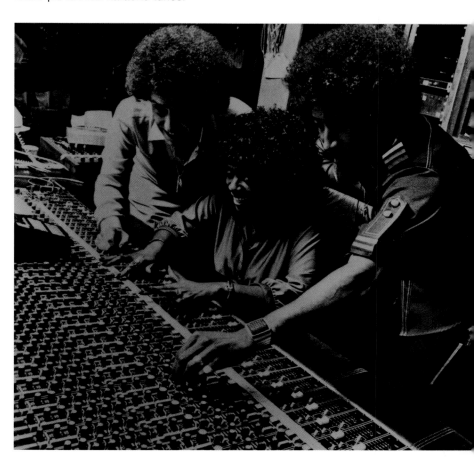

Pump It Up
Elvis Costello & The Attractions

Released May 1978
Not issued U.S. / Radar *ADA 10* (U.K. #24)

Emerging in 1977, Elvis Costello found himself included as part of the British punk scene but soon revealed himself to be a far more enduring and diverse talent. 'Pump It Up' is the best-loved of his early new-wave hits. Born Declan McManus in 1955, Costello grew up with The Beatles and Motown, and worked as a computer operator before signing to the influential independent Stiff Records late in 1976. He made the acclaimed *My Aim Is True* album the following year before recruiting a backing band, The Attractions, with whom he would work, on and off, for the next two decades. The Attractions gave a harder-edged backing to Costello's songs, which tended to overflow with artful, acerbic wordplay.

The first fruit of Costello's work with The Attractions was the sneering, ska-influenced '(I Don't Want To Go To) Chelsea,' which preceded the release of his second full-length, *This Year's Model*. 'Pump It Up' was next out of the blocks, a raucous crystallization of Costello's new sound that's driven by Steve Nieve's monotonous organ and Pete Thomas's snare-heavy backbeat. In true Costello style, the punchy, catchy tune is topped by a barbed lyric about the perils of rock'n'roll decadence, written in late 1977 while he was on tour with Stiff label-mates Ian Dury and The Damned.

Most of Costello's singles, 'Pump It Up' included, were not issued in the U.S., but their parent albums invariably reached the *Billboard* Top 30 – no mean feat for such an idiosyncratically British artist.

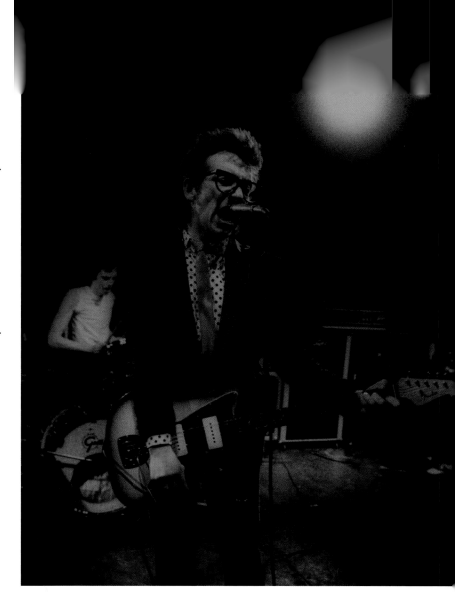

No One Is Innocent (A Punk Prayer By Ronald Biggs) / My Way
The Sex Pistols

Released June 1978
Not issued U.S. / Virgin *VS 220* (U.K. #7)

Public Image
Public Image Ltd

Released October 1978
Not issued U.S. / Virgin *VS 228* (U.K. #9)

Less than a year after releasing their landmark debut album, *Never Mind The Bollocks*, The Sex Pistols were in disarray. The group's last proper single was the double A-side release, 'No One Is Innocent' / 'My Way,' recorded after frontman John Lydon (a.k.a. Johnny Rotten) had quit to form Public Image Ltd (PiL).

'No One Is Innocent' is a throwaway 'punk prayer' featuring a guest vocal by Ronnie Biggs, the notorious Great Train Robber who spent many years exiled in Brazil. Of more interest is the flipside, a rendition of 'My Way,' earlier popularized by Frank Sinatra. Here it is sung, lugubriously, by Sex Pistols bassist Sid Vicious. The single would be seen as Sid's swan song after the events of the next few months: he was charged with the murder of his girlfriend, Nancy Spudgeon, in October 1978, and died of a drug overdose the following April before the matter

could be taken any further. By this stage the somewhat less volatile PiL had made its recorded debut with 'Public Image.' Like a lot of the group's best material, the single is driven by Jah Wobble's throbbing bass and the propulsive, Krautrock-derived drums, provided by Jim Walker, the first in a long line of apparently expendable kit men. Fighting for space atop the rhythm section are Keith Levene's sandblasted guitar and a ranting, raging vocal that could only have come from the larynx of a certain Mr. Lydon. It was the first in a line of great records from a group that, while lacking the sheer cultural impact of The Sex Pistols, created an equally impressive musical legacy.

Killing An Arab
The Cure

Released December 1978
Not issued U.S. / Small Wonder *SMALL 11* (U.K.)

Stark, minimalist, and hugely energetic, 'Killing An Arab' marked the start of The Cure's extraordinary career. Recorded on September 28, 1978, at Morgan Studios in London, England, it became their first single and, although it failed to chart, it plunged them into a worldwide debate about whether or not its lyric was racist. "It was a short poetic attempt at condensing my impression of the key moments in *L'Étranger* by Albert Camus," explained Cure mainman Robert Smith, clearly horrified by the interpretations of racism. The debate, fuelled by escalating Arab-Western tensions, still rumbles on – as does the one about whether The Cure are now, or ever were, Goths.

Ever Fallen In Love
(With Someone You Shouldn't've)
The Buzzcocks

Released September 1978
Not issued U.S. / United Artists *UP 36455* (U.K. #12)

This is the best-loved single by one of the enduring groups of the British punk era, marrying a melodic-minor chord progression with a frenetic performance and a lyric anyone could relate to. The group was formed in 1976 by singer-guitarists Pete Shelley and Howard Devoto, but Devoto appeared only on the Spiral Scratch EP before founding the more cerebral band Magazine. The first Buzzcocks single, 'Orgasm Addict.' was far too shocking for radio and didn't chart, but by the end of 1977 the group had built a wide and devoted following. 'Ever Fallen In Love' was one of five U.K. Top 30 hits they scored in 1978. It was not issued as a single in the U.S., but a cover version by Fine Young Cannibals reached Number 11 on the Billboard Hot Dance Music/Club Play chart in 1986.

Teenage Kicks
The Undertones

Released September 1978
Sire *49195* (U.S.) / Good Vibrations *GOT 4* (U.K. #30)

This seminal punk-influenced hit is perhaps best known for having been among the all-time favorites of the influential British DJ John Peel. The Undertones were formed in 1975 by vocalist Feargal Sharkey, guitar-playing brothers John and Damian O'Neill, bassist Mike Bradley, and drummer Billy Doherty. In the summer of 1978 they recorded 'Teenage Kicks,' their debut single, in a one-off deal for the small independent label Good Vibrations, based in their native Northern Ireland. Driven by a dirgey two-chord guitar riff, the song is peppered with handclaps and Sharkey's yearning cry: "I wanna hold her, wanna hold her tight / Get teenage kicks right through the night."

The single was immediately championed by Peel – who later named it as his favorite song of all time – and climbed into the U.K. charts, earning The Undertones a deal with the Sire label. The group had several other hits before splitting in 1983, while Sharkey topped the British charts two

years later with the solo single 'A Good Heart,' but nothing else that he or the group produced had the same visceral thrill as 'Teenage Kicks.'

Peel was, without exaggeration, the most important DJ in the history of British radio. He began his career in the U.S., where he worked using his real surname, Ravenscroft, for stations in Dallas, Oklahoma City, and San Bernardino. He returned to the U.K. in early 1967 and for several months had a show on the pirate station, Radio London, before landing a job with the newly created pop channel Radio One that summer.

For the next 34 years, until his sudden death in 2004, Peel regularly introduced listeners to new and exciting sounds. He was the first British DJ to play punk, reggae, and hip-hop, and an early champion of countless musical acts, from Captain Beefheart to T. Rex, The Sex Pistols to The Smiths, Pulp to The White Stripes. Notorious for playing records at the wrong speed, he was also the first British DJ to air the same record twice in a row. That record was, of course, 'Teenage Kicks.'

Hit Me With Your Rhythm Stick
Ian Dury & The Blockheads

Released November 1978
Epic *850726* (U.S.) / Stiff *BUY 38* (U.K. #1)

Milk And Alcohol
Dr. Feelgood

Released January 1979
Not issued U.S. / United Artists *UP 36468* (U.K. #9)

These two singles mark the commercial peak of pub-rock, the British music scene that laid the foundations for punk and then continued alongside it.

One of the most unlikely frontmen of the 1970s, Ian Dury taught painting at Canterbury College before turning to music. 'Hit Me With Your Rhythm Stick' followed the cult favorite 'Sex And Drugs And Rock And Roll' (1977) and displays all the hallmarks of Dury's best work, with its infectious combination of ramshackle rock'n'roll, the occasional hint of jazzy funk, and bawdy lyrical witticisms. Few people – including Dury himself – would have expected the single to top the U.K. charts, but it did so, for two weeks in early 1979, selling close to a million copies on the way.

Dury never matched that feat, but 'Reasons To Be Cheerful (Pt. 3)' did provide him with a successful British follow-up in 1979. He had high hopes for the caustic 'Spasticus Autisticus,' written in 1981 to commemorate the International Year of The Disabled, but it was banned by the BBC and, with little airplay, failed to chart.

In the same month that 'Hit Me With Your Rhythm Stick' topped the U.K. chart, Dr. Feelgood – who, like Dury, hailed from Essex, England – readied the irresistible 'Milk And Alcohol.' While the group never quite recovered from the departure of founding guitarist Wilko Johnson in 1977, this was their most successful single. It was co-written by Nick Lowe, the producer of a number of defining British albums of the era, including The Damned's *Damned Damned Damned* and several by Elvis Costello. 'Milk And Alcohol' features a suitably leering, cigarette-ravaged vocal delivery from frontman Lee Brilleaux over choppy, stop-start guitar and drums. It was issued as two different-colored 7-inch singles, one 'beery,' the other 'milky.'

Video Killed The Radio Star
Buggles

··

Released September 1979
Island *49114* (U.S. #40) / Island *WIP 6524* (U.K. #1)

'Video Killed The Radio Star' is the quintessential earworm: an irritatingly catchy novelty hit that gets stuck in the listener's head for days. It is also a perfectly crafted pop single and the first demonstration of the ingenious production talents of Trevor Horn, who went on to create some of the defining records of the 1980s.

British-born Horn formed Buggles in 1978 with keyboardist Geoff Downes, essentially as a vehicle for these two former session musicians to have a chart-topping hit. (Both had been members of the unsuccessful group Camera Club, which also included future pop star Thomas Dolby.)

'Video Killed The Radio Star' gave the duo exactly what they wanted at the first attempt, topping the U.K. singles chart and spending a total of 11 weeks in the listings. As well as Horn and Downes, the single featured keyboardist Hans Zimmer, who went on to become an Oscar-winning soundtrack composer, scoring movies including *Crimson Tide*, *Gladiator*, and *The Lion King*.

One of the great ironic pop hits, 'Video Killed The Radio Star' overflows with hook after hook, from the "ooh ooh" backing vocals to the many layers of overflowing keyboards. On close inspection, what at first sounds light and throwaway is revealed to be a cleverly constructed and rigorously detailed masterpiece of early synthesizer-pop. Similarly, the lyrics, far from being a string of half-baked phrases, are in fact a knowing deconstruction of the failings of the popular music industry.

Buggles followed 'Radio Star' with a handful of minor British hits over the next year, including 'The Plastic Age' and 'Clean Clean.' Neither Horn nor Downes had much interest in the further pursuit of pop stardom, however, and they split the group in 1980. The duo then joined the progressive rock group Yes, replacing departing members Rick Wakeman and Jon Anderson and producing the album *Drama*. After Yes disbanded in 1982, Downes formed Asia with Yes guitarist Steve Howe, Carl Palmer (the P in ELP), and John Wetton (once of King Crimson).

Horn meanwhile stepped away from the spotlight to embark on a highly successful career as a record producer. Among the countless acts whose rough diamonds he polished were ABC, Frankie Goes To Hollywood, Tina Turner, Pet Shop Boys, and tATu. He produced the charity hit 'Do They Know It's Christmas' for Band Aid and was a founding member of Art Of Noise, whose most notable releases include 'Close To The Edit' and 'Kiss,' a high-tech cover of the Prince original, recorded with Tom Jones.

Horn's style of production is difficult to categorize, not least because it has mutated over the years alongside the development of recording technology, but it is characterized by a sound that is rich and detailed but never cluttered. He will still be best remembered, however, for 'Video Killed The Radio Star,' which had the distinction – with fitting irony – of being the first song aired on MTV.

We Are Family
Sister Sledge

Released April 1979
Cotillion *44251* (U.S. #2) / Atlantic-Cotillion *K 11293* (U.K. #8)

Writer-producers Bernard Edwards and Nile Rodgers were at the top of their game following their success with Chic and, offered the pick of the Atlantic roster, decided to add their golden touch to Sister Sledge. Debbie, Kim, Joni, and Kathy Sledge had formed their group in Philadelphia in 1971 when the sisters were aged between 12 and 16, and they enjoyed some minor success, including a British Number 20 hit with 'Mama Never Told Me' in 1975. Edwards and Rodgers's subtly sparse production over catchy choruses gave the girls a trio of classic disco hits: 'He's The Greatest Dancer,' 'We Are Family,' and 'Lost In Music.' Both 'We Are Family' and 'Lost In Music' have returned to the U.K. charts on two separate occasions and 'He's The Greatest Dancer' formed the basis of Will Smith's 1998 U.S. chart-topper 'Gettin' Jiggy Wit It.' Unlike most disco hits of the era, the songs and production of Edwards and Rodgers had lasting quality that stands the test of time. Sister Sledge went on to more popularity in Britain, where they topped the charts in 1985 with 'Frankie,' which was not a hit in America.

Pop Muzik
M

Released April 1979
Sire *49033* (U.S. #1) / MCA *413* (U.K. #2)

In 1979 the synthesizer-sequencer explosion was yet to have a big impact in the U.K., although Gary Numan and Kraftwerk had made early inroads, and more than a few proto-New Romantic and hip-hop acts would be tweaking Wasp keyboards in the next year or two. This made M's splendid, utterly futuristic 'Pop Muzik' seem like a song from another galaxy, with its reverb-free percussion, relentless bassline, and those staccato lyrics, themselves something of a philosophical statement. 'Pop Muzik' was the brainwave of Robin Scott – educated at a London art school, even if the record sounded like it came from a bunker in Munich. The single made a huge splash and then dragged its maker down into obscurity.

Are 'Friends' Electric?
Tubeway Army

Released May 1979
Atco *7206* (U.S.) / Beggars Banquet *BEG 18* (U.K. #1)

Cars
Gary Numan

Released August 1979
Atco *7211* (U.S. #9) / Beggars Banquet *BEG 23* (U.K. #1)

Gary Numan was one of the first internationally successful exponents of synthesizer-pop, initially as the leader of Tubeway Army and then as a solo artist. Tubeway Army started out in a fairly perfunctory punk vein before Numan (born Gary Webb in London, England, in 1958) fell for the charms of the MiniMoog synthesizer, the pioneering mid-1970s work of Kraftwerk, and David Bowie's collaborations with Brian Eno. 'Are 'Friends' Electric?' was the group's fourth single. While the first three had failed to chart, this one went all the way to Number 1 in Britain, a

surprise given that it runs to more than five minutes, has no discernible chorus, and features several barely intelligible spoken-word sections. Its bleak, murky synth parts were later reworked to great effect by the 21st century girl group The Sugababes for their 2003 hit 'Freak Like Me.'

Within months of 'Friends' topping the U.K. chart, Numan had disbanded Tubeway Army and set out on his own. His first solo release, 'Cars,' gave him a second British Number 1 and his only U.S. Top 10 hit. Like its predecessor, 'Cars' has a bleak, post-modern lyric – in this instance inspired by a road-rage incident – but is set to a somewhat lighter musical backdrop. In the U.K. it has charted in three successive decades: first in its original form in '79; then with an 'E Reg' remix in 1987; and again in 1996, after its use on TV ads for beer.

Don't Stop 'Til You Get Enough
Michael Jackson

Released August 1979
Epic *50742* (U.S. #1) / Epic *EPC 7763* (U.K. #3)

This was Michael Jackson's first solo Number 1 as an adult and introduced the chic, Quincy Jones-produced sound that would soon see him dubbed the King Of Pop. A year earlier, however, the idea of Jackson producing a huge international smash hit seemed unlikely. He had left Motown, the label for which he had recorded since the late 1960s, and was last seen playing the Scarecrow in *The Wiz*, the big-screen adaptation of *The Wizard Of Oz* that failed miserably at the box office. Nonetheless *The Wiz* was crucial to Jackson's career because it introduced Jackson to Quincy Jones, who served as the movie's musical director before becoming the perfect foil for the singer's growing talents in songwriting and arranging.

Jackson wrote 'Don't Stop' in 1978, and his original home demo – included on the recent expanded reissue of the *Off The Wall* album – shows that he knew exactly what he wanted from the song. The jangling, cowbell-laden rhythm, distinctive bass and guitar licks, and Jackson's newly developed falsetto are all there; the only extra ingredient the song needed was Jones's polished, spacious production sheen.

Issued at the height of summer 1979, the resulting single took three months to climb slowly but surely to the Number 1 spot on the *Billboard* chart, initiating Jackson's domination of the pop world for the next decade. It was quickly followed by two further U.S. Top 5 hits, *Off The Wall*'s title track and 'Rock With You,' both written by Rod Temperton, formerly of the disco group Heatwave.

Bat Out Of Hell
Meat Loaf

Released January 1979
Not issued U.S. / Epic *EPC 7018* (U.K. #15)

When Jim Steinman and Meat Loaf began work on the songs that
became *Bat Out Of Hell*, they were intended for a futuristic musical
based on Peter Pan entitled *Neverland*. The ten-minute epic was one of
three videos specially commissioned by Columbia after witnessing Mr.
Loaf's stunning performance at a U.S. convention. The album, released
in America in October 1977, took about six months to take off and was a
success in Britain first. In early 1978, the video of the title track was
screened on the BBC's influential TV music show *The Old Grey Whistle
Test* to such acclaim that it had to be shown again the following week.
The album then hit the U.K. charts in March, some two months before its
American Top 40 debut.

The juggernaut title track, the centerpiece of the album, was described
by its writer as the result of his wish to create "the ultimate motorcycle
crash song." Which makes the highlight of the track, and indeed the
entire album, the motorcycle guitar effect played by producer Todd
Rundgren. Steinman had wanted this all along, but Rundgren hated the
idea, and it wasn't until the mixing stage that he plugged in his guitar
and played the effect live in the studio. He continued into the following
solo, to the utter amazement of all present – and all in one take.

Just about every adjective imaginable has been thrown at this track over
the years. 'Bombastic' seems to top the list. This doesn't bother Mr.
Steinman in the least. "Bombastic? Of course it's bombastic. I take that
as a compliment. Rock'n'roll is the most bombastic form ever –
heightened, oversized, gigantic, thrilling, and silly." 'Bat Out Of Hell' was
not a single in the U.S., but in Britain it became the biggest of three hits
from the LP, which went on to sell 37 million copies worldwide and
spend a remarkable nine years on the British album charts.

My Sharona
The Knack

Released June 1979
Capitol *CL 16087* (U.S. #6) / Capitol *4731* (U.K. #1)

Back in '79, The Knack were hated by the critics for their cynicism, their
refusal to speak to the serious music press, and the antediluvian (and
anti-punk) nature of their British Invasion fashions and power pop
sounds. A quarter of a century on, such passions seem barely
comprehensible about a band whose only real prevailing impact on
popular culture is this huge international hit. Written by their songwriting
axis of Fieger & Averre, it boasts everything that made people both love
and loathe them: it was naggingly catchy … at the same time as its
heartless professionalism and stop-start rhythms made it somehow
unlovely.

Goodbye Stranger
Supertramp

Released July 1979
A&M *2162* (U.S. #15) / A&M *AMS 7481* (U.K.)

"Just the thought of those sweet ladies / Sends a shiver through my
veins" confided U.K.-born Rick Davies in this paean to the women of the
world. Although the song sounded as if it had been written in a Chevy
on Route 66 as the singer worked his way through a parade of females,
in fact 'Goodbye Stranger' was stuffed with a very English reticence,
perhaps the very quality that made it so memorable. Although the song
didn't make much impact on the charts, Supertramp – whose line-up
fluctuated endlessly – did go on to enjoy vast sales. The legacy of their
work has endured, despite the fact that they themselves were among the
most faceless of stars.

I Don't Like Mondays
The Boomtown Rats

Released July 1979
Columbia *11117* (U.S.) / Ensign *ENY 30* (U.K. #1)

Lest we forget, before becoming 'the man who organized Live Aid,' Bob
Geldof was a pop star. 'I Don't Like Mondays' was his only Hot 100 hit
with The Boomtown Rats in the U.S. (it scraped in at Number 73) but in
Britain it was the second of two consecutive chart-toppers, following
late-1978's 'Rat Trap.'

Geldof formed the six-piece group in Ireland in 1975 before dragging the
whole lot of 'em across to London the following year, just in time for the
punk trend. But the sound of The Boomtown Rats was closer to 1960s-
style R&B than The Sex Pistols. The group was an immediate chart
success in the U.K. and had notched up four hit singles and a pair of
Top 20 albums before 'Rat Trap' reached Number 1.

'I Don't Like Mondays' is driven by sturdy piano chords pitched
somewhere between David Bowie's early-1970s output and something
from a stage musical. The lyrics were inspired by the murders committed
by 16-year-old Brenda Ann Spencer at Cleveland Elementary School in
San Diego, California, in January 1979. Spencer killed two adults and

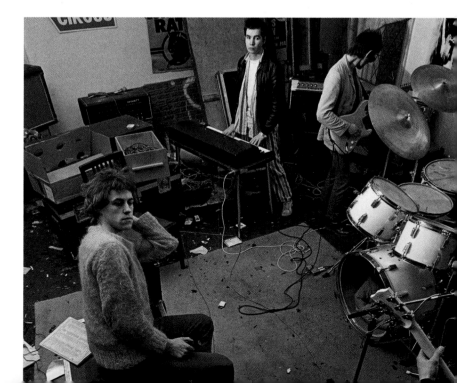

wounded eight children and a police officer with a rifle she had been given for Christmas. When asked to explain her actions, she replied simply: "I don't like Mondays." Perhaps surprisingly, it didn't appear to bother anybody too much that Geldof had turned the words of a killer into a pop song. In fact, the meaning seemed to escape most radio DJs altogether – it was played regularly on Monday mornings during the 1980s to ease the masses back to work.

Message In A Bottle
The Police

Released September 1979
A&M *2190* (U.S.) / A&M *AMS 7474* (U.K. #1)

'Message In A Bottle' was the first of five British Number 1s for the group consisting of Sting (sole writer of all their hits), Stewart Copeland, and Andy Summers. The lead single from their second album *Reggatta De Blanc*, it was also A&M's first official British chart-topping single. The group's breakthrough had been a 1979 Number 32 hit in America with 'Roxanne,' which preceded major U.K. success, but their second album (a British Number 1) received a disappointing response Stateside. While 'Message In A Bottle' was a U.K. Number 1 it only reached Number 74 in America.

Of the group's trademark white-reggae sound – *Reggatta De Blanc* is a nonsense translation of the term – Sting said: "They're not straight reggae songs. What I do is weld elements of reggae into a rock setting." 'Roxanne' had originally been a ballad, and it was drummer Stewart Copeland who suggested adding a reggae beat.

Sting said he usually begins a song by finding a title. "It's common sense, really, because the title of the tune coincides with your hook-line, your chorus. So I write titles and work backwards from there." He added: "I never begin a song unless I have a metaphor," and the modest songwriter said he's particularly proud of 'Message In A Bottle.' "It's quite a cleverly put together metaphor: it develops and has an artistic shape to it."

While the *Reggatta* album received mixed reviews in Britain, it became the first of five chart-topping collections and gave the group another U.K. Number 1 single with 'Walking On The Moon.' And just in case you're curious, towards the end of that song Sting does indeed sing "Sending out an Esso Blue." He has a habit of playing with lyrics on the fade-outs of his songs: Esso Blue was a popular brand of British paraffin (kerosene) in the 1960s.

Hey Hey, My My (Out Of The Blue) / My My, Hey Hey (Into The Black)
Neil Young With Crazy Horse

Released August 1979
Reprise *49031* (U.S.) / Reprise *K 14498* (U.K.)

Young wrote this song, which name-checks Johnny Rotten, after his generation was derided as irrelevant by punks in the late 1970s. Two versions exist: a hard-rock take and an acoustic version, released as A- and B-side of this single with slightly different titles. The acoustic version contains the line "It's better to burn out than to fade away," and this unusual lack of complacency endeared Neil to younger musicians, not least of whom was Nirvana's Kurt Cobain, king of grunge. Cobain quoted the line in his suicide note, much to Young's distress.

Another Brick In The Wall (Part 2)
Pink Floyd

Released November 1979
Columbia *11187* (U.S. #1) / Harvest *HAR 5194* (U.K. #1)

Arguably the oddest Christmas Number 1 ever, 'Another Brick In The Wall' was Pink Floyd's first single in 11 years and, horror of horrors for their prog-rock album-orientated fans, it was set to a thumping disco beat. Written by Floyd's bassist, Roger Waters, the powerfully anti-establishment song was extracted from their double concept album (this is more like it) *The Wall*.

The track was recorded in France and Los Angeles, but the atmospheric children's choir section was added without any Floyd member present. "I sent the tape to England and got an engineer to summon some kids," recalled guitarist David Gilmour. "I gave him a whole set of instructions – 10 to 15-year-olds from north London, mostly boys – and I said, 'Get them to sing in as many ways as you like.'" The original intention was that the choir should be in the background, but the results were so strong that it was decided to feature them on their own.

Another distinctive element is the weird sound emanating from Gilmour's guitar at the end. How many effects pedals did it take to achieve that sound? "That's just Dave direct, with a little compression," explained producer Bob Ezrin, adding that it was also the first take. The song spent five weeks at Number 1 in the U.K., four weeks in America, and, as if to prove Waters's point about repressive educational systems, it was banned by South Africa's apartheid regime when black children began to adopt it as their anthem.

Heart Of Glass
Blondie

Released January 1979
Chrysalis *2295* (U.S. #1, U.K. #1)

Atomic
Blondie

Released February 1980
Chrysalis *2410* (U.S. #39, U.K. #1)

Blondie's first chart-topping hit in the U.S. and the U.K., 'Heart Of Glass' cemented the group's position as the most commercially successful act of the punk/new wave era. Blondie was formed in 1974 by vocalist Debbie Harry – a former Playboy bunny – and her boyfriend, guitarist Chris Stein. The group burst out of the blocks in 1976 with the organ-led punk-Motown hybrid 'X Offender' and in 1978 scored a pair of U.K. Top 10 hits, 'Denis' and '(I'm Always Touched By Your) Presence Dear.' By this stage they had expanded to a sextet, with drummer Clem Burke, bassist Nigel Harrison, keyboardist Jimmy Destri, and guitarist Frank Infante.

'Heart Of Glass,' the second single from the group's third and best album, *Parallel Lines*, was driven by a sparse, disco-inspired arrangement and Harry's angelic vocal. Both single and album were produced by Mike Chapman who, alongside regular collaborator Nicky Chinn, had sat at the helm of numerous British hits of the early-to-mid 1970s by The Sweet, Suzi Quatro, and others. Chapman was able to strip away some of the rough edges of Blondie's sound without dulling the group's impact, in the process turning them into an unassailable chart force. The following year's 'Atomic' also pitched itself somewhere between new wave and disco, and was given a similarly striking production job by Chapman. Although not as successful in the U.S. as some of Blondie's other hits – 'Call Me,' 'The Tide Is High,' and 'Rapture' completed a quartet of *Billboard* chart-toppers – it remains one of the group's best-loved songs.

Rapper's Delight
The Sugarhill Gang

Released September 1979
Sugar Hill *542* (U.S. #36) / Sugar Hill *SHL 101* (U.K. #3)

Although 'King Tim III' by The Fatback Band has the strongest claim to the title of first rap single, 'Rapper's Delight' was the genre's first Top 40 hit and without doubt one of the most important hip-hop recordings of all time.

Sylvia Robinson was a singer-songwriter-producer based in Englewood, New Jersey. She began to take note of the growing popularity of hip-hop in New York City during the late 1970s, promptly founding Sugar Hill Records to give this new music a commercial outlet. With the help of her son Joey, Robinson recruited three rappers, Big Bank Hank, Wonder Mike, and Master Gee – better known to their mothers as Henry Jackson, Michael Wright, and Guy O'Brien. She dubbed them The Sugarhill Gang. (According to hip-hop legend, Joey auditioned Jackson outside a pizza place, and Jackson's two comrades heard the performance and asked if they could have a go, too.)

Robinson was the brains behind the trio's debut single, 'Rapper's Delight,' which, like many early hip-hop records, used as its instrumental backing the hook from a recent disco hit – in this case, Chic's masterful 'Good Times.' What she couldn't do, though, was rap. Fortunately, Mike, Hank, and Gee knew all about that. The three of them trade effortless, joyous rhymes, which today sound a world away from the harsh, profanity-laden bile of much modern hip-hop.

'Rapper's Delight' only caught on locally at first, but then spread across the seas, even reaching the Top 10s in South Africa and Israel. Some estimates suggest total worldwide sales of over eight million copies. More massive hip-hop hits arrived in the subsequent months and years, but this is where rap's dominance of the airwaves and pop charts started.

London Calling
The Clash

Released December 1979
Not issued U.S. / CBS *8087* (U.K. #11)

Released in the final weeks of 1979, the apocalyptic 'London Calling' brought a fitting close to an erratic decade. The title track and opener from the group's third album, it was The Clash's highest charting single in the U.K. until a reissued 'Should I Stay Or Should I Go' was propelled to Number 1 in 1991 after featuring in a television advertisement for jeans. The song was not released as an A-side in the U.S. but featured as the B-side to the more upbeat 'Train In Vain (Stand By Me),' which gave The Clash their debut American hit in the early months of 1980.

Having burst onto the British punk scene in 1977 with the incendiary 'White Riot,' The Clash soon began to demonstrate a musical awareness that far outshone the majority of their peers. The group's third and finest collection, the double-disc album *London Calling* (1979), shows off a range of non-punk influences from ska and reggae to rockabilly. But there is nothing more powerful on that album than the anthemic title track.

'London Calling' kicks off with staccato guitar chords and a steady backbeat, but those features are almost blown out of the water by a monstrous rolling bassline. Joe Strummer revels in a call-and-response vocal with the other members of the group, variously putting down "phony Beatlemania" and announcing that "the ice age is coming." After two minutes he almost allows the song to self-destruct in a barrage of yelps, feedback, and – yes, it's true – Mick Jones's brief guitar solo, but pulls it back from the brink for a defiant final verse.

Brass In Pocket
The Pretenders

Released November 1979
Sire *49181* (U.S. #14) / Real *ARE 11* (U.K. #1)

Springing into life just as the U.K. punk scene began to fizzle out, The Pretenders had a much more enduring, classic pop-rock sound than most of their contemporaries, and in Chrissie Hynde were possessed of one of the greatest frontwomen of the time. Hynde was born in Akron, Ohio, but moved to Britain during the mid 1970s and worked for several years as a journalist on the NME music paper there.

In 1977 a demo tape of Hynde's self-penned songs caught the attention of the fledgling Real label, which requested that she put together a band. The Pretenders have been through countless line-up changes over the years, but were initially settled on the quartet of Hynde plus three British men: James Honeyman-Scott (guitar), Pete Farndon (bass), and Martin Chambers (drums).

The group's debut was a strident cover of The Kinks' 'Stop Your Sobbing' produced by Nick Lowe, best known at the time for his work with Elvis Costello. This and 'Kid' were minor U.K. hits during the first half of 1979 but paled in comparison to the group's third effort. 'Brass In Pocket' is driven by clean, stop-start Telecaster chords and Hynde's cool, cocksure vocal, a declaration that "I'm special, so special / I got to have some of your attention." Her bandmates join in, cooing the word "special" back in response, in the process eliminating any doubt there might be that Hynde's confidence could be misplaced.

1980

Love Will Tear Us Apart
Joy Division

....

Released April 1980
Not issued U.S. / Factory *FAC 23* (U.K. #13)

The suicide of Joy Division's singer Ian Curtis in 1980 has cast a
perpetual ghostly hue over the band's slim volume of recorded work. Yet
even before his death there was something authentically other-worldly
about Joy Division. A band inspired by punk but never a punk band, Joy
Division initially favored a sort of monolithic rock, dominated by two-note
guitar riffs, rigid drum patterns, and Curtis's forbiddingly gloomy baritone,
with bassist Peter Hook providing most of the melody. The later addition
of rudimentary synthesizer parts seemed to bring out a hitherto buried
musicality in Curtis's voice, and on 'Love Will Tear Us Apart' the band
crafted what is most definitely a pop single, albeit a rather dark, forlorn
form of pop.

'Love Will Tear Us Apart' appeared in April 1980, just as the Joy Division
story reached crisis point. Curtis was an epileptic and sometimes had
seizures on stage. He cultivated a jerking, manically spasmodic dance
routine that seemed to mimic the seizures, and audiences grew
morbidly fascinated by his on-stage movements. Was he having a fit
or just dancing?

The band was working a punishing schedule in early 1980, despite
rumors of Curtis's declining health, exacerbated when some dates were
cancelled on a European tour in January. Nonetheless, on their return the
band started work immediately on the second album and released 'Love
Will Tear Us Apart.' It was heaped with critical adulation but failed to
reach beyond the independent charts. Then, on the eve of an American
tour in early May, Curtis hanged himself. That summer a re-release of
'Love Will Tear Us Apart' gave the band their first British hit. It has since
been covered by artists as unlikely as blue-eyed-soul boy Paul Young
and the 1960s trouser-splitter, P.J. Proby.

Turning Japanese
The Vapors

Released January 1980
United Artists *1364* (U.S. #36) / United Artists *BP 334* (U.K. #3)

This A-side, an up-tempo live anthem chock-full of vocal and guitar hooks with a funky tempo change in the middle, borrowed as much from rock as it did from new wave. All of this made it an obvious chart candidate, boosted by the rumor that the title referred to masturbation, and specifically the facial expression at the climax of that activity. This was never confirmed by the band, who were discovered by Bruce Foxton of The Jam, and who went on to join the long line of new wave one-hit wonders, leaving this excellent ditty behind them.

Going Underground
The Jam

Released March 1980
Not issued U.S. / Polydor *POSP 113* (U.K. #1)

These days, a single entering the British chart at Number 1 is commonplace. When 'Going Underground' achieved that feat in March 1980 it was the first time it had happened since 'Merry Xmas Everybody' by Slade in 1973. There was a whiff of manipulation about the accomplishment: it was a double-pack single featuring bonus live tracks, and there was a convenient delay of a week from its originally announced release date due to a supposed pressing problem.

The Jam had undeniably built up a commercial strength through superb singles like 'The Eton Rifles,' and the ascent of 'Underground' to the top marked the start of The Jam in their pomp – which lasted until their dissolution in 1982. During that time they fulfilled the promise of the punk movement, to which they had come rather late in the day.

Technically this single was a double A-side, but few remember 'Dreams Of Children' today. It was 'Going Underground' that captured the imagination of DJs and the public, with a fearsome guitar riff, songwriter-guitarist Paul Weller's spat-out vocal, the thunderous rhythm work of drummer Rick Buckler and bassist Bruce Foxton, and a nuclear-nightmare lyric (now dated, then very resonant). Weller's lyrics could often be cringe-worthy but the cherry on the icing here was the superb couplet: "You choose your leaders and place your trust / As their lies wash you down and their promises rust."

Whip It
Devo

Released August 1980
Warner Bros. *49550* (U.S. #14) / Virgin *VS 383* (U.K.)

Ludicrous it may have sounded, but 'Whip It' contained all the hallmarks of the burgeoning new-wave sound – and more comedy than anybody else around at the time. The American punk-industrial-electronic quintet made sure everyone knew about their slightly unnerving connections – the Church Of The SubGenius among them – and kept the joke going on their songs, many of which, like this one, were packed full of vaguely homo-erotic innuendo. And all with a catchy chorus and a slinky synth bassline that sounded, at the time, like all our futures: "No one gets away, until you … whip it" they promised, and how we agreed. 'Whip It' was Devo's only Top 40 hit on either side of the Atlantic. Vocalist Mark Mothersbaugh has since found success with his soundtrack work, which includes writing the theme to the animated TV series *Rugrats*.

a native of Indiana, but while in the air force in the 1960s he found himself stationed in East Anglia, England. There he took and slightly modified the name of Gino Washington, a minor American rhythm & blues star. He fooled U.K. promoters and record labels into believing he was the real Washington. Before long, Geno's gravelly delivery and stage charisma had made him a star in his own right, and he secured four moderate chart hits. He also secured the wide-eyed admiration of young Kevin Rowland who, we are told by this song's lyric, saw him "back in '68 in a sweaty club." Rowland continues: "You fed me, you bred me, I'll remember your name." Rowland, who co-wrote the song with Kevin Archer, couldn't resist informing his erstwhile hero that he thought their roles were now reversed: "And now just look at me as I'm looking down on you / No, I'm not being flash, it's what I'm built to do." Rowland's rather whining voice never quite lived up to the bombast of his lyrics and certainly did not live up to the breathtaking majesty of the Midnight Runners' horn charts, but the record was still stirring enough to storm its way up the charts, a genuine word-of-mouth smash.

Antmusic
Adam & The Ants

Released November 1980
Columbia *0204* (U.S.) / CBS *9352* (U.K. #2)

'Antmusic' was a clarion call of pure post-punk groove, complete with drumming patterned after the Burundi tribes of Africa, some guttural chanting, and the sweetly rebellious vocals of a charismatic frontman. MTV launched in 1981 and played the single on heavy rotation, making an early video star out of the nattily coiffed and painted Adam Ant (who masqueraded as a pirate). 'Antmusic' helped the group earn a Grammy Award nomination for Best New Artist in 1982, the same year that Ant had his first American Top 20 hit as a solo artist, 'Goody Two Shoes.'

Geno
Dexys Midnight Runners

Released March 1980
Not issued U.S. / Late Night Feelings *R 6033* (U.K. #1)

Dexys frontman Kevin Rowland infamously took his music and his image very seriously indeed. 'Geno' was an extension of this passion. The song's subject, Geno Washington – real name George Washington – was

SINGLE FUTURE: VINYL, CASSETTE, OR CD ?

The cassette single burst on to the scene in 1980, with help from the irrepressible Malcolm McLaren, former manager of The Sex Pistols. In 1980, he persuaded EMI to issue the first cassette single to launch his new act, Bow Wow Wow. Not only did 'C30, C60, C90, Go!' champion the cause of home taping, then considered by record labels to be a form of piracy that was "killing music," it only included one song. He left the other side blank for buyers to use for their own piratical activities, a calculated attempt to bite the hand that was feeding him.

Bow Wow Wow were manufactured by McLaren to promote the Burundi-meets-Captain-Hook concept he had originally designed for Adam & The Ants; prized away from Adam, the original Ants now backed Annabella Lwin, a 14-year-old Burmese schoolgirl whom McLaren had found working in a London dry-cleaners. The cassette single reached only Number 34 in the British charts, despite its novelty value. McLaren followed it up with Your Cassette Pet, an eight-song cassette-only release, then gave up the campaign and turned to vinyl for the band's first album. Bow Wow Wow's heady mix of adolescent sexuality and art-school camp carried them along for a few scandalous years and even gave them a couple of British hits.

McLaren's was not an entirely original idea. 'Cassette culture' had been something of a post-punk cult in Britain for several years, allowing artists to release music directly to their followers without using record companies. Bands would often mail out their music in exchange for a blank cassette and an addressed envelope. In America, however, the cassette single (sometimes known as the cassingle) had more prosaic origins. With cassette albums now dominating sales, record companies reasoned that there were now teenagers without turntables to play vinyl records.

The first major cassette single was Bryan Adams's 'In the Heat Of The Night,' issued on A&M in 1987. Later releases would have more than two songs, and for a time the cassette single did well. A poll by Arista that year showed that more than 40 per cent of cassette-single buyers had long given up buying 45s, but that 90 per cent said they would now start buying singles again. In 1989, De La Soul's 'Me Myself And I' became the first cassette-only single to enter the U.S. Top 40.

The cassette single's heyday was short. The introduction of the little 3-inch CD single, overpriced and initially unplayable on most machines, was a flop, but once CD singles began appearing on normal-sized discs, the commercial cassette single was doomed. By 2001 it had effectively died, along with its album-length predecessor. Blank CDs and file-sharing would replace it as an anti-commercial underground medium. The cassette has, however, achieved a kind of afterlife among enthusiasts and experimentalists.

Magic
Olivia Newton-John

Released May 1980
MCA *41247* (U.S. #1) / Jet *196* (U.K. #32)

Xanadu
Olivia Newton-John & Electric Light Orchestra

Released June 1980
MCA *41285* (U.S. #8) / Jet *185* (U.K #1)

Two years after her resounding success with both the movie and the soundtrack for *Grease*, Olivia Newton-John took on the silver screens of Hollywood once again with *Xanadu*. The feature film, directed by Robert Greenwald, co-stars Newton-John with leading man Michael Beck (fresh from his own success in *The Warriors*) and dancing legend Gene Kelly. The trailer promised that it would be "the most dazzling, romantic musical fantasy in years" with vibrant, disco-inspired dancing and roller-skating, a far-fetched plot line borrowing from Greek mythology, and a plethora of original songs done by Newton-John and Electric Light Orchestra (ELO) to fuel the performance sequences. *Xanadu*'s Greek muse Kira was a far-cry from *Grease*'s teenage Sandy, but each character that she played proved more than capable of belting out some lovely tunes.

Unfortunately, audiences didn't agree with the trailer's proclamation of excitement, and Universal Pictures had to swallow a well-publicized box office failure with *Xanadu*. Instead, the buying public confirmed its preference for Newton-John as a singer rather than a singer-actress, rewarding her efforts with platinum sales for the soundtrack and pop-chart placements for its two key songs, the smoldering ballad 'Magic' and the cosmic 'Xanadu,' both written by longtime Newton-John songwriter John Farrar plus ELO's Jeff Lynne. With sales of more than a million copies, 'Magic' topped the *Billboard* chart and gave Newton-John her first Gold single in America (and third Number 1) while U.K. fans made 'Xanadu' their Number 1 song from the movie.

(Just Like) Starting Over
John Lennon

Released October 1980
Geffen *49604* (U.S. #1) / Geffen *K 79186* (U.K. #1)

On December 8, 1980, the 20th century lost one of its most popular figures when John Lennon was shot dead outside his New York City apartment. Lennon was indeed starting over, having hardly touched a guitar during his five years as a house-husband bringing up Sean, his son with Yoko. Retiring to Bermuda in the summer of 1980 for a family holiday, Lennon began to write again. He said that all the songs on the *Double Fantasy* album came within a period of three weeks. He was without a record contract, and there was no lack of interest from bidding record companies, although John and Yoko signed with David Geffen because he offered to take on the record without hearing a note.

The album received mixed reviews, while '(Just Like) Starting Over,' a 1950s-sounding piece released shortly after his 40th birthday, was shaping up to be a moderate hit – it had already peaked at Number 8 in Britain before sliding to Number 21 – when tragedy struck. Ironically, Lennon had not had a British Number 1 since the demise of The Beatles,

but in the weeks following his death four of his songs would top the charts while another reached Number 2. First came '(Just Like) Starting Over,' which swiftly vaulted to Number 1, while a reissued 'Happy Xmas' rose to Number 2. In the new year, with accumulated back-orders of 300,000, 'Imagine' rose to the top, followed shortly afterwards by 'Woman,' the second single from *Double Fantasy*. Finally, in February 1981, Bryan Ferry and Roxy Music took 'Jealous Guy' to the top in a fitting tribute to one of the greatest icons in popular-music history.

There's No One Quite Like Grandma
St. Winifred's School Choir

Released November 1980
Not issued U.S. / Music For Pleasure *FP 900* (U.K. #1)

Among the longstanding U.K. yuletide traditions is the coveted Christmas Number 1. British bookmakers take millions in bets on the Christmas Day chart-topper. This phenomenon is peculiar to the U.K. charts, where national radio and television coverage enables a single released in early December to shoot to the top of the charts in a very short space of time. With records traditionally making great Christmas presents, there is also a history of offbeat middle-of-the-road singles topping the U.K. charts at Christmas, records that youngsters can buy as gifts for older relatives, of which 'There's No One Quite Like Grandma' by St Winifred's School Choir is perhaps the best-known example.

Remarkably, the choir had already appeared on another U.K. Number 1, Brian & Michael's 'Matchstalk Men And Matchstalk Cats And Dogs,' which topped the charts there in April 1978. 'Grandma' was the first single ever released on EMI's budget label Music For Pleasure, usually strictly albums only, and featured seven-year-old soloist Dawn Ralph. While they only had one hit single, St Winifred's had a lengthy career – albeit with numerous personnel changes – and recorded nine albums over a period of ten years.

9 To 5
Dolly Parton

Released December 1980
RCA *12133* (U.S. #1) / RCA *25* (U.K.)

Country legend Dolly Parton had one of the largest crossover hits of her career with this title song to the soundtrack of *9 To 5*, an irreverent comedy movie starring Jane Fonda, Lily Tomlin, and Parton herself as resourceful working women wreaking revenge on an oppressive boss. From bleary-eyed coffee making in the morning to the chaotic juggling of duties once at the job, the record is a sassy and remarkably detailed tribute to the blue-collar nation, and was embraced dearly to the heart of America, particularly by women. The elusive Oscar agreed: '9 To 5' earned an Academy Award for Best Song.

Vienna
Ultravox

Released January 1981
Chrysalis *6597* (U.S.) / Chrysalis *CHS 2481* (U.K. #2)

In 1981 Midge Ure and his band of less-than-merry men sucked in their cheeks, applied a dab of panstick, and slipped into long trenchcoats for 'Vienna,' still one of the finest moments of early-1980s electro and by far Ultravox's best-known song to this day – even if the group was more experimental and just as ambitious on other recordings.

The song stood out from the rest of the synthesizer-rock pack for several reasons, firstly because of its stripped-down, less-is-more atmosphere. If you bought into the gothic imagery that adorned the jacket of 'Vienna' – and thousands of spotty, angst-ridden teenagers did – you could well believe that Midge and his men spent their time lurking around the Austrian capital's celeb-laden cemetery pouting over the tombstones of Mozart, Brahms, and a flock of Strausses, drinking absinthe. Secondly, the song took its time to build up to an epic climax, held down by an unforgiving rhythm section, a vocal melody that insinuated itself into your brain and wouldn't leave, and the big snare sounds of the era.

But aside from all the film noir pretension, 'Vienna' is simply a highly hummable pop tune, with its ethereal synth wash anchoring *that* bass and kick-drum riff with nihilistic precision. There's a tempo change towards the end, too, underpinning some gorgeous, reverb'd piano tinkles and Midge's wail of "It means nothing to meeeee!" – the best singalong party line of all Ure's considerable oeuvre.

(We Don't Need This) Fascist Groove Thang
Heaven 17

Released March 1981
Not issued U.S. / Virgin *VS 400* (U.K.)

When singer Glen Gregory joined ex-Human League computer boffins Martyn Ware and Ian Marsh to form the British group Heaven 17 (named after a bar in Anthony Burgess's novel *A Clockwork Orange*) they initially produced tinny, lightweight electronica of the weakest order. Gregory's medium-range vocals leavened the mixture somewhat, and in the process improved this A-side – which, remarkably, was initially banned by the BBC for its title. It wasn't until their excellent 1983 single 'Temptation' that Heaven 17 really found their feet, but as an example of early-1980s anti-capitalist pop propaganda, 'Fascist Groove Thang' does the trick perfectly: naive, tuneful, and faintly trashy music to be used once and thrown away.

Tainted Love
Soft Cell

Released July 1981
Sire *49855* (U.S. #8) / Some Bizzare *BZS 2* (U.K. #1)

Soft Cell's debut hit is an example of both the role of technology in creating new sound and the way that a good song can endure. As synthesizers became readily available and affordable in the early 1980s, many seized the chance to try to emulate Kraftwerk and David Bowie's

'Berlin' trilogy of albums. Among them were Marc Almond and Dave Ball, who formed Soft Cell, the archetypal synth-pop duo. The band released an EP and two singles in 1980 and '81 that caused some interest but didn't sell. Then they came across 'Tainted Love.'

The song had been written by one Ed Cobb, a 1960s songwriter-producer-manager who had once been a member of the hit vocal harmony group The Four Preps. In his stable of artists was the garage-rock band The Standells. Cobb wrote what became their biggest hit, 'Dirty Water,' with which 'Tainted Love' shares a powerful four-to-the-floor beat. 'Dirty Water' was covered by British band The Inmates, while 'Tainted Love,' which had been recorded by soul singer Gloria Jones in 1964, became a favorite in Britain's Northern Soul clubs in the late 1970s. Soft Cell kept the best of the original version of 'Tainted Love' – the solid, stomping beat – thus ensuring that their version would work as a dance number. But the instrumentation was entirely electronic, over which Almond performed theatrical vocal histrionics. The duo went on to have many more hits, but it is with this song that they will be forever associated.

Don't You Want Me
Human League

Released November 1981
A&M/Virgin *2397* (U.S. #1) / Virgin *VS 466* (U.K. #1)

With its fine melody, duologue lyric, and soap opera storyline, 'Don't You Want Me' was destined to become a karaoke favorite. Its monster synthesizer riff etched itself into the listener's memory as much as any guitar lick, completing the radio-friendly picture. The League had come a long way since their Kraftwerk-like gloom of two years ago when the line-up had included future Heaven 17 members Martyn Ware and Ian Craig Marsh.

The song was based on a photo-strip in a girl's magazine. The depiction of a starmaker scooping a nobody into celebrity seemed to allude to the real-life romance between frontman and writer Phil Oakey and vocalist Susanne Sulley, although perversely it was the group's other singer, Joanna Catterall, who sang the female lines. Another perverse touch came in Oakey's narrative where the girl bites that hand that feeds her.

While 'Don't You Want Me' wasn't a first of any kind – the U.K. charts were already awash with synth-pop – it was certainly the record that confirmed to any remaining doubters that synth-pop did not have to be merely a watery, weedy version of rock. The path was being set for the unthinkable: the demise of rock, which in the space of the next 15 years would be reduced to a mere sub-genre of popular music.

Meanwhile, as Ware and Craig Marsh happily received one per cent of the royalties for 'Don't You Want Me' in part return for giving up the rights to the Human League name, the League itself slowly went broke in a vain attempt to make another record with the impact of this one.

Rapture
Blondie

Released January 1981
Chrysalis *CHS 2485* (U.S. #1, U.K. #5)

It seems somewhat perverse to declare a record by a bunch of nerdy (white) New Yorkers and a former Playboy bunny to be one of the key moments in the development and popularization of rap music. But 'Rapture' is exactly that. Blondie had spent the previous half-decade becoming and then cementing their position as the biggest group of the punk/new wave era. By this stage they had chalked up a number of memorable transatlantic hit singles, among them 'Heart Of Glass,' 'Atomic,' and 'Call Me,' a collaboration with the disco producer Giorgio Moroder.

'Rapture' was taken from Blondie's fifth full-length effort, *Autoamerican*, which saw release in late 1980. Although the album itself is considered to be the point at which Blondie began to decline, its singles showed no signs of ill health – 'Rapture' followed 'The Tide Is High' to the top of the *Billboard* Hot 100.

The first (overlooked) half of 'Rapture' features one of Debbie Harry's finest vocal melodies, which soars seductively amid chiming bells and funky bass. Midway through, she ups the ante further, launching into a cool, collected rap that – while dismissed by some hip-hop purists – has the measure of many of the genre's early MCs. While it might not have the musical pedigree of Afrika Bambaataa or The Sugarhill Gang, 'Rapture' brought rap to suburban America for the first time, and it even had a heavy metal style guitar solo, preempting later rap-rock.

Once In A Lifetime
Talking Heads

Released February 1981
Sire *40649* (U.S.) / Sire *SIR 4048* (U.K. #14)

Talking Heads' best-loved song, 'Once In A Lifetime' represents the high-water mark of the group's association with über-producer Brian Eno. In the three years since recording their debut LP, *Talking Heads 77*, the quartet's output had evolved from taut post-punk to a funky melting pot of sound that drew as much on African polyrhythms as it did on more traditional, rock-based forms. Much of this can be put down to the influence of Eno, and also to the band's acceptance of their own limitations as musicians and subsequent hiring of talented guest players like the guitar virtuoso Adrian Belew.

'Once In A Lifetime' is the most immediate of the eight songs on the group's fourth full-length album, *Remain In Light*. Its verses are dominated by leader David Byrne's questioning spoken-word vocal, in which he ruminates on a wealthy, materialistic – but ultimately empty – world, over a backdrop of stop-start bass and watery keyboards. There is no real hook to speak of until the chorus, which is surprisingly euphoric, given that Byrne sings of letting "the days go by" and "the water hold me down."

Part of the song's lasting appeal was the accompanying promo video, which features Byrne's crazy-man dancing in front of some endearingly simple special effects. It remains a staple of music-television programming, while the song itself is one of the most distinctive singles of the early 1980s. No subsequent Talking Heads release so successfully melded their pop sensibilities and artistic invention, although they had a bigger hit four years later with 'Road To Nowhere.'

Ghost Town
The Specials

Released June 1981
2-Tone *2525* (U.S.) / 2-Tone *CHSTT 17* (U.K. #1)

Among the finest U.K. chart-toppers of the 1980s, 'Ghost Town' was The Specials' defining moment: an intoxicating mix of eerie fairground organ, dub bass, and timely lyrics about inner city violence. Released in the midst of rioting in London and Liverpool, it proved in effect to be the group's swan song, as three of its founding members left soon afterwards.

The Specials formed in 1978 and were soon at the forefront of a ska revival in the U.K., releasing their records on keyboardist Jerry Dammers's own 2-Tone label. The group's eponymous debut LP, released at the tail end of 1979, was produced by Elvis Costello and mixed reggae, punk, ska, and pop with impassioned socio-political lyrics. Three U.K. Top 10 hits and a second album, *More Specials*, followed in 1980 before the group unleashed its crowning achievement in the summer of 1981.

'Ghost Town' leaps from wistful to foreboding and back again across its six minutes, as vocalists Terry Hall and Neville Staples wonder "why must the youth fight among themselves?" Integral to the group's sound, as ever, is trombonist Rico Rodriquez, plus the super-tight rhythm section of bassist Horace Gentleman and drummer John Bradbury. Despite the group reaching their artistic and commercial high point, they were already on their last legs: by the end of 1981, Hall, Staples, and guitarist Lynval Goulding had left to form Fun Boy Three. The remaining members and various replacements carried on to increasingly diminishing returns as The Special A.K.A. before splitting in 1984.

O Superman
Laurie Anderson

Released October 1981
Warner Bros. *49876* (U.S.) / Warner Bros. *K 17870* (U.K. #2)

'O Superman,' an eight-minute spoken-word piece backed by minimal synthesizer passages, is one of the most unusual one-hit wonders of all time. Underpinned by a monotonous vocal sample, it was extracted from a lengthy stage work, *United States*, which performance artist Laurie Anderson eventually issued as a five-disc live set in 1985. The single was originally issued a month earlier on the independent One-Ten label, but a rush of orders – mostly from the U.K. – led to a recording deal with Warners and the company's subsequent re-release of the record. But nothing else Anderson recorded ever had the same commercial impact.

Radio Free Europe
R.E.M.

Released July 1981
Hib-Tone *HT 0001* (U.S.) / IRS *IR 9916* (U.K.)

'Radio Free Europe' marks the moment when post-punk turned into alternative rock. But at the time, R.E.M. didn't much care for it. They'd first attempted to record the song in February 1981, tried again in April, agonized over remixes, and finally released a version that none of them really liked. Lyrically incomprehensible (because writer-singer Michael Stipe wanted it that way), 'Radio Free Europe' nevertheless boasted a sound that cleverly combined traditional and avant-garde elements into something mysterious and yet radio-friendly. It was, however, a third version – recorded for the album *Murmur* – that rocketed all the way to Number 78 in America in August 1983, starting R.E.M. on the road to fame and fortune.

In The Air Tonight
Phil Collins

Released January 1981
Atlantic *3824* (U.S. #19) / Virgin *VS 102* (U.K. #2)

With this single, Phil Collins stepped out from the behind the drum-kit of the progressive group Genesis to become one most unlikely solo stars of the 1980s. The vast international success of 'In The Air Tonight' was all the more surprising given that the song is a bitter message to Collins's ex-wife set to a sparse drum-machine pattern and funereal electric-organ chords.

In 1979, Collins returned home from the latest in a run of lengthy world tours with Genesis to find his personal life in tatters: his wife had left him and taken their children with her. Not knowing what else to do with himself, he set up a small home studio – which consisted of a Rhodes electric piano, a Prophecy synthesizer, a Roland drum machine, and an 8-track recorder – and started pouring his heart out onto tape.

Collins recorded very quickly what he thought would be just a demo of 'In The Air Tonight,' writing the words as he sang them. Unable to replicate the original recording in a 'proper' studio the following year, he instead reworked the existing version. The main addition is the closing, tension-releasing drum fill, which was recorded, somewhat serendipitously, through the studio's 'reverse talkback' feed by accident, giving it a distinctive, highly compressed sound.

The success of the single sent Collins's full-length solo debut album, *Face Value*, into the upper reaches of the charts on both sides of the Atlantic and established a lucrative second career for the drummer. He had further solo hits throughout the 1980s, including seven U.S. chart-toppers, among them 'Against All Odds' and 'Groovy Kind Of Love.'

0234 PHIL COLLINS/In The Air Tonight

Rock This Town
The Stray Cats

Released January 1981
EMI America *8132* (U.S. #9) / Arista *SCAT 2* (U.K. #9)

This smart 1980s update of the '50s rockabilly sound came from three larger-than-life personalities who stood out amongst the synth-driven groups of the time. The refreshing trio hit first with this 45 in Britain, opening the gateway to hit-making back home in America. Singer-guitarist Brian Setzer, drummer Slim Jim Phantom, and upright-bass man Lee Rocker took The Stray Cats from their Long Island roots to London to work with veteran producer-guitarist Dave Edmunds. MTV ate up the visual presentation of the Cats and turned them into some of the first video stars.

Endless Love
Diana Ross & Lionel Richie

Released July 1981
Motown *1519* (U.S. #1) / Motown *TMG 1240* (U.K. #7)

Motown was always looking for that extra dollar, and teaming together two of their top artists, one of whom was the supreme ballad writer of the period, seemed bound to produce a winner. And indeed it did: 'Endless Love' became the company's biggest selling single of all time, shifting three million copies in America alone and spending nine weeks as the country's Number 1. It was written for the Brooke Shields movie of the same name, which also marked Tom Cruise's screen debut, but the film was a fiasco. Richie had already enjoyed three U.S. Number 1s, with 'Three Times A Lady' and 'Still' for The Commodores and 'Lady' for country star Kenny Rogers. 'Endless Love' was first commissioned as an instrumental, but Richie was asked for lyrics, and finally a female vocalist was suggested. Conflicting schedules called for the recording to be made at 3:30am in a Nevada studio, and while Ms. Ross hadn't heard the song before, the finished recording was in the can an hour and a half later.

Under Pressure
Queen & David Bowie

Released October 1981
Elektra *47235* (U.S. #29) / EMI *5250* (U.K. #1)

This sparse, under-produced collaboration is best known for its bassline, perhaps one of the most memorable and infectious in popular music history. It was the product of a spontaneous jam session between Queen and David Bowie at Mountain Studios in Montreux, Switzerland, in July 1981. The origins of the famous bassline are somewhat confused. Both Queen bassist John Deacon and Bowie have, surprisingly, denied writing it, each claiming it to be the work of the other. In 1990 Vanilla Ice recycled both the bass riff and the main piano part for his landmark hit 'Ice Ice Baby,' but has since claimed that he did actually sample the original. While 'Under Pressure' was not a major U.S. hit on its release in 1981, it has become one of the best known songs in both Queen and Bowie's catalogs, and remains a staple of the latter's live performances.

Start Me Up
The Rolling Stones

Released August 1981
Rolling Stones 21003 (U.S. #2) / Rolling Stones *RSR 108* (U.K. #7)

The last truly great Rolling Stones single, 'Start Me Up' is a gargantuan rocker cut from the same cloth as 1960s classics like 'Honky Tonk Women' and 'Satisfaction.' It demonstrated that Mick Jagger and Keith Richards still had a knack for a great tune, and also the extent to which they needed each other. The pair spent much of the rest of the 1980s somewhere between bickering and feuding, and the quality of the group's work suffered as a result.

'Start Me Up' was the first single drawn from *Tattoo You*, the 19th studio album from the self-proclaimed World's Greatest Rock'n'Roll Band. Like much of the group's work, it was produced by Jagger and Richards under the name The Glimmer Twins. Stripped back to its constituent parts, the song is amazingly simple: there is little more here than a pair of guitar riffs and a couple of repeated lyrics, but anything else would feel like padding. Richards's muscular guitar-playing dominates without ever becoming showy, while Charlie Watts provides a typically steady backbeat.

'Start Me Up' stormed into the upper reaches of the British and American charts, as did its parent album, but it marked the end of the Stones' run as a creative force. Amid Jagger and Richards's bickering about the direction the group should take and the unhelpful distractions of solo work, they slowly evolved into a spectacular live group that occasionally makes so-so records. But this single remains a live favorite, on a par with pretty much anything in the Stones' canon.

beast altogether, a harsh, confrontational look inside urban poverty and desperation, given voice by Melle Mel's urgent delivery. It's an unforgiving telegram sent from the heart of the crumbling and deadly Bronx in New York City where the twin effects of Reaganomics and a proliferating crack trade were colliding in a display of mass destruction.

Before 'The Message,' hip-hop was largely a happy-go-lucky, partying style, where you'd expect to find escapism rather than reportage. After its release, however, the genre would never be the same. In fact, hip-hop has subsequently been praised and prized for its ability to shine a mainstream light on the underexposed conditions of oppression. Without this song, the entire course of the genre could have been very different indeed, and some of its most prominent voices might never have surfaced.

'The Message' did not have the muscle to reach the higher American pop charts, peaking at Number 62, but it did receive attention overseas, hitting Number 8 in the U.K. and enjoying platinum sales within a month of its official release. Notable Los Angeles rapper (and later actor) Ice Cube would sample the backing track of 'The Message' to form the basis of his own rap song, 1992's 'Check Yo Self,' which transferred the original song's lament for a suffering city into a tune about accountability in the wake of self-destruction. And five years later another famous rapper, Puff Daddy, used a similar sample for his song 'Can't Nobody Hold Me Down,' pairing instrumental elements from 'The Message' with a vocal interpolation of lyrics from Matthew Wilder's 1984 song 'Break My Stride.'

Both are tributes to the iconic status and continuing relevance of 'The Message,' which remains a pivotal and influential song in hip-hop, one that has permanently pulled back the curtain on urban blight in America. Solutions to severe crime and poverty haven't been easy, nor have they been forthcoming, but 'The Message' shows that it's necessary to try.

The Message
Grandmaster Flash & The Furious Five

Released May 1982
Sugar Hill *584* (U.S.) / Sugar Hill *SHL 117* (U.K. #8)

Popular New York DJ Joseph Saddler (a.k.a. Grandmaster Flash) is one of hip-hop's most respected architects, an innovator of many of the techniques still used by professional DJs and a catalyst who brought the culture above ground. Most importantly, the legendary Flash has taught DJs how to create a lasting groove out of spare elements by manipulating records with the use of a mixer – so it followed that he'd make a great producer.

Saddler landed a recording contract with the burgeoning Sugar Hill Records, which had introduced itself to audiences with The Sugarhill Gang's 'Rapper's Delight' in 1979. He joined with several MCs to form Grandmaster Flash & The Furious Five, with a line-up that included brothers Melvin Glover (Melle Mel) and Nathaniel Glover (Kid Creole) along with Keith Wiggins (Cowboy), Eddie Morris (Scorpio), and Guy Williams (Rahiem).

Flash had already begun to make a name for himself in the recording world with his cut-up disco mega-mixes of songs from record labels like Salsoul and Casablanca, but 'The Message' was an entirely different

Planet Rock
Afrika Bambaataa & The Soul Sonic Force

Released June 1982
Tommy Boy *823* (U.S.) / Polydor *POSP 497* (U.K.)

Afrika Bambaataa is often called the godfather of hip-hop, and while he has some notable company – such as Kool Herc and Grandmaster Flash – the man born Kevin Donovan in Bronx, New York City, proudly carries a lot of the weight for what would eventually become global youth culture. 'Planet Rock,' produced by Arthur Baker and performed with Bambaataa's group Soul Sonic Force, is an urban tribute to the song that inspired it: 1977's 'Trans-Europe Express' by the German group Kraftwerk. It is also Bambaataa's enduring signature song.

Not only is the electro funk style of 'Planet Rock' prevalent today in a large palette of dance music styles, from house and drum'n'bass to techno and breakbeat, but the central instrument used in its creation, Roland's TR-808 drum machine, known simply as the 808, still beats in the heart of hip-hop around America, particularly in the South. It's traceable through the booty shake of provocative Miami bass records to the brilliantly rowdy crunk music that soundtracks an energetic youth in Atlanta. Without 'Planet Rock' many different artists would be searching for a production blueprint half as influential.

The song's impact is not only technical but also spiritual. 'Planet Rock' has a lesson to share that is still important, an ideal of multicultural harmony, on and off the dancefloor. Bambaataa walked the talk he talked: before making music he was a gang member, but later he renounced that life and formed the peaceful Zulu Nation, a collective that has celebrated more than 20 birthdays.

Mickey
Toni Basil

Released February 1982
Chrysalis *2638* (U.S. #1) / Radialchoice *TIC 4* (U.K. #2)

At a time when Toni Basil was an aspiring triple threat to the worlds of acting, dancing, and singing, she blended her various talents in this memorable, cheer-like tune based on a 1979 song, 'Kitty,' by the British band Racey. The video for 'Mickey,' featuring Basil fronting a sassy team of cheerleaders, became a popular mainstay of MTV. She spoke of the excitement of fitting into her old Las Vegas High School cheerleading outfit for the performance. Often called a one-hit wonder, Basil enjoyed a successful career as a choreographer after 'Mickey,' creating memorable dance moves for David Bowie and David Byrne.

I Love Rock'n'Roll
Joan Jett & The Blackhearts

Released February 1982
Boardwalk *135* (U.S. #1) / Epic *EPC A 2152* (U.K. #4)

The Arrows originally wrote this song in 1975, and pop tartlet Britney Spears would cover it in a lackluster way almost 30 years later, but it was Joan Jett and her Blackhearts who shot 'I Love Rock'n'Roll' to the top of the charts for eight weeks. The fiery Jett, who first debuted in the all-woman band The Runaways, took two attempts to make the song into a hit: her first version with former Sex Pistols Paul Cook and Steve Jones didn't catch on in anything like the same way as the Blackhearts take.

Ebony And Ivory
Paul McCartney with Stevie Wonder

Released April 1982
Columbia *02860* (U.S. #1) / Parlophone *6054* (U.K. #1)

The Girl Is Mine
Michael Jackson / Paul McCartney

Released November 1982
Epic *03288* (U.S. #2) / Epic *EPC A 2729* (U.K. #8)

While it may be a contrived song, 'Ebony And Ivory' gave Paul McCartney his lengthiest stay at the top of the U.S. singles charts – he was there for seven weeks – and it gave Stevie Wonder his first visit to Number 1 in Britain. Recorded for McCartney's *Tug Of War* album, the song marked his reunion with former Beatles producer George Martin and was recorded at Martin's Air studios on the picturesque island of Montserrat.

Later that year, McCartney was invited to contribute vocals to a Michael Jackson composition that put him on the biggest selling album of all time. Released as the first single from *Thriller*, 'The Girl Is Mine' was a sugary duet that gave little indication of how much of a blockbuster the album would become (it has sales of 54 million at the time of writing). McCartney recorded another duet with Jackson, 'Say Say Say,' for his 1983 album *Pipes Of Peace* before the pair fell out – Jackson used his *Thriller* millions to outbid McCartney for the Beatles copyrights owned by ATV Music Publishing. Jackson paid $47.5 million (about £27 million) for the pleasure. Jackson had been calling McCartney and asking for financial advice; according to McCartney it was something of a running joke. "He'd say, 'I'm gonna buy your publishing, ya know!' I'd go, 'Ha! Good one, kid!' Then one day I get phoned up and they say, 'He's just bought your stuff!'" McCartney concluded: "All's fair in love, war, and business, I suppose. But it's a little galling now to find that I own less of 'Yesterday' than Michael Jackson. It's a thorn in my side."

Da Da Da
Trio

Released April 1982
Mercury *4019* (U.S.) / Mobile Suit Corporation *CORP 5* (U.K. #2)

In an era when synthesizers revved overtime and haircuts quickly fluffed and angled out of control, the German band known as Trio opted for more of a deconstructionist approach to their machine-driven ditties. The charm of the guiltily infectious 'Da Da Da' comes in its spare use of Casio beats and the vocal textures supporting a simple tune. The result has had a completely unexpected longevity for a Teutonic band that isn't Kraftwerk. Later, the song would enjoy a substantial new wind in America that blew it into the popular consciousness when it was picked up as a jingle for a car ad in 1997.

Eye Of The Tiger
Survivor

Released June 1982
Scotti Bros. *02912* (U.S. #1) / Scotti Bros. *SCT A 2411* (U.K. #1)

Survivor fan Sylvester Stallone asked the band to write a song for his certain-blockbuster movie *Rocky III*. But not even Stallone could have predicted the heavyweight knock down and drag out success of this monster song. The kudos included an Oscar nomination, a Grammy, a People's Choice Award, international chart placements, and Survivor's sole Number 1 hit. The sports world embraced 'Eye Of The Tiger,' which leaped from *Rocky* screens to real-life arenas, where it remained a motivational anthem. Strangely, in 1995 U.K. boxing champion Frank Bruno covered the song, which hit the Top 40 in Britain.

Do You Really Want To Hurt Me
Culture Club

Released September 1982
Epic *03368* (U.S. #2) / Virgin *VS 518* (U.K. #1)

The U.K.-based quartet that dubbed itself Culture Club was Boy George, Roy Hay, Mikey Craig, and Jon Moss. They began one of the most vibrant and successful careers in 1980s pop music with this sweet tune influenced by the easygoing rhythmic vibes of reggae toasters from the island of Jamaica. Boy George's honeyed soul voice went down the pop palate rather easily, and he managed to confound audiences on both sides of the Atlantic with his truly different androgynous look – braided long hair, lots of makeup, flashy outfits – and his ambiguously coy reactions to the constant questions about his sexuality.

Hungry Like The Wolf
Duran Duran

Released May 1982
Harvest *5134* (U.S. #3) / EMI *5295* (U.K. #5)

'Hungry Like The Wolf' was the fourth Top 20 hit in the group's native U.K. and the song that introduced Duran Duran to an eager America, ushering in a string of hits and hordes of female admirers. This potent,

extended sexual metaphor was a timely and unique combination of tough rock-guitar licks and frenetic beats, worthy of post-disco dancefloors – but was reportedly inspired by the innocent childhood fairy tale of *Little Red Riding Hood*. It also turned out to have an extended shelf life once the world embraced Duran Duran as a pop sensation.

Director Russell Mulcahy took Duran Duran to picturesque Sri Lanka to shoot the adventurous video, which most memorably features the thrilling tension of lead singer Simon LeBon pursued through a jungle by a painted she-wolf in heat. The quintet (originally Nick Rhodes, John Taylor, Andy Taylor, and Roger Taylor in addition to LeBon) fast became teen idols around the world, especially as the MTV audience devoured the video, which was considerably more filmic and action-packed than much of the competing material of the time. In 1984, 'Hungry Like The Wolf' won the Grammy for Best Video Shortform and made a notable contribution towards Duran Duran's second honor that year, for Best Video Album. Mulcahy would go on to shoot many of Duran Duran's most famous videos during the group's peak era of MTV superstardom.

Come On Eileen
Dexys Midnight Runners

Released June 1982
Mercury *76189* (U.S. #1) / Mercury *DEXYS 9* (U.K. #1)

Despite wearing clothes that were obsolete about ten minutes after they appeared and shooting a video that included the worst haircut crime ever committed – namely, the female mullet – Dexys Midnight Runners managed not to mess up their biggest hit. Depending on your point of view, 'Come On Eileen' was an elegantly catchy bit of pop folklore or a teeth-grindingly tinny gypsy lament: either way, it sank its teeth into everyone's cerebral cortex in 1982 and refused to let go for decades.

To this day, high school disco-themed dancefloors erupt as its first bars ring out – a stamping bass and drum intro followed by a whimsical violin melody – and people then either run for cover or celebrate its apparently eternal charm. Listen out for the many strokes of genius that punctuate the record, such as the chorus line, which drops down beguilingly from the verse, and the slow-shout-out break that builds to a fast ending.

Dexys, and specifically their maverick leader Kevin Rowland, couldn't have foreseen the song's enormous success – and failed to deal with it when it materialized, spiraling downward into eccentric inconsistency

after some decent singles ('Geno' was a triumph, as was 'Jackie Wilson Says') and a critically acclaimed album, *Don't Stand Me Down*. By that point the cowbilly wear had been ditched in favor of a preppy suit look that amused no one. But for a brief moment back there, Dexy and his Runners looked as if they might take over the world.

It Started With A Kiss
Hot Chocolate

Released July 1982
EMI America *8157* (U.S.) / RAK *344* (U.K. #5)

Formed in London in 1969, this multi-racial group's first recording was a reggae version of John Lennon's 'Give Peace A Chance' that they sent to The Beatles' Apple Records, who released it without success. They signed a new deal with Mickie Most in 1970 at the birth of his newly formed RAK label. Hot Chocolate went on to become the label's most consistently successful act, placing at least one hit on the U.K. charts every year between 1970 and 1984. They recorded a mixture of originals and custom-written material by contemporary writers. 'It Started With A Kiss' was composed by frontman and vocalist Errol Brown and was a U.K. hit on three separate occasions in 1982, 1993, and 1998, demonstrating the band's enduring popularity in Britain where their biggest international hit, 'You Sexy Thing,' also charted three times.

Sexual Healing
Marvin Gaye

Released October 1982
Columbia *03302* (U.S. #3) / CBS *A 2855* (U.K. #4)

'Sexual Healing' was a testimony to Marvin Gaye's continued talent after the glory years with the Motown label, earning two Grammys and an American Music Award and selling over a million copies. It introduced the legendary crooner to a fickle 1980s audience, who decided that this undeniably grooving ode to getting down was a goodie from an oldie. David Ritz wrote 'Sexual Healing' after witnessing the singer's pornographic magazine collection and went on to write *Divided Soul*, the revelatory biography about Gaye's life and his untimely death at the hands of his father in 1984.

Buffalo Gals
Malcolm McLaren & The World's Famous Supreme Team

Released November 1982
Island *99941* (U.S.) / Charisma *MALC 1* (U.K. #9)

The notoriously unctuous former manager of punk's defunct Sex Pistols re-emerged in an unusual way, as the impetus behind this hip-hop collaboration with two relatively unknown New York radio jocks called the World Famous Supreme Team. McLaren sniffed potential in the burgeoning rap scene and played a large role in transporting it to Britain. 'Buffalo Gals' has been sampled endlessly by hip-hop and electronica producers on both sides of the Atlantic. Certain snippets – including McLaren's introductory greeting, a Wild West-inspired "Helloooooooo!" – are iconic sounds in these genres, even though many listeners remain unaware of their origins.

1999
Prince

Released October 1982
Warner Bros. *29896* (U.S. #12) / Warner Bros. *W 9896* (U.K. #25)

In 1948 the great novelist George Orwell zeroed in on the year 1984 as the point of no return, but another visionary named Prince looked further ahead for his perpetually funky send-off to the end of time. Prince's first international hit expertly channels the pervasive panic about nuclear bombs, world wars, and other possibilities for Armageddon that gripped America in the 1980s under the presidential reign of Ronald Reagan (and the U.K.'s simultaneous rule by Margaret Thatcher). It is fitting that this lyrically and sonically innovative record served as a formal introduction to one of America's most singular soul talents since James Brown.

While his Minneapolis-bred backing band, The Revolution, were never meant to take center stage with the flamboyant Prince himself, '1999' is their biggest showcase – and particularly the duo known simply by their first names, Wendy & Lisa – as they sing and provide rhythmic counterpoints to his verses. The song was re-released in 1999 and managed the difficult feat of landing in the U.K. Top 10 and beating its original placement. Key lyrics such as "Two-thousand, zero zero / Party over / Oops, out of time" fit in perfectly with the end-of-the-world hysteria that surfaced just before the advent of Y2K, when there seemed to be some question marks over the world's future. Even in the 21st century club DJs continue to play '1999,' saving it for those moments when they want a large crowd reaction on the dancefloor.

Golden Brown
The Stranglers

Released January 1982
Not issued U.S. / Liberty *BP 407* (U.K. #2)

Is it about a brunette? Is it about heroin? No one knows, possibly not even head Strangler Hugh Cornwell, whose laconic vocals sung over a fiendishly complex harpsichord-driven backing are one of this single's many high points. 'Golden Brown' was an unlikely hit given its unusual instrumentation and time signature, but the fact that it remains the group's best-known song (with 'Peaches') speaks volumes about The Stranglers' status as punk icons. After all, would a 'real' punk band have added a dreamy, reverb'd vocal melody as the outro of the song, a clean jazz drone instead of a proper guitar solo, and a military snare pattern? Probably not.

More than this, 'Golden Brown' says a lot about the tastes of the music-buying British public back in 1982 as punk's second wave took off and the twin demons of New Romanticism and synth-pop found a foothold. In retrospect, it doesn't seem to have been an era in which fans would have shelled out for what was practically a piece of classical music masquerading as a pop single. But they did anyway – in droves – which makes The Stranglers' achievement all the more notable. Perhaps this underlines that good music will find its way to market no matter what the prevailing trends indicate. Certainly the group themselves never equaled it again, despite semi-pop love songs such as 'Skin Deep' that tried and failed to replicate the classy, almost 1960s West Coast vibe of this most unusual recording.

House Of Fun
Madness

Released May 1982
Not issued U.S. / Stiff *BUY 146* (U.K. #1)

Following hot on the heels of The Specials, Madness were the most successful of the British ska-revivalists of the late 1970s and early 1980s. 'House Of Fun' was the highest charting of the group's many memorable U.K. hits. They formed in early 1979 in London, England, and by the end of the year had appeared twice on the British singles chart, with 'The Prince' – a giddy tribute to ska legend Prince Buster – and 'One Step Beyond.' Led by cheeky-chappy vocalist Graham 'Suggs' McPherson, the seven-piece line-up included a permanent two-man horn section, and the group maintained a fine line in snappy suits and crazy dancing.

The group had already reached the U.K. Top 10 on nine occasions – notably with 'Baggy Trousers' in 1980 – before 'House Of Fun' became their only Number 1. A typically fun-filled tale of adolescence, the song is driven by syncopated drums, nagging piano, and rapturous bursts of sax and trumpet. Its fairground feel is vaguely reminiscent of The Specials' landmark 'Ghost Town' but without the doomy overtones.

Two further huge hits followed, 'Driving In My Car' and 'Our House,' which became the group's only U.S. Top 10 hit early the following year. Their fortunes began to fade soon after, however, when their material took on a more melancholic edge. Although they continue to record and tour sporadically, Madness have never since been able to reach the heights of their 1980s heyday.

Rock The Casbah
The Clash

Released June 1982
Epic *03245* (U.S. #8) / CBS *A 2479* (U.K. #30)

British punk royalty The Clash will forever be remembered in the pop world for this, their biggest hit in America. Its rebellious mock protestation of an Arabian government unsympathetic to the power of a good rock jam moved audiences across the globe. The original cover art for 'Rock The Casbah' finds an Arab and a Hasidic Jew dancing with each other to the same groove, a peaceful thought that some still wish for, almost a quarter-century later. The song was a classic-rock radio mainstay for years until officially banned by radio giant Clear Channel in the wake of the U.S. terrorist attacks of September 11, 2001.

White Wedding
Billy Idoll

Released October 1982
Chrysalis *42697* (U.S. #36) / Chrysalis *CHS 2656* (U.K.)

For a great many artists, re-invention is the name of the game. David Bowie is the master of this particular skill, but failed British 1960s teen idol Shane Fenton's re-birth as mysterious glam-rocker Alvin Stardust is perhaps a better reference point for the transformation of Billy Idol. Born William Broad in London, England, he renamed himself Billy Idol while a member of The Bromley Contingent, cult followers of The Sex Pistols, played for a while with punk band Chelsea, and then made a splash as frontman of Generation X.

Unable to hit the big time in Britain, Idol relocated to New York City in 1981 where he teamed up with Kiss manager Bill Aucoin and guitarist-songsmith Stevie Stevens. As a solo act he contrived a new image that was part-metal, part-punk, and 100 per cent MTV-friendly. Conveying a rebellious persona with slick bondage-chic videos playing heavily on his grotesquely over-the-top variation on the petulant Elvis-James Dean sneer, Idol was ideal heavy-rotation fodder, securing his first American Top 30 entry with 'Hot In The City.'

His blisteringly powerful but hardly innovative follow-up was 'White Wedding.' Cleverly juxtaposing rebellious sentiments with traditional values, this was the one that eventually exported Idol's success back home, delivering his first British Top 10 entry when reissued in 1985.

New Year's Day
U2

Released January 1983
Island *99915* (U.S.) / Island *WIP 6848* (U.K. #10)

This school band made it all the way to the top, so keep up the group practice – you never know. They formed as Feedback and later The Hype before becoming U2 and winning a CBS contract in Ireland following a talent contest sponsored by Guinness. Two Ireland-only CBS singles topped the home charts before they secured an international deal with Island in 1980. 'New Year's Day,' from their third album, *War*, was U2's first British Top 10 single and their first proper U.S. single to make the charts, although only to Number 53. The album did better, making Number 12. ('Gloria' from their second album, *October*, had charted at Number 81 in the U.S. on the basis of import sales alone.)

It would be 1987's *The Joshua Tree* that turned U2 into a world-class act, but it was around this time that they transformed themselves into major-league players. That came from continual U.S. touring, as well as *War*, their first focused collection, including politically charged songs such as 'New Year's Day' and 'Sunday Bloody Sunday,' complete with Bono's flag-waving routine. 'New Year's Day' nearly didn't make the album at all. Bass player Adam Clayton came up with the bass riff at a soundcheck, Edge polished it on piano, but Bono had considerable problems coming up with a finished lyric. It's essentially a love song that moves further into politics, and the group were happy to let listeners draw associations with Lech Walesa's Solidarity movement. The song's line "Under a blood red sky..." was later appropriated as the title of their live mini-album that also included 'New Year's Day.'

Every Breath You Take
The Police

Released May 1983
A&M *2542* (U.S. #1) / A&M *AM 117* (U.K. #1)

Sting wrote 'Every Breath You Take' on a piano once owned by Noel Coward, while holidaying on the island of Jamaica at Golden Eye, the former home of James Bond author Ian Fleming. According to Sting himself, his most popular song appeared to him in the middle of the night and virtually wrote itself. He rose, went to the piano, wrote the song within ten minutes, and returned to bed.

'Every Breath You Take' was inspired by the break-up of Sting's first marriage, to actress Frances Tomelty, and is a prime example of the old music-business adage that simple songs are often the best. As the writer himself has freely admitted, the lyrics are taken virtually "straight out of a rhyming dictionary" while the melody is about as basic as it gets.

At first listen it appears to be a love song, but Sting has emphasized its ominous side. He said: "I consider it a fairly nasty song. It's about surveillance and ownership and jealousy." Summing up his most popular work, he concluded: "It's very simple, laughably simple, and at the same time it does have some kind of emotional relevancy. It's kind of mysterious that way."

'Every Breath You Take' was named Song Of The Year at the 1984 Grammy Awards before being reworked, 13 years later, by Puff Daddy and Faith Evans as 'I'll Be Missing You,' a tribute to Notorious B.I.G., the murdered rap star.

Mr. Roboto
Styx

Released February 1983
A&M *2525* (U.S. #3) / A&M *AMS 8303* (U.K.)

Arena rockers Styx took an unpredictable turn of sound and ideas with 'Mr. Roboto,' the group's infectious version of machine funk that also proved to be their odd little swan song. The strangely dramatic ditty is the centerpiece of Styx's perplexing *Kilroy Was Here* album, a rock opera of sorts that finds the hero (Kilroy) attempting an escape from a prison populated by robotic correctional officers. American audiences did not take to the overall concept as put forth by lead singer Dennis DeYoung, but still they wholeheartedly embraced 'Mr. Roboto' as the quirky piece of pop wonderment that it is.

Total Eclipse Of The Heart
Bonnie Tyler

Released February 1983
Columbia *03906* (U.S. #1) / CBS *TYLER 1* (U.K. #1)

Another dose of pomp and circumstance from *Bat Out Of Hell* composer Jim Steinman provided a transatlantic Number 1 for Bonnie Tyler (born Gaynor Hopkins, in Wales). A throat operation in 1976 to remove nodules on her vocal cords resulted in Tyler's trademark husky voice, and she arrived in the U.K. charts soon afterwards with 'Lost In France' and 'It's A Heartache' (which also made the U.S. country charts). Ms. Tyler recalled: "I didn't have any control over what I was doing at all. I was signed to a production company and the guys who managed me were also songwriters. So they'd only let me record their material. They wanted me to sing country songs because they were aiming at the Nashville market. Some of the material was quite good, I suppose, but after I'd had seven flops in a row in a two-year period my heart went out of it. When my contract expired, I just walked out."

A new deal with CBS-Columbia opened up some new possibilities, and among producers considered were Jeff Lynne, Phil Collins, and Jim Steinman. Tyler said she pestered Steinman with phone calls and demos until he finally agreed to take her on. Featuring Steinman's trademark overblown production, 'Total Eclipse' was, like most of his work, a song you either loved or loathed. The track featured contributions from Max Weinberg and Roy Bittan of Bruce Springsteen's E-Street Band and guitar by Rick Derringer. The mother album *Faster Than The Speed Of Night* was a U.K. Number 1, and Tyler teamed up with Steinman again in 1984 for the *Footloose* track 'Holding Out For A Hero.' In 1994 'Total Eclipse' would climb to Number 5 on the U.K. charts in a re-make by Nicki French.

True
Spandau Ballet

Released March 1983
Chrysalis *42720* (U.S. #4) / Reformation *SPAN 1* (U.K. #1)

Spandau Ballet had enjoyed eight previous appearances on the British Top 40, but Tony Hadley's sensitive vocals helped propel 'True' beyond the group's homeland and into the international pop pantheon. This love song proved to have a prolonged shelf-life that couldn't possibly have

been premeditated by the quintet, consisting of Hadley plus brothers Gary and Martin Kemp, John Keeble, and Steve Norman. In 1991, New Jersey-based hip-hop group P.M. Dawn cleverly sampled vocal tones and melodies from 'True' to build the backbone of the breakout song 'Set Adrift On Memory Bliss,' which topped the American charts and landed at Number 3 in Britain.

Rockit
Herbie Hancock

Released July 1983
Columbia *04054* (U.S.) / CBS *A 3577* (U.K. #8)

The noted jazz artist Herbie Hancock was briefly yet significantly at the center of the nascent recorded hip-hop world with 'Rockit,' the song that in a long and varied career is still his best known single and the one that crossed most boundaries.

While audiences loved the robotic voices and fresh synthesizer groove unique to 'Rockit,' but center-stage really belonged to the scratching sounds of New York hip-hop DJ Grand Mixer D.ST. He is recognized as a main architect of the technique of manipulating a record back and forth on a turntable while using a mixer to cut the sound in and out and make short, choppy musical phrases. It made an ideal counterpoint to Hancock's keyboards and helped push 'Rockit' to Number 71 in *Billboard's* Hot 100.

Hancock had always embraced technology and experimentation in his compositions, as had bassist Bill Laswell, who co-produced the song with Michael Beinhorn. But 'Rockit' gave Hancock a street relevance and impact while simultaneously grabbing mainstream honors, such as the 1983 Grammy for Best R&B Instrumental Performance. It's a rather tricky feat that he was never able to repeat with any other song.

The humorous video for 'Rockit' features Hancock jamming along with a band of robots and strange, self-playing instruments; it quickly became an MTV mainstay. Hancock cleaned up at the 1984 MTV Video Music Awards with 'Rockit,' taking home five moon-men statuettes for Best Concept Video, Best Special Effects, Best Art Direction, Best Editing, and, most interestingly, the fleeting honor of Most Experimental Video.

Flashdance . . . What a Feeling
Irene Cara

Released April 1983
Casablanca *811440* (U.S. #1) / Casablanca *CAN 1016* (U.K. #2)

This is the title cut from the soundtrack for the runaway smash movie *Flashdance*, the inspirational story of a Pittsburgh factory worker who beats incredible odds to live out her dreams to dance. It brought some top honors to Irene Cara, a singer who was seeing her own dreams unfolding. To paraphrase the song, Cara was taking her passion and making it happen. The enviable accolades for 'Flashdance ... What A Feeling' included the Grammy for Best Female Pop Vocal and the Oscar for Best Song (awarded to *Flashdance* composer Giorgio Moroder). Cara had sung on another Academy Award-winning tune, 1980's 'Fame,' but 'Flashdance' swept the world.

Holiday
Madonna

Released October 1983
Sire *29478* (U.S. #16) / Sire *W 9405* (U.K. #2)

A buoyant, carefree ditty that seems tailor-made for Madonna, 'Holiday' was actually written by Lisa Hudson and Curtis Stevens with ex-Supremes singer Mary Wilson in mind. After Wilson declined the song, it was then recorded by the songwriters' friend, producer John 'Jellybean' Benitez, and the young Ms. Ciccone. 'Holiday' became the lead single from Madonna's debut self-titled album after it received tremendous response from the club DJs who had been sent promotional copies of the record (backed with another subsequent hit, 'Lucky Star'). To this day, DJs are an important part of the singer's career, often breaking each new song to the public. Her third single (following 'Everybody' and 'Burning Up' / 'Physical Attraction'), 'Holiday' guaranteed Madonna's spot on the global dancefloor, a position she still occupies.

Just a few years after the song's release, 'Holiday' was being sampled and re-used by others. In 1986, Dutch duo MC Miker G and DJ Sven used the instrumental of 'Holiday' for their own 'Holiday Rap,' a novelty track that improved on Madonna's original for pop-chart domination when it reached Number 1 in 34 countries.

'Holiday' has since been sampled by Australian dance act The Avalanches and provided the concept for the bassline to Stardust's international club hit 'Music Sounds Better With You,' a catchy song from 2000 that Madonna later referenced by sampling it on 'Get Together' from her 2006 album *Confessions On A Dancefloor*. Madonna's third single was still an influential dance hit more than two decades after its release – and even an influence on her own career.

Uptown Girl
Billy Joel

Released September 1983
Columbia *04149* (U.S. #3) / CBS *A 3775* (U.K. #1)

This snappy tune is one of many of the diverse gems in the multi-platinum-selling Piano Man's vast catalog of hits. For the benefit of befuddled listeners who didn't know exactly who Billy Joel's 'Uptown Girl' was in real life, the question was answered definitively in the iconic video made to promote the song, which was an MTV favorite. It finds Joel playing a grease monkey ogling a beautiful lady in a colorful dress. She turns out to be none other than supermodel Christie Brinkley, who would soon be Joel's wife (and later, sadly, his ex).

White Lines (Don't Don't Do It)
Grandmaster & Melle Mel

Released October 1983
Sugar Hill *465* (U.S.) / Sugar Hill *SH 130* (U.K. #7)

After the international attention generated by Grandmaster Flash & The Furious Five's 'The Message,' the pioneering New York DJ known as Flash teamed up with Furious Five MC Melle Mel to bring another type of message record from the heart of the nascent hip-hop world. While 'The Message' encapsulated the volatility of urban oppression in the Bronx onto a record that the mainstream could instinctively feel and embrace, 'White Lines' decried cocaine. Abuse of the drug was one of the most insidious problems ravaging the city. While the song was clear in its avocation, it had an undeniable funk and groove that helped the hard lessons go down with a spoonful of sugar.

Much of the instrumental inspiration for 'White Lines' came from another song: 'Cavern' by Liquid Liquid, the underground New York post-punk group fronted by singer Sal Principato. 'Cavern' features the bassline that is now principally associated with Flash, and Principato's vocal inflections seem to dictate the melodic direction employed by Melle Mel on 'White Lines.'

As with 'The Message,' 'White Lines' was not a hit on the American pop charts but was a success in the U.K. Top 10. It remains a staple of club DJs worldwide, from hip-hop to house music aficionados. As a notorious party anthem, its central theme has surely been misinterpreted thousands of times on non-sober dancefloors. Even with the song's success in Britain, it was still a shocker when U.K. pop act Duran Duran covered 'White Lines' for their 1995 album *Thank You* and brought it back to the British pop charts.

Billie Jean
Michael Jackson

Released January 1983
Epic *03509* (U.S. #1) / Epic *EPC A 3084* (U.K. #1)

The second, biggest, and best of seven singles from *Thriller*, 'Billie Jean' set a crown upon the head of the King Of Pop and made him the first superstar of the MTV generation. Of course, Michael Jackson was already a star long before 'Billie Jean.' From 1969 and 'I Want You Back' onwards, rarely did a few months pass without a new Jackson hit making a large dent on the charts. For the most part, however, the first dozen or so years of his career were dominated by his work with his brothers as The Jackson 5. Solo hits such as 'Rockin' Robin' and 'Ben' in the early 1970s and 'Don't Stop 'Til You Get Enough' at the end of the decade were exceptions, not the rule.

In late 1982, Jackson released his duet with Paul McCartney, 'The Girl Is Mine,' as the first single from *Thriller*. While it reached the Top 10 in Britain and the U.S., not all of his critics were convinced. But his next release raised the bar significantly higher. 'Billie Jean' opens with a stark two-beat drum loop and what Jackson considered to be "the perfect bassline," which is eventually augmented by swift stabs of synthesized strings. The main focus is, naturally, Jackson's vocal. Legend states that Jackson nailed the lead part first take, before painstakingly building up the multi-tracked backing vocals.

Like the rest of its parent album, 'Billie Jean' was produced by Quincy Jones, but the song and arrangement are very much Jackson's own, as demonstrated by his 1981 home demo version – included on the 20th anniversary reissue of *Thriller* – on which all of the key components are already in place. Jones's main contribution was to make each of the instrumental and vocal parts sound as good as they possibly could. He did, however, have two major objections to Jackson's vision for 'Billie Jean.' He felt that the 30-second intro was much too long for a pop single, and wanted the title to be changed, fearing that listeners would associate the song with the tennis player Billie Jean King – but lost out on both counts.

Jackson's determination to retain the song's original title was largely due to its real-life roots. This cautionary tale of predatory female fans is based on a woman who had begun to call herself 'Billie Jean Jackson' and claim that the singer was the father of one – but not both – of her twin sons. This particular 'Billie Jean' was eventually institutionalized, but Jackson has since intimated in interviews that she wasn't the only crazed fan that he has had to inform, in no uncertain terms, that "the kid is not my son."

Released at the end of January, 1983 – less than two months after the perfectionist Jackson completed the final mix – 'Billie Jean' quickly rose to the top of the *Billboard* singles chart and soon also reached Number 1 in the U.K. and across Europe. Just as important as its chart position was the accompanying promo video, directed by Steve Barron. MTV at the time was dominated by white artists and initially refused to air 'Billie Jean' until a timely ultimatum came from Jackson's record boss, CBS President Walter Yetnikoff: start showing the video or there will be no more white CBS acts on MTV. (CBS owned the Columbia and Epic labels.)

By March the station had relented, and Jackson was the first black star of MTV. Others soon followed, among them Prince and Lionel Richie. But the 'Billie Jean' promo did more than just break down racial barriers. It paved the way for a brand new kind of music video. Before, videos tended to be little more than a performance piece; this, on the other hand, was more like a short film, with high production values and something approaching a narrative storyline. Before the year was out, Jackson had taken the form even further with the epic, horror-movie-styled *Thriller* video.

'Billie Jean' introduced the world to another of Jackson's innovations: his moonwalk dance, which he debuted on the U.S. TV special *Motown 25: Yesterday, Today, And Forever* in front of an audience of over 47 million viewers. The performance was integral to *Thriller* becoming the biggest selling album of all time, while 'Billie Jean' – still the only song to which Jackson moonwalks – remains his best-selling single. He followed it with another *Billboard* chart-topper, 'Beat It,' the third of an unprecedented seven hit singles to be drawn from *Thriller* and the fifth of 12 career U.S. Number 1s at the time of writing.

QUINCY JONES: POPULAR MUSIC'S RENAISSANCE MAN

A true everyman of the entertainment industry, Chicago-born Quincy Jones would earn himself the reputation of living legend by the time he hit 60 in 1993 and continues to operate effectively within the music and film businesses.

Like many music-biz moguls, Jones paid his dues on stage, honing a mastery of the jazz trumpet through a scholarship at the nascent Berklee School of Music in Boston and playing in the orchestra of jazz bandleader Lionel Hampton at the age of only 20. After moving into arranging – he worked with luminaries such as Count Basie, Cannonball Adderley, Tommy Dorsey, and Dinah Washington – Jones led a band assembled by jazzman Dizzy Gillespie and recorded his own debut album, *This Is How I Feel About Jazz*. He studied in Paris, which led to production work for the French Barclay label, where he worked with Jacques Brel, Charles Aznavour, Billy Eckstine, and Sarah Vaughan.

This might have been a career's-worth for many men, but Jones had much more to offer and went behind the scenes, becoming the first black senior exec. for a major U.S. record company when he was hired as Mercury's vice-president in 1961. Two years later he moved into film work, composing the score for Sidney Lumet's controversial *The Pawnbroker* and going on to soundtrack no fewer than 33 movies. A fruitful alliance with Frank Sinatra saw him arrange and conduct sessions for Sinatra's *It Might As Well Be Swing* LP, arrange the legendary *Sinatra At The Sands* album (recorded with the Count Basie Orchestra), and did the same for the singer's 1984 set *L.A. Is My Lady*.

Meanwhile, jazz wasn't enough to contain Jones. Alongside his own successful solo career he stepped into the pop and soul fields, working with Aretha Franklin, Paul Simon, and others. He was responsible for a major jazz coup, however, when he persuaded the ailing Miles Davis to perform a gig at the Montreux Jazz Festival, just months before the star's death in 1991.

By this time, Jones had become a staple of the modern black music mainstream, working with stars such as Rufus & Chaka Khan and – most famously – Michael Jackson, whose epoch-shaping *Off The Wall*, *Thriller*, and *Bad* albums he produced. Jones also worked on the 'We Are The World' single by U.S.A. For Africa in 1985, a sickly composition that was notable despite its musical shortcomings for the commercial boost it gave many of the black artists who contributed to it.

In the last two decades Jones has moved into film production, bringing movies such as the Steven Spielberg-directed *The Color Purple* to the screen and co-creating the renowned Will Smith TV comedy series *The Fresh Prince Of Bel Air*. In the course of his career Jones has scooped no fewer than 26 Grammy awards, and at the time of writing he is still active at the age of 73.

Blue Monday
New Order

Released March 1983
Factory-Rough Trade *FACTUS 10* (U.S.) / Factory *FAC 73* (U.K. #9)

The biggest selling 12-inch single of all time, 'Blue Monday' is a near-perfect marriage of rock and dance music. After Joy Division frontman Ian Curtis committed suicide in 1980, few expected much from the group's three remaining members. Undeterred, guitarist (and now vocalist) Bernard Sumner, bassist Peter Hook, and drummer Stephen Morris regrouped the following year as New Order, recruiting keyboardist Gillian Gilbert and recording their debut album. *Movement* sounded too much like Joy Division Lite in places, but on the ensuing singles 'Everything's Gone Green' and 'Temptation' New Order started to experiment with electronic rhythms that bore the hallmarks of Kraftwerk and Afrika Bambaataa.

In late 1982 New Order started to work with Arthur Baker, the producer of Bambaataa's landmark single 'Planet Rock.' Baker helped crystallize the group's ambition, moving them towards a sound that fused 'real' and sequenced instrumentation. 'Blue Monday' was packaged in a stark, eye-catching jacket that resembled an oversized computer disk. It proved immediately that Sumner, Hook, and Morris could move out of the shadow of their former group.

Running to seven-and-a-half minutes and released only as a 12-inch, the single opens with a series of pulsating electronic rhythms, which are soon joined by sequenced bass and a synthesizer part evocative of Kraftwerk's 'Trans Europe Express.' Sumner's detached vocal arrives two minutes in, leading the song to its doomy epicenter with a lyric inspired by the recent Anglo-Argentinian Falklands War. The only live playing is Hook's melodic bassline, played high up the neck of the bass in what is now thought of as his trademark style. (Hook arrived at the style during the early days of Joy Division because he couldn't hear himself playing the lower notes, so weak was his amplifier.)

'Blue Monday' shot straight into the U.K. Top 10 on its release and became a huge club hit on both sides of the Atlantic. Part of its sales success was down to the fact that the group's concurrent album, *Power, Corruption And Lies*, contained an inferior demo version, making the 12-inch single an essential purchase. It was not a hit in the U.S. until the release five years later of 'Blue Monday 1988,' one of several subsequent remixes and reissues.

Sweet Dreams (Are Made Of This)
Eurythmics

Released January 1983
RCA *13533* (U.S. #1) / RCA *DA 2* (U.K. #2)

Vocalist Annie Lennox and multi-instrumentalist Dave Stewart, as Eurythmics, brought an emotional resonance to the often soulless sound of 1980s synth-pop. 'Sweet Dreams' was the duo's breakthrough hit and remains their most famous single. Lennox and Stewart formed the group in 1980; previously they were lovers as well as members of the modestly successful late-1970s pop act The Tourists. The duo's first album as Eurythmics featured contributions from Can's Holger Czukay and Jackie Liebezeit, and Blondie drummer Clem Burke, but was a critical and commercial failure. Stung by the reaction to their debut, the pair retreated to their London home studio and began experimenting with various analog synthesizers (even then seen as retro), alongside co-producer Andy Williams.

Stewart hit upon 'Sweet Dreams' almost by accident: the main riff came from the notes chimed out by a music box, replayed in reverse order on a rasping bass synth. Coupled with piston-like electronic drums, the instrumental track is strikingly minimalist and evocative of Kraftwerk's mid-1970s explorations, as such offering an effective contrast to Lennox's soulful vocal. It was her richly emotive voice that won over listeners from beyond the typical synth-pop market and made 'Sweet Dreams' a worldwide hit. Although the duo have had many more hits in the ensuing years, none has been as popular – or perhaps as good – as this song. 'Sweet Dreams' has since been recorded by a number of other artists, notably the shock-rocker Marilyn Manson (on his 1996 *Smells Like Children* EP).

Let's Dance
David Bowie

Released March 1983
EMI America *8158* (U.S. #1) / EMI America *EA 152* (U.K. #1)

A switch of record labels from RCA to EMI America saw Bowie revitalizing his career and delivering his most commercial piece since the early 1970s. Simplicity itself, 'Let's Dance' presented the bare bones of rock'n'roll and was remarkably positive and uplifting in comparison with much of Bowie's earlier material. It has the most straightforward lyric in his catalog, and while he certainly could do much better, one has to admire the calculated in-your-face commerciality of this track, one that was obviously going to Number 1. And it was precisely the right move for the times. Dumping all his previous personas, here the former chameleon of rock became David Bowie, slick, modern Rock Star.

His interest in soul and disco music goes back to his 'thin white duke' mid-1970s period, so it's no surprise that when he decided to make a cutting-edge dance album in 1983 he chose one of the genre's masters, ex-Chic guru Nile Rodgers, to oversee production. Glossy hi-tech studio work by Rodgers coupled with a cameo guitar appearance by Stevie Ray Vaughan and radio-friendly mixing by Bob Clearmountain resulted in a chart-topping single on both sides of the Atlantic – Bowie's second Number 1 in America and third in Britain (fourth if you count 'Under Pressure,' his 1981 collaboration with Queen).

'Let's Dance' is a much-used title in the annals of pop, with four major hits bearing that name in Britain: first came Chris Montez in 1962; Bowie's hit was in 1983; that was succeeded by Chris Rea in 1987; and finally came boy-band Five, whose version reached Number 1 in August 2001. They are all different songs.

Relax
Frankie Goes To Hollywood

Released October 1983
Island *99805* (U.S. #10) / ZTT *ZTAS 1* (U.K. #1)

For a few brief months during 1984 it looked as if Liverpool's Frankie Goes To Hollywood, fronted by Holly Johnson, could be the biggest band of the 1980s. The group had spent two years going nowhere before they were spotted by Trevor Horn, the British production guru behind hits by Yes, Spandau Ballet, and ABC. "What I liked about the song was its structure," explained Horn. "It was like a radio jingle or a chant, except that Holly sang it like a wild animal."

Horn re-recorded the group's demo with The Blockheads (Ian Dury's backing band), transforming their promising, erotically-charged rave into a monstrously huge production that integrated their classically Liverpudlian four-on-the-floor beat into a soundscape where Giorgio Moroder met Phil Spector, complete with orgasmic sound effects.

With a new Holly Johnson vocal in place, the single was released and, to everyone's dismay, went nowhere. 'Relax' was rescued from oblivion on January 11, 1984, when BBC Radio One DJ Mike Read, having just realized that the lyric offered step-by-step advice on how to delay an orgasm, pulled it off his turntable and declared it obscene.

The resulting ban rocketed the song to Number 1, and the Frankies brilliantly milked the controversy to chalk up two more British chart-toppers, 'Two Tribes' and 'The Power Of Love,' becoming only the second band ever to score three consecutive Number 1s with their first three releases. (The first to achieve that was Gerry & The Pacemakers.) However, 'Relax' did not chart in America until a year later, reaching only Number 10, and both follow-ups floundered dismally there. Then, as suddenly as they'd arrived, the Frankies disappeared.

This Charming Man
The Smiths

Released October 1983
Not issued U.S. / Rough Trade *RT 136* (U.K. #25)

Following their debut single, 'Hand in Glove,' The Smiths released 'This Charming Man,' the second 45 from one of Manchester, England's most famous international exports. The influential rock quartet consisted of singer Morrissey, guitarist Johnny Marr, bassist Mike Joyce, and drummer Andy Rourke, and the single is a classic example of the special chemistry between the band's songwriters, Morrissey and Marr, and their innovative techniques. Morrissey's masterful, maundlin voice, prone to great emotion and hyperbole, had no peers, while Marr's guitar work showed a generation of self-taught bedroom musicians how to push the boundaries of their instrument.

Morrissey's lyrics to 'This Charming Man,' full of sexual ambiguity, obscure literary and filmic references, and with a clever semantic flow, would probably have made his hero Oscar Wilde proud. Diametrically opposed on the surface to the flamboyance of, say, Culture Club, Morrissey's words were in fact not too far from those of Boy George in that they encouraged fans to speculate – even though the singer has never quite publicly declared a sexual orientation.

The song's opening question – "Punctured bicycle / On a hillside, desolate / Will nature make a man of me yet?" – perfectly reflects the song's duality, its multivalent outlook on life. Benign and innocent, or titillating and devious; the audience is left questioning Morrissey's intentions, and the witty frontman would surely want it no other way. The single's sleeve did precisely nothing to distract potential fans from this overall confusion: it's a still of dreamy actor Jean Marais lying in reflection, taken from Jean Cocteau's 1950 fantasy romance epic *Orphée*.

Wake Me Up Before You Go Go
Wham!

Released May 1984
Columbia *04552* (U.S. #1) / Epic *A 4440* (U.K. #1)

Careless Whisper
George Michael

Released July 1984
Columbia *04691* (U.S. #1) / Epic *A 4603* (U.K. #1)

Teen duo Wham! got off to a shaky start. Their debut single, 'Wham Rap!,' flunked on first release and only became a U.K. hit after the success of their second single, 'Young Guns (Go For It).' In America, none of their first four singles even tickled the Top 40. Hardened industry cynics were writing them off as lightweights. Macho mainstream rock acts such as Prince and Bruce Springsteen dominated the era and Wham!'s carefully contrived image – James Dean but squeaky clean – looked laughable by comparison.

'Wake Me Up Before You Go Go' turned everything around. With a title based on a sign hung on Wham! member Andrew Ridgeley's bedroom door, it was a vibrantly energetic 1960s-Motown pastiche, which the dynamic duo made larger than life by prancing around in shorts and summer shirts on Britain's influential TV show *Top Of The Pops*. Instead of backing off from their lightweight image, they'd turned it up to 11 and confounded the critics. Suddenly it was cool to be young again. The song took them to Number 1 on both sides of the Atlantic, starting a run of hits that lasted until the duo split up – but cracks in the partnership were evident within weeks.

'Careless Whisper,' a tear-jerking ballad from the very first demo that had secured their deal with Innervision Records, came out in the U.K. as a solo release under George Michael's name but in America was credited to Wham! Featuring George Michael. Two years later, Ridgeley would be history and Michael a megastar.

as an instrument and turning U2 into a world-class act. Like many of the band's best songs, 'Pride' was the result of soundcheck jamming. Bono's original focus for the lyrics had been the kind of pride that comes before a fall. To be more precise, he was thinking of what he called the "Reaganesque pride that might cause nuclear war." That idea didn't work, but he found inspiration during a visit to a Chicago peace museum and an exhibit on assassinated civil-rights leader Martin Luther King Jr.

There were problems in the studio. A 'finished' version of the track wasn't working and was scrapped at the last moment, with the band starting again from scratch the next day as Pretenders leader Chrissie Hynde sang backing vocals. There was some concern over Bono's choice of subject. Guitarist Edge recalled: "Because of the situation in our country, non-violent struggle was such an inspiring concept. Even so, when Bono told me he wanted to write about King, at first I said: 'Woah, that's not what we're about.' Then he came in and sang the song and it felt right; it was great. When that happens there's no argument. It just *was*."

This was the group's biggest U.K. hit to date, reaching Number 3, and in fact remained their best British chart placing until 1988, when 'Desire' reached Number 1. They would go on to enjoy two U.S. chart-toppers from their next album, *The Joshua Tree*, and conquer the world with their performance at Live Aid.

Radio Ga Ga
Queen

Released January 1984
Capitol *5317* (U.S. #16) / EMI *QUEEN 1* (U.K. #2)

This was Queen's 22nd British Top 40 hit and their 11th in America. The group are especially notable in that all the individual members were bona fide songwriters with major hits to their credit. Among these, 'Bohemian Rhapsody' was by Freddie Mercury, guitarist Brian May wrote 'We Will Rock You,' bass guitarist John Deacon was responsible for 'Another One Bites The Dust,' while 'Radio Ga Ga' was by drummer Roger Taylor.

Originally the song was under consideration for Taylor's second solo album, and the title was inspired by some baby talk from his young son. Taylor says he wrote it after locking himself in the studio with a synthesizer and a drum machine, but after playing it to the band, Deacon came up with a bassline and Mercury, who was convinced it had hit potential, did some work on the lyrics.

The video for this anthemic piece – described in a *Melody Maker* review as "arrogant nonsense" – contained sequences from Fritz Lang's futuristic 1927 silent movie *Metropolis* intercut with staged scenes of synchronised handclapping, later impressively copied by tens of thousands of fans at stadium concerts.

The lyrics about the power that MTV had over former radio listeners seemed ironic since it was Queen's own 'Bohemian Rhapsody' clip that had helped usher in the video age. Composer Taylor explained: "It deals with how important radio used to be, historically speaking, before television, and how important it was to me as a kid. Today it seems that video, the visual side of rock'n'roll, has become more important than the music itself." Held at Number 2 in Britain by Frankie Goes To Hollwood's 'Relax,' the song nevertheless reached Number 1 in 19 countries.

Pride (In The Name Of Love)
U2

Released September 1984
Island *99704* (U.S. #33) / Island *IS 202* (U.K. #3)

This was U2's first single from their fourth studio album, *The Unforgettable Fire*, the first to be produced by Brian Eno and Daniel Lanois. The production duo functioned as surrogate band members, using the studio

You Spin Me Round (Like A Record)
Dead Or Alive

Released November 1984
Epic *04894* (U.S. #11) / Epic *A 4861* (U.K. #1)

'You Spin Me Round' was the biggest of ten U.K. hits for the British quartet fronted by the sexually ambiguous Pete Burns. They'd already hit the Top 30 with a cover of KC & The Sunshine Band's 'That's The Way I Like It' before engaging the services of up-and-coming writer-producers Mike Stock, Matt Aitken, and Pete Waterman.

It was Burns, impressed by the trio's production on hi-energy disco hits by Divine and Hazell Dean, who made the call. Waterman recalled: "There have been maybe a dozen extraordinarily important moments that have made me what I am today. That phone call was one of them."

Stock Aitken & Waterman were contracted to produce three tracks for Dead Or Alive's upcoming album, although 'You Spin Me Round' wasn't one of them. However, Waterman was so convinced it would be a huge hit that he spent most of the budget on the track – and it paid off when the record company agreed to let them produce the entire *Youthquake* album. Originally released in November 1984, 'You Spin Me' took over three months to climb to the summit: a remix gave it the extra push, and it reached Number 1 in Britain, later Number 11 in America.

The track is especially notable as the first Stock Aitken & Waterman production to hit Number 1. Probably the most successful writer-producers that Britain has ever seen, the trio would over the following years deliver dozens of hits for the likes of Bananarama, Mel & Kim, Kylie Minogue, Jason Donovan, and Rick Astley, achieving a total of 13 U.K. Number 1s between 1985 and 1990.

Twenty years after his only Number 1, Pete Burns, who has allegedly undergone extensive cosmetic surgery, is still a well-known figure in Britain and recently appeared on the U.K. cult television show *Celebrity Big Brother*.

Jump
Van Halen

Released January 1984
Warner Bros. *29384* (U.S. #1) / Warner Bros. *W 9384* (U.K. #7)

Still a quintessential rock anthem, 'Jump' finds the multi-platinum selling Van Halen – brothers Eddie and Alex Van Halen, Michael Anthony, and scene-stealer David Lee Roth – at their most vibrant. Lead singer Roth's flowing blond locks and gravity-defying acrobatics in the video were not in vain: they undoubtedly helped the band earn a 1984 MTV Video Music Award for Best Stage Performance In A Video. 'Jump' spent five weeks at Number 1 and marked the only time that Van Halen scored a chart-topper. It has been covered many times since, with veteran lounge lizard Paul Anka providing a memorable take on the song in 2005.

Drive
The Cars

Released July 1984
Elektra *69706* (U.S. #3) / Elektra *E 9706* (U.K. #4)

A group named The Cars and a song called 'Drive' – it sounds like a marketing ploy from the Ford Motor Company, although of course the group had actually been around for some years and had enjoyed their first of a dozen U.S. hits back in 1978. 'Drive' became a worldwide hit in 1984 but enjoyed a considerable revival and another trip into the U.K. Top 5 the following year after it featured in a moving video sequence of famine suffering at Live Aid. Writer Ric Ocasek then donated all subsequent royalties from the song to the Band Aid Trust.

Born In The U.S.A.
Bruce Springsteen

Released November 1984
Columbia *04680* (U.S. #9) / CBS *A 6342* (U.K. B-side; A #5)

It's surprising, considering how successful the *Born In The U.S.A.* album was, that none of the singles drawn from it – seven in the U.S. – reached Number 1 on either side of the Atlantic. The title track was inspired by a screenplay of the same name Springsteen had been sent. He originally recorded it at home on a 4-track machine in January 1982, together with the songs that would appear on his *Nebraska* album. Springsteen re-recorded it with The E-Street Band for the sessions that produced his bestselling album, nailing it live in the studio on the third take. It was released as the third single from an album that at the time of writing has sold over 15 million copies in America alone. In Britain it was the B-side of 'I'm On Fire,' a song more likely to attract U.K. airplay than this apparent celebration of American citizenship.

Springsteen has always been troubled by the continued misinterpretation of what is one of his favorite songs. Seen by many (including Ronald Reagan) as a gung-ho patriotic anthem, 'Born In The U.S.A.' was in fact about the bad treatment of homecoming Vietnam veterans, a theme to which Springsteen has often returned. With patriotism in mind, Chrysler offered $12 million to front an ad campaign; Springsteen rejected the idea. He did, however, allow 2 Live Crew to sample it for their 1990 Top 20 single 'Banned In The U.S.A.'

Girls Just Want To Have Fun
Cyndi Lauper

Released January 1984
Portrait *04120* (U.S. #2) / Portrait *A 3943* (U.K. #2)

Before the Spice Girls brought along their manufactured version of Girl Power, Cyndi Lauper had already provided it, the decade before, with 'Girls Just Want To Have Fun' – only she had musicianship and natural charisma. Her wild look in the video (orange hair, a myriad of baubles, and funky, gypsy-like clothes) made Lauper an MTV star; the network gave her the Video Music Award for Best Female Video in 1984. Her debut LP *She's So Unusual* featured three more hit songs after 'Girls' – 'Time After Time,' 'She Bop,' and 'All Through the Night' – and helped her take home the Grammy for Best New Artist.

Hello
Lionel Richie

Released March 1984
Motown *1722* (U.S. #1) / Motown *TMG 1330* (U.K. #1)

The success of this plaintive and romantic ballad provided a fourth Number 1 hit for Lionel Richie as a solo artist, apart from his considerable work with The Commodores. It was buoyed by the video, still one of Richie's strangest efforts and often viewed as somewhat camp (although that wasn't the intention). A mini-movie of sorts, it depicts a love story between Richie and a blind leading-lady who sculpts an uncanny likeness of Richie out of clay, despite her inability to see. With or without visuals, this song is demonstrative of a man at the peak of his powers.

Close (To The Edit)
Art Of Noise

Released June 1984
Island *99754* (U.S.) / ZTT *ZTPS 01* (U.K. #8)

'Close To The Edit' might not have aged particularly well, but in 1984 many considered its digital hums and orchestral stabs to be the sound of the future. It was the work of an unusual collective led by the record producer Trevor Horn, who had hit Number 1 in the U.K., as half of Buggles, five years earlier with 'Video Killed The Radio Star.' The group also included music journalist Paul Morley and arranger Anne Dudley, who later won an Academy Award for her work on the soundtrack to *The Full Monty*. 'Close To The Edit' was one of the first hit records to make use of the pioneering Fairlight CMI digital sampler. Horn and Morley left the group shortly after its release, leaving Dudley to carry on with two of Horn's former studio assistants, Gary Langan and J.J. Jeczalic.

Caribbean Queen
Billy Ocean

Released August 1984
Jive *9199* (U.S. #1) / Jive *77* (U.K. #6)

Born in Trinidad and Tobago, R&B singer-songwriter Billy Ocean (born Leslie Sebastian Charles) found pop stardom in the U.K., where he and his parents moved when he was eight. Ocean's Caribbean heritage gave his voice a sweet distinction truly his own, with a tone capable of leaping from high and light to low and sexy. After debuting in 1976 with a few minor hits, Ocean saw his propulsive 'Caribbean Queen' catapult him into an MTV star. He had tried a few different versions of the song but, alas, neither 'African Queen' nor 'European Queen' had the same ring.

I Just Called To Say I Love You
Stevie Wonder

Released August 1984
Motown *1745* (U.S. #1) / Motown *TMG 1349* (U.K. #1)

'I Just Called To Say I Love You' provides a convenient dividing line in the career of Stevie Wonder. During the 1970s he produced a string of classic albums – including *Talking Book*, *Innervisions*, and *Songs In The Key Of Life* – that demonstrate the perfect blend of technological experimentation and pop nous. In later years, though, he has seemed content to focus his work more exclusively on melody and song, and to pass on the sonic innovation baton to a younger generation of musicians. On this, the most commercially successful single of Wonder's career, the hook is so strong and memorable that it doesn't need to be backed by anything particularly revolutionary. A killer chorus and beautiful vocal delivery are more than enough.

far right > Ultravox frontman Midge Ure (second left), who co-wrote 'Do They Know It's Christmas?,' at work on the charity single with musicians including Genesis's Mike Rutherford (left) and Phil Collins (second right).

Smooth Operator
Sade

Released September 1984
Portrait *04807* (U.S. #5) / Epic *A 4655* (U.K. #19)

Jazz purists may spit at the immaculately pedicured feet of crooner Sade Adu, but the rest of the world doesn't care: her best songs, such as the huge hit 'Smooth Operator,' go down a treat with the after-dinner coffee and mints, and always will. The Sade brand was built on her voice, her looks, and her production, all things of great beauty and the perfect package for the suave yuppie 1980s. But beneath the superslick exterior there was real talent, as evidenced by the long and fruitful career the singer nurtured on the back of hits such as this. It's a safe bet that the likes of Katie Melua and Norah Jones wouldn't be around today if it hadn't been for Sade.

Do They Know It's Christmas?
Band Aid

Released December 1984
Columbia *04749* (U.S. #13) / Mercury *FEED 1* (U.K. #1)

We Are The World
U.S.A. For Africa

Released March 1985
Columbia *04839* (U.S. #1) / CBS *USAID 1* (U.K. #1)

Like millions of other British television viewers, Bob Geldof was shocked when he saw a BBC documentary film about famine in Ethiopia in fall 1984. At first he set himself a target of raising £70,000 (about $90,000) but then decided to record a charity Christmas record. According to Geldof, he knocked off the lyric in the back seat of a taxi between meetings. Co-writer Midge Ure produced the entire backing track in his home studio, with the exception of Phil Collins's drums, which were added at the last minute, following the recording of the individual and massed vocals.

Geldof's methods of persuasion ensured one of the largest gatherings of stars ever seen in a recording studio, on November 25, 1984, including Sting, Bono, George Michael, Boy George, and David Bowie. Free studio time, manufacturing, and distribution were also arranged. The only body that failed to succumb to Geldof's tenacity was the British government, who refused to forgo their income from the V.A.T. (value-added tax) on sales of the record. Released on December 7, the disc immediately shot to Number 1 in Britain and sold over 3 million copies, while in America it reached Number 13 and sold a further million.

Following in the wake of Band Aid, Harry Belafonte began laying plans for a similar fund-raising project in America, named U.S.A. For Africa. Lionel Richie and Michael Jackson wrote 'We Are The World' in two-and-a-half hours, and it was recorded in Los Angeles on January 28, 1985, following the American Music Awards, which ensured that most of the top artists would be in town. Jones had sent a copy of the tape to all the participating musicians advising them in an accompanying letter to "check their egos at the door."

Contributors included Bob Dylan, Willie Nelson, Paul Simon, Ray Charles, Bruce Springsteen, and Diana Ross, in addition to Richie, Jackson, Stevie Wonder, and instigator Belafonte. Even Bob Geldof made the trip to appear on this American Band Aid offspring. Released on March 7, the single soon sold 7.5 million copies in America alone. In a remarkable demonstration of worldwide solidarity, on Easter Friday, April 5, 1985, at 15:50 GMT, 'We Are The World' was simultaneously broadcast by 5,000 radio stations around the globe.

Having got the ball rolling, Geldof then decided to go further by organizing a live-by-satellite worldwide concert. Staged on Saturday July 13, 1985, Live Aid, also known as The Global Juke Box, took place at London's Wembley Stadium and Philadelphia's JFK Stadium. Within a year, income from the various related projects had accumulated over $70 million in famine relief. Geldof was later rewarded for his efforts by a knighthood from the Queen, although he probably would have been more satisfied with a V.A.T. refund from the British government.

How Soon Is Now?
The Smiths

Released January 1985
Sire *S7155* (U.S.) / Rough Trade *RT 176* (U.K. #24)

'How Soon' was originally a B-Side to the 1984 single 'William It Was Really Nothing' but eventually became an A-side itself, as well as the most enduring song from the Manchester quartet (Morrissey, Johnny Marr, Andy Rourke, and Mike Joyce). It is a hallmark of the brief yet significant songwriting partnership of Morrissey and Marr, loved by guitar enthusiasts for Marr's adventurous, vibrato-laden technique (here including intricate multiple layers) and prized by lonely hearts across the globe for Morrissey's tender delivery. As with previous singles, the cover art depicted a young film actor – here Sean Barrett in 1958's *Dunkirk* – and Morrissey's ever-ambiguous lyrics continued to fuel speculation about the singer's sexuality.

'How Soon Is Now?' has enjoyed a strange afterlife among covers and songs that sample from it. In 1990, Marr's iconic opening chords were looped and sampled for Soho's 'Hippychick,' a female-led dance anthem that hit the U.K. Top 10 – higher than The Smiths ever got with the original. It was a strange choice given the isolationist nature of Morrissey's song, and a lot of Smiths fans despised it, but the considerably more upbeat 'Hippychick' solidified the versatility of Marr's singular talent.

A little over a decade later, 'How Soon Is Now?' received another unexpected revival when it was covered by Love Spit Love (an offshoot of British 1980s hit-makers The Psychedelic Furs) and used as the theme song to *Charmed*, an adventure show from TV mogul Aaron Spelling about young female witches.

Summer Of '69
Bryan Adams

Released June 1985
A&M *2739* (U.S. #5) / A&M *AM 267* (U.K.)

Born in 1959 in Kingston, Ontario, Bryan Adams signed to A&M Records in Canada in 1979 after they offered him $1 to record four songs. It was the best offer he could get at the time, and his first record for the company was the disco hit 'Let Me Take You Dancing,' which sold around 240,000 copies, mostly in the U.S. and Canada. The record was considerably speeded up to attain the required beats-per-minute for dancing purposes, and Adams ended up sounding like one of The Chipmunks. This is probably why 'Let Me Take You Dancing' is notable for its absence from Adams's many subsequent career collections. However, this initial success did enable him to splash out on his first car and, more importantly, won him a long-term contract with A&M.

It was his fourth album, *Reckless*, released in 1984, that gave Adams his big breakthrough, with a string of hits including 'Run To You' (originally submitted to Blue Öyster Cult), 'Heaven,' and 'Summer Of '69,' all composed with his first writing partner Jim Vallance. According to Adams, 'Summer Of '69' was mostly the work of Vallance and was "the hardest song on the album to write. The year is immaterial, although it was a great year – I was only ten, of course, but I remember the moon landing, the Beatles breaking up, Woodstock. ... That song took more rewrites than any of the others, and I only let it go on [the record] because I didn't know what else I could do with it."

Money For Nothing
Dire Straits

Released July 1985
Warner Bros. *28950* (U.S. #1) / Vertigo *DSTR 10* (U.K. #4)

Many of Mark Knopfler's songwriting ideas come from real life experiences, the passing comments of friends, remarks on television, from movies, or a phrase read in a book. 'Money For Nothing,' described in a *Rolling Stone* review as "Led-Zep for yuppies," was just such a song. "I was in New York," Knopfler recalled, "it was one of those big appliance shops – at the back there were big walls of TVs all tuned to MTV. There was this Joe 'six-pack' figure there with his big checked shirt on and he was holding forth to an audience of one or two about the performances on MTV. The kind of stuff he was saying was so classic. I managed to eavesdrop for a couple of minutes, then I went and got a piece of paper and started writing down the lines." The situation aroused Knopfler's writing talents, and he instinctively felt that this was the basis for a song. Much of the lyrical content of the resulting song consisted of direct quotes from the guy in the shop.

Later, while recording was taking place at Air studios on the island of Montserrat, Knopfler happened to bump into Sting, who was spending some leisure time with his family while also working on demos for his debut solo album *The Dream Of The Blue Turtles*. Inviting him to the session, Knopfler suggested adding the hook "I want my MTV," the music station's contemporary advertising slogan, to the melody of Sting's own Police hit 'Don't Stand So Close To Me.' Thus, Sting got a share of the writing credit and royalties, and an international hit was born.

CD SINGLES: THE CHANGE FROM BLACK TO SILVER

After CD albums hit the Japanese and European markets in late 1982 and U.S. stores early the following year, it was only a matter of time before singles started to appear on the same format.

The Compact Disc was first conceived in the late 1960s, but it took over a decade of development and squabbling between electronics and recording companies – in particular Sony and Philips – before the technology became available to the public. Finally, in 1979, a series of standard specifications were set for the new format: the 120mm (four-and-three-quarter inch) diameter discs, made from polycarbonate, would hold a maximum of 74 minutes of 16-bit audio with a sampling rate of 44.1 kHz.

CD album sales were initially slow, and particularly in the U.S. didn't really pick up until 1986, but some labels had already begun to experiment with the format for singles. The first widely available CD single was 'Brothers In Arms' by Dire Straits, the title track from the group's 25-million-selling album of 1985. It was vastly outperformed, however, by the U.S. Number 1 hit 'Money For Nothing,' and in any case the CD version – issued to coincide with a European stadium tour – accounted for only a small percentage of sales. Like its big brother the CD album, the CD single took some time to establish itself as a viable alternative to vinyl and cassette, but by the early 1990s had become the most prevalent format in the singles market.

For a brief period, record companies experimented with issuing CD singles as smaller, three-inch discs, sometimes known as the CD3. The format never really took off, in part because the discs were somewhat awkward to use. They often had to be fitted into a plastic adapter – which increased their diameter to the regular CD diameter – before they would cooperate with some CD players. Storage was also a problem. No unified packaging format was agreed, and even if one had been devised, the discs would still not sit neatly among a collection of regular CDs. The CD3 was popular in Japan, but even there it was soon seen as something of a novelty item. While CD3s are still occasionally produced – such as U2's 2005 hit 'Sometimes You Can't Make It On Your Own' – they tend to be limited-edition oddities, almost always sold as well as, rather than instead of, a conventional CD single edition.

The CD arrived with the promise of crystal clear sound that would last forever but, as it turned out, both of these bold claims were wildly exaggerated. It did, however, offer room for much more music than the traditional seven-inch vinyl. Thus the process that had begun with the introduction of the 12-inch 'maxi' single continued, and the number – and length – of songs included on the average single increased. Where singles were once no more than an A- and a B-side, it soon became common for them to feature three, four, or more songs, bringing them up to the length of what was once referred to as an EP. In some instances during the 1990s, singles contained more music than most albums of the 1950s and '60s.

During the 1990s, the singles market expanded further, particularly in the U.K., when record labels hatched the idea of issuing two CD versions of a single – "CD1" and "CD2" – containing the same A-side but different B-sides. While it was often intimated that this was a helpful and considerate way of offering the die-hard fan even more songs by his or her favorite band, it was little more than a marketing ploy. Not only did two different editions of a single increase the label's potential earnings from the release in question, it also facilitated a higher chart placing, since many listeners would feel compelled to buy both.

left > Dire Straits performing 'Money For Nothing' with Sting (center) during the Live Aid concert at Wembley Stadium, London, England, on July 13, 1985.

Everybody Wants To Rule The World
Tears For Fears

Released March 1985
Mercury *880659* (U.S. #1) / Mercury *IDEA 9* (U.K. #2)

'Everybody Wants To Rule The World,' a superbly produced pop single with a highly effective guitar motif, was the seventh hit in Britain for the west country synth-pop duo who took their name (and a good deal of lyrical inspiration) from a book on primal-scream therapy by Arthur Janov. Their first U.S hit, it went straight to Number 1, as did the follow-up, 'Shout,' more mainstream pop than their gloomy earlier material and therefore somewhat more America-friendly.

In 1985 U.K. acts would hold the Number 1 spot on the *Billboard* singles chart for an impressive 25 weeks, and for 24 on the albums chart, all part of a mid-1980s British invasion of the U.S. charts. Conversely, in 1986 there were only eight weeks of singles chart-topping glory, and two on the albums charts.

Tears For Fears had spent many months perfecting the grandiose 'Shout,' an anthemic piece with endless overdubs, but 'Rule The World' was apparently a last-minute addition to the *Songs From The Big Chair* album, a half-completed song they didn't rate highly and that they finished in just three days. The *Songs* album topped the *Billboard* album charts for five weeks, shifting eight million copies, enough to keep the band in keyboard polish for the five years it took them to make the follow-up. A slightly modified version of the song hit the U.K. Top 5 the following year as 'Everybody Wants To Run The World' in support of Band Aid offshoot Sport Aid, during which 20 million people ran for Africa and raised $100 million.

part of a pattern where Madonna's label does not always zero in on her key songs, only later catching up to the public's demand. But the song is forever associated with the deliciously mischievous personality of Madonna's Susan, one of the few well-liked characters she ever played. Susan danced and hustled her way through the Big Apple with a uniquely eclectic style and flair – much in the way the singer herself did in those early days of what has turned into a lengthy and iconic career.

Angel
Madonna

Released April 1985
Sire *29008* (U.S. #5) / Sire *W 8881* (U.K. #5)

Into The Groove
Madonna

Released June 1985
Sire *20335* (U.S. B-side) / Sire *W 8934* (U.K. #1)

Written by Madonna and Steve Bray, the breezy love song 'Angel' was produced by Nile Rodgers, legendary guitarist and hit-maker for disco superstars Chic (although 'Angel' itself is not heavy with guitar work). But it was 'Into the Groove,' the B-side of the 'Angel' 12-inch, taken from the 1985 film *Desperately Seeking Susan* (starring Madonna, Rosanna Arquette, and Aidan Quinn), that remains a more frequently visited Madonna classic. It's a pumping party jam styled after her earlier dance hits such as 'Burning Up' and beloved by her core home listening audience as well as professional DJs, who initially broke the song in nightclubs. 'Into the Groove' helped solidify Madonna's commitment to the dancefloor, something she has never abandoned.

Although 'Into the Groove' was in the film – the video was created from a montage of scenes – it's surprising to note that it wasn't on the released soundtrack for *Desperately Seeking Susan*. This seems to be

The Power Of Love
Jennifer Rush

Released June 1985
Epic *05754* (U.S.) / CBS *A 5003* (U.K. #1)

The Power Of Love
Huey Lewis & The News

Released July 1985
Chrysalis *42876* (U.S. #1) / Chrysalis *HUEY 1* (U.K. #11)

Jennifer Rush (born Heidi Stern) grew up in Queens, New York City, but launched the successful phase of her professional career in Germany with a series of minor European hits. She was the daughter of an opera singer, Maurice Stern, and earned international attention for her startling vocal cords with the remarkable octaves and dizzyingly long notes she reaches on 'The Power of Love.'

The song topped charts all over the world, yet did not advance past number 57 in America. The ballad, which became the U.K.'s best-selling single of 1985 and landed a place in *The Guinness Book Of Records*, has been a popular cover. It was re-made most notably by artists as varied as Air Supply, Laura Branigan, and Celine Dion. Branigan (1987) and Dion (1993) each took the song into the Top 40 with their respective versions and more or less kept to the ballad's original template.

Huey Lewis & The News, a pop-rock band from the San Francisco Bay Area, made their own song called 'The Power of Love' the same year as Rush's. Perhaps the title was lucky, or maybe the band was just talented, but it was also a remarkably successful song. A highlight and lead of the soundtrack for the Michael J. Fox time-travel comedy *Back To The Future* (in which Lewis made a cameo appearance), the group's 'Power of Love' was nominated for an Academy Award for Best Song.

Running Up That Hill
Kate Bush

Released August 1985
EMI America *8285* (U.S. #30) / EMI *KB 1* (U.K. #3)

Kate Bush's biggest international hit was one of the finest recordings of her career. 'Running Up That Hill' broke a three-year silence: as the first single from her landmark *Hounds Of Love* album, it was also her first offering since retreating to the English countryside to build a 48-track studio at the end of her garden. Bush spent much of her time off learning to work with new recording technology, particularly the cutting-edge Fairlight CMI, the first synthesizer to offer sampling and sequencing capabilities.

Opening as if it's emerging from thick fog, 'Running Up That Hill' makes good use of Bush's new toys, with unrelenting processed rhythms and disembodied, multi-layered synthesizer parts. Just as important, however, is the keen human element: a not-quite-persuasive-enough plea to God to fix a failing romantic relationship. The song was, in fact, originally called 'A Deal With God,' until Bush's label requested she change it, noting that songs that take the Lord's name in vain tended not to succeed on the American charts.

EMI had wanted to issue the more restrained 'Cloudbursting' as the first single from *Hounds Of Love*, but a change of name was as far as Bush was willing to compromise, arguing that 'Running Up That Hill' was a much truer reflection of the album as a whole. The relative performances of the two songs on the *Billboard* Hot 100 suggested she chose well: 'Running Up That Hill' became her biggest ever U.S. hit while 'Cloudbursting' failed to chart at all.

Dancing In The Street
David Bowie & Mick Jagger

Released September 1985
EMI America *8288* (U.S. #5) / EMI America *EA 204* (U.K. #1)

Bowie and Jagger's update of the classic Martha & The Vandellas 1964 hit 'Dancing In The Street' was that rare thing, a pop reworking of a soul classic that wasn't completely overshadowed by the original. It sold in vast quantities thanks to the emotional tie-in with Live Aid (which benefited from the record's sales revenue) and an iconic video in which the twosome, still in their prime, twirled the night away. The shouted, tension-building intro added value, and the song was not overproduced, a common mid-1980s studio blunder. Here then was firm evidence that spontaneous charitable ideas don't have to result in poor quality records, although the singers might now regret their choice of shirts in the video.

West End Girls
Pet Shop Boys

Released November 1985
EMI America *8307* (U.S. #1) / Parlophone *R 6115* (U.K. #1)

Pet Shop Boys frontman Neil Tennant worked for U.K. pop-music magazine Smash Hits (and, previously, for Marvel Comics) when he met future musical partner Chris Lowe in an equipment shop. The training in superheroes and teen idols was good for the duo, as their first single, 'West End Girls' (originally recorded by New York producer Bobby Orlando), eventually connected its charisma with a worldwide audience.

The song has disparate influences: Tennant's rap-like delivery and relative grittiness was inspired by 'The Message,' the raw hip-hop song about oppressive conditions in the Bronx by Grandmaster Flash & The Furious Five, and The Waste Land, a poem by T.S. Eliot. American gangster films also contributed to the vibe, but the lyrics dealt with the seediness of London's East End and the interaction of its ruffians with ladies from the posh West End.

After good club reaction but poor chart action, the song was reworked a year later by producer Stephen Hague, who lightened the Communist references, fattened up the sounds, and gave it an overall polish. The second time proved to be the charm: Hague's version shot to the top of the charts in America and in Britain, where 'West End Girls' was the first of four Number 1 hits from the album *Please*. The song's title has since inspired the names of at least two bands and a television show, and a steady stream of remixes has helped keep this dance classic alive in the clubs. It was crowned best song of the decade 1985-94 at the Ivor Novello awards, ahead of shortlisted singles by U2, Robert Palmer, Radiohead, and Massive Attack.

Kiss
Prince & The Revolution

Released February 1986
Paisley Park *28751* (U.S. #1) / Paisley Park *W 8751* (U.K. #6)

Manic Monday
The Bangles
Released January 1986
Columbia *05757* (U.S. #2) / CBS *A 6796* (U.K. #2)

Sign 'O' The Times
Prince
Released March 1987
Paisley Park *28399* (U.S. #3) / Paisley Park *W 8399* (U.K. #10)

Others might lay claim to having sold more records, but nobody wrote and recorded as many classic singles of the 1980s as Prince. 'Kiss' was the last of his great hits with his original backing group, The Revolution, while 'Sign 'O' The Times' marked the start of a new self-reliant and socially conscious phase of his career. He also provided the launching pad for another of the most successful acts of the late 1980s, The Bangles, when he wrote 'Manic Monday' for the all-girl quartet.

By 1986, Prince had reached the top of his game, both artistically and commercially, following a string of hit singles and albums that included '1999,' 'Little Red Corvette,' *Purple Rain*, and 'Raspberry Beret.' This remarkable run of success seemed to do nothing to dull his creativity or his perfectionism: he was never completely happy with 'Kiss,' and first gave it to the group Mazarati to record. On hearing their minimalist rendition, Prince realized the true worth of the song, claimed it back, and to the Mazarati recording added his own lead vocal and a stark acoustic guitar part.

The result is one of the finest songs in Prince's oeuvre and, like the earlier landmark single 'When Doves Cry,' another of his bass-less wonders: somehow, by removing the low-end, he managed to make it even funkier. Although 'Kiss' is credited to Prince & The Revolution, his backing band are missing in action, replaced by a simple drum-machine pattern and a subtle keyboard part. 'Kiss' quickly rose to Number 1 in the U.S., where it remained for three weeks, holding another Prince composition, 'Manic Monday' by The Bangles, off the top spot.

The Bangles had formed in 1982 as a garage-rock trio consisting of vocalist Susanna Hoffs and sisters Vicki and Debbi Peterson on guitar and drums. Despite adding a bassist, Micki Steele, and smoothing out the rough edges of their sound, the group struggled to crack the pop market with their full-length debut album, *All Over The Place* (1985). That soon changed when Prince – masquerading as 'Christopher' – donated this sure-fire hit, a knowing update of the classic Mamas & The Papas hit 'Monday Monday.' (Rumors that he gave up this instant classic – rather than record it himself – because of his interest in Hoffs have never been substantiated.)

'Manic Monday' soon climbed to Number 2 in Britain and America and propelled The Bangles' sophomore album, *Different Light*, into the upper reaches of the album charts on both sides of the Atlantic. After the lesser 'If She Knew What She Wants' came the group's first U.S. Number 1, 'Walk Like An Egyptian' – an irresistible novelty hit written by Liam Sternberg, who also wrote the theme to *21 Jump Street*. Several further memorable Bangles singles followed, including a cover of Simon

& Garfunkel's 'Hazy Shade Of Winter' and the transatlantic chart-topper 'Eternal Flame,' but nothing ever quite matched 'Manic Monday.'

Meanwhile, Prince spent most of the rest of 1986 touring with a stripped-down band in support of *Parade*, the album that included 'Kiss.' At the end of the year he started work on his epic, state-of-the-nation double album, *Sign 'O' The Times*. It was the first of his LPs since 1981's *Controversy* to be recorded without The Revolution and introduced a more refined, serious Prince sound.

The album's first single and title track is as stark musically as 'Kiss' – the bass is back, but there is little more alongside it than a drum-machine pulse and occasional snatches of guitar and keyboard. Prince constructed most of the music using the revolutionary Fairlight CMI synthesizer, which had become something of a holy grail for forward-thinking musicians in the 1980s, among them Kate Bush and Peter Gabriel.

'Sledgehammer,' which he described as "an attempt to re-create some of the spirit and style of the music that most excited me as a teenager – 1960s soul," was the first public unveiling of the new policy. Collins, of course, wasn't averse to remodeling 1960s soul styles for fun and profit, but where Collins favored Motown, Gabriel's inspiration was clearly the funkier, horn-driven grit of Stax. "Obviously there was a lot of sexual metaphor there," he explained. "I was trying to write in the old blues tradition, much of which is preoccupied with mating activities."

The song would have fared well on its own merits, but Gabriel's insurance policy came in the form of an innovative video helmed by young director Stephen R. Johnson, using a revolutionary new stop-motion technique that made real people appear to have been animated. Filmed over eight days at the famed Aardman studios in Bristol, England, the video immediately went into heavy rotation on MTV, propelling 'Sledgehammer' irresistibly to Number 1 on the *Billboard* chart. The accompanying album, *So*, quickly turned platinum, and on September 17, 1987, Johnson's video swept the board at the MTV Awards, winning in half of the 20 award categories.

Where 'Kiss' was a joyous, sexually charged affair, 'Sign 'O' The Times' is a doomy tirade against the dangers of drugs and the spread of AIDS – and is perhaps Prince's finest ever lyric. Despite its uncomfortable subject matter, the single soon climbed into the British and American Top 10s. It remains one of its creator's most important statements. Prince's purple period continued through to the end of the 1980s with further notable singles such as 'If I Was Your Girlfriend,' 'Alphabet St.,' and 'Batdance.'

Addicted To Love
Robert Palmer

Released March 1986
Island *99570* (U.S. #1) / Island *IS 270* (U.K. #5)

"We wanted to form the ultimate rock band," Duran Duran's John Taylor said with massive arrogance about his liaison in The Power Station with Robert Palmer. Yes, there was a time when Palmer's trebly, unthreatening pop was regarded as rock – in a kind of ageing-Lothario, upbeat-Bryan Ferry way. Surprisingly, 'Addicted To Love' is a credible supporting argument for these rock credentials, with the stop-start riff behind "You're gonna have to face it…" a triumphant live moment. The synth-brass sounds tinny today, and the video – featuring a bevy of guitar-playing ladies – is ludicrous rather than iconic, but the song's attractive, infectious qualities are still strong.

Sledgehammer
Peter Gabriel

Released April 1986
Geffen *28718* (U.S. #1) / Virgin *PGS 1* (U.K. #4)

For over two decades, as the frontman of Genesis and as a solo performer, Peter Gabriel's brilliance attracted massive critical acclaim without riches to match. In 1986, perhaps spurred by the solo success of Phil Collins, his replacement in Genesis, Gabriel made a conscious decision to become as successful as he was admired.

Take My Breath Away
Berlin

Released July 1986
Columbia *05903* (U.S. #1) / CBS *A 7320* (U.K. #1)

Veteran producers Giorgio Moroder and Tom Whitlock crafted this smoldering tune for Berlin, a Southern California band with a Teutonic name. Many will remember it as the theme to *Top Gun*, which starred Tom Cruise and Kelly McGillis in a romance taking flight. 'Take My Breath Away' helped propel sales in excess of one million copies for the *Top Gun* soundtrack, became an international hit, and earned both the Oscar and the Golden Globe Award for Best Song. Pop singer Jessica Simpson took the song back to the top of the charts in America when she covered it in 2004.

The Final Countdown
Europe

Released October 1986
Epic *06416* (U.S. #8) / Epic *A 7127* (U.K. #1)

With 'The Final Countdown' causing endless confusion in non-music media for years after its release – was it rock? was it metal? was it pop? – you'd be forgiven for thinking that the Swedish quintet responsible might wish to escape their best-known song. Not at all: Europe – now a laughing-stock in the U.K. but huge in their home country and Germany – released a whole album of songs featuring the parping synth horns of 'The Final Countdown' and even went so far as releasing a pre-millennium remix of the tune in late 1999. It's rock, Jim, but not as we know it.

RICK RUBIN: REVERED FOR RIFF AND RHYME

Jewish New Yorker Rick Rubin (born in 1963) reshaped the hip-hop and metal scenes several times over before settling into comfortable all-round maverick status in his middle age, and is the most influential producer on the American rock scene. Hiding behind a massive beard and shades, Rubin cultivates the appearance of an impassive guru – which makes it all the more remarkable that he started out as a classic rock nerd, citing Led Zeppelin as a big early influence.

Rubin made his first inroads into the record industry when he set up the Def Jam hip-hop label in 1984 with his college friend Russell Simmons. Their first big act was Run-DMC, led by Simmons's brother Joseph, but even this band was eclipsed by the enormous success of The Beastie Boys, a white Jewish act who performed rocked-up hip-hop. The

combination of riff and rhyme was key to much 1980s rock, with Rubin crossing another boundary when he produced Slayer's colossal *Reign In Blood* album in 1986, acknowledged by many as the finest thrash-metal record ever made.

Rubin continued to work with Slayer, Danzig, and other moshers into the 1990s, but took a further step into godhood when he hooked up with The Red Hot Chili Peppers for their epoch-defining *Blood Sugar Sex Magik* LP in 1991. Landmark recordings with a revitalized Neil Diamond and with Johnny Cash, just before the legendary singer's death, as well as enormous success with the alt.metal band System Of A Down, ensured that Rubin's legacy is now set in stone. He remains one of the industry's most revered figures.

Walk This Way
Run-DMC
....

Released July 1986
Profile *5112* (U.S. #4) / London *LON 104* (U.K. #8)

The original version of 'Walk This Way' appeared on Aerosmith's 1975 album *Toys In The Attic*, reaching the American Top 10 as a single upon its re-release the following year. But the song's true potential was realized nearly a decade after its initial showing when it became the inspiration for a rap song from an upstart trio from Queens, New York City.

Run-DMC's DJ, Jam Master Jay, often created an instrumental version of 'Walk This Way' by cutting back and forth between two vinyl copies so that MCs Run and DMC could rhyme over the top. Def Jam's Rick

Rubin, business partner of Run's brother Russell Simmons, suggested that Run-DMC release a single based on Aerosmith's original cut. It turned into a winner for Aerosmith as well as Run-DMC. Aerosmith's career was revitalized in the process, creating a second wind that helped sail the band towards at least another 20 years of multi-platinum success.

The song, from Run-DMC's seminal album *Raising Hell*, is remembered fondly for its music video, which was wildly popular on MTV. Mimicking the song's obvious sound-clash between rock and hip-hop, the video finds Run-DMC jamming in their own, enclosed room until the wall comes tumbling down at the behest of Aerosmith's Steven Tyler and Joe Perry.

Even 20 years later, artists and record company executives were still trying to recapture the magic of this merged-genres idea, but few have come close to the synergy of 'Walk This Way.'

Rock Me Amadeus
Falco

Released February 1986
A&M *2821* (U.S. #1) / A&M *AM 278* (U.K. #1)

Recorded by a quirky Austrian singer-songwriter resolutely determined to make his original mark on the international pop landscape, 'Rock Me Amadeus' stands as the only song in history sung in German that topped the charts in both the U.S. and Britain. For the lighthearted and colorful video, which was an MTV staple, Falco donned a powdered wig in tribute to his favorite original classical composer. It's true that Wolfgang Amadeus Mozart was never a rock star, but this rousing ditty did its part to immortalize him in a very 1980s way.

Venus
Banarama

Released May 1986
London *886056* (U.S. #1) / London *NANA 10* (U.K. #8)

Already a regular fixture on the Top 10 in their native U.K., Banarama were transformed into international superstars by the production trio Stock Aitken & Waterman, who worked their magic on over 200 British hits between the mid 1980s and the early 1990s. 'Venus' was originally a U.S. chart-topper in 1970 for the Dutch rock band Shocking Blue, but in the hands of S/A/W became a brash, glossy pop hit. The single's key element is the suspended chord with which it opens (and to which it periodically breaks down), which provided an effortless hands-in-the-air moment for clubgoers. The bass may now sound a little tacky, and the super-busy drum pattern is somewhat distracting, but perfect pop doesn't come much more perfect than this.

Nasty
Janet Jackson

Released May 1986
A&M *2830* (U.S. #3) / A&M *AM 316* (U.K. #19)

The youngest Jackson grew up in a show-business family and had been around the cameras since she was a small child, but her 1986 album *Control*, buoyed by this shockingly rebellious hit, marked Janet's coming-out party and launched her into the world of superstardom. 'Nasty' earned the American Music Award for Favorite Soul/R&B Single in 1987. That same year, Paula Abdul grabbed the MTV Video Music Award for Best Choreography for her work on the popular 'Nasty' video. Abdul would go on to enjoy her own relatively fruitful pop career, and later hosted the smash TV show *American Idol*.

The Lady In Red
Chris de Burgh

Released July 1986
A&M *2848* (U.S. #3) / A&M *AM 331* (U.K. #1)

Take a soupy bassline by Pino Palladino, a wash of smooth synth chords, and a rimshot-based drum pattern, add the happily-married musings of a blandly contented rocker on a day off, and you have the makings of a hugely successful suppertime love classic. Universally vilified by critics who really should know better, 'Lady In Red' is a success because it links a popular activity – looking at a pretty female – with a spine-chilling vocal melody. All in all, it's hard to argue with a song that topped the charts in 25 countries and remains, to this day, one of the most instantly recognizable love songs of all time.

Don't Get Me Wrong
The Pretenders

Released October 1986
Sire *28630* (U.S. #10) / Real *YZ 85* (U.K. #10)

A breeze through some of Chrissie Hynde's most optimistic sentiments, the unforgettable 'Don't Get Me Wrong' – with its gorgeous ascending title melody – seems at first to be a long way from The Pretenders' punk roots. But then you recall that the group began their recording career with a cover of The Kinks' 'Stop Your Sobbing' – swiftly followed by the catchy pop hooks of Hynde's own 'Kid' and 'Brass In Pocket' – and you're left with the distinct impression that behind all the mid-1970s punk snarl was a songwriter whose sympathies lay more with Joe Jackson than Joe Strummer.

You Give Love A Bad Name
Bon Jovi

Released August 1986
Mercury *884953* (U.S. #1) / Vertigo *VER 26* (U.K. #14)

'You Give Love A Bad Name' is the ultimate fist-pumping rock anthem, and the first of Bon Jovi's four U.S. Number 1 hits. It also marked the start of the New Jersey quintet's collaborations with songwriter Desmond Childs, who helped bring the group's pop sensibilities to the fore, and in the process turning a reasonably successful rock act into international superstars. (He has also given the same treatment to Aerosmith, Alice Cooper, and Ricky Martin.) While it's easy now to mock the big hair and spandex outfits, it's hard to find fault with Bon Jovi's mix of hard-rock guitars and singalong choruses – a winning combination that made them one of the most successful bands of the 1980s.

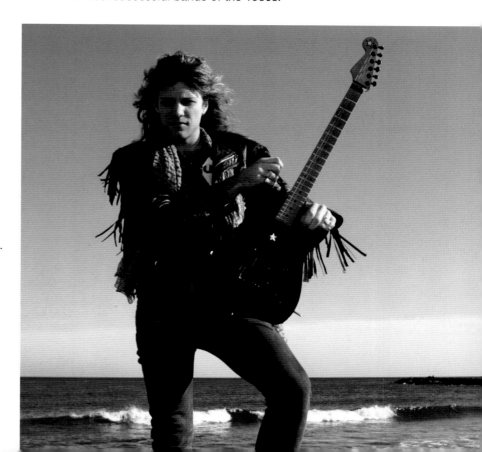

Bad
Michael Jackson

Released September 1987
Epic *07418* (U.S. #1) / Epic *651155* (U.K. #3)

When it was time for Michael Jackson's first release since *Thriller*, the pressure was on for it to be equal to or better than that blockbuster hit. 'Bad' was conceived as a collaboration with Prince, but that didn't happen, and fans embraced the new record even as they were perplexed by Jackson's continually changing appearance. His skin appeared lighter and his nose more sculpted. What had been a rather cuddly persona on the *Thriller* album had also changed: 'Bad' is Jackson in unabashedly confrontational mode.

The public already knew from epics such as 'Thriller' that Jackson simply does not do small video productions. So it wasn't a great shock when he enlisted top director Martin Scorcese (*Taxi Driver*, *Raging Bull*) to create the video for 'Bad,' a choreographed fight dance in a New York subway station that features future movie star Wesley Snipes. The clip runs to 17 minutes (more than four times longer than the average music video) and was filmed in black-and-white as well as color. The video featured in a highly anticipated network television premiere, broadcast to millions of viewers.

Weird Al Yankovic, no stranger to lampooning Jackson, then presented 'Fat,' his parody of 'Bad' that grabbed the Grammy in 1988 for Best Concept Video. Miami rapper Trina later made a tribute to Jackson with 'Da Baddest Bitch,' a song (with an album of the same name) that used 'Bad' as part of its backing track, veering into the brazenly sexual territory to which Jackson could only hint coyly in his original.

Nothing's Gonna Stop Us Now
Starship

Released February 1987
Grunt *5109* (U.S. #1) / Grunt *FB 49757* (U.K. #1)

Starship was a descendent of the legendary San Francisco rock band named first Jefferson Airplane, then Jefferson Starship, and, following a legal dispute with founding (and parting) member Paul Kantner, simply Starship. After waning popularity over the course of 20 or more years, the group had two surprise Number 1 hits in 1985 ('We Built This City' and 'Sara') and two years later followed up with 'Nothing's Gonna Stop Us Now.' It was the last chart-topper in the fruitful and influential musical career of singer Grace Slick, who harmonizes beautifully with co-lead singer Mickey Thomas on this memorable power ballad.

I Wanna Dance With Somebody (Who Loves Me)
Whitney Houston

Released May 1987
Arista *9598* (U.S. #1) / Arista *RIS 1* (U.K. #1)

The boppy 'I Wanna Dance With Somebody' was the first single from Houston's sophomore album, *Whitney*, coming at the heels of an astounding debut that has since sold in excess of 24 million units and earned the elusive Diamond certification (for sales over ten million). The vibrant song was prepared to weather such pressure and break some new ground of its own for the singer. It went to Number 1 in five countries and remains a snapshot of the singer in the happiest and seemingly most innocent presentation of her public persona.

When Smokey Sings
ABC

Released May 1987
Mercury *888604* (U.S. #5) / Neutron *NT 111* (U.K. #11)

ABC executed a mid-career change of direction with this deft homage to Smokey Robinson, refining the sub-James Bond, sub-New Romantic pop with which they had peaked so perfectly on 'The Look Of Love' and 'Poison Arrow.' Aside from vocalist Martin Fry's Motown-style harmonies and the title, there was very little that was consciously retro about the song. Slickly emitted by a band who had mastered the art of late-1980s pop, 'When Smokey Sings' was the perfect disco anthem – piano flourishes and all. It's no surprise, then, to learn that this instant-classic single was co-produced by Chic's Bernard Edwards.

Pump Up The Volume
M/A/R/R/S

Released August 1987
4th & Broadway *7452* (U.S. #13) / 4AD *AD 70* (U.K. #1)

When AR Kane and Colourbox renamed themselves M/A/R/R/S for a one-off recording project in 1987, the result was the unexpectedly successful 'Pump Up The Volume,' a piano, beatbox, and bassline composition of indeterminate structure that appeared in a multitude of remixes for various geographic regions. The song became famous on two counts: first, because it was reportedly the first U.K. chart-topper to contain samples; second, because one of those samples was an audio snippet from 'Roadblock' by Stock Aitken Waterman.

In fact, the song is less important than the impact it made on the record-buying public and the music industry. It demonstrated that sampling technology had evolved to the point where stealing other people's sounds could be a chart-topping stratagem – and that doing so could lead to a whole swathe of musicians, producers, lawyers, and accountants simultaneously frothing at the mouth about the possibility of their property being swiped. This proved significant when S.A.W. successfully sued M/A/R/R/S for infringement of copyright, forcing the band to remove the offending sample from later pressings of the single.

Within a couple of months, the sampling trend began to expand dramatically as musicians discovered the possibilities that the idea offered. Add this to the arrival of hip-hop and house music, which was almost entirely digital (or at least machine-based) in its production, and the potential represented by 'Pump Up The Volume' becomes clear. Music was becoming virtual, and songs such as this one told us all about that new fact.

Push It
Salt-n-Pepa

Released December 1987
Next Plateau *315* (U.S. #19) / ffrr *FFR 2* (U.K. #2)

The misleadingly named Salt-n-Pepa – there were actually three of them – was the first female hip-hop act of note. Cheryl 'Salt' James and Sandy 'Pepa' Denton worked together in a Sears department store in Queens, New York City, before scoring an underground hit with their 1985 debut single 'The Show Stopper' (a response to Doug E. Fresh and Slick Rick's 'The Show'). By the time they cut their first full-length album, *Hot, Cool & Vicious*, the group also included DJ Pamela Green, while the bulk of the trio's songs were written by James's boyfriend, Hurby 'Luv Bug' Azor, a fledgling record producer.

Hot, Cool & Vicious spawned three minor chart hits: 'My Mike Sounds Nice,' 'Chick On The Side,' and a cover of Otis & Carla's 1960s-soul classic 'Tramp.' 'Push It' originally existed as the B-side of 'Tramp,' but the version that became Salt-n-Pepa's mainstream breakthrough was in fact a remix by the San Francisco-based radio DJ Cameron Paul.

Driven more by its instrumental hook than by Salt-n-Pepa's raps, 'Push It' at first sounded suspiciously like a novelty hit, but was the first of eight of the duo's singles to reach the *Billboard* Top 40. Half a decade later, after Green had been replaced by Deidre 'Spindarella' Roper, Salt-n-Pepa improved on the success of 'Push It' with 'Shoop' and 'Whatta Man' (a collaboration with another female trio, En Vogue). In doing so, they became one of only a small handful of hip-hop acts to have significant hits in both the 1980s and the '90s.

With Or Without You
U2

Released March 1987
Island *99469* (U.S. #1) / Island *IS 319* (U.K. #4)

The Joshua Tree was U2's finest moment of the 1980s, an album chock-full of big-hearted anthems that drew in fans from all districts of the rock metropolis. None came bigger or more overblown than the third track, 'With Or Without You,' the point at which for the first time producers Brian Eno and Daniel Lanois excelled themselves on behalf of the Irish quartet.

What makes this song sing with relevance is its indication – visible nowadays with the acuity of 20/20 hindsight – that the world's most earnest Christian rock band were about to undergo not one but two big changes. The fragile, surprisingly intimate two-note drone that opens the track and continues all the way to its heart-wrenching close is guitarist Edge at his understated best: remember his maxim that if you play only the root and octave of a chord, its 'sex' – major or minor – remains hidden, allowing all kinds of expansion.

Bono's lyrics are powerful and his vocals are by turns keening and emotional, allowing the song to build and build until – at last – the old lantern-jawed U2 we know from the days of *War* and *Boy* reveals itself. With this kind of disguised rocking-out hidden for so long before exposing itself, we can foresee that Bono and his chums were paying serious attention to the question of their own identity.

Of course, we know now that they took the issue a long way, morphing into a faux blues-soul act for the utterly pretentious *Rattle And Hum* before spreading their wings to achieve full potential as a self-aware act of great sophistication, post-*Achtung Baby*. 'With Or Without You' is the sound of the first steps in that process.

La Bamba
Los Lobos

Released July 1987
Slash *28336* (U.S. #1) / Slash *LASH 13* (U.K. #1)

Throwing R&B, soul, Tex-Mex, and traditional Latin music into their songs with infectious enthusiasm, Los Angeles quintet Los Lobos (it means The Wolves) had been gigging for a decade before their smash hit. 'La Bamba' was an old Ritchie Valens song covered for the new *La Bamba* movie.

The film could have been cheesy, but it covered serious topics, namely the short life and tragic death of Valens, who was only 17 when he died in a plane crash along with Buddy Holly and the Big Bopper. It caught the attention of cinema fans, and the associated soundtrack was a hit, led off by this song.

The flavor of the tune, in line with Valens's status as the first Mexican-American rock star, is entirely Latin, with squealing horns, Spanish-sounding guitar riff, frantic percussion, and of course the stop-start call of the title phrase that makes it so memorable. Nowadays, the song evokes the atmosphere of a Mexican restaurant in a dull city suburb, but back in 1987 it provided a distinctly exotic vibe when it landed in the charts and became deservedly popular on radio.

(You Gotta) Fight For Your Right (To Party!)
Beastie Boys

Released January 1987
Def Jam *06595* (U.S. #7) / Def Jam *650418* (U.K. #11)

With a name using an acronym that only the most die-hard fans know means "Boys Entering Anarchistic States Towards Inner Excellence," the Big Apple trio known as Beastie Boys hold the most excellent distinction of having the first Number 1 rap album in America (although at the time their white skin made them targets of criticism for participating in a largely black genre).

Producer Rick Rubin, who had released their AC/DC-sampling 'She's On It' for the *Krush Groove* movie soundtrack, had signed The Beastie Boys – resident New Yorkers Michael 'Mike D' Diamond, Adam 'MCA' Yauch, and Adam 'Ad-Rock' Horovitz – to his young record label Def Jam. The runaway success of *Licensed To Ill*, which spent five weeks in the top slot, was unquestionably buoyed by the anthemic '(You Gotta) Fight For Your Right (To Party!).'

'Fight For Your Right' is a more than convincing parody of the type of beer-soaked, panty-raiding rock jam that rules fraternity houses and dingy bars alike, all power guitar chords and messily shouted chorus. The three Beasties had prior experience with hardcore punk bands (including Ad-Rock's stint in the memorably named The Young & The Useless), so they drew upon their roots in thrashing rock for this novelty hit. An appropriately hedonistic video for the song, depicting the party that is every suburban parent's worst nightmare, made new MTV stars out of the Boys, and the band would evolve its image over the next several years through the lens of the music network.

Los Lobos saw their career plateau after 'La Bamba,' and they would never equal it commercially. However they remain a respected club-level draw, with a Spanish-speaking audience that seems certain to provide the group with a fanbase as long as they choose to continue.

I Think We're Alone Now
Tiffany

Released September 1987
MCA *53167* (U.S. #1) / MCA *1211* (U.K. #1)

Foolish Beat
Debbie Gibson

Released April 1988
Atlantic *89109* (U.S. #1) / Atlantic *A 9059* (U.K. #9)

Formulas for pop success are many and varied. Among the most consistently lucrative is the Svengali-like manipulation of the limited vocal talents of pretty teenage girls. From Marianne Faithfull to Kylie Minogue and beyond, there always seem to be older, wiser music-biz professionals lurking in the background – almost invariably men.

Producer George Tobin, a graduate of the Brill Building, heard big-voiced 12-year-old Tiffany sing while she was recording demos in his San Fernando Valley studio. Two years later, he advised her to record 'I Think We're Alone Now,' a 1960s smash for Tommy James & The Shondells. Tiffany didn't like the song but, persuaded by Tobin, she let him record the musical tracks over which she laid her vocal. The magic worked and the song, despite Tiffany's wobbly vocals, became an international success.

Sometimes, however, what you see isn't what it seems. Just as Tiffany hit Number 1, another pretty and precocious teen, Debbie Gibson, was notching up her second U.S. Top 5 hit, 'Shake Your Love.' Inevitably, the pair became locked in a media-inspired battle for the title of America's teen pop queen. In reality they were worlds apart. Gibson wrote her first song at the age of four, won a $1,000 prize in a songwriting contest at 12, and composed, recorded, and produced her own material, including 'Foolish Beat,' which became her first U.S. Number 1.

Both girls notched up sizeable strings of hits, leading Carole King, whose career straddled both the Brill Building and the singer-songwriter eras, to single them out as "artists of the MTV generation who have also accumulated years as they accumulate success."

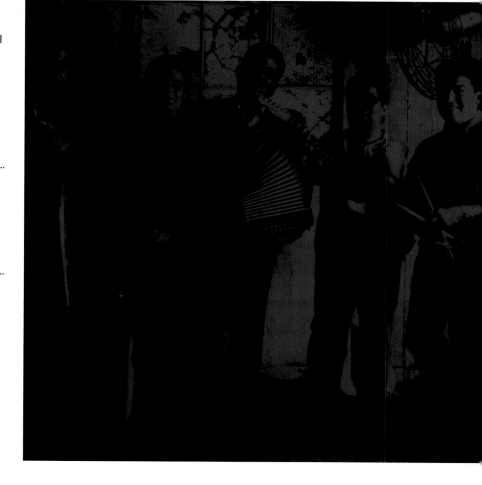

left > Teen idol Debbie Gibson strikes a pose in a New York diner at the height of her fame.
above right > Los Lobos.
opposite > Left to right: Mike D, Ad Rock, and MCA of the Beastie Boys on stage in New York in 1987.

Dude (Looks Like A Lady)
Aerosmith

Released October 1987
Geffen *28240* (U.S. #14) / Geffen *GEF 29* (U.K.)

Given the apparently homophobic tendencies that Middle America has been known to exhibit, a song called 'Dude (Looks Like A Lady)' might be a startling title for a hit. But it's helmed by the veteran rockers Aerosmith, who with this song proved that folks listen to lyrics just a little bit less than they do a massively rockin' guitar riff. The song, from the group's *Permanent Vacation* album, also resurfaced on the soundtrack for the 1993 movie *Wayne's World 2*. Aerosmith appeared in this sequel to the blockbuster comedy starring Mike Myers and Dana Carvey, a spin-off from the popular *Saturday Night Live* sketch.

Heaven Is A Place On Earth
Belinda Carlisle

Released October 1987
MCA *53181* (U.S. #1) / Virgin *VS 1036* (U.K. #1)

After multi-platinum success fronting the fierce female rock group The Go-Gos, the charismatic Belinda Carlisle ventured out and continued on her own. She surprised and delighted an international audience with this first single, a singalong tune decidedly more pop-orientated than the group's heavy beats and strumming guitars. While the meteoric rise of 'Heaven' promised a skyscraping career for Carlisle, it would later prove to be the zenith of her solo years. It is possible to look at this positively: otherwise, Carlisle may never have reunited later with The Go-Gos.

Don't Dream It's Over
Crowded House

Released February 1987
Capitol *5614* (U.S. #2) / Capitol *CL 438* (U.K. #27)

Crowded House, born after the 1984 dissolution of Split Enz, a cult favorite Australian rock act that featured New Zealand-born brothers Neil and Tim Finn, became one of the most successful international bands that either of those countries have produced. Guitarist Neil Finn enlisted Split Enz drummer Paul Hester, bassist Nick Seymour, and guitarist Craig Hooper to form a new band called The Mullanes. They secured a record deal, moved way out to Los Angeles (without Hooper), and soon changed their name to Crowded House, reflecting the cozy new conditions they encountered in California.

'Don't Dream It's Over' keenly captures the tough exterior and tender interior of a great rock ballad, with a wonderfully rousing chorus and substantive lyrics. With a lack of gimmickry and no dramatic stories of rock-star type hedonism with which to promote the band, Crowded House took this simply sweet song to the upper reaches of the American pop charts in a surprise maneuver.

In 1987, 'Don't Dream It's Over' won the MTV Video Music Award for Video of the Year; Crowded House also took home a moon-man statuette for Best New Artist. The band followed up with another hit in 'Something So Strong' and would record for a further ten years (later, significantly, with brother Tim Finn). But nothing reached the same heights of 'Don't Dream It's Over,' the song that holds firm in its place as an all-time Crowded House favorite.

The One I Love
R.E.M.

Released September 1987
IRS *53171* (U.S. #9) / IRS *IRM 46* (U.K.)

Despite its apparently good natured title, R.E.M.'s breakthrough single is a moody dismissal of an ex-lover. Previously, the Athens, Georgia, quartet had barely scraped into the *Billboard* Hot 100, their highest chart success being 'Radio Free Europe,' which had peaked at a lowly 78. Perhaps most listeners didn't notice the sardonic mockery in Michael Stipe's voice, or perhaps they didn't care and were swayed instead by the jangling guitars and Mike Mills's harmonic backing vocals. Whatever the reason, 'The One I Love' set R.E.M. on the way to becoming one of the biggest groups of the subsequent decade.

Fairytale Of New York
The Pogues featuring Kirsty MacColl

Released November 1987
Not issued U.S. / Pogue Mahone *NY 7* (U.K. #2)

'Fairytale Of New York' is one of the most unusual, not to mention one of the best, festive hits in the history of the British singles chart. It arrived in the middle of an unexpected period of commercial success for The Pogues, an unruly bunch of Irishmen who mixed punk and traditional Celtic folk to great effect.

Much of The Pogues' finest work features a female counterpoint to gin-soaked frontman Shane McGowan, and this single is no exception. In the group's first few years, McGowan's foil was bassist and backing vocalist Cate O'Riordan, but she departed in 1986 after marrying Elvis Costello (they met when he produced The Pogues' seminal *Rum, Sodomy, And The Lash* album). Here that role is played by Kirsty MacColl, who had previously charted twice as a solo artist in the U.K. with the endearingly idiosyncratic 'There's A Guy Works Down The Chipshop Swears He's Elvis' (1981) and 'A New England' (1985).

'Fairytale Of New York' begins as a wistful, piano-led ballad before launching into a celebratory jig, which peaks when McGowan and MacColl begin to trade playful insults. Most memorable is the couplet: "Happy Christmas your arse / I pray God it's our last." Unlike most other holiday hits, which tend towards phony, cloying sentimentality, the feelings behind this single are genuine and easy to relate to. But it was still a surprise to most – perhaps even The Pogues themselves – when it climbed to Number 2 on the U.K. chart. The only thing more surprising was the appearance of Brat Pack actor Matt Dillon in the accompanying promo video, playing a policeman who pushes McGowan – in a shopping cart! – around New York City.

left > Kirsty MacColl joins The Pogues for a performance of 'Fairytale Of New York' on the group's December 1988 tour of the U.K.

I Should Be So Lucky
Kylie Minogue

Released January 1988
Geffen 27922 (U.S. #28) / PWL 8 (U.K. #1)

Especially For You
Kylie Minogue & Jason Donovan

Released December 1988
Not issued U.S. / PWL 24 (U.K. #1)

These two records illustrate how far Kylie Minogue's star rose in the space of 12 months. When the actress from the Australian soap *Neighbours* first materialized in the studio of Matt Aitken and Mike Stock in 1987, she found that the duo had never heard of her and had not even been told of her appointment. The pair proceeded to knock together a song for her in the space of 20 minutes. Aitken wanted to give her a Bananarama reject; Stock said that she should be so lucky to receive one of their seconds. With the phrase amended, a song about a girl lamenting her mediocre love-life was born. Its breathless peppiness and Minogue's celebrity kept it at Number 1 in Britain for five weeks.

Come 1988, not only had the pair given Minogue three more U.K. Top 5s, but also they had created a chart career for her *Neighbours* co-star Jason Donovan. There were no plans to record a duet with the two until a zealous Woolworths buyer, erroneously informed that they planned a joint single, ordered 400,000 copies.

STOCK AITKEN & WATERMAN SHOULD BE SO LUCKY

There was a dichotomy about Mike Stock, Matt Aitken, and Pete Waterman. Many critics seemed to despise their music – but the millions upon millions of people who bought the records clearly loved them. The statistics speak for themselves: the trio wrote and/or produced around 70 Top 20 U.K. hits in the space of eight years.

So how do we explain these extremes of love and hate? A big factor is that the three men – billed on their records as Stock/Aitken/Waterman and often referred to in print as S/A/W – were part of a new breed of songwriter. Modern technology enabled them to spurn the use of session musicians. Playing all the instruments they could manage, and using sequencers and synthesizers for the rest, they made their singles remarkably quickly. This also engendered a certain sameness, as well as a high-pitched, glaring sonic quality that for many summed up the emptiness and trashiness of the 1980s.

Pete Waterman was not a member of the writing team. Composers Mike Stock and Matt Aitken were musicians who once played in covers bands and were happy to give Waterman a third credit and (eventually) royalty on their songs, because his abilities to spot talent and make deals meant they could concentrate on writing. Early collaborations included novelty records and a Eurovision Song Contest entry for Cyprus. Hazell Dean's 'Whatever I Do (Wherever I Go)' – a British Number 4 in 1984 – was the first proper S/A/W hit, although they were happy to secure a Number 1 with Dead Or Alive's 'You Spin Me Round (Like A Record)' a

few months later as mere producers. The team's further success with chanteuse Princess led the well-established girl trio Bananarama to request the services of S/A/W, who gave them a new lease on chart life that included the Top 10 U.K. hits 'Love In The First Degree' and 'I Want You Back.'

Black cockney sisters Mel & Kim were newcomers, however, and S/A/W made them famous with the sassy anthems 'Showing Out' and 'Respectable,' the latter becoming in 1987 S/A/W's first self-written chart-topper. Rick Astley – a fresh faced boy with an old man's voice – was another unknown to become a star under their aegis. He was one of the rare S/A/W American successes, scoring two Number 1s Stateside. Soon afterwards, S/A/W's Midas touch made actress Kylie Minogue the biggest selling singer in Britain.

The pivotal year was 1989. S/A/W started it with a Number 1 and closed it with the Christmas Number 1 (as producers) and Number 2, in between which had come two dozen U.K. Top 10s and half a dozen U.K. Number 1s. From that high point followed a gradual disintegration, starting with Aitken's departure from the team in 1991 and culminating in a bitter legal battle between Stock and Waterman over the latter's decision to sell the S/A/W recordings. At the time of writing it was announced that the three will be working together again. It remains to be seen whether they can pick up the thread of pure chart gold from the decade that they helped to define in Britain.

Doctorin' The Tardis
The Timelords

Released May 1988
TVT *4025* (U.S.) / KLF *003* (U.K. #1)

3:A.M. Eternal
The KLF

Released September 1989
Arista *2230* (U.S. #5) / KLF *005* (U.K. #1)

The Kopyright Liberation Front, to give it its full name, was the brainchild of Bill Drummond (who had earlier founded the Zoo record label in Liverpool, England) and Jim Cauty, a former member of Brilliant. The duo's first musical work together was an album, *1987 (What The Fuck Is Going On?)*, credited to The Justified Ancients Of Mu Mu. They chopped up – and mocked – records by artists including The Beatles, Led Zeppelin, and Abba, and the album's release was later blocked after the instigation of legal action by Abba.

Drummond and Cauty's next move was to aim a novelty hit at the top of the U.K. chart. 'Doctorin' The Tardis' was put together in a similar cut-and-paste fashion, and makes liberal use of two Gary Glitter songs – 'Rock And Roll (Part Two)' and 'Leader Of The Gang' – and the main theme to the British TV series *Dr. Who*. (Both the single's title and the alias Drummond and Cauty assumed for its release – The Timelords – refer to the long-running sci-fi show.) In a press release, Drummond described 'Doctorin' The Tardis' as "probably the most nauseating record in the world," noting that he and Cauty enjoyed "celebrating the trashier side of pop." The duo swiftly followed it with the mock how-to guidebook, *The Manual (How To Have A Number One The Easy Way)*.

Drummond and Cauty's biggest hits, however, came as The KLF around the turn of the decade. '3:A.M. Eternal' was initially issued in 1989 but didn't hit the charts until 1991. While the single hasn't aged particularly well, it does represent the cream of the contemporary U.K. house scene. It was followed by an improbable duet, 'Justified And Ancient,' recorded with "The First Lady Of Country: Tammy Wynette." All the while, Drummond and Cauty were still involved in various non-musical activities, which included sponsoring a prize for the worst British artist of the year, and – most controversially – setting fire to £1 million in banknotes, all in the name of art.

Roll With It
Steve Winwood

Released May 1988
Virgin *99326* (U.S. #1) / Virgin *VS 1085* (U.K.)

Steve Winwood is mainly remembered as the leader of the psychedelic rock group Traffic, with whom he recorded a number of hit singles and albums in the late 1960s and early 1970s. During the 1980s, however, the British singer and keyboardist carved out a new niche for himself as a solo star with a polished, soulful sound. 'Roll With It' was Winwood's second U.S. Number 1 (following 1986's 'Higher Love') and the biggest hit of his career. It was also his first single release since being tempted away from Island Records, for whom he had recorded since 1967, by a big-money deal from Virgin. Winwood's solo success started to dwindle soon afterwards, prompting him first to shrink from the media glare and then, in the mid 1990s, to return his attention to Traffic.

Never Tear Us Apart
INXS

Released June 1988
Atlantic *89038* (U.S. #7) / Mercury *INXS 11* (U.K. #24)

INXS had bigger hits, but 'Never Tear Us Apart' is arguably their finest moment, the fourth U.S. Top 10 entry from the Aussie world-beaters' multi-platinum album *Kick*. Keyboardist Andrew Farriss wrote the music in New Zealand while the rest of the band were playing tennis, but what he envisioned as an up-tempo Gene Vincent-style retro-rocker was dramatically slowed down by singer-lyricist Michael Hutchence. As a result, it presented them at their most poignantly tender, with Hutchence in fine voice, enhanced by Kirk Pengilly's haunting sax solo. At the funeral service following Hutchence's tragic death in 1997, his coffin was carried out to the sound of 'Never Tear Us Apart.'

Kokomo
The Beach Boys

Released July 1988
Capitol *69385* (U.S. #1) / Elektra *EKR 85* (U.K. #25)

When 'Kokomo' topped the charts, it was a landmark for The Beach Boys. As a group that had peaked over 20 years earlier, the song provided a fresh introduction to a generation gripped by new wave and heavy metal. The legendary group had last reached the Number 1 spot in 1966 with the Brian Wilson masterpiece 'Good Vibrations,' and indeed 'Kokomo' shared the mellifluous harmonies that are The Beach Boys' hallmark, but now spiced with some island flavor. The song, inspired by a resort in Montego Bay, Jamaica, made a filmic cameo with Tom Cruise in *Cocktail*.

Gigantic
The Pixies

Released August 1988
Not issued U.S. / 4AD *BAD 805* (U.K.)

Although it failed to chart, 'Gigantic' is a record of no small importance. While they never achieved widespread popularity at the time, Boston band The Pixies were a defining influence on many of those who followed in the late 1980s and early 1990s and have been acknowledged since as one of the most important rock groups of their time.

'Gigantic' is something of an oddity in their catalog in that it is sung by bassist Kim Deal (who tended then to go by the name Mrs. John Murphy). Most Pixies songs are front-ended by bandleader Black Francis's impassioned yelp, but here Deal offers up a smoother, softer vocal that wraps neatly around the song's four-chord riff. The other key element of 'Gigantic' is the change in dynamics from soft verse to loud chorus: less striking, perhaps, than in other Pixies songs of a similar vintage – 'Caribou,' for instance – but it was nonetheless this simple structure that provided the impetus for so many singles that followed, chief among them Nirvana's smash hit 'Smells Like Teen Spirit.'

The closest The Pixies came to a hit was when 'Planet Of Sound' scraped in at Number 27 on the U.K. chart in 1991. By that stage grunge, as it became known, was on its way to dominating the airwaves on both sides of the Atlantic, but the group that led the way was on the verge of splitting. The Pixies didn't achieve a level of commercial success to match the critical plaudits bestowed upon them until 2004, when they reformed for a world tour.

Kiss
Art Of Noise Featuring Tom Jones

Released October 1988
China *871038* (U.S. #31) / China *11* (U.K. #5)

In 1988 Tom Jones's commercial stock was low. The sometime Welsh love titan was more or less confined to Las Vegas residencies and country albums. However, during the long dark fog of near-obscurity that shrouded him post-Elvis, pre-*Reload* and indie credibility, Jones popped up on this corker of a Prince cover that made him cool again, albeit for about 20 minutes in 1988. The original clipped-funk stroke of genius was revamped and given new life courtesy of the Art Of Noise's studio technology, while Big Tom himself added some vaudeville macho-isms to the brew that made for a deserved international hit.

Sweet Child O' Mine
Guns N' Roses

Released June 1988
Geffen *27963* (U.S. #1) / Geffen *GEF 43* (U.K. #24)

Guns N' Roses were edgier and dirtier than all the tarted-up heavy metal groups that had preceded the band in Los Angeles, and they go down in history as one of the most distinctive rock bands ever to have walked the earth. GNR ferociously upped the ante for Sunset Strip debauchery with a decidedly more macho take on rock stardom than the spandex'd competition could muster. After making few waves with early singles 'It's So Easy' and 'Welcome To The Jungle' (which was later a massive hit), the mellow, almost gentle 'Sweet Child O' Mine' was the first Guns N' Roses Number 1 single and one of the best loved songs from the debut album, *Appetite For Destruction* – which, with more than 25 million copies sold (and the elusive Diamond certification in America), is one of the biggest sellers of all time.

The *Appetite* album was released in the summer of 1987 but 'Sweet Child O' Mine' wasn't a hit until 1988, demonstrating just a small piece of the longevity this album enjoyed in the popular landscape. The public loved the savage guitar grooves of Slash, the alluring, snarly warbles of wild frontman Axl Rose, and the social and pharmacological exploits of all of the band members (which, at this time, also included Duff McKagan, Izzy Stradlin, and Stephen Adler). An MTV favorite, the song earned the network's Video Music Award for Best Heavy Metal/Hard Rock Video as well as the American Music Award for Best Single Heavy Metal/Hard Rock.

Fast Car
Tracy Chapman

Released May 1988
Elektra *69412* (U.S. #6) / Elektra *EKR 73* (U.K. #5)

Tracy Chapman was born in Cleveland, Ohio, and went to university in Massachusetts, honing her performing and songwriting skills on the Boston folk circuit. She had begun writing poems and songs at the age of eight, and wrote the material on her debut album over a period of nine years. It was released in 1988 and earned excellent reviews, but the singer-songwriter was probably unprepared for the instant success she achieved with the record.

Chapman recalled that when she appeared at Nelson Mandela's 70th Birthday Concert at London's Wembley Stadium in 1988 "they didn't have a slot for me and I was kept waiting. It was just me and my acoustic guitar and I think they called me three times, hoping to put me on while the next act was getting ready." Sent back to her dressing room again, she was called out when Stevie Wonder was unable to appear after losing some computer software. It was all so sudden she had no time to feel the pressure of performing alone in front of the vast Wembley crowd and an enormous global television audience. Chapman delivered a show-stopping performance that sent her album soaring to the top of both the British and American charts.

'Fast Car' is about a couple trying to escape poverty for a better life, and would have sat well on any Bruce Springsteen album. It became the first of three hits from the album and won a Grammy award for Best Pop Vocal Performance. Chapman also won the Grammy for Best New Artist. Another of the album's highlights, 'Baby Can I Hold You,' written when she was just 18, became a huge international hit for Boyzone in early 1998.

Wild Thing
Tone Loc

Released December 1988
Delicious Vinyl *102* (U.S. #2) / Fourth & Broadway *BRW 121* (U.K. #21)

One of the most distinctive hip-hop hits of the late 1980s, 'Wild Thing' brought the deep-throated Tone Loc from underground obscurity to mainstream pop stardom in one giant leap. The record was written by Marvin Young, a.k.a. Young M.C., who went on to become a highly regarded producer and rapper in his own right, notably with his Grammy-winning single 'Bust A Move.'

'Wild Thing' was issued at the end of 1988 but didn't make it into the upper reaches of the *Billboard* chart until several months into the following year. It makes blatant – and unauthorized – use of a drum fill from Van Halen's 'Jamie's Cryin',' but the heavy-rock band didn't pursue the matter. Another hip-hop group of the time wasn't so lucky, however: the ever-controversial 2 Live Krew found themselves in a big bowl of legal hot water after taking guitar licks from Van Halen's 'Ain't Talkin' 'Bout Love' in 1989.

Tone Loc followed 'Wild Thing' with another *Billboard* Top 5 hit, 'Funky Cold Medina,' in the spring of 1989, but that was his last single of any real significance. In the 1990s he turned his attention to acting, appearing in a number of blockbuster hits, including *Heat* and *Ace Ventura: Pet Detective*.

Buffalo Stance
Neneh Cherry

Released November 1988
Virgin *99231* (U.S. #3) / Circa *YR 21* (U.K. #3)

The stepdaughter of jazz trumpeter Don Cherry, Neneh Cherry brought a tough and streetwise yet sassy and feminine vibe to 'Buffalo Stance,' an R&B song with a hip-hop swagger, back when such a thing did not exist. She performed the New York-flavored song on British TV chart show *Top Of The Pops* while pregnant, igniting a firestorm of judgment in the media. But the headstrong Cherry didn't seem to care one bit; her cut was a favorite of nightclub DJs everywhere, and even reached the top of the American dance-music chart.

Girl You Know It's True
Milli Vanilli

Released September 1988
Arista *9781* (U.S. #2) / Cooltempo *COOL 170* (U.K. #3)

High from the tremendous success of the guilty-pleasure R&B-dance hit 'Girl You Know It's True,' the duo known as Milli Vanilli won two American Music Awards, including Favorite Single Pop/Rock and Favorite New Artist. But the statuettes were returned in disgrace in a widely-broadcast press conference after it had been revealed that uncredited studio singers hired by producer Frank Farian were behind Milli Vanilli, rather than Fabrice Morvan and Rob Pilatus, the visual representation of the group. There has never been a bigger embarrassment in pop music. The scandal became comedic fodder for late-night TV and must surely have contributed to the events preceding Pilatus's suicide in 1998 at age 33.

Like A Prayer
Madonna

Released March 1989
Sire *27539* (U.S. #1) / Sire *W 7539* (U.K. #1)

After five years in the charts, Madonna Louise Vernon Ciccione saw her career at a plateau. The 'shocking' sex themes she had explored in 'Like A Virgin' and the ditzy dancefloor stuff she did so well along the lines of 'Get Into The Groove' were becoming outmoded. Her enormous fanbase would require something a little more intellectually satisfying to retain their attention, and so in due course Madonna explored her troubled Catholic background with 'Like A Prayer,' a gospel workout that would have been about a tenth as controversial without its accompanying video.

Over the excellent, bouncing rhythm – bass was supplied by sessioneer extraordinaire Guy Pratt – and the soaring, uplifting gospel-choir vocals, Madonna sings out: "Just like a prayer / I'll take you there," while walking through a candlelit church. In due course she approaches the altar and kneels to pray to the figure of Jesus, eyes closed on a crucifix. And lo! After a couple of seconds, Jesus opens his eyes and, stepping down from his rather uncomfortable position, embraces Madonna passionately – which sent middle America into a froth of self-righteous horror. The fact that Jesus was played by a black actor served only to strengthen the resulting Bible Belt protests.

All these years later it seems rather harmless, especially as Madonna has now settled into an inoffensive role as lady of the manor in ye olde England. But back in 1989 it seemed as if a good deal of America expected Madonna to be struck down by a thunderbolt from above.

People Hold On
Coldcut Featuring Lisa Stansfield

Released March 1989
Tommy Boy/Warner *922848* (U.S.) / Ahead Of Our Time *CCUT 5* (U.K. #11)

Lisa Stansfield had been a presenter on a U.K. TV show that was a weekly dance party, but her career jumped when she paired up with Coldcut's Matt Black and Jonathan More to record 'People Hold On.' This jubilant party anthem, evocative of the developing house music genre of the time, landed on the group's debut album *What's That Noise?* as its highlight. Stansfield would later chart with more hits and eventually won a Brit Award (the U.K. equivalent of a Grammy) while Coldcut launched their independent record label Ninja Tune and nurtured the careers of several hip-hop and electronica artists.

Me Myself And I
De La Soul

Released April 1989
Tommy Boy *7926* (U.S. #34) / Big Life *BLR 7* (U.K. #22)

In 1989 American hip-hop was the province of scary, sweary hood-dwellers such as Ice-T and NWA – who sold gazillions of records while threatening to beat up on you and insult your lady friend – or ridiculous party-rappers like Will Smith and M.C. Hammer, who did little other than dance inventively in large trousers. Someone clearly had to fill the gap, and while the U.K. scene soon supplied non-violent, non-trivial bands like Massive Attack and Soul II Soul, the U.S. provided the excellent De La Soul, who pioneered the 'Daisy Age' style of laidback beats and peaceful, intelligent rhymes.

Although Daisy Age was – like romo and cowbilly – an idiotic term dreamed up by some rookie journalist, it actually described the mellow, organic vibe of De La Soul's tunes rather well. Laying out their wares

with their debut single 'Me Myself And I' were the New York trio of Kelvin 'Posdnuos' Mercer, David 'Trugoy The Dove' Jolicoeur, and Vincent 'Maseo' Mason. They smothered the tasty samples and relaxed, unhurried beats with a conversational rapping style that drew its inspiration from nursery-rhyme surrealism and everyday observations rather than the bloody confrontations that illustrated the gangsta-rappers' work so vividly. They spoke too of black power and traditional relaxants such as marijuana, but without the penetrating, aggressive overtones that would populate albums by Dr Dre and Ice Cube.

Life for De La Soul was, you inferred from their music, about taking it easy rather than getting annoyed, and perhaps that is the reason why the public on both sides of the Atlantic took to them so readily.

Back To Life
Soul II Soul

Released June 1989
Virgin *99171* (U.S. #4) / 10-Virgin *TEN 265* (U.K. #1)

Londoner Jazzie B's collective of singers, musicians, and dancers made an international splash with this Caron Wheeler-fronted groove where Wheeler's tuneful vocals provide the perfect foil to the propulsive dance beats and soaring strings. Along with 'Keep On Movin',' the song is a highlight of Soul II Soul's debut album *Club Classics Vol. One*. The album title turned out to be an apt prediction for these Soul II Soul songs, particularly 'Back To Life,' which was later covered most notably by American R&B star Mary J. Blige and sampled by British electronica producer Wookie.

Soul II Soul continued to release albums and singles until 1995, but were never able to match the success of 'Back To Life.' The group's Nellee Hooper, though, has since carved out a niche as one the most acclaimed producers of recent times. His CV includes such high-profile acts as U2, Björk, Madonna, and Gwen Stefani, as well as a BAFTA Award – the British equivalent of an Oscar – for his work on the soundtrack to Baz Luhrmann's cinematic adaptation of *Romeo And Juliet*.

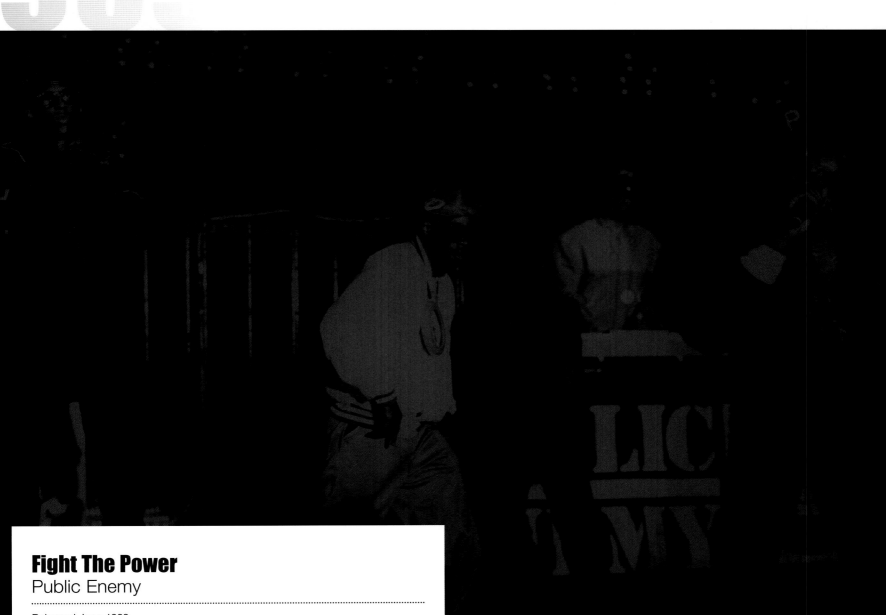

Fight The Power
Public Enemy

Released June 1989
Motown *MOT 4647* (U.S.) / Motown *ZB 42877* (U.K. #29)

The most important rap group of all time reached their apex with this era-defining single, which featured on the soundtrack to Spike Lee's similarly pivotal *Do The Right Thing*. The seeds of Public Enemy were sown in the early 1980s when rapper Chuck D and Hank Shocklee, leader of a local DJ crew, started performing regularly on a New York radio show hosted by Bill Stephney. Stephney became the group's publicist, while Shocklee formed a production team, The Bomb Squad, with his brother Keith and Eric 'Vietnam' Sadler. From the start, the membership of Public Enemy was closer to that of a political organization than a regular group. Next to join was a second rapper, Flavor Flav, DJ Terminator X, and 'Minister Of Information' Professor Griff.

The group launched in full force in 1987 with a debut album, *Yo! Bumrush The Show* on the influential Def Jam label, home to Run DMC. A year later Public Enemy unleashed *It Takes A Nation Of Millions To Hold Us Back* – regularly cited as the greatest hip-hop album ever – and its resplendent singles 'Bring The Noise' and 'Don't Believe The Hype.'

Borrowing its title from a 1975 Isley Brothers hit, 'Fight The Power' is a crystallization of the sound and ideas of *Nation Of Millions*. It was issued on the Motown label in a one-off deal, as was the *Do The Right Thing* soundtrack album. Like all of Public Enemy's singles it was only released as a DJ-friendly 12-inch, hence its failure to reach the *Billboard* pop chart. (It did, however, top the *Hot Rap* listings.)

The single is underpinned by a typically frantic Bomb Squad production, dominated by relentless drums, pulsating two-note bass, snatches of funk guitar, and intermittent wailing sirens. The state-of-the-nation lyrics are among Chuck D's finest. The first two verses are a call to his fellow black Americans to fight oppression and institutional racism; in the third, his tone becomes more incendiary as he rails against a list of what in his view were racist celebrity figures. Most striking is his put-down of Elvis Presley: "A hero to most, but he never meant shit to me." John Wayne and Bobby McFerrin are among his other targets.

Chuck D saw rap music as "the black CNN" – a voice for a section of the community generally ignored by the mainstream media. Both 'Fight The Power' and *Do The Right Thing* – which was set against a backdrop of inner-city racial conflict – demonstrated an open distaste for cozy, white America, and stirred up waves of controversy and debate. But Public Enemy's defining single was soon overshadowed by an interview that Professor Griff gave to the *Washington Times* later the same summer, in which he claimed Jews were to blame for "the majority of wickedness that goes on in the world." The ensuing storm drew attention away from one of the most powerful moments in rap history, and – even though Griff was eventually fired – cast an unfortunate shadow over the rest of Public Enemy's career. None of the group's subsequent releases – which include the Buffalo Springfield-sampling 'He Got Game' (1998) – have come close to matching the visceral thrill of 'Fight The Power.'

She Drives Me Crazy
Fine Young Cannibals

Released January 1989
IRS/MCA *53483* (U.S. #1) / London *LON 199* (U.K. #5)

The U.K. trio of singer Roland Gift and musicians David Steele and Andy Cox took their name from *All The Fine Young Cannibals*, a 1960 movie starring Robert Wagner and Natalie Wood. As part of the rhythm section of successful pop-ska act The (English) Beat, Steele and Cox brought hit-making know-how to Fine Young Cannibals, but it was the suave Gift who made the group stand out. Gift was capable of reaching into the falsetto range, and his inimitable vocal tone helped catapult the jangly guitars and boogie-inducing groove of 'She Drives Me Crazy' into the upper reaches of the pop charts.

Hangin' Tough
New Kids On The Block

Released July 1989
Columbia *68960* (U.S. #1) / CBS *BLOCK 3* (U.K. #1)

New Kids On The Block was the brainchild of Maurice Starr, the eccentric manager who first put himself on the industry map with the multi-platinum success of New Edition. Starr manufactured the white NKOTB in the same way as he had the black New Edition, even trawling the same city limits of Boston to find the right talented and adorable candidates in brothers Jordan and Jonathan Knight, Donnie Wahlberg, Joey McIntyre, and Danny Wood. After failing to hit pop gold with the self-titled debut album, a new hope emerged when MTV picked up 'You Got It (The Right Stuff),' the first single from NKOTB's second album *Hangin' Tough*. Greeted with a warm reception from its female audience, the network soon moved on to the title track. The *Hangin' Tough* album eventually sold more than 12 million copies, a staggering figure that set the standard for subsequent boy-bands to try to emulate.

Ride On Time
Black Box

Released August 1989
RCA *62003* (U.S.) / Deconstruction *PB 43055* (U.K. #1)

Italian dance producers Black Box reached into the annals of disco, beefing up earlier grooves for modern listeners in a winning formula that enjoyed exposure in nightclubs around the world and helped usher in the house music genre. While slinky, dark-skinned model Catherine Quinol provided the visual representation for the group on record jackets and videos, the vocals on Black Box's hits were made by sampling black vocalists Loleatta Holloway and Martha Wash. Snippets from Holloway's 1980 tune 'Love Sensation' formed the basis of 'Ride On Time,' a huge U.S. club hit and the U.K.'s best-selling single of 1989.

Love Shack
The B-52's

Released September 1989
Reprise *22817* (U.S. #3) / Reprise *W 9917* (U.K. #2)

Swing The Mood
Jive Bunny & The Mastermixers

Released July 1989
Music Factory/Atco *99140* (U.S. #11) / Music Factory Dance *MFD 001* (U.K. #1)

It seemed as if pop music was in safe hands early in 1990 as the gorgeously infectious 'Love Shack' from the perennially eccentric B-52's landed on the charts. Part 1950s hop anthem, part '60s surf jingle, and a looney tune of the most traditional stripe, 'Love Shack' was ostensibly the tale of "a little known place where we can get together" but in truth was an excuse for everyone to get highly silly, with more impressionable teens even adopting a beehive hairdo in the video's honor. The B-52's attempted more hits in the same vein but soon fell from grace as the joke wore off. They did retain some critical credibility thanks to the occasional kudos-enhancing move, such as singer Kate Pearson adding guest vocals to R.E.M.'s ultra-irksome but popular 'Shiny Happy People' a year later.

As we know, pop music is an evil mistress, and late in '89 came the devilish noise of Jive Bunny, a remix duo who sampled Bill Haley's 'Rock Around The Clock', added a cheap backbeat, and created a 'song.' The Bunny's 'Swing The Mood' caused grown men to weep after the third playback and reduced the work rate, the sperm count, and probably the will to live during its long, agonizing chart run. Air-headed radio DJs indulged the monster with far too much airplay, and for a while it seemed as if the future might not after all be an Orwellian boot stamping on a human face but the sound of the late, disembodied Haley stuttering "Ah one-one-one-one-one…" et cetera and repeat forever.

left > New Kids On The Block on tour in Holland in 1990. Clockwise from top right: Jordan Knight, Jonathan Knight, Joey McIntyre, Donnie Wahlberg, and Danny Wood.

It all came to a head one Friday evening in November 1989 when the British chart TV program *Top Of The Pops* staged an all-time coup by featuring Happy Mondays and The Stone Roses – two brand-new bands out of Manchester – on the same show. The Mondays, usually credited with pipping the Roses to the post and kick-starting the 'Madchester' scene, peaked a year later with 'Kinky Afro,' an insanely funky paean to not much in particular. The band's attraction centered on frontman Shaun Ryder – soon to emerge as drugs hoover for a generation – who mouthed his meaningless verse with high insouciance, while tambourine-player and all-round fifth wheel Bez did his strange funky-chicken dance.

The Stone Roses, meanwhile, were heavier and grumpier, lacking the Technicolor cartoon flash of Ryder and his chums but boasting supreme musicianship. Frontman Ian Brown kept his trancey, low-in-the-mix vocals understated (the birth of 'shoegazing'), while guitarist John Squire wah-wah'd up a storm and the expert rhythm section of Gary 'Mani' Mounfield and Alan 'Reni' Wren brought Motown to a new generation. The non-LP track 'Fool's Gold' may have been the better song, but the Mondays had the gift of the gab and, as it turned out, more staying power – despite the sea of drugs that nearly sank them on several occasions.

Like The Stone Roses without the attitude or Happy Mondays with an IQ, James rode the coat-tails of the Madchester movement with 'Sit Down,' a fantastic three-chord trick that in Britain became a student-disco staple for years. Anchored by a lolloping snare-drum pattern and an octave-laden bassline, it appeared at first glance to be no more than a request to, well, to take a seat. But frontman Tim Booth was always a clever fellow (he worked with cerebral soundtrack writer Angelo Badalamenti in later times) and had more up his sleeve, working in an almost political message, with lines such as: "Those who feel the breath of silence / Sit down next to me."

Standing somewhat to one side of all this was Primal Scream, the brainchild of sometime Jesus & Mary Chain drummer Bobby Gillespie. 'Loaded' was the perfect fusion of rock and dance beats, entering the indie-dance canon as an all-time classic tune of the era. Aided by the often surly Gillespie and his knack for a soundbite – he too enjoyed recreational substances, and saw no reason to hide the fact – the Scream founded a long and profitable career that continues to this day.

Fool's Gold
The Stone Roses

Released November 1989
Jive *1315* (U.S.) / Silvertone *ORE 13* (U.K. B-side; A #8)

Sit Down
James
Released June 1989
Not issued U.S. / Rought Trade *RT 225* (U.K.)

Loaded
Primal Scream
Released February 1990
Not issued U.S. / Creation *CRE 070* (U.K. #16)

Kinky Afro
Happy Mondays
Released July 1990
Not issued U.S. / Factory *FAC 302* (U.K. #5)

As the 1980s faded from view in Britain, permanently taking with it the post-punks and the New Romantics, a new sound was emerging from the Midlands. House music and hip-hop had begun to make their presence felt in clubland worldwide, but the 1960s pop of The Beatles and The Byrds was also experiencing a renaissance – particularly in Manchester and Liverpool. A small cadre of bands was emerging who liked house and pop, and didn't see why they should be mutually exclusive. Thus was the concept born of 'rock music you can dance to.'

Nothing Compares 2 U
Sinéad O'Connor

Released January 1990
Ensign/Chrysalis *23488* (U.S. #1) / Ensign *ENY 630* (U.K. #1)

This intensely heartfelt performance was too much for some: one reviewer called it "a pointless and embarrassing over-sentimental paw … a waste of talent." Millions of others clearly thought otherwise, making this single and the album *I Do Not Want What I Haven't Got reach* Number 1 on both sides of the Atlantic, an accomplishment Ms. O'Connor has found hard to follow. 'Nothing Compares' remains her only major hit single, and its huge success was undoubtedly assisted by a stark video shot in one take after a more lavish production didn't work. The tears are genuine.

O'Connor would become better known for her non-musical activities, such as tearing up a picture of the Pope John Paul II on live television, and has since claimed that she hated the fame that 'Nothing Compares' brought her. It was her manager who suggested she record what was until that point a little-known gem written by Prince in 1985. The man who seems to write ten songs before breakfast had given this song to The Family, a group signed to his Paisley Park label that included former members of The Revolution and future members of The New Power Generation. It was only an album track at the time, and the Purple One didn't perform or record it himself until after O'Connor had made it internationally popular. A live-in-the-studio duet with Rosie Gains recorded in 1992 appears on Prince's *The Hits/The B-Sides* three-CD collection.

U Can't Touch This
M.C. Hammer

Released February 1990
Capitol *15571* (U.S. #8) / Capitol *CL 578* (U.K. #3)

Ice Ice Baby
Vanilla Ice

Released September 1990
SBK *07335* (U.S. #1) / SBK *18* (U.K. #1)

These songs established recycling as an easy formula for hit-making – and a formula that would be revisited a decade later by Sean 'Diddy' Combs and others in pursuit of pop success. Two of the biggest blockbuster rap singles to date, these infectious tunes are known for their big, obvious samples lifted from other popular songs. 'U Can't Touch This' was made with the help of Rick James's saucy 'Super Freak,' while 'Ice Ice Baby' is built on the instrumental bed of 'Under Pressure' by Queen & David Bowie.

Vanilla Ice followed M.C. Hammer into the pop charts and would often be compared with him. They shared some surface similarities, such as the gift of dancing feet and a propensity for wearing parachute pants. But behind the scenes, Hammer's upbringing and outlook were very different from Ice's. M.C. Hammer had a reputation for benevolence and helping his community while Vanilla Ice quickly became known for a selfish, snobbish attitude.

M.C. Hammer was born Stanley Kirk Burrell and grew up on the rough streets of Oakland, California, but opted towards bubblegum when it came to his music. He simply had no interest in perpetuating the violent lifestyle he saw on the streets. Meanwhile, Vanilla Ice began life as Robert Van Winkle, a kid from suburban Texas who pretended to come from the inner city of Miami and professed to be hard on boastful songs like 'Ice Ice Baby.' Both 'U Can't Touch This' and 'Ice Ice Baby' helped their respective albums each sell over ten million copies.

Dub Be Good To Me
Beats International

Released February 1990
Elektra *64970* (U.S.) / Go! Beat *GOD 39* (U.K. #1)

Norman Cook was a former guitarist with The Housemartins now turned DJ-producer, and would later be known as multi-platinum artist Fatboy Slim. He scored an early Number 1 single in his native U.K. with this lively version of an American R&B hit. 'Dub Be Good To Me' is a cover of 1982's 'Just Be Good To Me' by Atlanta's S.O.S. Band. The original was crafted by Jimmy Jam and Terry Lewis, the super-producers credited for catapulting Janet Jackson into maverick pop stardom. Cook preserved much of the melodic integrity of their song, revving it up a little with a bassline borrowed from punk band The Clash.

The Power
Snap!

Released March 1990
Arista *2013* (U.S. #2) / Arista *113133* (U.K. #1)

Less than one year after the music world was outraged by the unmasking of Milli Vanilli as the secret studio project of German producers and not two spunky young black men, Germany would again concoct a hugely successful pop sham in Snap!, whose high-energy dance hit 'The Power' is unabashedly constructed from vocal samples. The samples were swiped (and uncredited) from the relatively unknown house music diva Jocelyn Brown ('I'm Gonna Get You') and rapper Chill Rob G ('Let The Words Flow'), although in 'live' performances and on the video, the singing and rapping is represented by stand-ins Jackie Harris and Turbo B, respectively.

Killer
Adamski

Released March 1990
MCA *24049* (U.S.) / MCA *1400* (U.K. #1)

Seal (Sealhenry Samuel) later became internationally famous, sold over 10 million albums, and married a supermodel. But on this record, he was a newcomer vocalist guesting on a haunting U.K. chart-topper, grabbing the spotlight through the sheer power of his raw, emotive voice. Adamski had been buoyed by the U.K. Top 20 success of his rave anthem 'N.R.G.,' but now the more subtle yet grooving 'Killer' became the producer's career highlight. While Adamski never stopped making music (latterly as Adam Sky), he never did repeat these chart feats and the success of his album *Doctor Adamski's Musical Pharmacy*. But from 'Killer' and Seal's later solo hit 'Crazy' a unique, enduring star was born.

World In Motion
ENGLANDneworder

Released May 1990
Not issued U.S. / Factory/MCA *FAC 293* (U.K. #1)

Oh, how the British public laughed when New Order – the warmer, clubbier reincarnation of the much darker and more depressing Joy Division – released this excellent song for England's World Cup team, one of only two decent soccer tunes in recorded history. (The other was Skinner & Baddiel's ludicrously singable 'Three Lions' in 1996.) Somehow, art activist Keith Allen was involved. Somehow, England player John Barnes was persuaded to perform a surprisingly on-point rap – and somehow agreed to do a lame (and mildly racist) visual gag in the video in which his cropped head was mistaken for a microphone. Somehow, it was all rather good – perhaps because of the song's unique selling point, the pronunciation of 'England' as 'En-ger-land.'

Groove Is In The Heart
Deee-Lite

Released August 1990
Elektra *64934* (U.S. #4) / Elektra *EKR 114* (U.K. #2)

Deee-Lite was a trio comprised of the vivacious American singer Lady Miss Kier Kirby and the turntable-studio wizards known as Supa DJ Dmitry Brill (from the former Soviet Union) and Jungle DJ Towa 'Towa'

Tei (of Japan). They captured the lovely utopian bubble of glamorous and internationally savvy New York City club life and brought it to the mainstream for everyone's enjoyment. 'Groove Is In The Heart' features guest vocals from Parliament-Funkadelic's inimitable Bootsy Collins and rapper Q-Tip from A Tribe Called Quest. The whimsical, bouncy beat hugs Lady Kier's pop-culture-packed lyrics tight and just right. The single was unlucky not to top the U.K. chart – it sold exactly the same number of copies as Steve Miller Band's 'The Joker,' but stalled at Number 2

because of an obscure (and never-before enforced) chart ruling, which states that, in the event of a tie, the single with the highest sales increase on the previous week should be awarded the Number 1 spot.

Unbelievable
EMF

Released October 1990
EMI *50350* (U.S. #1) / Parlophone *R 6273* (U.K. #3)

This first song from an unknown U.K. dance-rock group called EMF was a surprise hit on both sides of the Atlantic. 'Unbelievable' is a guitar-driven groover featuring odd vocal samples from the controversial American comedian Andrew 'Dice' Clay, attempting to convey just how shocking the song's main character is. EMF is said to stand for Epsom Mad Funkers, but many say it is really Ecstasy Mother Fuckers, the name of a secret song on EMF's debut album *Schubert Dip*. Given the band's place on the cusp of Britain's then-burgeoning acid-house rave scene, it's not hard to believe.

Sadeness Part 1
Enigma

Released November 1990
Charisma *98864* (U.S. #5) / Virgin International *DINS 101* (U.K. #1)

Gregorian chant set to a gentle dance beat: 'Sadeness' must surely rank as one of the strangest international hits in the history of popular music. It was the debut single by Enigma, the brainchild of the Romanian-born German-based composer Michael Cretu, who later re-christened himself Curly MC. Gregorian chant had been a regular component of new age music for some time, but the simple addition of an electronic backbeat brought these ancient sounds into the upper reaches of the charts across Europe and America. Alongside typically drippy synths and a panpipe melody, the single also features a breathless vocal from Cretu's wife, Sandra (calling herself F. Gregorian). Enigma have had several other big hits since, but none has had the surprise impact of 'Sadeness.'

There She Goes
The La's

Released October 1990
London *869370* (U.S.) / Go! Discs *GOLAS 5* (U.K. #13)

The La's (so named after the Merseyside slang for 'lads') crashed and burned in spectacular style after peaking with a near-perfect single, 'There She Goes.' Frontman Lee Mavers was dubbed "the Syd Barrett of the 1990s" by an over-excited press, although there are parallels between The La's man and the dotty old Pink Floyd bod, as Mavers too vanished from view, attaining an almost mythical status as a flawed genius who lost his way.

Rumors circulated for years that Mavers was on the point of returning with more perfect pop in the mold of 'There She Goes,' but we had to wait until 2005, when the band re-formed … a decade too late. However, their finest three minutes remains Mavers's legacy: 'There She Goes' boasts an unforgettable arpeggiated intro, the singer's gorgeous falsetto, and a surprisingly elegant bass part from John Power, who went on to form the briefly popular Britpop band Cast.

Enjoy The Silence
Depeche Mode

Released February 1990
Sire/Reprise *19885* (U.S. #8) / Mute *BONG 18* (U.K. #6)

Depeche Mode were one of the defining British groups of the 1980s, but their biggest and best-remembered hit didn't arrive until the start of the subsequent decade. Hailing from unfashionable Basildon, south-east England, the synth-pop quartet were a regular fixture on the charts in their homeland from 1981 onwards but didn't begin to make it into the American market until several years later. 'People Are People' (1984) looked like being the group's lone U.S. hit until (somewhat fittingly) the 1987 *Music For The Masses* album brought them into the mainstream. Depeche Mode ended the 1980s on a high note with the strident robotic blues vamp 'Personal Jesus,' a Top 30 hit on both sides of the Atlantic.

The follow-up was even better and even more successful. Produced by Flood – whose resumé includes U2, Smashing Pumpkins, and P.J. Harvey – 'Enjoy The Silence' is propelled along by neat, sequenced bass and drums and foreboding mock-choral synthesizer chords. Dave Gahan turns in one of the finest vocal performances of his career, his baritone delivery perfectly suited to multi-instrumentalist Martin Gore's despairing lyric. His message seems to be that the more you talk, the more you erode the magical mystery of a new romance – not the most positive of sentiments, but hard to dispute.

Epic
Faith No More

Released February 1990
Slash *19813* (U.S. #9) / Slash *LASH 21* (U.K. #37)

From San Francisco's Faith No More, 'Epic' was one of the most bizarre hybrid songs to hit the pop charts in the 1990s, a rock-rap-funk mixture similar to the hits of L.A.'s Red Hot Chili Peppers. The minor-key wails of frontman Mike Patton are effective at the same time as they seem a highly unusual choice for popular melodies. There was a ruckus among activists when the explosive performance video for 'Epic' was seen, including goldfish that have fallen out of their tank and gasp desperately for air, but the band helpfully tried to reassure everyone that no fish were harmed during the filming.

Tom's Diner
DNA Featuring Suzanne Vega

Released March 1990
A&M *1529* (U.S. #5) / A&M *AM 592* (U.K. #2)

The endearingly melancholic Suzanne Vega, a poet-turned-folk-singer raised in New York City, could never have predicted that she'd have one of her biggest hits with this club jam that originated as a bootleg release by a pair of creative British DJs. Vega wrote 'Tom's Diner' in the early 1980s and held onto it until '87, when she released the album *Solitude Standing*. The original is performed a cappella – simply Vega's voice, with no instrumentation to back her up, not even her trusty guitar. Three years later, DNA grafted the original onto a chugging beat by Soul II Soul and pressed up illegal white labels, vinyl records devoid of images or information. The recording's popularity among DJs spread quickly, and with Vega's permission an official release eventually emerged on her record label, A&M.

While DNA later released another mix of a Vega song ('Rusted Pipe'), the group never became known pop stars, instead fading back into the faceless dancefloor world from whence they came. In 1991, 'Tom's Diner' was celebrated with its own tributary compilation, *Tom's Album*, featuring versions from little-known bands like Bingo Hand Job, a special collaboration between R.E.M. and Billy Bragg. Tom's Restaurant, the real-life New York coffee shop where 'Tom's Diner' was written, would later return to the spotlight on television, starring as the local coffee shop for the gang on smash situation comedy *Seinfeld*. While the exterior of the real restaurant was shown, the interior was shot on a sound stage in Los Angeles.

Freedom
George Michael

Released October 1990
Columbia *73559* (U.S. #8) / Epic *GEO 3* (U.K. #28)

'Freedom' marked the point of George Michael's transformation from camp 1980s pop idol to serious musical artiste. That earlier role had served Michael well: after Wham!, his highly successful duo with Andrew Ridgeley, came to the end of its natural life, he embarked on a run of eight U.S. Top 5 hits – five of them chart-toppers – between 1987 and 1990, a feat not achieved by a British act since The Beatles. Those hits included the mildly controversial 'I Want Your Sex,' 'Faith,' 'Father Figure,' and 'Praying For Time.'

'Praying For Time' was the first single to be drawn from Michael's *Listen Without Prejudice: Vol. 1*, which introduced the pop world to a newly mature and sensitive version of the star – not to mention one capable, for the first time, of producing a solid, musically diverse album. An effortlessly funky, house-inflected affirmation of life, love, and liberty, 'Freedom' was the second single to be drawn from the album, and the second Michael single to bear that title (the first was a 1984 Wham! hit). It was obviously a matter of great importance to the singer to maintain his independence, and two years later he took his label, Sony, to court, citing restraint of trade. (He was dismayed at Sony's apparent reticence to back his newly serious material and image, which was borne out in lower chart placings from 'Freedom' onwards.) He lost the case but was eventually freed by Sony, and was able to resume his career almost as if nothing had happened after a four-year hiatus.

Wicked Game
Chris Isaak

Released November 1990
Reprise *19704* (U.S. #6) / London *LON 279* (U.K. #10)

Falling
Julee Cruise
Released November 1990
Warner Bros. *4346* (U.S.) / Warner Bros. *W 9544* (U.K. #7)

Go
Moby
Released March 1991
Instinct *EX 229* (U.S.) / Outer Rhythm *FOOT 15* (U.K. #10)

The common thread here is the cinematic auteur David Lynch: Isaak and Cruise were given a leg up by their prominence in his work, while Moby's first U.K. hit sampled the *Twin Peaks* theme.

Chris Isaak was already a cult favorite, having made three albums of gentle 1950s-style rock, but none had reached the charts. 'Wicked Game' is built around a slow, sensual slide-guitar line and Isaak's delicate, cracked croon, and was originally featured on the singer's 1989 set *Heart Shaped World*. It was given a new lease on life the following year when Lynch used it in the nightmarish road movie *Wild At Heart*, and he also directed the song's promo video.

Julee Cruise, by contrast, was something of a pet project for Lynch and his regular musical collaborator, Angelo Badalamenti. 'Falling' is a vocal version of the orchestral theme to Lynch's landmark television series *Twin Peaks* (in which Cruise also had a small, recurring role). It was a surprise

U.K. hit as *Peaks* became the most talked-about TV series in years.

Moby first issued an embryonic version of his *Twin Peaks*-sampling 'Go' while 'Falling' was still on the U.K. chart. A refined version of the ambient techno song reached the British Top 10 a year later. It was the first hit in a long and eclectic career for the New York-based electronic musician, who reached his commercial peak a decade later with his ten-million-selling *Play* album, which spawned the singles 'Porcelain,' 'Why Does My Heart Feel So Bad,' and 'South Side.'

Smells Like Teen Spirit
Nirvana

Released October 1991
DGC *19050* (U.S. #6) / DGC *DGCS 5* (U.K. #7)

'Smells Like Teen Spirit' confirmed the rumblings that had been emanating from Seattle since the spring of 1989. Something called grunge was happening up in that Northwestern backwater. Those in the know, having sniffed the air, now realized that grunge might have the same power as punk had a decade and a half earlier: the power to turn the music business upside down.

At first, the front-runner in the race to make grunge go global was Mudhoney, a raw but melodic quartet signed to the tiny Sub-Pop label. Before long, however, another Sub-Pop act, Nirvana, led by the enigmatic Kurt Cobain, was turning heads. The group's early singles and live shows confirmed them as a force to be reckoned with, and the British rock press in particular began hailing them as potential saviors of a corporate music scene that had grown bloated and out of touch with younger listeners.

In the year prior to the release of 'Teen Spirit,' the charts were dominated by slickly processed pop, rock, and dance from the likes of Mariah Carey, Bryan Adams, Madonna, Michael Bolton, Janet Jackson, Extreme, Whitney Houston, and Paula Abdul. Talented as these artists were, their music was calculated, sophisticated, and rooted in their ability to turn on a sanitized semblance of sincere emotion whenever they opened their mouths. Nirvana was the antithesis of almost everything these artists stood for. Nirvana's music was about chaos, confusion, and spontaneity.

So it was appropriate that 'Smells Like Teen Spirit' was sparked to life by a misunderstanding. Cobain and his friend Kathleen Hanna of punk-feminist band Bikini Kill had spent an evening together at his apartment on North Pear Street, Olympia, 60 miles south of Seattle. During the evening, Hanna spray-painted the graffiti "Kurt smells like Teen Spirit" on one of the walls. "I took that as a compliment," Cobain explained in a subsequent interview. "I thought she was saying that I was a person who could inspire. I just thought that was a nice little title." What Hanna meant, however, was much more literal: that Cobain smelled like the female under-arm deodorant Teen Spirit. "I didn't even know that deodorant existed," claimed Cobain, "until after the song was written."

Having found a title, Cobain next had to put some music together. "I was trying to write the ultimate pop song," he revealed in 1994. "I was basically trying to rip off The Pixies. … We used their sense of dynamics, being soft and quiet, then loud and hard." What he came up with gave a good indication of Cobain's eclectic musical tastes. To The Pixies' dynamics he added the primitive drive of The Kingsmen's 'Louie Louie,' a long-time favorite of Seattle rockers, combined with more than a hint of the chord changes of 'More Than A Feeling' by prog-rock giants Boston.

Lyrically, the song is – to be generous – impervious to logical examination. Cobain snarls out a long string of loosely rhyming non sequiturs, clearest of which is the phrase "Here we are now, entertain us," derived from a line Cobain used to break the ice at social gatherings. Elsewhere, he growls a terse and inscrutable list that runs: "A mulatto, an albino, a mosquito, my libido." Despite the lack of traditional meaning, the almost stream-of-consciousness words are delivered with a numbed conviction that spoke volumes about Cobain's state of mind – despairing, angry, vulnerable – and were a perfect match for the millions of disaffected teenagers who found it impossible to relate to the phony glamour that surrounded Whitney, Madonna, and their ilk.

Jonathan Poneman of Sub-Pop was there in Seattle's OK Hotel on April 17, 1991, when Nirvana played 'Smells Like Teen Spirit' live for the very first time. Poneman recalled: "I remember going, 'Wow, God, this is a really good song.' Then it comes to the chorus and everyone went, 'Oh my God, this is one of the greatest choruses of any songs I've ever heard!'" But Poneman didn't get the opportunity to release the song, because Nirvana moved to DGC Records, a subsidiary of Geffen, at the end of the month.

'Smells Like Teen Spirit' was recorded at the start of May 1991 in Sound City Studios, Van Nuys, California, during sessions with producer Butch Vig for the group's second album, *Nevermind*. Their indie debut, *Bleach*, had cost slightly over $600. This major-label follow-up ran to $120,000.

Like Sub Pop's Poneman, Vig was immediately blown away by the song. "I kept having them play it over and over again, because it was so fucking good," he revealed later, adding that the song was more or less complete by the time he heard it. He did admit, however, to having done "some minor tweaking of the arrangement" that included having Cobain repeat during each chorus a brief guitar ad-lib, which originally appeared only at the end of the song.

In advance of release, the single was sent out to American radio DJs on August 27, 1991, while the band was touring in Europe. Geffen's marketing team and Nirvana's management company, Gold Mountain, were completely taken aback by the response. "We thought it was gonna be the college/alternative-rock track," remembered Danny Goldberg of Gold Mountain, "and the feeling was that 'Come As You Are' was a more melodic song so it would be more of a pop song." Instead, 'Teen Spirit' took off immediately at all levels of rock and pop radio.

Director Sam Bayer's memorable video for 'Teen Spirit' had its first MTV play on September 29, but the song took off first in Britain, entering the U.K. singles chart at the end of November, swiftly followed by its U.S. chart debut on December 7. In both territories, the single stopped just outside the Top 5, but there was no mistaking its impact. A whole new generation of record buyers had been galvanized, and grunge was set to be rock's dominant force for the rest of the decade already underway.

Unfinished Sympathy
Massive Attack

Released February 1991
Virgin *DMD 1662* (U.S.) / Wild Bunch *WBRS 2* (U.K. #13)

Regularly cited among the greatest singles of the 1990s if not all time, 'Unfinished Sympathy' introduced the world to Massive Attack and the 'trip-hop' sound that the group pioneered. Robert Del Naja (a.k.a. '3D'), Adrian Vowles ('Mushroom'), and Grant Marshall ('Daddy G') were part of a music collective based in Bristol, England, known as The Wild Bunch, before forming Massive Attack in 1987.

This was the group's third single, and the second to be drawn from their milestone debut album, *Blue Lines*. Both album and single laid out the ground rules for what became known as trip-hop, the first legitimate British response to rap music, and inspired a host of similar artists, notably occasional Massive Attack member Tricky, and Portishead, both from the Bristol area.

'Unfinished Sympathy' is built around a jangly, slowed-down hip-hop beat and a moving, cinematic string arrangement. The remarkably soulful vocal is by Shara Nelson, who also stars in the memorable promo video for the song. In it she is filmed walking the backstreets of Los Angeles, apparently unaware of everything going on around her. It was one of the first music videos to be shot in one continuous take.

The single is something of an oddity in the group's catalog in that it was credited simply to Massive. They were persuaded to drop the "unpatriotic" Attack during the first Gulf War, a step that Del Naja continues to regret. He was a vocal critic of the second war in Iraq a decade later. In the intervening years Massive Attack had continued to make records of the highest quality, including the U.K. hit singles 'Protection,' 'Karmacoma,' and 'Teardrop,' which featured a gorgeously ethereal vocal by former Cocteau Twins mouthpiece Elizabeth Fraser.

Losing My Religion
R.E.M.

Released February 1991
Warner Bros. *19392* (U.S. #4) / Warner Bros. *W 0015* (U.K. #19)

After a decade building a slow success, R.E.M. was ready for the big time at the start of the 1990s. Surprisingly, however, the song that confirmed the group's status among rock music's elite was a morose ballad dominated by a mandolin, an instrument not usually considered as a leading voice in rock music. The only other notable hit to feature it prominently is 'Maggie May' by Rod Stewart, released two decades earlier. But in the hands of R.E.M.'s Peter Buck, the mandolin offers a fine counterpoint to sad strings and a maudlin Michael Stipe vocal – written, according to its author, as a follow-up to 'Every Breath You Take' by The Police.

'Losing My Religion' was helped along by a memorable video starring Stipe and Saint Sebastian, and it became the best-known song of the group's career, winning a Grammy for Best Pop Performance (By A Duo Or Group With Vocals). It went down well everywhere, in fact, except Ireland, where the single was banned because of its religious content – somewhat ironic, given that the offending word is used purely metaphorically.

R.E.M. scored another U.S. Top 10 hit several months later with 'Shiny Happy People,' a bouncy duet with Kate Pierson of The B-52's. The group quickly grew to hate that song, however, and has never performed it live, unless you count a rendition given on TV's *Sesame Street* more than a decade later, when it was re-christened 'Furry Happy Monsters.'

(Everything I Do) I Do It For You
Bryan Adams

Released June 1991
A&M *1567* (U.S. #1) / A&M *AM 789* (U.K. #1)

This epic ballad was written for and featured in the movie *Robin Hood: Prince Of Thieves*, and spent a record 16 weeks at Number 1 in the U.K. during the summer of 1991.

Adams was originally commissioned simply to add words to a theme written by Michael Kamen, whose work encompasses numerous film scores, 11 ballets, and guest appearances with musicians ranging from Kate Bush to Metallica. In the end, though, Adams and his producer, Mutt Lange, came up with a song that bore little relation to Kamen's music for the movie (but for which Kamen nonetheless retained a co-writing credit).

Neither Kamen nor the producers of *Robin Hood: Prince Of Thieves* were keen on Adams's song, and relegated it to the movie's end credits. The public disagreed, however, and sent 'Everything I Do' to the top of the charts on both sides of the Atlantic and 28 other countries around the world. In the U.S. – where it spent seven weeks at Number 1 – it ranks second only to the charity hit 'We Are The World' by U.S.A. for Africa among the biggest-selling singles of all time.

Despite its huge international success, 'Everything I Do' is loathed as much as it is admired, in part because of its apparent disinclination towards leaving the charts – not to mention the airwaves – and also, perhaps, because of Adams's clean cut looks and squeaky-clean persona. What is undeniable, though, is that the song contains a strong vocal melody, an expertly assembled build-up, and a weighty, lighters-aloft ending that gets people cheering around the jukebox every time. Love it or hate it, 'Everything I Do' is one of the biggest and most easily recognizable records of the 1990s.

Enter Sandman
Metallica

Released August 1991
Elektra *64857* (U.S. #16) / Vertigo *METAL 7* (U.K. #5)

'Enter Sandman' finds Metallica at their most approachable, but without losing any of the band's famous metal edge they had carefully cultivated in their first ten years of ear-blistering life. The lead single off the album *Metallica*, the infamous multi-platinum selling effort colloquially known as *The Black Album*, it helped propel that record into the band's most popular effort ever. The song gained new life once adopted into the sports world as a steely anthem of intimidation, and a popular professional wrestler named Jim Fullington even adopted the moniker of The Sandman.

Do The Bartman
The Simpsons

Released January 1991
Not issued U.S. / Geffen *GEF 87* (U.K. #1)

'Do The Bartman' was a spin-off from the long running animated TV series *The Simpsons* and is the work of the pseudonymous John Jay Smith, better known to the world as Michael Jackson. Series creator Matt Groening finally admitted at the 1998 Second Annual World Animation Celebration that Jackson had written the song, expressing his surprise that nobody had discovered the truth earlier.

'Do The Bartman' bears many of the hallmarks of Jackson's work of the time, and the backing vocals sound suspiciously like him . . . mainly because they are by him (and the song's producer, Bryan Loren). If those weren't big enough clues, our Mr. Smith is also name-checked in the lyrics: "If you can do the Bart you're bad like Michael Jackson."

'Do The Bartman' was the opening track on *The Simpsons Sing The Blues*, an album of songs sung by different characters from the series. The lead vocal here is rapped by Nancy Cartwright, the regular voice of bratty pre-teen Bart. The single was not granted a physical release in the U.S., although the album cut made Number 11 on *Billboard*'s Airplay chart, and the video was still Number 1 on MTV for the first three months of 1991. A single was released in the U.K., where it topped the chart, despite the fact that *The Simpsons* was shown only on satellite television in Britain until 1996. Its enduring legacy – aside from the story of its mysterious author – is that anybody aged six to 16 at the time of the song's release can most likely still recite Bart's rap.

The Shoop Shoop Song (It's In His Kiss)
Cher

Released January 1991
Geffen *19659* (U.S. #33) / Epic *6566737* (U.K. #1)

Covering a 1963 hit by Merry Clayton was a masterstroke by sliced-and-diced cyborg pop lady Cher, once of Sonny & Cher fame, especially as it also appeared on the soundtrack for the *Mermaids* movie, in which she starred as mum of wayward goth brat Winona Ryder. Cher had previously tried her hand at watered-down hair-rock – remember the hideous 'If I Could Turn Back Time,' in whose video she appeared in almost nothing but greenish tattoos? – and would eventually strike it big with house-trance in the late 1990s. But this classic bit of soul was a triumph, not to be repeated.

Mama Said Knock You Out
LL Cool J

Released January 1991
Def Jam *73706* (U.S. #17) / Def Jam *6564470* (U.K. B-side)

"Don't call it a comeback!" shouts a rugged LL Cool J on this American Top 20 hit. "I've been here for years!" He was born James Todd Smith but his new name stood for Ladies Love Cool James, and he was one of the first world-famous rappers as well as one of the first artists on New York City's legendary Def Jam label.

After debuting as a hard-edged teenager with obvious sex-symbol potential, he had become known for entertaining the ladies just a bit more than the men as he started to grow up and come across with near-ballads like 'I Need Love.' The fickle streets had started to turn away from him until the reaffirmation of 'Mama Said Knock You Out,' a pounting, unrelenting song and the title track of his fourth album. In the rap world, one's inner-city credibility is paramount, and this song was the sound of LL vehemently taking back that credibility and never letting it go.

With the help of legendary hip-hop DJ-producer Marley Marl at the controls, 'Mama Said' is anything but soft and is indelibly complimented by its gorgeous black-and-white video featuring LL in a boxing ring. The *Mama Said* album featured a further hit in 'Around The Way Girl' while songs like 'The Boomin' System' and 'Jingling Baby' earned heavy club rotation. The album went double-platinum and cemented LL Cool J's place in the hip-hop pantheon for years to come.

Summertime
DJ Jazzy Jeff & The Fresh Prince

Released June 1991
Jive *1465* (U.S. #4) / Jive *JIVECD 279* (U.K. #8)

This Philadelphia hip-hop duo, which debuted in 1987 and enjoyed the fruits of multi-platinum sales, had its last major hit in 1991 with the enduring jam 'Summertime.' The song, perfect for outdoor barbecues, pool parties, and slow cruising in a caravan of cars, is decidedly more laidback than their earlier successes with cheeky songs like 'Parents Just Don't Understand.' Alongside these achievements, the charismatic Will Smith (a.k.a. The Fresh Prince) had started an acting career with his lead role in the popular situation comedy *The Fresh Prince Of Bel-Air*. The transition was so successful that by the end of the 1990s Smith would no longer be known principally as a rapper: he became a full-fledged blockbuster movie star demanding millions of dollars.

The group's relative silence off the small screen (*Bel-Air* enjoyed frequent cameos from Jazzy Jeff) had built up anticipation for the 1991 release of the *Homebase* album, which was nicely buoyed by the reception for 'Summertime.' To paraphrase the rap star LL Cool J, people called it a comeback, although DJ Jazzy Jeff and the Fresh Prince had been there for years. In one of the ultimate honors for any song,

'Summertime' grabbed a Grammy for Best Rap Performance By A Group. Not a bad way to put a cap on a successful career, for while Jazzy Jeff and Will Smith have remained the tightest of friends and talked about future collaborations, they've never released another proper album together since *Homebase*.

I'm Too Sexy
Right Said Fred

Released July 1991
Charisma *98671* (U.S. #1) / Tug *SNOG 1* (U.K. #2)

When we first heard 'I'm Too Sexy' we all said no, this can't be a real song, it's a nursery rhyme, or a parody of a gay disco anthem. In fact, Right Said Fred's debut single was both, becoming iconic for its proud-to-be-out associations and its none-more-simple bass and drums motif with a bit of brass tacked on top. The shaven-headed, muscular British band – baritone singer Richard Fairbrass, his songwriter-instrumentalist brother Fred, and guitarist Rob Manzoli – added to the song's impact with their unique look and defied all criticism by sustaining their career a lot longer than they should have done. Remarkable.

Set Adrift On Memory Bliss
PM Dawn

Released August 1991
Gee Street *866094* (U.S. #1) / Gee Street *GEE 33* (U.K. #3)

It's certainly a long way from Jersey City to London, but brothers Prince Be (Attrell Cordes) and DJ Minute Mix (Jarrett Cordes) bridged many international gaps of sound and style with their hippified take on hip-hop as PM Dawn. They scored a massive crossover hit with the creative 'Set Adrift on Memory Bliss,' which lifts the familiar melodic stabs from 'True,' the 1983 hit ballad from U.K. pop group Spandau Ballet. 'Set Adrift' was included on PM Dawn's loftily named and sampladelic 1991 album *Of The Heart, Of The Soul And Of The Cross: The Utopian Experience*.

O.P.P.
Naughty By Nature

Released September 1991
Tommy Boy *988* (U.S. #6) / Big Life *BLR 74* (U.K. #35)

The New Jersey trio had an international hit with this hilarious ode to fooling around. Rappers Treach (Anthony Criss) and Vinnie (Vincent Brown) plus DJ Kay Gee (Keir Gist) hail from the ghetto of East Orange and shared tough childhood experiences, heavily reflected in the group's songs. But 'O.P.P.' is different, almost bubblegum, largely because of the song it samples heavily: 'ABC' by The Jackson 5. While the polite explanation for the acronym 'O.P.P.' is that it stands for Other People's Property, the more crass definition replaces the last word with names for male and female genitalia. Committing adultery never sounded so funky.

Finally
Ce Ce Peniston

Released October 1991
A&M *1586* (U.S. #5) / A&M *AM 858* (U.K. #2)

The gorgeous and poised Cecelia Peniston was simply not satisfied to rest on the laurels earned from her title as Miss Black Arizona of 1989. Instead, just a few short years later she'd be known as the queen of the dancefloor with one of the most infectious and bestselling club hits of the 1990s. 'Finally' is a love song with oomph, a sassy anthem with universal appeal. The album of the same name generated two more pop hits ('We Got a Love Thang' and 'Keep On Walkin") and earned Peniston two *Billboard* Music Awards.

Don't Let The Sun Go Down On Me
George Michael & Elton John

Released November 1991
Columbia *74086* (U.S. #1) / Epic *657646* (U.K. #1)

There was no reason why a live version of Elton John's 1974 hit 'Don't Let The Sun Go Down On Me' should become a hit now, but this didn't deter his chum George Michael, who pulled out a spiffing version of the old chestnut and watched it race up the charts like a rat up a drainpipe. The song is unremarkable if you're familiar with the original melodic piano-ballad, other than the money-shot moment when Big George says to the fawning audience: "Ladies and gentlemen … mister Elton John!" The venue goes berserk, Reg comes on and does his stuff, hugs are exchanged, and another trillion dollars go into the accounts of Messrs. Panayiotou and Dwight.

Black Or White
Michael Jackson

Released November 1991
Epic *74100* (U.S. #1) / Epic *657598* (U.K. #1)

After Michael Jackson was *Bad*, the emboldened artist took a step further and became *Dangerous*, speaking out more loudly against his self-inflicted oppression and alienation from the rest of the world. While he continued to have hits, Jackson's public persona only grew stranger.

Regular television network Fox and the three major American music cable networks (MTV, VH1, and BET) premiered the memorable video, which features a morphing of the faces of a diverse group of people (much like the famous video for Godley and Creme's 'Cry'). Protestors subsequently forced the excising of one violent scene of Jackson smashing a car window, but it's less clear why the scene featuring Fox cartoon characters Homer and Bart Simpson hit the cutting room floor. Perhaps it was just to get Fox on board in the early stages?

In a way that has been repeated countless times in his obstacle-laden career, Jackson's intentions for this song ended up hideously twisted against him in what could be considered a major backfire. "It don't matter if you're black or white," he sings, clearly troubled. But no sooner had the song hit the airwaves than late-night talk-show hosts and aspiring stand-up comedians alike had concocted dozens and dozens of jokes, questioning Jackson's strangely morphing skin color. He claimed it was due to the melanin-depleting skin disorder vitiligo, but folks weren't so sure.

Baby Got Back
Sir Mix-A-Lot

Released April 1992
Def American *18947* (U.S. #1) / Def American *DEFA 20* (U.K.)

The urban music world, which stars the complementary genres of R&B and hip-hop, has a fondness – even an unabashed joy – for a woman's backside. While it is a frequent subject of songs and in videos, it was Seattle's most famous rapper Sir Mix-A-Lot (born Anthony Ray) who broke the ice with 'Baby Got Back,' his chart-topping paean to the beauty of the big ol' booty.

In his raucously funny lyrics, Mix-A-Lot takes pains to detail the type of posterior he finds most appealing. He wants a lady with an "LA face and an Oakland booty." No skinny girls with flat rumps are desired over here; that type of woman is only for the pages of *Cosmo*, not black men with real needs. "36-24-36?" he asks, somewhat sarcastically. "Only if she's five three!"

The accompanying video for 'Baby Got Back' couldn't possibly be more descriptive of the song itself, with its giant ass mountains, suggestively moving fruit and vegetables, and, perhaps most importantly, a voluptuous, gyrating dance troupe to drive home the point. 'Baby Got Back' stayed in the Number 1 slot for four weeks and shocked critics when it won an elusive Grammy for Best Rap Solo Performance. Sir Mix-A-Lot later attempted to be a breast man with the racy 'Put 'Em On the Glass,' which featured a soapy car-wash video, but neither that song nor any other overshadowed his butt of a joke.

Jump
Kris Kross

Released April 1992
Ruffhouse *74197* (U.S. #1) / Ruffhouse *657847* (U.K. #2)

In their early teens, Atlanta's Chris Kelly and Chris Smith were respectively dubbed Mack Daddy and Daddy Mack, and they shot to fame with the catchy hip-pop song 'Jump.' But it wasn't the rapid-fire lyrical delivery that got Kris Kross noticed, it was the truly odd way they would wear their clothes: all completely backwards. The young artists were an early success story for Jermaine Dupri, the producer and music executive who launched his own hit-making record label, So So Def, and later created multi-platinum work with artists such as Mariah Carey and his girlfriend Janet Jackson.

Jump Around
House Of Pain

Released July 1992
Tommy Boy *7526* (U.S. #3) / Ruffness *XLS 43* (U.K. #8)

The rap community is not typically characterized as having Irish pride, yet House Of Pain briefly changed that with this enduring anthem from MCs Everlast (Erik Schrody) and Danny Boy (Dan O'Conner) plus DJ Lethal (Leor Dimant). They came from the same underground Los Angeles scene that gave us compatriots Cypress Hill, but 'Jump Around' is a raucous party jam that still, years after its release, can ramp up the energy on any dancefloor. After House Of Pain disbanded, Everlast enjoyed a moderately successful solo career, while DJ Lethal joined multi-platinum rock group Limp Bizkit.

End Of The Road
Boyz II Men

Released July 1992
Motown *2178* (U.S. #1) / Motown *TMG 1411* (U.K. #1)

I Will Always Love You
Whitney Houston

Released November 1992
Arista *12490* (U.S. #1) / Arista *120657* (U.K. #1)

For 36 years, nobody was able to match Elvis Presley's 11-week stint at Number 1 on the *Billboard* singles chart with his 1956 hit 'Hound Dog' / 'Don't Be Cruel.' Then his record was broken twice in the space of four months by two of the biggest R&B acts of the 1990s.

Boyz II Men (Nathan Morris, Wayna Morris, Shawn Stockman, and Michael McCary) formed in 1989 at the High School Of The Creative And Performing Arts in Philadelphia, Pennsylvania. After auditioning backstage at a New Edition gig, the group signed to Motown, and hit Number 2 in the U.S. with their debut single, 'It's So Hard To Say Goodbye To Yesterday,' in 1991. By the following fall, the group had perfected their smooth, soulful sound, and had found the perfect collaborator in the form of songwriter Kenneth 'Babyface' Williams. He provided them with 'End Of The Road,' which spent 13 weeks at Number 1 on the *Billboard* Hot 100 and is Motown's most successful single of all time.

A few months later, Houston's cover of Dolly Parton's enduring country hit 'I Will Always Love You' was the soaring crescendo to *The Bodyguard*, which starred Houston and Kevin Costner in a musically-driven romance. With 14 weeks at Number 1 in the U.S., the song shattered the record set by 'End Of The Road.' Houston later won Grammys for Record Of The Year and Best Pop Vocalist, Female. But her record would be surpassed a few years later by another Boyz II Men single, this time a collaboration with Mariah Carey, 'One Sweet Day,' which topped the charts for an incredible 16 weeks.

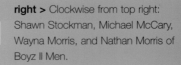

right > Clockwise from top right: Shawn Stockman, Michael McCary, Wayna Morris, and Nathan Morris of Boyz II Men.

Mr. Loverman
Shabba Ranks

Released July 1992
Epic *74257* (U.S. #40) / Epic *659 0782* (U.K. #3)

Oh Carolina
Shaggy

Released November 1992
Virgin *12672* (U.S.) / Greensleeves *GRE 361* (U.K. #1

With his cover of the 1960 Folkes Brothers song 'Oh Carolina,' Shaggy (born Oroville Richard Burrell) might be the only artist ever to have hit the pop charts who served as a soldier in the Gulf War. And along with Shabba Ranks, then a label-mate of Michael Jackson, Shaggy was one of the few 1990s reggae artists originally from Jamaica to have enjoyed success away from the island. Not since the days of Bob Marley, that is. Both artists played up their accents, their deep voices, and their all-around masculine sex appeal to generate hordes of adoring female fans. Men liked them too, even if they didn't want to admit it too loudly, mainly because these sizzling songs from exotic sex symbols probably helped them get women.

Not long after the success of 'Mr. Loverman,' Shabba Ranks (known to his loving mother as Rexton Rawlson Fernando Gordon) fell out of favor with the general public on both sides of the Atlantic, coming under fire for his unabashedly homophobic lyrics in some other songs. Apparently it wasn't enough to cultivate an image as a ladies' man; it was also imperative to declare a stubborn intolerance for difference. This was all quite badly timed, what with the rise of political correctness. The combination proved damaging to Shabba, and we did not hear much more from him.

Would I Lie To You
Charles & Eddie

Released September 1992
Capitol *44809* (U.S. #13) / Capitol *CL 673* (U.K. #1)

It seems not to matter how weak a song's production is or how insipid its sentiments, as long as the top-line melody is catchy enough to stay in the listener's head until old age sets in. This was certainly the case for 'Would I Lie To You,' the career high of Edward Chacon and the late Charles Pettigrew, a soul duo whose knack for a super-bland R&B lick made them stars. The song is notable for the singers' keening falsettos – always a reliable banker in these diluted days – and the interchange of improvised lines that the men throw in from time to time. It's that simple.

Connected
Stereo MC's

Released September 1992
Gee Street *864744* (U.S. #20) / Fourth & Broadway *BRW 262* (U.K. #18)

British pop music has been popular in America since The Beatles, but it has been markedly difficult for the isle's urban sounds to make an impact beyond its shores. Stereo MC's shook up American dance floors and hit the Top 20 in their native U.K. with 'Connected,' which has a catchy shuffle beat provided by Nick Hallam and the mellifluous tones of singer-rapper Rob Birch. While not the big breakthrough that the band and the genre itself might have banked on, its simultaneous presence on radio, clubs, and MTV is exactly the strategy for success that more recent urban artists from Britain have adopted abroad.

Tears In Heaven
Eric Clapton

Released January 1992
Duck-Reprise *19038* (U.S. #2) / Reprise *W 0081* (U.K. #5)

Songs about real-life tragedies are usually mawkish and embarrassing, but Eric Clapton pulled off a coup with 'Tears In Heaven,' which he wrote in the aftermath of the death of his five-year-old son Conor. The song was both catchy enough to pull in public attention and sober enough to serve the subject, with Clapton never making it sound routine or forced, although he admitted that it was sometimes difficult to perform.

The wider impact of 'Tears In Heaven' was twofold. First, it demonstrated that Clapton, who had been in career doldrums for at least two decades after the scintillating work he put in with John Mayall, Cream, and others in the 1960s, could still be a chart-topper. As a piece of songwriting, 'Tears' is perfect. Second, it showed that Clapton could deliver the goods as an acoustic musician as well as in electric mode. His preferred method over the years had always been with the help of a battered electric guitar, but his command of the acoustic instrument here was flawless.

It should also be noted that 'Tears In Heaven,' released as a single alongside Clapton's bestselling MTV *Unplugged* album, ushered in a new awareness of the acoustic medium to the grunge generation of 1992. The album showed that Clapton could rearrange his classic hits for a largely acoustic set and still sound cool (try the revised version of 'Layla'), and was among the first in an unplugged fad that lasted a few years but never produced an album as good as Clapton's, with the possible exceptions of those by Nirvana and Neil Young.

The Drowners
Suede

Released May 1992
Not issued U.S. / Nude *NUD 1S* (U.K.)

Suede never matched the commercial success or the lasting appeal of contemporaries such as Blur, Pulp, and Oasis, but they were first out of the blocks when it came to reinvigorating British guitar-based music in

the early 1990s. The group's androgynous, post-glam sound and image – a mixture of The Smiths and David Bowie – stirred up an instant media storm, and put them on the cover of key U.K. music paper *NME* before they'd even released a single. Dominated by Bernard Butler's bruising guitar chords and Brett Anderson's arch vocal, 'The Drowners' more than matched the hype, scraped in at Number 49 on the chart, and opened the floodgates for the ensuing Britpop tide.

Friday I'm In Love
The Cure

Released May 1992
Elektra *64742* (U.S. #18) / Fiction *FIC 42* (U.K. #6)

The entire blame for the drunken crab dance that is The Cure's rise from post-punk upstarts to international goth megastars can be laid at the feet of Robert Smith. His near-schizophrenic musical eclecticism has enabled the band to thrash out a cacophonous maelstrom on albums like *Pornography* and *Faith*, then craft chart hits spanning everything from electro-pop ('Let's Go To Bed') to jaunty swing ('The Love Cats') and nightmarish goth ('Lullaby').

'Friday I'm In Love' was the second single from the Number 1 album *Wish* and, once again, it rang the changes. "It's a dumb pop song," Smith admitted cheerfully, "but it's quite excellent, actually, because it's so absurd. It's so out of character – very optimistic and really out there in happy land."

Examined clinically, it's just one of hundreds of songs that use the days of the week as a starting point – others include 'Friday On My Mind' by The Easybeats and 'Thursday's Child' by David Bowie. But Porl Thompson's jangly guitar lines and the song's irrepressibly happy mood made 'Friday' The Cure's second biggest British hit single, peaking at Number 6. "People think we're leaders of some sort of gloom movement," Smith complained. "I could sit and write gloomy songs all day long, but I just don't see the point."

Creep
Radiohead

Released September 1992
Capitol *44932* (U.S. #34) / Parlophone *6078* (U.K. #7)

Radiohead's breakthrough hit 'Creep' became something of an albatross from which the group struggled to escape for the next few years. Like a lot of the group's early material it is heavily indebted to the loud-soft dynamics and bleak lyrical sentiments of The Pixies and Nirvana. This meant that the quintet from Oxford, England, had a ready-made fan-base in the U.S., where the single gave them a debut hit. But back home 'Creep' was deemed too miserable for radio in 1992 and didn't chart until it was reissued a year later. Even then, Radiohead were sneered at as a faux-grunge band that had lucked out in America.

Radiohead referred to 'Creep' as "our Scott Walker song," but "our Hollies song" might have been more appropriate. Distinct similarities to 'The Air That I Breathe' meant that its credits were retroactively altered to include Albert Hammond and Mike Hazelwood, composers of the 1960s hit.

Supposed unintentional plagiarism aside, the most memorable moment in 'Creep' is the atonal crunch of Jonny Greenwood's guitar before each chorus. According to legend he arrived at the sound by accident as a way of expressing his irritation at a slow song he didn't much care for. He wasn't alone: frontman Thom Yorke used the band's next single, 'My Iron Lung,' to express his disdain for live audiences who turned up wanting to hear this song but no others. He needn't have worried too much: by 1997 Radiohead were the most important band on the planet.

Jeremy
Pearl Jam

Released September 1992
Epic *77935* (U.S.) / Epic *658 2582* (U.K. #15)

On January 8, 1991, Jeremy Wade Delle, a distraught 16-year-old student at Richardson High School in Dallas, Texas, shot himself dead in front of his classmates during an English lesson. After reading about it in a newspaper, Eddie Vedder of recently formed Seattle-based grunge hopefuls Pearl Jam found himself moved to write a song about it that very night.

Drawing on his own recollections of a fellow student in junior high school in San Diego, California, who had gone on a shooting spree, Vedder came up with a lyric that Pearl Jam guitarist Jeff Ament realized would fit with "two pieces of music that I wrote on acoustic guitar with the idea I would play them on a Hamer 12-string bass I had just ordered." The song evolved further during the recording process at Seattle's London Bridge studio. "I had an idea for the outro," said Ament. "I overdubbed a 12-string bass part and we added a cello part – big-time production for us."

Released as the third single from their multi-platinum debut album *Ten*, 'Jeremy' failed to chart significantly in America, but the award-winning video by director Chris Cafaro became a long-running staple on MTV. "The message of the video was a warning of the exact thing that happened at Columbine," explained Ament, referring to the 1999 U.S. school massacre. "Parents and teachers don't always pay attention to what's going on." It's a testament to the increasing power of MTV that, despite its humble chart record, 'Jeremy' remains the song most closely identified with Pearl Jam.

1992

One
U2

Released March 1992
Island *866533* (U.S. #10) / Island *IS 515* (U.K. #7)

Driven by Edge's subtle, soulful guitar chords and Bono's plaintive vocal delivery, 'One' remains among U2's finest singles. It was the third of three classic singles drawn from the group's sixth studio album, *Achtung Baby*, all released in the space of four months (the other two were 'The Fly' and 'Mysterious Ways').

Achtung Baby is famous as the album where U2 cast off their trad-rock shoes and restyled themselves as post-modern, electro-tinged experimentalists. This is clear enough on songs such as 'Fly,' which bears the hallmarks of producer Brian Eno's work in the late 1970s with David Bowie. The album as a whole is rather impressively layered with multi-tracked, effects-laden guitars, towering synthesizers, and forceful rhythms inspired by (then) cutting-edge dance beats. 'One,' however, is a much more simple, stately affair, anchored not by tinkering with the latest studio gadgetry but by an elegant four-chord riff, everyman lyrics, and a magisterial singalong chorus.

The song's words are ambiguous enough to apply to any situation (which represents a large part of its appeal), but the fact that profits from sales of the single were given to AIDS charities suggests that it might have been written with those suffering from the disease in mind. In later years, Bono has often found himself castigated for sanctimoniously pontificating about global issues, but it's hard to find fault with his genuinely affecting tone here. The lasting popularity of 'One' was demonstrated in 2006 when the lyrics were chosen as the greatest of all time by viewers of the music-TV channel VH1 in Britain.

Are You Gonna Go My Way
Lenny Kravitz

Released February 1993
Not issued U.S. / Virgin America *VUS 65* (U.K. #4)

From the album of the same name, 'Are You Gonna Go My Way' finds superstar Lenny Kravitz in the purest and most rockin' moment of his career. Four years since his startling debut album *Let Love Rule* shocked the world, here he was revved up to full throttle. And once he had everyone's attention, Kravitz wasn't about to let go for anything. From the signature guitar riffs and the way the song's structure builds up and releases tension to Kravitz's inimitably sexy and soulful snarls, the track is solid from top to bottom – with maximum tenacious funk.

Linger
The Cranberries

Released February 1993
Island *862800* (U.S. #8) / Island *IS 559* (U.K. #14)

Proof that suspended drone chords will always elevate a song from the mundane to the magical, 'Linger' is a mournful ballad that bears many listens before becoming too mawkish to bear. The Cranberries, later known for their political angst and singer Dolores O'Riordan's tabloid antics, hit an early creative peak with their debut single, which dealt expertly with the ruins of a relationship without ever employing maudlin imagery or petty rent-a-ballad tricks. In fact, the song arrives with a beautiful guitar figure, hits you with a clutch of heart-stopping choruses, and goes away without outstaying its welcome. Shame they never equaled it again.

Everybody Hurts
R.E.M.

Released April 1993
Warner Bros. *18638* (U.S. #29) / Warner Bros. *W 0169* (U.K. #7)

Having climbed to the top of the pop ladder two years earlier with 'Losing My Religion,' R.E.M. consolidated their position among the key rock bands of the 1990s with another moving ballad. The unusually direct lyrics of 'Everybody Hurts' were later used by the British charity Samaritans in advertising aimed to discourage young men from committing suicide.

In the liner notes to *The Best Of R.E.M.*, bandleader Michael Stipe reflected on the song, concluding that "the reason the lyrics are so atypically straightforward is because it was aimed at teenagers. ... I've never watched *Buffy The Vampire Slayer*, but the idea that high school is a portal to hell seems pretty realistic to me. It's hard for everyone."

The song features one of the finest vocal performances of Stipe's career; the music was written by drummer Bill Berry, although he was supplanted for the recording by a Univox drum machine. The strings were arranged by former Led Zeppelin bassist John Paul Jones. Aside from the almost-raucous bridge, the rest of the arrangement is as spartan as the lyric, with only gentle electric guitar arpeggios, a simple electric organ figure, and on-beat bass. Like 'Losing My Religion,' the single's success was aided by an affecting promo video.

Cats In The Cradle
Ugly Kid Joe

Released March 1993
Stardog *864888* (U.S. #6) / Mercury *MER 385* (U.K. #7)

And so it was decreed in the Book Of Rock that any band worth its salt shall release a ballad as their third single. Lo! This proved to be the case with Ugly Kid Joe, whose big hit – 'Everything About You' – had been mildly diverting in 1992, and who now wanted to show off their sensitive side with a cover of Harry Chapin's 'Cats In The Cradle.' In fact their version wasn't half bad, with singer Whitfield Crane showcasing a sensitive, sub-Cobain bark that perfectly suited the song's father-and-son theme. Acoustic motifs lent the record sophistication and the future looked temporarily bright for UKJ, although they folded in due course.

What's Up
4 Non Blondes

Released May 1993
Interscope *98430* (U.S. #14) / Interscope *A 8412* (U.K. #2)

Iron-lunged Linda Perry and her band, 4 Non Blondes, did well to nick the chord sequence for this song from a million old hits (including Bobby McFerrin's 'Don't Worry, Be Happy'). Adding a vocal hook consisting of variations on the word "yeah" ensured that Generation X didn't have to work too hard to get the message and, behold, 'What's Up' was a huge hit. It helped, too, that Perry's repeated question of "What's going on?" wasn't aimed at anything in particular. Unfortunately, grunge was on its way out in 1994 and nu-metal was on its way in, which made the neither-here-nor-there 4 Non Blondes instantly unfashionable.

I'd Do Anything For Love (But I Won't Do That)
Meat Loaf

Released September 1993
MCA *54626* (U.S. #1) / Virgin *VSCDT 1443* (U.K. #1)

Meat Loaf's massive success with this song, which topped the charts in no fewer than 28 countries across the globe, is an ideal case study for a comeback that was utterly against the odds and yet surpassed all previous efforts. In his nearly 20-year career, Meat was never as big as he was after 'I Will Do Anything For Love (But I Won't Do That).'

Most critics and armchair pundits had already declared the singer's career long over, gone with the heyday of the *Bat Out Of Hell* album and his rendition of 'Hot Patootie' as the Eddie character in cult classic flick *The Rocky Horror Picture Show*. But his dedication to staying on the road and performing live helped keep his name out there, and people became increasingly interested.

'I Will Do Anything' was certainly a leftfield selection for the hell-raising Mr. Loaf, whose mother named him Marvin Lee Aday when he was born in Dallas, Texas, in 1947. The song's almost operatic arrangement and its regal vocal feel were accurately captured by the dark environs of the video. It helped the *Bat Out Of Hell II* album go on to sell over ten million copies – and, to top it all off, Meat Loaf took home a Grammy for Best Rock Solo Performance in 1994.

No Limit
2 Unlimited

Released January 1993
Radikal-Critique *15499* (U.S.) / PWL Continental *PW 256* (U.K. #1)

Dutch techno had its oh-so-brief moment in the global spotlight when 2 Unlimited took a simple, bleepy tune called 'No Limit' and spun it into world pop success. 'No Limit' did not land in the *Billboard* Hot 100 in America – which wasn't such a surprise, since few techno songs did. However, this oversight might have seemed rather strange to the rest of the world, given that 35 countries embraced the song as a Number 1 hit. Despite that success, 2 Unlimited never became pop stars with any sustainable appeal or longevity.

Nuthin' But A "G" Thang
Dr. Dre

Released February 1993
Death Row *53819* (U.S. #2) / Death Row *A 8328* (U.K. #31)

Dr. Dre was easily the most important hip-hop producer of the 1990s, and he brought his innovative G-Funk sound to the mainstream with 'Nuthin,' which also introduced the wider world to a certain Snoop Doggy Dogg. Before striking out on his own, both as producer and solo artist, Dre was a founding member of the late-1980s West Coast hip-hop group N.W.A., with whom he made the seminal *Straight Outta Compton* LP.

Built around a sample from 'I Want'a Do Something Freaky To You' by smooth 1970s funk artist Leon Haywood, 'Nuthin But A "G" Thang' was the finest example yet of the production style Dre had begun to develop around the turn of the decade. All the hallmarks of his best work are here: the Funkadelic-inspired beats, the stop-start liquid bass, the subtle funk guitar, and the heavy-breathing backing vocals. Dre's talents were many and varied, and he was one of the most clued-up talent spotters around, for 'G Thang' also marks the first time that Snoop Doggy Dogg made it into the *Billboard* Hot 100. Within a year Snoop would reach the Top 10 with two singles of his own, 'What's My Name' and 'Gin & Juice,' in the process becoming the first widely recognized gangsta rapper.

'Nuthin' But A "G" Thang' remains the biggest of Dr. Dre's solo hits, although he did guest on BLACKstreet's 1996 chart-topper 'No Diggity' (which he also produced). Since then, Dre has spent most of his career behind the mixing desk, fashioning hits for such hip-hop heavyweights as 2Pac and Eminem, as well as doling out more pop-orientated fare to the likes of Mary J. Blige and Gwen Stefani.

Whoomp! (There It Is)
Tag Team

Released June 1993
Life *79500* (U.S. #2) / Club Tools *SHXCD 1* (U.K. #34)

The Atlanta-bred duo of DC The Brain Supreme and Steve Roll'n are not exactly household names, but their one hit 'Whoomp! (There It Is)' did win the curiously widespread fame enjoyed by other big 1990s novelties such as 'Macarena' and even 'Achy Breaky Heart.' Tag Team's hit was part of the club-driven, hip-hop-wise style of bass that was springing out of both Atlanta and Miami, and manages perfectly to encapsulate the frenetic energy of the genre. DC The Brain Supreme can still be found holding it down as the DJ at various Atlanta-area strip clubs, the very spots where many urban hits are discovered.

Human Behaviour
Björk

Released June 1993
Elektra *66299* (U.S.) / One Little Indian *112* (U.K. #36)

Venus As A Boy
Björk

Released August 1993
Elektra *66273* (U.S.) / One Little Indian *122* (U.K. #29)

'Human Behaviour' and 'Venus As A Boy' launched the solo career of one of the most idiosyncratic talents of the late 20th century. Born and raised in Iceland, Björk had sung in various bands since her teens, most notably The Sugarcubes, who had a U.K. Top 20 hit with the aptly titled 'Hit' in late 1991. Within a year, however, the group's vocalist, nearing the end of her 20s, decided to relocate to London, England, and strike out on her own. There she began working with the cream of the U.K.'s dance music musicians and producers, including keyboardist and programmer Marius De Vries and Soul II Soul founder Nellee Hooper.

The first fruits of their work together was 'Human Behaviour,' a vibrant, up-tempo tune driven by striking, multi-timbral percussion and Björk's cooing vocal and faux-naive lyrics, which according to the singer detail "an animal's point of view on humans." The accompanying promo video was the first of a number of memorable collaborations between Björk and the French director Michel Gondry, and was named Best Breakthrough Promo at the 1994 MTV Awards.

Björk followed 'Human Behaviour' with the similarly exuberant 'Venus As A Boy,' which was the only one of her early singles to feature on the *Greatest Hits* disc of her career-spanning *Family Tree* box set. It's easy to see why – with its sensuous blend of bottle-like percussion sounds, lilting strings, and simple but effective lyrics, 'Venus' has aged much more gracefully than the rest of Björk's early 1990s material and, indeed, the majority of the pop music of the time.

Dreamlover
Mariah Carey

Released August 1993
Columbia *77080* (U.S. #1) / Columbia *6594445* (U.K. #9)

Mariah Carey's summertime ditty borrows familiar melodic elements from 'Genius of Love' by Tom Tom Club. Of the dozens of songs that have sampled that 1982 hit, Carey's 'Dreamlover' remains the Club's favorite. "She must have been quite a little girl when [our] song came out, like eight or ten years old," said Tom Tom Club's Tina Weymouth. "I think it reminds her of a happy time in her life, and what she's done with it is very sweet." Weymouth and fellow Tom Tom Club member/husband Chris Frantz are fond too of Carey's remix, which features a guest rap from the late Ol' Dirty Bastard.

Loser
Beck

Released March 1994
DGC-Bong Load *21930* (U.S. #10) / Geffen *GFS 67* (U.K. #15)

'Loser' was the defining moment in the popularization of lo-fi music and introduced the world to one of the most eclectic, multi-talented performers of the 1990s. Lo-fi is an umbrella term for music recorded using somewhat primitive means but that nonetheless succeeds despite the relatively low production values. Its emergence coincided with the arrival of cheap 4-track tape recorders in the 1980s, which allowed musicians to make recordings at home on a low budget. But it did not filter into the mainstream until the likes of Beck, Pavement, and Elliott Smith began to make waves in the first half of the '90s.

Born in 1970 in Los Angeles, Beck Hansen spent some time within the New York avant-folk East Village coffee-house scene in the late 1980s before returning to the West Coast and making a clutch of one-off singles for various independent labels in the early '90s. One of these was 'Loser,' first recorded for the tiny Bong Load imprint. It was among the earliest of the genre-bending experiments for which he became famous, mixing his love for Delta Blues with a keen admiration for hip-hop, particularly Public Enemy. (Beck went on to make his finest album, *Odelay*, with that legendary group's production team, The Bomb Squad.)

Musically, 'Loser' is remarkably simple, consisting of little more than a looped drumbeat and a couple of dirty, bluesy guitar lines. It was recorded, fittingly, on a 4-track machine by Beck and co-author Carl Stephenson, another musician clearly schooled in the lo-fi aesthetic. The vocal is an ironic half-spoken, half-sung semi-rap about being a social outcast. The mocking tag-line – "I'm a loser baby / So why don't you kill me?" – was a jokey response to the singer's inability to rap like Public Enemy's Chuck D. He can't, of course, but that doesn't limit the appeal of a song that eventually became known as the anthem of a supposed 'slacker generation' – ironic given that the pre-fame Beck worked long, low-paid hours to support his musical endeavors.

The initial 1993 release of 'Loser' by Bong Load had been a small-scale affair and had resulted in little airplay and no chart success. But it did spark a bidding war between major labels. Beck ultimately signed to Geffen, who offered him the freedom to carry on making occasional lower-profile albums for smaller labels. (In fact this only happened once, in 1995, when *One Foot In The Grave* was released by K Records. Beck had intended his 1998 set, *Mutations*, to be given a similarly low-key release, but Geffen intervened, and the label has since taken charge of all the singer's subsequent work.)

The first thing Geffen did after signing Beck in 1994 was to reissue 'Loser,' and with major label money behind it, the single was a memorable, inspirational international hit. Beck has since recorded a number of other highly acclaimed albums and singles, but none will be as fondly remembered as this.

She Don't Use Jelly
The Flaming Lips

Released August 1994
Warner Bros. *218131* (U.S.) / Warner Bros. *W 0246* (U.K.)

'She Don't Use Jelly' was a surprise one-off hit (Number 55 in the U.S.) for one of the few truly original bands of modern times. The Flaming Lips started out from Oklahoma in the mid 1980s as an outré psychedelic act but had mellowed sufficiently to sign a deal with Warners in 1992. Even so, few would have expected this alt-bubblegum curio to reach the charts. An even more surreal touch came as the band rode the crest of their 15-minute fame-wave by performing the song on *Beverly Hills 90210* and receiving the backing of the teen soap's Steve Sanders (played by Ian Ziering), who announced: "I've never been a big fan of alternative music, but these guys rocked!"

Girls And Boys
Blur

Released March 1994
SBK *58115* (U.S.) / Food *47* (U.K. #5)

Parklife
Blur

Released August 1994
Not issued U.S. / Food *53* (U.K. #10)

With these two singles, Blur announced themselves as the leading lights of Britpop, the dominant trend in British music and culture during the mid 1990s. The London-based group's second album, *Modern Life Is Rubbish* (1993), was essentially a template for the bands that followed. Often thought of as a response to grunge, Britpop grouped together a loose affiliation of bands inspired by British guitar-led pop of the 1960s and 1970s.

Blur, however, were always a step ahead of their contemporaries, whose records were often mere carbon copies of The Small Faces, The Beatles, and others. 'Girls And Boys,' the first single from the group's third full-length effort, *Parklife,* has a disco backbeat and funky bassline reminiscent of Blondie and provided by the under-appreciated rhythm section of Dave Rowntree and Alex James. Guitarist Graham Coxon adds spiky, staccato chords, while vocalist Damon Albarn offers the main hook, an infectious, tongue-twisting chorus about "Girls who are boys / Who like boys to be girls …"

'Girls And Boys' was Blur's highest-charting single in the U.K. so far, and gave the group a rare U.S. hit (Number 59), but it was 'Parklife' that confirmed the quartet as the darlings of British music. A joyous faux-cockney romp, it features a guest spoken-word vocal by Phil Daniels, star of the movie version of The Who's *Quadrophenia*. His dulcet tones perfectly compliment Albarn's arch lyric, which includes such gems as: "John's got brewer's droop / He gets intimidated by the dirty pigeons."

Black Hole Sun
Soundgarden

Released August 1994
Not issued U.S. / A&M *5807532* (U.K. #12)

With its spacious, dreamy verses and bruising chorus, 'Black Hole Sun' was one of the finest alternative rock singles of the decade. Because they were from Seattle and making heavy, guitar-based music, Soundgarden were lumped in with grunge, but had actually been in existence for several years before Nirvana, Pearl Jam, and the others

came along. Like the majority of the group's singles, 'Black Hole Sun' – which features on their fourth album, *Superunknown* – was not issued as a physical single in America, but the album cut made Number 24 on *Billboard*'s Airplay chart and was a huge MTV hit.

All I Wanna Do
Sheryl Crow

Released June 1994
A&M *0702* (U.S. #2) / A&M *580842* (U.K. #4)

This breezy, carefree hit, tailor-made for summer afternoons on the open highway, provided the launch-pad for one of the most popular adult-orientated rock acts of the 1990s. Before achieving her chart breakthrough with 'All I Wanna Do,' Sheryl Crow worked as a session singer, most notably touring with Michael Jackson. She sought a record deal of her own but found that the imagination of most major labels extended little further than wanting to turn her into a grown-up Debbie Gibson.

Crow signed to A&M in 1991 and made an aborted first attempt at recording her debut with Police producer Hugh Padgham, whose polished pop sheen was not to her taste. Instead she started working informally with a group of seasoned session musicians, including her boyfriend, Kevin Gilbert, and producer-guitarist Bill Bottrell. These clever creative types named their Tuesday-night musical evenings the *Tuesday Night Music Club*, and gave the same name to the record they recorded together, which became Crow's debut. The album did little business until 'All I Wanna Do' was sent out to radio stations. Carefully driven by lilting slide-guitar and handclaps, the single was – somewhat ironically, given Crow's dismay at the earlier attempts to make her album – much more slick and polished than the rest of *Tuesday Night*. Crow found the lyrics in a book of poetry by Wyn Cooper, who earned an unexpected fortune from the song when it became one of the biggest hits of 1994.

Sabotage
Beastie Boys

Released July 1994
Capitol *58171* (U.S.) / Capitol *CL 716* (U.K. B-side; A #19)

From the fourth album *Ill Communication*, 'Sabotage' wasn't exactly what one would call a runaway chart-topping sensation for the Beastie Boys, that wacky rapping trio of Ad-Rock, MCA, and Mike D who first stormed the world in the late 1980s with drunken antics and clever rhymes. But it has a fond place in the hearts of so many fans because it was a tune that proclaimed in no uncertain terms that the group was not only here to stay, it planned on causing some serious damage as well. The song's power guitar chords and squelchy scratches are perfectly matched by the urgency of the vocal delivery.

The downright silly music video for 'Sabotage' made it an instant favorite on MTV, which aired it as if the Beastie Boys were one of the only bands on the planet. Directed by longtime cohort Spike Jonze (who has worked with artists such as Björk and Fatboy Slim), it parodies 1970s cop dramas like *Chips* and *Starsky & Hutch* with hilarious pomp and circumstance. Handlebar mustaches, loud suits, and spirited chases – it's all there, and then some. Other songs such as 'Sureshot' and 'Get It Together' were consistent enough to keep Beastie Boys fans excited about the album, but 'Sabotage' ultimately provided the rocket-fuel blast to take *Ill Communication* through sales of more than three million copies in the United States alone.

Gin & Juice
Snoop Doggy Dogg

Released February 1994
Death Row *98318* (U.S. #8) / Death Row *A 8316* (U.K. #39)

Regulate
Warren G & Nate Dogg

Released May 1994
Death Row *98280* (U.S. #2) / Death Row *A 8290* (U.K. #5)

These two hip-hop mega-hits are bound together by family ties. Snoop Doggy Dogg was discovered by and worked closely with hip-hop super-producer Dr. Dre, the half brother of Warren G – who launched his own musical career with a collaboration with Snoop's cousin, Nate Dogg. Both singles are rooted in the G-funk sound Dre developed to such striking effect on his own U.S. Number 2 hit 'Nuthin' But A "G" Thang' and the accompanying album, *The Chronic*.

'Gin & Juice' is the second and most memorable of Snoop Doggy Dogg's early hits, which wisely stick closely to the sound of the two Dr. Dre singles on which he had previously appeared, 'Deep Cover' and the 'G Thang.' With 'Gin & Juice,' Dogg was confirmed as one of the most distinctively talented rappers of his generation. His laidback and apparently effortless style seemed somewhat at odds with his image, defined by his complicity in a gang-related shooting the previous year. (Dogg was acquitted, on grounds of self-defense, but related charges hung around him for the next few years.)

Like his half-brother, Warren G is a skilled rapper and producer (although both are more adept at the latter than the former). 'Regulate' is smoother and slicker than the bulk of Dre's work. Similarly, at a time when angry, confrontational gangsta rap was becoming increasingly widespread, the lyrics and delivery here hark back to the gentler themes of early-1980s hip-hop and are complemented neatly by Nate Dogg's soulful vocal delivery.

Bump N' Grind
R. Kelly

Released February 1994
Jive *42207* (U.S. #1) / Jive *368* (U.K. #8)

From the freakily titled album *12 Play* came this breakthrough single from Chicago singer Robert Kelly. He had already made waves as part of the R&B group Public Announcement before striking out with this overtly sexual opus. "I don't see nothing wrong with a little bump'n'grind," he sings suggestively, and neither did the legions of loyal female fans that the song and video netted for Kelly. Given his later troubles with the law relating to charges of child pornography, 'Bump N' Grind' and related songs like 'Downlow' seem all the more ironic with the benefit of hindsight.

The Most Beautiful Girl In The World
The Artist Formerly Known As Prince

Released March 1994
NPG-Bellmark *72514* (U.S. #3) / NPG *60155* (U.K. #1)

With its video evoking the sheer goodness of Mother's Day celebrations, 'Most Beautiful Girl' is a sweet ballad in praise of women that stands in stark innocence when compared to the remarkably unbridled and risqué songs that are liberally sprinkled through Prince's catalog. The song was inspired by Prince's lust for Vanessa Marcil, a gorgeous American actress known primarily for her roles in *General Hospital*, *Melrose Place*, and most recently *Las Vegas*.

Although the song earned Prince his first Number 1 hit in Britain, it is more significant to note 'Beautiful Girl' as a useful marker for his change of name to The Artist Formerly Known As Prince – or simply The Artist, represented by his own proprietary logo, which fused the male and female signs together with a flourish. This infamous shift was a result of Prince's dissatisfaction with his prohibitively long-term recording and publishing contracts at Warner Brothers. It was an upset so profound that he took to writing the word 'slave' on his face in public and comparing his plight to segregationist times. He began to speak of "emancipation from the chains that bind" and ceased promoting earlier work issued under the Prince name. Ironically, his publishing contract with Warner-Chappell expired on December 31, 1999, giving the Artist his name back and, no doubt, the urge to party like it's 1999.

7 Seconds
Youssou N'Dour Featuring Neneh Cherry

Released June 1994
Sony *77482* (U.S.) / Columbia *660508* (U.K. #3)

The combination of washed-up female rapper and Afrobeat star doesn't sound promising on paper, but when Senegalese singer Youssou N'Dour teamed with Neneh Cherry for this ambient trip-hop composition, the world stopped to listen. For '7 Seconds' they took a Bach-originated descending bassline, smothered it in a nice warm synth-wash, and added alternating vocals for the verse before a dramatic drop to the chorus line – so simple it had to be a hit.

'7 Seconds' equalled Cherry's highest ever chart placing in the U.K., although she bettered it early the following year when she appeared on the British Number 1 charity single 'Love Can Build A Bridge' alongside Eric Clapton and The Pretenders' Chrissie Hynde. She had a further U.K. Top 10 hit in 1996 with 'Woman,' which evoked '7 Seconds' in its use of a similar descending chord progression. N'Dour, meanwhile, never troubled the charts again, but continues to make records, and maintains a devoted following across Europe and Africa.

Love Is All Around
Wet Wet Wet

Released May 1994
London *856194* (U.S.) / Precious *JWL 23* (U.K. #1)

Rock observers had been waiting for years for some canny pop chancers to update the excellent 1967 Troggs hit 'Love Is All Around' and knew that when it came it would hit big. But no one could have predicted the impact in Britain of Wet Wet Wet's sickly-sweet version of Reg Presley's cheery tune, assisted by the *Four Weddings And A Funeral* soundtrack on which it appeared. The song went on to become the longest-reigning Number 1 single in the U.K., notching up no fewer than 15 weeks at the top (although it made only Number 41 in America). Pellow and his pals deserved the success: they added a cunning orchestration and an upgraded vocal melody on the last chorus, adding up to a big improvement on the original.

Kiss From A Rose
Seal

Released July 1994
ZTT-Sire *17896* (U.S. #1) / ZTT *ZANG 52* (U.K. #4)

After the runaway success of Seal's first self-titled album in 1991, expectations were high for the follow-up. When it arrived – another eponymous set – 'Kiss From A Rose' was an immediate high point, even if the rest of the album struggled to match up.

It's clever stuff. Although 'Kiss From A Rose' masquerades quite efficiently as a mere lover's ballad from start to finish, Seal throws in every sub-Bacharach & David trick he can think of to make it fly. For starters, there's that lovely clarinet theme; then he opens each chorus with a highly hummable wail of "Bay-bee!" that covers close to an octave in a word; then for good measure he throws in a vocal round composed of multiple croons of "I've been kissed by a rose". The man has obviously studied the fine art of songwriting, and is a master musician too.

Surprisingly, 'Kiss From A Rose' was only a minor hit in the U.K. on its initial release in 1994, and was not issued at all in the U.S. at the time. Then, the following summer, it was used on the soundtrack to *Batman Forever*, its glittering production well matched by the movie's glossy look, and gained a new lease of life on both sides of the Atlantic. Seal's slick music fell out of vogue shortly afterwards, but songs such as this remain among the finest singer-songwriter records of the decade.

Here Comes The Hotstepper
Ini Kamoze

Released October 1994
Columbia *77614* (U.S. #1) / Columbia *6610472* (U.K. #4)

Ini Kamoze (born Cecil Campbell) remains one of the few Jamaican dancehall acts to make an impact on the charts in America and Britain. Disco aficionados recognized the instrumental in 'Hotstepper' as that of 'Heartbeat' by Taana Gardner, a song released in 1981 through New York's West End Records. Unfortunately, Kamoze was about a decade too early to fully capitalize on the dancehall craze that later hit America hard, thanks to artists such as Sean Paul and Elephant Man. Instead, he brought a brief flash of island fire to transatlantic airwaves with this international smash – and was never heard from again.

Back For Good
Take That

Released April 1995
Arista *12848* (U.S. #7) / RCA *1271462* (U.K. #1)

"I wrote 'Back For Good' in 10 minutes," grinned Take That songwriter Gary Barlow after the song became a gigantic success. He might well grin: the tune used the same ascending chord sequence as a stack of other hits. Cleverly, he used the same chords in the verse and the chorus but separated the two with a simple bridge, adding a standard middle-eight. The only other touch of sophistication was the alternating lead and backing vocals, which flipped around for the outro. So that's how to write a hit.

Barlow and his crew (Jason Orange, Howard Donald, Mark Owen, and some show-off kid called Robbie Williams) are still the supreme boy-band in Britain, following their 2005 comeback, even as the genre passes its first decade in business. Among the first of the newer breed of deliberately manufactured pop acts, Take That manage to retain some credibility by writing many of their own hits and possessing genuine vocal talent. And they launched Williams's phenomenally successful solo career.

Only the Irish quintets Boyzone and Westlife came close to unseating Take That from their British throne, although innumerable acts such as East 17 have tried and failed to do so. This is because Take That have the songs, no matter how anodyne the delivery or ludicrous the dance routines – a lesson that wannabe boy-bands should note. 'Back For Good,' although it's cheesier than a bowl of Parmesan, and is the group's only U.S. hit, is the gold standard that the kids and their managers should aim for.

Buddy Holly
Weezer

Released April 1995
Not issued U.S. / Geffen *GFS 88* (U.K. #12)

"Oo-wee-oo, I look just like Buddy Holly / Oh-oh, and you're Mary Tyler Moore," warbled Weezer singer Rivers Cuomo in the L.A. quartet's breakthrough single, 'Buddy Holly,' an entertaining mish-mash of influences that would inspire a whole raft of nerdy oh-so-ironic alternative-rock bands (There was no physical single in the U.S., but the album cut made Number 18 on *Billboard*'s Airplay chart.)

It was probably the extremely popular video that was responsible for the band's subsequent rise to a respectable B-league status in alt.rock. Thanks to the magic of movie technology, Weezer were superimposed onto the stage of Arnolds, the diner in the old *Happy Days* sitcom. Cuomo and band walked through the song dressed in the 1950s preppie wear that characters such as the young Ron Howard had worn in the original series – in other words, they looked like geeks of the highest order.

The song was inspired by the band's incessant comments about Cuomo's then-girlfriend, a highly eccentric Korean, hence the line "Your tongue is twisted, your eyes are slit." It became something of a teen anthem, helped by the resolution to a payoff line: "I don't care what they say about us anyway." The evolving emo generation bought into the song with enthusiasm, responding in droves to the 'geeks rule' ethos and Weezer's tongue-in-cheek approach. Thousands even bought a pair of horn-rimmed glasses – as it happened, the one essential nerd accessory that Cuomo didn't use in the 'Buddy Holly' video. Is that ironic irony, or irony squared? Either way, Weezer are responsible for a lot, even if their career never again rose to these same heights.

Free As A Bird
The Beatles

Released December 1995
Apple *58497* (U.S. #6) / Apple *R 6422* (U.K. #2)

'Free As A Bird' was built around an opaque demo vocal from the 15-years-late John Lennon and was The Threetles' sort-of-comeback single, issued to tie in with the start of the remarkable *Anthology* compilation albums and TV series. Lennon's vocal sounded disappointingly weak and thin – an inevitable result of the passage of time and the condition of the pre-digital tapes – and doubly so in comparison with that of Paul McCartney, who chipped in on the middle section and elsewhere. But the production was fat, warm, and organic, with Ringo's drum sound right on the money, Macca's bass as huggable as always (and he didn't overdo the fills), and George's guitar as ever a thing of beauty, especially the masterful slide intro.

What of the song itself? The structure was based on a descending chord sequence straight out of Beatles cliché, but worked well enough and could have come from any of a dozen 1960s bands with a knack for a semi-classical progression. The sentiments that 'Free As A Bird' expressed were more or less contained in the title. But this was that unique thing – at least until the follow-up single 'Real Love' came along – *a new song by The Beatles*. Very few people were going to argue with that. And in case anyone wasn't sure, they stuck a fade-out on the end that could have come straight off *Revolver*. You half expected McCartney to mutter "cranberry sauce" two octaves too low.

Alright
Supergrass

Released July 1995
Capitol *82277* (U.S.) / Parlophone *R 6413* (U.K. #2)

As Britpop flourished and grunge waned, the cheekiest of the cheeky new British bands was Supergrass, who seemed to leap straight out of the radio, simultaneously warm and dated like the 1970s and new and glistening like the '90s. Kicking off with a wonky piano break and adding a melodic bass lick, the song bounded along like an overenthusiastic puppy, weaseling its way into everyone's psyche and making Supergrass, three scamps from Oxford, into willing stars. In due course all this cheeky-chappy foolishness began to wear thin and the band adopted a more grown-up approach, but 'Alright' remains a prime early candidate for 'grass greatness.

Common People
Pulp

Released May 1995
Island *7138* (U.S.) / Island *CID 613* (U.K. #2)

The Britpop years may have been dominated by Blur and Oasis, but the era's finest single came from Pulp. A nerdy anti-hero in the Buddy Holly mold, Jarvis Cocker formed Pulp in 1981 but didn't achieve anything approaching success for over a decade. That finally changed with 'Common People,' his amusing almost-true story of a snooty Greek art student who couldn't quite bring herself to rough it. Pitched somewhere between krautrock and glam-pop, the single became an instant classic in the U.K. but did little business elsewhere. It was given a bizarre new reading in 2004 when it was covered by *Star Trek*'s William Shatner.

Wonderwall
Oasis

Released October 1995
Epic *78216* (U.S. #8) / Creation *CRE 215* (U.K. #2)

Love 'em or hate 'em, Oasis were the biggest British group of the 1990s, and their 'Wonderwall' one of the decade's defining singles. Led by the irrepressible Gallagher brothers – vocalist Liam and songwriter-guitarist Noel – Oasis came bursting out of Manchester in 1994 with the U.K.'s fastest-selling debut album ever, *Definitely Maybe*, which drew on the best bits of the past three decades of British music: The Beatles, T. Rex, The Sex Pistols, etc.

The following year the group became embroiled in a high-profile, press-orchestrated feud that pitched the five working class lads from the industrial north of England against Blur, four former art students from down south. The rivalry reached its peak in August when both issued new singles on the same day: and Blur's chirpy 'Country House' beat Oasis's tepid 'Roll With It' to Number 1.

Had Oasis chosen to release this instead, Blur might not have been so lucky. Taking its name from the 1968 film of the same name, which featured a soundtrack by George Harrison, 'Wonderwall' is one of the finest and most elegant songs in the Noel Gallagher songbook, and features one of his younger brother's strongest and most affecting vocal performances. Eight other Oasis singles have gone one better on the U.K. chart – including 'Don't Look Back In Anger' (1996) and 'All Around The World' (1998) – but this remains the group's defining moment. It has become a regular fixture on British polls to find the greatest singles of all time and is the band's only significant U.S. hit to date.

Don't Stop (Wiggle Wiggle)
The Outhere Brothers

Released February 1995
Aureus *AU1200-1* (U.S.) / Eternal *YZ 917* (U.K. #1)

This year, concern about obscene lyrics on rap and heavy-rock records resulted in potentially offensive releases being stickered with parental advisory warnings. Unexpectedly, sales went up, because we now knew which records were cool without having to listen to them first.

Perhaps worried that their single might not get stickered, foul-mouthed Chicago rap duo The Outhere Brothers made the parental warning an integral part of their single's cover design. 'Don't Stop' zoomed to Number 1 in the U.K., but it wasn't until the equally naughty follow-up, 'Boom Boom Boom,' had spent four weeks at Number 1 that the authorities finally noticed and banned it, which of course enhanced sales still further.

Scatman (Ski-Ba-Bop-Ba-Dop-Bop)
Scatman John

Released May 1995
RCA *64379* (U.S.) / RCA *281712* (U.K. #3)

Surely the combination of jazz scatting and house-trance could never work? That's what many thought in horror as 'Scatman (Ski-Bap-Bop-Ba-Dop-Bop)' ascended the British charts in 1995. But it did work, with Scatman John – an American, John Paul Larkin, who had learned to scat to overcome a stutter – doing his rapid-fire thing over a euphoric house groove that in fact worked rather well on the dancefloor. The rapped verses were nothing special and the song grated after a couple of listens, but if you were 13 years old it probably sounded like the best thing ever recorded. Larkin didn't have long to enjoy his newfound fame, succumbing to lung cancer in 1999.

Waterfalls
TLC

Released June 1995
LaFace *24107* (U.S. #1) / LaFace *298812* (U.K. #4)

From the blockbuster album *CrazySexyCool*, which spawned multiple hits and has sold over ten million copies in America, this is considered by many fans to be the signature song from Tionne 'T-Boz' Watkins, Lisa 'Left Eye' Lopes, and Rozonda 'Chilli' Thomas, the R&B supernova known as TLC. Although the life of the Atlanta-bred outfit was cut short with Left Eye's tragic death in a car accident in Honduras in 2002, TLC are one of the most successful female groups of all time.

Most of their songs tended towards the lighter and funkier side, but 'Waterfalls' is a cautionary tale ("Don't go chasing waterfalls / Please stick to the rivers and the lakes that you're used to"), ushering in new respect as the group proved they could bring substance to their songs. The memorable video features computer-generated sequences of the ladies dancing on water as various characters are shown traveling the wrong paths, leading to destruction and untimely ends.

'Waterfalls' was nominated for two Grammys and helped TLC take home the award for Best R&B Album for *CrazySexyCool*. The song was produced by Organized Noize (Patrick 'Sleepy' Brown, Ray Murray, and Rico Wade), the studio wizards credited for nurturing and developing the career of another wildly successful group, Atlanta hip-hop duo OutKast. In fact, it was TLC who gave OutKast their first visible guest appearance in the early 1990s thanks to the remix of the TLC single 'What About Your Friends.'

I Got 5 On It
Luniz

Released June 1995
Noo Trybe *38474* (U.S. #8) / Virgin America *VUSCD 101* (U.K. #3)

The San Francisco Bay Area has been a fertile ground for hip-hop music of all flavors, but this ode to smoking marijuana has transcended local fame while remaining a homegrown staple. Oakland's Luniz (Yukmouth and Numskull) twisted up their original version, which features a hook from R&B singer Michael Marshall, and made a remix, legendary for its inclusion of top Bay Area rap stars Shock G, E-40, Spice 1, Dru Down, and Richie Rich, all together on one track. There was U.S. Top 40 success for the original (Number 8) as well as the remix (Number 28).

I Wish
Skee-Lo

Released July 1995
Sunshine *78032* (U.S. #13) / Wild Card *5777752* (U.K. #15)

Rappers by nature are usually much more boastful than shy, but not Skee-Lo (a.k.a. Antoine Roundtree). His sole U.S. hit 'I Wish' is quite possibly the most unegotistical tune ever to have been set to a hip-hop beat. Over a multi-layered pastiche of clever samples and a patented West Coast bounce, he rhymes: "I wish I was a little bit taller / I wish I was a baller / I wish I had a girl who looked good / I would call her." The song was pervasive enough to earn the album of the same name a Grammy nomination for Best Rap Album.

One Of Us
Joan Osborne

Released December 1995
Mercury *852368* (U.S. #4) / Blue Gorilla *JOACD 1* (U.K. #6)

Once in a blue moon, pop music's perennial concerns about love, intoxication, and dancing in the moonlight are briefly joined by a one-off hit single that seems to swim in deeper waters. 'One Of Us,' written by Eric Bazilian of The Hooters, was that record for this year.

Osborne, very much in the prevailing mode of Alanis Morissette and Sheryl Crow, invited us to ponder how it might be "if God was one of us … just a stranger on a bus." The single went gold, the accompanying album, *Relish*, went triple platinum, and Prince described it as "a great melody and an important statement." What more can you ask?

Gangsta's Paradise
Coolio Featuring L.V.

Released August 1995
MCA Soundtracks *55104* (U.S. #1) / Tommy Boy *MCSTD 2104* (U.K. #1)

What could actress Jodie Foster and music legend Stevie Wonder possibly have to do with a West Coast gangsta rap song? Plenty, for hip-hop artist Coolio (a.k.a. Artis Ivey) and L.V. (a wheelchair-using R&B singer) recorded this song for the soundtrack of *Dangerous Minds* (a movie starring Foster as a teacher at a troubled school), basing it on Wonder's 'Pastime Paradise.' Coolio had worked the same trick a year earlier on 'Fantastic Voyage,' which drew on The Ohio Players' song of the same name and hit Number 3 on *Billboard*.

'Gangsta's Paradise' earned Coolio a Grammy for Best Rap Solo Performance and topped the charts on both sides of the Atlantic, making it the U.K.'s first gangsta rap chart-topper and the first hip-hop single to sell over a million copies there. Like many big hits before – among them 'Beat It' by Michael Jackson and Nirvana's 'Smells Like Teen Spirit' – the most successful single of Coolio's career received the dubious honor of being parodied by Weird Al Yankovich, who re-titled the song 'Amish Paradise.'

You Are Not Alone
Michael Jackson

Released August 1995
Epic *78002* (U.S. #1) / Epic *662 3102* (U.K. #1)

Scream
Michael Jackson & Janet Jackson

Released June 1995
Epic *78000* (U.S. #5) / Epic *662 0222* (U.K. #3)

Constant controversy was still a staple of Michael Jackson's diet by 1995, even if he felt he hadn't done much to heat up the oven. Written by R&B crooner R. Kelly, 'You Are Not Alone' is mainly remembered for its accompanying visuals. At the time Jackson was married to Lisa Marie Presley, daughter of Elvis, and the video is an awkward physical display – semi-nude – of a relationship that continues to puzzle the general public. Many commented on how Jackson's skin tone appears almost as milky white as his wife's.

The 1989 single 'Leave Me Alone' had been Jackson's first overt attack on the paparazzi and media that feasted on all the truths and half-truths of his life, which at that time included stories like buying the bones of the Elephant Man and sleeping in a hyperbaric chamber. With the help of sister Janet, 'Scream' revisits the same topic in much more confrontational form ("Just stop pressuring me / Makes me want to scream").

'Scream' was produced by Jimmy 'Jam' Harris and Terry Lewis, the Minneapolis duo who had groomed Janet for international superstardom with her 1986 album *Control*. Where the animated video for 'Leave Me Alone' softened the message of the song with its cuteness, the black-and-white flick for 'Scream' featured the Jackson siblings scowling and executing aggressive choreography. It reportedly cost $7 million to film – a price which, more than a decade on, still seems staggering and extravagant. To put it into perspective, Michael Jackson's breakthrough video for 'Thriller' cost a mere $800,000.

Missing (remix)
Everything But The Girl

Released October 1995
Atlantic *87124* (U.S. #2) / Blanco y Negro *NEG 84CD* (U.K. #3)

DJs and remixers have been responsible for giving previously unseen success to some unlikely artists through dancefloor hits. Such is the case with the U.K.'s Everything But The Girl (partners Tracey Thorn and Ben Watt). No one would have expected the mellow twosome to craft songs for dance parties, but the band's only American hit was a club-friendly take on EBTG's original acoustic song 'Missing,' souped up with a lively beat by New York house music legend Todd Terry. Watt later turned much of his attention to DJing, starting a British club night called Lazy Dog and touring all over the world.

One Sweet Day
Mariah Carey & Boyz II Men

Released November 1995
Columbia *78074* (U.S. #1) / Columbia *6626035* (U.K. #6)

Judged on musical content alone, 'One Sweet Day' doesn't sound like a particularly remarkable single, but this duet by two of the hottest R&B acts of the decade holds the record for the longest stint at the top of the *Billboard* Hot 100.

The song itself was borne out of tragedy. In January 1995, David Cole, one half of C&C Music Factory and a close friend and frequent collaborator of Carey's, died following an unspecified illness. At the same time as Carey's grief began to blossom into a song, Boyz II Men were working on a musical tribute to their murdered road manager, Khalil Roundtree. On hearing that they were both working on similar efforts, the two acts decided to pool their resources, resulting in this collaborative effort.

'One Sweet Day' shot straight in at Number 1 on the U.S. charts and remained there for a total of 16 weeks. Neither act was a stranger to long stays at the top: Boyz II Men had twice held the same record, with 'End Of The Road' (13 weeks) and 'I'll Make Love To You' (14 weeks); two of Carey's previous singles, 'Dreamlover' and 'Fantasy,' had sat at the top of the pile for eight weeks each. 'One Sweet Day' was up for Record Of The Year and Best Pop Collaboration (With Vocals) at the 1996 Grammy Awards, bringing Carey's total nominations for the year to six. She left empty-handed, however, but not before she had made her humiliation very clear, and declined to attend another Grammy event until 2006.

Spaceman
Babylon Zoo

Released January 1996
EMI *10485* (U.S.) / EMI *CDEM 416* (U.K. #1)

Boosted by its use in a TV ad for Levi's jeans, 'Spaceman' was the kind of one-hit-wonder single that polarizes opinion. Babylon Zoo singer Jas Mann, a sort of proto-Marilyn Manson, had the right look, a killer PR campaign, and a fairly decent song in 'Spaceman.' But the decision to switch the song mid-way through from sub-Depeche Mode miserabilia to shrieking, warp-speed fast-forward gimmickry provoked delight and disdain in equal measure. The double-speed section of the song was in fact not part of the original, but was taken from a remix by the legendary American DJ and record producer Arthur Baker.

Firestarter
The Prodigy

Released March 1996
Maverick *17387* (U.S. #30) / XL *70CD* (U.K. #1)

Born Slippy
Underworld
Released July 1996
TVT *8731* (U.S.) / Junior Boy's Own *JBO 44CDS* (U.K. #2)

Setting Sun
Chemical Brothers
Released October 1996
Astralwerks *6176* (U.S.) / Freestyle Dust-Virgin *CHEMSD 4* (U.K. #1)

For a brief period, as the Britpop scene began to implode in a cocaine fog, British music was dominated by electronic acts, who at one point even threatened to break into the U.S. mainstream. The biggest of these was The Prodigy, whose harsh but hook-laden techno hits had made regular appearances on the U.K. chart since the early 1990s.

On 'Firestarter,' the group's former concert dancer Keith Flint takes center stage, delivering a John Lydon-style rant about his not-so-latent pyromania, over a barrage of ferocious beats and distorted guitar samples. The accompanying promo video, set on a disused London Underground line, drew countless complaints, but that did nothing to halt the single's unstoppable rise to the top of the U.K. chart. The similarly menacing 'Breathe' repeated the feat, while the subsequent Prodigy album, *The Fat Of The Land*, was a transatlantic Number 1.

Several months after 'Firestarter' came the definitive hit by the more cerebral techno trio Underworld. The group had existed in various forms since 1983 but was thrust into the mainstream when 'Born Slippy' – an infectious blend of freeform vocals, delayed piano chords, and frenetic programmed rhythms – was featured on the soundtrack to the cult hit movie *Trainspotting*. The Chemical Brothers, meanwhile, were the kings of big beat, an upbeat strand of electronica. 'Setting Sun' featured a guest vocal by Oasis's Noel Gallagher, giving him a second U.K. Number 1 hit of 1996 (and U.S. Number 80) following his own group's 'Don't Look Back In Anger.'

Ironic
Alanis Morissette

Released March 1996
Maverick-Sire *17698* (U.S. #4) / Maverick *W 0343CD* (U.K. #11)

While Alanis Morissette doesn't appear to understand the titular concept of her biggest hit – "rain on your wedding day" might be irritating, but there's nothing explicitly ironic about it – she certainly knows her way around a radio-friendly pop chorus. The success of this single – and its follow-up, 'You Learn' – helped make her *Jagged Little Pill* the biggest-selling debut album of all time. (She had made an earlier dance-pop record as a teenager but that sold only in her native Canada.)

Morissette first caught the attention of rock audiences in summer 1995 with the release of the furious, vengeful 'You Oughta Know.' The song's lyric became the cause of much speculation when it was revealed to be about the lecherous, manipulative behavior of an unnamed music-industry figure. The singer has never revealed his identity, aside from whispering it to Larry David in an episode of *Curb Your Enthusiasm*.

Impressive as 'You Oughta Know' was, Morissette needed something gentler and more melodic to facilitate her mainstream breakthrough. 'Ironic' was just the ticket, and its jangly guitars and angsty – but not too angsty – vocals became a regular fixture on rock and pop radio stations throughout the spring and summer of 1996. With this proper smash hit in the bag, Morissette cemented her position on the crest of the wave of female alternative rock performers – Tori Amos, Jewel, Joan Osborne, and the rest – who flooded the market during the mid 1990s.

Macarena
Los Del Rio

Released May 1996
RCA *64407* (U.S. #1) / RCA *1345372* (U.K. #2)

'Macarena' sees an obscure Spanish song gets reworked into an international dance smash. One of the biggest novelty hits of all time, the Latin song introduces the world's easiest and most inane dance. Its sheer simplicity helped catapult the song into worldwide domination, with a shelf life far longer than it deserved (it charted for well over a year in some countries). The unlikely hit stayed in the Number 1 spot in America for 14 weeks, a feat achieved by very few artists, among them the mighty Elvis Presley.

Wannabe
The Spice Girls

Released July 1996
Virgin 38579 (U.S. #1) / Virgin VSCDX 1588 (U.K. #1)

The Spice Girls' remarkable debut and instant signature song 'Wannabe' was put together by Richard Stannard and Matt Rowe, a successful songwriting team. The duo had written three hits for East 17, the British boy-band of the moment, and agreed to work with the five-woman vocal group after seeing a showcase performance they gave late in 1994.

The Girls' claims of self-determination went too far when publicists insisted that the group – none of whom played musical instruments – wrote all of the lyrics and most of the music for their records, which is clearly untrue. Certainly it's unlikely that, despite the formal credits, they co-wrote 'Wannabe,' but their personalities and outlook can surely be discerned in the lyric and sentiment of this, the second song that Stannard and Rowe devised for the Girls. (The first, 'Feed Your Love,' was ultimately rejected as too raunchy for their intended audience.)

Rowe set up a drum loop, and its strutting nature reminded him of 'You're The One That I Want' from the movie Grease, which in turn led to a song with a certain feistiness. It's hard not to imagine the composers bombarded with ideas by their eager charges among the song's tidal wave of catchphrases and sarcastic remarks. A few hard-rock guitar riffs and the most inane euphemism ever devised for sexual congress, "Zig-a-zig-ahh," completed the ridiculously catchy and quotable anthem.

The song's key phrase is "If you wanna be my lover / You gotta get with my friends," a declaration that no man will come between the girls and their female mates. It's easy to mock The Spice Girls' toytown feminism manifested in that line and in their slogan Girl Power (appropriated from now-forgotten girl duo Shampoo). British journalist Julie Burchill pointed out that a predilection for wearing skimpy outfits is a freedom that men have never tried to deny women.

But the group struck a chord with (largely pre-pubescent) women around the world – and apparently with many others. For a while, everyone seemed to go Spice Girls mad. They had five U.S. Top 10 hits. In Britain, the only one of their ten singles that didn't make Number 1 ('Stop') got to the second spot.

Many people were troubled by the group because they pretended to be something they were not. They were not the significant talents they claimed or any sort of liberationists, but a classic bubblegum pop band, ciphers who by hard work, physical attractiveness, and engaging personalities sold the art of their highly-skilled backroom boys with massive success. Just like proto bubblegum band The Monkees, it may take the space of a generation for those who resent the fraudulence of The Spice Girls to forget that baggage and recognize their records as pop of the highest quality.

Lovefool
The Cardigans

Released September 1996
Not issued U.S. / Stockholm 5710502 (U.K. #2)

Abba proved that Swedish pop could capture the fickle hearts of an international audience and put them in a trance, and this was reinforced by the success of The Cardigans' single 'Lovefool.' It is filled with the irresistible coos of lead singer Nina Persson, then a delicate blonde with limitless sex-symbol appeal singing "Love me, love me." The song made a memorable addition to the soundtrack of Baz Luhrmann's Romeo + Juliet, with Clare Danes and Leonardo DiCaprio as the star-crossed lovers. ('Lovefool' made Number 2 as an album cut on the U.S. airplay chart but wasn't a single.)

California Love
2Pac Featuring Dr. Dre And Roger Troutman

Released April 1996
Death Row *854652* (U.S. #6) / Death Row *DRWCD 3* (U.K. #6)

No Diggity
BlackSTREET Featuring Dr. Dre

Released October 1996
Interscope *97007* (U.S. #1) / Interscope *IND 95003* (U.K. #9)

By 1996 it looked possible that the promising career trajectories of producers Teddy Riley and Dr. Dre had already reached their peaks. Riley (of Virginia Beach, VA) had been known as the father of new jack swing, a streetwise brand of R&B. It was best represented by his protégé Bobby Brown, a former singer from New Edition who hit the multi-platinum jackpot with the Riley-produced album *Don't Be Cruel* (1990). And Dr. Dre (Andre Young) had been known as the hip-hop producer with the Midas touch, first in bringing his group NWA to the forefront and then doing the same with rapper Snoop Doggy Dogg. But now their hits failed to flow so freely as they had in the past.

'No Diggity' and 'California Love' changed all that, putting both back into the pop spotlight. Riley's R&B group BlackSTREET performed 'No Diggity' with all the swagger of street rappers, which proved successful when combined with guest hip-hop verses from Dre and female MC Queen Pen. The song went on to win a Grammy for Best R&B Performance By A Duo Or Group.

Meanwhile, Dre had a special song cooked up to celebrate the release from prison of controversial rapper Tupac Shakur (a.k.a. 2Pac), in collaboration with Dre himself and Roger Troutman, the funkily vocoder'd frontman of Zapp. 'California Love' remains one of the best-loved songs from 2Pac and was unfortunately one of his last hits. The rapper died tragically in September 1996 after being shot in Las Vegas.

DON'T FORGET ABOUT DRE

Simply put, Dr. Dre is the platinum standard in hip-hop, the pinnacle of success that millions dream of yet never achieve. His songwriting virtuosity, which samples and draws from soul, rock, and funk in equal measures, parallels the skills of some of the greatest writers in music, and has won him accolades from just about every corner of the music industry, including the Grammys, which named him Producer Of The Year in 2000. Those unfamiliar with this titan of urban sounds may draw an easy analogy: Dr. Dre is the Quincy Jones of hip-hop, setting trends and staying ahead of the curve at all times.

After forming the controversial gangster-rap supergroup NWA (it stands for the incendiary Niggaz With Attitude) with Ice Cube, Eazy E, MC Ren, and Yella, he left to become an accomplished solo star in his own right with one of the most celebrated hip-hop albums, *The Chronic* (1992). He is also known for nurturing and developing the careers of some of pop music's brightest modern stars, including Snoop Dogg, Tupac Shakur, Eminem, and 50 Cent, whose work is indelibly associated with Dre's magic. Dre's ever-evolving sound, rooted in George Clinton's messy funk and given a spicy twist all his own, is easily the most emulated and the most ripped-off in the history of the genre.

The man born Andre Young began his musical career when he DJ'd in his hometown of Compton, in the rough South Central portion of Los

Angeles, peddling mixtapes at flea markets and swap meets. He went on to regional success with his first two groups, the World Class Wrecking Cru and, later, NWA. The P-Funk flavored hits of *The Chronic* such as 'Nuthin' But a "G" Thang' and 'Let Me Ride' were anthems that put Dre in the public eye through constant video, radio, and club rotation. But Dre seemed only too happy to retreat from the solo spotlight to focus all his energies into the studio as he crafted the careers of others.

His first major artist was Snoop Dogg (born Cordozar 'Calvin' Broadus), a young rapper introduced to Dre by his own stepbrother Warren G (Warren Griffin III), who was in a group called 213 with Snoop. Their perfect chemistry began right from the start, when Snoop and Dre recorded Dre's debut solo single 'Deep Cover' on the first day they worked together. Dre's perfectionist approach and ear for talent would allow him to repeat this feat again with both Eminem and 50 Cent.

Some of Dre's most promising studio assistants and protégés have gone on to lucrative careers of their own – including Scott Storch, the man behind hits for artists such as Beyoncé, Lil Kim, and Fat Joe. Meanwhile, Dre's Aftermath label, which he established after famously leaving Suge Knight's Death Row Records, continues to dictate industry standards in hip-hop with such popular artists as Busta Rhymes and The Game.

Virtual Insanity
Jamiroquai

Released August 1996
Sony *OSK 0857* (U.S.) / Sony *S2 663613* (U.K. #3)

British group Jamiroquai were long reviled as lukewarm poster-boys for those members of the Gap generation who found acid jazz too funky. But the group at last found their commercial and critical groove with 'Virtual Insanity,' a nifty bit of coffee-table fatback with a nod to Stevie Wonder that everyone could enjoy. Sucked in by that stop-start line, "Future … feels like … virtual insanity," plus a dose of strings and, of course, Stuart Zender's unparalleled bass playing, millions endorsed mouthy little Jay Kay's band and elevated them to the super-league. The award-winning video and Kay's enviably cool dancing helped, of course, and a career in modern funk was assured.

Un-Break My Heart
Toni Braxton

Released October 1996
LaFace *24200* (U.S. #1) / LaFace *1410632* (U.K. #2)

Gorgeous singer Toni Braxton commanded the American pop charts for 11 weeks with this Number 1 hit ballad. Penned by Diane Warren, whose songs have been recorded by everyone from Natalie Cole to Kiss, 'Un-Break My Heart' is both poignant and hopeful. The song helped to bring multi-platinum honors to Braxton's second album, *Secrets*. Unfortunately, less secret was the fact that within two years of this triumph, Braxton would file for bankruptcy. But ten years later she became a star on Broadway who maintained a reasonably successful position in R&B.

I Believe I Can Fly
R. Kelly

Released December 1996
Jive *42422* (U.S. #2) / Jive *JIVECD 415* (U.K. #1)

Most would agree that rabbits can't take flight, but please don't tell that to the veteran cartoon character Bugs Bunny, who believes not only that he could fly, but that he could touch the sky. One of the dear hare's favorite songs must be 'I Believe I Can Fly,' the theme song to *Space Jam*, a movie starring Bugs and basketball megastar Michael Jordan (among other *Looney Tunes* and NBA icons). While Jordan battles to regain his prodigious talent – which has been taken by Bugs and friends – there's an epic song of empowerment guiding him along to victory over his awfully cute alien abductors.

This inspirational ode to positive achievement from Chicago-born singer-songwriter Robert Kelly stands apart from the bulk of his musical catalog, which is laden with an abundance of sexual innuendo. Despite his certain specialty, the prolific Kelly does have a proven talent for writing sports-oriented songs. He would later provide 'The World's Greatest,' a theme to go along with the movie *Ali*, about boxer Muhammad Ali.

The song netted three Grammy Awards (Best R&B Song, Best Original Song From A Soundtrack, and Best R&B Male Vocal Performance). The impeccably rowdy cover band Me First & The Gimme Gimmes (best known for their 'Somewhere Over the Rainbow' theme song for HBO's *Taxicab Confessions*) later tackled 'I Believe I Can Fly' in their own inimitable style, transforming a ballad to something far more visceral.

Killing Me Softly
Fugees

Released June 1996
Not issued U.S. / Columbia-Ruffhouse *663343* (U.K. #1)

The Fugees offered a welcome alternative to the trend among 1990s hip-hop acts for tales of drug runnin', gun totin' gangstas. This, their most memorable single release, was a heartfelt modernization of Roberta Flack's soulful 1973 chart-topper 'Killing Me Softly With His Song.' The Fugees' version is dominated by Lauryn Hill's powerful, emotive vocal delivery, underpinned by subtle instrumentation and augmented by the occasional encouragement – "One time!" – from her fellow Fugees, Pras Michel, and Wyclef Jean.

Michel and Jean, both Haitian immigrants, formed the group with Hill in her native East Orange, New Jersey, in the early 1990s. The trio made its recorded debut in 1994 with *Blunted On Reality*, an album that set socially conscious lyrics against jazz and reggae-inflected music. It didn't sell well, but was followed two years later by the *Billboard* chart-topper, *The Score*. 'Killing Me Softly' was one of four international hits drawn from the album (although some, like 'Killing Me,' were U.S. airplay hits and not physical singles); the others were the upbeat calling card 'Fu-Gee-La,' the darker 'Ready Or Not,' and a cover of Bob Marley's 'No Woman, No Cry.'

Back in 1996, just as 'Killing Me Softly' started to take over the airwaves, Lauryn Hill's voice was the key ingredient of another notable hip-hop R&B hit, 'If I Ruled The World' by Nas. Since the release of his 1994 debut, *Illmatic*, Nas has been one of the prominent figures in the rap world, chalking up a number of hit singles and albums. He is perhaps most famous for a heated public feud with Jay-Z, although the pair had reconciled their differences by 2005, and at the time of writing were rumored to be working on a collaborative album.

Meanwhile, with the world seemingly at their feet, the Fugees had in fact drifted apart within a year of the release of 'Killing Me Softly.' The trio spent the best part of a decade working on solo projects to varying levels of critical and commercial success before reuniting in 2005 for the so-so 'Take It Easy.'

I'll Be Missing You
Puff Daddy & Faith Evans Featuring 112

Released June 1997
Bad Boy *79097* (U.S. #1) / Puff Daddy *1499102* (U.K. #1)

Mo Money Mo Problems
The Notorious B.I.G. Featuring Puff Daddy & Ma$e

Released July 1997
Bad Boy *79100* (U.S. #1) / Puff Daddy *1492492* (U.K. #6)

'I'll Be Missing You' is, quite simply, one of the biggest hip-hop records of all time. Released in tribute to the recently murdered Notorious B.I.G. – and featuring a guest vocal by his widow, Faith Evans – it made a global star of Sean 'Puffy Daddy' Combes, his close friend and Bad Boy Records label boss. It also inaugurated a new kind of hit-making. Going above and beyond mere sampling, the single is based almost entirely on The Police's 1983 hit 'Every Breath You Take.'

Rap in the mid 1990s was dominated by a feud between a pair of record labels from either side of the U.S. – Puff Daddy's New York-based Bad Boy imprint and Marion 'Suge' Knight's L.A.-centric Death Row. The bad blood stemmed from Death Row artist 2Pac Shakur's claims that he had slept with Faith Evans; by the time the hostilities had ended, both 2Pac and B.I.G. had been shot dead, six months apart, by assailants still unidentified to this day.

Puff Daddy had already topped the U.S. singles chart several months before B.I.G.'s death with his debut release, 'Can't Nobody Hold Me Down.' But 'I'll Be Missing You' took him into a completely new league. It spent 11 weeks atop the *Billboard* Hot 100 and was a Number 1 hit in the U.K. and countless other territories. Nominally composed by another rapper, Sauce Money, the single's main chord progression and chorus vocal-melody are lifted straight out of 'Every Breath You Take.'

Puff Daddy made no bones about this brazen act of musical recycling, and the original song's composer, Sting, didn't mind much either as he

received the lion's share of the ensuing royalties on ten-million-plus sales. It did, however, provoke heated debate within the music industry, with many critics questioning the artistic value of a record that added little to The Police's original, aside from Puff Daddy's rap. That didn't stop many other artists using the same trick to huge commercial success. Puff Daddy himself repeated the feat in 1998 with 'Been Around The World' – essentially 'Let's Dance' by David Bowie – and 'Come With Me,' which modeled itself on Led Zeppelin's 'Kashmir' and guest-starred that group's guitarist, Jimmy Page.

With a sad inevitability, The Notorious B.I.G.'s career reached its high-water mark in the months after his death. His second album – titled, with grim foresight, *Life After Death* – topped the U.S. chart in the week of his death, while its first two singles were also American Number 1 hits.

'Mo Money Mo Problems' was his biggest and most memorable single, and like 'I'll Be Missing You' it made liberal – although not quite so liberal – use of a sample, this time 'I'm Coming Out' by Diana Ross. To that it added a fat, dirty bassline, funky guitar, guest raps by Puff Daddy and Bad Boy stable-mate Ma$e, and a prescient chorus vocal line: "The more money we come across / The more problems we see." In the self-destructive gangsta-rap wars of the time, little could be mo' true.

Candle In The Wind 1997
Elton John

Released September 1997
Rocket *568108* (U.S. #1) / Rocket *PTCD 1* (U.K. #1)

As unlikely as it might seem now, so long after the event, in 1997 the world was briefly united in grief following the death of Diana, Princess Of Wales. It drove many of the normally stoic and reserved populace of her native Britain into an unprecedented state of public mourning, which in turn led Elton John to rewrite and reissue his 'Candle In The Wind' and, in the process, notch up the biggest-selling single of all time.

The original version of the song, written in tribute to the actress Marilyn Monroe, was a U.K. Number 11 hit for Elton early in 1974. He later became a close friend and confidante of the princess and, in the days immediately following her death (on August 31, 1997) asked his regular collaborator Bernie Taupin to rework the lyric to reflect her life and the impact of her death.

The new version was ready in time for Elton to perform it at Diana's funeral on September 6 at Westminster Abbey, London, and to record it with former Beatles producer George Martin that same day. 'Candle In The Wind 1997' went on sale exactly one week later, hitting Number 1 in pretty much every country with a singles chart, paving the way to eventual worldwide sales of over 33 million copies. Incredibly, the single spent three years in the Canadian singles chart, where it clung to the top spot for 45 weeks. And it was important in the rejuvenation of Elton's career, pushing his well-timed solo album *The Big Picture* into the U.S. and U.K. Top 10s.

left > Notorious B.I.G. (left) with friend and label boss Puff Daddy.
right > Elton John performing at the funeral of Princess Diana.

Your Woman
White Town

Released January 1997
Chrysalis-EMI *58638* (U.S. #23) / Chrysalis *CDCHS 5052* (U.K. #1)

'Your Woman' was one of the most unlikely U.K. chart-toppers ever. It was a kitsch pop bedroom recording by a British Asian student, Jyoti Mishra, built around a trumpet part sampled from a 1930s recording. The single was given a limited release in 1996 on an EP entitled *Abort, Retry, Fail?*. Mishra sent out only five promotional copies. One landed on the desk of a late-night radio DJ, Mark Radcliffe, who played it while filling in as presenter of the BBC Radio 1 breakfast show. The resulting major-label reissue gave Mishra a one-off Number 1 hit and a very fleeting – and ultimately unwanted – taste of fame.

Da Funk
Daft Punk

Released February 1997
Virgin *38587* (U.S.) / Virgin *VSCDT 1625* (U.K. #7)

Sexy Boy
Air

Released February 1998
Caroline *06645* (U.S.) / Virgin *VSCDT 1672* (U.K. #13)

In the late 1990s, a strange thing happened: all of a sudden, French music was cool outside France. The seeds were sown with the 1996 compilation album *Super Discount*, put together by the house DJ Etienne de Crecy, and mainstream success came early the following year with Daft Punk's major-label debut.

'Da Funk' is, essentially, low-tech techno. A prime example of the less-is-more philosophy, it is made up of little other than a squelching synth melody, one-note bass, and a beat that sounds as if it were recorded out of a passing car window. Parisians Thomas Bangalter – the son of a disco producer – and Guy-Manuel De Homem Christo first issued the single on the dance label Soma in 1995, but the Virgin reissue was a U.K. Top 10 hit, thanks it part to a memorable promo video, directed by Spike Jonze and starring a walking, talking dog. The follow-up, 'Around The World,' was a minor U.S. hit, and in 1998 Bangalter recorded one of the European club hits of the summer, 'Music Sounds Better With You,' under the alias Stardust.

By the time that single had hit the charts, Daft Punk had a rival as kings of French pop in the shape of another Parisian duo, Air. Nicholas Godin and Jean-Benoit Dunckel released three singles between 1995 and 1996, later reissued collectively as *Premiers Symptomes*. 'Sexy Boy' was their first for Virgin, following hot on the heels of their acclaimed full-length debut, *Moon Safari*. Like the rest of the album, the single is built around warm, retro synths, gentle beats, and charming Franglais vocals.

right > The French electronica duo Daft Punk, who insist on wearing masks for all publicity photos.

Bitch
Meredith Brooks

Released May 1997
Capitol *58634* (U.S. #2) / Capitol *CDCL 790* (U.K. #6)

In 1995, Alanis Morrissette's notorious single 'You Oughta Know' made it the rage for women to show rage in pop. Meredith Brooks was a singer from Oregon known for making much milder music, but when she hit the pop charts with 'Bitch' two years later the song was instantly charged as derivative of Morrissette's amped-up paean to failed love. However, 'Bitch' doesn't have the bitter ring – it's a feminist-positive anthem. Brooks reclaims the word as a term of empowerment, not degradation. The Grammy Awards didn't think Ms. Brooks was such a bitch, giving her a nomination for Best Vocal Peformance.

Tubthumping
Chumbawamba

Released August 1997
Republic *56146* (U.S. #6) / EMI *CDEM 486* (U.K. #2)

English group Chumbawamba, an ultra-left-wing collective that had slogged through the morass of activist-pop for years with little commercial impact, surprised absolutely everybody when they hit the Top 10 with 'Tubthumping,' a highly catchy shoutalong that temporarily mesmerized everyone. Unfortunately, Britpop Britain only heard the line "He drinks a vodka drink … he drinks a cider drink" and assumed it was a simple drinking song, missing out entirely on the subtext of escapist futility. Other than singer Danbert Nobacon chucking a bucket of water over U.K. deputy prime minister John Prescott at the 1998 Brit Awards, 'Tubthumping' was Chumbawamba's only moment in the sun.

Paranoid Android
Radiohead

Released May 1997
Not issued U.S. / Parlophone *CDODATAS 01* (U.K. #3)

Issued to great fanfare as "the 'Bohemian Rhapsody' of the 1990s," this six-minute epic was one of the most ambitious British rock singles of the decade. According to vocalist and songwriter Thom Yorke, however, it was inspired by the cut-and-paste feel of The Beatles' 'Happiness Is A Warm Gun' and not Queen's rock operatics. Bassist Colin Greenwood corroborated the story in a contemporary interview, claiming that 'Paranoid Android' was about "taking things apart and sticking them back together again to see if they made any sense."

It started life as three separate songs: the tricksy, time-shifting opening; a maudlin, choral centerpiece; and, sandwiched either side of that, a jerky, Pixies-style freak-out dominated by Jonny Greenwood's ferocious lead guitar. Yorke's lyric was, by all accounts, inspired by a nightmarish night-out in the media glitz of Los Angeles. Despite being – in the words of its critics – pompous, overblown, and much too long, 'Paranoid Android' debuted at Number 3 on the U.K. singles chart. It served as the perfect introduction to Radiohead's third album, *OK Computer*, which reset the parameters within which a modern rock band could or was supposed to operate. Also, it finally gave the group a more fitting legacy than "that band who did 'Creep.'"

Bitter Sweet Symphony
The Verve

Released June 1997
Hut-Virgin *38634* (U.S. #12) / Hut *HUTDG 82* (U.K. #2)

This swirling, string-driven epic, topped off by a chest-beating vocal, was one of the decade's greatest singles. True to its title, it was also something of a bitter-sweet success for The Verve, who didn't earn a penny in publishing royalties from the record. The problem stemmed from a four-bar sample of an orchestral rendition of The Rolling Stones's 'The Last Time,' discovered by Verve frontman Richard Ashcroft on an album by The Andrew Loog Oldham Orchestra.

Ashcroft then wrote the rest of the music himself – including the main orchestral hook – but despite clearing the Oldham sample, he was then sued by Allen Klein, whose ABKCO Records holds the rights to all of the Stones's material from the 1960s. Following an out-of-court settlement, all copyright on 'Bitter Sweet Symphony' reverted to ABKCO – despite Mick Jagger and Keith Richards giving The Verve's song their blessing, and the fact that it bore no resemblance to 'The Last Time.'

Regardless of the legal wrangling, however, few could deny that The Verve had created a modern classic. The song climbed into the upper reaches of the charts on both sides of the Atlantic; in Britain its rise to the top was halted only by another landmark 1990s single, 'I'll Be Missing You' by Puff Daddy. The Verve followed up with a stirring ballad, 'The Drugs Don't Work,' which gave them their only British Number 1 hit, and then their third and final studio album, *Urban Hymns*.

Torn
Natalie Imbruglia

Released November 1997
Not issued U.S. / RCA *1527982* (U.K. #2)

It seems rather unlikely that a former Australian soap actress would hit international pop-music paydirt by covering an obscure song by a band from Los Angeles, but such is the tale of Natalie Imbruglia's first and most popular single 'Torn.' After appearing on the popular Aussie television serial *Neighbours* – a veritable feeding ground of homegrown talent that has gone on to worldwide success – Imbruglia tried her hand at a music career and released a cover version of a song from Ednaswap, the now defunct band fronted by Anne Preven, whose lyrics immaculately captured the contradictory dilemmas of everyday life.

TO CHART OR NOT TO CHART?

During the 1990s, a number of hugely popular records failed to make it onto the *Billboard* Hot 100 because they were not given a commercial release in a physical format. Sales of singles had been in decline since the 1970s, prompting many record labels not to bother manufacturing them at all, and instead to release tracks to radio stations only. The labels also hoped that, by not making a single available to the public, they would encourage greater sales for their artists' albums (which, of course, made more money). A direct result of this, however, was that many of the decade's most memorable songs, including Alanis Morissette's 'You Oughta Know,' The Cardigans' 'Love Fool,' and 'Torn' by Natalie Imbruglia, were not in fact Hot 100 hits in the U.S. (the latter song did, however, top the *Billboard* Airplay chart). Eventually, in December 1998, the regulations by which the Hot 100 chart is compiled were altered to reflect the declining importance of the physical single so that, for the first time, records could enter the chart without a single copy being sold.

On & On
Erykah Badu

Released January 1997
Kedar-Universal *56002* (U.S. #12) / Universal *UND 561117* (U.K. #12)

Erykah Badu – born Erica Wright in Dallas, Texas – remains one of the most startling talents the world of soul music has ever seen, a virtuoso in a sea of conformity. Her breakthrough single 'On & On' has a fresh, bluesy feel and an immediacy of emotion lacking in much contemporary R&B, as well as a low-end groove to appeal to modern ears. The song helped propel her debut album *Baduizm* to Number 2 in America, and its video gave a visual introduction to the eccentric singer with the throwback voice and the otherworldly look.

Return Of The Mack
Mark Morrison

Released March 1997
Atlantic *84868* (U.S. #2) / WEA *040CD* (U.K. #1)

Alas, the Mack known as Mark Morrison never revisited the chart glory of this catchy chart-topper. But it wasn't his lack of talent or a dearth of well-crafted tunes that prevented Morrison – born in Germany and brought up in England – from reaching similar heights. Rather, his cluttered arrest record reveals a range of charges from assault to weapons violations. Morrison's run-ins with the law made him a notorious 'bad boy' in the eyes of the British press, but that and his constant assertions of innocence failed to help him continue to sell records.

MMMBop
Hanson

Released May 1997
Mercury *574261* (U.S. #1) / Mercury *5745012* (U.K. #1)

'MMMBop' was a peppy, infectious tune that catapulted young brothers Isaac, Taylor, and Zachary Hanson from making kid-friendly cover songs of oldies into massive international fame. But it might not have reached its heights of glory if some experienced underground producers hadn't made a savvy remix. The song was originally conceived as a ballad, but in the hands of The Dust Brothers – Los Angeles production duo John King and Mike Simpson – it turned into an infectious pop hit with the briefest touch of hip-hop breakbeat momentum.

King and Simpson were responsible for giving the critically acclaimed Beastie Boys album *Paul's Boutique* its sampladelic flair, and later helped bring new success to singer Beck. Their production for 'MMMBop' is comparatively spare, accented by scratchy noises and the brothers' punchy, high-note harmonies and their prodigious work on keys, guitar, and drums. Not since the Jacksons has America seen such a talented family, although the Hansons have more unity.

'MMMBop' helped them earn three Grammy nominations, for Record Of The Year, Best Pop Performance By A Duo Or Group, and Best New Artist. The memorable video features a bevy of performance sequences and was directed by the famous youth-culture film director Tamra Davis (*CB4*, *Half Baked*, *Crossroads*). Almost a decade after their first hit,

Hanson continue to enjoy a successful career, releasing albums together through their own independent record label, 3CG (it stands for 3 Car Garage).

How Do I Live
LeAnn Rimes

Released July 1997
Curb *73022* (U.S. #2) / Curb *CUBCX 30* (U.K. #7)

A simple, moderately affecting ballad from identikit blonde country singer LeAnn Rimes, 'How Do I Live' was the postman's whistling choice for much of 1997 thanks to its killer title melody and the chance – fully exploited by Rimes – to launch a lung-busting epic climax at its end. As with so much modern country-pop (think Shania Twain, The Dixie Chicks), it's the precision-engineered production that makes the song so shiny, with all the melodies waterfall-perfect and the vocals a thing of great beauty. Yes, it's covered in a layer of pure cheese, but as modern country goes, you could do much worse.

You Make Me Wanna ...
Usher

Released August 1997
LaFace *24265* (U.S. #2) / LaFace *1560652* (U.K. #1)

Usher was an entertainer more or less since birth, made his recorded debut at age 14, and went on to establish himself as a nationally-known teen heartthrob by the time he was 19 with 'You Make Me Wanna.' As an R&B singer with extraordinary pipes – and dance moves that seem as if handed down by Michael Jackson himself – Usher still relishes the heartthrob role a decade or so later. Even before he was legal he was a ladykiller, crooning slick lines like this song's infectious chorus: "You make me wanna leave the one I'm with / And start a new relationship / With you ... ."

Barbie Girl
Aqua

Released September 1997
MCA *55392* (U.S. #7) / Univeral *UMD 80413* (U.K. #1)

By 1997 techno had been hijacked by the Nickelodeon kids' channel and other cultural media aimed at the under-12s, and children's music has been based on Eurobeats ever since. But all this plinky-plinky rubbish never seemed destined to break through into the adult world until the advent of Danish-Norwegian quartet Aqua, who made you listen to it whether you wanted to or not.

The quartet – singer Lene Nystrøm Rasted, rapper-comic stooge René Dif, and keyboard players Søren Nystrøm Rasted and Claus Norreen – nailed a moderately clubby beat to a sickly Barbie-and-Ken love story, delivered in helium vocals, and made a bazillion euros out of it.

How could this happen, and how was it permitted? The secret lay in the fine looks of singer Lene, the daft interplay between her and rapper Dif,

It's worth considering the fate of a host of girl bands in the late 1990s. Remember B*Witched from Ireland, a kind of Corrs for kids? Once thought to be The Next Big Thing, they in fact became The Next Forgotten Thing, despite a signature tune ('C'est La Vie') and a selling point (Irishness). All Saints avoided this fate, narrowly, because they had 'Never Ever' – a real song.

Angels
Robbie Williams

Released December 1997
Capitol *7788192* (U.S.) / Chrysalis *CHSLH 5072* (U.K. #4)

As the world moved toward the 21st century, it seemed as if rock music was an art form that would be left in the 20th, a relic of a bygone age and superseded by house, techno, rap, and other musical styles. Then in Britain along came an artist who seemed to embody both in spirit and output all the attributes of that once all-powerful, now marginalized genre.

Robbie Williams affected rock'n'roll irreverence and cheeky likeability while releasing records infused with the great melodies, memorable licks, knowing lyrics, and potential for communal live singalongs that always characterized the greatest rock music. Remarkably, he was a former member of a boy-band, and hitherto had seemed a talentless twerp.

'Angels' was the song that weakened the resistance of those who could not take seriously as a legitimate rock artist someone who had been in Take That. Although Guy Chambers provided the melodic foil to Williams's lyrics, the song started life as a collaboration between the artist and budding songwriter Ray Heffernan, who provided the verse and its melody. But it was the combination of Chambers's grand, sweeping chorus melody and Williams's affectingly vulnerable words that gave 'Angels' the air of a modern classic. No Williams concert would now be complete without a mass singalong of the chorus with its climactic phrase that nobody quite understands: "I'm loving angels instead."

and the none-more-unforgettable line "I'm a Barbie girl / In the Barbie world" that you had to sing, like it or not. The bat-like vocal frequencies remained stuck in the listener's head – and inspired much conjecture as to whether Lene's natural range was really that high.

When two more singles appeared, the broadly similar 'Doctor Jones' and the much more acceptable ballad 'Turn Back Time,' they revealed just how much studio treatment had been required to give 'Barbie Girl' its day-glo, amphetamine feel. Unfortunately, that same near-psychotic look and sound made the band rapidly obsolete, and they split in 2001, although the song is probably still played to this day at Copenhagen infant-school discos.

Never Ever
All Saints

Released November 1997
London *570178* (U.S. #4) / London *LONCD 407* (U.K. #1)

After endless accusations of being "the new Spice Girls" (which, rightly, they laughed away), London quartet All Saints delivered this classy chunk of gospel and saw their detractors fall silent and their stock go stratospheric. Most people didn't realize why it sounded so familiar, but then it didn't occur to them that the girls had adapted a hymn, 'Amazing Grace.' Luckily, their perfect harmonies disguised the lift.

As with Take That's 'Back For Good' – the gold standard in boy-band pop – 'Never Ever' has gone down as the manufactured-girl-band song to beat, alongside '2 Become 1' by the aforementioned Spice ladies. It's a simple, affecting ballad, which bandleader Shaznay Lewis had written in the aftermath of a failed relationship, and boasts the chorus line: "Never ever have I ever felt so low," which itself is a catchy tongue-twister.

The song was the boost that the band needed, although their progress faltered with the next two singles, a weak remake of the Chili Peppers' 'Under The Bridge' and the R&B-by-numbers 'Bootie Call.' But then in 2000 All Saints triumphed with two excellent singles produced by William Orbit before quitting in the following year.

Robbie Williams //
Angels

. . . Baby One More Time

Britney Spears

Released November 1998
Jive 42545 (U.S. #1) / Jive 0522752 (U.K. #1)

This arresting, instantly memorable mega-hit provided the perfect introduction to the most iconic popular music star of the turn of the century. While the global resurgence of teen-orientated pop had begun several years earlier with the rise of The Spice Girls and The Backstreet Boys, no one else could match the near-global ubiquity of young Britney Spears.

Like all great pop prodigies, Britney – born in Kentwood, Los Angeles – started singing and dancing locally almost as soon as she could string a sentence together. In 1990, at the age of eight, she appeared on a nationally televised *Star Search*. As with future pop starlets Christina Aguilera and Justin Timberlake – with whom she had a very public and allegedly chaste relationship for several years – she then worked as a mouseketeer on the Disney Channel's *New Mickey Mouse Club*.

In between times, Spears had studied at the Professional Performing Arts School in New York City. At 15 she signed a deal with Jive Records – nominally an independent label, but home to such big sellers as R. Kelly and The Backstreet Boys – and began work on a debut album with a number of hot songwriters and producers, including Eric Foster White and Max Martin. It was Martin who wrote and produced 'Baby One More Time,' the song that gave Spears an international Number 1 hit at the first attempt and provided the perfect springboard to her ensuing superstardom. Like The Spice Girls and their 'Wannabe,' Britney's debut is somewhat unconventional in structure. It doesn't rely on a big, hook-laden chorus, but instead is made up of several interlocking parts that, while not particularly remarkable on their own, add up to one of the most striking, catchy pop hits of recent times.

The key elements are the vocal melodies and Britney's coy, suggestive delivery; the instrumental parts – rock-ballad drums, vaguely funky bass, washes of synth strings – are rarely more than perfunctory, aside perhaps from the juddering piano chords that open each verse. The lyrics, too, are unusual: "I must confess / That my loneliness is killing me" seems on paper as if it belongs to an angst-ridden rock song, not a bright, bouncy pop single.

Just as important to the success of 'One More Time' was the accompanying music video, which cast the 17-year-old Spears as a modern-day Lolita in skimpy school uniform. Integral to the Britney Spears phenomenon was the intriguing juxtaposition of the singer's regular espousal of her good, pure values – particularly sexual abstinence – and her raunchy, provocative music and image.

The furious debate about what was and wasn't decent peaked the following summer when Britney made a scantily-clad appearance on the cover of *Rolling Stone*. By then, 'Sometimes' and '(You Drive Me) Crazy' had followed 'Baby One More Time' into the upper reaches of the charts across the Western world, and Britney had cemented her position as the biggest solo female artist of her time.

MAX MARTIN: POP'S SWEDISH CHEF

When the Britney Spears hit '. . . Baby One More Time' took over the airwaves in late 1998 and into '99, many were surprised to discover that the song was the handiwork of a songwriter-producer based in Sweden. Max Martin (born Martin Sandberg in Stockholm in 1971) started working for the Swedish pop label Cheiron at the age of 21. Alongside the label's founder, Denniz PoP, he co-wrote and produced a string of European hit singles and albums in the mid 1990s for artists including Ace Of Base and Rednex.

The duo's big break came in 1996 with an invitation from the American record company Jive to contribute to the eponymous debut album by the label's boy-band, The Backstreet Boys. Both Backstreet Boys and the singles 'Quit Playing Games (With My Heart)' and 'As Long As You Love Me' were remarkably successful across mainland Europe and, eventually, in the U.S. too.

Over the next few years Martin and PoP consolidated a highly successful relationship with Jive. In 1997 they provided The Backstreet Boys with several more international hits, notably the self-mythologizing 'Everybody (Backstreet's Back),' which paired their trademark dance-pop with a theatrical Phantom Of The Opera feel. After launching the Swedish singer Robyn out into the pop world with 'Show Me Love,' Martin and PoP worked on the debut by another American Jive act, *Nsync.

In 1998, PoP succumbed to cancer, leaving Martin to assume the reigns of Cheiron. Now he wrote and produced the majority of his hits alongside another fellow Swede, by the name of Rami. One of this new pairing's first collaborations was '. . . Baby One More Time,' Britney Spears's debut single, which gave Martin his first U.S. Number 1 hit.

Over the course of the following year, Max Martin became the world's most in-demand songwriter-producer for hire, helming further hits for Britney and The Backstreet Boys as well as new clients, among them Celine Dion, Bryan Adams, and former Take That star Gary Barlow. In 1999 and 2000 Martin was named Songwriter Of The Year by the American Society Of Composers, Authors, & Publishers.

At the start of the 21st century Martin closed down Cheiron and formed a new hit factory, Maratome. Despite the change of name and support personnel, the hits kept coming. Chief among them was 'Since U Been Gone,' which transformed 2002 *American Idol* winner Kelly Clarkson from pop puppet to almost-serious artiste in 2004.

While Hill's solo success was phenomenal, and certainly the loudest of the three at the time, it is Wyclef Jean who has emerged as the soloist with longevity, both in his own work and in producing others (such as the Columbian megastar Shakira). Jean's catchy, jangly hip-pop tune 'Gone Till November' asserted that his own career was definitely on the up.

Gettin' Jiggy Wit It
Will Smith

Released February 1998
Columbia *78804* (U.S. #1) / Columbia *6655605* (U.K. #3)

The indefatigable Will Smith based 'Gettin' Jiggy Wit It' on a fantastic three-chord sample from 'He's The Greatest Dancer' by Sister Sledge. Smith peaked as a hip-hop artist in 1998, just before acting became his main career, and never did do better than this cheerful, up-tempo piece of nonsense. Although the title was in hip-hop lingo and Smith has always made much of his Philly-ghetto roots, the production and promotion of this single screamed 'major-label act!' His credibility among the genuine hip-hop elite has always been tarnished by his populist vibe and cheesy grin. But do we need another too-serious, too-violent rapper? No. Which is why we love Big Will.

Gone Till November
Wyclef Jean

Released February 1998
Ruffhouse *78752* (U.S. #7) / Columbia *6658712* (U.K. #3)

Doo Wop (That Thing)
Lauryn Hill
Released September 1998
Ruffhouse *78868* (U.S. #1) / Ruffhouse *6665152* (U.K. #3)

Ghetto Supastar (That Is What You Are)
Pras Michel Featuring Ol' Dirty Bastard & Introducing Mya
Released June 1998
Interscope *95021* (U.S. #15) / Interscope *INC 95593* (U.K. #2)

After the phenomenal success of the Fugees, whose sophomore album *The Score* remains one of the most successful hip-hop albums of all time, the group slowly began to show cracks in its foundation and decided to part ways. In 1998, all three members (Lauryn Hill, Wyclef Jean, and Pras Michel) set out to recapture that achievement – only they did it individually, as solo artists.

Led by the rap-R&B hybrid hit 'Doo Wop (That Thing),' Hill's multi-platinum *The Miseducation Of Lauryn Hill* was nominated for a staggering 11 Grammys and grabbed five, including Best New Artist, Best R&B Song, and Best R&B Vocal Performance. Michel, meanwhile, came out with his debut album *Ghetto Supastar*, lending its title cut to the soundtrack for the Warren Beatty movie *Bulworth*. R&B ingenue Mya sang the hook – an odd lift from 'Islands In The Stream,' the 1983 chart-topping duet between Dolly Parton and Kenny Rogers – while the Wu-Tang Clan's madcap Ol' Dirty Bastard traded rap verses. It gave Michel another taste of mainstream success, but this would prove fleeting.

It's Like That
Run-D.M.C. Vs. Jason Nevins

Released March 1998
Columbia *665293* (U.S.) / Sm:)e *SM 90652* (U.K. #1)

This updated version of Run-D.M.C.'s 'It's Like That' didn't dent the American pop charts but soared to the top in the U.K. and almost 30 other countries. It was also a smash on dancefloors around the world, employed by DJs of many genres who were looking to inject a little hip-hop flavor into the mix. Detractors griped that Jason Nevins, the New York-based DJ-remixer responsible for the song's second-time-around, did little more than add a peppier, metronomic beat while leaving the 1983 original largely untouched. But Nevins's skill was to unearth a classic at precisely the right time and reap the benefit.

Feel It
The Tamperer Featuring Maya

Released April 1998
Jive *46506* (U.S.) / Pepper *0530032* (U.K. #1)

With its unforgettable chorus line – "what's she gonna look like with a chimney on her?" – 'Feel It' was one of the finest European dance-pop hits of the late 1990s. The musical backdrop of jangling bells and up-tempo house rhythms was the work of a pair of Italian DJs, Alex Farfoli and Mario Fargetta. Their female compatriot, Maya, provided the empowering vocal, which is centered on an oddly playful threat of revenge against somebody foolish enough to have slept with her man. The single was hugely successful across Europe, as was the follow-up, 'If You Buy This Record Your Life Will Be Better,' although it seems doubtful they could have proved such a bold sales pitch.

Dance The Night Away
The Mavericks

Released April 1998
MCA *72056* (U.S.) / MCA Nashville *MCSTD 48081* (U.K. #4)

Led by the jovial, goateed Raoul Malo, The Mavericks are a U.S. country band with Tex-Mex influences. Their music is melodic, radio-friendly, and highly inoffensive – the three golden qualities for modern commercial success, some might say. The very catchy 'Dance The Night Away' was a worldwide hit, even if its blandness was almost breathtaking. But nobody complained because the band had worked to earn their recognition – 'Dance' was taken from their fifth album. Two further singles scraped the British Top 50 but The Mavericks never had such success in their home country.

The Boy Is Mine
Brandy & Monica

Released May 1998
Atlantic *84089* (U.S. #1) / Atlantic *AT 0036CD* (U.K. #2)

This sassy and technically superior pop anthem finds vocalists Brandy Norwood and Monica Arnold in a fictional clash of fierce lyrics and trilling diva ad-libs. Both had been popular R&B stars since their early teenage years, and 'The Boy is Mine' (released on both of their albums of the time) brought the singers to new heights of mainstream recognition. Amid rumors that they were not getting along too well, at the time of writing this record unfortunately marked the last collaboration from these two young talents. But the tale has a happy ending: they've both since blossomed into mothers and maintained successful solo careers.

What Can I Do
The Corrs

Released August 1998
Atlantic *84444* (U.S.) / Atlantic *AT 0044CD* (U.K. #3)

A relative flop on its first release but a big old smash hit after a brush-up and a remix from Tin Tin Out, 'What Can I Do' is a highly attractive three minutes of pop fluff from the perennially attractive Corrs, the prettiest band (excluding their brother) ever to have come out of Ireland. Andrea Corr fronts the quartet and supplies tin whistle, her two sisters Sharon and Caroline are on violin and drums, and brother Jim is on guitar. They struck gold by providing the Celtic-friendly music-buying public with a resolutely Irish sound – a clever move in America and the UK.

'What Can I Do' was in fact the fifth single from The Corrs – the world had been slow to catch on, at least initially – and the band gave the impression in interviews that the way to stardom had been no easy ride. However, once this single hit in Britain it became obvious that the time was ripe for 'Irish pop,' and The Corrs capitalized with a series of similarly chirpy tunes that boasted the latest in crisp production and a media-friendly home-country image that neither overdid the Irish angle nor neglected it entirely. There was always a violin or tin whistle solo lurking in the background.

'What Can I Do' had such a commercial whack in Britain that a leading bank used it to soundtrack a TV ad, with Andrea and the family changing the lyrics to "What can we do to make you happy?"

I Don't Want To Miss A Thing
Aerosmith

Released August 1998
Columbia *78952* (U.S. #1) / Columbia *6664082* (U.K. #4)

Like the proverbial bolt from the blue, this power-ballad gave Aerosmith a third peak in a sporadic four-decade career of extreme ups and downs. After an initial period of success in the mid 1970s, several members of the group had battled hard-drugs addiction prior to a Run-D.M.C.-inspired comeback in the mid-to-late 1980s. But it appeared that their popularity – and creativity – had begun to wane by the time they issued a career retrospective, *Big Ones*, in 1994.

Then came 'I Don't Want To Miss A Thing,' written for the band by the phenomenally successful songwriter Diane Warren. A huge international hit, the song was given a further boost by its inclusion on the soundtrack to the movie *Armageddon*, which, coincidentally, starred Aerosmith vocalist Steven Tyler's daughter, Liv.

Rosa Parks
OutKast

Released November 1998
LaFace *4367* (U.S.) / Not issued U.K.

One of the most successful hip-hop groups of all time, Atlanta's OutKast (Andre 'Andre 3000' Benjamin and Antwan 'Big Boi' Patton) have also touched on many controversial moments in their career, whether by accident or design. OutKast's third album Aquemini, a masterpiece of soul and hip-hop otherworldliness, is now best remembered for featuring the single 'Rosa Parks.'

The lively and funky song is named after Rosa Parks, the civil rights activist. In 1955 in Montgomery, Alabama, Parks famously refused to move to the back of the segregated bus she was on, which sparked a nationwide uproar. The song makes reference to this event in part of the chorus ("Ah ha / Hush that fuss / Everybody move to the back of the bus . . ."), but otherwise the song is not about her. 'Rosa Parks' was nominated for a Grammy for Best Rap Performance By A Duo Or Group, and the song would later surface as part of an emotional battle.

OutKast's huge success during the coming years was not enough to shield its members from the certain pain of an unlikely lawsuit. Representatives for Parks launched a suit against the group and its record companies in 1999, claiming that the song was both a copyright infringement and defamed her character. After a battle with many dramatic twists and turns that managed to reach all the way up to the U.S. Supreme Court, the case was settled out of court in April 2005, just six months before Parks's death at age 92.

My Heart Will Go On
(Love Theme From 'Titanic')
Celine Dion

Released February 1998
550 Music-Epic *78825* (U.S. #1) / Epic *6655472* (U.K. #1)

When director James Cameron unleashed his mega-movie *Titanic* in 1997 – then the most expensive film ever made – he required a suitably epic song to soundtrack its key subplot (the relationship between the two leads) with plenty of hooks to deploy at key moments throughout the film.

Thus, Swiss-American chanteuse Celine Dion – one of the world's biggest singing stars following the success of her albums *Falling Into You* (1996) and *Let's Talk About Love* (1997), which between them sold over 60 million copies worldwide – performed 'My Heart Will Go On.' The single sold in enormous quantities thanks to its winsome Hollywood-Celtic flute melody, slick orchestration, and money-shot line of "Near … far … whereeeeeeeeeever you are." This last songwriting conceit, an operatic moment of almost Wagnerian pomp, had the delivery boys whistling for months.

Even the song's creators must have been startled by its success – Dion herself didn't think much of the song to begin with, and took some convincing to record it. While some might have found 'My Heart Will Go On' to be rather too overwrought and overblown, the record did nonetheless deserve its fame. Composer James Horner came up with a melody to die for, and while the title meant very little, moviegoers certainly got the message as Leonardo DiCaprio sank into the icy depths. The single won an Academy Award for Best Original Song – just one of a record-equalling 11 Oscars picked up by *Titanic*.

Ray Of Light
Madonna

Released April 1998
Maverick *17206* (U.S. #5) / Maverick *W 0444CD* (U.K. #2)

By the mid 1990s it looked as if Madonna's career was on its last legs after just over a decade at the top of the pop ladder. She was pushing 40 – about 120 in pop years – and with singles such as 'Human Nature' ('95) and 'One More Chance' ('96) she seemed unable to match the luster of earlier mega-hits.

Then came perhaps the most surprising change of direction in her chameleon-like career. Madonna decided to star in the cinematic adaptation of Andrew Lloyd Webber's *Evita*. The movie was a big box-office hit, but more importantly seemed to reignite her passion for music.

The singing lessons she took prior to accepting the role didn't hurt, either: her 1998 'comeback' single, the icy ballad 'Frozen,' showed off one of the best vocal performances of her career.

The follow-up, the pulsating future-disco cut 'Ray Of Light,' was even better. For the first time in years it seemed that Madonna had broken free from the shackles of controversy – the church-baiting 'Like A Prayer' or the over-sexed 'Justify My Love' – and made the music itself her focus once again. Not that 'Ray of Light' was entirely free of controversy. Soon after it rose into the British and American Top 5, the song was found to be based quite substantially on 'Sepheryn,' a 1970s song written by Curtis Muldoon and Dave Curtiss. Both were more than a little miffed at the way Madonna's producer William Orbit had co-opted their song but cheered up somewhat when they were awarded a large chunk of the royalties.

Believe
Cher

Released October 1998
Warner *17119* (U.S. #1) / WEA *175CD* (U.K. #1)

Cherilyn Sarkisian, a sprightly 53 but looking 20 years younger when her career was saved by 'Believe,' had struggled for credibility since the 1980s. The one-time Mrs. Sonny Bono had scored a few minor hits with a soft-rock approach that made much of her surgically-enhanced youthfulness, but by 1998, Top 5 hits had become thin on the ground since 'If I Could Turn Back Time,' a grisly rock ballad from 1989.

Cher then stunned her detractors with the massive-selling 'Believe,' a song that fell somewhere between kitchen-sink techno, cheesy house-trance, and plain old sugary pop. Its success came from two key elements: the chorus line of "Do you believe in life after love?" specifically the yodel in the middle of the word "believe," and the masterful decision by the producers to employ a vocoder-like effect on her voice towards the end of the song. Although this turned her voice into a digitized soup and was slightly nauseating for some listeners, many loved it and the song shot up the charts. The whole thing shifts upwards in key at one point, a classic maneuver that nearly always makes a struggling song sound suddenly fresher. So, Cher was on a career high again, and capitalized on the success with – yes! – another house tune, 'Strong Enough,' that also featured a pitch-shifted vocal.

If You Had My Love

Jennifer Lopez

Released May 1999
Epic-Work *79163* (U.S. #1) / Columbia *6675772* (U.K. #4)

There are countless examples of movie stars making lame attempts to record a pop song, usually resulting in the actor in question quickly retreating to his or her primary occupation in the midst of negative reviews and poor sales. There are also musicians who make dire big-screen appearances. Jennifer Lopez, however, appears equally adept in both roles. Having established herself as the world's highest-paid Latin American actress with *Out Of Sight*, in which she starred with George Clooney in 1998, she decided the following year to launch a pop career. 'If You Had My Love' was the first of many smash hit singles that, as well as establishing Lopez as one of the most famous women in the world, helped to bring Latin-flavored pop into the mainstream.

Genie In A Bottle

Christina Aguilera

Released June 1999
RCA *65692* (U.S. #1) / RCA *1705482* (U.K. #1)

Following the pattern of all great pop idols, once Christina Aguilera hit the popular consciousness, she seemed as if she was there to stay and had always been a big household name. It happened for Aguilera in the summer of 1999, when America became blanketed by the ubiquity of 'Genie In A Bottle.' The young woman from near Pittsburgh served time as a pre-teen in TV's *Mickey Mouse Club* with future stars Justin Timberlake and Britney Spears and went on to sing the key song 'Run To You' in the Disney movie *Mulan*. All that and her extraordinary pipes helped net a recording contract with RCA.

One of the more overt songs on her debut album *Christina Aguilera*, 'Genie' features the chorus: "If you want to be with me / Baby there's a price to pay / I'm a genie in a bottle / You gotta rub me the right way." While Aguilera seemed to spend much time in her early interviews disputing the meaning of the song, it seemed to be contradicted by her

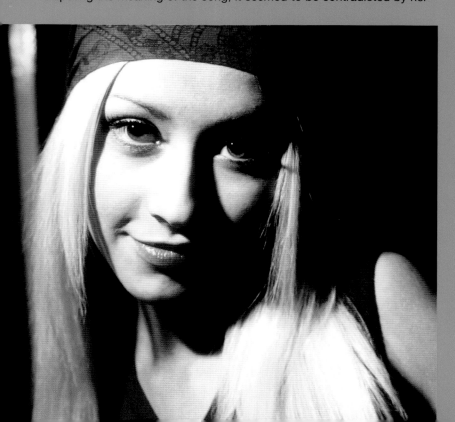

sexy dance moves and bottle-blonde looks displayed in the video and her performances. All of a sudden, Britney Spears had a significant threat to the throne of teen queen, and the two former mouseketeers continued to skyrocket to worldwide fame. Aguilera took home the coveted Grammy Award for Best New Artist in 2000.

I Try

Macy Gray

Released October 1999
Epic album cut (U.S. #5) / Epic *6681832* (U.K. #6)

From the time when Erykah Badu's first album broke in 1997 until about 2003, neo-soul looked like a force to be reckoned with. Badu, Jill Scott, and Macy Gray boosted the trend, mixing up vintage Motown influences with hip-hop sounds and urban production. Gravelly voiced Gray scored one of the genre's biggest hits with 'I Try,' a gospel-infused hymn to a broken heart anchored by a simple piano and bass rhythm that, in combination, made a pure torch anthem. The single was nominated for three Grammys at the 2001 awards ceremony, at which it won in the category of Best Female Pop Vocal Performance.

Caught Out There

Kelis

Released November 1999
Virgin *38677* (U.S.) / Virgin *VUSCD 158* (U.K. #4)

Got Your Money

Ol' Dirty Bastard Featuring Kelis

Released November 1999
Elektra *67022* (U.S. #33) / Elektra *E 7077CD* (U.K. #11)

Harlem's own Kelis Rogers may not be the most successful R&B singer in America but she is one of the true modern innovators in the genre – and one of the musicians others turn to when they're ready to rip off someone. She has only partially been recognized for her ability to set the pace. Kelis's debut single 'Caught Out There' brought some Alanis Morrissette-style rage to the urban pop world with the snarled chorus of "I hate you so much right now!" The video helped contextualize the aggression, fronted by a cute and diminutive female with a giant, colorful Afro, and got people talking about this different new artist.

Ol' Dirty Bastard (or ODB; born Russell Jones) was a key part of the acclaimed New York rap group Wu-Tang Clan until his death in late 2004. He was an incomparable figure of unabashed craziness known for fathering many children, ingesting many confusicants, and releasing groundbreaking records. For his biggest solo hit he recruited Kelis to sing the hilarious R&B hook ("Hey, Dirty / Baby, I got your money / Don't you worry") that helped portray ODB as a comically ruthless pimp.

The popularity of the song, and its blaxploitation-styled video, kick-started a great demand for Kelis to guest on other songs, starting a side career of sorts for the singer. She would later grace tunes by hip-hop stars such as Busta Rhymes, Clipse, and P. Diddy, and married the Big Apple rap star Nas.

My Name Is
Eminem

Released February 1999
Aftermath 95040 (U.S. #36) / Interscope INC 95638 (U.K. #2)

A few short months after Britney Spears and her 'Baby One More Time' gave the imminent millennium a new queen of pop, this landmark single announced the king. A calling card for the most successful white rapper of all time, Eminem's debut single had all the hallmarks of his best work. Its creator is one of a very small handful of performers who can honestly claim to have irreversibly altered the landscape of popular music in the past two decades.

According to hip-hop legend, Dr. Dre – a founding member of NWA and producer of countless other rap acts of the 1990s – found Eminem's demo tape on the floor of the garage of Interscope Records head Jimmy Iovine. The young rapper, born Marshall Mathers in 1973 in Kansas City, had been struggling to find a record deal; he assumed this was largely because of the color of his skin. His main antecedent, Vanilla Ice, had come to be seen as something of a laughing stock, and few other white rappers had managed any notable success. But Dr. Dre saw something special in Eminem and, after watching him perform at the 1997 Rap Olympics, brought the rapper to Interscope and started production work on what eventually would become The Slim Shady LP.

In 1998 Eminem made his first, tentative steps to fame, first appearing on Kid Rock's Devil Without A Cause and then issuing a low-profile taster for his debut album proper, 'Just Don't Give A Fuck.' As soon as 'My Name Is' reached radio at the tail end of the year, however, any plans that Interscope had to slowly ease Eminem into the mainstream quickly disappeared.

In just three rapid-fire verses, the rapper – in his Slim Shady guise – sets out his bitter, angry stall, railing against his mother (who, famously, "smokes more dope than I do"), teachers ("I smacked him in the face with an eraser, chased him with a stapler"), record company executives, and a host of celebrities, from The Spice Girls to Pamela Anderson. By the time of the subsequent release of The Slim Shady LP, Eminem had added a catalog of songs about rape, murder, child molestation, drug abuse, and more. This naturally provoked widespread controversy and moral condemnation, as well as furious debate about whether there could be any artistic value in music that focused on such repellent subject matter.

The rapper soon found himself labeled a misogynist, a homophobe, and, generally speaking, a vile, immoral, bad influence on youth. In his defense, he always maintained that the lyrics are from the perspective of his Slim Shady character and that he doesn't advocate rape, murder, and the rest – duh! – but that his freedom of speech should allow him to rap about whatever he chooses. Race seems to be the only contentious area he generally avoids, perhaps because, as his 2002 single 'Without Me' suggests, he feels a modicum of guilt for "being the worst thing since Elvis Presley" for using "black music so selfishly."

Inevitably with Eminem records, the focus tends to fall on the lyrical content – as jaw-dropping as ever here both for clever wordplay and unspeakable nastiness – while Dr. Dre's stellar production work is all but ignored. On 'My Name Is' Dre underpins the vocal tracks with an uncluttered backdrop of stark, stop-start bass and drums and occasional bursts of keyboard. The song embodies elements of the 1975 recording 'I Got The . . .' by the British-African poet and musician Labi

Siffre (who insisted Eminem remove certain homophobic lyrics from 'My Name Is' before clearing the sample).

As well as having a remarkably catchy single on his hands, Eminem also began to reap the benefits, for the first time, of being white. Where before the color of his skin had proved a stumbling block to acceptance in the hip-hop world, now that he'd got there he found it opened up an unparalleled market for rap music across white America.

Within weeks of its release, 'My Name Is' found its way into the U.S. Top 40 and peaked at Number 2 in Britain. It was followed by a single that many critics felt was even better. 'Guilty Conscience' casts Dr. Dre as the rapper's good side, as bad Marshall rants about problems with his wife, Kim, and the various unpleasant ways he would respond to finding her in bed with another man. (These two childhood sweethearts went through a very messy, very public divorce in the early 2000s, only to remarry in 2006.)

As with Britney Spears, Eminem's musical worth began to falter the more he became a 'media star,' but few – if any – other rappers of the time could match the artistic and commercial success of his early work. Even when the controversial lyrics and odious Slim Shady persona are stripped from 'My Name Is,' what remains is, indisputably, a great record.

Cowboy
Kid Rock

....

Released October 1999
Lava-Atlantic *84520* (U.S.) / Atlantic *AT 0076CD* (U.K. #36)

Detroit-bred Kid Rock, born Robert Ritchie, began his music career as a DJ and rapper under the tutelage of veteran artist Too $hort, but remained an underground artist until he incorporated a wider palette of rock and country-inspired sounds into his strangely original mix – just as he does on 'Cowboy.' Thankfully this combination, true to his roots, was what people wanted to hear, otherwise he might have suffered the indignant fate of Vanilla Ice and other neglected white rappers. Strangely, while 'Cowboy' wasn't a runaway pop smash, the album on which it appeared, *Devil Without A Cause*, sold more than 11 million copies.

All The Small Things
Blink-182

....

Released November 1999
MCA *155606* (U.S. #6) / MCA *MCSTD 40223* (U.K. #2)

Never mind the bollocks, this is the new punk, circa 1999. Courtesy of accomplished producer Jerry Finn, this song from Southern California's Blink-182 (from the cheekily titled album *Enema Of The State*) was the perfect companion to Blink's rough but cuddly image. Even the British, purveyors of fine punk bands like The Clash and The Sex Pistols, were quick to accept Blink-182's 'All The Small Things' as the new pop incarnation of a formerly rebellious musical genre. The video, which lampoons the vids of antiseptic boy bands such as Backstreet Boys and *NSYNC, made it a certified MTV hit.

Praise You
Fatboy Slim

Released January 1999
Astralwerks *66254* (U.S. #36) / Skint *42CD* (U.K. #1)

Fatboy Slim is one of several aliases used over the years by Norman Cook (Quentin to his mum), one of very few British electronic musicians to achieve widespread success in America. He began his musical career in the mid 1980s as bassist in The Housemartins, then formed Beats International, whose 'Dub Be Good To Me' was a U.K. Number 1 hit in 1990, and had further success later in the decade as Freak Power and Pizzaman.

In 1996 Cook signed to the cult Brighton-based label Skint and became Fatboy Slim, issuing a debut album of brash, infectious techno, *Better Living Through Chemistry*, that spawned an entire genre of its own, dubbed big beat. In 1998 his remix of 'Brimful Of Asha' by the British Asian indie group Cornershop was an unexpected U.K. Number 1, setting the stage for two huge Fatboy Slim hits later in the year, 'The Rockafeller Skank' and 'Gangster Trippin'.'

Both were soon eclipsed by 'Praise You,' which added infectious piano chords and a powerful, stop-start breakbeat to a gospel vocal sample. It remains the most successful and most memorable single of Cook's career, in part because of the accompanying promo video. In it, director Spike Jonze leads a pretend dance troupe through a series of ironic moves outside a California theatre. Despite its minimal production values, the promo was a multiple award-winner, and proved instrumental in establishing Fatboy Slim as a mainstream pop success in America.

Kiss Me
Sixpence None The Richer

Released February 1999
Squint *79101* (U.S. #2) / Elektra *E 3750CD* (U.K. #4)

Texas quintet Sixpence None The Richer took their name from a phrase used in a C.S. Lewis book and are one of the ultimate one-hit-wonder bands. They enjoyed a huge hit with the excellent 'Kiss Me' and then vanished from public view faster than you can say "universally ignored La's cover version." The single was a breath of fresh air in the nu-metal-plagued music scene of 1999, all winsome vocals and super-fragile guitars. Perhaps on paper this doesn't sound like the combination for a potential hit, but the song is proof that a winning melody will always comes through. SNTR's version of the aforementioned 'There She Goes' was dull, however, so it was bye-bye from them forever, with or without a kiss.

Windowlicker
Aphex Twin

Released March 1999
Sire *35007* (U.S.) / Warp *WAP 105* (U.K. #16)

'Windowlicker' remains the finest individual statement by one of the late 20th century's greatest musical innovators. The English eccentric Richard D. James began working as Aphex Twin in the early 1990s, producing a run of highly acclaimed albums and singles that run from soothing ambient tones to mind-melting drum'n'bass. 'Windowlicker' mixes hyperactive programmed drum rhythms and bass pulses with ironically moaning and cooing vocal samples. The latter element was intended to parody the overt sexualization of modern pop music, as was the promo video, which stars a group of half-naked dancers with faces manipulated to resemble a grotesque variation of James's own.

You Get What You Give
New Radicals

Released March 1999
MCA album cut (U.S. #36) / MCA *MCSTD 48111* (U.K. #5)

'You Get What You Give' was one of the biggest international hits of the summer of 1999, a bright, shiny, unashamedly *pop* single clearly inspired by 1970s rock and soul. In 2004 it was praised by Joni Mitchell, who included it on an *Artist's Choice* compilation of favorite songs, for "rising from the swamp of 'McMusic' like a flower of hope."

A rallying cry to disaffected youth, it was the work of Gregg Alexander (born Grosse Pointe, Michigan), who formed New Radicals with the express purpose of scoring a big worldwide hit single. Having achieved that at the first attempt, he split the 'band' – he was the sole member – and turned his attention to writing for and producing other artists. He has since worked with Rod Stewart, Hanson, and Ronan Keating, among others, and won a Grammy for his song 'The Game Of Love,' performed by Santana and Michelle Branch.

'You Get What You Give' is driven by emphatic piano chords, melodic guitar licks, and an instantly memorable vocal line. While most of the lyric is inoffensive feel-good fare, the closing lines were designed by Alexander to test the priorities of the music media.

As he expected, little attention was given to the couplets about what he deemed important political issues – "health insurance, rip-off lying / FDA, big bankers buying" – but his petty faux-sniping at fellow celebrities Courtney Love, Marilyn Manson, and Beck drew countless unwarranted column inches of muck-raking.

Flat Beat
Mr. Oizo

Released March 1999
Not issued U.S. / F Communications-Pias *F 104CD* (U.K. #1)

This deliciously frantic techno song by an inventive French electronica artist will forever be identified with a creature named Flat Eric. The cute and cuddly yellow puppet served as the mascot for a memorable commercial for jeans in Europe where Flat Eric happily jerks and shimmies to Mr. Oizo's thumping beat. Later, Oizo's Paris-based record label F Communication privately questioned its decision to license this song to the Levi's corporation after receiving dozens of phone calls per week inquiring not about Oizo but where they could get their very own Flat Eric to take home.

Everybody's Free (To Wear Sunscreen)
Baz Luhrmann

Released June 1999
EMI *887176* (U.S.) / EMI *CDBAZ 001* (U.K. #1)

Perhaps the only well-known film director to release a chart-topping single – and definitely the only such person from Australia – Baz Luhrmann, 37 years old in 1999, recorded 'Everybody's Free (To Wear Sunscreen)' partly as an elaborate joke and partly as a serious health message. The song takes its lyrics from a *Chicago Tribune* article that provided a list of practical advice, including the use of sun protection, although the lyrics were erroneously attributed to the novelist Kurt Vonnegut. Pop pickers watched in confusion as the song became a summer hit in '99 while Luhrmann prepared to hit the headlines with his extravagant *Moulin Rouge* movie. It seems highly improbable that he will attempt to invade the charts again.

Smooth
Santana Featuring Rob Thomas

Released July 1999
Arista *13718* (U.S. #1) / Arista *1748762* (U.K. #3)

This song was Number 1 in the U.S. for an astonishing 12 weeks – something that the legendary Bay Area guitarist Carlos Santana might never have conceived possible in his long and storied career. For his album *Supernatural*, Santana sought the contributions of a youthful mix of guest artists, including R&B singer-rappers Lauryn Hill (formerly of Fugees) and Cee-Lo (of Goodie Mob). But it was 'Smooth' and its smolderingly sexy vocals courtesy of Matchbox 20 lead singer Rob Thomas that provided the fuel *Supernatural* needed to win the Grammy for Album Of The Year.

Sing It Back
Moloko

Released August 1999
Warner Bros. *44687* (U.S.) / Echo *ECSCD 82* (U.K. #4)

This U.K. dance act, fronted by the gorgeous and talented Irish lead singer Roisin Murphy, became pop stars as this song from their second album went from club hit to mainstream hit, all thanks to a funky remix from German DJ-producer Boris Dlugosch. While not a chart-buster in America, where the video received almost no airplay, 'Sing It Back' won loyal fans for Moloko amongst U.S. dance-music aficionados. The song received many additional remix treatments, all extending its shelf-life in the clubs well beyond the woefully short span of a typical house-music tune.

Steal My Sunshine
Len

Released November 1999
Under The Covers *9906* (U.S. #9) / Columbia *6685062* (U.K. #8)

Whaddya know, a Canadian alt.rock band. When siblings Marc and Sharon Costanzo released a blend of hip-hop beats, attitude, and simple pop humability in 1999 and named it after its persistent chorus line, they had no idea that it would be a global hit and that they would dematerialize from the limelight shortly afterwards. Bizarrely, Marc delivered his raps in a hoarse, almost death-metal grunt while Sharon sang her chorus line in a flat tone that seemed to indicate a complete lack of interest. But the public didn't care and watched keenly for a follow-up. Sadly, nothing of note was forthcoming, and Len were history.

Re-Rewind The Crowd Say Bo Selecta
Artful Dodger Featuring Craig David

Released December 1999
Republic *156916* (U.S.) / Public Demand-Relentless *RELENT 1CDS* (U.K. #2)

Fill Me In
Craig David

Released April 2000
Wildstar-Atlantic *88101* (U.S. #15) / Wildstar *CDWILD 28* (U.K. #1)

Although U.K. garage was viable by the end of the 1990s, the genre lacked personalities, in stark contrast to the superstar DJs and MCs in drum'n'bass, hip-hop, and R&B. Many urban-music fans wondered if garage might languish behind the scenes as a result, but those fears were dispelled by the production duo known as Artful Dodger. With effortless aplomb, their snappy beats and bass underpinned the nonsensical line from prodigy Craig David: "When the crowd say bo – selecta."

The Artful Dodger vanished shortly afterwards, but David became a megastar, albeit with an entirely different musical approach. Stripping his solo recordings of the hard, urban production of 'Re-Rewind,' David took a more soulful tack, and one aimed more directly at mainstream ears. His move to a softer sound paid immediate dividends as he topped the British singles chart twice in 2000, with 'Fill Me In' and '7 Days.' Both reached the American Top 20 in early 2001 – no mean feat for a previously unknown British singer.

Independent Women Part 1
Destiny's Child

....

Released September 2000
Columbia *79493* (U.S. #1) / Columbia *6705932* (U.K. #1)

It was ironic that Destiny's Child – a Supremes for the 21st century – reached their artistic and commercial peak during the most tumultuous phase of their career. 'Independent Women Part 1' climbed to Number 1 on the *Billboard* Hot 100 – and stayed there for 11 weeks – just months after two former members of the group, LaTavia Roberson and LeToya Luckett, took legal action against their ex-colleagues and their manager, Matthew Knowles, citing breach of partnership.

Houston, Texas-based Knowles had started the group in 1990 when his daughter, Beyoncé, and Roberson were both only nine years old. By 1993 he had added Luckett and his niece, Kelly Rowland, to the group. After several years of performing in the Houston area, the teenage group signed to Columbia in 1997. The quartet scored a number of international hits, including 'No, No, No' and 'Bills, Bills, Bills,' but by the time 'Say My Name' topped the U.S. singles chart in March 2000, Roberson and Luckett were on their way out. Both disliked the way Knowles handled the group's affairs and his apparent favoritism towards his daughter and niece. They didn't intend to quit – but found themselves suddenly replaced by Michelle Williams and, briefly, Farrah Franklin (who only lasted five months before leaving for unspecified reasons).

In the meantime, with lawsuits pending from Roberson and Luckett, Destiny's Child released the lesser 'Jumpin' Jumpin'' before the trio of Knowles, Rowland, and Williams hit their stride on 'Independent Women Part 1.' A glorious slab of R&B-pop reminiscent of Michael Jackson at his peak in the late-1970s and early-'80s, the single was included in the remake of *Charlie's Angels*, guaranteeing it worldwide exposure. A transatlantic Number 1 hit, it was also included on the group's third full-length effort, *Survivor* (2001) – as was 'Part 2,' a slightly slower reading of 'Independent Women' with different lyrics and space-age sound-effects. By the time of the album's release, Roberson and Luckett had settled out of court with their former bandmates but continued to pursue their former manager.

Part of the settlement between the four original members of Destiny's Child was an agreement that neither side would criticize the other publicly, but this didn't stop the new-look trio issuing *Survivor*'s title track as their next single. Most listeners realized that the not-so-subtle call-and-response lyrics were aimed squarely at Roberson and Luckett ("You thought that I'd be weak without you / But I'm stronger … You thought I wouldn't sell without you / Sold nine million"). That's what the axed duo themselves thought, too, prompting a further lawsuit.

Nevertheless, 'Survivor' gave Destiny's Child another massive international hit, which they followed with the similarly successful 'Bootylicious,' a storming ode to the power of the rump. In 2002, each member of the trio started work on individual projects. Inevitably, it was Beyoncé who achieved the greatest solo success, first as an actress – in *Austin Powers In Goldmember* – and then with her ubiquitous 2003 hit 'Crazy In Love.'

The Bad Touch
The Bloodhound Gang

Released March 2000
Polygram International *497267* (U.S.) / Geffen *4972672* (U.K. #4)

A comedy band with comedy songs, The Bloodhound Gang have somehow managed to sustain a reasonably successful career since 1992, when alternative rock and nu-metal were still in their infancy. At the end of the 1990s the rock-buying public seemed to go mad for lightweight, irreverent pop acts – such as Weezer – and pop-punk bands – like Green Day. In the midst of all that, this Pennsylvanian quintet's amusing frat-boy blend of smutty humor and synth-rock provided them with a batch of hits. The biggest, 'The Bad Touch,' was an ode to sex ("You and me baby, we ain't nothing but mammals / Let's do it like they do on the Discovery Channel") accompanied by a 'funny' video.

Porcelain
Moby

Released June 2000
V2 *27650* (U.S.) / Mute *CDMUTE 252* (U.K. #5)

South Side
Moby Featuring Gwen Stefani

Released January 2001
V2 *27665* (U.S. #11) / Not issued U.K.

The New York-based producer Moby (born Richard Melville Hall, a descendent of the author of *Moby Dick*) is one of America's most notable and outspoken artists in the field of electronic music. He is known as much for trying a vast array of sounds and styles as he is for talking about social and political issues, showing that an artist can be

both entertaining and intelligent. With his propulsive techno anthems, Moby has been a fixture on the international scene since the 1990s heyday of rave culture.

He took a distinct left-turn with his 2000 album *Play*, where he took recordings of blues musicians by sound anthropologist Alan Lomax into his sample palette. *Play* pleasantly surprised critics and fans, opening up his audience base with a thoughtful balance of classic and modern elements.

A British Top 10 hit, 'Porcelain' did not fare nearly as well on the American pop charts for Moby (which seemed to suit him well). But it was an undeniable hit with executives on Madison Avenue: 'Porcelain,' like most of *Play*, was licensed throughout the world for use in film and television and was used to sell a number of brands and products – a car, a department store, a liqueur – which seemed like a

testimonial to its versatility and broad appeal. With several hundred licenses for a multitude of applications, *Play* has since been cited and studied by the music industry and the advertising industry as a test-case of potential salesmanship.

Early in 2001 Moby redressed the failure of *Play*'s singles on the U.S. *Billboard* chart with the release of a re-recorded version of the album's 'South Side.' A key element in its mainstream success was the guest vocal by Gwen Stefani of the ska-pop group No Doubt, whose past hits included 'Just A Girl' and 'Don't Speak.' It was the first of two smash-hit collaborations for Stefani in early 2001: she also sang on Eve's U.S. Number 2 hit 'Let Me Blow Ya Mind.'

I'm Outta Love
Anastacia

Released September 2000
Epic *79354* (U.S.) / Epic *6695782* (U.K. #6)

Although Anastacia is a strikingly beautiful woman with a powerful stage show and an equally impressive set of lungs, her brash, slightly aggressive demeanor has caused more than a few fans to back away in fear over the years. Nonetheless, there's no denying the power of her voice and songwriting, and this single was a remarkable introduction to both. Labeled by many critics as "the new Tina Turner" for her bulging-neck-veins fortissimo, Anastacia gave it maximum power in 'I'm Outta Love,' a very hum-able tune with a stamping beat and wall-of-sound backing that resembled a hybrid of The Supremes and Cher. Surprisingly, despite achieving smash-hit status across Europe, the single stuttered in at a lowly 92 in her native America.

Since I Left You
The Avalanches

Released September 2000
Modular *010* (U.S.) / XL Recordings *XLS 134CD* (U.K. #16)

Australian electronica quartet The Avalanches (Robbie Chater, Tony Diblasi, Gordon McQuilten, and Darren Seitmann) gained international attention with this creative and lively slice of sampladelia that is reminiscent of U.K. pop band St. Etienne.

A hit in the land down under, the song missed the American pop charts but still managed to make an impression among underground tastemakers in both regions as a significant club hit. It's a versatile tune that won favor among DJs of varying styles. In Britain, the single was successfully reissued on XL Recordings, home of techno terrorists Prodigy, while in America they signed with the major label Sire.

The Avalanches were cheekily vocal about the fact that the *Since I Left You* album was made possible with the liberal use of over 900 samples from records of just about every style imaginable, and they promoted the record with a special DJ mix that dipped into everyone from Hall & Oates to some obscure German electronica. It was impossible to legally clear all of the album's samples for use, so listeners were left guessing about the correct origins of many of the eclectic sounds. As far as we can tell, the song seems inspired by bright 1960s pop, but it could just as easily have been made by pillaging modern country songs.

B.O.B. (Bombs Over Baghdad)
OutKast

Released September 2000
LaFace *24500* (U.S.) / LaFace-Arista *1822942* (U.K.)

Ms. Jackson
OutKast

Released November 2000
LaFace *24516* (U.S. #1) / LaFace-Arista *1836822* (U.K. #2)

OutKast's fourth album *Stankonia* showed the group in transition into popular consciousness, and the lead single 'B.O.B. (Bombs Over Baghdad)' burst onto the scene with a techno-like pace, moving with the ferocity of a roaring train. A metaphor for the group's bombastic potency, the song was a hit on radio as well as MTV, although it was later banned by the corporate radio giant Clear Channel in the aftermath of the attacks on the U.S. in September 2001.

'Ms. Jackson,' on the other hand, strips the group of a considerable amount of its machismo, something few rappers like to have taken away. An ode to their "babymama's mamas," the song is written as an apology to the mothers of their former girlfriends (and mothers of their children), because they broke up with the girl even after they had a child together. Many still believe the main inspiration for the character of 'Ms. Jackson' to be the mother of soul singer Erykah Badu, with whom OutKast's André Benjamin had a son named Seven.

'Ms. Jackson' later received the Grammy for Best Rap Performance By A Duo Or Group, the award that had earlier eluded the pair for 'Rosa Parks.' OutKast also achieved Grammy nominations for 'Ms. Jackson' for Best Shortform Video and for Record Of The Year, the latter a rare feat for any hip-hop artist. *Stankonia*, meanwhile, won the Grammy for Best Rap Album and was nominated for Album Of The Year – an honor the group would grab in 2004 for the follow-up double album *Speakerboxxx / The Love Below*.

Stan
Eminem

Released November 2000
Interscope album cut (U.S.) / Interscope *97470* (U.K. #1)

Thank You
Dido

Released January 2001
Arista *13922* (U.S. #3) / Cheeky-Arista *1853042* (U.K. #3)

A haunting tale of obsessive fandom, 'Stan' captures Eminem at the height of his fame and the peak of his creative powers. It also helped the British singer-songwriter Dido, whose 'Thank You' is sampled in the chorus.

Eminem's proper debut single, 'My Name Is,' was issued less than two years earlier, but in the intervening period he had achieved more than most performers do in their entire careers – and generated more controversy. 'Stan' was the third single to be drawn from *The Marshall Mathers LP*, which sold over two million copies in its first week on sale and was the first rap album ever to be nominated for Album Of The Year at the Grammys.

But it took 'Stan' to cement Eminem's role as one of the biggest stars of the popular-music mainstream. The single is more considered and melodic than his previous releases, mostly through its liberal use of the chorus vocals and instrumental backing from 'Thank You.' Over shuffling acoustic guitars and subtle programmed drums, Eminem performs the first three verses in the character of Stan, a devoted fan who becomes so enraged by the rapper's failure to respond to a series of letters that he kills himself and his pregnant wife by driving off a bridge. The final verse contains the rapper's belated response as he realizes all-too-late that the Stan to whom he is replying is the same fan whose suicide he has just heard about.

Despite its bleak, unsettling lyrical content, 'Stan' was a huge international hit and in the week before Christmas 2000 gave Eminem his second British chart-topping single ('The Way I Am' had been a U.K. Number 1 six months earlier). As was the case with the majority of the rapper's singles, 'Stan' was not released commercially in the U.S. but quickly became a staple of music television and radio programming, and made Number 51 on the *Billboard* Hot 100.

At the 2001 Grammy Awards ceremony, Eminem performed the song with Elton John singing Dido's parts, in response to widespread criticism of the rapper's lyrics by the Gay And Lesbian Alliance Against Defamation (who still picketed the event). The duet with Elton raised a few eyebrows, but in many ways the combination of Eminem – America's most controversial rapper – and Dido – a hippy-dippy English songbird – was just as surprising.

Dido made her first appearances on record in the mid to late 1990s with the dance-pop group Faithless, fronted by her brother, Rollo. Born Florian Cloud de Bounevialle Armstrong, Dido studied at the Guildhall School Of Music in London from the age of six before completing a law degree.

Her full-length solo debut, *No Angel* (1999), was helped first when 'Here With Me' was used as the main theme to the sci-fi TV series *Roswell* and then by Eminem's adoption of 'Thank You.' By the middle of 2001, 'Thank You' had become a British and American hit in its own right, while the gentle, ethereal songs of *No Angel* found their way into over 13 million record collections across the world.

Yellow
Coldplay

Released July 2000
EMI *889077* (U.S.) / Parlophone *CDR 6538* (U.K. #4)

Can it really be this long since Chris Martin and his band released their second proper single, the fragile 'Yellow'? Nowadays the quartet are a globally successful chart act, walking into America with a shy smile and a keyboard flourish and hobnobbing with the great and the good of Hollywood thanks to Martin's marriage to A-league actress Gwyneth Paltrow. Yet it all started so quietly. This single crept into the U.S. charts at Number 48.

'Yellow' is a simple song, elevated to the realms of the extraordinary by three key attributes. First, there is Martin's killer falsetto in the bridge. Everyone likes a romantic, spiralling boy-wail (in this case on the line "Your *skin*, oh yeah your skin and bones") and Coldplay's version was no exception. Second, the clever decision at the end of the song to play the same chords that have made up the whole song so far – but switching them from major to minor: not a common move, but here a stroke of genius. Finally, the band filmed an excellent less-is-more video featuring Martin ambling along a beach as dawn breaks, mouthing the words in slow motion (in fact he had to sing it at double speed for the shoot). Although he resembled the science geek you used to pick on at school, the song's sheer quality ensured classic status for the video. More hit singles and three hit albums followed, and the rest is history.

Beautiful Day
U2

Released September 2000
Island *562972* (U.S. #21) / Island *CID 766* (U.K. #1)

Although the 1990s had started well for U2 – when, as now, they were the biggest band in the world – they had lost their way by the *Pop* album of 1997 and needed to reclaim some relevance as the new decade began. Fortunately, 'Beautiful Day' and its parent album *All That You Can't Leave Behind* were just what was needed, ushering in a whole new sound, steeped in vintage vibes, exuding middle-aged cheerfulness, and attracting a new generation of listeners.

Astoundingly, 'Beautiful Day' marked the first time that Bono, Edge, Adam Clayton, and Larry Mullen Jr. displayed a tendency towards plagiarism, inadvertently or otherwise. As Bono's vocal broke into "Touch me ... take me to that place" and then "Teach me ... I know I'm not a hopeless case" it was obvious that the melody was similar to the 1985 hit 'The Sun Always Shines On TV' by Norwegian trio A-Ha. But it's safe to assume that everyone's favorite Irish rockers wouldn't have deliberately pinched the idea. Indeed, Bono had once sarcastically dedicated a live rendition of their hit 'One' to British garage man Craig David, whose song 'Walking Away' had borrowed the chord sequence of the U2 tune with cheeky nonchalance.

'Beautiful Day' marked the resumption of U2's keen performance in the singles charts, and it isn't too much to say that without it they might have gone down a steady route into obscurity – one to which their arch experiments with electronica on *Pop* could only lead. As it is, they seem now to be well set for the rest of their lives.

Rollin'
Limp Bizkit

Released October 2000
Flip/Interscope *06406* (U.S.) / Interscope *IND 97474* (U.K. #1)

Taken from the Number 1 multi-platinum-selling album *Chocolate Starfish And The Hotdog Flavored Water*, 'Rollin'' is one of Limp Bizkit's most memorable anthems. The Florida band, fronted by angsty lead singer Fred Durst (a tabloid favorite for his escapades), had burst into the pop world three years earlier with a bombastic cover of George Michael's ditty 'Faith.'

Limp Bizkit followed up two years later with the crass 'Nookie' and the hip-hop savvy 'N Together Now,' a song produced by legendary DJ Premier and featuring rapper Method Man of Wu-Tang Clan. But 'Rollin'' – a perfect anthem for SUV road rage – rocks the hardest.

Feel Good Hit Of The Summer
Queens Of The Stone Age

Released November 2000
Interscope *497443* (U.S.) / Interscope *497455* (U.K.)

Stoner-rock had been something of a niche interest before Queens Of The Stone Age came along. Genre pioneers Kyuss and Monster Magnet were reliable festival draws but hardly troubled the charts. That changed when the notoriously hard-partying QOTSA landed in the lower U.K. charts with the very cheeky 'Feel Good Hit Of The Summer,' a one-note grind featuring as its sole lyric the line "Nicotine, valium, vicodan, marijuana, ecstasy, and alcohol" and the one-word chorus of "C-c-c-c-c-cocaine!" Rob Halford of Judas Priest lent his robust vocals to the song, which became much-loved for its simplicity and catchiness and its controversial subject – a killer combination.

Modern Age
The Strokes

Released January 2001
Beggars Banquet *85024* (U.S.) / Rough Trade *RTRADCD 010* (U.K.)

Hotel Yorba
The White Stripes

Released November 2001
XL Recordings *XLS 139* (U.S., U.K. #26)

New York quartet The Strokes and Detroit duo The White Stripes had been performing and recording since the late 1990s, but their first widely successful releases came in 2001 – and boy, did they make an impact. The two bands are rather different in style but were lumped together initially thanks to their stripped-down music, ineffably cool pouts, and the fact that their names began with 'The' (hysteria began to build when The Hives joined in the fuss).

The Strokes' signature song remains the fantastic 'Last Nite,' which leads off the *Modern Age* EP. It's a combination of simple, trancey blues-rock riffing, a look that was pure marketing heaven, and a lean, economical sound akin to Blondie and the other tight, funky post-punk acts. With their gorgeous curls and skin-tight black jeans, they looked as if they'd been pulled straight from 1981 and the oh so fashionable bars of New York's Lower East Side, where they had made their name. Frontman Julian Casablancas personified their appeal with his Italian-American sneer and a penchant for flinging the mic-stand about between puffs on his Marlboro. Fortunately, all this was backed up by some solid songwriting.

The more enigmatic Jack and Meg White (vocals-guitar and drums respectively – there is no bassist in The White Stripes) were less immediately digestible but appear to be the more durable act. With their raw, powerful sound derived from vintage American blues, the duo struck gold with 'Hotel Yorba,' their first proper single. Massive success came in 2003 with the Stripes' biggest song to date, 'Seven Nation Army,' and their future seemed assured.

Clint Eastwood
Gorillaz

Released March 2001
EMI *879050* / Parlophone *CDR 6552* (U.K. #4)

The idea of a cartoon rock band wasn't exactly original – remember The Archies? – but with his animated Gorillaz project, sometime Blur frontman Damon Albarn offered up some of the most innovative pop music of the new millennium. 'Clint Eastwood' mixes the haunting, minor-key melodicism of The Specials with producer Dan 'The Automator' Nakamura's slick rhythms and an icy cool rap by Del Tha Funkee Homosapien.

Albarn and Jamie Hewlett, creator of the cult comic-book series *Tank Girl*, first conceived of the idea of a "virtual hip-hop group" in the late 1990s. While Hewlett came up with the visuals, Albarn started putting the music together with a host of collaborators from the worlds of rock and rap, including Nakamura, DJ Kid Koala, and the former Talking Heads rhythm section of Chris Frantz and Tina Weymouth.

The resulting *Gorillaz* album was filled to the brim with genre-blending, thoroughly modern pop, and the most joyous music Albarn had made since the early days of Blur. 'Clint Eastwood' was the second single to be drawn from the album, following the low-key release of 'Tomorrow Comes Today' in late 2000 (for which the musicians behind Gorillaz tried but failed to keep their identities secret). 'Clint Eastwood' continued Albarn's run of chart success in the U.K. but more crucially provided the first step towards the kind of U.S. success that had always eluded him with Blur, with a Number 57 entry on the *Billboard* Hot 100.

Where's Your Head At
Basement Jaxx

Released November 2001
Astralwerks *38803* (U.S.) / XL Recordings *XLS140CD* (U.K. #9)

Based on a big distorted keyboard riff sampled from Gary Numan, Basement Jaxx's most memorable single to date was a blast right from its first bars. The song was loaded with sirens from the DAT tape marked 'Chemical Brothers' and had an infectious four-to-the-floor beat in a clubland groove nailed to some amusing vocals – and that was it. Crowds loved the single, especially when it was coupled with the rather outrageous rock act that the band put on. However, 'Head' wouldn't have done half as well without its accompanying video, a genuinely unnerving clip in which an unsuspecting laboratory visitor is threatened by half-human half-monkey mutants.

Get Ur Freak On
Missy Elliott

Released March 2001
Elektra *67190* (U.S. #7) / East West-Elektra *E 7206CD* (U.K. #4)

In four breathtaking minutes, 'Get Ur Freak On' demonstrates exactly why Missy Elliott was one of the hottest musical talents of the late 1990s and early 2000s. It was also one of the first major hits to blend cutting-edge hip-hop with Middle Eastern instrumentation.

After working with Jodeci and New Edition, Elliott got her break half a decade earlier when she and long-standing collaborator Timbaland contributed seven songs to teen R&B star Aaliyah's big-selling *One In A Million* (1996). Missy's own debut, *Supa Dupa Fly*, arrived a year later and was soon propelled up the charts on the strengths of the sterling single 'The Rain,' which made clever use of an Ann Peebles sample. The multi-talented, larger-than-life star soon became something of a style icon, too, appearing in ad campaigns for Gap and Sprite as singles like 'She's A Bitch' and 'Hot Boyz' became hits.

Over the years Elliott has racked up a host of hits as a solo performer, among them 'Work It' (2002), and produced chart smashes for numerous other artists. It's unlikely, however, that anything else she does will be able to eclipse the scattershot rhythms, tricksy tabla patterns, and cocksure vocals of 'Get Ur Freak On.' The only drawback for Elliott is that, since the release of this single and the accompanying *Miss E . . . So Addictive* album, expectations for her subsequent releases have been impossibly high – although she almost topped 'Get Ur Freak On' with 'Work It.'

Family Affair
Mary J. Blige

Released July 2001
MCA *155859* (U.S. #1) / Uptown-MCA *MCSTD 40267* (U.K. #8)

The sensational soul singer Mary Jane Blige (originally from Yonkers, New York) has been consistently praised for her heartfelt lyrics and phenomenal vocal tone, but 'Family Affair' made longtime fans want to know who produced the equally strong instrumentation behind her. The answer is Dr. Dre, the legendary hip-hop producer who's largely responsible for the careers of blockbuster artists such as Snoop Dogg and Eminem. This pairing of two supernovas in the urban music world shot straight to the top of the American pop charts thanks to Dre's funk-infused strings and Mary's uplifting and celebratory singing.

Fallin'
Alicia Keys

Released June 2001
J Records *21041* (U.S. #1) / J Records *1903692* (U.K. #3)

Alicia Keys (born Alicia Cook) has traveled a long and hard road in the music business, from years spent playing a small piano in a cramped apartment she shared with her mother Terri in the rough Hell's Kitchen section of Manhattan, to the pinnacle of international pop success and humanitarian activism. After the heartbreak of a failed record deal that collapsed on itself before she was even old enough to drive, Keys caught the attention of wizened Arista Records music executive Clive Davis, who had launched the careers of serious legends like Whitney Houston and Santana. After leaving Arista, Davis kicked off his new venture J Records with the startling talent of this extraordinary singer-songwriter wise beyond her tender years.

With simple yet deep lyrics that resonate with anyone who has wrestled with the rollercoaster emotions of love, the aching piano ballad 'Fallin'' made Alicia Keys an instant heartthrob and a household name in record time. The song cleaned up at the 2002 Grammy Awards, where she brought home statuettes for Song Of The Year, Best R&B Song, and Best R&B Vocal Performance. The song was also a catalyst for the rest of Keys's multi-platinum-selling debut album *Songs In A Minor*, which gathered a host of gongs from the NAACP Image Awards, the *Billboard* Awards, the Soul Train Awards, and the Teen Choice Awards.

Rock The Boat
Aaliyah

Released September 2001
Priority *46109* (U.S. #14) / Blackground-Virgin *VUSCD 243* (U.K. #12)

'Rock The Boat' was not Aaliyah Haughton's biggest hit. That may have been 'One In A Million' in 1996, or 2000's 'Try Again,' both Number 1 singles in America – and both produced by Virginia studio wizard Timbaland for the young star, who got her start as a protégé (and secret love interest) of R. Kelly. But 'Rock The Boat' accidentally became more than just a sultry song with a barely veiled nautical metaphor for sexual intercourse. The Detroit-born R&B star died tragically in a plane crash – along with some of her employees and personnel from her label, Virgin Records – after video director Hype Williams shot the song's beautiful performance video on Abaco Island in the Bahamas. Aaliyah's star power had been soaring high in music and in film alike, with starring roles in *Romeo Must Die* and *Queen Of The Damned*, and she was just 22 years old.

At the time of the accident, Aaliyah had been quietly dating New Yorker Damon Dash, an outspoken man who was then the business partner of rapper Jay-Z in the Roc-A-Fella empire, a massive, multi-tiered company that earned millions in the clothing and music industries. The typically vocal Dash remained respectful and relatively quiet about the shock of her death, although he admitted frankly that he couldn't listen to the radio or watch television because of the heavy airplay that 'Rock The Boat' was enjoying.

Can't Get You Out Of My Head
Kylie Minogue

Released September 2001
Capitol *77685* (U.S. #7) / Parlophone *CDRS 6562* (U.K. #1)

'Can't Get You Out of My Head' was a comeback single for the former soap-opera actress who most people thought had run the full course of her European pop success. But it proved that Australian beauty Kylie Minogue could be remembered for more than covering 1960s hit 'The Locomotion' and having the most prized posterior this side of bootylicious American actress-singer-dancer Jennifer Lopez. A household name in Europe, Kylie turned this song into her introduction to most American audiences, who had barely made a note of 'The Locomotion' when she trotted it out in the 1990s.

'Can't Get You Out of My Head' received dozens of unofficial, underground remixes from aspiring bedroom producers all over the world. These versions, sometimes called mash-ups, helped extend the shelf-life of the original song, which was played well beyond its original point of expiration. (One version memorably paired Minogue's solo voice with the instrumental backing to New Order's 'Blue Monday.') The song was penned by the British duo of Rob Davis, formerly the bassist in 1970s glam-rock band Mud, and Cathy Dennis, who had international chart success in the '90s as part of dance act D Mob. This global hit for Minogue gave Dennis a second wind, and she later wrote more pop hits, including 'Toxic,' the biggest song so far for another modern pop sensation, Britney Spears.

Get The Party Started
Pink

Released October 2001
Arista *15074* (U.S. #4) / LaFace-Arista *1913372* (U.K. #2)

Beautiful
Christina Aguilera

Released December 2002
RCA *98364* (U.S. #2) / RCA *6502462* (U.K. #1)

The colorfully-dressed all-female rock band from the San Francisco Bay Area known as 4 Non Blondes are remembered, sometimes derisively, as a one-hit wonder for their unusual 1992 hit 'What's Up.' But a decade later, former 4NB guitarist Linda Perry went on to craft memorable hits for young pop stars Pink and Christina Aguilera, and earned a distinction as one of America's most promising and in-demand 'new' producers.

Perry's 'Get The Party Started' was one of two songs she wrote for Pink's sophomore album *M!ssundaztood*. It helped Pink transform her image from lightweight R&B crooner to gutsy rock singer with a slice of sassy and jangly guitar pop. Pink has since been viewed as an artist capable of a much more versatile range than many had thought possible, something the artist herself had been telling her record-label executives from day one.

After shocking the public with the raunchy single 'Dirrty,' Christina Aguilera followed it up with Perry's 'Beautiful,' a plaintive ballad for self-esteem with its stirring chorus: "You are beautiful / No matter what they say / Words can't bring you down." The song brought back what people loved best about Aguilera: her remarkable voice, but not her somewhat childish attempt to be a sex kitten. 'Beautiful' was nominated for a Grammy for Song Of The Year.

Pop
*NSYNC

Released June 2001
Jive *42933* (U.S. #19) / Jive *9252422* (U.K. #9)

I'm a Slave 4 U
Britney Spears
Released October 2001
Jive *42967* (U.S. #27) / Jive *9252892* (U.K. #4)

Lapdance
N*E*R*D Featuring Lee Harvey & Vita
Released May 2001
Virgin *38786* (U.S.) / Virgin *VUSCD 196* (U.K. #33)

Mouseketeers have to grow up eventually, and 2001 was a key year in the development of the lives of former Mickey Mouse Club members Britney Spears and Justin Timberlake, then the lead singer of boy-band *NSYNC. The former couple in puppy love were morphing into young adults under the extreme heat of the world's spotlight. Instead of remaining in creative stasis, they tried to make records in a more mature style that broke away a little from the earlier work. *NSYNC's 'Pop' was a breakbeat-heavy tune directed by American electronica producer BT (Brian Transeau) and it gave the band a new edge with DJs on the club scene – just as its members were becoming old enough to get into clubs and drink legally.

By 2001, The Neptunes (Pharrell Williams and Chad Hugo) had built their name as producers with the gold and platinum touch, largely in the hip-

hop world with artists such as N.O.R.E. and Jay-Z. Working with pop princess Britney Spears on the successful single 'I'm A Slave 4 U' forced a broader definition of their capabilities across musical boundaries. Spears was intrigued by the growing reputation of The Neptunes as hitmakers, but few could have predicted how utterly combustible their collaboration would be. Where Spears's earlier recorded efforts hinted at sex in the hands of an innocent sweetheart, the video for 'I'm A Slave 4 U' found her in hot pink leather and chaps, writhing around a sweaty room with an erotic arrangement of equally drenched dancers. Her contrived goody-two-shoes image was gone for good, but thankfully the song's lyrics were not entirely explicit and still left a little something to the imagination.

'I'm A Slave 4 U' was not Spears's biggest hit by a long shot, stalling at Number 27 on the *Billboard* Hot 100. But its water-cooler potential – the ability to generate office talk and other forms of mainstream buzz – exceeded that of every song she had put out so far, and it remains one of her most controversial cuts. The second single from the *Britney* album was 'I'm Not a Girl, Not Yet a Woman,' but the imagery and lyrics Spears portrayed with 'I'm A Slave 4 U' had many fans unsure if that was a true statement.

So shocking was Britney Spears's song upon its release that another steamy Neptunes production was almost lost in the shuffle. The soaring chords and urgently plucky rhythms of 'Lapdance,' recorded under Williams and Hugo's relatively shortlived guise as N.E.R.D. (standing for No one Ever Really Dies), features the little-known female rapper Vida singing the spicy hook: "Baby, you want me? / Well, you can get this lapdance here for free." But compared to Spears, who had the sweat literally licked off of her in her video, the more urban-focused 'Lapdance' failed to raise quite as many eyebrows in America.

IN SEARCH OF THE NEPTUNES

Poseidon, who also answers to the catchy little name of Neptune, is the eternal god of the sea, the overlord of all things aquatic and fluid. He's an unlikely mascot for a town, yet Neptune is the centerpiece of a myriad of activities in Virginia Beach, VA. His gargantuan statue likeness watches over the Virginia Beach boardwalk with commanding grace, while turtles, fish, and other sea creatures cling on for dear life.

He was no doubt a powerful icon to the young Virginia Beach natives Pharrell Williams and Chad Hugo, for when they officially formed a studio production team they called themselves The Neptunes, later the recipients of a Grammy Award for Producer Of The Year (2004). They learned throughout the 1990s under the wing of R&B producer Teddy Riley (known as the inventor of new jack swing for artists such as Bobby Brown), but by the turn of the century Williams and Hugo would come to eclipse Riley's significant achievements in the recording industry and set off into the deep end of superstardom, crafting hits for a diverse array of artists.

The Neptunes' electronic bleeps, punchy rhythms, and sweet soul hooks became signature stamps that many wanted to collect. This meant not only a heavy demand for Williams and Hugo but also resulted in a slew of inferior copycat productions by amateurish producers who wanted to cash-in on an apparent formula for victory.

Williams and Hugo first started creating a buzz with rap songs like N.O.R.E.'s 'Superthug' (1998), Mystikal's 'Shake Ya Ass' (2000), and Jay-Z's 'I Just Wanna Love U (Give It 2 Me)' (2000), but by 2001 they were crafting songs for pop tartlet Britney Spears, the best example being her controversially mature 'I'm A Slave 4 U.' They've since gone on to record with Usher, Beyoncé, Toni Braxton, Gwen Stefani, Mariah Carey, and others in the pop world, but have maintained a close tie with their beloved hip-hop and R&B flavors, fostering groups such as the street-edged Clipse and the singer Kelis, for whom they've produced several memorable songs including her hits 'Caught Out There' (1996) and 'Milkshake' (2004). They've worked with hip-hop stars like Nelly, Busta Rhymes, Fabolous, and LL Cool J, although they explored the fringes of rock with their N.E.R.D. group, a project that spawned one album, *In Search Of*. They've also given rap icon Snoop Dogg the biggest hits of his career with 'Beautiful' (2003) and 'Drop It Like It's Hot' (2004).

Despite having a population of less than half a million, Virginia Beach has come to be known as a breeding ground for distinctively different musical talent. Besides The Neptunes and their mentor Teddy Riley, the town is also the place where rap-R&B superstars Jodeci, Missy Elliot, and Timbaland all grew up. Maybe there really is something in those waters of Neptune.

It Wasn't Me
Shaggy

Released January 2001
MCA *155782* (U.S. #1) / MCA *1558022* (U.K. #1)

Because I Got High
Afroman

Released August 2001
Universal *015310* (U.S. #13) / Universal *MCSTD 40266* (U.K. #1)

Two of the most hilarious odes to non-accountability in music emerged in 2001 – and became not just cult hits but international hits. 'It Wasn't Me' was the bestselling song in the U.K. that year and the largest in Jamaican singer Shaggy's career, while 'Because I Got High' was a surprise triumph from a relatively unknown rap artist. Shaggy's anthem is about not being a cheater, even in the face of obvious and damning evidence such as being caught red-handed in the sexual act, and is as gut-bustingly funny as Afroman blaming everything in his life on smoking too much marijuana.

Izzo (H.O.V.A.)
Jay-Z

Released July 2001
Roc-A-Fella *588701* (U.S. #8) / Roc-A-Fella *5888152* (U.K. #21)

From the critically acclaimed and multi-platinum-selling album *The Blueprint*, 'Izzo (H.O.V.A.)' was produced by Chicago's Kanye West, who later became an internationally acclaimed solo artist on the level of a blockbuster rapper like Jay-Z (the alias of Brooklyn-born Sean Carter). Loyal to the man who gave him his greatest fame as a producer, West signed to Jay-Z's label Roc-A-Fella. 'Izzo' samples and loops the briefest snippet of Michael Jackson in his Jackson 5 days and speeds it up even faster than the young chipmunk could do on his own, exemplifying the creative production style that became West's signature. Several years later, it was still being 'borrowed' by countless hip-hop producers worldwide in their fruitless quest to capture his winning formula. West's first solo breakout hit, 2003's 'Through The Wire,' applied the technique to Chaka Khan's hit 'Through The Fire.'

But 'Izzo' is not just simply a showcase for the prodigious Kanye West; musical titan Jay-Z is spotlighted rather well here, too. Lyrically, the song demonstrates Jay-Z's considerable talent for wordplay: 'H.O.V.A.' is an abbreviation for "Jay-Hova," a play on Jehovah to indicate his rap-god status; 'Izzo' appropriates a type of West Coast hip-hop slang that throws the 'izz' sound in the middle of words, a style popularized by L.A. rapper Snoop Dogg. 'Izzo (H.O.V.A.)' earned Jay-Z a Grammy nomination for Best Rap Solo Performance.

Gotta Get Thru This
Daniel Bedingfield

Released December 2001
Island *570976* (U.S. #10) / Relentless *RELENT 27CD* (U.K. #1)

The New Zealand-born and British-bred singer-producer Daniel Bedingfield scored an international hit with this catchy take on the rollicking, funky dance music that's been referred to variously as U.K. garage and 2-step. Listeners who first heard 'Gotta Get Thru This' were not immediately aware that vocalist Bedingfield was male, since the singing was considerably speeded up. It was a surprise hit in America, a country that didn't take to the genre the way it took to this song.

Hero
Enrique Iglesias

Released October 2001
Interscope *497613* (U.S. #3) / Interscope *IND 97671* (U.K. #1)

Whenever, Wherever
Shakira

Released November 2001
Sony International *672196* (U.S. #6) / Epic *6724262* (U.K. #2)

The turn of the century brought a new appreciation for Latin American pop stars in Britain and America, a phenomenon that brought new success for Spain's Enrique Iglesias and Columbia's Shakira, singers who had already enjoyed success in the Spanish-speaking world.

After scoring his first American chart-topper in 1999 with 'Bailamos,' Enrique, son of legendary singer Julio Iglesias, returned to the Top 10 in 2001 with 'Hero' from his album *Escape*. That same year, Shakira – a star in her native Columbia since she was a pre-teen – debuted her first U.K. album *Laundry Service* and the breakout hit 'Whenever, Wherever.' Both artists have had hits by mixing Spanish and English in the same songs, but of course their mainly English versions have done best in the English-speaking territories.

It hurts neither Iglesias nor Shakira that each has become a sex symbol, which they both exploited fully in their videos for these songs as well as in their careers generally. The video for 'Hero' features an adventure plot with the damsel in distress played by Iglesias's then-girlfriend Jennifer Love Hewitt, an attractive American movie actress who got her start as a star of the Fox television drama *Party Of Five*. Meanwhile, Shakira's visual take for 'Whenever, Wherever' has her rolling around in mud and shaking her body suggestively while wearing a tight leather bikini top.

Ain't It Funny
Jennifer Lopez Featuring Ja Rule & Caddillac Tah

Released January 2002
Epic *672390* (U.S. #1) / Epic *6724922* (U.K. #4)

Foolish
Ashanti

Released March 2002
Murder Inc. *588986* (U.S. #1) / Murder Inc. / Mercury *0639942* (U.K. #4)

During the first half of 2002, the hip-hop label Murder Inc. and it's biggest star, Ja Rule, held an 18-week stranglehold on the *Billboard* Hot 100's Number 1 spot.

Born Jeffrey Atkins in Queens, New York City, Ja Rule wrote and produced several hits with R&B hooks – and lent his lyrical talents to a few R&B songs and helped make them hits as well. The first time he had success with the formula was with New Jersey singer Christina Milian on the sexy 'Between Me & You' and then with Baltimore's Lil' Mo on 'Put It On Me,' but his next single, 'Always On Time,' brought it straight to the top. A burgeoning chanteuse from Long Island, New York, named Ashanti Douglas sang the 'Always On Time' hook, and by the time the two performers appeared together in the video, yet another star was born, and Ja Rule had his first Number 1 single.

After two weeks at the top, 'Always On Time' was replaced by an even bigger hit, 'Ain't It Funny,' the first of two hip-hop-savvy collaborations between Ja Rule and the Bronx-born actress-dancer-singer Jennifer Lopez. Both 'Ain't It Funny' and 'I'm Real' appeared on a remix album called *J To Tha L-O! The Remixes*. The songs, which sampled classic hip-hop joints like Craig Mack's 'Flava In Your Ear,' lent the critically panned Lopez some credibility in the hip-hop world, which she had long tried to join. (She continued to espouse her "street" credentials with 'Jenny From The Block,' a Number 3 hit on the *Billboard* Hot 100 later in 2002.)

In the meatime, Ashanti had signed to Murder Inc. and been busying herself working on a record of her own, with help from label boss Irv Gotti and, naturally, the omnipresent Mr. Rule. Follwing 'Ain't It Funny''s six-week stint at Number 1, Ashanti's solo debut, 'Foolish,' hit the top spot, and hung on in there for a total of ten weeks. Ja Rule didn't feel the need to put in an appearance on this particular record, but did pop up in the video, which was fashioned after the much-loved gangster movie *Goodfellas*.

Hot In Herre
Nelly

Released May 2002
Fo' Real *279* (U.S. #1) / Universal *MCSTD 40289* (U.K. #4)

Dirrty
Christina Aguilera Featuring Redman

Released October 2002
RCA *97635* (U.S. #48) / RCA *1962722* (U.K. #1)

St. Louis-based rapper Nelly had a runaway hit with 'Hot In Herre,' a catchy and flirty tune produced by Pharrell Williams of The Neptunes that spent seven weeks atop the American charts and snagged a Grammy for Best Male Rap Solo Performance. In addition to ruling clubs, radio, MTV, and BET for months, the song unintentionally inspired a hit from another pop artist (Christina Aguilera) and a film from an internationally famous fashion photographer (David LaChappelle).

After Nelly's anthem started to wane just a little, Canadian electro DJ Tiga followed it up with his own version of 'Hot in Herre.' Tiga ended up with an international club hit and released a memorable video featuring marionette puppets singing the lyrics. 'Hot' also inspired songbird Christina Aguilera in the slangified spelling of her own 'Dirrty' later that year. Musically, Aguilera's surprisingly raunchy tune derives from 'Let's Get Dirty,' a song by East Coast rapper Redman, produced by Rockwilder.

Aguilera's camp secured production by Rockwilder and a guest appearance by Redman to make 'Dirrty.' Her song is indelibly associated with its David LaChappelle-directed video in which Aguilera, clad in skimpy underwear and chaps, writhes with female dancers in a muddy underworld replete with illicit fighting and strange fetishes. Among the cast of performers are dancers from South Central Los Angeles who practice a style called krumping. LaChappelle's experience shooting 'Dirrty' inspired him to create his award-winning documentary Rize in 2005, a chronicle of krumping (and its predecessor, clowning).

Gimme The Light
Sean Paul

Released October 2002
VP *6400* (U.S. #7) / VP-Atlantic *AT 0146CD* (U.K. #5)

The sounds of Jamaica were pivotal in creating the foundation for American hip-hop, but styles such as reggae and its lively sub-strain of dancehall have traditionally only been popular in U.S. cities with sizeable Caribbean populations, such as New York and Miami. Sean Paul Henriques kicked the door down with 'Gimme The Light,' a smash with club DJs that broke through to radio and video outlets.

The chart-topping follow-up single 'Get Busy' and album *Dutty Rock* (which got the Grammy for Best Reggae Album) helped cement dancehall as a viable sound within the American urban-music scene in 2003. That year he also added his vocals to two of the biggest international hits of the summer – Beyoncé's 'Baby Boy' and 'Breathe' by Blu Cantrell.

A Moment Like This
Kelly Clarkson

Released October 2002
RCA *6022* (U.S. #1) / RCA *60622* (U.K. B-side)

Kelly Clarkson was catapulted to fame as the winner of the first season of *American Idol*, the U.S. version of the British TV talent show *Pop Idol*. There is nothing particularly remarkable about the Texan singer's debut single, but there didn't need to be. Given the platform of such a successful television series, there was no question that 'A Moment Like This' would become a smash-hit on the *Billboard* charts, establishing a pattern that has since been followed by each of the subsequent *American Idol* winners.

To her credit, Clarkson seems like one of the few winners of *Idol* with the talent to last more than a couple of polished, throwaway pop ditties. By 2004 she had re-cast herself as rock chick par excellence with the international hit 'Since U Been Gone,' which was written for her by Max Martin, the Swedish composer of Britney Spears's breakthrough hit '. . . Baby One More Time.'

Cry Me A River
Justin Timberlake

Released December 2002
Jive *40073* (U.S. #3) / Jive *9254612* (U.K. #2)

As the most sought-after member of the blockbuster boy-band *NSYNC, Memphis-born Justin Timberlake was always touted as the one from the group who was most likely to have a successful solo career. But the extent of the multi-platinum success of Timberlake's debut effort *Justified,* an album that generated several hits, was still largely a surprise.

Most of *Justified* was breezy and fun, but the most talked about and easily the most scathing song on the record is 'Cry Me A River.' Produced by and featuring Timbaland (a.k.a. Tim Mosley, the Virginia-based producer of R&B hits for Aaliyah and Missy Elliot), the song is a tale of a cheating, dumped girlfriend and the ways of dealing with the consequences of her misguided actions.

It was widely rumored that 'Cry Me A River' was based on Timberlake's own tumultuous breakup with fellow pop-star Britney Spears (who allegedly cheated on him with her choreographer, Wade Robson). Their relationship had been dissected in the media for years, down to every last little detail, and Timberlake did nothing to discourage the widely held interpretation of the song. The video only added fuel to the already raging flames of the scandal by featuring a blonde Britney look-alike model as the target of Timberlake's hurtful revenge. It should come as no surprise that it was a favorite of the MTV video countdown program *Total Request Live* and a regular subject visited in gossip magazines such as *U.S. Weekly* and *Star*.

TV IDOLS: A NEW OLD WAY TO FABRICATE POP STARS

The idea of the manufactured pop act is nothing new – it dates back almost as far as pop music itself – but *Pop Idol*, *American Idol*, and the various spin-off TV shows that air around the globe have made the ploy even more transparent, not to mention even more successful.

The basic premise of the show – which in the U.K. was superseded by *The X-Factor* – is that a series of open auditions are held from which a "final 12" performers are selected to compete to become that year's idol. Every week, each of them sings a song before a panel of judges, who offer instant criticism. Viewers vote for their favorite, and the least popular act is voted off, until only one remains. Over the course of the series the performers are taught singing techniques and dance steps,

often by visiting guest musicians eager to put in an appearance – and plug their latest product – on what has become the top-rated show on American television.

Each year's winner is guaranteed a hit or two straight away, but few seem destined for enduring success – after all, it's never too long before the next *Idol* comes along. The true, lasting star is Simon Cowell, the main judge on both the British and American versions of the show, who is loved and hated in equal measure for his blunt put-downs of most of the performers. On the strength of this he has become one of the highest-paid stars in the history of American television, not to mention one of the most influential figures in the popular music industry.

Hate To Say I Told You So
The Hives

Released February 2002
Burning Heart *60157* (U.S.) / Burning Heart *BHR 1059* (U.K. #23)

Garage-rock had already been re-re-established in the U.K. thanks to
The Strokes and The White Stripes by the time that Swedish quintet The
Hives arrived with this addictive single, which scraped in at Number 86
in America. But it was this song that made many listeners aware of the
power of punked-up rock'n'roll, especially when pumped out by
Scandinavians in suits. Led off by an overdriven guitar (and breaking
down at one point to a similarly distorted bass part), 'Hate To Say I Told
You So' is powered by a simple four-note riff and fueled by the deranged
wails of Howlin' Pelle Almqvist. Impeccably good; unforgettably raw.

Freak Like Me
Sugababes

Released April 2002
Universal International *582898* (U.S.) / Island *CID 798* (U.K. #1)

'Freak Like Me' is the most commercially successful example of the
mash-up, a club remix that combines the musical elements of one song
with the vocal parts of another – and one of the most memorable U.K.
hits of recent times. In this case, the three Sugababes sing the lyrics to
Adina Howard's 1995 single of the same name against the powerful
synthesizer frame of Gary Numan's 1979 British Number 1 'Are Friends
Electric,' as reworked by the DJ-producer Richard X. The single helped
to establish Sugababes, who despite their ever-changing line-up were
among the most successful British girl-bands of the new millennium.
Numerous hits followed, including 'Round Round,' 'Hole In The Head,'
and 'Push The Button,' all U.K. Number 1s.

Toxicity
System Of A Down

Released March 2002
American album cut (U.S.) / Columbia *6725022* (U.K. #25)

Having prepared the way with the stunning 'Chop Suey!,' America's
finest Armenian metal quartet shed the last remaining vestiges of the nu-
metal tag with this epic song, which was also the title of their second
and most accessible album. Singer Serj Tankian laid his heavily vibrato'd
vocals over a dense but funky guitar soup, with the listener's ears drawn
inexorably to the stop-start riff in the bridge and the chorus line: "The
toxicity / Of our cities." The tune ends rather insanely with a snatch of
Eastern melody and Tankian's mad yelp. The future would be even
madder for this ambitious, unique band. While their singles were not
major chart hits in the U.S. – this one peaked at Number 70 – *Toxicity*
was the first of the group's three Number 1s on the *Billboard* album chart.

Let's Push Things Forward
The Streets

Released April 2002
Not issued U.S. / Locked On-679 *679L 005CD* (U.K. #30)

Aside perhaps from the likes of Massive Attack, there was little in the
way of a viable U.K. alternative to hip-hop during the 1980s and 1990s.
At the dawn of the 21st century, however, British urban music found a
new lease on life with the sounds of 2-step and U.K. garage – essentially
vocal versions of earlier, less mainstream strands of jungle and
drum'n'bass. This new music made its first impact on the charts with
hits by The Artful Dodger, Oxide & Neutrino, and the shortlived So Solid
Crew (essentially a poor man's Wu Tang Clan). But the genre's first true
star was Mike Skinner, a.k.a. The Streets.

Born in 1978, Skinner grew up on the outskirts of the typically British city
of Birmingham and started experimenting with music at a young age.
The title of his second single, 'Let's Push Things Forward,' is

representative of his music-making philosophy: the instrumental parts are clean, sleek, ultra-modern, and the words describe British urban life in a way never before heard on record. Steering clear of the sensationalism of a lot of U.S. hip-hop, Skinner instead reports on the mundane matters of life – cans of beer, Indian take-outs, darts – in a striking mock-cockney voice. Making explicit the comparison between his lyrics and those of his American counterparts, he said: "Around here, we say birds, not bitches." Skinner continued from strength to strength over the next few years, confirming his mainstream pop-star status with his first U.K. Number 1, 'Dry Your Eyes,' in late 2004.

House Of Jealous Lovers
The Rapture

Released April 2002
DFA *2121* (U.S.) / Output *OPRDFA 001* (U.K.)

Losing My Edge
LCD Soundsystem

Released July 2002
DFA *2123* (U.S.) / Output *OPRDFA 002* (U.K.)

It was only a matter of time, following the arrival of The Strokes, The Hives, and the rest, for a new bunch of bands to mine the dancier, funkier end of late-1970s and early-'80s punk and new wave. Two of the first and best of these were The Rapture and LCD Soundsystem. Both issued their defining singles in 2002, but it took a little longer for them to achieve noteworthy commercial success.

The Rapture had been in existence since the late 1990s but didn't begin to hit their stride until they made the *Out Of The Races And Onto The Tracks* EP, which echoed the work of Public Image Ltd and Talking Heads two decades earlier. 'House Of Jealous Lovers' took things a step further, adding an irresistibly funky backbeat and singalong chorus to the usual angular guitars and throbbing bass.

A 2003 reissue of 'Jealous Lovers' on Mercury Records reached Number 23 on the U.K. singles chart. The original version had been put out by the fledgling DFA Records, founded in 2001 by the New York-based producer James Murphy and his regular English collaborator Tim Goldsworthy (formerly of U.N.K.L.E.). Part of the reason for forming the label was to create a platform for Murphy's own recordings as LCD Soundsystem. His debut, 'Losing My Edge,' is a sarcastic send-up of too-cool-for-school music fans – most of the lyrics are simply the names of hip bands – set to a gritty, electro-punk backing.

A Little Less Conversation
Elvis Vs. JXL

Released June 2002
RCA *060575* (U.S. #50) / RCA *1943572* (U.K. #1)

It wasn't entirely surprising that a classic such as Elvis Presley's 1968 ditty 'A Little Less Conversation' would be remixed for current ears by someone like Junkie XL, a.k.a. Tom Holkenborg, a Dutch-born DJ-producer known for bombastic techno and breakbeat cuts. Hip-hop and electronica artists often look to the past for present inspiration. What was more shocking was that a remix such as this was picked up to be a part of an official Elvis release (the *30 #1 Hits* album) after the single became a Number 1 hit in several countries as, essentially, a bootleg. It then became the theme to TV's *Las Vegas*.

Ignition–Remix
R. Kelly

Released December 2002
Jive *40065* (U.S. #2) / Jive *9254972* (U.K. #1)

Even as controversial R&B singer R. Kelly (Chicago-born Robert Kelly) faced international scandal stemming from numerous counts of child pornography against him in Illinois and Florida, his pop music mettle and his status as an urban legend grew ever stronger. Nowhere was this more in evidence than with the radio and video release of 'Ignition–Remix' from Kelly's two-million-plus-selling album *Chocolate City*.

Following the dramatically repentant 'Heaven, I Need a Hug,' a radio-circulated song apparently in direct response to the charges, and never formally released, 'Ignition–Remix' found the singer returning to his more salacious roots with a unapologetically infectious song that bored into pop psyches like a worm on a mission, just as his best melodies always have. Once again pondering his all-time favorite topic – sex, of course – Kelly sets up this mid-tempo bouncer with a simple (and totally inane) metaphor about male and female anatomy and car keys and ignitions.

Kelly's instincts for putting out 'Ignition–Remix' at this time were frighteningly on target. Stoked by the real-life headlines, the titillating motor of this song ran strong, stopping just shy of the top spot in America but netting Kelly his second-ever U.K. Number 1 (the first was 1996's 'I Believe I Can Fly'). More than that, however, it symbolized Kelly's continued foothold in pop music, no matter how the details of his personal life unfurled.

Hey Ya!
OutKast

Released November 2003
LaFace *54962* (U.S. #1) / Arista *6579532* (U.K. #3)

An inescapable slice of experimental pop infectiousness, 'Hey Ya!' may well be one of the biggest crossover records in history. It was released only as a DVD single in the U.S., but the deceptively simple tune has introduced countless ears around the world to the mercurial sound of OutKast, where hip-hop is really only a starting point for musical fun.

'Hey Ya!' peaked at the top of the *Billboard* Hot 100 and at Number 3 in the U.K., and was a fixture on global dance floors and radio airwaves for at least a year following its release. The song was instrumental in the meteoric and sparkling performance of the unique long-player *Speakerboxxx / The Love Below*, a double-album showcasing the individual and collective talents of OutKast members Andre '3000' Benjamin and Antwan 'Big Boi' Patterson.

'Hey Ya!' is nonsensical at times but offers a somewhat twisted take on the clichés of the love song, questioning what makes love real and true. But the song's lyrics and overall message were quickly relegated to the background amid the public fervor for the catchy keys and booming bass of the backing track, although Benjamin's requests to "shake it like a Polaroid picture" became an oft-repeated phrase from the song, much to the delight of the camera corporation.

Directed by Bryan Barber, the video for 'Hey Ya!' casts the song in a new, imaginative light. Both amusing and technologically tricky, it is a

cheeky parody of The Beatles' iconic 1964 TV appearance on *The Ed Sullivan Show*. But instead of the fab four, the band performing is The Love Below – all its members are played by Benjamin himself, including the sassy backup singers, The Love Haters, who are all clad in jockey garb. Since Benjamin wrote, produced, sang, and played most of the instruments on the song, the depiction is not really such a stretch. Barber also directed 'The Way You Move' – released as a joint DVD single with 'Hey Ya!' – and *My Life In Idlewild*, OutKast's HBO-funded movie musical inspired by The Love Below. Almost a mini-movie in itself, the 'Hey Ya!' video is a whimsical introduction to Benjamin's genuine love for acting, which he has gone on to explore more formally, notably in John Singleton's movie *Four Brothers* (2005).

'Hey Ya!' was well celebrated, grabbing Video Music Awards from MTV and MTV Europe. It also copped the 2004 Grammy for Best Urban/ Alternative Performance, although the band's live performance of the song at the ceremony was criticized by several Native American organizations, who opposed the Indian-styled costuming and choreography. Undeterred by what might have been a momentary lapse of judgment, the song went on to top critics' polls at *Village Voice* and *Rolling Stone*, the latter saving it a place in its 500 Greatest Songs Of All-Time list.

In Da Club
50 Cent

Released January 2003
Interscope *497856* (U.S. #1) / Interscope *4978742* (U.K. #3)

By the time 'In Da Club' journeyed from the streets of New York City to top the *Billboard* Hot 100, where it stayed for nine weeks and became the bestselling single of 2003, 50 Cent had already gained and lost a record deal and been at death's door. Born Curtis Jackson in Queens, the former drug dealer was contracted to Columbia and startled the hip-hop industry with the sizable hit 'How To Rob,' an antagonistic song about stealing respect – and possessions – from rap stars. After recording *Power Of The Dollar* (2000), and following an incident in which he was shot nine times, 50 Cent was dropped before he could release the album, and he returned to his old life in the rap underground.

The attack added to the rapper's growing legend in New York, which he capitalized on over the next two years through his own independent mix-tape releases. These caught the attention of hip-hop luminaries Eminem and Dr. Dre, who signed him and produced his debut album *Get Rich Or Die Tryin'*. The upbeat first single 'In Da Club' became an inescapable presence on radio and MTV as well as in the clubs. But the most enduring legacy of 50 Cent's first hit may be its infectious chant, which has now become standard drunken-birthday-party fare: "Go shorty, it's your birthday / We go'n' party like it's your birthday."

Milkshake
Kelis

Released August 2003
Star Trax-Arista *54243* (U.S. #3) / Virgin *VSCDX 1863* (U.K. #2)

With this playfully suggestive single, the American R&B singer Kelis finally found success in her homeland, having already established a strong following in Europe. After graduating in 1998 from New York City's Fiorello H. LaGuardia High School of Music & Art and Performing Arts, Kelis Rodgers met and started working with The Neptunes, who had just started on their way to becoming the most sought-after production duo of modern times.

The Neptunes produced Kelis's first two albums, *Kaleidoscope* (1999) and *Wanderland* (2001), but both floundered in America. She scored minor British hits with the singles 'Caught Out There' (with its memorable chorus line of "I hate / You so much right now"), 'Good Stuff' (both 1999), and 'Young, Fresh, N' New' (2001), but her only taste of chart success in the U.S. was with her guest appearance on Ol' Dirty Bastard's 'Got Your Money.'

Three things contributed to the reversal of Kelis's fortunes in America. The first was her relationship with and subsequent marriage to the high-profile rapper Nas; the second was a move to The Neptunes' Star Trax label, who put more effort into promoting her; and the third was the release of her finest single to date. 'Milkshake' bounces along on warm synths, stop-start drums, and a vocal that sounds like a warped playground chant. The lyrics – a not-very-veiled declaration of just how great are the singer's breasts – stirred up a heap of conjecture and controversy, but in the end that served only to help Kelis to her biggest international success so far. (Two further European smash hits followed: 'Trick Me' and 'Millionaire,' a duet with OutKast's Andre 3000.)

Crazy In Love
Beyoncé

Released June 2003
Columbia *79949* (U.S. #1) / Columbia *6740672* (U.K. #1)

'Crazy In Love' launched the solo career of erstwhile Destiny's Child singer Beyoncé, and immediately made her one of the biggest popular-music stars of the early 21st century.

Columbia Records executives were initially unsure about Beyoncé's choice of the song as her first proper solo single, fearing its harder-edged sound might alienate sections of her existing fan base. They were eventually convinced, however, by the addition of a rap from the singer's beau, hip-hop renaissance man Jay-Z, which gave the song indisputable star power. Earlier in the year Beyoncé had appeared on his U.S. Number 2 hit ''03 Bonnie And Clyde.' Here he returns the favor, first announcing that the duet is "history in the making," and then taking the opportunity to declare himself to be "cut from a different cloth / My texture is the best fur / Of chinchilla."

The main musical hook of 'Crazy In Love' is a thrusting horn sample, taken from the Chi-Lites' 1971 hit 'Are You My Woman.' The backing track – which flits, rhythmically, between a jangling, hi-hat-heavy breakbeat in the verses to four-to-the-floor disco in the chorus – was the work of a then struggling producer, Rich Harrison.

After working on Mary J. Blige's 1999 full-length *Mary*, Harrison found himself in something of a slump until Beyoncé chanced upon an embryonic version of what became 'Crazy In Love.' The singer enlisted him to finish off the music, adding the bulk of the lyrics and melody herself. The main vocal highlight arrives in the bridge, the "uh oh uh oh uh oh no no" neatly encapsulating the rest of the lyric's theme of romantic insanity.

'Crazy In Love' was an instant smash hit, climbing high up the charts in Britain, North America, Japan, Australia, and across Europe. Within a month of its release, Beyoncé had become the first female artist to simultaneously top the album and singles charts in the U.S.A. and the U.K. when her full-length debut, *Dangerously In Love*, joined it at Number 1. The single was also one of the first true successes of legal downloading, chalking up 100,000 sales in the U.S.A. alone. It won Grammy Awards for Best R&B Song and Best Rap/Sung Collaboration; a club mix by Maurice Joshua, 'Krazy In Luv,' was named Best Remixed Recording. Its success was further boosted by an extravagant promo clip, directed by Jake Nava, which features an exploding car and numerous costume changes.

All in all, the single and its star became so ubiquitous that it afforded Beyoncé that ultimate signifier of fame: she was able to drop her surname – Knowles, by the way.

opposite > OutKast's Andre 3000 performing 'Hey Ya!' on February 17th, 2004 at the Brit Awards in London, England. Beyoncé then joined the stage for a rendition of her 'Crazy In Love.'

Mundian To Bach Ke
Panjabi MC

Released January 2003
Sequence *8012* (U.S. #32) / Showbiz-Instant Karma *KARMA 28CD* (U.K. #5)

'Mundian To Bach Ke' was the first major U.K. hit to fuse modern hip-hop and electronica with bhangra, a form of Indian and Pakistani dance music. A remix by Jay-Z then helped the song into the U.S. Top 40. Western ears had begun to warm to Middle Eastern and Indian sounds, most notably with the success of Missy Elliott's tabla-laden smash-hit 'Get Ur Freak On.' The British-Asian electronic musician Talvin Singh had a brief period of fame in Britain when his solo debut album *OK* (1998), which fused Hindi classical music with drum'n'bass, won the U.K.'s Mercury Music Prize.

Panjabi MC (born Rajinder Rai) made the Indian influence more explicit in his music, rapping and singing in both English and Punjabi and using traditional bhangra instruments such as dhol drums and a one-string instrumental called the tumbi. Rai had started his musical career in the early 1990s and found widespread success within Asian communities across Europe. 'Mundian To Bach Ke' – which translates as 'Beware Of The Boys' – was originally issued in 1998 on the Big Star label but was re-released and first charted five years later, at a time when other British-Asian musicians, including the producer Rishi Rich, were finding fame. Key to the song's success is its use of the distinctive bassline and other musical figures from the theme to the TV series *Knight Rider*. After topping the singles chart in Germany and reaching the Top 5 in Britain, 'Mundian' caught the attention of Jay-Z, who liked the song so much that he remixed it, adding his own rap to the new version.

All The Things She Said
t.A.T.u.

Released January 2003
Interscope *019354* (U.S. #20) / Interscope *0196972* (U.K. #1)

"Sex sells" is a well-known axiom in just about every industry there is, but with t.A.T.u., the music business hadn't seen such an overstated attempt to embody the phrase since Brooklyn rapper Lil Kim's oversexed antics made headlines in the 1990s. Until t.A.T.u., Russian pop artists had very little success on the international charts. 'All The Things She Said' brought water to that desert-like drought, and it was not too surprising when the public thirstily drank it up.

But the success of 'All The Things' was not simply because the song resonated with the public. Full of high notes but little in the way of a catchy hook or melody, it is not the sort of tune that normally dominates pop charts. Instead, record-buyers picked up on the implied lesbian relationship between members Elena Sergeevna Katina and Yulia Olegovna Volkova, which was precisely what t.A.T.u.'s calculating manager Ivan Shapovalov intended them to notice.

Photographs showing the pair kissing, cuddling, and holding hands, their antics in live performances, and the video for 'All The Things She Said' all played up this pretend imagery, with two very young-looking performers clad in even younger-looking clothing meant to evoke the classic Catholic schoolgirl. It was not a lasting formula for success – especially when they 'came out' to say that they are both heterosexual women who date men.

Hurt
Johnny Cash

Released April 2003
Universal *779982* (U.S.) / American-Lost Highway *0779982* (U.K. #39)

In the last years of his life Johnny Cash achieved an entirely unpredicted last dose of fame thanks to the motivating force of the equally great Rick Rubin. Beginning with *American Recordings* in 1994, the pair recorded several albums mixing Cash originals with often surprising covers.

Among the most incongruous of these, seemingly, was Cash's reading of 'Hurt' by the industrial rock group Nine Inch Nails. Nails mainstay Trent Reznor has been something of an unsung hero in modern metal, discovering and nurturing Marilyn Manson, for example, before watching his protégé eclipse him totally. Reznor had struck a gloomy strain of gold with 'Hurt,' which dealt with the keen misery of life through a miasma of drug withdrawal and gothic darkness. Cash sang Reznor's lines in his gruff, beautiful voice and gave the song renewed meaning, ironically introducing Cash to a new generation of listeners just months before his wife died. He followed her four months later. Of course, in this modern age, the song's starkest impact came in the accompanying video clip, which had Cash in a darkened room at home. In one unforgettable shot he sits before a piano with closed lid – a sign, or even an admission, that his life was drawing to a close. The video won several awards as the industry tried to pay Cash due recognition before it was too late.

I Luv U
Dizzee Rascal

Released May 2003
Not issued U.S. / XL Recordings *XLS 165CD* (U.K. #29)

Hot on the heels of The Streets came the prodigiously talented rapper and producer Dizzee Rascal, still only 17 when 'I Luv U' made its way into the British Top 30. Born Dylan Mills in 1985 to Ghanaian immigrants, Dizzee learned to make music on school computers and at 15 started MC-ing at raves and on London pirate-radio stations. 'I Luv U' is typical of the grime style, of which Dizzee Rascal is the chief exponent: the beats are harsh and unvarnished and sound more like malfunctioning underground trains than drums; the lyrics, which detail an accidental teenage pregnancy, are fittingly spat out rather than rapped.

Where Is The Love
Black Eyed Peas

Released June 2003
A&M *000714* (U.S. #8) / A&M *9810996* (U.K. #1)

A guest appearance here by former *NSYNC lead Justin Timberlake helped establish Black Eyed Peas as one of the most popular hip-pop groups of the early 21st century. The Los Angeles based trio of will.i.am, aple.de.ap, and taboo – who all sign their names in kd lang-style lowercase – went on to recruit the sassy, sexy vocalist Fergie as a permanent fourth member of the band, and she seemed to be the key ingredient in the sustained popular success that the group has enjoyed since. Fergie made her debut on the naggingly insistent follow-up 'Shut Up,' a British Number 2 hit.

Bring Me To Life
Evanescence

Released June 2003
Wind-Up *673573* (U.S. #5) / Epic *6739762* (U.K. #1)

Although gothic metal had previously been a strictly niche interest with little or no commercial effect, Evanescence – a kind of slightly darker Linkin Park with the amazing vocals of the 22-year-old Amy Lee – took the recipe straight to the charts with this melodic, anthemic slice of gloom. 'Bring Me To Life' was accompanied by a video in which Lee jumped off a building and sang the song on her way down, scoring with its combination of Lee's soaring larynx and some rapped interludes, plus the requisite big guitars and some wicky-wack scratching. The gates duly opened for a flood of Evanescence-style female-fronted bands such as Lacuna Coil and Nightwish.

I Believe In A Thing Called Love
The Darkness

Released September 2003
Atlantic *301349* (U.S.) / Must Destroy *DARK 01CD* (U.K. #2)

We still don't know whether England's hair-metal heroes The Darkness are supposed to be a joke or not, but it's an irrelevant point when their songs sound this charismatic. 'I Believe In A Thing Called Love' was delivered with an ironic wink by singer Justin Hawkins in bat-alarming falsetto tones, but avoided misinterpretion as mere comic vaudeville by the strength of the riffs that he and his brother Dan delivered. 'Older' rock fans were delighted by the band's espousal of AOR/chart-metal sounds from the 1980s – think Whitesnake, Foreigner, Boston – while younger listeners were kept amused by Hawkins's catsuit.

Mad World
Michael Andrews Featuring Gary Jules

Released December 2003
Universal *9816488* (U.S.) / Sanctuary *SANXD 250* (U.K. #1)

The movie *Donnie Darko*, a kind of teen *American Beauty* loaded with gothic miserablism and an exciting new face in Jake Gyllenhaal, was briefly the toast of the critics in 2003, spurring this soundtrack song into the charts. Gary Jules and Michael Andrews's piano-and-vocal cover of Tears For Fears' excellent 1981 hit 'Mad World' was bleak, disturbing, and very catchy, although Jules's voice – like Michael Stipe with added vibrato – became somewhat irksome after a few hearings. In due course *Donnie* fever subsided, the song slipped away, and the twosome dematerialized, leaving us all free to enjoy *American Pie 2* and *Terminator 3* instead.

Maps
The Yeah Yeah Yeahs

Released September 2003
Interscope *207322* (U.S.) / Dress Up-Polydor *9811413* (U.K. #26)

At first, The Yeah Yeah Yeahs appeared to be heading for success purely by virtue of coming from New York City and peddling a punky, garage-rock-derived sound. With the thoughtful, expansive 'Maps,' however, they proved themselves to be a fine band in their own right. Like The White Stripes the group lacks a bassist, but they more than make up for this with the effects-laden guitar work of Nick Zinner and Brian Chase's sturdy backbeat. The real star of the show is vocalist Karen O, a mutant cross-breed of P.J. Harvey and Chrissie Hynde. Her fearful vocal plea on 'Maps' – "they don't love you like I love you" – was aimed at her then-boyfriend, Angus Andrew of the avant-rock group Liars.

Take Me Out
Franz Ferdinand

Released February 2004
Sony *76774* (U.S.) / Domino *RUG 172CD* (U.K. #3)

Scottish quartet Franz Ferdinand are not at all apologetic for co-opting the styles of Talking Heads and Gang Of Four for their trademark brittle, arty sound. The band were immediately popular on their arrival on the indie scene in 2004 and caused a whole generation to consult the 20th-century history books. 'Take Me Out' was a glorious blast through a simple chord progression heard a trillion times before, but it still worked perfectly – perhaps because it was so jerky and awkward.

The Ferdinands plunged into the song with unrestrained abandon – listen to the laughing tone of the "I say, you don't know…" lines – and deliver a committed performance on stage, while the slightly garage-style production values of the record make it sound as if it should have been delivered in a middle-American college campus in 1981 – or perhaps a club in Manchester, England, in 1990. Listen too for the all-band tempo change in the intro, which lends some hands-in-the-air excitement, and the sudden stop-and-shout moments that come straight from vintage post-punk.

The song was a huge hit in Britain (but only made Number 66 in the U.S.), revitalizing the U.K. art-rock circuit (or what was left of it in our corporate era) and arousing a brief revival of the pencil moustache. With their skinny frames, sensible haircuts, decidedly intellectual tastes, and oh-so-crisp post-mod fashion sense, Franz Ferdinand seemed for a while to be the future of British pop. Indeed they continue to ascend the chart of cool – unlikely progress for a band who started so explosively.

Take Your Mama
Scissor Sisters

Released April 2004
Universal *21236* (U.S.) / Polydor *9866277* (U.K. #17)

Scissor Sisters highlighted a softening attitude during the mid 2000s towards music that drew unashamedly and pretty much entirely on the past. There's nothing particularly innovative about 'Take Your Mama' – it sounds like two parts Elton John, one part Bee Gees, and George Michael stirred-in to taste – but innovation is not what's required. The brash, glam New York quintet – they started out playing at burlesques – realized early in their career that the most important ingredient in the recipe for pop success is a cool, catchy chorus. And 'Take Your Mama,' which could well have fallen off the back of Elton's 1972 opus *Goodbye Yellow Brick Road,* certainly has that component firmly in place.

Scissor Sisters are also in possession of two fine focal points in the form of extravagant co-vocalists Jake Shears and Ana Matronic. 'Take Your Mama' was the biggest of five U.K. hits from the group's eponymous debut, which ended up as Britain's best-selling album of 2004. Scissor Sisters didn't achieve the same level of success in the U.S., although one of several follow-ups to 'Take Your Mama,' 'Filthy / Gorgeous,' topped the Hot Dance Club Play chart.

Irish Blood, English Heart
Morrissey

Released May 2004
Attack-Sanctuary *86000* (U.S.) / Attack *ATKXS 002* (U.K. #3)

'Irish Blood, English Heart' began a highly successful comeback for the former Smiths frontman, following almost a decade in the musical wilderness. After the band split in 1987, Morrissey stepped effortlessly into a solo career with the singles 'Suedehead' and 'Every Day Is Like

THE FUTURE OF THE DIGITAL SINGLE

Commentators often speak in long, hyperbolic sentences about revolutions in the music industry, many of which never survive to make the long-term history books. But there can be little doubt of the huge impact that download technology is having on how music is discovered, purchased, and listened to.

Many people think of online downloads as synonymous with MP3, the most prevalent of a number of audio file formats. The term MP3 is derived from the long-winded MPEG-1 Audio Layer 3, the third iteration of an audio-visual file compression format that dates back to the late 1970s. It wasn't until 1994, however, that a series of standardized specifications for MP3 were devised by a group of European audio engineers headed by a German, Karlheinz Brandenberg.

Put simply, MP3 technology allows sound to be stored digitally in a fraction of the space required by CD audio files. (The smaller file sizes do have an effect on the resulting sound quality, but not as noticeably as some of the format's detractors would suggest.) MP3 was important because, firstly, it allowed users to store a greater number of song files on their computers' hard drives, which back then were a fraction of the gargantuan sizes of today. Secondly and even more importantly, the technology made it possible for music to be 'shared' over the internet.

MP3 files – 'MP3s' – first came into use in 1995 but did not begin to enter the public consciousness until the turn of the century. Partly this was because of the controversy surrounding the Napster software program, which allowed its growing army of users to share their newly digitized record collections. Most record companies were very slow to respond to the capabilities of digital audio, but they woke up when fans began freely and illegally to download their product. After much outcry and declarations about the end of the music industry as we know it, Napster and other similar file-sharing systems were forced to close in their then current form.

What the slothful music industry lacked was a way of making their music available for sale over the internet. In 2003, that gap in the market was filled by Apple Computer's iTunes Music Store, which allowed users to buy individual tracks by a growing number of artists for 99¢ each (79p in the U.K.). Other similar download music retailers followed, but Apple continues to dominate both the market for this and for portable digital audio players, with its acclaimed iPod (a Walkman-sized personal jukebox, capable of holding thousands of songs).

So what effect has this had on the single? Certainly not as much as it has on the album, which remains in a state of flux as web-savvy consumers opt to download one or two favorite tracks rather than forking out for a full set of 13-or-so songs and finding many of them to be mediocre. Since singles by their very nature are almost always focused on one song alone, how you listen to it (or purchase it), whether on your gramophone or your iPod, is not a matter of huge consequence. Naturally, B-sides are now of less importance, both to consumers and record labels – but they have been for many years, at least since there became no need to turn over a slab of vinyl to hear them.

Since 2003, singles charts in the U.S. and the U.K. have been modified to reflect the growing number of download sales. The effect of this is harder to judge in the U.S. since chart placings on the *Billboard* Hot 100 are generally more a reflection of airplay than record sales. *Billboard* added a Hot Digital Tracks listing to its vast roster of charts in 2003 but did not begin to incorporate download sales into its main charts until February 2005. The first digital download single to sell over a million copies in the U.S. was Gwen Stefani's 'Hollaback Girl' (2004). At the time of writing, the biggest-selling download has been 2005's 'Since U Been Gone' by 2002 *American Idol* winner Kelly Clarkson.

In the U.K., a specific download chart was introduced in September 2004. Those who expected this to become a platform for less commercial music were somewhat disappointed to find that the first act to top this particular chart was the bland Irish boy-band Westlife, with an unremarkable live rendition of 'Flying Without Wings.'

Until recently, chart regulations in Britain were more stringent than in the U.S., requiring a physical product to be on sale before a record is allowed entry into the main Top 40. The rules were finally relaxed in 2006, just in time for hip-hop duo Gnarls Barkley to fly in at Number 1 with what became the year's biggest hit in Britain, 'Crazy.'

Sunday' and the accompanying album *Viva Hate* (all 1988). The 1990s were less kind to him, however: his recorded output was spotty, he was labeled a racist by the media after several vague – and perhaps misunderstood – statements and an onstage appearance draped in the Union Jack flag, and he was sued, successfully, by former bandmate Mike Joyce over a royalty dispute. By the end of the decade he had lost his recording contract with Island Records and relocated to Los Angeles, where he led a solitary, almost reclusive existence.

Morrissey started his road back to success in 2003 with a world tour – which he embarked upon, unusually, without a record to promote – and a new deal with Sanctuary (or, more precisely, the label's former reggae imprint, Attack, which the singer now controls). To the surprise of many, he then started work with Jerry Finn, the producer best known for his work with pop-punk act Blink-182. Finn, however, lends 'Irish Blood, English Heart' a powerful, polished sheen: the perfect backdrop for a typically defiant lyric, in which the poet-laureate of pop declares: "There is no one on earth I'm afraid of / And no regime can buy or sell me."

Vertigo
U2

Released November 2004
Island *9868183* (U.S. #31) / Island *CIDX 878* (U.K. #1)

The Irish rock behemoth's finest single for a decade, 'Vertigo' returned some much-needed raw power to U2's sound after too long a deviation with dance beats and group-up balladry. Arriving with the odd cry of "uno, dos, tres, catorce!" ("one, two, three, fourteen!"), this is an uptempo rocker power-driven by sheet-metal guitars and fuzzy bass. Bono turns in a fine vocal, complete with one or two more apparently off-the-cuff lines of Spanglish thrown in for good measure, and there is a typically strident performance from unsung hero Larry Mullen Jr. on drums. 'Vertigo' won three awards at the 2005 Grammys, and was notable as part of a widespread cross-promotional ad campaign with Apple's iTunes Music Store, which sold a download of the single before it was available anywhere else.

Yeah!

Usher Featuring Lil' Jon & Ludacris

Released January 2004
Arista *59149* (U.S. #1) / Arista *6606002* (U.K. #1)

This high-energy R&B-rap song blared out of radios, dominated dance floors, and enjoyed heavy video rotation on MTV, VH1, and BET (a rare feat). Singer Usher was well used to accolades, but this record gave him his longest-running American chart-topper. He also acquired some needed street credibility from the collaboration with producer and pop culture star Lil Jon and rapper-actor Ludacris. All three made their careers in the urban music mecca of Atlanta, and this song pays tribute to that city through lyrical references to other songs amid calls to perform some lively dance steps invented in Atlanta.

'Yeah!' was just one of four huge U.S. Number 1 hits for Usher in 2004. It spent 12 weeks atop the *Billboard* Hot 100 during the spring; the only record able to take away the top spot was his own follow-up, 'Burn,' which clung on for a further seven weeks. With the release of his third chart-topper of the year, 'Confessions Part II,' Usher became the first solo artist to have three singles in the *Billboard* Top 10 at once. The similarly successful 'My Boo,' a duet with Alicia Keys, followed, meaning that in 2004 Usher spent a record-breaking total of 28 weeks at Number 1.

Toxic

Britney Spears

Released February 2004
Jive *59214* (U.S. #9) / Jive *6602092* (U.K. #1)

This was a year of scandal and regular tabloid appearances for Britney Spears. The young pop tartlet married twice, first in January to a childhood pal in a 55-hour Las Vegas gag, and later in the year to backup dancer Kevin Federline, whom she had dated for about three months. 'Toxic' fell right between the nuptials.

Britney owed much of her earlier success to songs penned and produced by a Swede, Max Martin, and now she again looked to Sweden for hits. Bloodshy and Avant (Christian Karlsson and Pontus Winnberg) had

enjoyed European success with American pop singer Christina Milian and hit the spot again with this track, which has club-inspired breakbeats, and violin lines reminiscent of James Bond films. British songwriter Cathy Dennis, who co-wrote Kylie Minogue's 'Can't Get You Out Of My Head,' signed on to pen the catchy lyrics.

Fans who reckoned she would never top her racy video for 'I'm A Slave 4 U' had to think again: this one has her donning many disguises as a female assassin, and plays on her supposed promiscuity by placing the singer in multiple situations with different men. 'Toxic' has proved to be Spears's greatest musical triumph, netting her a Grammy for Best Dance Recording.

This Love

Maroon5

Released March 2004
J Records *63388* (U.S. #5) / J Records *6608452* (U.K. #3)

Los Angeles-based band Maroon5 took home the coveted Grammy Award for Best New Artist in 2005, owing largely to this remarkably infectious pop single from an album released almost three years earlier. 'This Love' is a simple yet clever power-guitar tune with near universal appeal, and it proved inescapable throughout 2004 on American radio and on MTV. The band has, to its possible regret, become noted for its extracurricular activities: singer Adam Levine has the rugged good looks and the fickle attitude of a famous Hollywood bachelor, and has since been a fixture in tabloid magazines, linked to young celebrities such as Jessica Simpson and Lindsay Lohan.

Drop It Like It's Hot

Snoop Dogg

Released September 2004
Geffen *357411* (U.S. #1) / Geffen *2103461* (U.K. #10)

Rapper-actor Snoop Dogg is about as American as apple pie. He's been an iconic figure of popular culture since his recorded debut early in the 1990s, but the top spot on the American pop charts eluded him until the release of the sizzling, snappy, and Snoopendous 'Drop It Like It's Hot' in 2004, made with the help of the hit-making producer Pharrell Williams (of Neptunes/N.E.R.D. fame). The song received numerous awards in America (including two Grammy nominations) while in Britain it took home the 2005 MOBO for Best Video thanks to its clever black-and-white treatment.

You Had Me

Joss Stone

Released November 2004
EMI *867482* (U.S.) / Relentless-Virgin *RELDX 13* (U.K. #9)

Dusty Springfield aside, Britain has produced few female soul vocalists of particular note, and even fewer with the talent and popular appeal to achieve longstanding international success. A rare potential exception to that rule arrived in 2003, from rural Devon, England, at just 16 years old. Joss Stone had traveled a year earlier to New York City where she caught the eye – and ears – of S-Curve Records founder Steve Greenberg. During the spring of 2003 he took charge of Stone's debut album, *The Soul Sessions*, alongside singer-producer Betty Wright. That album spawned a minor U.K. hit early the following year with a re-reading of a White Stripes song, 'Fell In Love With A Boy,' which showed off the remarkably mature voice that Stone had developed while listening to soul legends such as Aretha Franklin. An even better single followed later in the year. 'You Had Me,' the first track drawn from her second album, *Mind, Body & Soul*, is a strident, mid-tempo funk number reminiscent of 1970s Stevie Wonder that contains the kind of chorus that buries itself deep in the listener's head after even a single listen. Stone's first U.K. Top 10 hit, it did not chart in the U.S. but was nonetheless instrumental in helping Mind, Body & Soul climb to Number 11 on the Billboard albums chart there, making the singer's future look decidedly rosy.

Goodies
Ciara

Released May 2004
LaFace *57550* (U.S. #1) / BMG *6665881* (U.K. #1)

The teenage R&B singer and dancer Ciara Harris was discovered in Atlanta by Jazze Pha (Phalon Alexander), a DJ and producer whose father, James Alexander, had been a founding member of soul greats The Bar-Kays. Jazze Pha produced most of Ciara's debut album *Goodies*, but the title track was crafted by Lil Jon (Jonathan Smith). Lil Jon was another producer known for a local style of hyped-up dancefloor records termed 'crunk' after an energetic Atlanta youth culture that had been bubbling for some time. The song features a guest performance from platinum-selling North Carolina rapper Petey Pablo, who tried valiantly to contain his passion for the sexy Ciara in his verse, mainly because she wasn't quite 18 when they recorded it.

The combination of Ciara's R&B vocals and Lil Jon's crunk beats were initially described as 'crunk & B,' but use of the term faded after Ciara's subsequent singles showed her ability to move beyond that sound. Video director Benny Boom gave the public their visual introduction to Ciara. He set 'Goodies' in an Atlanta car wash for a dance performance showcasing her formidable moves, including a back bend reminiscent of the slow motion action dodging executed by Keanu Reeves in *The Matrix*. 'Goodies' brought Ciara to the top of the American charts for seven weeks, a goal she had envisioned while still in high school. She might not necessarily have predicted that she'd repeat the feat in the U.K. and Canada as well, but this proved a harbinger of international sucess.

What You Waiting For
Gwen Stefani

Released September 2004
Interscope *00350711* (U.S.) / Interscope *9864986* (U.K. #4)

"Take a chance, you stupid ho'," shouts Gwen Stefani on her first single, 'What You Waiting For.' Strangely, she's chastising herself – for a lack of confidence that's manifesting itself as writers' block. It must've been frightening for the lead singer of the award-winning Southern California-reared No Doubt to go solo at the height of her band's success; that inner turmoil is reflected in the frenetic tick-tock pace of the song. The video introduces her memorable Harajuku Girls, brightly dressed and sassy Japanese dancers whom she would use on subsequent singles and the tour for her *Love Angel Music Baby* album.

Unwritten
Natasha Bedingfield

Released December 2004
BMG download only (U.S. #1) / Phonogenic-BMG *6663522* (U.K. #6)

Prior to achieving success of her own, Natasha Bedingfield looked on as her older brother, Daniel, scored a run of international hits in the early 2000s, notably the U.K. Number 1 'Gotta Get Thru This.' She studied psychology – in part, apparently, because "I knew it'd make me a better songwriter" – before making *Unwritten*, an album of breezy up-tempo pop-dance songs. It spawned three British hits in 2004, including the chart-topping 'These Words,' which put Natasha and Daniel in the *Guinness Book Of Records* as the only brother and sister to both achieve solo Number 1s in the U.K.

It took over a year, though, for 'Unwritten' to receive any significant attention in America. As with several other slow-burning hits of recent times, it was given a boost when performed by a contestant on *American Idol*. It was also used as the theme to the MTV reality show *The Hills*. By the spring of 2006, the single had been certified five times platinum in the U.S. as one of only a handful of records so far to sell over a million copies as a download-only single. Even more impressively, Bedingfield was the first British woman to top the Hot 100 since *Billboard* magazine began compiling its various musical hit parades in 1940.

Jailhouse Rock
Elvis Presley

Released January 2005
Not issued U.S. / RCA *6667152* (U.K. #1)

In The Kitchen / Trapped In The Closet
R. Kelly

Released April 2005
Jive *69126* (U.S.) / Not issued U.K.

In 2005, RCA hit upon an inventive way of celebrating 50 years of Elvis hits in Britain. Over the course of 18 weeks, the label reissued each of the king's Number 1 singles, one per week, in chronological order. The first of these was 'All Shook Up,' but it was ineligible for the chart because it was packaged within a collectors-edition box big enough to house all 18 singles. (Had it been allowed to chart, it would have hit Number 2.) The following week's 'Jailhouse Rock' then provided the first U.K. chart-topper of 2005; it was followed a week later by a reissue of the double A-side 'One Night' / 'I Got Stung,' which now has the distinction of being the 1,000th record to top the British singles chart.

Not all of the subsequent 15 Elvis singles released made it to the pole position, but each of them made it into the Top 5, demonstrating – as if there were any need – that Elvis remains among the most enduringly popular performers in the history of music. RCA's clever reissue strategy was asking to be copied, and it was perhaps inevitable that the first artist to attempt to match Elvis's feat came from the king of pop, Michael Jackson, during the spring and early summer of 2006.

Jackson did not fare nearly as well, however: none of his repackaged hits made it into the Top 10 (and most lingered around the Number 15 spot before dropping off the chart after a week). Perhaps this was partly bad timing: RCA had commenced the Elvis singles series in January, traditionally the easiest time to score a British Number 1 hit, given the lack of major releases in the post-Christmas lull. Also, Jackson's sequence of past hits made the stores less than a year after his trial on several counts of child molestation and abduction. Although he was acquitted on all counts, the case did little for his reputation.

Meanwhile, on the other side of the Atlantic, R. Kelly – a man who could at times rival Michael Jackson both for unsavory media stories and sheer madness – issued the first in a different kind of multi-part series. The B-side to his rather mundane single 'In The Kitchen' offered up the first 'Chapter' of 'Trapped In The Closet,' a series of 12 narrative songs all set to the same musical backing. None of the 'Closet' series made a serious indentation on the *Billboard* charts, but they became a fixture on urban radio as fans waited to hear the next installment of Kelly's soap-opera-style relationship drama.

Kelly's summer 2005 *TP.3 Reloaded* album collected the first five parts of the series and offered up a promo video for each of them, in which he and some friends act out the story. Both the audio and video Closets are frequently hilarious, but it's not always clear if this is intentional, such is the apparent determination in both his wordplay and acting. At the end of the year the prolific singer released a DVD of all 12 chapters, complete with bonus material and an enlightening director's commentary.

Ghetto Gospel
2Pac Featuring Elton John

Released June 2005
Not issued U.S. / Interscope *9882168* (U.K. #1)

Nasty Girl
The Notorious B.I.G. Featuring Diddy, Nelly, Avery Storm, & Jagged Edge

Released December 2005
Bad Boy *94143* (U.S.) / Bad Boy *ATO229CDX* (U.K. #1)

Dozens of musicians can say that they worked with the late Tupac Shakur (a.k.a. 2Pac), either on collaborations when he was alive or songs constructed after his violent death in 1996 at age 25. But there was surely no collaboration more unusual than the unlikely ballad 'Ghetto Gospel,' constructed using a sample from Elton John's 1971 composition 'Indian Sunset' for the documentary *2Pac: Resurrection*. Like Elvis Presley, 2Pac has had a thriving career in the afterlife, with millions of posthumous record sales. Unlike Elvis, however, 2Pac had a sense of impending doom and worked tirelessly to amass a catalog of material that could see the light after his demise.

On the day that 2Pac was shot and killed, his great rival The Notorious B.I.G. denied any involvement, stating that he had been busy in the studio, working on a song called 'Nasty Girl.' A few months later, B.I.G. was murdered too. 'Nasty Girl' remained unfinished for almost a decade. It was eventually completed in 2005 for inclusion on the posthumous collection *Duets: The Final Chapter*, and on the finished version B.I.G. vies for time on the mic with Diddy (a.k.a. Puff Daddy, his former friend and label boss), Nelly, the hotly tipped Avery Storm, and the R&B vocal group Jagged Edge. (The accompanying all-star promo video also features Usher, Pharrell Williams, and the supermodel Naomi Campbell.) Ironically, neither 2Pac nor Notorious B.I.G. had topped the British singles chart during their lifetimes, but both managed to achieve the feat posthumously with these singles, less than a year apart.

Candy Shop
50 Cent Featuring Olivia

Released July 2005
Universal *9880609* (U.S. #1) / Interscope *9881293* (U.K. #2)

Superstar rapper 50 Cent's trip to the 'Candy Shop' earned him his third U.S. Number 1 and added to the growing list of controversies in his fast-moving career. He'd been incarcerated for drug-related offenses, he'd been shot at, and he'd engaged in countless feuds with other hip-hop performers. Now he was criticized for the thinly veiled sexual connotations of this hit that paraphrased commercials for M&Ms, the candy that "melts in your mouth, not in your hand." Widespread parental disapproval did little to halt the success of 'Candy Shop,' which, like his 2003 breakthrough hit 'In Da Club,' spent nine weeks at the top of the *Billboard* Hot 100. (In between, he'd spent five weeks at Number 1 with '21 Questions,' a collaboration with Nate Dogg.)

Perhaps more surprising than any of his gritty, foul-mouthed songs was 50 Cent's political stance. He backed George W. Bush in the 2004 U.S. election and defended the president's widely criticized response to the destruction caused by 2005's Hurricane Catrina. While Kanye West, his rival at the top of the rap game, declared on live television that George Bush "doesn't care about black people," 50 Cent proclaimed him to be "incredible … a gangsta. I wanna meet George Bush, just shake his hand and tell him how much of me I see in him." The president would surely agree.

We Belong Together
Mariah Carey

Released July 2005
Def Jam-Island *000516211* (U.S. #1) / Def Jam-Island *9883483* (U.K. #2)

During the 1990s it became customary for Mariah Carey to spend weeks at the top of the *Billboard* Hot 100. At the start of the new decade, however, her career looked all but over. The singer started 2001 well, signing a deal with Virgin Records worth a reported $80 million. But by the end of that year her semi-autobiographical movie and album project, *Glitter*, was a huge critical and commercial failure, and the singer was reported to have suffered a physical and emotional breakdown. This followed several promotional appearances that could only be described as unusual. In one instance she turned up on MTV's *Total Request Live* handing out popsicles before performing something akin to a striptease; in others she just rambled on about nothing in particular.

In 2002 Carey suffered the indignity of being bought out of her contract by Virgin. She subsequently signed to Def Jam, but it seemed that her days of dominating the singles chart were well and truly over. Then, seemingly out of nowhere, came her smash comeback album *The Emancipation Of Mimi* and 'We Belong Together,' which provided Carey with the 16th Number 1 hit of her career. The record spent nearly a quarter of 2005 in that top pop spot. Crafted by Atlanta-based music mogul and longtime friend Jermaine Dupri (along with his secret weapon, young songwriter Johnta Austin), it has a savvy hip-hop feel in the way that Carey makes her lyrics flow, but it is still a sweet love song. It's a combination that proved irresistible and opened up a world of possibilities for a talented artist still finding her considerable voice.

Gold Digger
Kanye West

Released August 2005
Roc-A-Fella *000511811* (U.S. #1) / Universal International *5885699* (U.K. #2)

Kanye West was at first known as the highly skilled producer behind artists such as Jay-Z but has since stepped out from behind the mixing board to establish himself as one of the finest and most successful hip-hop performers of the early 21st century. One of several excellent singles to be drawn from his acclaimed second album *Late Registration*, 'Gold Digger' spent ten weeks at Number 1 in America. It also stands at the time of writing as the fastest-selling download ever.

Somewhat strangely, 'Gold Digger' features both a repeated vocal sample from Ray Charles's 'I've Got A Woman' and, in its intro, an imitation of the jazz-soul legend's voice by the actor-singer Jamie Foxx. (Foxx had recently won the Academy Award for Best Actor for his portrayal of Charles in the biopic *Ray*.) The rest of the song is dominated by a sparse, irresistibly funky backing track and West's somewhat tongue-in-cheek lyrics about gold-diggin' women who "ain't messin' with no broke niggas." It is often remarked that West's skills as a rapper fall far short of his abilities as a producer, but it's difficult to fault his vocal performance on 'Gold Digger,' which ended up as big a crossover smash as OutKast's 'Hey Ya' had been two years previously.

West followed up with two more sterling singles – 'Heard 'Em Say' and 'Touch The Sky' – that showed off the gifts of *Late Registration*'s unexpected co-producer, Jon Brion, previously best known for his work with Fiona Apple and on the soundtracks to such movies as *Magnolia* and *Eternal Sunshine Of The Spotless Mind*.

2005

Speed Of Sound
Coldplay

Released May 2005
EMI *8729862* (U.S. #8) / Parlophone *CDR 6664* (U.K. #2)

Axel F
Crazy Frog

Released May 2005
Gusto *21495* (U.S.) / Gusto *CDGUS 17* (U.K. #1)

In May 2005 an unusual battle raged for the top spot on the U.K. singles chart. In the left corner, representing good, honest – if a little dull – rock music, was the London-based quartet Coldplay; in the right corner, a spin-off from one of the most irritating TV ad campaigns in history, and the most potent example of the power of the ringtone. It had become apparent shortly into the new millennium that consumers didn't just want their music available on CD and as a download, but wanted to consume music through their cell phone, translated into a polyphonic series of bleeps or as a 'realtone,' in which actual music blared from your mobile.

Coldplay had by this stage become one of the biggest bands in the world. Their importance was such that shares in their parent label, EMI, dropped significantly when it was announced that the forthcoming album *X&Y* – from which 'Speed Of Sound' was taken – would be delayed.

Driven by stately guitar and piano amid big, roomy drums, the single is one of the group's finer efforts, but not exactly the kind of grandstanding musical rebirth hinted at before its release. It does have the notable distinction of being the first single for 37 years by a British group to go straight into the U.S. Top 10. The last one to achieve such a feat was The Beatles' 'Hey Jude.'

As successful as it was in America, in the U.K. 'Speed Of Sound' couldn't match the commercial clout of 'Axel F,' which was issued on the same day and sold four times as many copies in its first week as Coldplay's single (mostly to kids who didn't know any better). Almost certainly the most diabolical release to top the British chart – to call it a song is stretching the point – 'Axel F' had a strange and convoluted genesis. The main musical element is a souped-up version of the theme to the 1984 Eddie Murphy movie *Beverly Hills Cop*. Layered over the top are a series of migraine-inducing vocal parts, chief among them a feat of strained vocal gymnastics originally performed in 1997 by a Swedish teen, Daniel Malmedahl.

Despite its dubious musical merit, 'Axel F' and the accompanying Crazy Frog video had become ubiquitous in the U.K., largely because of the blanket advertising bought up on its behalf by the new media company Jamba! According to *The Guardian* newspaper, Crazy Frog-related ads were shown over 2,000 times a day on British television in May 2005. Their main aim was to sell Crazy Frog ringtones. The success of the single was secondary; it was recorded on Jamster!'s behalf by the German duo Bass Bumpers, who wisely chose to release it under a pseudonym. The ringtone itself remains, to date, the most lucrative of all time; it has earned Jamster! over £14 million in Britain alone (about $26 million) and untold additional riches across the U.S. and Europe.

Jamster! found itself censured soon after 'Axel F' topped the charts (it made only Number 50 in America). The U.K. Advertising Standards Authority upheld countless complaints that it wasn't entirely clear that the ringtone sale led to a subscription service and not simply a one-off payment. Also, the animated Crazy Frog's genitalia was visible. The result was that the vile creature was banned from the airwaves until after 9:00pm.

You're Beautiful
James Blunt

Released June 2005
Custard download only (U.S. #1) / Atlantic *AT 0207CD* (U.K. #1)

A lovelorn ballad about glimpsing an ex-girlfriend on the subway, 'You're Beautiful' unexpectedly became one of the biggest hits across Europe during the summer of 2005. Early the following year it rose to the top of the *Billboard* Hot 100, making Blunt the first British artist to have an American Number 1 since Elton John topped the charts with 'Candle In The Wind' in 1997. Given the fey, lightweight feel of this breakthrough hit for Blunt, it came as a surprise to some to discover that he had served in the British Army prior to embarking on a musical career. Although repeated exposure to 'You're Beautiful' seemed to invoke feelings of despair and irritation in many listeners, the single remained a radio staple on both sides of the Atlantic for the best part of a year. The great Weird Al Yankovic was sufficiently moved by Blunt's song to record his own special kind of tribute: 'You're Pitiful.'

Bad Day
Daniel Powter

Released July 2005
Warner Bros. download only (U.S. #1) / WEA *W 682CD* (U.K. #2)

Like James Blunt's similarly themed 'You're Beautiful,' 'Bad Day' was a British hit in the summer of 2005 but took a further year to top the U.S. chart. Its slow climb to Number 1 harked back to an earlier age, when records would slowly pick up momentum as they spread into different radio markets. It has become more common today for singles to perform well for a few weeks but then quickly slide down the charts. Surprisingly, Powter's breakthrough hit stalled at Number 3 in his native Canada, where it was a hit in early 2005. It then found widespread success across Europe, but was largely ignored in the U.S. until it was chosen as the song to be played whenever a contestant was voted off the 2006 season of *American Idol*. It was also heard often during the 2006 NBA playoffs following the elimination of several teams on their home courts. Despite these intrinsic links with failure, 'Bad Day' provided Powter with one of the biggest-selling downloads of all time in the U.S., where over a million internet-savvy music fans have paid for the privilege of saving the song onto their hard drives.

I Bet You Look Good On The Dance Floor
Arctic Monkeys

Released October 2005
Domino *3533392* (U.S.) / Domino *RUG 212* (U.K. #1)

'I Bet You Look Good On The Dance Floor' was one of the biggest British grassroots successes of recent times. Before even releasing a record, the band had built up a wide fanbase through word-of-virtual-mouth on the internet and on the strength of live performances in the north of England. The teenage quartet's first widespread release, 'Dance Floor' entered the U.K. singles chart at Number 1 and made Arctic Monkeys the most talked about British band in years.

It's a measure of the group's innocence that, just a couple of years earlier, school friends Alex Turner and Jamie Cook had asked for guitars for Christmas, and then started learning their trade by picking out the chords to songs by The White Stripes and The Vines with the help of

bassist Andy Nicholson and drummer Matt Helders. In the blink of an eye, the four lads from Sheffield were well on the way to joining their idols in the big league, thanks largely to the promise shown in a set of demos the band made available for free on the internet.

'Dance Floor' is pitched midway between the early-21st-century vogue for scratchy new wave and the confident swagger of 1990s favorites Oasis. The record is dominated by jagged guitar chords and Turner's stream-of-consciousness-style vocal about "dancing to electro-pop like a robot from 1984" along with typically teenage feelings of romantic insecurity. It was followed to the top of the British chart by 'When The Sun Goes Down' in January 2006. A week later, Arctic Monkeys' first full-length became the fastest-selling debut album of all time in the U.K. It reached Number 24 in America, where the group is beginning to make a considerable mark.

King Of The Mountain
Kate Bush

Released November 2005
EMI *45087* (U.S.) / EMI *EM 674* (U.K. #4)

After all but disappearing for more than a decade, Kate Bush returned with this elegiac homage to Elvis Presley, the most successful solo artist in chart history. Bush's last single release had been 'And So Is Love,' from her underwhelming seventh album *The Red Shoes* (1993), which amounted to her only 1990s output. In the intervening years, her stock continued to rise. She was regularly named among the most innovative and influential women in pop and name-checked by other artists, from John Lydon to OutKast. Earlier in 2005, the British new-wave group The Futureheads hit the U.K. Top 10 with a well-received cover of Bush's 'Hounds Of Love,' the title track from her much-loved 1985 opus.

One of the year's most hotly anticipated releases, 'King Of The Mountain' is built around mournful synths, reggae bass, and lightly flicked guitar chords. It develops slowly over its four-and-a-half minutes, never quite reaching the expected climax. The lyrics reference *Citizen Kane* as well as Elvis, to whom Bush remarks that "another Hollywood waitress / Is telling us she's having your baby." A taster for the double-disc set *Aerial*, the single was issued on CD, as a digital download, and – harking back to an earlier time – a seven-inch picture disc, with artwork by Bush's son, Bertie.

So Sick
Ne-Yo

Released January 2006
Def Jam 000619011 (U.S. #1) / Def Jam 9854185 (U.K. #1)

Ne-Yo was still in his early 20s when 'So Sick' became a transatlantic chart-topper, but he had already carved out a career as a notable R&B songwriter, generating hits for artists such as Mary J. Blige, Jamie Foxx, and Rihanna. Born Shaffer Chimere Smith of African-American, Puerto Rican, and Chinese descent, he was given the nickname Ne-Yo by a friend who compared his ability to 'see' music to the visionary skills of Keanu Reeves's character Neo in the *Matrix* movie trilogy. It was therefore surprising when he called upon the Norwegian production team Stargate to craft 'So Sick,' restricting his own contribution to the lyrics, which declare him to be "so sick of your love songs / So sad and slow / But I just can't turn off the radio." Perhaps in response to this, Ne-Yo unleashed countless remixes of 'So Sick' to radio stations across the U.S., featuring duets with the likes of LL Cool J and 2Pac (the latter surely one of the most prolific dead men ever).

S.O.S.
Rihanna

Released February 2006
Def Jam 00631511 (U.S. #1) / Universal 9877821 (U.K. #2)

The latest in a line of teen-pop superstarlets, Rihanna was one of the biggest hits on the American and British singles charts in the first half of 2006. The Barbadian singer earned a deal with Def Jam at just 16 years old after auditioning for the label's CEO, the sometime rapper Jay-Z, who snapped her up on the spot. She hit Number 2 in the U.S. and the U.K. in 2005 with her debut single, 'Pon De Replay,' which merged R&B-pop with elements of Jamaican dancehall and West Indian calypso rhythms.

Its success was soon eclipsed by 'S.O.S.,' which is derived from a sample of Soft Cell's 1981 electro-pop classic 'Tainted Love,' itself a cover of a 1960s song by northern-soul singer Gloria Jones. The enduring chart success of 'S.O.S.' was such that, a few months later, Rihanna achieved the rare feat of having two songs in the *Billboard* Top 10 at once, when the smooth ballad 'Unfaithful' was released in June.

Beep
Pussycat Dolls Featuring will.i.am

Released February 2006
Universal 9852859 (U.S. #13) / Universal 9852861 (U.K. #2)

For the last two decades, the flow of countless hip-hop records has been interrupted by the beeping-out or muting of profanity. Often, this ends up making the radio edit of a single sound like a cell phone call from Outer Mongolia in which every other word is just about intelligible. 'Beep' takes a rather more amusing, self-referential tack, building the interruptions into the framework of the song.

Each line of the vocal ends with a beep – "you got a real big heart, but I'm lookin' at your [beep]," for instance – leaving it to the listener to

decide which choice expletive should fill in the gap. The combination of this smutty gimmickry, a guest appearance by Black Eyed Peas vocalist will.i.am, and an infectious, stop-start backing track ensured that 'Beep' was an international hit. (Perhaps surprisingly, the single was most successful in New Zealand, where it spent eight weeks at Number 1.)

'Beep' was the third U.S. hit for Pussycat Dolls, who started life in the mid 1990s as a burlesque dance troupe. With an ever-changing line-up, they performed a Thursday night residency at The Viper Room in Los Angeles from 1995 to 2001 before the group's creator, choreographer Robin Antin, decided to try his hand at pop music. Prior to focusing on music, the Dolls were regularly joined onstage at the Viper by high-profile female celebrities, from Britney Spears to Paris Hilton, all keen to unleash their wild side and become a pussycat for the night.

'Crazy' took advantage of a slackening in U.K. chart regulations that, for the first time allowed singles to enter the Top 40 without being available in a physical format. It subsequently spent nine weeks at Number 1 – making it the longest-reigning British chart-topper since Wet Wet Wet's 'Love Is All Around' hung on to pole position for 15 weeks in 1994.

Crazy
Gnarls Barkley

Released March 2006
Downtown *70002* (U.S. #2) / WEA *401CD* (U.K. #1)

'Crazy' became one of the most talked-about records of 2006 because it was the first song to top the British singles chart on the strength of downloads alone. It was also one of the most memorable hits of recent times, with Danger Mouse's widescreen-technicolor production style providing the perfect foil for singer-rapper-songwriter Cee-Lo Green's infectious, gospel-inspired vocal melody.

The success of 'Crazy' was a career high for both parties. Green had found sporadic success since the mid 1990s as a member of the hip-hop group Goodie Mob, as a solo artist, and as a writer and producer of hits for other artists, including Busta Rhymes and Pussycat Dolls. Danger Mouse, meanwhile, first drew attention for the illicit *Grey Album*, which mixed a cappella versions of Jay-Z's *Black Album* with instrumental tracks from The Beatles (a.k.a. *The White Album*). He then co-produced the acclaimed *Demon Days* by Gorillaz, which spawned the British hits 'Feel Good Inc.,' 'Dare,' and 'Dirty Harry.'

I Wish I Was A Punk Rocker (With Flowers In My Hair)
Sandi Thom

Released May 2006
Hungry Dog-Legacy *03* (U.S.) / RCA *6843422* (U.K. #1)

At first, 'I Wish I Was A Punk Rocker' seemed to be a true grassroots success, the result of innovative, independent self-promotion. A former student of the Liverpool Institute Of Performing Arts in England, Sandi Thom webcasted a series of 21 performances from her basement in south London in February and March 2006. The first of these was watched over the internet by fewer than a hundred people, but by the last one Thom had an audience of over 50,000.

Some of the gloss was taken off Thom's achievements when it was alleged that the webcasting idea had been devised and funded by RCA, part of the monolithic Sony organization. Wherever it originated, Thom's PR stunt had the desired effect, pushing 'Punk Rocker' to the top of the U.K. singles chart (the single had previously been given a limited release by an independent label at the end of 2005). While Thom's marketing tactics were decidedly high-tech, the song itself was no more than an inoffensive acoustic-guitar-led tune reminiscent of dozens of 1970s singer-songwriters.

Picture Credits

The photographs in this book are reproduced with permission from the following copyright holders, and we are grateful for their help. All of the images were supplied by Redfern's (indicated below by the initials XX/RF, where XX denotes the photographer) and Rex Features (XX/RX). On pages with multiple images, pictures are listed clockwise from top left.

Key to photographers: Richard E. Aaron RA; All Action AA; Cyrus Andrews CA; Jorgen Angel JA; Howard Barlow HB; Roberta Bayley RBA; Paul Bergen PB; Stephanie Chernikowski SC; George Chin GC; Roger Coles RC; Fin Costello FC; Andre Csillag AC; Grant Davis GD; Phil Dent PD; Ian Dickson ID; Kevin Dunn KD; Neville Elder NEL; David Warner Ellis DWE; Erica Echenberg EE; EMI Archives EMI; Brigitte Engl BE; David Farrell DF; Yann Feron YF; Tabatha Fireman TF; GAB Archives GAB; Charlie Gillett CG; Globe Photos GP; Harry Goodwin HG; Tom Hanley TH; Ron Howard RH; Mick Hutson MH; Steve Hurrell SH; Salifu Idriss SI; JM International JM; Ivan Keeman IK; Bob King BK; Elliott Landy EL; Beverly Lebarrow BL; Herman Leonard HL; Michael Linssen ML; John Lynn Kirk JL; David Magnus DM; George Mankowitz GM; Jim McCrary JMC; Keith Morris KM; Leon Morris LM; Steve Morley SMO; Chris Mills CMI; Chris Morphet CM; Stuart Mostyn SM; New Eyes NE; Petra Niemeier PN; Linda Nylind LN; Michael Ochs Archives MOA; K&K Ulf Kruger Ohg KK; Peter Pakvis PP; Don Paulsen DPA; Erik Pendzich EP; Jan Persson JP; David Peters DP; Mike Prior MP; Andrew Putler AP; Christina Radish CR; Brian Rasic BR; David Redfern DR; David Reed DRE; Simon Ritter SR; Ebet Roberts ER; Kerstin Rodgers KR; Jim Sharpe JS; Nicky J. Sims NS; Sipa Press SP; Chuck Stewart CS; Peter Still PS; Billy Tompkins BT; Virginia Turbett VT; Michael Uhil MU; Lex Van Rossen LVR; Michael Young RY; Charlyn Zlotnik CZ.

Jacket front JS/RF; FC/RF; MOA/RF; GAB/RF; MOA/RF; 1 MOA/RF; 2–3 KK/RF; 4–5 JA/RF; 6–7 CS/RF; 8 MOA/RF; 10 MOA/RF; JP/RF; 12 MOA/RF; 12–13 MOA/RF; 14 GAB/RF; 15 BL/RF; MOA/RF; 16 /RF; 16–45 MOA/RF; 46 MOA/RF; RB/RF; 47 RB/RF; 48 GEMS/RF; 49 MOA/RF; 50 HG/RF; 51 MOA/RF; 52 RB/RF; 53 DP/RF; 55 MOA/RF; 56–7 RF; 58 CA/RF; 60–3

MOA/RF; 64 EMI/RF; 65 DR/RF; 66 DPA/RF; 67 CG/RF; 68 HG/RF; DF/RF; 67 MOA/RF; 70–1 MOA/RF; 72 GAB/RF; 73 GM/RF; 74 CA/RF; 75 MOA/RF; 78–9 MOA/RF; 80 JP/RF; GAB/RF; 81 MOA/RF; GAB/RF; 82–4 MOA/RF; 86 DR/RF; 87 MOA/RF; 88 DM/RX; 89 RX; 90 EL/RF; 91 MOA/RF; RH/RF; 93 JP/RF; 94 AW/RF; 95 SP/RX; 97–9 MOA/RF; 102–3 MOA/RF; 104 JP/RF; 105 IK/RF; 106 MOA/RF; 107 RB/RF; MOA/RF; 108 JP/RF; 109 MOA/RF; 110 MOA/RF; MOA/RF; 120 GEMS/RF; 123 MOA/RF; RH/RF; 124–5 MOA/RF; 126–7 TH/RF; 128 CM/RF; RH/RF; 129 KM/RF; 130 MOA/RF; 131 TH/RF; 133 JMC/RF; 134 JP/RF; 135 DR/RF; 136 HG/RF; RH/RF; 137 MOA/RF; DRE/RF; 138–9 PN/RF; 141 MOA/RF; JL/RF; 142 BBC/RF; RH/RF; 143 DWE/RF; 145 ID/RF; 146 MOA/RF; 147 GEMS/RF; 148 BBC/RF; 149 HG/RF; 151 GAB/RF; 152–3 BBC/RF; 155 MOA/RF; 156 DR/RF; 157 SMO/RF; 158 KM/RF; 159 AP/RF; 160 DR/RF; 162–3 PN/RF; 164 RBA/RF; ID/RF; 165 ER/RF; 166 GP/RX; RY/RX; 167 ID/RF; ER/RF; 168 MOA/RF; 169 RA/RF; 170 FC/RF; 171 MOA/RF; 172 CZ/RF; 173 RA/RF; 174 GEMS/RF; 176–7 MP/RF; 178–9 MOA/RF; 180 KM/RF; 181 FC/RF; BBC/RF; 182 GMA/RF; 184–5 FC/RF; 186 RBA/RF; 187 FC/RF; ER/RF; 188–9 CMI/RF; 190 VT/RF; 191 HG/RF; 192 GAB/RF; 193 FC/RF; 194 MOA/RF; 195 SC/RF; ER/RF; 197 JP/RF; 198 MOA/RF; 199 LM/RF; 201 FC/RF; 202–3 ER/RF; 204 RA/RF; 205 EE/RF; 206 ER/RF; 207 NE/RF; 208 ER/RF; 209 MOA/RF; 210 BBC/RF; 211 KR/RF; ID/RF; 212 PD/RF; 213–5 BK/RF; 216 PD/RF; 217 SH/RF; 218–9 PS/RF; 220 DR/RF; 221 RB/RF; 222–5 ER/RF; 226 GD/RF; 227 GAB/RF; 228 ER/RF; 229 GAB/RF; ER/RF; 230 BR/RX; 231–2 BBC/RF; 233 MU/RF; 234 NE/RF; 235 AA/RF; 236 ID/RF; 237 ID/RF; 238–41 ML/RF; 242 GAB/RF; 243 MH/RF; 244 GAB/RF; MH/RF; 245 MH/RF; ID/RF; 246–7 PP/RF; 249 MU/RF; 250 GAB/RF; 252 ML/RF; 253 PB/RF; 255 GC/RF; PB/RF; 256–7 PB/RF; 258–61 MH/RF; 262 ER/RF; 263 GC/RF; 264 RC/RF; ER/RF; 265 MH/RF; 266 ER/RF; 267 DW/RF; 269 ER/RF; 270 SR/RF; 271 MH/RF; 273 MH/RF; 274 EP/RX; 275 RX; 276 PB/RF; 279 ML/RF; 281 GD/RF; 282–3 PB/RF; 284 PD/RF; 285 ML/RF; 286–7 SI/RF; 289 PB/RF; 290–1 JM/RF; 292 JS/RF; 293 BE/RF; 294 JS/RF; 295 NS/RF; 296 SI/RF; PP/RF; 297 SM/RF; 299 PB/RF; 300 KD/RF; 301 SM/RF; 302 NS/RF; 304 JM/RF; 305 NEL/RF; 307 TF/RF; 308 TF/RF; PP/RF; 310 PP/RF; 311 LN/RF; CR/RF; 313 LVR/RF; JM/RF; MH/RF; 314 MH/RF; 316 YF/RX; 317 AC/RX; jacket back MOA/RF; SI/RF; EMI/RF; BT/RF; ML/RF; HB/RF.

Publisher's Thanks

Stephen Atkinson (Rex Features), Jack Barnett, Nigel Osborne, Julian Ridgway (Redfern's), John Ryall. Many of the record labels and jackets used in this book were provided by Bob Solly, to whom we are particularly grateful.

Headings for each single show the A-side title (and occasionally the B-side), followed on the next line by the name of the artist and/or group. The label and catalogue number are shown for U.S. and U.K. releases, where appropriate, and if the single peaked at Number 40 or higher on first release then that position is given in brackets after a # (number) symbol. Chart information for U.S. releases comes from the various Billboard books, principally Joel Whitburn's Top 40 Hits, and for U.K. releases from the Guinness publications, primarily British Hit Singles.

The publisher would like to acknowledge the following sources, which have proved invaluable in the research and compilation of this book: The AllMusic Guide; Atlantic & Godfathers Of Rock'n'Roll, Justine Picardie & Dorothy Wade; Beat Instrumental; Behind The Hits, Bob Shannon & John Javna; Billboard; Chuck Berry – The Autobiography, Chuck Berry; Classic Rock Stories, Tim Morse; The Encyclopaedia Of Pop, Rock, And Soul; Entertainment Weekly; Good Vibrations, Mark Cunningham; The Great Rock Discography, Martin C. Strong; Guitar World; The Guys Who Wrote 'Em, Sean Egan; History of Rock; I Wish I Was Me, Pete Waterman; Kerrang!; Making Music; McCartney – The Biography, Chet Flippo; Melody Maker; Mojo; Modern Drummer; Music Week; New Musical Express; Off The Record: An Oral History of Popular Music, Joe Smith; Only The Lonely, Alan Clayson; Record Collector; Record Producers, John Tobler & Stuart Grundy; Rock Record, Terry Hounsome; Rolling Stone; Songwriters On Songwriting, Paul Zollo; Spin; Starmakers & Svengalis, Johnny Rogan; Story Of Rock; Strange Days, Strange Sounds, Mark Brend; Stone Alone, Bill Wyman; Street Life; Sweet Soul Music, Peter Guralnick; Trax; Village Voice

"It was a shock to hear that back. I must have had help from upstairs."
Brian Wilson on the completion of The Beach Boys' 'Good Vibrations'.